Safety Symbols

These symbols appear in laboratory activities. They ⟨...⟩ in the laboratory and remind you to wo⟨...⟩

 Safety Goggles Wear safety goggles to protect your eyes in any activity involving chemicals, flames or heating, or glassware.

 Lab Apron Wear a laboratory apron to protect your skin and clothing from damage.

 Breakage Handle breakable materials, such as glassware, with care. Do not touch broken glassware.

 Heat-Resistant Gloves Use an oven mitt or other hand protection when handling hot materials such as hot plates or hot glassware.

 Plastic Gloves Wear disposable plastic gloves when working with harmful chemicals and organisms. Keep your hands away from your face, and dispose of the gloves according to your teacher's instructions.

 Heating Use a clamp or tongs to pick up hot glassware. Do not touch hot objects with your bare hands.

 Flames Before you work with flames, tie back loose hair and clothing. Follow instructions from your teacher about lighting and extinguishing flames.

 No Flames When using flammable materials, make sure there are no flames, sparks, or other exposed heat sources present.

 Corrosive Chemical Avoid getting acid or other corrosive chemicals on your skin or clothing or in your eyes. Do not inhale the vapors. Wash your hands after the activity.

 Poison Do not let any poisonous chemical come into contact with your skin, and do not inhale its vapors. Wash your hands when you are finished with the activity.

 Fun⟨...⟩ ⟨...⟩en harmful vapors may be involved. Avoid inhaling vapors directly. Only test an odor when directed to do so by your teacher, and use a wafting motion to direct the vapor toward your nose.

 Sharp Object Scissors, scalpels, knives, needles, pins, and tacks can cut your skin. Always direct a sharp edge or point away from yourself and others.

 Animal Safety Treat live or preserved animals or animal parts with care to avoid harming the animals or yourself. Wash your hands when you are finished with the activity.

 Plant Safety Handle plants only as directed by your teacher. If you are allergic to certain plants, tell your teacher; do not do an activity involving those plants. Avoid touching harmful plants such as poison ivy. Wash your hands when you are finished with the activity.

 Electric Shock To avoid electric shock, never use electrical equipment around water, or when the equipment is wet or your hands are wet. Be sure cords are untangled and cannot trip anyone. Unplug equipment not in use.

 Physical Safety When an experiment involves physical activity, avoid injuring yourself or others. Alert your teacher if there is any reason you should not participate.

 Disposal Dispose of chemicals and other laboratory materials safely. Follow the instructions from your teacher.

 Hand Washing Wash your hands thoroughly when finished with the activity. Use antibacterial soap and warm water. Rinse well.

 General Safety Awareness When this symbol appears, follow the instructions provided. When you are asked to develop your own procedure in a lab, have your teacher approve your plan before you go further.

California
Focus on
Physical
Science

PEARSON
Prentice
Hall

Boston, Massachusetts
Upper Saddle River, New Jersey

CALIFORNIA SCIENCE EXPLORER

Program Print Resources

Student Edition
Teacher's Edition
Teaching Resources
Color Transparencies
Reading and Note Taking Guide Level A
Reading and Note Taking Guide Level B
Inquiry Skills Activity Books I–III
Vocabulary Flashcards
Laboratory Manual
Laboratory Manual, Teacher's Edition
Virtual Physical Science Lab Record Sheets
Probeware Lab Manual
Standards Review Workbook
Standards Review Transparencies
Progress Monitoring Assessments
Chapter Tests Level A and B
Teaching Guidebook for Universal Access

Program Technology Resources

Lab zone™ Easy Planner
Virtual Physical Science CD-ROM
PresentationExpress CD-ROM
Student Express with Interactive Textbook CD-ROM
TeacherExpress™ CD-ROM
ExamView® Computer Test Bank
Student Edition in MP3
Probeware Lab Manual CD-ROM

Program Video Resources

Lab Activity DVD
Discovery Channel DVD Library

Spanish Program Resources

Spanish Student Edition
Spanish Reading and Note Taking Guide
Spanish Teacher's Guide with Answer Keys
Spanish Student Edition in MP3

Acknowledgments appear on pages 691–693, which constitute an extension of this copyright page.

D0026436

ISBN 0-13-201270-7
7 8 9 10   11 10 09 08

Program Authors

Michael J. Padilla, Ph.D.
Professor of Science Education
University of Georgia
Athens, Georgia

Michael Padilla is a leader in middle school science education. He has served as President of the National Science Teachers Association and as a writer of the National Science Education Standards. As lead author of Science Explorer, Mike has inspired the team in developing a program that meets the needs of middle grade students, promotes science inquiry, and is aligned with the National Science Education Standards.

Ioannis Miaoulis, Ph.D.
President
Museum of Science
Boston, Massachusetts

Originally trained as a mechanical engineer, Ioannis Miaoulis is in the forefront of the national movement to increase technological literacy. As dean of the Tufts University School of Engineering, Dr. Miaoulis spearheaded the introduction of engineering into the Massachusetts curriculum. Currently he is working with school systems across the country to engage students in engineering activities and to foster discussions on the impact of science and technology on society.

Martha Cyr, Ph.D.
Director of K–12 Outreach
Worcester Polytechnic Institute
Worcester, Massachusetts

Martha Cyr is a noted expert in engineering outreach. She has over nine years of experience with programs and activities that emphasize the use of engineering principles, through hands-on projects, to excite and motivate students and teachers of mathematics and science in grades K–12. Her goal is to stimulate a continued interest in science and mathematics through engineering.

Book Authors

David V. Frank, Ph.D.
Head, Department of
   Physical Sciences
Ferris State University
Big Rapids, Michigan

T. Griffith Jones, Ph.D.
Science Department Chair
P. K. Yonge Developmental
Research School
College of Education—
University of Florida
Gainesville, Florida

John G. Little
Science Teacher
St. Mary's High School
Stockton, California

Beth Miaoulis
Technology Writer
Sherborn, Massachusetts

Steve Miller
Science Writer
State College, Pennsylvania

Jay M. Pasachoff, Ph.D.
Professor of Astronomy
Williams College
Williamstown, Massachusetts

Reading Consultants

Kate Kinsella
Kate Kinsella, Ed.D., is a faculty member in the Department of Secondary Education at San Francisco State University. A specialist in second-language acquisition and adolescent literacy, she teaches coursework addressing language and literacy development across the secondary curricula. Dr. Kinsella earned her master's degree in TESOL from San Francisco State University and her Ed.D. in Second Language Acquisition from the University of San Francisco.

Kevin Feldman
Kevin Feldman, Ed.D., is the Director of Reading and Early Intervention with the Sonoma County Office of Education (SCOE) and independent educational consultant. At the SCOE, he develops, organizes, and monitors programs related to K-12 literacy. Dr. Feldman has a master's degree from the University of California, Riverside, in Special Education, Learning Disabilities, and Instructional Design. He earned his Ed.D. in Curriculum and Instruction from the University of San Francisco.

Mathematics Consultant

William Tate, Ph.D.
Professor of Education and
   Applied Statistics and
   Computation
Washington University
St. Louis, Missouri

Contributing Writers

Linda Blaine
Science Teacher
Millbrook High School
Raleigh, North Carolina

Mary Sue Burns
Science Teacher
Pocahontas County High School
Dunmore, West Virginia

Mark Illingworth
Teacher
Hollis Public Schools
Hollis, New Hampshire

Thomas L. Messer
Science Teacher
Foxborough Public Schools
Foxborough, Massachusetts

Thomas R. Wellnitz
Science Instructor
The Paideia School
Atlanta, Georgia

Reviewers

California Master Teacher Board

Joel Austin
Roosevelt Middle School
San Francisco, California

Donna Baker
Riverview Middle School
Bay Point, California

Luz Castillo
Prairie Vista Middle School
Hawthorne, California

Laura Finco
Stone Valley Middle School
Alamo, California

Tawiah Finley
Central Middle School
Riverside, California

Glen Hannerman
San Lorenzo Middle School
King City, California

Al Janulaw
Sonoma State University (retired)
Rohnert Park, California

Sharon Janulaw
Sonoma County Office of Education
Santa Rosa, California

Cindy Krueger
Washington Middle School
La Habra, California

Diane Maynard
Vineyard Junior High
Alta Loma, California

Catherine Nicholas
Rio Norte Junior High School
Santa Clarita, California

Susan Pritchard, Ph.D.
Washington Middle School
La Habra, California

Ingrid Salim
Harper Junior High School
Davis, California

Tia Shields
Nicolas Junior High School
Fullerton, California

Mimi Wentz
TeWinkle Middle School
Costa Mesa, California

Jocelyn Young
El Dorado High School
Placentia, California

California Content Reviewers

Richard Berry, Ph.D.
Department of Geological Sciences
San Diego State University
San Diego, California

Londa Borer-Skov, Ph.D.
Department of Chemistry
California State University Sacramento
Sacramento, California

Eugene Chiang, Ph.D.
Department of Astronomy
University of California Berkeley
Berkeley, California

Susan Collins, Ph.D.
Department of Chemistry and Biochemistry
California State University Northridge
Northridge, California

Debra Fischer, Ph.D.
Department of Physics and Astronomy
San Francisco State University
San Francisco, California

James Hetrick, Ph.D.
Department of Physics
University of the Pacific
Stockton, California

Rita Hoots
Department of Science
Woodland College
Woodland, California

Janet Kruse
Discovery Museum
Sacramento, California

Michael Mastrandrea, Ph.D.
Center for Environmental
    Science and Policy
Stanford University
Stanford, California

George Matsumoto, Ph.D.
Senior Education and Research Specialist
Monterey Bay Aquarium Research Institute
Moss Landing, California

Robert Mellors, Ph.D.
Department of Geological Sciences
San Diego State University
San Diego, California

Donald Merhaut, Ph.D.
Department of Botany and Plant Science
University of California Riverside
Riverside, California

Eric Norman, Ph.D.
Lawrence Berkeley National Lab
University of California Berkeley
Berkeley, California

John Platt
Department of Earth Sciences
University of Southern California
Los Angeles, California

James Prince, Ph.D.
Department of Biology
California State University Fresno
Fresno, California

Gerald Sanders, Sr.
Department of Biology
San Diego State University
San Diego, California

Susan Schwartz, Ph.D.
Department of Earth Sciences
University of California Santa Cruz
Santa Cruz, California

Lynn Yarris, M.A.
Lawrence Berkeley National Lab
University of California Berkeley
Berkeley, California

Content Reviewers

Paul Beale, Ph.D.
Department of Physics
University of Colorado
Boulder, Colorado

Jeff Bodart, Ph.D.
Chipola Junior College
Marianna, Florida

Michael Castellani, Ph.D.
Department of Chemistry
Marshall University
Huntington, West Virginia

Eugene Chiang, Ph.D.
Department of Astronomy
University of California – Berkeley
Berkeley, California

Charles C. Curtis, Ph.D.
Department of Physics
University of Arizona
Tucson, Arizona

Daniel Kirk-Davidoff, Ph.D.
Department of Meteorology
University of Maryland
College Park, Maryland

Diane T. Doser, Ph.D.
Department of Geological Sciences
University of Texas at El Paso
El Paso, Texas

R. E. Duhrkopf, Ph.D.
Department of Biology
Baylor University
Waco, Texas

Michael Hacker
Co-director, Center for
   Technological Literacy
Hofstra University
Hempstead, New York

Michael W. Hamburger, Ph.D.
Department of Geological Sciences
Indiana University
Bloomington, Indiana

Alice K. Hankla, Ph.D.
The Galloway School
Atlanta, Georgia

Donald C. Jackson, Ph.D.
Department of Molecular Pharmacology,
   Physiology, & Biotechnology
Brown University
Providence, Rhode Island

Jeremiah N. Jarrett, Ph.D.
Department of Biological Sciences
Central Connecticut State University
New Britain, Connecticut

David Lederman, Ph.D.
Department of Physics
West Virginia University
Morgantown, West Virginia

Becky Mansfield, Ph.D.
Department of Geography
Ohio State University
Columbus, Ohio

Elizabeth M. Martin, M.S.
Department of Chemistry and Biochemistry
College of Charleston
Charleston, South Carolina

Joe McCullough, Ph.D.
Department of Natural and
   Applied Sciences
Cabrillo College
Aptos, California

Robert J. Mellors, Ph.D.
Department of Geological Sciences
San Diego State University
San Diego, California

Joseph M. Moran, Ph.D.
American Meteorological Society
Washington, D.C.

David J. Morrissey, Ph.D.
Department of Chemistry
Michigan State University
East Lansing, Michigan

Philip A. Reed, Ph.D.
Department of Occupational & Technical
   Studies
Old Dominion University
Norfolk, Virginia

Scott M. Rochette, Ph.D.
Department of the Earth Sciences
State University of New York, College at
   Brockport
Brockport, New York

Laurence D. Rosenhein, Ph.D.
Department of Chemistry
Indiana State University
Terre Haute, Indiana

Ronald Sass, Ph.D.
Department of Biology and Chemistry
Rice University
Houston, Texas

George Schatz, Ph.D.
Department of Chemistry
Northwestern University
Evanston, Illinois

Sara Seager, Ph.D.
Carnegie Institution of Washington
Washington, D.C.

Robert M. Thornton, Ph.D.
Section of Plant Biology
University of California
Davis, California

John R. Villarreal, Ph.D.
College of Science and Engineering
The University of Texas – Pan American
Edinburg, Texas

Kenneth Welty, Ph.D.
School of Education
University of Wisconsin–Stout
Menomonie, Wisconsin

Edward J. Zalisko, Ph.D.
Department of Biology
Blackburn College
Carlinville, Illinois

Safety Reviewers

W. H. Breazeale, Ph.D.
Department of Chemistry
College of Charleston
Charleston, South Carolina

Ruth Hathaway, Ph.D.
Hathaway Consulting
Cape Girardeau, Missouri

Douglas Mandt
Science Education Consultant
Edgewood, Washington

Teacher Reviewers

David R. Blakely
Arlington High School
Arlington, Massachusetts

Jane E. Callery
Two Rivers Magnet Middle School
East Hartford, Connecticut

Melissa Lynn Cook
Oakland Mills High School
Columbia, Maryland

James Fattic
Southside Middle School
Anderson, Indiana

Dan Gabel
Hoover Middle School
Rockville, Maryland

Wayne Goates
Eisenhower Middle School
Goddard, Kansas

Katherine Bobay Graser
Mint Hill Middle School
Charlotte, North Carolina

Darcy Hampton
Deal Junior High School
Washington, D.C.

Karen Kelly
Pierce Middle School
Waterford, Michigan

David Kelso
Manchester High School Central
Manchester, New Hampshire

Benigno Lopez, Jr.
Sleepy Hill Middle School
Lakeland, Florida

Angie L. Matamoros, Ph.D.
ALM Consulting, INC.
Weston, Florida

Tim McCollum
Charleston Middle School
Charleston, Illinois

Bruce A. Mellin
Brooks School
North Andover, Massachusetts

Ella Jay Parfitt
Southeast Middle School
Baltimore, Maryland

Evelyn A. Pizzarello
Louis M. Klein Middle School
Harrison, New York

Kathleen M. Poe
Fletcher Middle School
Jacksonville, Florida

Shirley Rose
Lewis and Clark Middle School
Tulsa, Oklahoma

Linda Sandersen
Greenfield Middle School
Greenfield, Wisconsin

Mary E. Solan
Southwest Middle School
Charlotte, North Carolina

Mary Stewart
University of Tulsa
Tulsa, Oklahoma

Paul Swenson
Billings West High School
Billings, Montana

Thomas Vaughn
Arlington High School
Arlington, Massachusetts

Susan C. Zibell
Central Elementary
Simsbury, Connecticut

Activity Field Testers

Nicki Bibbo
Witchcraft Heights School
Salem, Massachusetts

Rose-Marie Botting
Broward County Schools
Fort Lauderdale, Florida

Colleen Campos
Laredo Middle School
Aurora, Colorado

Elizabeth Chait
W. L. Chenery Middle School
Belmont, Massachusetts

Holly Estes
Hale Middle School
Stow, Massachusetts

Laura Hapgood
Plymouth Community
   Intermediate School
Plymouth, Massachusetts

Mary F. Lavin
Plymouth Community
   Intermediate School
Plymouth, Massachusetts

James MacNeil, Ph.D.
Cambridge, Massachusetts

Lauren Magruder
St. Michael's Country
   Day School
Newport, Rhode Island

Jeanne Maurand
Austin Preparatory School
Reading, Massachusetts

Joanne Jackson-Pelletier
Winman Junior High School
Warwick, Rhode Island

Warren Phillips
Plymouth Public Schools
Plymouth, Massachusetts

Carol Pirtle
Hale Middle School
Stow, Massachusetts

Kathleen M. Poe
Fletcher Middle School
Jacksonville, Florida

Cynthia B. Pope
Norfolk Public Schools
Norfolk, Virginia

Anne Scammell
Geneva Middle School
Geneva, New York

Karen Riley Sievers
Callanan Middle School
Des Moines, Iowa

David M. Smith
Eyer Middle School
Allentown, Pennsylvania

Gene Vitale
Parkland School
McHenry, Illinois

Unit 1

Chemical Building Blocks

Focus on the BIG Idea

How do scientists investigate the natural world?

Chapter 1

Introduction to Physical Science xl

Build Science Vocabulary: High-Use Academic Words ... 2

How to Read Science: Preview Text Structure 4

Standards Investigation: Design and Build a Density-Calculating System 5

1 What Is Physical Science? 6
2 Scientific Inquiry 10
3 Measurement 16
   Skills Lab: Making Sense of Density 27
4 Mathematics and Science 30
5 Graphs in Science 34
   Analyzing Data: Car Travel 39
   Skills Lab: Density Graphs 42
6 Science Laboratory Safety 43

Focus on the BIG Idea

What is chemistry?

Chapter 2

The Nature of Matter 52

Build Science Vocabulary: Prefixes 54

How to Read Science: Identify Main Ideas 56

Standards Investigation: Classify Changes in Matter 57

1 Describing Matter 58
2 Changes in Matter 68
   Analyzing Data: Is Matter Conserved? 72
3 Energy and Matter 73
   Analyzing Data: Comparing Energy Changes 75
   Skills Lab: Isolating Copper by Electrolysis 78

Chapter 3

Solids, Liquids, and Gases 84

    Build Science Vocabulary: Suffixes 86

    How to Read Science: Create Outlines 88

    Standards Investigation:
    A Story of Changing States 89

1 States of Matter 90

2 Changes of State 96

    Analyzing Data: Temperature and Changes of State .. 100

    Skills Lab: Melting Ice 102

3 The Behavior of Gases 103

    Analyzing Data: Graphing Gas Behavior 111

    Skills Lab: It's a Gas 112

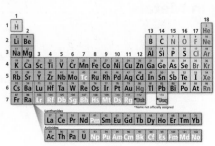

Chapter 4

Elements and the Periodic Table 118

    Build Science Vocabulary: Greek Word Origins 120

    How to Read Science: Preview Visuals 122

    Standards Investigation:
    Survey Properties of Metals 123

1 Introduction to Atoms 124

2 Organizing the Elements 131

3 Metals 138

    Analyzing Data:
    Melting Points in a Group of Elements 141

    Consumer Lab: Copper or Carbon?
    That Is the Question 146

4 Nonmetals, Inert Gases, and Semimetals 148

    Skills Lab: Alien Periodic Table 156

5 Radioactive Elements 158

Unit 1 Review 168

Focus on the
BIG Idea

How do solids,
liquids, and
gases differ in
the motion of
their particles?

Focus on the
BIG Idea

How is the
periodic table
organized?

Unit 2

Chemical Interactions

Focus on the
BIG Idea

How do compounds form?

Chapter 5

Atoms and Bonding 170

Build Science Vocabulary:
High-Use Academic Words 172

How to Read Science: Compare and Contrast 174

Standards Investigation: Models of Compounds 175

1 Atoms, Bonding, and the Periodic Table 176
Skills Lab: Comparing Atom Sizes 183

2 Ionic Bonds 184
Skills Lab: Shedding Light on Ions 190

3 Covalent Bonds 192
Analyzing Data: Comparing Molecular
and Ionic Compounds 195

4 Bonding in Metals 198

Focus on the
BIG Idea

What happens during a chemical reaction?

Chapter 6

Chemical Reactions 208

Build Science Vocabulary: Identify Multiple Meanings .. 210

How to Read Science: Take Notes 212

Standards Investigation: Demonstrate
Conservation of Matter 213

1 Observing Chemical Change 214
Analyzing Data: Energy in Chemical Changes 220
Skills Lab: Where's the Evidence? 222

2 Describing Chemical Reactions 224
Analyzing Data: Balancing Chemical Equations 229

3 Controlling Chemical Reactions 234
Skills Lab: Temperature and Enzyme Activity 240

4 Fire and Fire Safety 242

Chapter 7

Acids, Bases, and Solutions 250

Build Science Vocabulary:
Use Related Words 252

How to Read Science: Create Outlines 254

Standards Investigation:
Make Your Own Indicator 255

1 **Understanding Solutions** 256
2 **Concentration and Solubility** 262
   Analyzing Data: Temperature and Solubility 266
3 **Describing Acids and Bases** 268
4 **Acids and Bases in Solution** 274
   Consumer Lab: The Antacid Test 280

Focus on the
BIG Idea

What are some
characteristics
of acids
of bases?

Chapter 8

Carbon Chemistry 286

Build Science Vocabulary:
Use Clues to Determine Meaning 288

How to Read Science: Compare and Contrast 290

Standards Investigation: Check Out the Fine Print . . . 291

1 **Properties of Carbon** 292
2 **Carbon Compounds** 296
   Analyzing Data: Boiling Points of Hydrocarbons 300
   Skills Lab: How Many Molecules? 305
3 **Polymers and Composites** 306
4 **Life With Carbon** 316
   Consumer Lab:
   Are You Getting Your Vitamins? 324

Unit 2 Review 330

Focus on the
BIG Idea

Why does carbon
have a central
role in the
chemistry
of living
organisms?

Unit 3

Motion, Forces, and Energy

Chapter 9

Motion and Energy **332**

　　Build Science Vocabulary:
　　High-Use Academic Words 334

　　How to Read Science: Identify Main Ideas 336

　　Standards Investigation:
　　Show Some Motion 337

1 Describing Motion **338**

2 Speed and Velocity **342**

　　Skills Lab: Inclined to Roll 348

3 Acceleration **350**

　　Skills Lab: Stopping on a Dime 356

4 Energy **358**

Focus on the
BIG Idea

How can you describe an object's motion?

Chapter 10

Forces 368

Build Science Vocabulary: Latin Word Origins 370

How to Read Science: Take Notes 372

Standards Investigation: Newton Scooters 373

1 The Nature of Force 374

Consumer Lab: Sticky Sneakers 378

2 Friction, Gravity, and Elastic Forces 380

Analyzing Data: Free Fall 386

3 Newton's First and Second Laws 389

4 Newton's Third Law 393

Skills Lab: Forced to Accelerate 400

5 Rockets and Satellites 402

Focus on the
BIG Idea

What causes an object's velocity to change?

Chapter 11

Forces in Fluids 410

Build Science Vocabulary:
Identify Multiple Meanings 412

How to Read Science: Sequence 414

Standards Investigation: Staying Afloat 415

1 Pressure 416

Design Your Own Lab: Spinning Sprinklers 423

2 Floating and Sinking 424

Skills Lab: Sink and Spill 430

3 Pascal's Principle 432

Analyzing Data: Comparing Hydraulic Lifts 435

4 Bernoulli's Principle 437

Unit 3 Review 448

Interdisciplinary Exploration From Vines to Steel .. 450

Focus on the
BIG Idea

How can you predict if an object will sink or float in a fluid?

Unit 4

Focus on the
BIG Idea

What events are caused by the motion of Earth and the moon?

Astronomy

Chapter 12
Earth, Moon, and Sun **458**
    Build Science Vocabulary: Latin Word Origins 460
    How to Read Science: Sequence 462
    Standards Investigation: Track the Moon 463
1 Earth in Space **464**
    Skills Lab: Reasons for the Seasons 472
2 Gravity and Motion **474**
    Analyzing Data: Gravity Versus Distance 476
3 Phases, Eclipses, and Tides **478**
    Skills Lab: A "Moonth" of Phases 486
4 Earth's Moon **488**

Focus on the
BIG Idea

How do scientists learn more about the solar system?

Chapter 13
Exploring Space **496**
    Build Science Vocabulary: High-Use Academic Words .. 498
    How to Read Science: Relate Cause and Effect 500
    Standards Investigation:
    Design and Build a Space Exploration Vehicle 501
1 The Science of Rockets **502**
    Analyzing Data: Rocket Altitude 505
    Technology Lab: Design and Build a
    Water Rocket 508
2 The Space Program **510**
3 Exploring Space Today **515**
4 Using Space Science on Earth **520**
    Consumer Lab: Space Spinoffs 525

Chapter 14

The Solar System 532

Build Science Vocabulary: Greek Word Origins 534
How to Read Science: Create Outlines 536
Standards Investigation: Build a Model
of the Solar System 537
1 Observing the Solar System 538
   Analyzing Data: Planet Speed Versus Distance 542
2 The Sun 545
   Skills Lab: Stormy Sunspots 551
3 The Inner Planets 552
4 The Outer Planets 562
   Design Your Own Lab: Speeding Around the Sun 570
5 Comets, Asteroids, and Meteors 572
6 Is There Life Beyond Earth? 576

Chapter 15

Stars, Galaxies, and the Universe 584

Build Science Vocabulary: Suffixes 586
How to Read Science: Identify Supporting Evidence 588
Standards Investigation: Star Stories 589
1 Telescopes 590
   Technology Lab: Design and Build a Telescope 597
2 Characteristics of Stars 598
   Skills Lab: How Far Is That Star? 606
3 Lives of Stars 608
4 Star Systems and Galaxies 614
5 The Expanding Universe 622
   Analyzing Data: Speeding Galaxies 624

Unit 4 Review 632

Reference Section

Skills Handbook 634
Appendix A Laboratory Safety 650
Appendix B Using a Laboratory Balance 652
Appendix C List of Chemical Elements 653
Appendix D Astronomical Data 654
Appendix E Star Charts 656
English & Spanish Glossary 658
Index 676
Acknowledgments 691

Focus on the
BIG Idea

What types of objects are found in the solar system?

Focus on the
BIG Idea

What is the structure and composition of the universe?

xv

Activities

Lab zone Standards **Warm-Up**   Exploration and inquiry before reading

How Does a Ball Bounce? 6

Can You Make a Shadow Disappear? . . .10

Which Has More Mass? 16

How Many Marbles Are There? 30

What's in a Picture? 34

Where Is the Safety Equipment
in Your School? 43

What Is a Mixture? 58

Is a New Substance Formed? 68

Where Was the Energy? 73

What Are Solids, Liquids, and
Gases? 90

What Happens When You
Breathe on a Mirror? 96

How Can Air Keep Chalk
From Breaking? 103

What's in the Box? 124

Which Is Easier? 131

Why Use Aluminum? 138

What Are the Properties of
Charcoal? 148

What Happens When an Atom
Decays? 158

What Are the Trends in the
Periodic Table? 176

How Do Ions Form? 184

Can Water and Oil Mix? 192

Are They "Steel" the Same? 198

How Does Matter Change? 214

Do You Lose Anything? 224

Can You Speed Up or Slow
Down a Reaction? 234

How Does Baking Soda Affect
a Fire? 242

What Makes a Mixture a Solution? . . . 256

Does It Dissolve? 262

What Colors Does Litmus
Paper Turn? 268

What Can Cabbage Juice Tell You? 274

Why Do Pencils Write? 292

What Do You Smell? 296

What Did You Make? 306

What Is in Milk? 316

How Fast and How Far? 338

How Slow Can It Flow? 342

Will You Hurry Up? 350

How High Does a Ball Bounce? 358

Is the Force With You? 374

The Flexible Meter Stick 380

What Changes Motion? 389

How Pushy Is a Straw? 393

What Makes an Object
Move in a Circle? 402

Does Water Push Back? 416

What Can You Measure With
a Pencil? 424

Why Does the Cartesian Diver
Sink? 432

Does the Movement of Air
Create Unbalanced Forces? 437

What Causes Day and Night? 464

How Does the Moon Move? 478

What Force Moves a Balloon? 502

Where on the Moon Did Astronauts
Land? 510

What Do You Need to Survive in
Space? 515

Which Tool Would Be More Useful in
Space? 520

What Is at the Center? 538

How Can You Safely Observe the Sun? 545

How Does Mars Look From Earth? . . .552

How Big Are the Planets? 562

Which Way Do Comet Tails Point? 572

Is Yeast Alive or Not? 576

How Does Distance Affect an Image? 590

How Does Your Thumb Move? 598

What Determines How Long Stars Live? 608

Why Does the Milky Way Look Hazy? 614

How Does the Universe Expand? 622

Lab zone Try This Activity — Reinforcement of key concepts

As Thick as Honey 94

Keeping Cool 98

Under Pressure 105

How Far Away? 128

Show Me the Oxygen 152

Crystal Clear 188

What Do Metals Do? 200

Observing Change 216

Mostly Cloudy 219

Is Matter Conserved? 226

Scattered Light 258

pH Predictions 276

Dry or Wet? 299

Alphabet Soup 318

Like Oil or Water? 320

Spinning Plates 382

Around and Around 390

Colliding Cars 397

Card Trick 418

Faucet Force 438

Sun Shadows 468

Be a Rocket Scientist 504

A Loopy Ellipse 541

Viewing Sunspots 548

Greenhouse Effect 556

Remote Control 558

Micrometeorites 574

Locating Radio Waves 593

Star Bright 601

A Spiral Galaxy 619

Lab zone Skills Activity — Practice of specific science inquiry skills

Interpreting Data 60

Classifying 136

Predicting 161

Interpreting Data 187

Interpreting Data 237

Designing Experiments 260

Predicting 264

Classifying 301

Calculating 308

Calculating 385

Making Models 482

Calculating 512

Calculating 543

Making Models 566

Communicating 577

Inferring 600

Predicting 610

Lab zone — At-Home **Activity** — Quick, engaging activities for home and family

Quantitative or Qualitative? 9

Which Falls Fastest? 15

Which Line Is Best? 41

Tracking Energy Changes 77

Squeezing Liquids and Gases 95

Finding Graphs 111

Modeling Atoms 130

Everyday Metals 145

Halogen Hunt 155

Looking for Elements 182

Laundry Chemistry 197

Comparing Reaction Rates 239

Family Safety Plan 245

Passing Through 261

pH Lineup .279

Mix It Up 304

Walkabout .341

Hot Wire 363

House of Cards 377

Swing the Bucket 405

Water and Weight 422

Changing Balloon Density 429

Paper Chimney 441

Tracking the Tides 485

Moonwatching 491

Landmarks in Space Flight 514

Spinoffs at Home 524

Sun Symbols 550

Observing Meteors 575

Make a Message 579

Observing Orion 605

Stargazing .627

Math — Point-of-use math practice

Sample Problems

Calculating Density 24

Calculating Acceleration 353

Calculating Force 392

Calculating Momentum 396

Math Skills

Area 32

Ratios 64

Calculating a Concentration 263

Exponents 359

Area 417

Calculating Density 425

Circumference 568

Scientific Notation 620

Math Practice

Calculating Density 24

Calculating Density 26

Area 33

Ratios 67

Balancing Equations 231

Calculating a Concentration 267

Calculating Acceleration 353

Calculating Acceleration 355

Exponents 363

Area 373

Calculating Force 392

Calculating Momentum 396

Calculating Momentum 399

Circumference 569

Scientific Notation 621

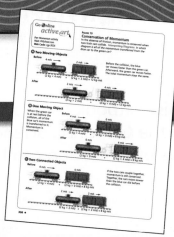

active art. Illustrations come alive online

The Nature of Inquiry 11

Plotting a Line Graph 37

Conserving Matter 71

Gas Laws 108

Periodic Table 134, 178

Radioactive Tracers 162

Balancing Equations 228

Salt Dissolving in Water 259

Carbon Bonding 295

Graphing Motion 346

Energy Transformations 362

Momentum 398

Hydraulic Systems 434

Seasons 469

Moon Phases and Eclipses 483

Multistage Rocket 507

Solar System 543

The Lives of Stars 611

Video Field Trip
Discovery Channel School

Go Online
Web Links

Enhance understanding through dynamic video.

Preview Get motivated with this introduction to the chapter content.

Field Trip Explore a real-world story related to the chapter content.

Assessment Review content and take an assessment.

Get connected to exciting Web resources in every lesson.

SciLINKS Find Web links on topics relating to every section.

Active Art Interact with selected visuals from every chapter online.

Planet Diary® Explore news and natural phenomena through weekly reports.

Science News® Keep up to date with the latest science discoveries.

Experience the complete text-book online and on CD-ROM.

Activities Practice skills and learn content.

Videos Explore content and learn important lab skills.

Audio Support Hear key terms spoken and defined.

Self-Assessment Use instant feedback to help you track your progress.

CALIFORNIA Science Content Standards

This textbook is organized to support your understanding of the California Science Content Standards. Understanding this organization can help you master the standards.

Focus on the BIG Idea

S 8.5

What happens during a chemical reaction?

Every chapter begins with a Focus on the Big Idea question that is linked to a California Science Standard. Focus on the Big Idea poses a question for you to think about as you study the chapter. You will discover the answer to the question as you read.

CALIFORNIA Standards Focus

S 8.9 Scientific progress is made by asking meaningful questions and conducting careful investigations.

 What skills do scientists use to learn about the world?

What do physical scientists study?

Each section begins with a Standards Focus. You will learn about these California Science Standards as you read the section.

The Standards Focus is broken down into two to four Key Concept questions. You will find the answers to these questions as you read the section.

Standards Key

Grade Level   Standard Set and Standard

S 8.2.a

Content Area
S for Science
E-LA for English-Language Arts
Math for Mathematics

The *Science Content Standards for California Public Schools* was adopted in 1998. The California Grade 8 strand is organized into nine general standard sets. The standard sets are Motion, Forces, Structure of Matter, Earth in the Solar System, Reactions, Chemistry of Living Systems, Periodic Table, Density and Buoyancy, and Investigation and Experimentation. Each standard set is divided into a series of specific topic standards. Use this section as a preview for your physical science course and as a review guide when you study for exams.

STANDARD SET 1

Motion

1. **The velocity of an object is the rate of change of its position. As a basis for understanding this concept:**

   1. a. *Students know* know position is defined in relation to some choice of a standard reference point and a set of reference directions.
   1. b. *Students know* that average speed is the total distance traveled divided by the total time elapsed and that the speed of an object along the path traveled can vary.
   1. c. *Students know* how to solve problems involving distance, time, and average speed.

What It Means to You
Understanding position, distance, and speed is key to learning about motion. You describe the position and distance of an object relative to a reference point. For example, you could measure your bike to be 50 meters east of the flagpole. The flagpole is the reference point.

Speed describes how much distance an object travels in a given time period. If you pedal quickly on your bike, you will travel a greater distance in a certain time period than if you pedal slowly. You will learn how to use position, distance, and speed to describe the motion of objects.

Where You Will Learn It
This material is covered in Chapter 9.

STANDARD SET 1, continued

1. d. *Students know* the velocity of an object must be described by specifying both the direction and the speed of the object.
1. e. *Students know* changes in velocity may be due to changes in speed, direction, or both.
1. f. *Students know* how to interpret graphs of position versus time and graphs of speed versus time for motion in a single direction.

What It Means to You

To accurately describe the motion of an object, you must include speed and direction. For example, if you want to get to a baseball game on time, you'll need to know how fast you must travel and in what direction. Velocity describes both the speed and direction of an object. For example, a car might have a speed of 30 miles per hour but a velocity of 30 miles per hour north. You will learn how to describe the velocity of objects.

You can graph the position and speed of an object over time. You can then analyze these graphs to determine if an object is moving at a constant speed, or if it is speeding up or slowing down. You will learn how to graph an object's motion. You will also learn how to interpret motion graphs.

Where You Will Learn It

This material is covered in Chapter 9.

2. Unbalanced forces cause changes in velocity. As a basis for understanding this concept:

2. a. *Students know* a force has both direction and magnitude.

2. b. *Students know* when an object is subject to two or more forces at once, the result is the cumulative effect of all the forces.

2. c. *Students know* when the forces on an object are balanced, the motion of the object does not change.

2. d. *Students know* how to identify separately the two or more forces that are acting on a single static object, including gravity, elastic forces due to tension or compression in matter, and friction.

What It Means To You

A force is a push or a pull. You will learn about the force of gravity, elastic forces, and friction. Usually there are at least two forces acting on an object at any given time. You will learn how to find the net force acting on an object.

If the net force on an object is zero, the forces acting on the object are balanced. The object's motion will not change. The forces on a parked car are balanced. The car's motion will not change until an unbalanced force acts on it. You will learn how to use net force to make predictions about an object's motion.

Where You Will Learn It

This material is covered in Chapter 10.

CALIFORNIA Science Content Standards

STANDARD SET 2, continued

2. e. *Students know* that when the forces on an object are unbalanced, the object will change its velocity (that is, it will speed up, slow down, or change direction).

2. f. *Students know* the greater the mass of an object, the more force is needed to achieve the same rate of change in motion.

2. g. *Students know* the role of gravity in forming and maintaining the shapes of planets, stars, and the solar system.

What It Means To You

Unbalanced forces cause an object's motion to change. When an object's motion changes, the object either speeds up or slows down. For example, when you release a ball, it accelerates to the ground. You will learn how to use net force and mass to calculate the acceleration of an object. You will also learn the effect of increasing force and increasing mass on the acceleration of an object.

Gravity causes objects to fall to Earth. It is also the force responsible for the formation of the solar system, stars, and galaxies. The moon revolves around Earth because of gravity. You will learn about gravity's role in the universe.

Where You Will Learn It

This material is covered in Chapters 10, 11, 12, and 14.

3. **Each of the more than 100 elements of matter has distinct properties and a distinct atomic structure. All forms of matter are composed of one or more of the elements. As a basis for understanding this concept:**

   3. a. *Students know* the structure of the atom and know it is composed of protons, neutrons, and electrons.

   3. b. *Students know* that compounds are formed by combining two or more different elements and that compounds have properties that are different from their constituent elements.

   3. c. *Students know* atoms and molecules form solids by building up repeating patterns, such as the crystal structure of NaCl or long-chain polymers.

   3. d. *Students know* the states of matter (solid, liquid, gas) depend on molecular motion.

   3. e. *Students know* that in solids the atoms are closely locked in position and can only vibrate; in liquids the atoms and molecules are more loosely connected and can collide with and move past one another; and in gases the atoms and molecules are free to move independently, colliding frequently.

   3. f. *Students know* how to use the periodic table to identify elements in simple compounds.

What It Means to You

All matter is made up of atoms. An atom consists of a positively charged nucleus surrounded by negatively charged electrons. There are more than 100 different types of atoms. Their unique atomic structures define elements. The periodic table organizes elements according to their atomic structures. You will learn about atomic structure and the periodic table.

Through the process of bonding, elements combine to form compounds. For example, hydrogen and oxygen bond together to form water. You will learn how elements bond in solids, liquids, and gases.

Where You Will Learn It

This material is covered in Chapters 2, 3, 4, and 5.

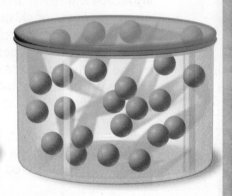

STANDARD SET 4

Earth in the Solar System (Earth Sciences)

4. **The structure and composition of the universe can be learned from studying stars and galaxies and their evolution. As a basis for understanding this concept:**

   4. a. *Students know* galaxies are clusters of billions of stars and may have different shapes.

   4. b. *Students know* that the Sun is one of many stars in the Milky Way galaxy and that stars may differ in size, temperature, and color.

   4. c. *Students know* how to use astronomical units and light-years as measures of distances between the Sun, stars, and Earth.

   4. d. *Students know* that stars are the source of light for all bright objects in outer space and that the Moon and planets shine by reflected sunlight, not by their own light.

   4. e. *Students know* the appearance, general composition, relative position and size, and motion of objects in the solar system, including planets, planetary satellites, comets, and asteroids.

What It Means to You

When you look up at the sky at night, you see many points of light. Some of these points are stars, while others are galaxies. Galaxies consist of clusters of stars. The sun is one of the many stars in the Milky Way galaxy. You will learn how to recognize different types of stars and galaxies.

The sun is the source of all light in the solar system. The planets and the planetary satellites are visible because they reflect sunlight. You will learn about the sun, the planets, and planetary satellites.

Where You Will Learn It

This material is covered in Chapters 12, 13, 14, and 15.

5. Chemical reactions are processes in which atoms are rearranged into different combinations of molecules. As a basis for understanding this concept:

5. a. *Students know* reactant atoms and molecules interact to form products with different chemical properties.

5. b. *Students know* the idea of atoms explains the conservation of matter: In chemical reactions the number of atoms stays the same no matter how they are arranged, so their total mass stays the same.

5. c. *Students know* chemical reactions usually liberate heat or absorb heat.

5. d. *Students know* physical processes include freezing and boiling, in which a material changes form with no chemical reaction.

5. e. *Students know* how to determine whether a solution is acidic, basic, or neutral.

What It Means to You

Have you ever observed what happens when you drop an effervescent tablet in water? The tablet starts to disappear just as bubbles rise to the surface. This is an example of a chemical reaction. The water and the tablet are interacting to form products with different chemical properties. You will learn about chemical reactions.

Conservation of matter states that, in a chemical reaction, the mass of reactants equals the mass of products. You will apply this principle when you balance chemical equations and perform chemical reactions in the laboratory.

Where You Will Learn It

This material is covered in Chapters 2, 3, 6, and 7.

CALIFORNIA

6. Principles of chemistry underlie the functioning of biological systems. As a basis for understanding this concept:

6. a. *Students know* that carbon, because of its ability to combine in many ways with itself and other elements, has a central role in the chemistry of living organisms.

6. b. *Students know* that living organisms are made of molecules consisting largely of carbon, hydrogen, nitrogen, oxygen, phosphorus, and sulfur.

6. c. *Students know* that living organisms have many different kinds of molecules, including small ones, such as water and salt, and very large ones, such as carbohydrates, fats, proteins, and DNA.

What It Means to You

Six elements combine to form most of the mass in living systems. These elements are carbon, hydrogen, nitrogen, oxygen, phosphorus, and sulfur. These elements combine to form large molecules such as DNA and carbohydrates and simpler compounds such as salt and water. You will learn about these molecules and compounds.

Carbon has a unique role in the functioning of biological systems because it can bond to itself and to many other elements. You will learn about the various carbon molecules and their roles. You will also construct models of carbon-based molecules.

Where You Will Learn It

This material is covered in Chapter 8.

	1												18					
1	1 H	**2**												**13**	**14**	**15**	**16**	**17**	2 He
2	3 Li	4 Be												5 B	6 C	7 N	8 O	9 F	10 Ne
3	11 Na	12 Mg	**3**	**4**	**5**	**6**	**7**	**8**	**9**	**10**	**11**	**12**	13 Al	14 Si	15 P	16 S	17 Cl	18 Ar
4	19 K	20 Ca	21 Sc	22 Ti	23 V	24 Cr	25 Mn	26 Fe	27 Co	28 Ni	29 Cu	30 Zn	31 Ga	32 Ge	33 As	34 Se	35 Br	36 Kr
5	37 Rb	38 Sr	39 Y	40 Zr	41 Nb	42 Mo	43 Tc	44 Ru	45 Rh	46 Pd	47 Ag	48 Cd	49 In	50 Sn	51 Sb	52 Te	53 I	54 Xe
6	55 Cs	56 Ba	71 Lu	72 Hf	73 Ta	74 W	75 Re	76 Os	77 Ir	78 Pt	79 Au	80 Hg	81 Tl	82 Pb	83 Bi	84 Po	85 At	86 Rn
7	87 Fr	88 Ra	103 Lr	104 Rf	105 Db	106 Sg	107 Bh	108 Hs	109 Mt	110 Ds	111 Rg	112 *Uub	114 *Uuq					

*Name not officially assigned

Lanthanides

57 La	58 Ce	59 Pr	60 Nd	61 Pm	62 Sm	63 Eu	64 Gd	65 Tb	66 Dy	67 Ho	68 Er	69 Tm	70 Yb

Actinides

89 Ac	90 Th	91 Pa	92 U	93 Np	94 Pu	95 Am	96 Cm	97 Bk	98 Cf	99 Es	100 Fm	101 Md	102 No

STANDARD SET 7

Periodic Table

7. The organization of the periodic table is based on the properties of the elements and reflects the structure of atoms. As a basis for understanding this concept:

7. a. *Students know* how to identify regions corresponding to metals, nonmetals, and inert gases.

7. b. *Students know* each element has a specific number of protons in the nucleus (the atomic number) and each isotope of the element has a different but specific number of neutrons in the nucleus.

7. c. *Students know* substances can be classified by their properties, including their melting temperature, density, hardness, and thermal and electrical conductivity.

What It Means to You

The periodic table is an invaluable tool for chemists. It organizes the elements according to their atomic structures. For example, the atomic number of elements increases from left to right and down one row at a time. You will use the periodic table to find the atomic numbers of elements.

In the periodic table, metals are on the left, semimetals are in the middle, nonmetals are on the right, and inert gases are on the far right. You will use the periodic table to classify a substance as a metal, semimetal, nonmetal, or inert gas.

Where You Will Learn It

This material is covered in Chapters 4 and 5.

8. All objects experience a buoyant force when immersed in a fluid. As a basis for understanding this concept:

8. a. *Students know* density is mass per unit volume.

8. b. *Students know* how to calculate the density of substances (regular and irregular solids and liquids) from measurements of mass and volume.

8. c. *Students know* the buoyant force on an object in a fluid is an upward force equal to the weight of the fluid the object has displaced.

8. d. *Students know* how to predict whether an object will float or sink.

What It Means to You

Suppose you have a steel ball and a foam ball of the same size. The steel ball has a greater density. It has more mass per unit of volume than the foam ball. The volume of the foam ball would have to be many times greater than that of the steel ball in order for the two balls to have the same mass.

You will learn how to calculate the densities of different objects. You will also learn how to use density to predict whether an object will sink or float in a fluid.

Where You Will Learn It

This material is covered in Chapters 1 and 11.

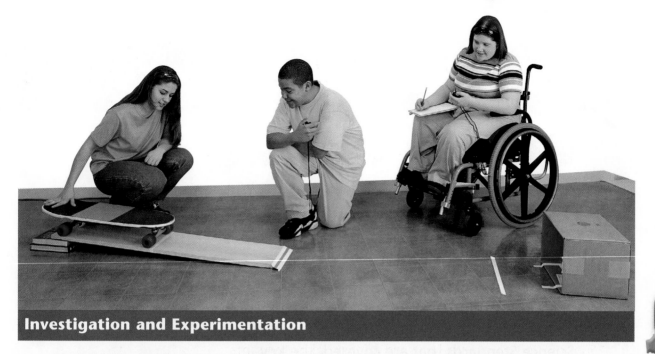

Investigation and Experimentation

9. **Scientific progress is made by asking meaningful questions and conducting careful investigations. As a basis for understanding this concept and addressing the content in the other strands, students should develop their own questions and perform investigations. Students will:**

  9. a. Plan and conduct a scientific investigation to test a hypothesis.

  9. b. Evaluate the accuracy and reproducibility of data.

  9. c. Distinguish between variable and controlled parameters in a test.

  9. d. Recognize the slope of the linear graph as the constant in the relationship $y = kx$ and apply this principle in interpreting graphs constructed from data.

  9. e. Construct appropriate graphs from data and develop quantitative statements about the relationships between variables.

  9. f. Apply simple mathematic relationships to determine a missing quantity in a mathematic expression, given the two remaining terms (including speed = distance/time, density = mass/volume, force = pressure X area, volume = area X height).

  9. g. Distinguish between linear and nonlinear relationships on a graph of data.

What It Means to You

In this program, you will do activities that demonstrate the concepts in the text. You will design and build a vehicle that moves without the use of electricity, gravity, or a person pushing or pulling on it. You will conduct tests to compare how various antacids neutralize acid.

This program contains various types of activities. The *Standards Warm-Ups* introduce the concepts in a section. The *Skills Activities*, *Try This*, and *At-Home Activities* reinforce key concepts from the sections. The Labs reinforce both inquiring skills and science concepts. All of the activities in the text will lead you through the process of discovering meaningful ideas about physical science.

Where You Will Learn It

This material is covered in the labs and activities in the Student Edition.

Your Keys to Success

Read for Meaning

This textbook has been developed to fully support your understanding of the science concepts in the California Science Standards. Each chapter contains built-in reading support.

Before You Read

Use the Standards Focus to preview the California Science Standards that are covered, the key concepts, and key terms in the section.

Standards Focus
The California Science Standards that you will learn are listed at the beginning of each section.

Key Concepts
Each science standard is broken down into smaller ideas called Key Concepts.

Key Terms
Use the list of key terms to preview the vocabulary for each section.

Section 1

What Is Physical Science?

CALIFORNIA
Standards Focus

S 8.9 Scientific progress is made by asking meaningful questions and conducting careful investigations.

- What skills do scientists use to learn about the world?
- What do physical scientists study?

Key Terms
- science
- observing
- inferring
- predicting
- chemistry
- physics

Lab zone **Standards Warm-Up**

How Does a Ball Bounce?

1. Your teacher will give you three balls and a meter stick. Hold the meter stick with the zero end touching the floor.
2. Hold one ball beside the top of the meter stick so it doesn't touch. Drop the ball. Have a partner record the height of the first bounce.
3. Repeat Step 2 twice using the same ball.
4. Repeat Steps 2 and 3 for each of the other balls.

Think It Over
Predicting Can you use your data to predict accurately how each ball will bounce in the future? Explain.

As you walk around an amusement park, you may wonder how the rides work. How does a ferris wheel spin? How do the bumper cars work? What makes the neon lights so colorful? Why don't people fall out of the roller coaster as it completes a loop? These are all questions that physical science can help to answer. The designers of amusement parks must know a great deal about physical science to make sure that visitors experience fun and thrills while staying safe.

An amusement park is a ▶ great place to observe physical science in action.

As You Read

Key Concepts in boldface sentences allow you to focus on the important ideas of the chapter.

> Look for the green and yellow keys to find the key concepts in each section.

Skills Scientists Use

Science is the study of the natural world. Science includes all of the knowledge gained by exploring nature. To think and work like a scientist, you need to use the same skills that they do. **Scientists use the skills of observing, inferring, and predicting to learn more about the natural world.**

Observing Scientists observe things. **Observing** means using one or more senses to gather information. Your senses include sight, hearing, touch, taste, and smell. Each day of your life, you observe things that help you decide what to eat, what to wear, and whether to stay inside or go out.

Scientists usually make observations in a careful, orderly way. They make both qualitative and quantitative observations. Qualitative observations are descriptions that don't involve numbers or measurements. Noticing that a ball is round, that milk smells sour, or that a car is moving is a qualitative observation. Quantitative observations are measurements. You make a quantitative observation when you measure your height or weight. In science, observations may also be called evidence, or data.

Inferring When you explain your observations, you are **inferring**, or making an inference. Inferences are based on reasoning from what you already know. You make inferences all the time without thinking about it. For example, your teacher gives lots of surprise quizzes. So if your teacher walks into the room carrying a stack of paper, you may infer that the pages contain a quiz. But inferences are not always correct. The papers could be announcements to be taken home.

Predicting Every day, people make statements about the future. **Predicting** means making a forecast of what ... n past experience or ... cientists predict the ... and current infor- ... is based on data, ...

... s based on?

FIGURE 1 Inferring
When you explain or interpret your observations, you are making an inference. Inferring *How do you think these young women obtained the stuffed bear? Explain your reasoning.*

Temperature

As you head out the door each morning, one of the first things you might notice is the temperature. Is it cold out this morning? How high will the temperature rise?

Units of Temperature Scientists commonly use the Celsius temperature scale. On the **Celsius Scale,** water freezes at 0°C and boils at 100°C. There are exactly 100 degrees between the freezing point and boiling point of water. Normal human body temperature is about 37°C.

In addition to the Celsius scale, scientists also use another temperature scale, called the **Kelvin scale.** Units on the Kelvin scale are the same size as those on the Celsius scale. **The kelvin (K) is the SI unit of temperature.**

The temperature 0 K on the Kelvin scale is called **absolute zero.** Nothing can get colder than this temperature. Absolute zero is equal to −273°C on the Celsius scale.

Measuring Temperature You can measure temperature using a thermometer. Most thermometers consist of a sealed tube that contains a liquid. The liquid expands or contracts as the temperature changes.

Celsius (°C)   Kelvin (K)

Boiling Point of Water — 100 — 373
Freezing Point of Water — 0 — 273
Absolute Zero — −273 — 0

FIGURE 16
Measuring Temperature
Scientists use the Celsius and Kelvin scales to measure temperature.

After You Read

The Section Assessment tests your understanding of the Key Concepts. Each bank of Reviewing Key Concepts questions here focuses on one of the Key Concepts.

> If you can't answer these items, go back and review the section.

Section 3 Assessment

S 8.8.a, 8.8.b, E-LA: Reading 8.2.0, Math: 7NS1.2

Target Reading Skill Preview Text Structure Complete the graphic organizer for this section. What question did you ask about Weight and Mass? What was your answer?

Reviewing Key Concepts

1. **a. Identifying** What is the standard measurement system used by scientists around the world?
   b. Predicting Suppose that two scientists use different measurement systems in their work. What problems might arise if they shared their data?

2. **a. Listing** What are the SI units of length, mass, volume, density, time, and temperature?

   b. Estimating Estimate the length of a baseball bat and mass of a baseball in SI units. How can you check how close your estimates are?
   c. Describing Outline a step-by-step method for determining the density of a baseball.

Math Practice

Two solid cubes have the same mass. They each have a mass of 50 g.

3. **Calculating Density** Cube A has a volume of 2 cm × 2 cm × 2 cm. What is its density?

4. **Calculating Density** Cube B has a volume of 4 cm × 4 cm × 4 cm. What is its density?

Your Keys to Success

How to Read Science

 The target reading skills introduced on this page will help you read and understand information in this textbook. Each chapter introduces a reading skill. Developing these reading skills is key to becoming a successful reader in science and other subject areas.

Preview Text Structure By understanding how textbooks are organized, you can gain information from them more effectively. This textbook is organized with red headings and blue subheadings. Before you read, preview the headings. Ask yourself questions to guide you as you read. **(Chapter 1)**

Preview Visuals The visuals in your science textbook provide important information. Visuals are photographs, graphs, tables, diagrams, and illustrations. Before you read, take the time to preview the visuals in a section. Look closely at the title, labels, and captions. Then ask yourself questions about the visuals. **(Chapter 4)**

Sequence Many parts of a science textbook are organized by sequence. Sequence is the order in which a series of events occurs. Some sections may discuss events in a process that has a beginning and an end. Other sections may describe a continuous process that does not have an end. **(Chapters 11 and 12)**

Compare and Contrast Science texts often make comparisons. When you compare and contrast, you examine the similarities and differences between things. You can compare and contrast by using a table or a Venn diagram. **(Chapters 5 and 8)**

Analyze Cause and Effect A cause makes something happen. An effect is what happens. When you recognize that one event causes another, you are relating cause and effect. **(Chapter 13)**

Identify Main Ideas As you read, you can understand a section or paragraph more clearly by finding the main idea. The main idea is the most important idea. The details in a section or paragraph support the main idea. Headings and subheadings can often help you identify the main ideas. **(Chapters 2 and 9)**

Identify Supporting Evidence Science textbooks often describe the scientific evidence that supports a theory or hypothesis. Scientific evidence includes data and facts, information whose accuracy can be confirmed by experiments or observation. A hypothesis is a possible explanation for observations made by scientists or an answer to a scientific question. **(Chapter 15)**

Create Outlines You can create outlines to help you clarify the text. An outline shows the relationship between main ideas and supporting details. Use the text structure—headings, subheadings, key concepts, and key terms—to help you figure out information to include in your outline. **(Chapters 3, 7, and 14)**

Take Notes Science chapters are packed with information. Taking good notes is one way to help you remember key ideas and to see the big picture. When you take notes, include key ideas, a few details, and summaries. **(Chapters 6 and 10)**

Target Reading Skills

Each chapter provides a target reading skill with clear instruction to help you read and understand the text. You will apply the skill as you read. Then you will record what you've learned in the section and chapter assessments.

Before You Read
Each chapter introduces a target reading skill and provides examples and practice exercises.

As You Read
As you read, you can use the target reading skill to help you increase your understanding.

After You Read
You can apply the target reading skill in the Section Assessments and in the Chapter Assessments.

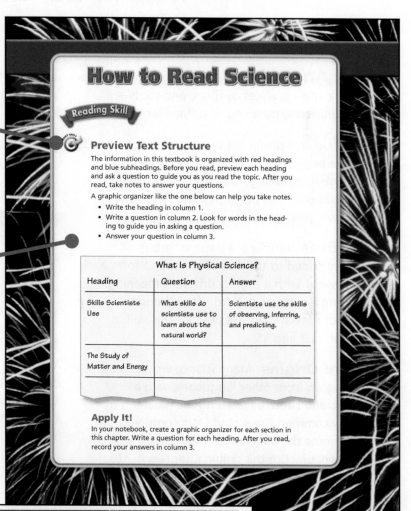

How to Read Science

Reading Skill

Preview Text Structure

The information in this textbook is organized with red headings and blue subheadings. Before you read, preview each heading and ask a question to guide you as you read the topic. After you read, take notes to answer your questions.

A graphic organizer like the one below can help you take notes.

- Write the heading in column 1.
- Write a question in column 2. Look for words in the heading to guide you in asking a question.
- Answer your question in column 3.

What Is Physical Science?

Heading	Question	Answer
Skills Scientists Use	What skills do scientists use to learn about the natural world?	Scientists use the skills of observing, inferring, and predicting.
The Study of Matter and Energy		

Apply It!

In your notebook, create a graphic organizer for each section in this chapter. Write a question for each heading. After you read, record your answers in column 3.

Section 3 Assessment S 8.8.a, 8.8.b, E-LA: Reading 8.2.0, Math: 7NS1.2

Target Reading Skill Preview Text Structure
Complete the graphic organizer for this section. What question did you ask about Weight and Mass? What was your answer?

Reviewing Key Concepts

1. a. **Identifying** What is the standard measurement system used by scientists around the world?
   b. **Predicting** Suppose that two scientists use different measurement systems in their work. What problems might arise if they shared their data?
2. a. **Listing** What are the SI units of length, mass, volume, density, time, and temperature?
   b. **Estimating** Estimate the length of a baseball bat and mass of a baseball in SI units. How can you check how close your estimates are?
   c. **Describing** Outline a step-by-step method for determining the density of a baseball.

Math Practice

Two solid cubes have the same mass. They each have a mass of 50 g.

3. **Calculating Density** Cube A has a volume of 2 cm × 2 cm × 2 cm. What is its density?
4. **Calculating Density** Cube B has a volume of 4 cm × 4 cm × 4 cm. What is its density?

Your Keys to Success

Build Science Vocabulary

Vocabulary Skill

Studying science involves learning a new vocabulary. Here are some vocabulary skills to help you learn the meaning of words you do not recognize.

Word Analysis You can use your knowledge of word parts—prefixes, suffixes, and roots—to determine the meaning of unfamiliar words.

Prefixes A prefix is a word part that is added at the beginning of a root or base word to change its meaning. Knowing the meaning of prefixes will help you figure out new words. You will practice this skill in Chapter 2.

Suffixes A suffix is a letter or group of letters added to the end of a word to form a new word with a slightly different meaning. Adding a suffix to a word often changes its part of speech. You will practice this skill in Chapters 3 and 15.

Word Origins Many science words come to English from other languages, such as Greek and Latin. By learning the meaning of a few common Greek and Latin roots, you can determine the meaning of new science words. You will practice this skill in Chapters 4, 10, 12, and 14.

Use Clues to Determine Meaning

When you come across a word you don't recognize in science texts, you can use context clues to figure out what the word means. First look for clues in the word itself. Then look at the surrounding words, sentences, and paragraphs for clues. You will practice this skill in Chapter 8.

Identify Multiple Meanings

To understand science concepts, you must use terms precisely. Some familiar words may have different meanings in science. Watch for these multiple-meaning words as you read. You will practice this skill in Chapters 6 and 11.

Identify Related Word Forms

You can increase your vocabulary by learning related forms of words or word families. If you know the meaning of a verb form, you may be able to figure out the related noun and adjective forms. You will practice this skill in Chapter 7.

atmos + sphaira = atmosphere
vapor   sphere   a layer of
gas   vapor or
                   gases that
                   surrounds
                   Earth

Vocabulary Skills

One of the important steps in reading this science textbook is to be sure that you understand the Key Terms. Your book shows several strategies to help learn important vocabulary.

Build Science Vocabulary

The images shown here represent some of the key terms in this chapter. You can use this vocabulary skill to help you understand the meaning of some key terms in this chapter.

Vocabulary Skill

Suffixes

A suffix is a letter or group of letters added to the end of a word to change its meaning and often its part of speech. For example, the suffix *-ation* added to a verb can form a noun that means "process of" or "action of."

| prepare | + | ation | = | preparation |
| | | process of | | the process of preparing |

In this chapter, you will learn key terms that end in the suffixes *-ation*, *-ine*, and *-sion*.

Suffix	Meaning	Part of Speech	Key Terms
-ation	State of, process of, act of	Noun	Vaporization, evaporation, condensation, sublimation
-ine	Consisting of	Adjective	Crystalline
-sion	State of, process of, act of	Noun	Surface tension

Apply It!

Vapor is another word for gas. Use the chart above to predict the meaning of *vaporization*. Revise your definition as needed.

When you come across an unfamiliar word, look at the suffix to help you determine the meaning. Then check the definition in the glossary or a dictionary.

gas

Before You Read

Each chapter introduces a Vocabulary Skill with examples and practice exercises. Key Terms come alive through visuals. The beginning of each section lists the Key Terms.

Changes Between Solid and Gas

If you live where the winters are cold, you may have noticed that snow seems to disappear even when the temperature stays well below freezing. This change is the result of sublimation. **Sublimation** occurs when the surface particles of a solid gain enough energy that they form a gas. **During sublimation, particles of a solid do not pass through the liquid state as they form a gas.** As a solid substance sublimates into a gas, the relative freedom of motion of its particles increases.

One example of sublimation occurs with dry ice. Dry ice is the common name for solid carbon dioxide. At ordinary atmospheric pressures, carbon dioxide cannot exist as a liquid. So instead of melting, solid carbon dioxide changes directly into a gas. As it changes state, the carbon dioxide absorbs thermal energy. If warmer materials are placed near dry ice, they will lose thermal energy and become colder. For this reason, dry ice can be used to keep things cold when a refrigerator is not available. When dry ice becomes a gas, it cools water vapor in the nearby air. The water vapor then condenses into a liquid, forming fog around the dry ice.

FIGURE 13
Dry Ice
When solid carbon dioxide, called "dry ice," sublimates, it changes directly into a gas. *Predicting If you allowed the dry ice to stand at room temperature for several hours, what would be left in the glass dish? Explain.*

Reading Checkpoint What physical state is skipped during the sublimation of a substance?

As You Read

Each Key Term is highlighted in yellow, appears in boldfaced type, and is followed by a definition.

Section 2 Assessment

S 8.3.d, 8.5.d, E-LA: Reading 8.1.0, Writing 8.2.0

Vocabulary Skill Suffixes Complete the sentences using the correct word form (*vaporize/vaporization*). As a pot of water boils, the liquid will ____ and form a gas. Boiling and evaporation are two types of ____.

Reviewing Key Concepts

1. a. Reviewing What happens to the particles of a solid as it becomes a liquid?
   b. Applying Concepts How does the thermal energy of solid water change as it melts?
   c. Making Judgments You are stranded in a blizzard. You need water to drink, and you're trying to stay warm. Should you melt snow and then drink it, or just eat snow? Explain.
2. a. Describing What is vaporization?
   b. Comparing and Contrasting Name the two types of vaporization. Tell how they are similar and how they differ.

   c. Relating Cause and Effect Why does the evaporation of sweat cool your body on a warm day?
3. a. Identifying What process occurs as pieces of dry ice gradually get smaller?
   b. Interpreting Photos What is happening in the air around the dry ice in Figure 13? Why does the fog form?

Writing in Science

Using Analogies Write a short essay in which you create an analogy to describe particle motion. Compare the movements and positions of people dancing with the motions of water molecules in liquid water and in water vapor.

After You Read

You can practice the Vocabulary Skill in the Section Assessments. You can apply your understanding of the Key Terms in the Chapter Assessments.

Your Keys to Success

Build Science Vocabulary

High-Use Academic Words

High-use academic words are words that are used frequently in classroom reading, writing, and discussions. They are different from Key Terms because they appear in many subject areas.

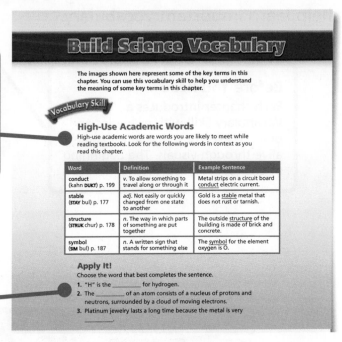

Learn the Words

Each unit contains a chapter that introduces high-use academic words. The introduction describes the words, provides examples, and includes practice exercises.

Practice Using the Words

You can practice using the high-use academic words in Apply It! and the section assessments.

Focus on Physical Science High-Use Academic Words

Learning the meaning of these words will help you improve your reading comprehension in all subject areas.

accelerate	consist	distribute	locate	region
accurate	constant	ensure	maintain	release
alter	construct	estimate	method	reliable
area	consumer	evidence	minimize	require
assume	contact	expand	neutral	research
benefit	contract	expel	obvious	resource
category	contrast	explore	occurred	revolution
complex	define	factor	operate	series
concentrate	definite	flexible	potential	significant
concept	detect	formula	predict	similar
conclude	develop	individual	principle	source
conduct	displace	interact	recover	stable

Investigations

You can explore the concepts in this textbook through inquiry. Like a real scientist, you can develop your own scientific questions and perform labs and activities to find answers. Follow the steps below when doing a lab.

1 Read the whole lab.

5 Record your data.

2 Write a purpose. What is the purpose of this activity?

3 Write a hypothesis. What is a possible explanation? Hypotheses lead to predictions that can be tested.

4 Follow each step in the procedure. Pay attention to safety icons.

Lab zone Skills Lab

Making Sense of Density

S 8.8.b, 8.9.b

Problem
Does the density of a material vary with volume?

Skills Focus
drawing conclusions, measuring, controlling variables

Materials
• balance • water • paper towels
• metric ruler • graduated cylinder, 100-mL
• wooden stick, about 6 cm long
• ball of modeling clay, about 5 cm wide
• crayon with paper removed

Procedure

1. Use a balance to find the mass of the wooden stick. Record the mass in a data table like the one shown above right.
2. Add enough water to a graduated cylinder so that the stick can be completely submerged. Measure the initial volume of the water.
3. Place the stick in the graduated cylinder. Measure the new volume of the water.
4. The volume of the stick is the difference between the water levels in Steps 2 and 3. Calculate this volume and record it.
5. The density of the stick equals its mass divided by its volume. Calculate and record its density.
6. Thoroughly dry the stick with a paper towel. Then carefully break the stick into two pieces. Repeat Steps 1 through 5 with one piece. Then, repeat Steps 1 through 5 with the other piece.
7. Repeat Steps 1 through 6 using the clay rolled into a rope.
8. Repeat using the crayon.

Data Table			
Object	Mass (g)	Volume Change (cm³)	Density (g/cm³)
Wooden stick			
Whole			
Piece 1			
Piece 2			
Modeling clay			
Whole			
Piece 1			
Piece 2			
Crayon			
Whole			
Piece 1			
Piece 2			

Analyze and Conclude

1. **Measuring** For each object you tested, compare the density of the whole object with the densities of the pieces of the object.
2. **Drawing Conclusions** Use your results to explain how density can be used to identify a material.
3. **Controlling Variables** Why did you dry the objects in Step 6?
4. **Communicating** Write a paragraph explaining how you would change the procedure to obtain more data. Tell how having more data would affect your answers to Questions 1 and 2 above.

Design an Experiment

Design an experiment you could use to determine the density of olive oil. With your teacher's permission, carry out your plan. Use the library or the Internet to find the actual density of olive oil. Compare your experimental value with the actual value, and explain why they may differ.

Oral presentations should include all of the information that you would include in a lab report.

6 Analyze your results. Answering the questions will help you draw conclusions.

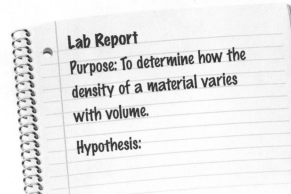

Lab Report
Purpose: To determine how the density of a material varies with volume.

Hypothesis:

7 Communicate your results in a written report or oral presentation. Your report should include:
◆ a hypothesis ◆ a purpose
◆ the steps of the procedure
◆ a record of your results
◆ a conclusion

For more information on Science Inquiry, Scientific Investigations and Safety refer to the Skills Handbook and Appendix A.

This scientist is busy at work ▶
in a laboratory.

Focus on the

S 8.9

BIG Idea

How do scientists investigate the natural world?

Check What You Know

Suppose you want to test whether sugar dissolves more quickly in cold water or hot water. How would you find out? How would you know if your answer is reliable?

Build Science Vocabulary

The images shown here represent some of the Key Terms in this chapter. You can use this vocabulary skill to help you understand the meaning of some Key Terms in this chapter.

High-Use Academic Words

Academic words are terms that are frequently used in classroom reading, writing, and discussions. These words are different from Key Terms because they appear in many science chapters as well as in other subject areas. Look for these words in context as you read this chapter.

Word	Definition	Example Sentence
constant (KAHN stunt) p. 12	*adj.* Staying the same	The temperature was kept <u>constant</u> in the experiment.
procedure (proh SEE jur) p. 44	*n.* The method of doing some action, especially the sequence of steps to be followed	Follow the <u>procedure</u> explained in the laboratory manual.
significant (sig NIF uh kunt) p. 32	*adj.* Having importance or meaning	A <u>significant</u> number of people voted against the bill.

Apply It!

From the table above, choose the word that best completes each sentence.

1. The amount of energy needed to move a piano is _____.
2. Be sure to follow the correct _____ during a fire drill.
3. The driver maintained a _____ speed.

model

chemistry

volume

density

Change in Shadow Height

graph

Height of Shadow (cm) vs. Distance Between Object and Light (cm)

weight

Chapter 1 Vocabulary

Section 1 (page 6)

science predicting
observing chemistry
inferring physics

Section 2 (page 10)

scientific inquiry controlled experiment
hypothesis data
parameter communicating
manipulated variable model
  scientific theory
responding variable scientific law

Section 3 (page 16)

SI density
weight Celsius scale
mass Kelvin scale
volume absolute zero
meniscus

Section 4 (page 30)

estimate significant
accuracy   figures
reproducibility precision

Section 5 (page 34)

graph line of best fit
horizontal axis linear graph
vertical axis slope
origin nonlinear graph
coordinate
data point

interactive
Textbook

Build Science Vocabulary
Online
Visit: PHSchool.com
Web Code: cxj-1010

How to Read Science

Preview Text Structure

The information in this textbook is organized with red headings and blue subheadings. Before you read, preview each heading and ask a question to guide you as you read the topic. After you read, take notes to answer your questions.

A graphic organizer like the one below can help you take notes.

- Write the heading in column 1.
- Write a question in column 2. Look for words in the heading to guide you in asking a question.
- Answer your question in column 3.

What Is Physical Science?

Heading	Question	Answer
Skills Scientists Use	What skills do scientists use to learn about the natural world?	Scientists use the skills of observing, inferring, and predicting.
The Study of Matter and Energy		

Apply It!

In your notebook, create a graphic organizer for each section in this chapter. Write a question for each heading. After you read, record your answers in column 3.

Standards **Investigation**

S 8.8.a

Design and Build a Density-Calculating System

How do you find the density of something if you don't have a balance to measure its mass? Suppose you can't use a graduated cylinder to measure the volume of such items as honey or table sugar. Can you build your own balance and devise a way to find the volume of items that are not easily measured with a ruler?

Your Goal

To design and build a device for collecting data that can be used to calculate the density of powdered solids and liquids

To complete the investigation, you must

- build a device to measure accurately the masses of powdered solids and liquids
- develop a method to measure volume without using standard laboratory equipment
- obtain data you can use to calculate the density of items
- follow the safety guidelines in Appendix A

Plan It!

Preview the chapter to find out how mass, volume, and density are related. Research how balances are constructed and how they work. Build a balance out of the materials supplied by your teacher. Then devise a container with a known volume that you can use to find the volumes of your test materials. When your teacher approves your plan, test your system. Redesign and retest your system to improve its accuracy and reliability.

What Is Physical Science?

CALIFORNIA
Standards Focus

S 8.9 Scientific progress is made by asking meaningful questions and conducting careful investigations.

- What skills do scientists use to learn about the world?
- What do physical scientists study?

Key Terms

- science
- observing
- inferring
- predicting
- chemistry
- physics

Lab zone Standards **Warm-Up**

How Does a Ball Bounce?

1. Your teacher will give you three balls and a meter stick. Hold the meter stick with the zero end touching the floor.
2. Hold one ball beside the top of the meter stick so it doesn't touch. Drop the ball. Have a partner record the height of the first bounce.
3. Repeat Step 2 twice using the same ball.
4. Repeat Steps 2 and 3 for each of the other balls.

Think It Over
Predicting Can you use your data to predict accurately how each ball will bounce in the future? Explain.

As you walk around an amusement park, you may wonder how the rides work. How does a ferris wheel spin? How do the bumper cars work? What makes the neon lights so colorful? Why don't people fall out of the roller coaster as it completes a loop? These are all questions that physical science can help to answer. The designers of amusement parks must know a great deal about physical science to make sure that visitors experience fun and thrills while staying safe.

An amusement park is a ▶ great place to observe physical science in action.

Skills Scientists Use

Science is the study of the natural world. Science includes all of the knowledge gained by exploring nature. To think and work like a scientist, you need to use the same skills that they do. ● **Scientists use the skills of observing, inferring, and predicting to learn more about the natural world.**

Observing Scientists observe things. **Observing** means using one or more senses to gather information. Your senses include sight, hearing, touch, taste, and smell. Each day of your life, you observe things that help you decide what to eat, what to wear, and whether to stay inside or go out.

Scientists usually make observations in a careful, orderly way. They make both qualitative and quantitative observations. Qualitative observations are descriptions that don't involve numbers or measurements. Noticing that a ball is round, that milk smells sour, or that a car is moving is a qualitative observation. Quantitative observations are measurements. You make a quantitative observation when you measure your height or weight. In science, observations may also be called evidence, or data.

Inferring When you explain your observations, you are **inferring,** or making an inference. Inferences are based on reasoning from what you already know. You make inferences all the time without thinking about it. For example, your teacher gives lots of surprise quizzes. So if your teacher walks into the room carrying a stack of paper, you may infer that the pages contain a quiz. But inferences are not always correct. The papers could be announcements to be taken home.

Predicting Every day, people make statements about the future. **Predicting** means making a forecast of what will happen in the future based on past experience or evidence. For example, some scientists predict the weather based on past experience and current information. Because a weather forecast is based on data, it is a prediction rather than a guess.

 **Reading Checkpoint** What are inferences based on?

Go Online
PHSchool.com

For: More on scientific thinking
Visit: PHSchool.com
Web Code: cgd-6011

FIGURE 1 Inferring
When you explain or interpret your observations, you are making an inference. **Inferring** *How do you think these young women obtained the stuffed bear? Explain your reasoning.*

▲ A chemist is removing a liquid from a flask.

▲ This physicist is experimenting with lasers.

FIGURE 2
Careers in Physical Science

People who work in physical science study changes in matter and energy. Chemists, physicists, and engineers are examples of people who work in physical science.

The Study of Matter and Energy

🔑 **Physical science is the study of matter, energy, and the changes they undergo.** Matter is all around you. It is anything that has mass and occupies space. Energy is the ability to do work or cause change.

Branches of Physical Science Physical science is divided into two main branches: chemistry and physics. **Chemistry** is the study of the properties of matter and how matter changes. When you study chemistry, you will learn about the particles that make up matter and why different forms of matter have different properties. You will find out how matter can change and why. For example, you'll learn why some materials burn while others do not.

Physics is the study of matter, energy, motion, and forces, and how they interact. When you study physics, you will learn about the different forms of energy and the physical laws that govern energy. You will also find out how the laws of physics apply to Earth, the solar system, and the universe beyond.

All of the people shown in Figure 2 work in some area of physical science. Some careers involve scientific research. Other careers, such as photography, piano tuning, or firefighting, require that you understand physical science. You may be thinking that physical science is important only if you work in careers like these. But you use physical science all the time. For example, when you blow on a spoonful of soup to cool it down, you are using physical science. In this book, you will learn about many more everyday events involving physical science.

▲ Two engineers are installing communications equipment on a mountaintop.

Big Ideas of Physical Science Physical scientists apply certain big ideas in their work. As you read this book, you will begin to grasp four concepts that help to unify physical sciences:

- force and energy;
- the laws of conservation;
- atoms, molecules, and the atomic theory;
- the behavior of particles of matter in solids, liquids, and gases.

These big ideas serve as important organizers that will be required as you continue to learn science. Keep reading to find out how these concepts apply to you and the world around you!

 **Reading Checkpoint** **What is physics?**

Section 1 Assessment

S 8.9, E-LA: Reading 8.2.0

⟳ **Target Reading Skill** Preview Text Structure Complete the graphic organizer for this section. How did you answer your question about The Study of Matter and Energy?

Reviewing Key Concepts

1. a. **Listing** Name three skills that scientists use to learn more about the natural world.
   b. **Comparing and Contrasting** How do observing and inferring differ?
   c. **Classifying** Is this statement an observation or an inference? *It must be raining outside.* Explain.
2. a. **Defining** What is physical science?
   b. **Identifying** What are the two main areas of physical science?
   c. **Inferring** How would a knowledge of physical science be useful to a musician? To a photographer?

Lab zone **At-Home Activity**

Quantitative or Qualitative? Look around your room at home. Write down three qualitative and three quantitative observations. How do these two types of observations differ from one another?

Scientific Inquiry

CALIFORNIA
Standards Focus

S 8.9.a Plan and conduct a scientific investigation to test a hypothesis.
S 8.9.c Distinguish between variable and controlled parameters in a test.

How do scientists investigate the natural world?

What role do models, theories, and laws play in science?

Key Terms
- scientific inquiry
- hypothesis
- parameter
- manipulated variable
- responding variable
- controlled experiment
- data
- communicating
- model
- scientific theory
- scientific law

A shadow puppet ▼

Lab zone Standards **Warm-Up**

Can You Make a Shadow Disappear?
1. Using a piece of clay as a base, set up a straw so that it stands up straight.
2. Shine a flashlight on the straw from as many directions as you can. Observe the different shadows you create. Record your observations.
3. Determine whether you can make the shadow disappear while using the light. If you can, describe how you did it.

Think It Over
Posing Questions If you had a meter stick among your materials, what are two other questions you could investigate?

Have you ever made shadow puppets on a wall? Shadows are produced when something blocks light from shining on a surface. Making shadow puppets might make you wonder about light and shadows. Your curiosity can be the first step in scientific inquiry. **Scientific inquiry** refers to the different ways scientists study the natural world. It is the ongoing process of discovery in science.

Just like you, scientists often find that being curious is the first step in scientific inquiry. Scientists have other habits of mind as well: honesty, open-mindedness, skepticism, and creativity. Honesty means reporting observations truthfully. Open-mindedness is accepting new and different ideas. Skepticism is being doubtful about information presented without evidence. Creativity involves coming up with new ways to solve problems.

The Process of Inquiry
Scientific inquiry does not always occur in the same way. But, certain processes are often involved. **The processes that scientists use in inquiry include posing questions, developing hypotheses, designing experiments, collecting and interpreting data, drawing conclusions, and communicating ideas and results.** Figure 3 shows some of the ways that these processes can happen.

FIGURE 3
The Nature of Inquiry

There is no set path that a scientific inquiry must follow. Different scientists may choose different paths when studying the same event.

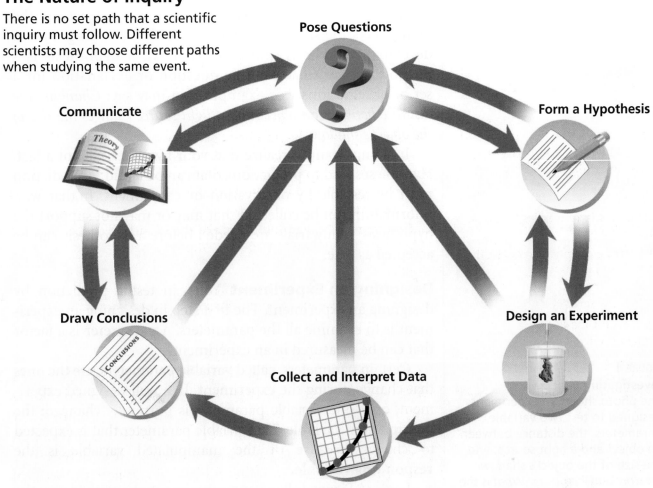

Pose Questions

Communicate

Form a Hypothesis

Draw Conclusions

Design an Experiment

Collect and Interpret Data

Posing Questions Suppose you want to learn more about light and shadows. You might ask, Does the size of a shadow depend on the distance between the light and the object? How is a shadow affected by the light's position? Will you get shadows if you have several light sources?

All those questions about light and shadows are scientific questions because you can answer them by making observations. For example, by observing the shadow of a tree over several hours during the day, you can see how the shadow changes with the sun's position.

Not all questions are scientific, however. For example, suppose you ask, "Which is the most interesting photo in a photography contest?" The answer to that question is based on personal opinion, not on evidence. Scientific inquiry cannot answer questions based on opinions, values, or judgments.

Go Online
active art

For: The Nature of Inquiry activity
Visit: PHSchool.com
Web Code: cgp-6012

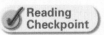
Reading Checkpoint) **What scientific questions can you ask about light and shadows?**

Developing Hypotheses Scientific inquiry moves forward when ideas can be tested. For example, suppose you want to find out how the distance between the object and the light affects the size of a shadow. Your first step might be to develop a hypothesis (plural: *hypotheses*). A **hypothesis** is a possible answer to a scientific question or explanation for a set of observations. For example, you may say: *Changing the distance between an object and a light source changes the size of the object's shadow.*

It is important to realize that your hypothesis is not a fact. Hypotheses lead to predictions that can be tested. A prediction must be testable by observation or experiment. In that way, information can be collected that may or may not support the hypothesis. Many trials are needed before a hypothesis can be accepted as true.

Designing an Experiment You can test a prediction by designing an experiment. The first step in designing an experiment is to examine all the parameters. A **parameter** is a factor that can be measured in an experiment.

Certain parameters, called variable parameters, are the ones that change during the experiment. In a well-designed experiment, only one variable parameter is purposely changed: the **manipulated variable.** The variable parameter that is expected to change because of the manipulated variable is the **responding variable.**

Look at Figure 4. For your experiment about shadows, the manipulated variable is the distance between the light source and the object. The responding variable is the height of the shadow.

To be sure that changes in the manipulated variable are causing the changes in the responding variable, scientists keep all the other parameters controlled—that is, kept constant. Figure 4 shows some parameters that need to be controlled in your shadow experiment: the type of light, the height and angle of the light, and the distance between the object and the wall. An investigation in which only one parameter is manipulated at a time is called a **controlled experiment.**

Reading Checkpoint **What is a hypothesis?**

FIGURE 4
Investigating Shadows
The photo shows an experiment designed to test two variable parameters: the distance between an object and a light source, and the size of the object's shadow.
Interpreting Diagrams *What is the manipulated variable in the experiment?*

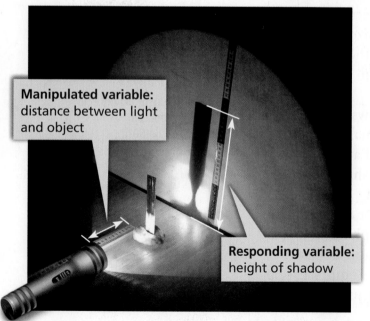

Manipulated variable: distance between light and object

Responding variable: height of shadow

Shadow Experiment	
Distance Between Object and Light (cm)	Height of Shadow (cm)
10	32
15	27
20	25
25	23
30	22
35	21
40	20

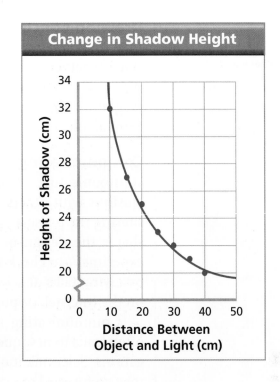

Change in Shadow Height

FIGURE 5
Showing Experimental Results
The results of the shadow experiment are shown here as a data table and as a graph.
Interpreting Graphs *What relationship do the data show?*

Collecting and Interpreting Data Before scientists begin an experiment, they usually create a data table for recording their data. **Data** are the facts, figures, and other evidence gathered through observations. A data table provides an organized way to collect and record observations. Figure 5 shows a data table that you might have made during your shadow experiment.

Recall that observations can be qualitative or quantitative. Data can also be qualitative or quantitative. Qualitative data can be recorded as notes in a journal or log. Quantitative data consist of measurements. Notice that the measurements in the data table are expressed in centimeters (cm), a unit of length.

After the data are collected, they need to be interpreted, or explained. Graphs are a useful way to analyze quantitative data because they can reveal trends or patterns in the data. Look at the graph in Figure 5. It shows that as the distance between the object and the light increased, the height of the shadow decreased. You can learn more about using data tables and graphs in the Skills Handbook.

 **Reading Checkpoint** How can a graph help you analyze data?

Video Field Trip

Discovery Channel School

The Work of Scientists

FIGURE 6
A Scientific Model
This illustration is a model of the solar system. The solid blue lines represent the paths followed by the planets as they revolve around the sun.

Drawing Conclusions After scientists interpret their data, they draw a conclusion about their hypothesis. A conclusion states whether or not the data support the hypothesis. For the data in the shadow experiment, you would conclude that the height of a shadow decreases as the light is moved farther away from an object.

Communicating An important part of scientific inquiry is communicating. **Communicating** is sharing ideas and conclusions with others through writing and speaking. It is also sharing the process you used in your inquiry. When a scientist shares the design of an experiment, others can repeat that experiment to check the results. Scientists often communicate by giving talks at scientific meetings, exchanging information on the Internet, or publishing articles in scientific journals.

Communicating information about scientific discoveries often leads to new questions, new hypotheses, and new investigations. Scientific inquiry is a process with many paths. Work may go forward or even backward when testing out new ideas.

How Science Develops

Over the years, as scientists studied the natural world, they did more than collect facts. They developed more complete explanations for their observations. ● **Scientists use models and develop theories and laws to increase people's understanding of the natural world.**

Scientific Models Sometimes, it may be impossible to observe certain objects and natural processes. So a scientist will make a model. A **model** is a picture, diagram, computer image, or other representation of an object or process. Physical models, such as a representation of the solar system, may look like the real thing. Other models can be generated by computers, such as the flight plan of a space vehicle. Still others can be mathematical equations or words that describe how something works. Certain models, such as models of atoms (the particles that make up matter), have been especially important in building up our understanding of the natural world.

Reading Checkpoint What is a model?

Scientific Theories In some cases, many observations can be connected by one explanation. This can lead to the development of a scientific theory. A **scientific theory** is a well-tested explanation for a wide range of observations or experimental results. For example, according to the atomic theory, all substances are composed of tiny particles called atoms. The atomic theory helps explain many observations, such as why water freezes or boils at certain temperatures, and why it can dissolve many other materials.

Scientists accept a theory only when there is a large body of evidence that supports it. However, future evidence may not support the theory. If that happens, scientists may modify the theory or discard it altogether.

Scientific Laws Have you ever heard someone say, "What goes up must come down"? When scientists repeatedly observe the same result in specific circumstances, they may develop a scientific law. A **scientific law** is a statement that describes what scientists expect to happen every time under a particular set of conditions.

A scientific law describes an observed pattern in nature without attempting to explain it. You can think of a scientific law as a rule of nature. For example, the law of gravity states that all objects in the universe attract each other. This law has been verified over and over again.

FIGURE 7
A Scientific Law
According to the law of gravity, this parachutist will eventually land back on Earth.

Section 2 Assessment

S 8.9.a, 8.9.c,
E-LA: Reading 8.1.0

Vocabulary Skill High-Use Academic Words In an experiment, why would you keep certain parameters *constant*?

Reviewing Key Concepts

1. a. **Defining** What is scientific inquiry?
   b. **Listing** Name six processes that are often involved in scientific inquiry.
   c. **Inferring** How can an experiment that disproves a hypothesis be useful?
2. a. **Defining** What is a scientific theory? A scientific law?
   b. **Comparing and Contrasting** How do scientific theories differ from scientific laws?
   c. **Classifying** The students who conducted the shadow length experiment concluded that their results supported their hypothesis. Can their supported hypothesis be called a scientific theory? Why or why not?

Lab zone At-Home Activity

Which Falls Fastest? Design an experiment to determine which falls fastest—an unfolded sheet of paper, a sheet of paper folded in fourths, or a crumpled sheet of paper. Be sure to develop a hypothesis, design a controlled experiment, and collect data. Do your data support your hypothesis? Discuss your results with a family member.

3 Measurement

CALIFORNIA
Standards Focus

S 8.8.a Students know density is mass per unit volume.

S 8.8.b Students know how to calculate the density of substances (regular and irregular solids and liquids) from measurements of mass and volume.

🔑 Why do scientists use a standard measurement system?

🔑 What are the SI units of measure for length, mass, volume, density, time, and temperature?

Key Terms

- SI
- weight
- mass
- volume
- meniscus
- density
- Celsius scale
- Kelvin Scale
- absolute zero

Lab zone Standards **Warm-Up**

Which Has More Mass?

1. Your teacher will provide you with some small objects. Look at the objects, but do not touch them.
2. Predict which object is lightest, which is second lightest, and so on. Record your predictions.
3. Use a triple-beam balance to find the mass of each object.
4. Based on the masses, list the objects from lightest to heaviest.

Think It Over

Drawing Conclusions How did your predictions compare with your results? Are bigger objects always heavier than smaller objects? Do objects of the same size always have the same mass? Why or why not?

Did you ever ask a relative for an old family recipe? If so, the answer might have been, "Use just the right amount of flour and water. Add a spoonful of oil and a pinch of salt. Bake it for awhile until it looks just right."

Instructions like these would be difficult to follow. How much flour is "just the right amount"? How big is a spoonful or a pinch? You could end up with disastrous results.

In tasks such as cooking, ▶ measurements can be critical to success!

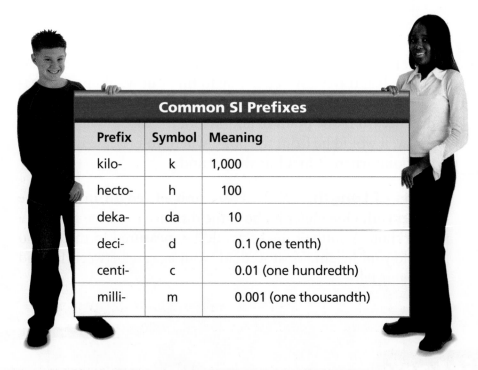

Common SI Prefixes		
Prefix	Symbol	Meaning
kilo-	k	1,000
hecto-	h	100
deka-	da	10
deci-	d	0.1 (one tenth)
centi-	c	0.01 (one hundredth)
milli-	m	0.001 (one thousandth)

FIGURE 8
SI units, based on multiples of 10, are easy to use. Knowing what the prefixes mean can help you judge how big or small a measurement is.
Calculating *How much larger is a* kilo- *than a* deka-?

A Standard Measurement System

The recipe example illustrates the importance of using a standard system of measurement. This is especially true in science. Using the same system of measurement minimizes confusion among scientists all over the world.

More than 200 years ago, most countries used their own measurement systems. Sometimes two or more different systems were used in the same country. In the 1790s, scientists in France developed a universal system of measurement called the metric system. A metric system is a system of measurement based on the number 10.

Modern scientists use an expanded metric system called the International System of Units, abbreviated as **SI** (for the French, *Système International d'Unités*). Scientists all over the world use SI units to measure length, volume, mass, density, temperature, and time. ⊂ **Using SI as the standard system of measurement allows scientists to compare data and communicate with each other about their results.** In this book, you will use both SI and other metric units.

Figure 8 lists the prefixes used to name the most common SI units. You may have seen these prefixes before in units such as centimeters or kilograms. Because SI units are based on multiples of 10, you can easily convert from one unit to another. For example, 1 meter equals 100 centimeters. You can learn about converting between SI units in the Skills Handbook.

 **Reading Checkpoint** SI units are based on multiples of what number?

Common Conversions for Length	
1 km	= 1,000 m
1 m	= 100 cm
1 m	= 1,000 mm
1 cm	= 10 mm

Length

How far can you throw a softball? Can you estimate by eye how far the ball travels? A better way to find out would be to measure the distance, or length, that the ball travels. Length is the distance from one point to another. In the case of your softball throw, it would be from the point where you release the ball to the point where it first hits the ground.

Units of Length 🔑 **The basic unit of length in SI is the meter (m).** One meter is about the distance from the floor to a doorknob. A softball throw would be measured in meters. So would your height. Most students your age are between 1.5 and 2 meters tall.

Science and **History**

Measurement Systems
Like so much else in science, systems of measurement developed gradually over time in different parts of the world.

1400 B.C.
A Simple Balance
The ancient Egyptians developed the first known weighing instrument, a simple balance with a pointer. Earlier, they had been the first to standardize a measure of length. The length, called a cubit, was originally defined as the distance between the elbow and the tip of the middle finger.

640 B.C.
Standard Units of Weight
Merchants in the Middle East and Mediterranean used units of weight to be sure that they received the correct amount of gold and silver in trade and to check the purity of the metal. A *talent* was about 25 kilograms, and a *mina* was about 500 grams. The Lydians minted the first true coins to have standard weight and value.

200 B.C.
Standard Measures
Shih Huang Ti, the first emperor of China, set standards for weight, length, and volume. He also improved travel conditions by setting standards for the widths of roads and for the distance between chariot wheels.

1500 B.C.	1000 B.C.	500 B.C.	A.D. 1

To measure objects smaller than a meter, scientists use units called the centimeter (cm) or the millimeter (mm). The prefix *centi-* means "one-hundredth," while the prefix *milli-* means one-thousandth. One meter, then, is equal to 100 centimeters or 1,000 millimeters. The length of a typical sheet of loose-leaf paper is 28 centimeters, which is equal to 280 millimeters.

What unit would you use to measure a long distance, such as the distance between two cities? For such measurements, scientists use a unit known as the kilometer (km). The prefix *kilo-* means one thousand. There are 1,000 meters in a kilometer. If you were to draw a straight line between San Francisco and Boston, the line would measure about 4,300 kilometers.

Writing in Science

Research and Write While scientists rely on SI units, people use different measurement units for other purposes. Research the units used in sailing, horse breeding, diamond cutting, farming, or another activity that interests you. Write a few paragraphs about your findings.

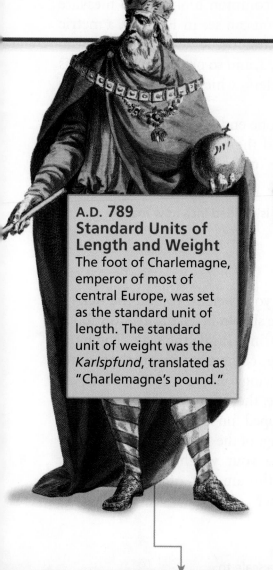

A.D. 789
Standard Units of Length and Weight
The foot of Charlemagne, emperor of most of central Europe, was set as the standard unit of length. The standard unit of weight was the *Karlspfund*, translated as "Charlemagne's pound."

A.D. 1714
Thermometer
Gabriel Fahrenheit invented the thermometer, a temperature-measuring device that relies on the expansion of mercury with heat. His name later came to be used as the name for a temperature scale.

A.D. 1983
International Standards
The International Bureau of Weights and Measures in France defined a single set of standard units. Scientists throughout the world use these units in their work. The official kilogram measure, shown above, is kept in a vacuum chamber.

A.D. 500   **A.D. 1000**   **A.D. 1500**   **A.D. 2000**

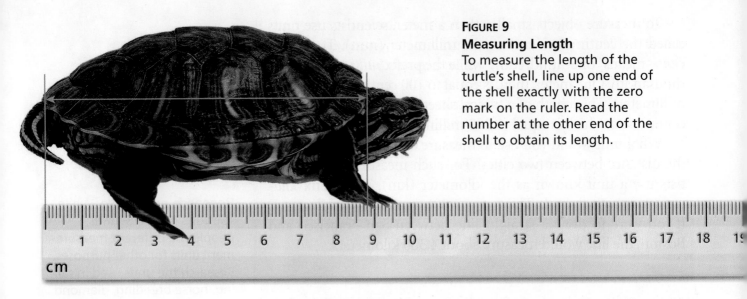

FIGURE 9
Measuring Length
To measure the length of the turtle's shell, line up one end of the shell exactly with the zero mark on the ruler. Read the number at the other end of the shell to obtain its length.

Measuring Length A very common tool used to measure length is the metric ruler. As you can see in Figure 9, a metric ruler is divided into centimeters. The centimeter markings are the longer lines numbered 1, 2, 3, and so on. Each centimeter is then divided into 10 millimeters, which are marked by the shorter lines.

To use a metric ruler, line one end of the object up exactly with the zero mark. Then read the number at the other end of the object. The shell of the turtle in Figure 9 is 8.8 centimeters, or 88 millimeters, long.

 **Reading Checkpoint** One centimeter is divided into how many millimeters?

Weight and Mass

Suppose you want to measure your weight. To find the weight, you step on a scale like the one shown in Figure 10. Your body weight presses down on the springs inside the scale. The more you weigh, the more the springs compress, causing the pointer on the scale to turn farther, giving a higher reading. However, your scale would not indicate the same weight if you took it to the moon and stepped on it. You weigh less on the moon, so the springs of the scale would not be compressed as much by your weight. How can your weight change if the amount of matter in your body stays the same?

FIGURE 10
Measuring Weight
You can stand on a scale to measure your body weight.

Weight Your **weight** is a measure of the force of gravity on you. Weight is measured in units such as newtons or pounds. The newton (N) is an SI unit. If you weigh 90 pounds, your weight in SI units is about 400 newtons.

On Earth, all objects are attracted toward the center of the planet by the force of Earth's gravity. On another planet, the force of gravity on you may be more or less than it is on Earth. On the moon, you would weigh only about one-sixth of your weight on Earth.

Mass Why do you weigh less on the moon than on Earth? The force of gravity depends partly on the mass of an object. **Mass** is a measure of the amount of matter an object contains. If you travel to the moon, the amount of matter in your body—your mass—does not change. But, the mass of the moon is much less than the mass of Earth, so the moon exerts much less gravitational force on you. Unlike weight, mass does not change with location, even when the force of gravity on an object changes. For this reason scientists prefer to measure matter by its mass rather than its weight.

Units of Mass 🔑 **The SI unit of mass is the kilogram (kg).** If you weigh 90 pounds on Earth, your mass is about 40 kilograms. Although you will see kilograms used in this textbook, usually you will see a smaller unit—the gram (g). There are exactly 1,000 grams in a kilogram. A nickel has a mass of 5 grams, and a baseball has a mass of about 150 grams.

Common Conversions for Mass		
1 kg	=	1,000 g
1 g	=	1,000 mg

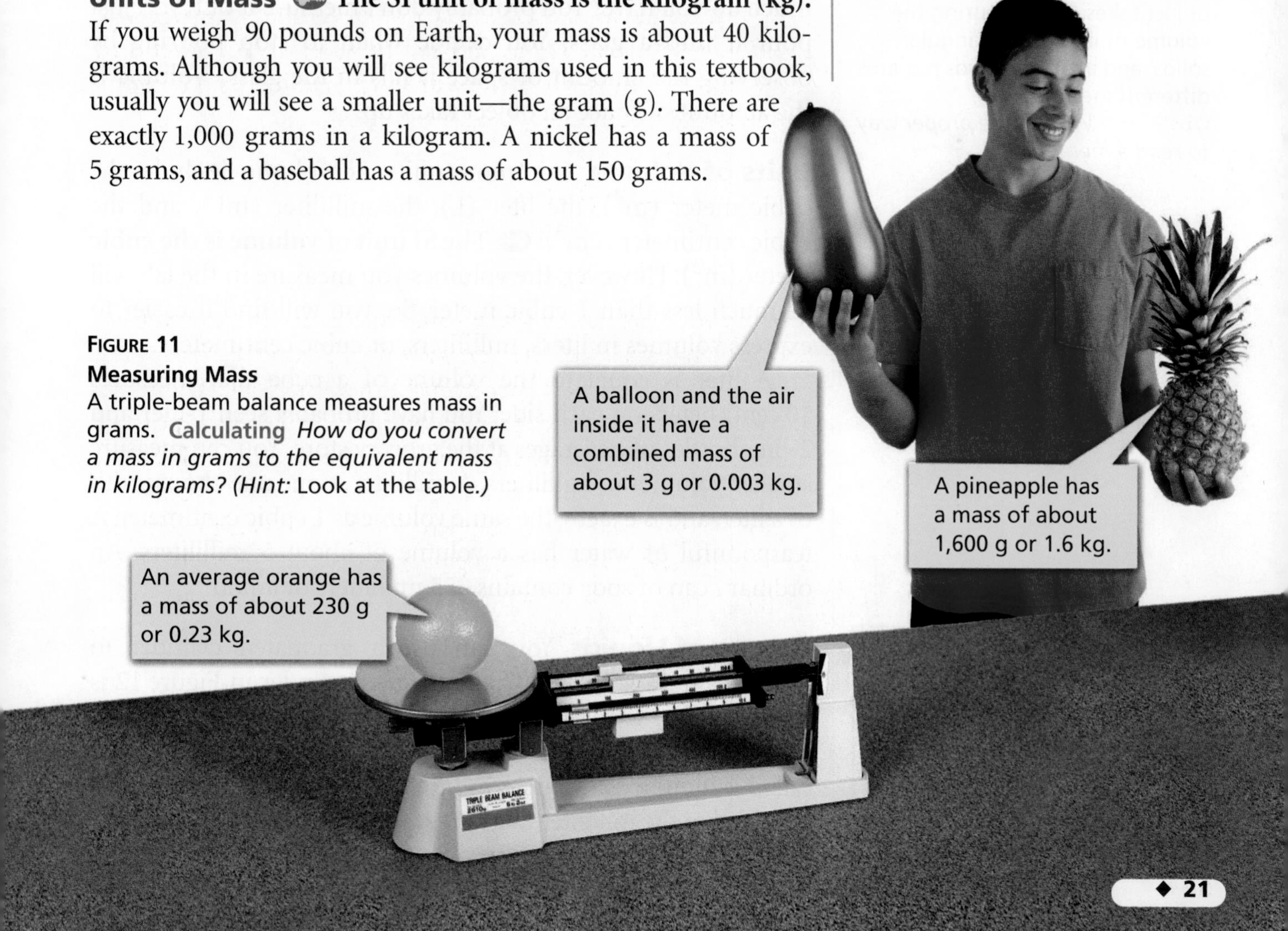

FIGURE 11
Measuring Mass
A triple-beam balance measures mass in grams. **Calculating** *How do you convert a mass in grams to the equivalent mass in kilograms? (Hint: Look at the table.)*

A balloon and the air inside it have a combined mass of about 3 g or 0.003 kg.

A pineapple has a mass of about 1,600 g or 1.6 kg.

An average orange has a mass of about 230 g or 0.23 kg.

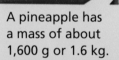

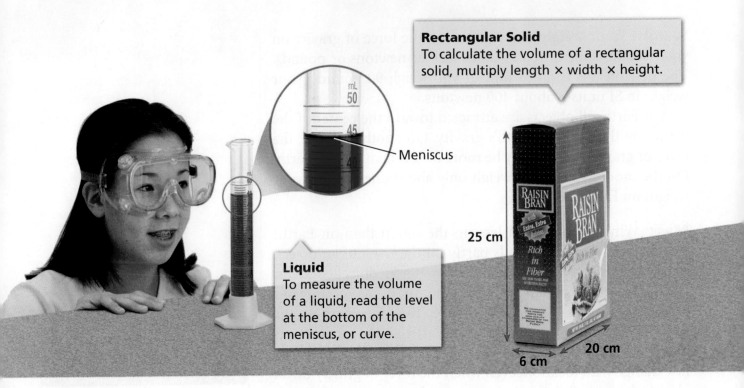

Rectangular Solid
To calculate the volume of a rectangular solid, multiply length × width × height.

Meniscus

25 cm

Liquid
To measure the volume of a liquid, read the level at the bottom of the meniscus, or curve.

20 cm

6 cm

FIGURE 12
Measuring Volume

Volume is the amount of space an object takes up. Measuring the volume of liquids, rectangular solids, and irregular solids requires different methods.
Observing *What is the proper way to read a meniscus?*

Common Conversions for Volume	
1 L	= 1,000 mL
1 L	= 1,000 cm³
1 mL	= 1 cm³

Volume

Do you drink milk or orange juice with breakfast? If so, how much do you have? You probably don't measure it out; you just pour it into a glass. You decide when to stop pouring by observing the amount of space it fills in the glass. **Volume** is the amount of space an object takes up.

Units of Volume Common units of volume include the cubic meter (m^3), the liter (L), the milliliter (mL), and the cubic centimeter (cm^3). ⊙ **The SI unit of volume is the cubic meter (m^3).** However, the volumes you measure in the lab will be much less than 1 cubic meter. So, you will find it easier to express volumes in liters, milliliters, or cubic centimeters.

A liter is equal to the volume of a cube that measures 10 centimeters on each side. You have probably seen 1-liter and 2-liter bottles of beverages at the grocery store. You can measure smaller volumes in milliliters. A milliliter is one one-thousandth of a liter, and is exactly the same volume as 1 cubic centimeter. A teaspoonful of water has a volume of about 5 milliliters. An ordinary can of soda contains 355 milliliters of liquid.

Volume of Liquids You can use a graduated cylinder to measure liquid volumes. The graduated cylinder in Figure 12 is marked off in 1-milliliter segments. Notice that the top surface of the water in the graduated cylinder is curved. This curve is called a **meniscus.** To determine the volume of the water, you should read the milliliter marking at the bottom of the meniscus.

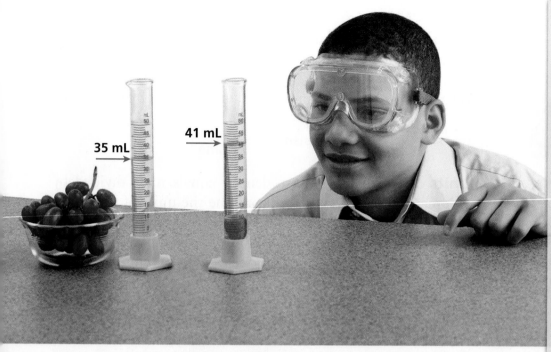

Irregular Solids
To measure the volume of an irregular solid, use the water displacement method.

1 Record the volume of water in the graduated cylinder.

2 Carefully place the irregular solid into the water. Record the volume of the water plus the object.

3 Subtract the volume of the water alone from the volume of the water plus the object.

35 mL

41 mL

Volume of Rectangular Solids How can you determine the volume of a cereal box? Volumes of rectangular solids or containers are often given in cubic centimeters. A cubic centimeter is equal to the volume of a cube that measures 1 centimeter on each side. This is about the size of a sugar cube.

You can calculate the volume of a rectangular object by using this formula:

Volume = Length × Width × Height

$\underbrace{\hspace{3cm}}_{\text{Area}}$

Because the area of a rectangle equals length times width, another way to write this formula is Volume = Area × Height.

Suppose that a cereal box is 20 centimeters long, 6 centimeters wide, and 25 centimeters high. The volume of the box is

Volume = $\underbrace{\text{20 cm × 6 cm}}_{\text{Area}}$ × $\underbrace{\text{25 cm}}_{\text{Height}}$ = 3,000 cm^3

Measurements always have units. So, when you multiply the three measurements, you must remember to multiply the units (cm × cm × cm) as well as the numbers (20 × 6 × 25 = 3,000).

Volume of Irregular Solids How can you measure the volume of an irregular object, such as a piece of fruit or a rock? One way is to submerge the object in water in a graduated cylinder. The water level will rise by an amount that is equal to the volume of the object in milliliters. This method is shown in Figure 12.

Go Online
PHSchool.com

For: More on measurement
Visit: PHSchool.com
Web Code: cgd-6021

Density

As you can see in Figure 13, two objects of the same size can have very different masses. This is because different materials have different densities. **Density** is mass per unit volume. To calculate the density of an object, divide its mass by its volume.

$$\text{Density} = \frac{\text{Mass}}{\text{Volume}}$$

Units of Density Because density equals mass divided by volume, the units for density combine the units of those two measurements. 🔑 **The SI unit of density is the kilogram per cubic meter (kg/m^3).** In this textbook, you will often see density expressed in grams per cubic centimeter (g/cm^3) for solids and grams per milliliter (g/mL) for liquids. In each case, the numerator is a measure of mass, and the denominator is a measure of volume.

FIGURE 13
Comparing Densities
Although the bowling ball and beach ball have the same volume, one contains much more mass than the other.
Inferring Which item has the greater density?

Reviewing Math: Number Sense 7.1.2

Math ▶ Sample Problem

Calculating Density
Suppose that a metal object has a mass of 57 g and a volume of 21 cm^3. Calculate its density.

1 Read and Understand
What information are you given?
Mass of metal object = 57 g
Volume of metal object = 21 cm^3

2 Plan and Solve
What quantity are you trying to calculate?
The density of the metal object = ■

What formula contains the given quantities and the unknown quantity?

$$\text{Density} = \frac{\text{Mass}}{\text{Volume}}$$

Perform the calculation.

$$\text{Density} = \frac{\text{Mass}}{\text{Volume}} = \frac{57\ g}{21\ cm^3} = 2.7\ g/cm^3$$

3 Look Back and Check
Does your answer make sense?
The answer tells you that the metal object has a density of 2.7 g/cm^3. The answer makes sense because it is the same as the density of a known metal—aluminum.

Math ▶ Practice

1. What is the density of a wood block with a mass of 57 g and a volume of 125 cm^3?

2. What is the density of a liquid with a mass of 45 g and a volume of 48 mL?

Densities of Common Substances The table in Figure 14 lists the densities of some common substances. The density of a substance is the same for all samples of that substance. For example, all samples of pure gold—no matter how large or small—have a density of 19.3 g/cm³.

Once you know an object's density, you can predict whether the object will float or sink in a given liquid. If the object is less dense than the liquid, it will float. If the object is more dense than the liquid, it will sink. For example, the density of water is 1 g/cm³. A piece of wood with a density of 0.8 g/cm³ will float in water. A ring made of pure silver, which has a density of 10.5 g/cm³, will sink.

Reading Checkpoint Will an object with a density of 0.7 g/cm³ float or sink in water?

Time

The crowd cheers wildly as you near the finish line. You push your legs to run even faster in the final moments of the race. From the corner of your eye, you see your opponent catching up to you. At moments like this, just one second can mean the difference between winning and losing.

Units of Time ⬦ **The second (s) is the SI unit of time.** Your heart beats about once per second—when you are not running, that is! The second can easily be divided by multiples of 10, like the other SI units. For example, a millisecond (ms) is one-thousandth of a second. Longer periods of time are expressed in minutes or hours. There are 60 seconds in a minute, and 60 minutes in an hour.

Measuring Time You use clocks and watches to measure time. Some digital stopwatches, which are used to time races, can measure time accurately to one hundredth of a second.

Densities of Some Common Substances

Substance	Density (g/cm³)
Air	0.001
Ice	0.9
Water	1.0
Aluminum	2.7
Gold	19.3

FIGURE 14
The density of a substance stays the same no matter how large or small a sample of the substance is. **Applying Concepts** *How could you use density to determine whether a bar of metal is pure gold?*

FIGURE 15
Measuring Time
You can use a stopwatch to measure time.

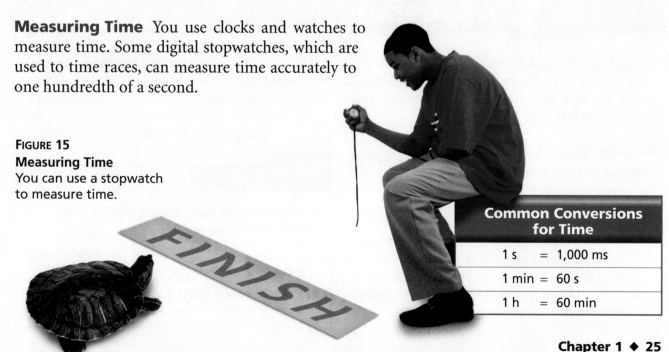

Common Conversions for Time

1 s	= 1,000 ms
1 min	= 60 s
1 h	= 60 min

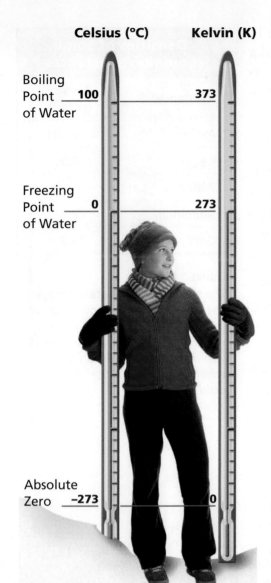

Celsius (°C)   **Kelvin (K)**

Boiling Point of Water   **100**   **373**

Freezing Point of Water   **0**   **273**

Absolute Zero   **−273**   **0**

Temperature

As you head out the door each morning, one of the first things you might notice is the temperature. Is it cold out this morning? How high will the temperature rise?

Units of Temperature Scientists commonly use the Celsius temperature scale. On the **Celsius Scale,** water freezes at 0°C and boils at 100°C. There are exactly 100 degrees between the freezing point and boiling point of water. Normal human body temperature is about 37°C.

In addition to the Celsius scale, scientists also use another temperature scale, called the **Kelvin scale.** Units on the Kelvin scale are the same size as those on the Celsius scale. **The kelvin (K) is the SI unit of temperature.**

The temperature 0 K on the Kelvin scale is called **absolute zero.** Nothing can get colder than this temperature. Absolute zero is equal to −273°C on the Celsius scale.

Measuring Temperature You can measure temperature using a thermometer. Most thermometers consist of a sealed tube that contains a liquid. The liquid expands or contracts as the temperature changes.

FIGURE 16
Measuring Temperature
Scientists use the Celsius and Kelvin scales to measure temperature.

Section 3 Assessment

S 8.8.a, 8.8.b, E-LA: Reading 8.2.0, Math: 7NS1.2

Target Reading Skill Preview Text Structure
Complete the graphic organizer for this section. What question did you ask about Weight and Mass? What was your answer?

Reviewing Key Concepts

1. a. Identifying What is the standard measurement system used by scientists around the world?
   b. Predicting Suppose that two scientists use different measurement systems in their work. What problems might arise if they shared their data?

2. a. Listing What are the SI units of length, mass, volume, density, time, and temperature?

   b. Estimating Estimate the length of a baseball bat and mass of a baseball in SI units. How can you check how close your estimates are?
   c. Describing Outline a step-by-step method for determining the density of a baseball.

Math **Practice**

Two solid cubes have the same mass. They each have a mass of 50 g.

3. Calculating Density Cube A has a volume of 2 cm × 2 cm × 2 cm. What is its density?

4. Calculating Density Cube B has a volume of 4 cm × 4 cm × 4 cm. What is its density?

Making Sense of Density

S 8.8.b, 8.9.b

Problem

Does the density of a material vary with volume?

Skills Focus

drawing conclusions, measuring, controlling variables

Materials

- balance • water • paper towels
- metric ruler • graduated cylinder, 100-mL
- wooden stick, about 6 cm long
- ball of modeling clay, about 5 cm wide
- crayon with paper removed

Procedure

1. Use a balance to find the mass of the wooden stick. Record the mass in a data table like the one shown above right.

2. Add enough water to a graduated cylinder so that the stick can be completely submerged. Measure the initial volume of the water.

3. Place the stick in the graduated cylinder. Measure the new volume of the water.

4. The volume of the stick is the difference between the water levels in Steps 2 and 3. Calculate this volume and record it.

5. The density of the stick equals its mass divided by its volume. Calculate and record its density.

6. Thoroughly dry the stick with a paper towel. Then carefully break the stick into two pieces. Repeat Steps 1 through 5 with one piece. Then, repeat Steps 1 through 5 with the other piece.

7. Repeat Steps 1 through 6 using the clay rolled into a rope.

8. Repeat using the crayon.

Data Table			
Object	Mass (g)	Volume Change (cm³)	Density (g/cm³)
Wooden stick			
Whole			
Piece 1			
Piece 2			
Modeling clay			
Whole			
Piece 1			
Piece 2			
Crayon			
Whole			
Piece 1			
Piece 2			

Analyze and Conclude

1. **Measuring** For each object you tested, compare the density of the whole object with the densities of the pieces of the object.

2. **Drawing Conclusions** Use your results to explain how density can be used to identify a material.

3. **Controlling Variables** Why did you dry the objects in Step 6?

4. **Communicating** Write a paragraph explaining how you would change the procedure to obtain more data. Tell how having more data would affect your answers to Questions 1 and 2 above.

Design an Experiment

Design an experiment you could use to determine the density of olive oil. With your teacher's permission, carry out your plan. Use the library or the Internet to find the actual density of olive oil. Compare your experimental value with the actual value, and explain why they may differ.

Should the United States Go Metric?

On a long car ride, have you ever asked, "Are we there yet?" If the driver answered, "We're 30 kilometers away," would you know whether you were close to your destination or far away?

As a U.S. resident, you probably have no trouble understanding English units, which include miles, feet, pounds, and gallons. Metric units, however, may be more unfamiliar. But most countries in the world use the metric system. Should the United States convert to metric or continue using the English system?

The Issues

Why Change?

People in the United States are comfortable with the English system of measurement. If the country converted to metric, citizens might have a hard time buying products or calculating distances. These problems may not disappear overnight.

Businesses in the United States rely on the English system. Many of the tools and machines that manufacture goods are based on the English system, as are the goods themselves. To go metric, machines would have to be replaced and the goods repackaged. This could cost millions of dollars.

Why Not Change?

Supporters of the metric system point out how easy it is to learn. Because metric units are based on the number 10, converting from kilometers to meters, for example, is simple. In contrast, converting miles to feet, or gallons to ounces, is more complicated. Schoolchildren could master the metric system much more quickly than the English system.

Furthermore, conversion may help the United States stay competitive in foreign trade. Many U.S. businesses sell their products in other countries. But people worldwide prefer products labeled in units they know—in this case, metric units. They may avoid products that are not made to metric standards. In fact, by 2010, products sold in Europe must be labeled in metric units only.

Why Not Compromise?

The next time you drink a bottle of juice, look at its label. Most likely, it includes both English and metric units. Labels like these are a compromise. They allow users of both measurement systems to know exactly what they are buying.

Some people feel that such a compromise works well enough. People who need to use the metric system, such as those in science and industry, should be able to use it. However, those who prefer to use English units should be able to do so as well.

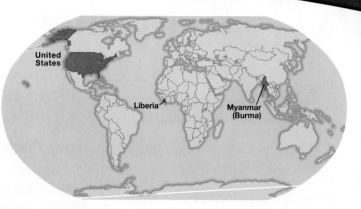

The countries in red currently use the English system of measurement.

You Decide

1. Identify the Problem
In your own words, state the advantages and disadvantages of converting to the metric system.

2. Analyze the Options
Do some research on countries that have recently gone metric. What problems did these countries face? How did they overcome the problems? Did the benefits of converting to the metric system outweigh the costs?

3. Find a Solution
Take a stance on this issue. Then engage in a class debate about whether or not the United States should convert to the metric system. Support your opinion with facts from this feature and from your research.

For: More on going metric
Visit: PHSchool.com
Web Code: cgh-6020

Mathematics and Science

S 8.9.b Evaluate the accuracy and reproducibility of data.

What math skills do scientists use in collecting data and making measurements?

Key Terms
- estimate
- accuracy
- reproducibility
- significant figures
- precision

Standards Warp-Up

Lab zone

How Many Marbles Are There?

1. Your teacher will give you a jar full of marbles.
2. With a partner, come up with a way to determine the number of marbles in the jar without actually counting all of them.
3. Use your method to determine the number of marbles. Write down your answer.
4. Compare the method you used to that of another group.

Think It Over

Predicting Which method do you think led to a more accurate answer? Why?

What are some tools that scientists use? You might think of microscopes, thermometers, and calculators. There are also scientific tools that you won't find on a lab bench. Curiosity, skepticism, creativity—these are attitudes that serve as useful tools in scientific inquiry. Knowledge is another important tool. One form of knowledge that is particularly useful in the study of science is mathematics. Mathematics is essential for asking and answering questions about the material world.

Estimation

Have you ever been on stage and wondered how many people there were in the audience? Maybe you counted the number of people in one row and multiplied by the number of rows. This would be one way to arrive at an estimate. An **estimate** is an approximation of a number based on reasonable assumptions. Estimating is not the same as guessing because an estimate is based on known information.

Scientists must sometimes rely on estimates when they cannot obtain exact numbers. Astronomers, for example, can't actually measure the distance between stars. An astronomer's estimate might be based on indirect measurements, calculations, and models.

Go Online
SC*i*LINKS **NSTA**

For: Links on math and science
Visit: www.SciLinks.org
Web Code: scn-1622

Accuracy and Reproducibility

Suppose you were to meet a friend at 4:00 P.M. Your friend arrives at 4:15 and says, "But it's 4:00 according to all the clocks in my house." The problem is that your friend's clocks do not show the accurate, or correct, time. **Accuracy** refers to how close a measurement is to the true or actual value. An accurate clock would read 4:00 P.M. Your friend's clocks may be working properly, but because they are set 15 minutes late, they are always inaccurate.

Reproducibility What would happen if you never told your friend that he was late? Your friend would always be late by 15 minutes. If the two of you tried to meet at 4:00 P.M. on consecutive days, your friend would arrive at 4:15 P.M. each day. Your friend's clocks may be inaccurate, but when used for repeated measurements, they yield consistent results.

The times measured with your friend's clocks can be said to be reproducible. **Reproducibility** refers to how close a group of measurements are to each other.

Accuracy and reproducibility do not mean the same thing. To help you understand the difference, think about a game of darts. As Figure 17 shows, accurate throws land close to the bull's-eye. Reproducible throws, on the other hand, land close to one another. Your friend's clocks show times that are reproducible but inaccurate, like the arrangement of darts in the middle dartboard.

Accuracy and Reproducibility in Measurements

Suppose you want to measure your friend's height. The measurement needs to be accurate, or close to your friend's actual height. The measurement also needs to be reproducible. This means that if you measured your friend's height several times, you would get the same measurement again and again.

👁 **Scientists aim for both accuracy and reproducibility in their measurements.** To ensure accuracy, you need to make your measurements carefully using the appropriate instruments. To ensure reproducibility, you need to repeat the measurement a few times.

FIGURE 17
Accuracy and Reproducibility
In a game of darts, it's easy to see the difference between accurate throws and reproducible throws. In order to hit the bull's-eye consistently, you need both accuracy and reproducibility!

▲ **Neither Reproducible nor Accurate**

▲ **Reproducible but Not Accurate**

▲ **Both Reproducible and Accurate**

I am certain of the "5" but am estimating the "3." Therefore, my measurement can be expressed to only two significant figures, 5.3 cm.

FIGURE 18
Significant Figures
A measurement should contain only those numbers that are significant. *Measuring Why can you report the length of the tile to only two significant figures?*

Area

To find the area of a surface, multiply its length by its width. Suppose a sheet of paper measures 27.5 cm by 21.6 cm.

Area = 27.5 cm × 21.6 cm

= 594 cm²

Practice Problem What is the area of a ticket stub that measures 3.5 cm by 2.2 cm?

Significant Figures and Precision

Figure 18 shows a tile next to a ruler marked off in 1-centimeter segments. Suppose you measure the length of the tile as 5.3 centimeters. This measurement has two digits that are "significant." The **significant figures** in a measurement include all of the digits that have been measured exactly, plus one digit whose value has been estimated. In measuring the tile to be 5.3 centimeters long, you are certain of the 5, but you have estimated the 3. So, the measurement 5.3 centimeters has two significant figures.

What if the ruler had been marked off in 1-millimeter segments? You would be able to make a more precise measurement. **Precision** is a measure of the exactness of a measurement. With a more precise ruler, you might measure the length of the tile as 5.32 centimeters. The measurement 5.32 centimeters (three significant figures) is more precise than 5.3 centimeters (two significant figures). ⟳ **Scientists use significant figures to express precision in their measurements and calculations.**

Adding or Subtracting When you add or subtract measurements, the answer should have the same number of decimal places as the measurement with the least number of decimal places. For example, suppose you add a tile that is 5.3 centimeters long to a row of tiles that is 21.94 centimeters long.

5.3 cm (1 decimal place)
+ 21.94 cm (2 decimal places)

27.24 cm ≈ 27.2 (1 decimal place)

In this calculation, the measurement with the least number of decimal places is 5.3 centimeters (one decimal place). So the answer, 27.2 centimeters, should be written to only one decimal place. The correct answer has three significant figures.

 **What are significant figures?**

32 ◆

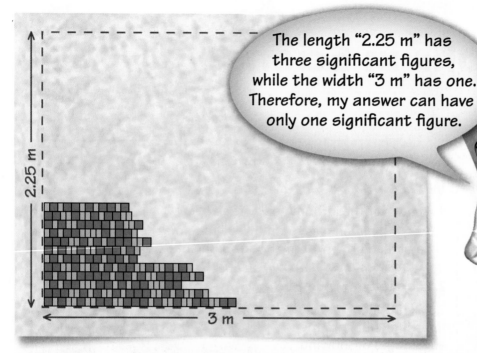

The length "2.25 m" has three significant figures, while the width "3 m" has one. Therefore, my answer can have only one significant figure.

Multiplying or Dividing When multiplying or dividing measurements, the answer should have the same number of significant figures as the measurement with the least number of significant figures. Suppose you need to tile a space that measures 2.25 meters by 3 meters. The calculated area would be:

$$\begin{array}{r}\text{2.25 m (3 significant figures)}\\ \times\ \underline{\text{3 m (1 significant figure)}}\\ \text{6.75 m}^2 \approx \text{7 m}^2 \text{ (1 significant figure)}\end{array}$$

The answer has one significant figure because the measurement with the least number of significant figures (3 meters) has one significant figure.

FIGURE 19
Multiplying Measurements
When you multiply measurements, your answer can have only the same number of significant figures as the measurement with the fewest significant figures.

Section 4 Assessment

S 8.9.b, E-LA: Reading 8.1.0, Math: 7MG2.1

Vocabulary Skill High-Use Academic Words What is the meaning of the word *significant* in the term *significant figures*?

🔑 Reviewing Key Concepts

1. a. **Identifying** What math skill do scientists rely on when they cannot obtain exact numbers?
   b. **Explaining** How can you be sure that your measurements are both accurate and reproducible?
   c. **Interpreting Data** Using a metric ruler with millimeter markings, a friend measures the width of a book to be 14.23 cm. How many digits can you be certain of? Explain.

Math Practice

2. **Area** To win a prize at a fair, you must throw a coin into a space that is 7.0 cm long and 4.0 cm wide. What is the area of the space you are aiming for? Express your answer to the correct number of significant figures.

Graphs in Science

S 8.9.d Recognize the slope of the linear graph as the constant in the relationship $y = kx$ and apply this principle in interpreting graphs constructed from data.

S 8.9.g Distinguish between linear and nonlinear relationships on a graph of data.

- What type of data can line graphs display?

- How do you determine a line of best fit or the slope of a graph?

- Why are line graphs powerful tools in science?

Key Terms

- graph
- horizontal axis
- vertical axis
- origin
- coordinate
- data point
- line of best fit
- linear graph
- slope
- nonlinear graph

Lab zone Standards **Warm-Up**

What's in a Picture?

1. Read over the information written below.

At age 1, Sarah was 75 cm tall. By the time she turned 2, Sarah had grown 10 cm. By age 3, she had grown another 10 cm. At age 4, Sarah was 100 cm tall.

2. Look at the "picture" below.

Think It Over

Inferring What are the advantages of showing information in a visual way, rather than with words in paragraph form? What trend do you see in the picture?

It's been a long day and all you can think about is food. You toss down your gym bag and head into the kitchen. Now for some pasta! You set a pot of water on the stove, turn on the heat, and wait eagerly for the water to boil.

Several minutes later, you are still waiting for the first sign of bubbles. Could the saying "A watched pot never boils" really be true? Or is the water taking longer to boil today because you filled the pot more than usual? Is the volume of water related to boiling time? You could do an experiment and collect some data to find out.

The Importance of Graphs

In Section 2, you learned why it is important to organize the data you collect in an experiment. Creating a data table is one way to organize experimental data. Another way to show data is in the form of a graph. You can think of a **graph** as a "picture" of your data. Have you ever heard the saying, "A picture is worth a thousand words"? This is exactly why graphs are such useful tools. Because of their visual nature, graphs can reveal patterns or trends that words and data tables cannot.

The three types of graphs that scientists commonly use are bar graphs, circle graphs, and line graphs. You can learn about these graphs in the Skills Handbook. This section focuses specifically on line graphs—how to create them and how to interpret the patterns they reveal.

Why Are Line Graphs Useful? Suppose you set up the experiment in Figure 20. You record in a data table the time it takes each pot of water to boil. From your data table, you can tell that as the volume of water increases, the boiling time seems to increase as well. But a line graph could reveal more clearly how these two variables are related.

🔑 **Line graphs are used to display data to show how one variable (the responding variable) changes in response to another variable (the manipulated variable).** In the water-boiling experiment, the responding variable is the time it takes for the water to boil. The manipulated variable is the volume of water in the pot.

FIGURE 20
Collecting Data
How long does it take different volumes of water to boil? You can collect data and plot a line graph to see the relationship between volume and boiling time.
Inferring *Why might a line graph be more useful than a data table?*

Data Table	
Volume of Water (mL)	Boiling Time
500	7 min 48 s (7.8 min)
1,000	16 min 37 s (16.6 min)
1,500	26 min 00 s (26.0 min)
2,000	33 min 44 s (33.7 min)

1,500 mL

2,000 mL

Plotting a Line Graph When should you plot a line graph? The answer is, when your manipulated variable is *continuous*—that is, when there are other points between the ones that you tested. In the water-boiling experiment, volumes of 501 mL, 502 mL, and so on exist between 500 mL and 2,000 mL. Time and mass are other continuous variables.

To plot a line graph of your data, follow these steps.

1 **Draw the axes.** The **horizontal axis,** or *x*-axis, is the graph line that runs left to right. The **vertical axis,** or *y*-axis, is the graph line that runs up and down.

2 **Label the axes.** Label the horizontal axis with the name of the manipulated variable. Label the vertical axis with the name of the responding variable. Be sure to include units of measurement on each axis.

3 **Create a scale.** On each axis, create a scale by marking off equally-spaced intervals that cover the range of values you will show. Both scales should begin at zero when possible. The point where the two axes cross is called the **origin** of the graph. On this graph, the origin has coordinates of (0,0), which represents "0 milliliters and 0 minutes." A **coordinate** is a pair of numbers used to determine the position of a point on a graph.

4 **Plot the data.** Plot a point for each piece of data. The dotted lines show how to plot your first piece of data (500, 7.8). Follow an imaginary vertical line extending up from the horizontal axis at the 500 mL mark. Then follow an imaginary horizontal line extending across from the vertical axis at the 7.8 minutes mark. Plot a point where these two lines cross, or intersect. The point showing the location of that intersection is called a **data point.**

5 **Draw a "line of best fit."** A **line of best fit** is a smooth line that reflects the general pattern of a graph. Though your first instinct might be to simply connect all the dots, that's not the correct approach to drawing a line graph. Rather, you should first stop and look at the points you plotted to identify a general trend in the data. Then draw a smooth line between the points to reflect that general pattern.

Notice that the resulting line of best fit for this graph is a straight line. A line graph in which the data points yield a straight line is called a **linear graph.**

6 **Add a title.** The title should identify the variables or relationship shown in the graph.

Data Table	
Volume of Water (mL)	Boiling Time (min)
500	7.8
1,000	16.6
1,500	26.0
2,000	33.7

 **Reading Checkpoint** What is a coordinate?

FIGURE 21

Plotting a Line Graph

You can obtain a picture of your experimental data by following these six steps.

Go Online
active art

For: Plotting a Line Graph activity
Visit: PHSchool.com
Web Code: cgp-6023

① Draw the Axes

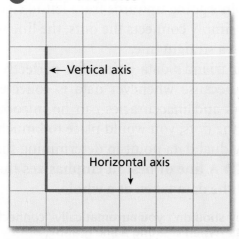

④ Plot the Data

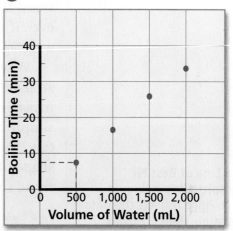

② Label the Axes

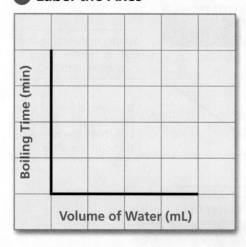

⑤ Draw a Line of Best Fit

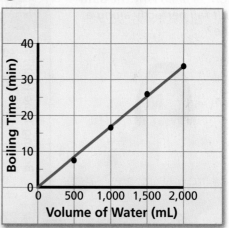

③ Create a Scale

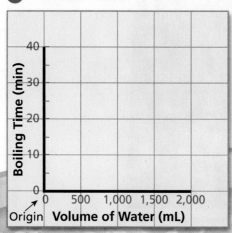

⑥ Add a Title

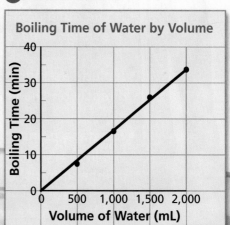

Why Draw a Line of Best Fit?

You may be wondering why you cannot simply connect all your data points with a line to create a line graph. To understand why this is the case, consider the following situation. Suppose your friend performs the same water-boiling experiment as you did and plots the graph shown in Figure 22.

Notice that your friend's graph shows the same general trend as yours—points going upwards from left to right. However, if your friend simply connects the dots, the line would be a zigzag, rather than a straight line.

Why don't your friend's data points fall perfectly along a straight line? It is because whenever data is collected, small measurement errors and inaccuracies can be introduced. By simply connecting the dots, you would place too much importance on each individual data point in determining the overall shape of the line. ⚭ **A line of best fit emphasizes the overall trend shown by all the data taken as a whole.**

 **Reading Checkpoint** **Why shouldn't you automatically "connect the dots" when creating a line graph?**

FIGURE 22
Drawing a Line of Best Fit
For this graph, a line going up from left to right reflects the data more accurately than a zigzag line does.
Relating Cause and Effect *What factors might explain why the data points don't fall perfectly along a straight line?*

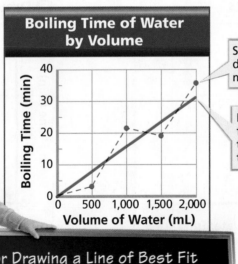

Simply connecting the dots is incorrect and may be misleading.

Drawing a line of best fit is the proper way to reflect the overall trend in the data.

Tips for Drawing a Line of Best Fit

• If the data points seem to follow along a straight line, draw a straight line.

• Include as many data points as possible directly on the line.

• For data points that don't easily fit on the line, try to have the same number of points above the line as below the line.

Math Analyzing Data

Distance Traveled Over Time

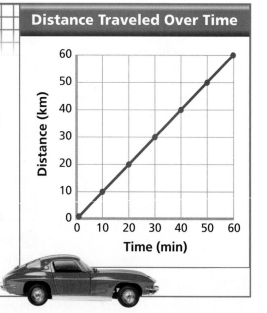

Car Travel

The graph shows the distance a car travels in a one-hour period. Use the graph to answer the questions below.

1. **Reading Graphs** What variable is plotted on the horizontal axis? The vertical axis?

2. **Interpreting Data** How far does the car travel in the first 10 minutes? In 40 minutes?

3. **Predicting** Use the graph to predict how far the car would travel in 120 minutes. Assume the car continues to travel at the same speed.

4. **Calculating** Calculate the slope of the graph. What information does the slope provide?

Slope

When a line graph is linear, you can determine a value called slope. One way to define **slope** is the steepness of the graph line. 🔑 **The slope of a graph line tells you how much y changes for every change in x.**

$$\text{Slope} = \frac{\text{Rise}}{\text{Run}} = \frac{y_2 - y_1}{x_2 - x_1}$$

To calculate slope, pick any two points on the line and write down the coordinates. In Figure 23, suppose you chose the points $(20, 10)$ and $(50, 25)$.

$$\text{Slope} = \frac{25 \text{ km} - 10 \text{ km}}{50 \text{ min} - 20 \text{ min}} = \frac{15 \text{ km}}{30 \text{ min}} = 0.5 \text{ km/min}$$

In the case of Figure 23, the slope represents the distance the car travels per unit of time, or its speed. So the speed of the car is 0.5 km/min. Note that the speed is constant. On a linear graph, the slope is constant.

If the straight line of a linear graph goes through the origin $(0, 0)$, the graph can be expressed as the following equation:

$$y = kx$$

In this equation, x is the manipulated variable, y is the responding variable, and the constant k is the slope.

Look again at Figure 23. Substituting for the variables x (time), y (distance), and k (0.5 km/min), you can now write:

$$\text{Distance} = (0.5 \text{ km/min})(\text{Time})$$

FIGURE 23
Slope
The slope of a line indicates how much y changes for every change in x. **Calculating** *What is the slope of this line?*

Distance Traveled Over Time

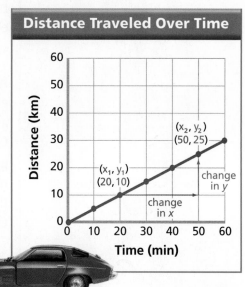

FIGURE 24
Trends in Graphs
Data may yield one of the trends shown in these graphs.
Reading Graphs *Which graph shows no relationship between the two variables?*

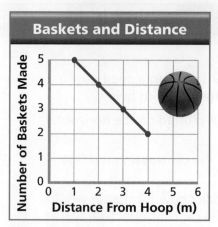

Baskets and Distance

Number of Baskets Made / Distance From Hoop (m)

A **Linear Trend** As the distance from the hoop increases, the number of baskets made decreases. The graph line descends to the right.

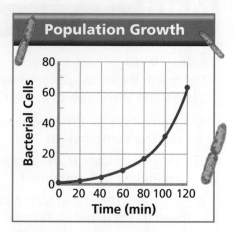

Population Growth

Bacterial Cells / Time (min)

B **Nonlinear Trend** Bacteria reproduce by dividing in two every 20 minutes. The number of bacterial cells increases sharply. The graph is a steep curve.

Using Graphs to Identify Trends

Your data won't always give you a graph with a straight line. A line graph in which the data points do not fall along a straight line is called a **nonlinear graph.**

Whether a graph is linear or nonlinear, the information it contains is very useful. 👉 **Line graphs are powerful tools in science because they allow you to identify trends and make predictions.**

Linear Trends When a graph is linear, you can easily see how two variables are related. For instance, Graph A in Figure 24 shows that the farther one student stands from a basketball hoop, the fewer baskets she can make.

You can also use the graph to make predictions. For example, how many baskets can she make at a distance of 5 meters? If you extend the graph line, you can see that your prediction would be one basket.

Nonlinear Trends There are several kinds of nonlinear graphs. In some nonlinear graphs, the data points may fall along a curve. A curve may be shallow, or it may be steep, as in Graph B. Other nonlinear graphs show different trends. A graph may rise and then level off, as in Graph C. Or, a graph may show a repeating pattern, as in Graph D. Because each of these graphs reveals a trend in the data, they are useful in understanding how the variables are related.

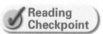 **Reading Checkpoint** What is a nonlinear graph?

Distance Biked

C **Nonlinear Trend** On a bike ride, the distance you bike increases with time. If you stop to rest, the distance remains the same and the graph levels off.

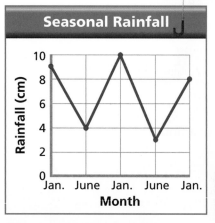

Seasonal Rainfall

D **Nonlinear Trend** In many places, rainfall varies with the seasons. The graph shows a repeating, or cyclical, pattern.

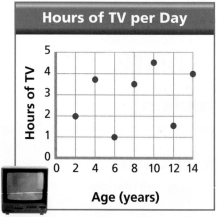

Hours of TV per Day

E **No Trend** The amount of television children watch and their ages are not related. The data points are scattered, and the graph shows no recognizable pattern.

No Trend In other nonlinear graphs, the data points may be scattered about in no recognizable pattern, as in Graph E. Would you be surprised to learn that even such graphs are useful? When there are no identifiable trends in a graph, it most likely means that there is no relationship between the two variables.

Section **5** **Assessment**

S 8.9.d, 8.9.g, E-LA: Reading 8.2.0

↩ **Target Reading Skill** Preview Text Structure Complete the graphic organizer for this section. What question did you ask about Slope? What was your answer?

🔑 **Reviewing Key Concepts**

1. a. **Reviewing** What can graphs reveal that data tables cannot?
   b. **Describing** What can a line graph tell you about the relationship between the variables in an experiment?
   c. **Interpreting Data** Could you use a line graph to show data about how body mass (the responding variable) changes with height (the manipulated variable)? Explain.
2. a. **Defining** What is a line of best fit?
   b. **Explaining** What does calculating the slope of a graph line tell you about the data?
   c. **Comparing and Contrasting** How does a graph line with a steeper slope compare to one with a shallower slope?

3. a. **Listing** List two things that line graphs allow scientists to do.
   b. **Reading Graphs** Describe how Graphs A and D in Figure 24 differ.

Lab zone **At-Home Activity**

Which Line Is Best? Show a family member how to "draw" a line of best fit by plotting the data points from Figure 22 onto a piece of graph paper. Tape the graph paper onto a thick piece of cardboard. Insert a pushpin into each data point. Then arrange a piece of string so that it best reflects the data. Once you have determined the line of best fit, tape the string to the graph. Explain why a line of best fit need not go through each data point.

Go Online
PHSchool.com

For: Data sharing
Visit: PHSchool.com
Web Code: cgd-6023

Density Graphs

S 8.8.b, 8.9.d

Problem

How can you determine the density of a liquid?

Skills Focus

graphing, calculating

Materials

- graduated cylinder
- balance • graph paper
- 3 sample volumes of the same liquid

Procedure

1. Measure the mass of an empty graduated cylinder. Record the mass in a data table.

2. Pour one of the liquid samples into the graduated cylinder. Measure and record the mass of the graduated cylinder plus the liquid.

3. Calculate the mass of the liquid alone by subtracting the mass of the empty graduated cylinder from the mass in Step 2.

4. Determine the volume of the liquid by reading the level at the bottom of the meniscus.

5. Repeat Steps 2–4 with the two other samples.

Analyze and Conclude

1. **Graphing** Use the data in your data table to create a graph. Graph volume on the horizontal axis (x-axis) and mass on the vertical axis (y-axis).

2. **Interpreting Data** Look at the points you plotted to identify a general trend in the data. Then draw a line of best fit that reflects the trend in the data.

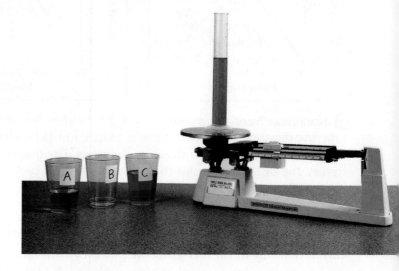

3. **Calculating** Select two points on the graph line and calculate the slope of the line.

$$\text{Slope} = \frac{\text{Rise}}{\text{Run}} = \frac{y_2 - y_1}{x_2 - x_1}$$

4. **Drawing Conclusions** Repeat Step 3 using a different pair of points on the graph line. Compare the two values calculated for the slope. What does the slope represent?

5. **Communicating** Explain why mass and volume measurements for any sample of the liquid should fall along the graph line.

Design an Experiment

Propose a plan to determine which is more dense—a marble, a plastic spoon, or the liquid used in this lab. *Obtain your teacher's permission before carrying out your investigation.*

Data Table				
Sample	Mass of Empty Graduated Cylinder	Mass of Liquid and Graduated Cylinder	Mass of Liquid Alone	Volume of Liquid
A				
B				
C				

Science Laboratory Safety

S 8.9 Scientific progress is made by asking meaningful questions and conducting careful investigations.

- Why is preparation important when carrying out scientific investigations in the lab and in the field?

- What should you do if an accident occurs?

Lab zone Standards **Warm-Up**

Where Is the Safety Equipment in Your School?

1. Look around your classroom or school for any safety-related equipment.
2. Draw a floor plan of the room or building and clearly label where each item is located.

Think It Over
Predicting Why is it important to know where safety equipment is located?

Suppose you and your family decide to go rock climbing. What plans should you make? You'll need to bring rope, some snacks to eat, and water to drink. But you'll also need to plan for everyone's safety.

For the climb to go smoothly, you'll want to make sure that everyone has the proper clothing and safety gear, such as helmets, harnesses, and climbing shoes. You'll check to see whether the equipment is in good condition. You'll also want to make sure that everyone follows proper procedures and knows their role as others take their turn climbing.

FIGURE 25
Climbing Safely
Climbing rocks safely requires careful preparation and the use of proper equipment.

FIGURE 26
Safety in the Lab

Good preparation for an experiment helps you stay safe in the laboratory. **Observing** *List three precautions each student is taking while performing the labs.*

Safety in the Lab

Just as when you go camping, you have to be prepared before you begin any scientific investigation. **Good preparation helps you stay safe when doing science activities in the laboratory.**

Thermometers, balances, and glassware—these are some of the equipment you will use in science labs. Do you know how to use these items? What should you do if something goes wrong? Thinking about these questions ahead of time is an important part of being prepared.

Preparing for the Lab Preparing for a lab should begin the day before you will perform the lab. It is important to read through the procedure carefully and make sure you understand all the directions. Also, review the general safety guidelines in Appendix A, including those related to the specific equipment you will use. If anything is unclear, be prepared to ask your teacher about it before you begin the lab.

Tie back long hair to keep it away from flames, chemicals, or equipment.

Wear safety goggles to protect your eyes from chemical splashes, glass breakage, and sharp objects.

Wear plastic gloves to protect your skin when handling chemicals.

Wear an apron to protect yourself and your clothes from chemicals.

Performing the Lab Whenever you perform a science lab, your chief concern must be the safety of yourself, your classmates, and your teacher. The most important safety rule is simple: Always follow your teacher's instructions and the textbook directions exactly. You should never try anything on your own without asking your teacher first.

Labs and activities in this textbook series include safety symbols like those at the right. These symbols alert you to possible dangers in performing the lab and remind you to work carefully. They also identify any safety equipment that you should use to protect yourself from potential hazards. The symbols are explained in detail in Appendix A. Make sure you are familiar with each safety symbol and what it means.

Another thing you can do to make your lab experience safe and successful is to keep your work area clean and organized. Also, do not rush through any of the steps. Finally, always show respect and courtesy to your teacher and classmates.

Reading Checkpoint What is the most important safety rule?

	Safety Symbols
	Safety Goggles
	Lab Apron
	Breakage
	Heat-Resistant Gloves
	Plastic Gloves
	Heating
	Flames
	No Flames
	Corrosive Chemical
	Poison
	Fumes
	Sharp Object
	Animal Safety
	Plant Safety
	Electric Shock
	Physical Safety
	Disposal
	Hand Washing
	General Safety Awareness

Wear heat-resistant gloves when handling hot objects.

Keep your work area clean and uncluttered.

Make sure electric cords are untangled and out of the way.

Wear closed-toe shoes when working in the laboratory.

End-of-Lab Procedures Your lab work does not end when you reach the last step in the procedure. There are important things you need to do at the end of every lab.

When you have completed a lab, be sure to clean up your work area. Turn off and unplug any equipment and return it to its proper place. It is very important that you dispose of any waste materials properly. Some wastes should not be thrown in the trash or poured down the drain. Follow your teacher's instructions about proper disposal. Finally, be sure to wash your hands thoroughly after working in the laboratory.

Safety in the Field

The laboratory is not the only place where you will conduct scientific investigations. Some investigations will be done in the "field." The field can be any outdoor area, such as a schoolyard, a forest, a park, or a beach.  **Just as in the laboratory, good preparation helps you stay safe when doing science activities in the field.**

There can be many potential safety hazards outdoors. For example, you could encounter severe weather, traffic, wild animals, or poisonous plants. Advance planning may help you avoid some potential hazards. For example, you can listen to the weather forecast and plan your trip accordingly. Other hazards may be impossible to anticipate.

Whenever you do field work, always tell an adult where you will be. Never carry out a field investigation alone. Ask an adult or a classmate to accompany you. Dress appropriately for the weather and other conditions you will encounter. Use common sense to avoid any potentially dangerous situations.

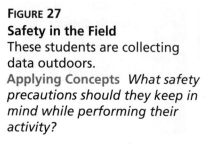 **Reading Checkpoint** What are some potential outdoor hazards?

FIGURE 27
Safety in the Field
These students are collecting data outdoors.
Applying Concepts *What safety precautions should they keep in mind while performing their activity?*

In Case of an Accident

Good preparation and careful work habits can go a long way toward making your lab experiences safe ones. But, at some point, an accident may occur. A classmate might accidentally knock over a beaker or a chemical might spill on your sleeve. Would you know what to do?

When any accident occurs, no matter how minor, notify your teacher immediately. Then, listen to your teacher's directions and carry them out quickly. Make sure you know the location and proper use of all the emergency equipment in your lab room. Knowing safety and first aid procedures beforehand will prepare you to handle accidents properly. Figure 28 lists some first-aid procedures you should know.

FIGURE 28
First-Aid Tips
These first-aid tips can help guide your actions during emergency situations. Remember, always notify your teacher immediately if an accident occurs.

In Case of Emergency

ALWAYS NOTIFY YOUR TEACHER IMMEDIATELY

Injury	What to Do
Burns	Immerse burns in cold water.
Cuts	Cover cuts with a clean dressing. Apply direct pressure to the wound to stop bleeding.
Spills on Skin	Flush the skin with large amounts of water.
Foreign Object in Eye	Flush the eye with large amounts of water. Seek medical attention.

Section 6 Assessment

S 8.9, E-LA: Reading 8.1.0, Writing 8.2.4

Vocabulary Skill High-Use Academic Words
What should you do after you complete a laboratory activity? Make a list with at least five steps. Use the term *procedures* in the title of your list.

Reviewing Key Concepts

1. a. Listing List two things you should do ahead of time to prepare for a lab.

b. Interpreting Diagrams Suppose a lab included the safety symbols below. What do these symbols mean? What precautions should you take?

c. Making Generalizations Why is it more difficult to prepare for a lab activity in the field than for one in a laboratory?

2. a. Reviewing Suppose during a lab activity you get a cut and start to bleed. What is the first thing you should do?

b. Sequencing Outline in order the next steps you would take to deal with your injury.

c. Making Judgments Some people feel that most accidents that occur really could have been prevented with better preparation or safer behaviors. Do you agree or disagree with this viewpoint? Explain your reasoning.

Writing in Science

Safety Poster Make a poster of one of the safety rules in Appendix A to post in your lab. Be sure to include the safety symbol, clear directions, and additional illustrations.

Study Guide

**The BIG Idea** Scientists investigate the natural world by posing questions, developing hypotheses, designing experiments, analyzing data, drawing conclusions, and communicating results.

1 What Is Physical Science?

Key Concepts S 8.9

- Scientists use the skills of observing, inferring, and predicting to learn about the natural world.
- Physical science is the study of matter and energy, and the changes that they undergo.

Key Terms

science	inferring	chemistry
observing	predicting	physics

2 Scientific Inquiry

Key Concepts S 8.9.a, 8.9.c

- Processes used in inquiry include posing questions, developing hypotheses, designing experiments, collecting and interpreting data, drawing conclusions, and communicating.
- Scientists use models and develop laws and theories to increase people's understanding of the natural world.

Key Terms

scientific inquiry	data
hypothesis	communicating
parameter	model
manipulated variable	scientific theory
responding variable	scientific law
controlled experiment	

3 Measurement

Key Concepts S 8.8.a, 8.8.b

- Using SI allows scientists to compare data and communicate with each other about results.
- SI units include: m, kg, m^3, kg/m^3, s, and K.
- Volume = Area × Height
- Density = $\dfrac{Mass}{Volume}$

Key Terms

SI	volume	Celsius scale
weight	meniscus	Kelvin scale
mass	density	absolute zero

4 Mathematics and Science

Key Concepts S 8.9.b

- When collecting data and making measurements, scientists use math skills involving estimation, accuracy and reproducability, significant figures, and precision.

Key Terms

estimate	significant figures
accuracy	precision
reproducibility	

5 Graphs in Science

Key Concepts S 8.9.d, 8.9.g

- Line graphs are used to display data to see how one variable (the responding variable) changes in response to another variable (the manipulated variable).
- A line of best fit emphasizes the overall trend shown by all the data taken as a whole.
- Slope = $\dfrac{Rise}{Run} = \dfrac{y_2 - y_1}{x_2 - x_1}$
- Line graphs are powerful tools in science because they allow you to identify trends and make predictions.

Key Terms

graph	data point
horizontal axis	line of best fit
vertical axis	linear graph
origin	slope
coordinate	nonlinear graph

6 Science Laboratory Safety

Key Concepts S 8.9

- Good preparation helps you stay safe when doing science activities in the laboratory or the field.
- When any accident occurs, no matter how minor, notify your teacher immediately. Then, listen to your teacher's directions and carry them out quickly.

Review and Assessment

Go Online
PHSchool.com

For: Self-Assessment
Visit: PHSchool.com
Web Code: cxa-1010

Target Reading Skill

Preview Text Structure Review Section 4 of the chapter. Then, complete the graphic organizer on Mathematics and Science.

Mathematics and Science		
Heading	**Question**	**Answer**
Estimation	What is an estimate?	
Accuracy and Reproducibility	How does accuracy differ from reproducibility?	
Significant Figures and Precision		

Reviewing Key Terms

Choose the letter of the best answer.

1. A logical interpretation based on reasoning from prior experience is called
   a. scientific inquiry.
   b. a prediction.
   c. an inference.
   d. an observation.

2. In an experiment where you change only the temperature, temperature is the
   a. responding variable.
   b. manipulated variable.
   c. hypothesis.
   d. controlled parameter.

3. The amount of matter an object contains is its
   a. length.   b. mass.
   c. weight.   d. volume.

4. Repeated measurements that are close to one another demonstrate
   a. accuracy.
   b. reproducibility.
   c. scientific inquiry.
   d. significant figures.

5. In the event that a glass beaker breaks during a lab, the first thing you should do is
   a. wash your hands.
   b. clean up the broken glass.
   c. alert your teacher.
   d. obtain another beaker.

Complete the following sentences so that your answers clearly explain the key terms.

6. When a meteorologist **predicts** the weather, she makes a _____.

7. A key process in the scientific method is the collection of **data,** which are _____.

8. You can predict whether an object will float or sink in water if you know the object's **density,** which is _____.

9. The measurement 5.22 centimeters has three **significant figures,** which means that _____.

10. One way to analyze a linear graph of data is to calculate the **slope,** which tells _____.

Writing in Science

Interview You are a sports reporter interviewing an Olympic swimmer who lost the silver medal by a few hundredths of a second. Write a one-page interview in which you discuss the meaning of time and the advanced instruments used to measure time.

Video Assessment

Discovery Channel School
The Work of Scientists

Review and Assessment

Checking Concepts

11. In your own words, briefly explain what physical science is.

12. Why must a scientific hypothesis be testable?

13. In a controlled experiment, why is it important to change just one variable parameter at a time?

14. Why must scientists use standard units of measure in their experiments?

15. Why is it important to be both accurate and precise when you make measurements?

16. When graphing, why should you draw a smooth line that reflects the general pattern, rather than simply connect the data points?

17. List three things you can do to prepare for a lab experiment.

Thinking Critically

18. **Comparing and Contrasting** Which of the objects below has a greater volume? Explain.

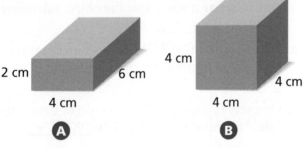

19. **Applying Concepts** When water freezes, it expands. Use this statement and your knowledge of density to explain why ice cubes float in water.

20. **Relating Cause and Effect** In a lab activity that involves many measurements and calculations, you and your lab partner rush through the procedures. In the end, you obtain a percent error of 50 percent. Explain what may have led to such a high percent error.

21. **Making Judgments** Why do you think that, as a general precaution, you should never bring food or drink into a laboratory?

Math Practice

22. **Calculating Density** A 12.5-g marble displaces 5.0 mL of water. What is its density?

23. **Area** Calculate the area of a picture frame that measures 17 cm × 12 cm.

Applying Skills

Use the graph to answer Questions 24–26.

A scientist measured the distance a lava stream flowed over 5 minutes.

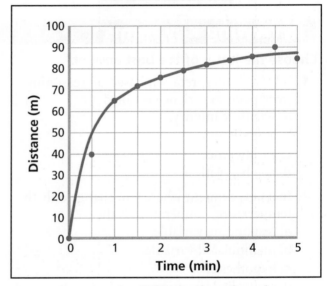

24. **Reading Graphs** What is plotted on the horizontal axis? The vertical axis?

25. **Interpreting Data** Did the stream travel the same distance every minute? Explain.

26. **Predicting** Predict the movement of the stream between 5 and 6 minutes.

Lab zone Standards Investigation

Performance Assessment Present a brief summary of your experience while building your density-calculating system. Describe the most difficult part of construction. What steps were easiest? Defend the accuracy and reliability of your system, and describe its limitations.

Choose the letter of the best answer.

1. Ranida measured the length of a string several times as 21.5 cm, 21.3 cm, 21.7 cm, and 21.6 cm. The actual length is 25.5 cm. Which statement best describes Ranida's measurements?

   A The measurements were accurate.

   B The measurements were not accurate, but they were reproducible.

   C The measurements were both accurate and reproducible.

   D The measurements were neither accurate nor reproducible.   **S 8.9.b**

2. A sample of sulfur has a mass of 12 g and a volume of 6.0 cm^3. What is the density of sulfur?

   A 0.5 g/cm^3

   B 2.0 g/cm^3

   C 2.0 cm^3/g

   D 72 g/cm^3 **S 8.8.b**

The graph below shows the masses of five different volumes of liquid. Use the graph and your knowledge of science to answer Question 3.

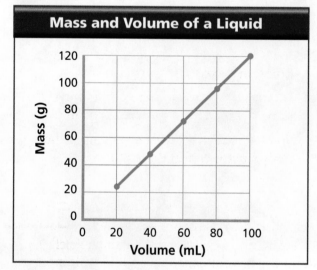

Mass and Volume of a Liquid

3. What is the slope of the graph line?

   A −1.0 g/mL

   B 1.0 g/mL

   C 1.2 mL/g

   D 1.2 g/mL   **S 8.9.d**

The graph below compares how well two different brands of insulated mugs retain heat. Each mug was filled with the same volume of boiling water. Use the graph and your knowledge of science to answer Questions 4–5.

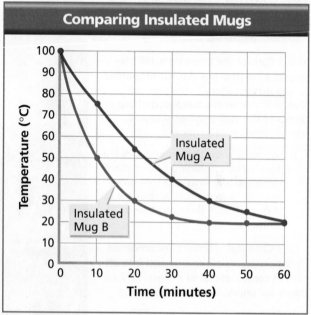

Comparing Insulated Mugs

4. Which parameter in this experiment was the responding variable?

   A the temperature of the water

   B the location of the insulated mug

   C the brand of insulated mug

   D the length of time the water was allowed to cool   **S 8.9.c**

5. What conclusion can you draw from this experiment?

   A There is no difference between Brand A and Brand B.

   B Brand A keeps water warmer than Brand B.

   C Brand B keeps water warmer than Brand A.

   D Brand B seems to add heat to the water.   **S 8.9.a**

Apply the BIG Idea

6. Suppose you are given a sample of a liquid. How can you predict the mass of a much larger sample of the same liquid? Describe the measurements and calculations required to make your prediction.   **S 8.8.a, S 8.9.a**

Chapter 2

The Nature of Matter

This "junk sculpture" of an armadillo is ▶ made entirely of metal can lids.

Focus on the
BIG Idea

S 8.3

What is chemistry?

Check What You Know

Suppose you have a whole cookie. You break the cookie into tiny pieces and crumbs. Then, you weigh all the pieces and crumbs. How do you think the weight of the whole cookie compares to the total weight of all the cookie crumbs?

Build Science Vocabulary

The images shown here represent some of the key terms in this chapter. You can use this vocabulary skill to help you understand the meaning of some key terms in this chapter.

Vocabulary Skill

Prefixes

A prefix is a word part that is added at the beginning of a root word to change its meaning. For example, the prefix *com-* means "with," or "together." In the word *combine*, the prefix *com-* is added to the root word *bind* to form *combine*, meaning "to bind together."

com	+	bind	=	combine
together		tie		bind or tie together

The following prefixes will help you learn new words in this chapter.

Prefix	Meaning	Example Word
com-	With, together	Compound
hetero-	Different	Heterogenous
homo-	Same	Homogenous
endo-	In, within	Endogenous
exo-	Out	Exothermic

Apply It!

The Greek root *therm* means "heat." Use the table to learn the meaning of the prefix *endo-*. Then predict the meaning of the adjective *endothermic*. Read Section 1 to see if your predicted definition is accurate or needs to be changed.

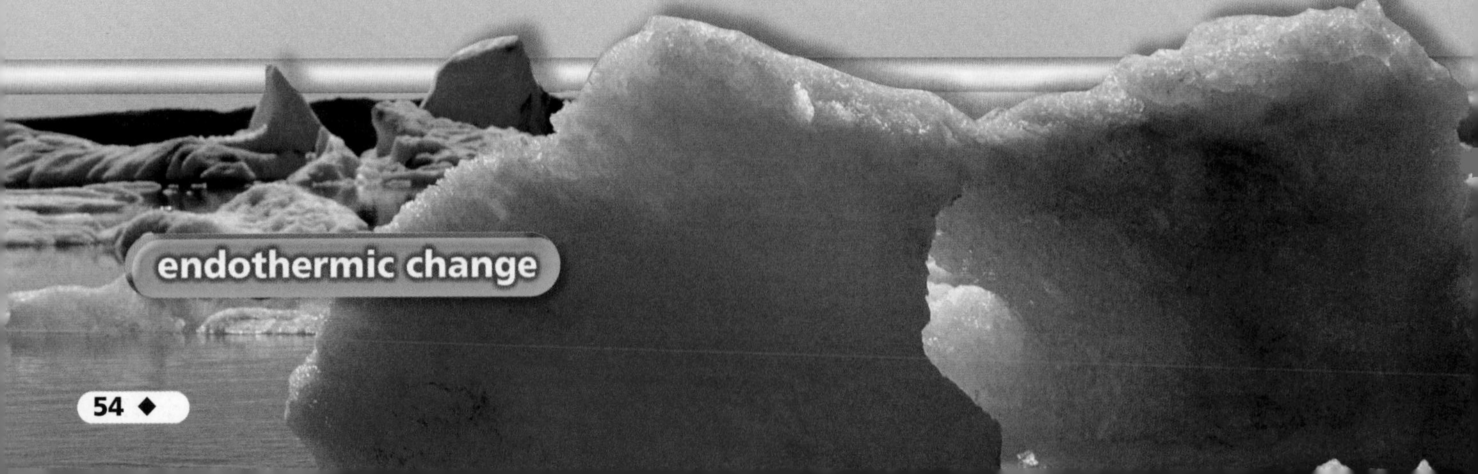

endothermic change

matter

thermal energy

physical change

chemical property

Chapter 2
Vocabulary

Section 1 (page 58)
matter
substance
physical property
chemical property
element
atom
chemical bond
molecule
compound
chemical formula
mixture
heterogeneous mixture
homogeneous mixture
solution

Section 2 (page 68)
physical change
chemical change
law of conservation of matter

Section 3 (page 73)
energy
temperature
thermal energy
endothermic change
exothermic change
chemical energy
electromagnetic energy
electrical energy
electrode

Interactive Textbook

Build Science Vocabulary
Online
Visit: PHSchool.com
Web Code: cxj-1020

How to Read Science

Identify the Main Idea

The main idea is the most important—or biggest—idea in a passage of text. Sometimes the main idea is stated directly. At other times, you must identify the main idea yourself.

Here are some tips.

- Look at the heading or subheading.
- Distinguish the important information.
- Identify a few important details about the topic.
- State the main idea of the passage.

Read the paragraph on page 58. Identify the main idea and supporting details. You can keep track of this information by using a graphic organizer like the one below.

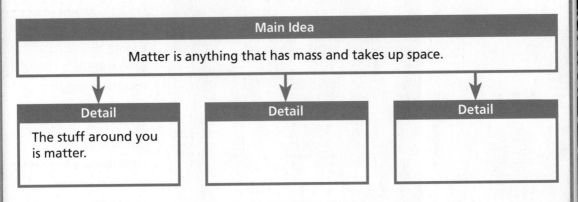

Main Idea
Matter is anything that has mass and takes up space.

Detail	Detail	Detail
The stuff around you is matter.		

Apply It!

In your notebook, copy and complete the graphic organizer.

As you read the chapter, look for the main ideas and supporting details in paragraphs.

S 8.3.b

Classify Changes in Matter

Look around. All sorts of changes are taking place. You might observe a fence rusting or a puddle of water evaporating. As you will learn in this chapter, changes in matter can be physical or chemical. In this investigation, you will keep a log of the changes that occur around you.

Your Goal

To identify and observe physical and chemical changes in your daily life and to record evidence for those changes

To complete the investigation, you must

- determine what evidence indicates that a change has taken place
- record observations of the different changes you notice in your life during one week
- classify the changes you observe as physical or chemical
- follow the safety guidelines in Appendix A

Plan It!

Preview the chapter to learn what physical and chemical changes are. With a group, discuss some changes you observe regularly. Try to decide if each change is a physical or chemical change.

Describing Matter

S 8.3.b Students know that compounds are formed by combining two or more different elements and that compounds have properties that are different from their constituent elements.

- What kinds of properties are used to describe matter?
- What are elements, and how do they relate to compounds?
- What are the properties of a mixture?

Key Terms

- matter • substance
- physical property
- chemical property • element
- atom • chemical bond
- molecule • compound
- chemical formula • mixture
- heterogeneous mixture
- homogeneous mixture
- solution

Lab zone Standards **Warm-Up**

What Is a Mixture?

1. Your teacher will give you a handful of objects, such as checkers, marbles, and paper clips of different sizes and colors.

2. Examine the objects. Then sort them into at least three groups. Each item should be grouped with similar items.

3. Describe the differences between the unsorted handful and the sorted groups of objects. Then make a list of the characteristics of each sorted group.

Think It Over

Forming Operational Definitions The unsorted handful of objects represents a mixture. Your sorted groups represent substances. Using your observations, infer what the terms *mixture* and *substance* mean.

You have probably heard the word *matter* many times. Think about how often you hear the phrases "As a matter of fact, …" or "Hey, what's the matter?" In science, this word has a specific meaning. **Matter** is anything that has mass and takes up space. All the "stuff" around you is matter, and you are matter too. Air, plastic, metal, wood, glass, paper, and cloth—all of these are matter.

▼ **Paper, ceramic, wood, metal, and foam are all forms of matter.**

Properties of Matter

Even though air and plastic are both matter, no one has to tell you they are different materials. Matter can have many different properties, or characteristics. Materials can be hard or soft, rough or smooth, hot or cold, liquid, solid, or gas. Some materials catch fire easily, but others do not burn. Chemistry is the study of the properties of matter and how matter changes.

The properties and changes of any type of matter depend on its makeup. Some types of matter are substances and some are not. In chemistry, a **substance** is a single kind of matter that is pure, meaning it always has a specific makeup—or composition—and a specific set of properties. For example, table salt has the same composition and properties no matter where it comes from—seawater or a salt mine. On the other hand, think about the batter for blueberry muffins. It contains flour, butter, sugar, salt, blueberries, and other ingredients shown in Figure 1. While some of the ingredients, such as sugar and salt, are pure substances, the muffin batter is not. It consists of several ingredients that can vary with the recipe.

🔑 **Every form of matter has two kinds of properties— physical properties and chemical properties.** A physical property of oxygen is that it is a gas at room temperature. A chemical property of oxygen is that it reacts with iron to form rust. You'll read more about physical and chemical properties in the next two pages.

FIGURE 1
Substances or Not?
Making muffin batter involves mixing together different kinds of matter. The batter itself is not a pure substance. **Classifying** *Why are salt, sugar, and baking soda pure substances?*

Pure Substances
Table salt, table sugar, and baking soda are pure substances.

Not Substances
Flour, baking powder, milk, eggs, and fruit are not pure substances.

FIGURE 2
Physical Properties

The physical properties of matter help you identify and classify matter in its different forms.
Applying Concepts *Why is melting point a physical property?*

▲ **Density and Melting Point**
The density of ice at 0°C is 0.917 g/cm³. Above 0°C, ice will change to liquid water.

◄ **Texture and Color**
Bumpy texture and bright colors are physical properties of this hungry chameleon.

▲ **Flexibility**
Metal becomes a shiny, flexible toy when shaped into a flat wire and coiled.

Lab zone Skills Activity

Interpreting Data

Melting point is the temperature at which a solid becomes a liquid. Boiling point is the temperature at which a liquid becomes a gas. Look at the data listed below. Identify each substance's physical state at room temperature (approximately 20°C). Is it a gas, a liquid, or a solid? Explain your conclusions.

Substance	Melting Point (°C)	Boiling Point (°C)
Water	0	100
Ethanol	−117	79
Propane	−190	−42
Table salt	801	1,465

Physical Properties of Matter A **physical property** is a characteristic of a pure substance that can be observed without changing it into another substance. For example, a physical property of water is that it freezes at a temperature of 0°C. When liquid water freezes, it changes to solid ice, but it is still water. Density, hardness, texture, and color are some other physical properties of matter. When you describe a substance as a solid, a liquid, or a gas, you are stating another physical property. Whether or not a substance dissolves in water is a physical property, too. Sugar will dissolve in water, but iron will not. Stainless steel is mostly iron, so you can stir sugar into your tea with a stainless steel spoon.

Physical properties can be used to classify matter. For example, two properties of metals are luster and the ability to conduct heat and electricity. Some metals, such as iron, can be attracted by a magnet. Metals are also flexible, which means they can be bent into shapes without breaking. They can also be pressed into flat sheets and pulled into long, thin wires. Other materials such as glass, brick, and concrete will break into small pieces if you try to bend them or press them thinner.

FIGURE 3
Chemical Properties

The chemical properties of different forms of matter cannot be observed without changing a substance into a new substance.

◄ **New Substances, New Properties**
Gases produced during baking create spaces in freshly made bread.

◄ **Flammability**
Wood fuels a fire, producing heat, gases, and ash.

Ability to React ►
Iron can form rust, turning a once shiny car into a crumbling relic.

Chemical Properties of Matter Unlike physical properties of matter, some properties can't be observed just by looking at or touching a substance. A **chemical property** is a characteristic of a pure substance that describes its ability to change into different substances. To observe the chemical properties of a substance, you must try to change it to another substance. Like physical properties, chemical properties are used to classify substances. For example, a chemical property of methane (natural gas) is that it can catch fire and burn in air. When it burns, it combines with oxygen in the air and forms new substances, water and carbon dioxide. Burning, or flammability, is a chemical property of methane as well as the substances in wood or gasoline.

One chemical property of iron is that it will combine slowly with oxygen in air to form a different substance, rust. Silver will react with sulfur in the air to form tarnish. In contrast, a chemical property of gold is that it does *not* react easily with oxygen or sulfur. Bakers make use of a chemical property of the substances in bread dough. With the help of yeast added to the dough, some of these substances can produce a gas, which causes the bread to rise.

 **Reading Checkpoint** What is a chemical property?

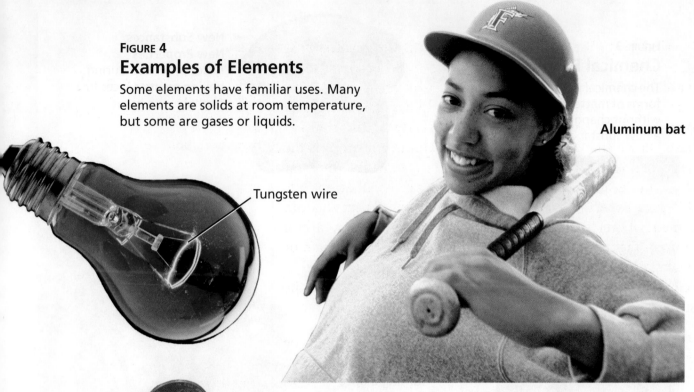

FIGURE 4
Examples of Elements

Some elements have familiar uses. Many elements are solids at room temperature, but some are gases or liquids.

Aluminum bat

Tungsten wire

Copper coating on pennies

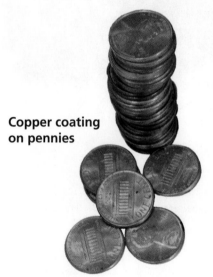

**Go Online**
SCI
LINKS™ NSTA

For: Links on describing matter
Visit: www.SciLinks.org
Web Code: scn-1111

Elements

What is matter made of? Why is one kind of matter different from another kind of matter? Educated people in ancient Greece debated these questions. Around 450 B.C., a Greek philosopher named Empedocles proposed that all matter was made of four "elements"—air, earth, fire, and water. He thought that all other matter was a combination of two or more of these four elements. The idea of four elements was so convincing that people believed it for more than 2,000 years.

What Is an Element? In the late 1600s, experiments by the earliest chemists began to show that matter was made up of many more than four elements. Now, scientists know that all matter in the universe is made of slightly more than 100 different substances, still called elements. An **element** is a pure substance that cannot be broken down into any other substances by chemical or physical means. **Elements are the simplest substances.** Each element can be identified by its specific physical and chemical properties.

You are already familiar with some elements. Aluminum, which is used to make foil and outdoor furniture, is an element. Pennies are made from zinc, another element. Then the pennies are given a coating of copper, also an element. With each breath, you inhale the elements oxygen and nitrogen, which make up 99 percent of Earth's atmosphere. Elements are often represented by one- or two-letter symbols, such as C for carbon, O for oxygen, H for hydrogen, and Zn for zinc.

Particles of Elements—Atoms What is the smallest possible piece of an element? Suppose you could keep tearing a piece of aluminum foil in half over and over again. Would you reach a point where you have the smallest possible piece of aluminum? The answer is yes. Since the early 1800s, scientists have known that all matter is made of atoms. An **atom** is the basic particle from which all elements are made. Different elements have different properties because their atoms are different. Experiments in the early 1900s showed that an atom is made of even smaller parts. Look at the diagram of a carbon atom in Figure 5. The atom has a positively charged center, or nucleus, that contains smaller particles. It is surrounded by a "cloud" of negative charge. You will learn more about the structure of atoms in Chapter 4.

When Atoms Combine Atoms of most elements have the ability to combine with other atoms. When atoms combine, they form a **chemical bond,** which is a force of attraction between two atoms. In many cases, atoms combine to form larger particles called **molecules** (MAHL uh kyoolz)—groups of two or more atoms held together by chemical bonds. A molecule of water, for example, consists of an oxygen atom chemically bonded to two hydrogen atoms. Two atoms of the same element can also combine to form a molecule. Oxygen molecules consist of two oxygen atoms. Figure 6 shows models of three molecules. You will see similar models throughout this book.

 **What is a molecule?**

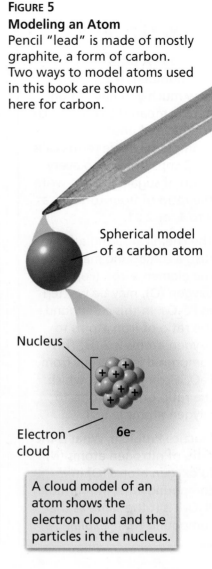

FIGURE 5
Modeling an Atom
Pencil "lead" is made of mostly graphite, a form of carbon. Two ways to model atoms used in this book are shown here for carbon.

Spherical model of a carbon atom

Nucleus

Electron cloud   6e⁻

A cloud model of an atom shows the electron cloud and the particles in the nucleus.

FIGURE 6
Modeling Molecules
Models of molecules often consist of colored spheres that stand for different kinds of atoms.
Observing *How many atoms are in a molecule of carbon dioxide?*

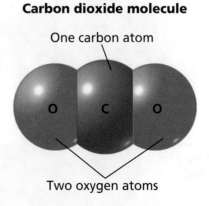

Water molecule

Two hydrogen atoms

H

O   H

One oxygen atom

Oxygen molecule

O   O

Two oxygen atoms

Carbon dioxide molecule

One carbon atom

O   C   O

Two oxygen atoms

Math Skills

Ratios A ratio compares two numbers. It tells you how much you have of one item compared to how much you have of another. For example, a cookie recipe calls for 2 cups of flour to every 1 cup of sugar. You can write the ratio of flour to sugar as 2 to 1, or 2 : 1.

The chemical formula for rust, a compound made from the elements iron (Fe) and oxygen (O), may be written as Fe_2O_3. In this compound, the ratio of iron atoms to oxygen atoms is 2 : 3. This compound is different from FeO, a compound in which the ratio of iron atoms to oxygen atoms is 1 : 1.

Practice Problem What is the ratio of nitrogen atoms (N) to oxygen atoms (O) in a compound with the formula N_2O_5? Is it the same as the compound NO_2? Explain.

Compounds

All matter is made of elements, but most elements in nature are found combined with other elements. A **compound** is a pure substance made of two or more elements chemically combined in a set ratio. A compound may be represented by a **chemical formula,** which shows the elements in the compound and the ratio of atoms. For example, part of the gas you exhale is carbon dioxide. Its chemical formula is CO_2. The number *2* below the symbol for oxygen tells you that the ratio of carbon to oxygen is 1 to 2. (If there is no number after the element's symbol, the number *1* is understood.) If a different ratio of carbon atoms and oxygen atoms are seen in a formula, you have a different compound. For example, carbon monoxide—a gas produced in car engines—has the formula CO. Here, the ratio of carbon atoms to oxygen atoms is 1 to 1.

When elements are chemically combined, they form compounds having properties that are different from those of the uncombined elements.** For example, the element sulfur is a yellow solid, and the element silver is a shiny metal. But when silver and sulfur combine, they form a compound called silver sulfide, Ag_2S. You would call this black compound *tarnish.* Table sugar ($C_{12}H_{22}O_{11}$) is a compound made of the elements carbon, hydrogen, and oxygen. The sugar crystals do not resemble the gases oxygen and hydrogen or the black carbon you see in charcoal.

Reading Checkpoint What information does a chemical formula tell you about a compound?

FIGURE 7
Compounds From Elements
This snail's shell is made mostly of calcium carbonate—a compound made from calcium, carbon, and oxygen.

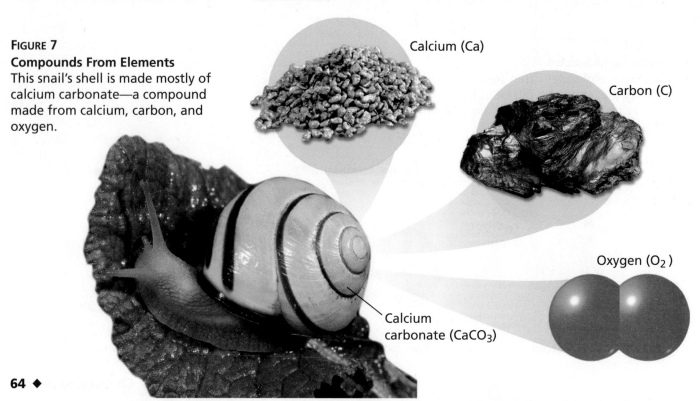

Calcium (Ca)

Carbon (C)

Oxygen (O_2)

Calcium carbonate ($CaCO_3$)

Mixtures

Elements and compounds are pure substances, but most of the materials you see every day are not. Instead, they are mixtures. A **mixture** is made of two or more substances—elements, compounds, or both—that are together in the same place but are not chemically combined. Mixtures differ from compounds in two ways. ⟳ **Each substance in a mixture keeps its individual properties. Also, the parts of a mixture are not combined in a set ratio.**

Think of a handful of moist soil such as that in Figure 8. If you look at the soil through a magnifier, you will find particles of sand, bits of clay, maybe even pieces of decaying plants. If you squeeze the soil, you might force out a few drops of water. A sample of soil from a different place probably won't contain the same amount of sand, clay, or water.

Heterogeneous Mixtures A mixture can be heterogeneous or homogeneous. In a **heterogeneous mixture** (het ur uh JEE nee us), you can see the different parts. The damp soil described above is one example of a heterogeneous mixture. So is a salad. Just think of how easy it is to see the pieces of lettuce, tomatoes, cucumbers, and other ingredients that cooks put together in countless ways and amounts.

Homogeneous Mixtures The substances in a **homogeneous mixture** (hoh moh JEE nee us), are so evenly mixed that you can't see the different parts. Suppose you stir a teaspoon of sugar into a glass of water. After stirring for a little while, the sugar dissolves, and you can no longer see crystals of sugar in the water. You know the sugar is there, though, because the sugar solution tastes sweet. A **solution** is an example of a homogeneous mixture. A solution does not have to be a liquid, however. Air is a solution of nitrogen gas (N_2) and oxygen gas (O_2), plus small amounts of a few other gases. A solution can even be solid. Brass is a solution of the elements copper and zinc.

FIGURE 8
Heterogeneous Mixture
Soil from a flowerpot in your home may be very different from the soil in a nearby park.
Interpreting Photographs
What tells you that the soil is a heterogeneous mixture?

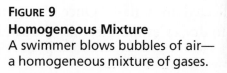

FIGURE 9
Homogeneous Mixture
A swimmer blows bubbles of air—a homogeneous mixture of gases.

FIGURE 10

Separating a Mixture

The different physical properties of iron, sulfur, and table salt help in separating a mixture of these substances.

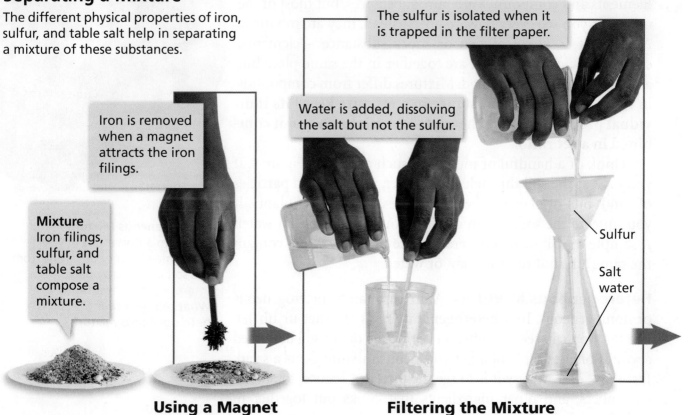

Iron is removed when a magnet attracts the iron filings.

Mixture Iron filings, sulfur, and table salt compose a mixture.

Using a Magnet

The sulfur is isolated when it is trapped in the filter paper.

Water is added, dissolving the salt but not the sulfur.

Sulfur

Salt water

Filtering the Mixture

Video Field Trip

Discovery Channel School

Introduction to Matter

Separating Mixtures Compounds and mixtures differ in yet another way. A compound can be difficult to separate into its elements. But, a mixture is usually easy to separate into its components because each component keeps its own properties. Figure 10 illustrates a few of the ways you can use the properties of a mixture's components to separate them. These methods include magnetic attraction, filtration, distillation, and evaporation.

In the Figure, iron filings, powdered sulfur, and table salt start off mixed in a pile. Iron is attracted to a magnet, while sulfur and salt are not. Salt can be dissolved in water, but sulfur will not dissolve. So, pouring a mixture of salt, sulfur, and water through a paper filter removes the sulfur.

Now the remaining solution can be distilled. In distillation, a liquid solution is boiled. Components of the mixture that have different boiling points will boil away at different temperatures. As most of the water boils in Figure 10, it is cooled and then collected in a flask. Once the remaining salt water is allowed to dry, or evaporate, only the salt is left.

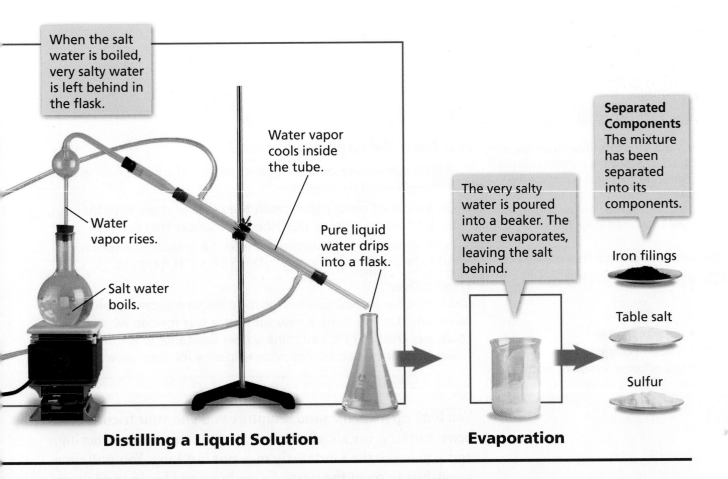

When the salt water is boiled, very salty water is left behind in the flask.

Water vapor cools inside the tube.

Water vapor rises.

Salt water boils.

Pure liquid water drips into a flask.

The very salty water is poured into a beaker. The water evaporates, leaving the salt behind.

Separated Components The mixture has been separated into its components.

Iron filings

Table salt

Sulfur

Distilling a Liquid Solution

Evaporation

Section 1 Assessment

S 8.3.b, E-LA: Reading: 8.1.0

Vocabulary Skill Prefixes How does knowing the meaning of the prefixes *hetero-* and *homo-* help you remember the Key Terms *heterogeneous mixture* and *homogeneous mixture*?

Reviewing Key Concepts

1. a. Explaining What is the difference between chemical properties and physical properties?
  b. Classifying A metal melts at 450°C. Is this property of the metal classified as chemical or physical? Explain your choice.
  c. Making Judgments Helium does not react with any other substance. Is it accurate to say that helium has no chemical properties? Explain.

2. a. Reviewing How are elements and compounds similar? How do they differ?
  b. Applying Concepts Plants make the sugar glucose, which has the formula $C_6H_{12}O_6$. What elements make up this compound?

3. a. Identifying How does a heterogeneous mixture differ from a homogeneous mixture?
  b. Drawing Conclusions Why is it correct to say that seawater is a mixture?
  c. Problem Solving Suppose you stir a little baking soda into water until the water looks clear again. How could you prove to someone that the clear material is a solution, not a compound?

Math Practice

4. Ratios Look at the following chemical formulas: H_2O_2 and H_2O. Do these formulas represent the same compound? Explain.

Changes in Matter

S 8.5.b Students know the idea of atoms explains the conservation of matter: In chemical reactions the number of atoms stays the same no matter how they are arranged, so their total mass stays the same.

- What is a physical change?
- What is a chemical change?

Key Terms

- physical change
- chemical change
- law of conservation of matter

Is a New Substance Formed?

1. Obtain a piece of chalk about the size of a pea. Observe it and record its properties.
2. On a piece of clean paper, crush the piece of chalk with the back of a metal spoon. Describe the changes that occur.
3. Place some of the crushed chalk into the bowl of the spoon. Add about 8 drops of vinegar. Describe what happens.

Think It Over

Drawing Conclusions Chalk is mostly a single substance, calcium carbonate. Do you think a new substance was formed when the chalk was crushed? Do you think a new substance was formed when vinegar was added? Provide evidence for your answers.

You look up from the sand sculpture you and your friends have been working on all afternoon. Storm clouds are gathering, and you know the sand castle may not last long. You pull on a sweatshirt to cover the start of a sunburn and begin to pack up. The gathering of storm clouds, the creation of sand art, and your sunburn are examples of changes in matter. Chemistry is mostly about changes in matter. In this section, you will read about some of those changes.

Sand has been ▶ transformed into art.

Physical Change

In what ways can matter change? A **physical change** is any change that alters the form or appearance of matter but does not make any substance in the matter into a different substance. For example, a sand artist may change a formless pile of sand into a work of art. However, the sculpture is still made of sand. ⊙ **A substance that undergoes a physical change is still the same substance after the change.**

Changes of State   As you may know, matter occurs in three familiar states—solid, liquid, and gas. Suppose you leave a small puddle of liquid water on the kitchen counter. When you come back two hours later, the puddle is gone. Has the liquid water disappeared? No, a physical change happened. The liquid water changed into water vapor (a gas) and mixed with the air. A change in state, such as from a solid to a liquid or from a liquid to a gas, is an example of a physical change.

Changes in Shape or Form   Is there a physical change when you dissolve a teaspoon of sugar in water? To be sure, you would need to know whether or not the sugar has been changed to a different substance. For example, you know that a sugar solution tastes sweet, just like the undissolved sugar. If you pour the sugar solution into a pan and let the water dry out, the sugar will remain as a crust at the bottom of the pan. The crust may not look exactly like the sugar before you dissolved it, but it's still sugar. So, dissolving is also a physical change. Other examples of physical changes are bending, crushing, breaking, chopping, and anything else that changes only the shape or form of matter. The methods of separating mixtures—filtration and distillation—that you read about in Section 1 also involve physical changes.

 **Reading Checkpoint**   **Why is the melting of an ice cube called a physical change?**

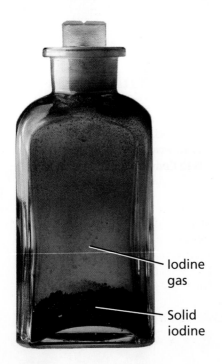

FIGURE 11
Change of State
At room temperature, the element iodine is a purple solid that easily becomes a gas.
Classifying Why is the change in the iodine classified as a physical change?

Iodine gas

Solid iodine

Table sugar

Aluminum

FIGURE 12
Change in Form
Crushing aluminum soda cans doesn't change the aluminum into another metal (left). When table sugar dissolves in a glass of water, it is still sugar (right).

Chemical Change

A second kind of change occurs when a substance is transformed into a different substance. A change in matter that produces one or more new substances is a **chemical change,** or a chemical reaction. In some chemical changes, a single substance simply changes to one or more other substances. For example, when hydrogen peroxide is poured on a cut on your skin, it breaks down into water and oxygen gas.

In other chemical changes, two or more substances combine to form different substances. For example, iron metal combines with oxygen from the air to form the substance iron oxide, which you call rust. ⊖ **Unlike a physical change, a chemical change produces new substances with properties different from those of the original substances.**

Examples of Chemical Change One familiar chemical change is the burning of natural gas on a gas stove. Natural gas is mostly the compound methane, CH_4. When it burns, methane combines with oxygen in the air and forms new substances. These new substances include carbon dioxide gas, CO_2, and water vapor, H_2O, which mix with air and are carried away. Both of these new substances can be identified by their properties, which are different from those of the methane. The chemical change that occurs when fuels such as natural gas, wood, candle wax, and gasoline burn in air is called combustion. Other processes that result in chemical change include electrolysis, oxidation, and tarnishing. The table in Figure 13 describes each of these kinds of chemical changes.

FIGURE 13
Four examples of chemical change are listed in the table.
Interpreting Photographs What fuel is undergoing combustion in the photograph?

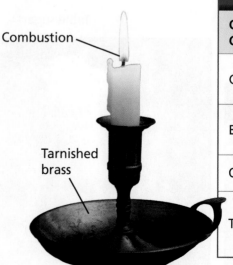

Combustion

Tarnished brass

Examples of Chemical Change		
Chemical Change	**Description**	**Example**
Combustion	Rapid combination of a fuel with oxygen; produces heat, light, and new substances	Gas, oil, or coal burning in a furnace
Electrolysis	Use of electricity to break a compound into elements or simpler compounds	Breaking down water into hydrogen and oxygen
Oxidation	Slow combination of a substance with oxygen	Rusting of an iron fence
Tarnishing	Slow combination of a bright metal with sulfur or another substance, producing a dark coating on the metal	Tarnishing of brass

Conservation of Matter A candle may seem to "go away" when it is burned, or water may seem to "disappear" when it changes to a gas. However, scientists long ago proved otherwise. In the 1770s, a French chemist, Antoine Lavoisier, carried out experiments in which he made accurate measurements of mass both before and after a chemical change. His data showed that no mass was lost or gained during the change. The fact that matter is not created or destroyed in any chemical or physical change is called the **law of conservation of matter.** Remember that mass measures the amount of matter. So, this law is sometimes called the law of conservation of mass.

Suppose you could collect all the carbon dioxide and water produced when methane burns, and you measured the mass of all of this matter. You would find that it equaled the mass of the original methane plus the mass of the oxygen that was used in the burning. No mass is lost, because during a chemical change, atoms are not lost or gained, only rearranged. A model for this reaction is shown in Figure 15.

 **Reading Checkpoint** Why is combustion classified as a chemical change?

FIGURE 14
Using Methane
Natural gas, or methane, is the fuel used in many kitchen ranges. When it burns, no mass is lost.

Go **O**nline
active art

For: Conserving Matter activity
Visit: PHSchool.com
Web Code: cgp-1013

FIGURE 15
Conserving Matter
The idea of atoms explains the law of conservation of matter. For every molecule of methane that burns, two molecules of oxygen are used. The atoms are rearranged in the reaction, but they do not disappear.

Methane molecule | **Two oxygen molecules** | | **Carbon dioxide molecule** | **Two water molecules**

H C H H H | O O   O O | | O C O | H O H   H O H

1 carbon atom
4 hydrogen atoms
4 oxygen atoms

1 carbon atom
4 hydrogen atoms
4 oxygen atoms

Math Analyzing Data

Is Matter Conserved?

Propane (C_3H_8) is a fuel that is often used in camping stoves. When propane burns, it reacts with oxygen, producing carbon dioxide gas and water vapor. The data table shows how much carbon dioxide is produced when different amounts of propane burn in oxygen.

Propane Combustion		
Mass of C_3H_8 Reacted (g)	Mass of O_2 Reacted (g)	Mass of CO_2 Produced (g)
44	160	132
250	909	750
400	1,455	1,200
465	1,691	1,395

1. **Interpreting Data** Based on the data in the table, how do you know that carbon dioxide is not the only substance formed in this chemical change?

2. **Calculating** Copy the data table and add a new column on the right. In the new column, enter how much water vapor is produced for each amount of propane burned.

3. **Graphing** Use the data in the table to make a graph. Plot the mass of C_3H_8 reacted on the horizontal axis, and the mass of CO_2 produced on the vertical axis.

4. **Reading Graphs** Use the graph to predict how much CO_2 would be produced if 100 grams of propane burned in oxygen.

Section 2 Assessment

S 8.5.b, E-LA: Reading 8.2.4, Writing 8.2.4

Target Reading Skill Identify Main Ideas
Review the text about Conservation of Matter on page 71. Identify two or three details that support the main idea that matter is conserved.

Reviewing Key Concepts

1. a. **Listing** Identify three different kinds of physical change that could happen to a plastic spoon.
   b. **Explaining** Why is the boiling of water considered a physical change?
   c. **Making Judgments** Which of the following processes is not a physical change: drying wet clothes, cutting snowflakes out of paper, lighting a match from a matchbook?

2. a. **Defining** What evidence would you look for to determine whether a chemical change has occurred?

   b. **Applying Concepts** Why is the electrolysis of water classified as a chemical change but the freezing of water is not?
   c. **Problem Solving** Explain why the mass of a rusted nail would be greater than the mass of the nail before it rusted. Assume that all the rust is still attached to the nail. (*Hint:* The nail rusts when exposed to the air.)

Writing in Science

Persuasive Letter Write a letter to persuade a friend that the formation of a gas does not necessarily mean that a chemical change has occurred.

Energy and Matter

- What are some forms of energy that are related to changes in matter?
- How is chemical energy related to chemical change?

Key Terms

- energy
- temperature
- thermal energy
- endothermic change
- exothermic change
- chemical energy
- electromagnetic energy
- electrical energy
- electrode

Lab zone Standards **Warm-Up**

Where Was the Energy?

1. Add 20 mL of tap water to an empty soda can. Measure the temperature of the water with a thermometer. (*Hint*: Tilt the can about 45 degrees to cover the bulb of the thermometer with water.)
2. Bend a paper clip into the shape shown in the photograph.
3. Stick a small ball of modeling clay into the center of an aluminum pie pan. Then stick the straight end of the paper clip into the ball.
4. Place one mini marshmallow on the flat surface formed by the top of the paper clip. Light the marshmallow with a match.
5. Use tongs to hold the can about 2 cm over the burning marshmallow until the flame goes out.
6. Measure the water temperature.

Think It Over
Drawing Conclusions How can you account for any change in the water's temperature? What evidence of a chemical change did you observe?

Do you feel as if you are full of energy today? **Energy** is the ability to do work or cause change. Every chemical or physical change in matter includes a change in energy. A change as simple as bending a paper clip requires energy. When ice changes to liquid water, it absorbs energy from the surrounding matter. When candle wax burns, it gives off energy.

Like matter, energy is never created or destroyed in chemical reactions. Energy can only be transformed—that is, changed from one form to another.

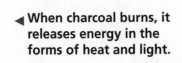
◄ When charcoal burns, it releases energy in the forms of heat and light.

FIGURE 16
Flow of Thermal Energy
Thermal energy from a hot cup of cocoa can warm cold hands on a chilly day.
Developing Hypotheses
How will the flow of thermal energy affect the cocoa?

FIGURE 17
An Endothermic Change
An iceberg melting in the ocean absorbs thermal energy from the surrounding water.

Forms of Energy

How do you know when something has energy? You might think that a battery has energy because it keeps a wristwatch working. And you would be right. Maybe you would think that the sun has energy because it gives off light. Again you would be right.

Energy is all around you, and it comes in many forms. 🔑 **Forms of energy related to changes in matter include thermal energy, chemical energy, electromagnetic energy, and electrical energy.**

Thermal Energy Think of how it feels when you walk inside an air-conditioned building from the outdoors on a hot day. Whew! Did you exclaim about the change in temperature? **Temperature** is a measure of the average energy of random motion of particles of matter. The particles of gas in the warm outside air have greater average energy of motion than the particles of air in the cool building.

Thermal energy is the total energy of all of the particles in an object. Most often, you experience thermal energy when you describe matter—such as the air in a room—as feeling hot or cold. Temperature and thermal energy are not the same thing, but temperature is related to the amount of thermal energy an object has. Thermal energy always flows from warmer matter to cooler matter.

When matter changes, the most common form of energy released or absorbed is thermal energy. For example, ice absorbs thermal energy from its surroundings when it melts. That's why you can pack food and drinks in an ice-filled picnic cooler to keep them cold. The melting of ice is an **endothermic change,** a change in which energy is taken in. Changes in matter can also occur when energy is given off. An **exothermic change** releases energy. Combustion is a chemical change that releases energy in the form of heat and light. You've taken advantage of an exothermic change if you've ever warmed your hands near a wood fire.

Math Analyzing Data

Comparing Energy Changes

A student observes two different chemical reactions, one in beaker A and the other in beaker B. The student measures the temperature of each reaction every minute. The student then plots the time and temperature data and creates the following graph.

1. **Reading Graphs** What do the numbers on the x-axis tell you about the length of the experiment?

2. **Comparing and Contrasting** How did the change in temperature in beaker B differ from that in beaker A?

3. **Interpreting Data** Which reaction is exothermic? Explain your reasoning.

4. **Calculating** Which reaction results in a greater change in temperature over time?

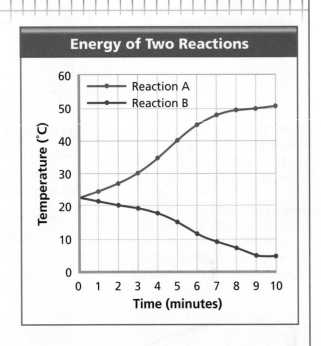

Energy of Two Reactions

Reaction A
Reaction B

Temperature (°C)

Time (minutes)

Chemical Energy The energy stored in the chemical bonds between atoms is a form of energy called **chemical energy.** Chemical energy is stored in the foods you eat, in the gasoline used to fuel cars, and even in the cells of your body.

When a chemical change occurs, chemical bonds are broken and new bonds are formed. If the change is exothermic, some of the chemical energy is transformed and released in a variety of other forms. Chemical changes usually involve transformations between chemical energy and thermal energy. For example, when a match burns, some of the chemical energy contained in the compounds of the match is transformed into thermal energy.

 **Reading Checkpoint** Where is chemical energy stored?

FIGURE 18
Chemical Energy
The particles in these grapes contain chemical energy. Your body can use this energy after you eat them.

Electromagnetic Energy You probably know that energy reaches Earth in the form of sunlight. Energy from the sun can increase the temperature of the surface of a sidewalk or change your skin by burning it. Visible light is one example of **electromagnetic energy** (or electromagnetic radiation), a form of energy that travels through space as waves. Radio waves, infrared "rays" from heat lamps, the waves that heat food in a microwave oven, ultraviolet rays, and X-rays are other types of electromagnetic energy.

Chemical changes can give off electromagnetic energy, such as the light from a wood fire. Also, both chemical and physical changes in matter may be *caused* by electromagnetic energy. For example, a microwave oven can change a frozen block of spaghetti and sauce into a hot meal—a physical change.

 **What is electromagnetic energy?**

Electrical Energy Recall from Section 1 that an atom consists of a positively charged nucleus surrounded by a negatively charged cloud. This "cloud" symbolizes moving, negatively charged particles called electrons. **Electrical energy** is the energy of electrically charged particles moving from one place to another. Electrons move from one atom to another in many chemical changes.

Electrolysis—a chemical change you first read about in Section 2—involves electrical energy. In electrolysis, two metal strips called **electrodes** are placed in a solution, but the electrodes do not touch. Each electrode is attached to a wire. The wires are connected to a source of electrical energy, such as a battery. As electric current flows through the wires, atoms of one kind lose electrons at one electrode in the solution. At the other electrode, atoms of a different kind gain electrons. New substances form at both of the electrodes as a result.

FIGURE 19
Electrolysis of Water
Electrical energy can be used to break down water, H_2O, into its elements. Bubbles of oxygen gas and hydrogen gas form at separate electrodes.
Drawing Conclusions *Why is the volume of hydrogen formed twice that of oxygen?*

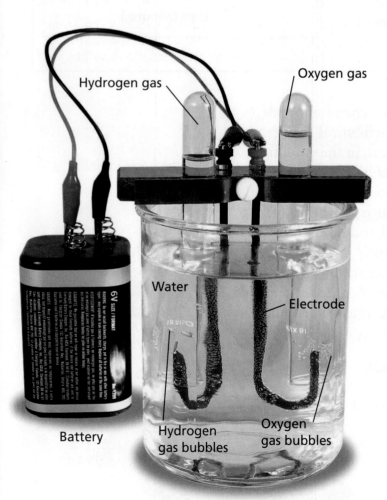

Hydrogen gas

Oxygen gas

Water

Electrode

Battery

Hydrogen gas bubbles

Oxygen gas bubbles

Transforming Energy

The burning of a fuel is a chemical change that transforms chemical energy and releases it as thermal energy and electromagnetic energy. When you push a bike (and yourself) up a hill, chemical energy from foods you ate is transformed into energy of motion. Similarly, other forms of energy can be transformed, or changed, *into* chemical energy. 👄 **During a chemical change, chemical energy may be changed to other forms of energy. Other forms of energy may also be changed to chemical energy.**

One of the most important energy transformations on Earth that involves chemical energy is photosynthesis. During photosynthesis, plants transform electromagnetic energy from the sun into chemical energy as they make molecules of sugar. These plants, along with animals and other living things that eat plants, transform this chemical energy once again. It becomes the energy needed to carry out life activities. The carrots you have for dinner may supply the energy you need to go for a walk or read this book.

FIGURE 20
Photosynthesis
Photosynthesis is a series of chemical changes in which plants convert electromagnetic energy from the sun into chemical energy.

> **Reading Checkpoint** **What type of energy transformation occurs during photosynthesis?**

Section 3 Assessment

S 8.5.c, E-LA: Reading 8.1.0, Math: 7AF1.5

Vocabulary Skill Prefixes Use what you've learned about the prefixes *endo-* and *exo-* to explain the difference between *endothermic change* and *exothermic change*.

👄 Reviewing Key Concepts

1. **a.** Listing What are four forms of energy related to changes in matter?
   b. Explaining What is thermal energy? How can you tell whether one glass of water has more thermal energy than another, identical glass of water?
   c. Inferring How might you cause an endothermic chemical change to begin and keep going?
2. **a.** Reviewing What happens to chemical energy during a chemical change?
   b. Relating Cause and Effect What are the two main forms of energy given off when paper burns, and where does the energy come from?
   c. Sequencing Describe the energy changes that link sunshine to your ability to turn a page in this book.

Lab zone At-Home Activity

Tracking Energy Changes
Volunteer to help cook a meal for your family. As you work, point out energy transformations, especially those that involve chemical energy. Explain to a family member what chemical energy is and what other forms of energy it can be changed into. Talk about energy sources for cooking and other tools and appliances used to prepare food. Try to identify foods that change chemically when they are cooked.

Lab zone Skills Lab

Isolating Copper by Electrolysis

S 8.3.b, 8.9.a

Problem

How can electrical energy be used to isolate copper metal?

Skills Focus

making models, inferring, observing, interpreting data

Materials

- glass jar, about 250 mL
- two metal paper clips
- 6-volt battery
- index card
- wires with alligator clips or a battery holder with wires
- copper chloride solution (0.6 *M*), 100 mL

Procedure

1. Unbend a paper clip and make a hook shape as shown in the diagram. Push the long end through an index card until the hook just touches the card.

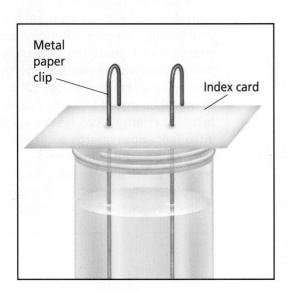

Metal paper clip

Index card

2. Repeat Step 1 with another paper clip so that the paper clips are about 3 cm apart. The paper clips serve as your electrodes.

3. Pour enough copper chloride ($CuCl_2$) solution into a jar to cover at least half the length of the paper clips when the index card is set on top of the jar. **CAUTION:** *Copper chloride solution can be irritating to the skin and eyes. Do not touch it with your hands or get it into your mouth. The solution can stain skin and clothes.*

4. Place the index card on top of the jar. If the straightened ends of the paper clips are not at least half covered by the copper chloride solution, add more solution.

5. Attach a wire to one pole of a battery. Attach a second wire to the other pole. Attach each of the other ends of the wires to a separate paper clip, as shown in the diagram. Do not allow the paper clips to touch one another.

6. Predict what you think will happen if you allow the setup to run for 2 to 3 minutes. (*Hint:* What elements are present in the copper chloride solution?)

7. Let the setup run for 2 to 3 minutes or until you see a deposit forming on one of the electrodes. Also look for bubbles.

8. Disconnect the wires from both the battery and the paper clips. Bring your face close to the jar and gently wave your hand toward your nose. Note any odor.

9. Note whether the color of the solution has changed since you began the procedure.

10. Note the color of the ends of the electrodes.

11. Discard the solution as directed by your teacher, and wash your hands.

Analyze and Conclude

1. **Making Models** Make a labeled diagram of your laboratory setup. Indicate which electrode is connected to the positive (+) side of the battery and which is connected to the negative (–) side.

2. **Inferring** Based on your observations, what substances do you think were produced at the electrodes? On which electrode was each substance produced? Recall that one of the substances was a solid you could see and the other was a gas you could smell.

3. **Observing** Compare the properties of the substances produced to those of the copper chloride in solution.

4. **Interpreting Data** If the color of the solution changed, how can you explain the change?

5. **Inferring** Based on your observations, does electrolysis produce a chemical change? Explain your reasoning.

6. **Communicating** Write a paragraph describing what you think happened to the copper chloride solution as the electric current flowed through it.

Design an Experiment

What do you think would happen if you switched the connections to the battery without disturbing the rest of the equipment? Design an experiment to answer this question. *Obtain your teacher's permission before carrying out your investigation.*

The BIG Idea Chemistry is the study of the properties of matter and how matter changes.

❶ Describing Matter

🔑 Key Concepts S 8.3.b

- Every form of matter has two kinds of properties—physical properties and chemical properties.
- Elements are the simplest substances.
- When elements are chemically combined, they form compounds having properties that are different from those of the uncombined elements.
- Each substance in a mixture keeps its individual properties. Also, the parts of a mixture are not combined in a set ratio.

Key Terms

matter	compound
substance	chemical formula
physical property	mixture
chemical property	heterogeneous
element	mixture
atom	homogeneous
chemical bond	mixture
molecule	solution

❷ Changes in Matter

🔑 Key Concepts S 8.5.b

- A substance that undergoes a physical change is still the same substance after the change.
- Unlike a physical change, a chemical change produces new substances with properties different from those of the original substances.

Key Terms

physical change
chemical change
law of conservation of matter

❸ Energy and Matter

🔑 Key Concepts S 8.5.c

- Forms of energy related to changes in matter include chemical, electromagnetic, electrical, and thermal energy.
- During a chemical change, chemical energy may be changed to other forms of energy. Other forms of energy may also be changed to chemical energy.

Key Terms

energy
temperature
thermal energy
endothermic change
exothermic change
chemical energy
electromagnetic energy
electrical energy
electrode

Review and Assessment

Target Reading Skill

Identify Main Idea Review Section 3 on Energy and Matter. Then, complete the graphic organizer to the right.

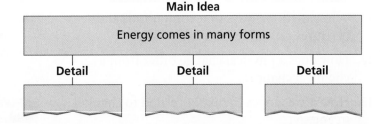

Main Idea

Energy comes in many forms

Detail	Detail	Detail

Reviewing Key Terms

Choose the letter of the best answer.

1. The ability to dissolve in water and to conduct electricity are examples of
   a. physical properties.
   b. chemical changes.
   c. chemical properties.
   d. chemical bonding.

2. Water is an example of
   a. an element.
   b. a homogeneous mixture.
   c. a compound.
   d. a heterogeneous mixture.

3. When matter changes, the most common form of energy released or absorbed is
   a. electrical energy.
   b. thermal energy.
   c. chemical energy.
   d. electromagnetic energy.

4. New substances are always formed when matter undergoes a
   a. change in shape.
   b. physical change.
   c. change in temperature.
   d. chemical change.

5. Chemical energy is the energy
   a. of temperature.
   b. stored in the bonds between atoms.
   c. of moving, electrically charged particles.
   d. that travels through space as waves.

Complete the following sentences so that your answers clearly explain the key terms.

6. The pencil you write with is an example of **matter**, which is defined as anything that _____ .

7. Different substances can be classified by their **chemical properties**, or properties that _____ .

8. All matter is made up of slightly more than 100 different **elements**, which are pure substances that _____ .

9. Chemist Antoine Lavoisier's experiments demonstrated the **law of conservation of matter**, which states that _____ .

10. The melting of ice is an example of an **endothermic change**, or a change in which _____ .

Writing in Science

How-to Paragraph Suppose you are preparing for a long journey on the ocean or in space. Write a journal entry that describes your plan for having fresh, drinkable water throughout your entire trip.

Video Assessment

Discovery Channel School
Introduction to Matter

Review and Assessment

Checking Concepts

11. What are three ways that compounds and mixtures differ?

12. How does a physical change differ from a chemical change?

13. How are changes in matter related to changes in energy?

14. How do you know that the burning of candle wax is an exothermic change?

Thinking Critically

15. Classifying Which of the following is a solution: pure water, fruit punch, cereal and milk in a bowl? Explain how you know.

16. Problem Solving Suppose you dissolve some table salt in a glass of water. How could you prove to someone that the dissolving was a physical change, not a chemical change?

17. Interpreting Graphs A student has two liquids at the same temperature. The liquids react with one another when mixed. The graph below shows the change in temperature after the two liquids are mixed. Did the reaction absorb or release thermal energy? Explain your answer.

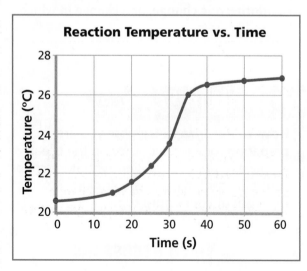

Reaction Temperature vs. Time

Math Practice

18. Ratios The elements phosphorus and oxygen form a compound with the formula P_2O_5. What is the ratio of phosphorus atoms to oxygen atoms in the compound?

Applying Skills

Use the information and the diagrams below to answer Questions 19–22.

Each diagram below represents a different kind of matter. Each ball represents an atom. Balls of the same color represent the same kind of atom.

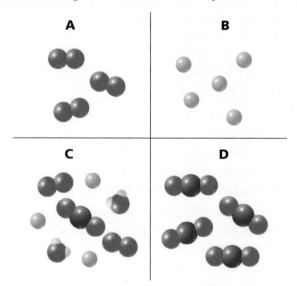

19. Interpreting Diagrams Which diagrams represent a single element? Explain.

20. Classifying Which diagrams represent pure substances? Explain.

21. Interpreting Data How do the molecules in diagram A differ from those in diagram D?

22. Interpreting Diagrams Which diagram represents a mixture? Explain.

Lab zone Standards Investigation

Performance Assessment Compare the changes you recorded in your log with those of your classmates. Defend your opinions as to whether or not your observations describe physical or chemical changes.

Choose the letter of the best answer.

1. What is the best title for the chart below?
   A Chemical Properties of Some Compounds
   B Physical Properties of Some Elements
   C The Periodic Table of the Elements
   D Gases Found in Air   **S 8.3.b**

?	
Helium	Colorless; less dense than air
Iron	Attracted to a magnet; melting point of 1,535°C
Oxygen	Odorless; gas at room temperature

A scientist did an experiment, described by the words and symbols below. Use the information to answer Questions 2 to 4.

hydrogen + oxygen → water + energy

2. The scientist found that 2 grams of hydrogen reacted completely with 16 grams of oxygen. What was the total mass of water produced?
   A 8 grams   C 18 grams
   B 14 grams   D 32 grams
                              S 8.5.b

3. The properties of the water produced by the reaction are
   A different from the properties of both hydrogen and oxygen.
   B the same as the properties of both hydrogen and oxygen.
   C the same as the properties of hydrogen, but different from the properties of oxygen.
   D the same as the properties of oxygen, but different from the properties of hydrogen.
                              S 8.3.b

4. Which pair of terms best describes the type of change that occurred in the reaction?
   A chemical and exothermic
   B chemical and endothermic
   C physical and exothermic
   D physical and endothermic   **S 8.5.c**

5. The fact that matter is neither created nor destroyed in any chemical or physical change is called the
   A law of exothermic change.
   B law of endothermic change.
   C law of thermal change.
   D law of conservation of matter.   **S 8.5.b**

6. How would you classify the burning of natural gas?
   A exothermic chemical change
   B endothermic chemical change
   C exothermic physical change
   D endothermic physical change   **S 8.5.c**

7. Which diagram best represents a mixture of two kinds of gas molecules?
                              S 8.3.b

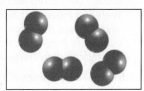
A   B

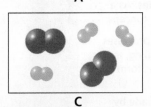
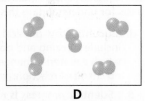
C   D

Apply the BIG Idea

8. Water is a compound with the chemical formula H_2O. Compare a physical change involving water with a chemical change involving water. How do the changes differ?
                              S 8.3.b

Solids, Liquids, and Gases

CALIFORNIA
Standards Preview

S 8.3 Each of the more than 100 elements of matter has distinct properties and a distinct atomic structure. All forms of matter are composed of one or more of the elements. As a basis for understanding this concept:

d. Students know the states of matter (solid, liquid, gas) depend on molecular motion.

e. Students know that in solids the atoms are closely locked in position and can only vibrate; in liquids the atoms and molecules are more loosely connected and can collide with and move past one another; and in gases the atoms and molecules are free to move independently, colliding frequently.

S 8.5 Chemical reactions are processes in which atoms are rearranged into different combinations of molecules. As a basis for understanding this concept:

d. Students know physical processes include freezing and boiling, in which a material changes form with no chemical reaction.

S 8.9 Scientific progress is made by asking meaningful questions and conducting careful investigations. As a basis for understanding this concept and addressing the content in the other three strands, students should develop their own questions and perform investigations. Students will:

b. Evaluate the accuracy and reproducibility of data.

e. Construct appropriate graphs from data and develop quantitative statements about the relationships between variables.

In and around this hot spring, ▶
water exists as a liquid, solid, and gas.

Focus on the

S 8.3.e

BIG Idea

How do solids, liquids, and gases differ in the motion of their particles?

Check What You Know

Suppose you leave a towel out on the beach on a hot, sunny day. After a few hours, you return to get the towel. How would the temperature of the towel have changed?

Build Science Vocabulary

The images shown here represent some of the key terms in this chapter. You can use this vocabulary skill to help you understand the meaning of some key terms in this chapter.

Suffixes

A suffix is a letter or group of letters added to the end of a word to change its meaning and often its part of speech. For example, the suffix *-ation* added to a verb can form a noun that means "process of" or "action of."

prepare	+	ation	=	preparation
		process of		the process of preparing

In this chapter, you will learn key terms that end in the suffixes *-ation, -ine,* and *-sion.*

Suffix	Meaning	Part of Speech	Key Terms
-ation	State of, process of, act of	Noun	Vaporization, evaporation, condensation, sublimation
-ine	Consisting of	Adjective	Crystalline
-sion	State of, process of, act of	Noun	Surface tension

Apply It!

Vapor is another word for gas. Use the chart above to predict the meaning of *vaporization*. Revise your definition as needed.

When you come across an unfamiliar word, look at the suffix to help you determine the meaning. Then check the definition in the glossary or a dictionary.

gas

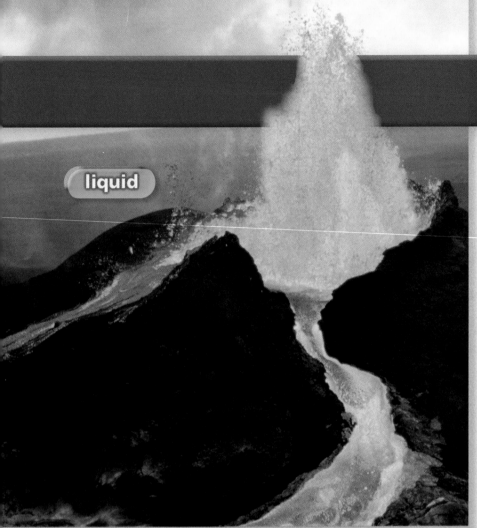

liquid

Chapter 3
Vocabulary

Section 1 (page 90)
solid
crystalline solid
amorphous solid
liquid
fluid
surface tension
viscosity
gas

Section 2 (page 96)
melting
melting point
freezing
vaporization
evaporation
boiling
boiling point
condensation
sublimation

Section 3 (page 103)
pressure
directly proportional
inversely proportional

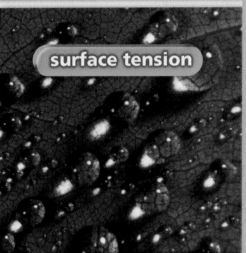

surface tension

crystalline solid

sublimation

Build Science Vocabulary
Online
Visit: PHSchool.com
Web Code: cxj-1030

How to Read Science

Create Outlines

An outline shows the relationship between main ideas and supporting details. An outline is set up like the one below. Roman numerals show the main topics or headings. Capital letters show the subheadings. Numbers show supporting details and key terms.

Look at the sample outline of the first part of Section 1.

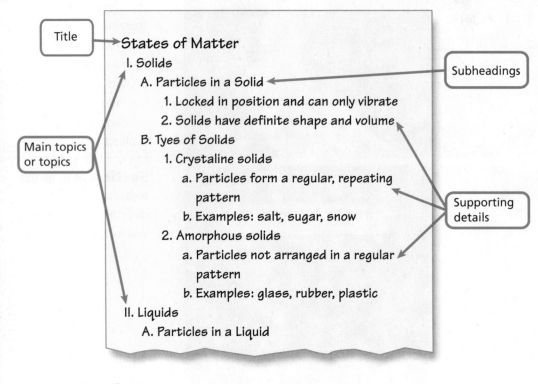

Title

States of Matter

I. Solids

   A. Particles in a Solid — Subheadings

      1. Locked in position and can only vibrate

      2. Solids have definite shape and volume

   B. Tyes of Solids

      1. Crystaline solids

         a. Particles form a regular, repeating pattern

         b. Examples: salt, sugar, snow

      2. Amorphous solids

         a. Particles not arranged in a regular pattern

         b. Examples: glass, rubber, plastic

II. Liquids

   A. Particles in a Liquid

Main topics or topics

Supporting details

Apply It!

1. What are the main topics in this outline?
2. What details support Types of Solids?

Copy the outline above into your notebook. Use the headings, subheadings, and key terms to help you select information to complete the outline for Section 1. Create an outline for Section 3.

S 8.3.d

A Story of Changing States

In this chapter, you will learn how particles of matter change from a solid to a liquid to a gas. As you read this chapter, you will build a model that shows these changes.

Your Goal

To create a skit or cartoon that demonstrates how particles of matter behave as they change from a solid to a liquid to a gas and then from a gas to a liquid to a solid

To complete the investigation, you must

- describe what happens to the particles during each change of state
- outline your skit or cartoon in a storyboard format
- illustrate your cartoon or produce your skit

Plan It!

With a group of classmates, brainstorm a list of the properties of solids, liquids, and gases. You'll be working on this investigation as you study this chapter. When you finish Section 2, describe the motion of particles in solids, liquids, and gases, and begin preparing a storyboard. Add information when you finish Section 3, and complete your cartoon or skit at the end of the chapter. Finally, present your completed skit or cartoon to the class.

States of Matter

CALIFORNIA
Standards Focus

S 8.3.e Students know that in solids the atoms are closely locked in position and can only vibrate; in liquids the atoms and molecules are more loosely connected and can collide with and move past one another; and in gases the atoms and molecules are free to move independently, colliding frequently.

- How can you describe the motion of particles in a solid?
- How can you describe the motion of particles in a liquid?
- How can you describe the motion of particles in a gas?

Key Terms

- solid
- crystalline solid
- amorphous solid
- liquid
- fluid
- surface tension
- viscosity
- gas

Lab zone Standards **Warm-Up**

What Are Solids, Liquids, and Gases?

1. Break an antacid tablet (fizzing type) into three or four pieces. Place them inside a large, uninflated balloon.

2. Fill a 1-liter plastic bottle about halfway with water. Stretch the mouth of the balloon over the top of the bottle, taking care to keep the tablet pieces inside the balloon.

3. Jiggle the balloon so that the pieces fall into the bottle. Observe what happens for about two minutes.

4. Remove the balloon and examine its contents.

Think It Over
Forming Operational Definitions Identify examples of the different states of matter—solids, liquids, and gases—that you observed in this activity. Define each of the three states in your own words.

What are the speed skaters in Figure 1 skating on? You probably answered "ice." But you may have also answered "water." So which is the right answer?

In fact, both answers are correct. "Water" refers to the substance that makes up the skating rink—a compound with the chemical formula H_2O. Depending on the temperature and pressure, water can exist as a solid, liquid, or gas. "Ice" refers to frozen water, or water in solid form.

FIGURE 1

Water as a Solid
Ice, or water in solid form, makes a great surface for skating.
Observing *What useful property does the frozen water have here?*

Your everyday world is full of substances that can be classified as solids, liquids, or gases. Another state of matter, called plasma, is common on the sun and other stars, but does not often occur naturally on Earth. Certain technologies, such as fluorescent lightbulbs, make use of plasma.

Solids, liquids, and gases may be elements, compounds or mixtures. One of the solid forms of the element carbon is diamond. Water is a compound you've seen as both a solid and a liquid. Air is a mixture of gases. Although it's easy to list examples of these three states of matter, defining them is more difficult. To define solids, liquids, and gases, you need to examine their properties.

Solids

What would happen if you were to pick up a solid object, such as a pen or a comb, and move it from place to place around the room? What would you observe? Would the object ever change in size or shape as you moved it? Would a pen become larger if you put it in a bowl? Would a comb become flatter if you placed it on a tabletop? Of course not. A **solid** has a definite shape and a definite volume. If your pen has a cylindrical shape and a volume of 6 cubic centimeters, then it will keep that shape and volume in any position and in any container.

FIGURE 2
Liquid Lava, Solid Rock
Hot, liquid lava flows from a volcano. When it cools to a solid, new rock will be formed.

FIGURE 3

Particle View of a Solid
Particles of a solid vibrate back and forth but are closely locked in position.

Particles in a Solid The particles in a solid are packed very closely together. In addition, each particle is tightly fixed in one position. This fixed, closely packed arrangement causes a solid to have a definite shape and volume.

Do the particles that make up a solid move at all? Yes, but not much.  **The particles in a solid are closely locked in position and can only vibrate.** This means that the particles move back and forth slightly, like a group of people running in place. In a solid, the particles have enough energy to vibrate, but not enough to slide past one another.

Types of Solids In many solids, the particles form a regular, repeating pattern. These patterns create crystals. Solids that are made up of crystals are called **crystalline solids** (KRIS tuh lin). Salt, sugar, and snow are examples of crystalline solids. When a crystalline solid is heated, it melts at a specific temperature.

In **amorphous solids** (uh MAWR fus), the particles are not arranged in a regular pattern. Plastics, rubber, and glass are amorphous solids. Unlike a crystalline solid, an amorphous solid does not melt at a distinct temperature. Instead, it may become softer and softer or change into other substances.

✓ Reading Checkpoint **How do crystalline and amorphous solids differ?**

FIGURE 4
Types of Solids
Solids are either crystalline or amorphous.

Go Online
*sci*LINKS
For: Links on solids
Visit: www.SciLinks.org
Web Code: cxn-1031

◄ Quartz is a crystalline solid. Its particles are arranged in a regular pattern.

◄ Butter is an amorphous solid. Its particles are not arranged in a regular pattern.

Liquids

A **liquid** has a definite volume but no shape of its own. Without a container, a liquid spreads into a wide, shallow puddle. Like a solid, however, a liquid does have a fixed volume. Suppose you have 100 milliliters of a liquid in a graduated cylinder, as shown in Figure 5. If you pour the liquid into a flask, you still have 100 milliliters. The liquid has the same volume no matter what shape its container has.

Particles in a Liquid In general, the particles in a liquid are packed almost as closely as in a solid. However, the particles in a liquid move freely. ● **Compared to particles in a solid, the particles in a liquid are more loosely connected and can collide with and move past one another.** As a result, a liquid flows and has no definite shape. A liquid is an example of a **fluid,** meaning a "substance that flows."

You can compare the movement of particles in a liquid to the way you might move a group of marbles around in your hand. Like the particles of a liquid, the marbles slide around one another but stay in contact. In solid or liquid form, the atoms of a substance stay at about the same average distance. So the density of the liquid remains very close to that of the solid.

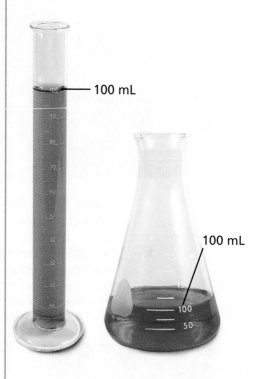

FIGURE 5
Equivalent Volumes
A liquid takes the shape of its container but its volume does not change.

100 mL

100 mL

FIGURE 6
Particle View of a Liquid
Particles in a liquid are packed close together, but can collide and move past one another, allowing liquids to flow. **Comparing and Contrasting** *How are liquids and solids alike? How do they differ?*

FIGURE 7
Surface Tension
Water beads up on a leaf due to attractions between the water molecules. Surface tension in water is strong enough to support the weight of an insect.

Properties of Liquids One characteristic property of liquids is surface tension. **Surface tension** is the result of an inward pull among the molecules of a liquid that brings the molecules on the surface closer together. Perhaps you have noticed that water forms droplets and can bead up on many surfaces, such as the leaf shown in Figure 7. That's because water molecules attract one another strongly. These attractions cause molecules at the water's surface to be pulled slightly toward the water molecules beneath the surface.

Due to surface tension, the surface of water can act like a sort of skin. For example, a sewing needle floats when you place it gently on the surface of a glass of water, but it quickly sinks if you push it below the surface. Surface tension enables the insect in Figure 7 to "walk" on the calm surface of a pond.

Another property of liquids is **viscosity** (vis KAHS uh tee)— a liquid's resistance to flowing. A liquid's viscosity depends on the size and shape of its particles and the attractions between the particles. Some liquids flow more easily than others. Liquids with high viscosity flow slowly. Honey is an example of a liquid with a particularly high viscosity. Liquids with low viscosity flow quickly. Water and vinegar have relatively low viscosities.

 **Reading Checkpoint** What property of liquids causes water to form droplets?

Gases

Like a liquid, a gas is a fluid. Unlike a liquid, however, a **gas** can change volume very easily. If you put a gas in a closed container, the gas particles will either spread apart or be squeezed together as they fill that container. Take a deep breath. Your chest expands, and your lungs fill with air. Air is a mixture of gases. When you breathe in, air moves from your nose to your windpipe to your lungs. In each place, the air has a different shape. When you breathe out, the changes happen in reverse.

If you could see the particles that make up a gas, you would see them moving in all directions, as shown in Figure 8. As they move, gas particles spread apart, filling all the space available. Thus, a gas has neither definite shape nor definite volume.

Compared to particles in a liquid, the particles in a gas have more energy of motion. 🔑 **In gases, the atoms and molecules are free to move independently, colliding frequently.** The distance between particles in a gas is much larger than the distance between particles in a solid or a liquid. You will read more about the behavior of gases in Section 3.

FIGURE 8
Particle View of a Gas
Gas particles move about freely and collide randomly with the walls of a container and with each other. **Predicting** *What will happen if the container lid is removed?*

Section 1 Assessment

S 8.3.e, E-LA: Reading 8.2.0

🔄 **Target Reading Skill** Create Outlines In your notebook, complete your outline for Section 1. What supporting details did you include under Properties of Liquids?

🔑 **Reviewing Key Concepts**

1. **a. Defining** What is a solid?
   b. Describing How can the motion of particles in a solid be described?
   c. Comparing and Contrasting How do crystalline solids differ from amorphous solids?

2. **a. Describing** How may liquids be described in terms of shape and volume?
   b. Explaining How do the positions and movements of particles in a liquid help to explain the shape and volume of the liquid?
   c. Relating Cause and Effect Explain why a sewing needle can float on the surface of water in a glass.

3. **a. Describing** How can the motion of particles in a gas be described?
   b. Reviewing What determines the shape and volume of a gas inside a container?
   c. Applying Concepts Use what you know about the particles in a gas to explain why a gas has no definite shape or volume.

Lab zone **At-Home Activity**

Squeezing Liquids and Gases Show your family how liquids and gases differ. Fill the bulb and cylinder of a turkey baster with water. Seal the end with your finger and hold it over the sink. Have a family member squeeze the bulb. Now empty the turkey baster. Again, seal the end with your finger and have a family member squeeze the bulb. Did the person notice any difference? Use what you know about liquids and gases to explain your observations.

Changes of State

CALIFORNIA
Standards Focus

S 8.3.d Students know the states of matter (solid, liquid, gas) depend on molecular motion.

S 8.5.d Students know physical processes include freezing and boiling, in which a material changes form with no chemical reaction.

🔑 What happens to a substance during changes between solid and liquid?

🔑 What happens to a substance during changes between liquid and gas?

🔑 What happens to a substance during changes between solid and gas?

Key Terms
- melting
- melting point
- freezing
- vaporization
- evaporation
- boiling
- boiling point
- condensation
- sublimation

Lab zone Standards **Warm-Up**

What Happens When You Breathe on a Mirror?

1. Obtain a hand mirror. Clean it with a dry cloth. Describe the mirror's surface.
2. Hold the mirror about 15 cm away from your face. Try to breathe against the mirror's surface.
3. Reduce the distance until breathing on the mirror produces a visible change. Record what you observe.

Think It Over

Developing Hypotheses What did you observe when you breathed on the mirror held close to your mouth? How can you explain that observation? Why did you get different results when the mirror was at greater distances from your face?

Picture an ice cream cone on a hot summer day. The ice cream quickly starts to drip onto your hand. You're not surprised. You know that ice cream melts if it's not kept cold. But why does the ice cream melt?

Particles of a substance at a warmer temperature have more thermal energy than particles of that same substance at a cooler temperature. You may recall that thermal energy always flows as heat from a warmer substance to a cooler substance. So, when you take ice cream outside on a hot summer day, it absorbs thermal energy from the air and your hand. The added energy changes the ice cream from a solid to a liquid.

▶ **Increased thermal energy turns an ice cream cone into a gooey mess!**

Solid silver   Liquid silver

FIGURE 9
Solid to Liquid
In solid silver, the atoms are in a regular, cubic pattern. The atoms in liquid (molten) silver have no regular arrangement.
Applying Concepts *How can a jewelry maker take advantage of changes in the state of silver?*

Changes Between Solid and Liquid

Particles of a liquid have more thermal energy than particles of the same substance in solid form. As a gas, the particles have even more thermal energy. So, a change from solid to liquid involves an increase in thermal energy. A change from liquid to solid is just the opposite: It involves a decrease in thermal energy.

Any change in thermal energy means a change in molecular motion. States of matter depend on molecular motion. For any substance, the freedom of motion of its particles increases from solids to liquids to gases. Resisting this motion are forces of attraction among the particles. The balance between the particles' motions and attractive forces determines the state of matter.

Melting The change in state from a solid to a liquid is called **melting.** In most pure substances, melting occurs at a characteristic temperature called the **melting point.** The melting point of pure water is 0°C. The melting point of table salt is 800.7°C. Note that melting point changes with air pressure.

☞ **When a substance melts, the particles in the solid vibrate so fast that they break free from their fixed positions.** Think of an ice cube taken from the freezer. The energy to melt the ice comes mostly from the air in the room. At first, the added thermal energy increases the average molecular motion of the water. The molecules vibrate faster, and the temperature of the ice increases. But at 0°C, the temperature of the ice stops increasing. Any added energy causes the water molecules to break out of their positions in crystals and to collide with one another. The ice melts into liquid water.

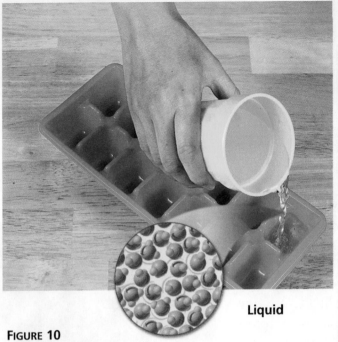

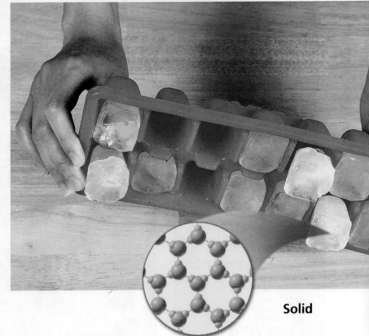

Liquid

Solid

FIGURE 10
Liquid to Solid
Just a few hours in a freezer will change liquid water into a solid.

Freezing The change from a liquid to a solid is called **freezing**. It is just the reverse of melting. **When a substance freezes, the particles in the liquid move so slowly that they begin to take on fixed positions.** Suppose you put liquid water into a freezer. The water loses energy to the cold air in the freezer. The water molecules move more slowly as they lose energy. The freedom of motion of the molecules decreases. Over time, the water becomes solid ice. When water begins to freeze, its temperature remains at 0°C until freezing is complete. The freezing point of water, 0°C, is the same as its melting point.

Note that both melting and freezing are reversible physical changes. They are not chemical changes. Liquid water that freezes is still water. Likewise, ice that melts is still water. Physical changes can usually be undone to recover the original materials unchanged. For example, after melting an ice cube, you can freeze the liquid water to recover the original solid.

Reading Checkpoint What happens to the particles of a liquid as they lose more and more energy?

Changes Between Liquid and Gas

Have you ever wondered how clouds form or how puddles dry up after a rain shower? To answer these questions, you need to look at the changes that occur between liquid and gas states.

The change from a liquid to a gas is called **vaporization** (vay puhr ih ZAY shun). **Vaporization takes place when the particles in a liquid gain enough energy to move independently, forming a gas.** As a substance changes from liquid to gas, the relative freedom of motion of its atoms or molecules increases. There are two main types of vaporization—evaporation and boiling.

Evaporation Vaporization that takes place only on the surface of a liquid is called **evaporation** (ee vap uh RAY shun). A shrinking puddle is an example. Water in the puddle gains energy from the ground, the air, or the sun. The added energy enables some of the water molecules on the surface of the puddle to escape into the air, or evaporate.

Boiling Have you ever watched a pot of water boiling on a stove? **Boiling** occurs when a liquid changes to a gas below its surface as well as at the surface. When water boils, vaporized water molecules form bubbles below the surface. The bubbles rise and eventually break the surface of the liquid.

The temperature at which a liquid boils is called its **boiling point.** The boiling point of a substance depends on the pressure of the air above it. The lower the pressure, the less energy needed for the particles of the liquid to escape into the air. In places close to sea level, the boiling point of water is 100°C. In the mountains, however, the air pressure is lower, and so is the boiling point of water. In Denver, Colorado, where the elevation is 1,600 meters above sea level, water boils at 95°C. Boiling point is a characteristic property of a substance.

Go Online

For: Links on changes of state
Visit: www.SciLinks.org
Web Code: cxn-1032

FIGURE 11
Evaporation and Boiling
Liquids can vaporize in two ways.
Interpreting Diagrams *How do these processes differ?*

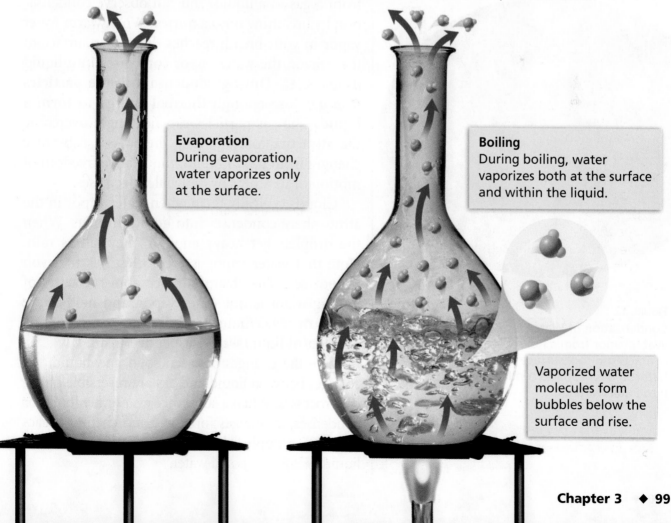

Evaporation
During evaporation, water vaporizes only at the surface.

Boiling
During boiling, water vaporizes both at the surface and within the liquid.

Vaporized water molecules form bubbles below the surface and rise.

Math Analyzing Data

Temperature and Changes of State

A beaker of ice at −10°C was slowly heated to 110°C. The graph shows how the temperature of the water changed over time.

1. **Reading Graphs** What two variables are plotted on the graph?

2. **Reading Graphs** What is happening to the temperature of the water during segment C of the graph?

3. **Interpreting Data** What does the temperature value for segment B represent? For segment D?

4. **Drawing Conclusions** What change of state is occurring during segment B of the graph? During segment D?

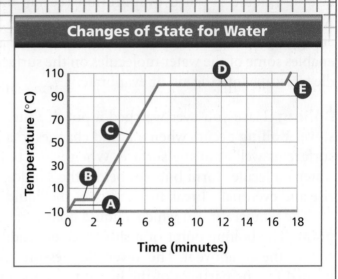

Changes of State for Water

5. **Inferring** In which segment, A or E, do the water molecules have more thermal energy? Explain your reasoning.

FIGURE 12

Condensation of Water
Water vapor from a hot shower contacts the cool surface of a bathroom mirror and condenses into liquid water.

Condensation The reverse of vaporization is condensation. **Condensation** is the change in state from a gas to a liquid. You can observe condensation by breathing onto a mirror. When warm water vapor in your breath reaches the cooler surface of the mirror, the water vapor condenses into liquid droplets. **During condensation, the particles in a gas lose enough thermal energy to form a liquid.** The gas particles can no longer overcome the attractive forces among them. As a substance changes from gas to liquid, the relative freedom of motion of its atoms or molecules decreases.

Clouds typically form when water vapor in the atmosphere condenses into liquid droplets. When the droplets get heavy enough, they fall as rain. Note that water vapor is a colorless gas that you cannot see. The steam you see above a kettle of boiling water is not water vapor, and neither are clouds or fog. What you see in those cases are tiny droplets of liquid water suspended in air.

Like the changes between solid and liquid, the changes between liquid and gas are reversible physical processes. When a substance evaporates, boils, or condenses, it changes form with no chemical reaction. For example, when water vapor condenses, the liquid that forms is still water.

Changes Between Solid and Gas

If you live where the winters are cold, you may have noticed that snow seems to disappear even when the temperature stays well below freezing. This change is the result of sublimation. **Sublimation** occurs when the surface particles of a solid gain enough energy that they form a gas. ● **During sublimation, particles of a solid do not pass through the liquid state as they form a gas.** As a solid substance sublimates into a gas, the relative freedom of motion of its particles increases.

One example of sublimation occurs with dry ice. Dry ice is the common name for solid carbon dioxide. At ordinary atmospheric pressures, carbon dioxide cannot exist as a liquid. So instead of melting, solid carbon dioxide changes directly into a gas. As it changes state, the carbon dioxide absorbs thermal energy. If warmer materials are placed near dry ice, they will lose thermal energy and become colder. For this reason, dry ice can be used to keep things cold when a refrigerator is not available. When dry ice becomes a gas, it cools water vapor in the nearby air. The water vapor then condenses into a liquid, forming fog around the dry ice.

FIGURE 13
Dry Ice
When solid carbon dioxide, called "dry ice," sublimates, it changes directly into a gas. **Predicting** *If you allowed the dry ice to stand at room temperature for several hours, what would be left in the glass dish? Explain.*

Reading Checkpoint What physical state is skipped during the sublimation of a substance?

Section 2 Assessment

S 8.3.d, 8.5.d, E-LA: Reading 8.1.0, Writing 8.2.0

Vocabulary Skill Suffixes Complete the sentences using the correct word form (*vaporize/ vaporization*). As a pot of water boils, the liquid will ____ and form a gas. Boiling and evaporation are two types of ____.

● **Reviewing Key Concepts**

1. a. **Reviewing** What happens to the particles of a solid as it becomes a liquid?
   b. **Applying Concepts** How does the thermal energy of solid water change as it melts?
   c. **Making Judgments** You are stranded in a blizzard. You need water to drink, and you're trying to stay warm. Should you melt snow and then drink it, or just eat snow? Explain.

2. a. **Describing** What is vaporization?
   b. **Comparing and Contrasting** Name the two types of vaporization. Tell how they are similar and how they differ.

   c. **Relating Cause and Effect** Why does the evaporation of sweat cool your body on a warm day?

3. a. **Identifying** What process occurs as pieces of dry ice gradually get smaller?
   b. **Interpreting Photos** What is the fog you see in the air around the dry ice in Figure 13? Why does the fog form?

Writing in Science

Using Analogies Write a short essay in which you create an analogy to describe particle motion. Compare the movements and positions of people dancing with the motions of water molecules in liquid water and in water vapor.

Go Online
PHSchool.com

For: Data sharing
Visit: PHSchool.com
Web Code: cgd-1022

Melting Ice S 8.3.d, 8.9.b

Problem

How does the temperature of the surroundings affect the rate at which ice melts?

Skills Focus

predicting, interpreting data, inferring

Materials

- stopwatch or timer
- thermometer or temperature probe
- 2 plastic cups, about 200 mL each
- 2 stirring rods, preferably plastic
- ice cubes, about 2 cm on each side
- warm water, about 40°C–45°C
- water at room temperature, about 20°C–25°C

Procedure

1. Read Steps 3–8. Based on your own experience, predict which ice cube will melt faster.

2. In your notebook, make a data table like the one below.

3. Fill a cup halfway with warm water (about 40°C to 45°C). Fill a second cup to the same depth with water at room temperature.

4. Record the exact temperature of the water in each cup. If you are using a temperature probe, see your teacher for instructions.

5. Obtain two ice cubes that are as close to the same size as possible.

6. Place one ice cube in each cup. Begin timing with a stopwatch. Gently stir each cup with a stirring rod until the ice has completely melted.

7. Observe both ice cubes carefully. At the moment one of the ice cubes is completely melted, record the time and the temperature of the water in the cup.

8. Wait for the second ice cube to melt. Record its melting time and the water temperature.

Analyze and Conclude

1. **Predicting** Was your prediction in Step 1 supported by the results of the experiment? Explain why or why not.

2. **Interpreting Data** In which cup did the water temperature change the most? Explain.

3. **Inferring** The ice absorbed energy as it melted. What was the source of that energy? How did the added energy affect the relative freedom of motion of the water molecules?

4. **Communicating** Write a paragraph describing how errors in measurement could have affected your conclusions in this experiment. Tell what you would do differently if you repeated the procedure. (*Hint:* How well were you able to time the exact moment that each ice cube completely melted?)

Design an Experiment

When a lake freezes in winter, only the top turns to ice. Design an experiment to model the melting of a frozen lake during the spring. *Obtain your teacher's permission before carrying out your investigation.* Be prepared to share your results with the class.

Data Table			
Cup	Beginning Temperature (°C)	Time to Melt (s)	Final Temperature (°C)
1			
2			

The Behavior of Gases

CALIFORNIA
Standards Focus

S 8.3.d Students know the states of matter (solid, liquid, gas) depend on molecular motion.

S 8.9.e Construct appropriate graphs from data and develop quantitative statements about the relationships between variables.

- What types of measurements are useful when working with gases?

- How are the volume, temperature, and pressure of a gas related?

Key Terms
- pressure
- directly proportional
- inversely proportional

Lab zone Standards **Warm-Up**

How Can Air Keep Chalk From Breaking?

1. Stand on a chair and drop a piece of chalk onto a hard floor. Observe what happens to the chalk.

2. Wrap a second piece of chalk in wax paper or plastic food wrap. Drop the chalk from the same height used in Step 1. Observe the results.

3. Wrap a third piece of chalk in plastic bubble wrap. Drop the chalk from the same height used in Step 1. Observe the results.

Think It Over

Inferring Compare the results from Steps 1, 2, and 3. What properties of the air in the bubble wrap accounted for the results in Step 3?

How do you prepare a hot-air balloon for a morning ride? First, you inflate the balloon, using powerful air fans. Then you heat the air inside with propane gas burners. For the balloon and its cargo to rise, the air inside the balloon must be less dense than the air outside the balloon. How does this happen? How can you keep the balloon floating safely through the atmosphere? How can you make it come down when you are ready to land? To answer these questions, you need to understand the relationships among the temperature, pressure, and volume of a gas.

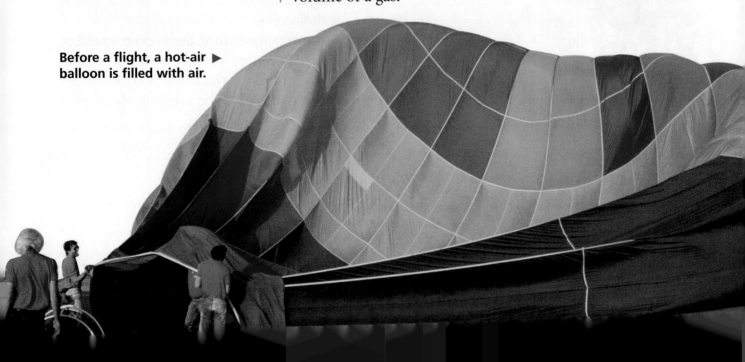

Before a flight, a hot-air ▶ balloon is filled with air.

Measuring Gases

How much helium is in the tank in Figure 14? If you don't know the mass of the helium, will measuring the volume of the tank give you the answer? Gases easily contract and expand. To fill the tank, helium was compressed—or pressed together tightly—to decrease its volume. When you use the helium to fill balloons, it fills a total volume of inflated balloons much greater than the volume of the tank. The resulting volume of helium, however, depends on the temperature and air pressure that day. **When working with a gas, it is helpful to know its volume, temperature, and pressure.** So what exactly do these measurements mean?

Volume From Chapter 1, you know that volume is the amount of space that matter fills. Volume is measured in cubic centimeters (cm^3), milliliters (mL), liters (L), and other units. Because gas particles move and fill the space available, the volume of a gas is the same as the volume of its container.

Temperature Hot soup, cold ice packs, warm hands, cool breezes—you are familiar with matter at different temperatures. But what does temperature tell you? Recall that all atoms and molecules are constantly moving. Temperature is a measure of the average energy of motion of the particles of matter. The faster the particles are moving, the greater their energy and the higher the temperature. You might think of a thermometer as a speedometer for molecules.

Even at room temperature, the average speed of particles in a gas is very fast. At about 20°C, the particles in a typical gas travel about 500 meters per second—more than twice the cruising speed of a jet plane!

FIGURE 14
How Much Helium?
A helium tank the height of this girl can fill over 500 balloons!
Interpreting Photos *How is the helium in the tank different from the helium in the balloons?*

Pressure Gas particles constantly collide with one another and with the walls of their container. As a result, the gas pushes on the walls of the container. The **pressure** of the gas is the force of its outward push divided by the area of the walls of the container. Pressure is measured in units of pascals (Pa) or kilopascals (kPa). (1 kPa = 1,000 Pa)

The firmness of a gas-filled object comes from the pressure of the gas. For example, the air inside a fully pumped basketball has a higher pressure than the air outside. This higher pressure is due to a greater number of gas particles per unit volume inside the ball than in the surrounding air.

What would happen if you punctured a hole in the basketball? Air would leak out of the ball through the hole. The pressure inside the ball would decrease, and the ball would become softer. Why does the air inside the ball leak out, rather than the surrounding air flow into the ball?

The higher pressure inside the ball results in gas particles hitting the inner surface of the ball more often. Therefore, gas particles inside the ball reach the hole and escape more often than gas particles outside the ball reach the hole and enter. Thus, many more particles go out than in. The pressure inside drops until it is equal to the pressure outside.

 **Reading Checkpoint** What units are used to measure pressure?

Lab zone Try This Activity

Under Pressure
1. Obtain a round, inflatable party balloon and a pushpin.
2. Inflate the balloon and knot the end.
3. Carefully prick a hole in the balloon with a pushpin. Observe what happens.

Inferring Was the air pressure higher inside or outside the balloon? Why did the balloon deflate?

FIGURE 15

A Change in Pressure

A punctured basketball deflates as the gas particles begin to escape.

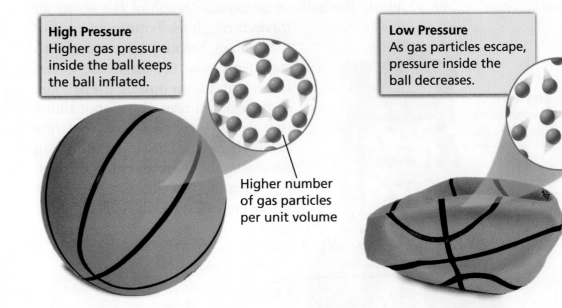

High Pressure
Higher gas pressure inside the ball keeps the ball inflated.

Higher number of gas particles per unit volume

Low Pressure
As gas particles escape, pressure inside the ball decreases.

Lower number of gas particles per unit volume

A A tied, gas-filled balloon is at room temperature.

B The balloon is lowered into liquid nitrogen at −196°C.

C The balloon shrinks as gas volume decreases.

FIGURE 16
Cooling a Balloon
The volume of a gas-filled balloon decreases as temperature decreases, and then increases as temperature increases.

FIGURE 17
Charles's Law
When the temperature of a gas increases at constant pressure, its volume increases.
Inferring What happens to the gas particles as the temperature increases?

Temperature and Volume

Figure 16 shows what happens when a balloon is slowly lowered into liquid nitrogen at nearly −200°C, then removed. As the air inside the balloon cools, its volume decreases. When the air warms up again, its volume increases. The pressure remains more or less constant because the air is in a flexible container.

Charles's Law French scientist Jacques Charles examined the relationship between the temperature and volume of a gas that is kept at a constant pressure. He measured the volume of a gas at various temperatures in a container that could change volume. ☞ **When the temperature of a gas is increased at constant pressure, its volume increases. When the temperature of a gas is decreased at constant pressure, its volume decreases.** This principle is called Charles's law.

Now think again about a hot-air balloon. Heating causes the air inside the balloon to expand. Some of the warm air leaves through the bottom opening of the balloon, keeping the pressure constant. But now the air inside is less dense than the air outside the balloon, so the balloon rises. If the pilot allows the air in the balloon to cool, the reverse happens. The air in the balloon contracts, and more air enters through the opening. The density of the air inside increases, and the balloon sinks.

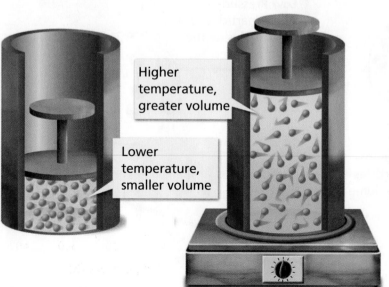

Higher temperature, greater volume

Lower temperature, smaller volume

D When removed from the nitrogen, the gas warms and the balloon expands.

E The balloon is at room temperature again.

Graphing Charles's Law Suppose you do an experiment to test Charles's law. Figure 18 shows a gas contained in a cylinder with a movable piston. The piston allows the gas to change volume at constant pressure. The experiment begins with 50 mL of the gas in an ice-water bath at 0°C. Then the water is slowly heated. Each time the temperature increases by 10°C, the gas volume is recorded. Note that the temperatures in the data table have been converted into kelvins, the SI unit of temperature. To convert from Celsius degrees to kelvins (K), add 273.

As you can see in the graph of the data, the data points yield a straight line. In fact, if you extended the line downward, it would pass through the origin. When a graph of two variables is a straight line passing through the origin, the variables are said to be **directly proportional** to each other. The graph of Charles's law shows that the volume of a gas is directly proportional to its kelvin temperature under constant pressure.

 **Reading Checkpoint** How do you convert from Celsius degrees to kelvins?

FIGURE 18
Linear Trend
As the water bath heats up, the gas inside the cylinder expands. The data show a linear trend. At constant pressure, the volume of a gas is directly proportional to its kelvin temperature.

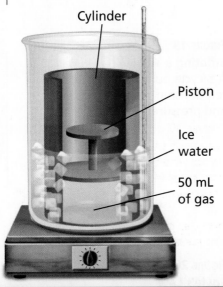

Temperature		Volume
(°C)	(K)	(mL)
0	273	50
10	283	52
20	293	54
30	303	56
40	313	58
50	323	60
60	333	62
70	343	63
80	353	66
90	363	67
100	373	69

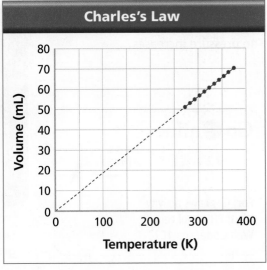

Pressure and Volume

Suppose you use a bicycle pump to inflate a tire. By pressing down on the plunger, you force the gas inside the pump through the rubber tube and out the nozzle into the tire. What happens to the volume of air inside the pump cylinder as you push down on the plunger? What happens to the pressure?

Boyle's Law In the 1600s, the scientist Robert Boyle conducted experiments in an effort to improve air pumps. He measured the volumes of gases at different pressures. Boyle's experiments showed that gas volume and pressure were related. ⊙ **When the pressure of a gas at constant temperature is increased, the volume of the gas decreases. When the pressure is decreased, the volume increases.** This relationship is called Boyle's Law.

Boyle's law applies to situations in which the volume of a gas is changed. The pressure then changes in the opposite way. For example, as you push down on the plunger of a bicycle pump, the volume of air inside the pump cylinder gets smaller, and the pressure inside the cylinder increases. The increase in pressure forces air into the tire.

Another example of Boyle's law in action involves high-altitude balloons, which are used in the study of the atmosphere. Researchers fill the balloons with only a small fraction of the helium gas that the balloons can hold. As a balloon rises through the atmosphere, the air pressure around it decreases and the balloon expands. If the balloon were fully inflated at takeoff, it would burst before it got very high.

FIGURE 19
Inflating a Tire
A bicycle pump makes use of the relationship between the volume and pressure of a gas.

FIGURE 20
Boyle's Law
As weights are added, the gas particles occupy a smaller volume. The pressure increases.

Go Online
active art

For: Gas Laws activity
Visit: PHSchool.com
Web Code: cgp-1023

Least pressure, greatest volume

Increasing pressure, decreasing volume

Greatest pressure, least volume

Volume (mL)	Pressure (kPa)
300	20
250	24
200	30
150	42
100	58
50	120

FIGURE 21
Pressure and Gas Volume
Pushing on the top of the piston decreases the volume of the gas. The pressure of the gas increases. **Predicting** *What would happen if you pulled up on the piston?*

Graphing Boyle's Law Suppose you conduct an experiment to test Boyle's law. Figure 21 shows a gas contained in a cylinder with a movable piston. A gauge indicates the pressure of the gas inside the cylinder. The experiment begins with the volume of the gas at 300 mL. The pressure of the gas is 20 kPa. Next, the piston is pushed into the cylinder, making the gas volume smaller. The pressure of the gas is recorded after each 50-mL change in volume. Temperature remains constant.

In this experiment, the manipulated variable is volume. In Figure 22, volume is shown on the scale of the horizontal axis from 0 mL to 300 mL. The responding variable is pressure. Pressure is shown on the scale of the vertical axis from 0 kPa to 120 kPa.

As you can see in the graph, the plotted points lie on a curve, not a straight line. Notice that the curve slopes downward from left to right. It is steep at lower volumes, but it becomes less steep as volume increases. If you multiply the two variables at any point on the curve, you will find that the product does not change.

$$300 \text{ mL} \times 20 \text{ kPa} = 6{,}000 \text{ mL} \cdot \text{kPa}$$

$$250 \text{ mL} \times 24 \text{ kPa} = 6{,}000 \text{ mL} \cdot \text{kPa}$$

$$200 \text{ mL} \times 30 \text{ kPa} = 6{,}000 \text{ mL} \cdot \text{kPa}$$

When the product of two variables is a constant, the variables are **inversely proportional** to each other. The graph for Boyle's law shows that gas pressure is inversely proportional to volume at constant temperature.

 **Reading Checkpoint** What is the manipulated variable in the pressure-volume experiment?

FIGURE 22
Nonlinear Trend
The graph of the data from Figure 21 shows a nonlinear trend. The gas pressure is inversely proportional to the volume when temperature is constant. **Calculating** *If you reduced the volume of the gas to 25 mL, what would its pressure be?*

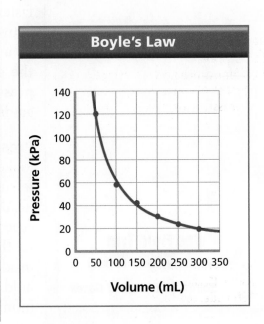

Boyle's Law

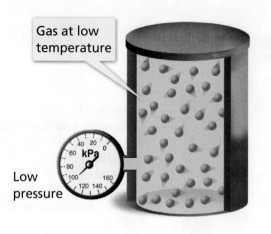

Gas at low temperature

Low pressure

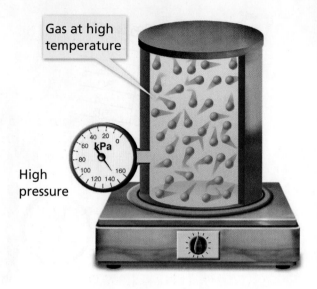

Gas at high temperature

High pressure

FIGURE 23
Temperature and Gas Pressure
When a gas is heated, the particles move faster and collide more often with each other and with the walls of their container. The pressure of the gas increases.

Pressure and Temperature

If you dropped a few grains of sand onto your hand, you would hardly feel them. But what if you were caught in a sandstorm? Ouch! The sand grains fly around very fast, and they would sting if they hit you. The faster the grains travel, the harder they hit your skin.

Although gas particles are much smaller than sand grains, a sandstorm is a good model for gas behavior. Like grains of sand in a sandstorm, gas particles travel individually and at high speeds (but randomly). The faster the gas particles move, the more frequently they collide with the walls of their container and the greater the force of the collisions.

Increasing Temperature Raises Pressure Recall from Section 2 that the higher the temperature of a substance, the faster its particles are moving. Now you can state a relationship between temperature and pressure. **When the temperature of a gas at constant volume is increased, the pressure of the gas increases. When the temperature is decreased, the pressure of the gas decreases.** Constant volume means that the gas is in a closed, rigid container.

Pressure and Temperature in Action Have you ever looked at the tires of an 18-wheel truck? Because the tires need to support a lot of weight, they are large, heavy, and firm. The inside volume of these tires doesn't vary much. On long trips, especially in the summer, a truck's tires can become very hot. As the temperature increases, so does the pressure of the air inside the tire. If the pressure becomes greater than the tire can hold, the tire will burst. For this reason, truck drivers need to monitor and adjust tire pressure on long trips.

Video Field Trip
Discovery Channel School
Solids, Liquids, and Gases

Math Analyzing Data

Graphing Gas Behavior

In an experiment, the temperature of a gas at a constant volume was varied. Gas pressure (in kilopascals) was measured after each 5-kelvin change in temperature. The data from the experiment are shown in the table.

Temperature (K)	Pressure (kPa)
273	8
278	11
283	14
288	17
293	20
298	23

1. **Graphing** Use the data to make a line graph. Plot temperature on the horizontal axis with a scale from 270 K to 300 K. Plot pressure on the vertical axis with a scale from 0 kPa to 25 kPa. (1 kPa = 1,000 Pa)

2. **Interpreting Data** What was the manipulated variable in this experiment?

3. **Interpreting Data** What kind of trend do the data show?

4. **Drawing Conclusions** What happens to the pressure of a gas when temperature is increased at constant volume?

Section 3 Assessment

S 8.3.d, 8.9.e, E-LA: Reading 8.2.0, Math: 7AF1.5

Target Reading Skill Create Outlines Review your outline on the Behavior of Gases. What are three important supporting ideas that you should know about measuring gases?

Reviewing Key Concepts

1. a. **Defining** How is gas pressure defined?
   b. **Describing** Describe how the motions of gas particles are related to the pressure exerted by the gas.
   c. **Relating Cause and Effect** Why does pumping more air into a basketball increase the pressure inside the ball?

2. a. **Reviewing** How does Boyle's law describe the relationship between gas pressure and volume?
   b. **Explaining** Explain why increasing the temperature of a gas in a closed, rigid container causes the pressure in the container to increase.

c. **Applying Concepts** Suppose it is the night before a big parade, and you are in charge of inflating the parade balloons. You just learned that the temperature will rise 15°C between early morning and the time the parade starts. How will this information affect the way you inflate the balloons?

Lab zone At-Home Activity

Finding Graphs Look for graphs in your newspaper or in magazines. Point out to members of your family which variable is the manipulated variable and which is the responding variable for each graph. Then compare any line graphs you have found to the graphs in this section. Which of your graphs show two variables that are directly proportional to each other? Do any show variables that are inversely proportioned?

It's a Gas

S 8.3.e, 8.9.e

Problem

How does the pressure you exert on a syringe affect the volume of the air inside it?

Skills Focus

graphing, predicting, interpreting data, drawing conclusions

Materials

- strong plastic syringe (with no needle), at least 35-cm³ capacity
- modeling clay
- 4 books of uniform weight

Procedure

1. Make a data table in your notebook like the one below.

2. Lift the plunger of the syringe as high as it will move without going off scale. The volume inside the syringe will then be as large as possible.

3. Seal the small opening of the syringe with a piece of clay. The seal must be airtight.

4. Hold the syringe upright with the clay end on the table. With the help of a partner, place one book on top of the plunger. Steady the book carefully so it does not fall.

5. With the book positioned on the plunger, read the volume shown by the plunger and record it in your data table.

6. Predict what will happen as more books are placed on top of the plunger.

7. Place another book on top of the first book resting on the plunger. Read the new volume and record it in your data table.

8. One by one, place each of the remaining books on top of the plunger. After you add each book, record the volume of the syringe in your data table.

9. Predict what will happen as books are removed from the plunger one by one.

10. Remove the books one at a time. Record the volume of the syringe in your data table after you remove each book.

Data Table			
Adding Books		Removing Books	
Number of Books	Volume (cm³)	Number of Books	Volume (cm³)
0		4	
1		3	
2		2	
3		1	
4		0	

Analyze and Conclude

1. **Graphing** Make a line graph of the data obtained from Steps 5, 7, and 8. Show the number of books on the horizontal axis and the volume in cubic centimeters (cm^3) on the vertical axis. Title this Graph 1.

2. **Graphing** Make a second line graph of the data obtained from Step 10. Title this Graph 2.

3. **Predicting** Did the results you obtained support your predictions in Steps 6 and 9? Explain.

4. **Interpreting Data** Compare Graph 2 with Graph 1. How can you explain any differences in the two graphs?

5. **Drawing Conclusions** What does Graph 1 tell you about how the volume of a gas changes with increasing pressure?

6. **Communicating** Write a paragraph explaining how the volume of the gas changed as books were added one by one. Base your explanation on what was happening to the gas particles in the syringe.

Design an Experiment

How could you use ice and warm water to show how the temperature and volume of a gas are related? Design an experiment to test the effect on the volume of a gas when you change its temperature. *Obtain your teacher's permission before carrying out your investigation.*

The **BIG Idea**

In solids, the particles vibrate in closely packed, fixed positions. In liquids, the particles are loosely connected and collide with one another. In gases, the particles are free to move independently.

1 States of Matter

🔑 **Key Concepts**   ⬛ S 8.3.e

- The particles that make up a solid are closely locked in position and can only vibrate.

- Compared to particles in a solid, the particles in a liquid are more loosely connected and can collide with and move past one another.

- In gases, the atoms and molecules are free to move independently.

Key Terms

solid
crystalline solid
amorphous solid
liquid
fluid
surface tension
viscosity
gas

2 Changes of State

🔑 **Key Concepts**   ⬛ S 8.3.d, 8.5.d

- When a substance melts, the particles in the solid vibrate so fast that they break free from their fixed positions.

- When a substance freezes, the particles in a liquid move so slowly that they begin to take on fixed positions.

- Vaporization takes place when the particles in a liquid gain enough energy to move independently, forming a gas.

- During condensation, the particles in a gas lose enough thermal energy to form a liquid.

Key Terms

melting
melting point
freezing
vaporization
evaporation
boiling
boiling point
condensation
sublimation

3 The Behavior of Gases

🔑 **Key Concepts**   ⬛ S 8.3.d, 8.9.e

- When working with a gas, it is helpful to know its volume, temperature, and pressure.

- When the temperature of a gas is increased at constant pressure, its volume increases. When the temperature of a gas is decreased at constant pressure, its volume decreases.

- When the pressure of a gas at constant temperature is increased, the volume of the gas decreases. When the pressure is decreased, the volume increases.

- When the temperature of a gas at constant volume is increased, the pressure of the gas increases. When the temperature is decreased, the pressure of the gas decreases.

Key Terms

pressure
directly proportional
inversely proportional

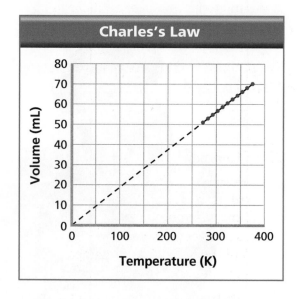

Charles's Law

Review and Assessment

Target Reading Skill

Create Outlines Review Section 2: *Changes of State.* In your notebook, complete the unfinished outline shown to the right. What important supporting ideas should you know about melting and freezing?

Changes of State
I. Changes Between Solid and Liquid
A. Melting
1.
2.
B. Freezing
1.
2.
II. Changes Between Liquid and Gas
A. Evaporation

Reviewing Key Terms

Choose the letter of the best answer.

1. A substance with a definite volume but no definite shape is a(n)
   a. crystalline solid.
   b. liquid.
   c. gas.
   d. amorphous solid.

2. Unlike solids and liquids, a gas will
   a. keep its volume in different containers.
   b. keep its shape in different containers.
   c. expand to fill the space available to it.
   d. have its volume decrease when the temperature rises.

3. The process in which a gas cools and becomes a liquid is called
   a. evaporation.
   b. sublimation.
   c. boiling.
   d. condensation.

4. The pressure of a gas is the force of its outward push divided by the
   a. volume of its container.
   b. mass of its container.
   c. area of the walls of its container.
   d. mass of the gas.

5. Under constant pressure, the volume of a gas and its kelvin temperature are
   a. inversely proportional.
   b. directly proportional.
   c. always equal.
   d. not related.

Complete the following sentences so that your answers clearly explain the key terms.

6. Water vapor and vegetable oil are examples of **fluids,** which are defined as _____ .

7. An example of a characteristic property of a substance is its **melting point,** which is ____ .

8. The reverse process of melting is **freezing,** in which a liquid _____ .

9. Evaporation and boiling are two types of **vaporization,** in which a liquid _____ .

10. At constant temperature, the volume of a gas and its pressure are **inversely proportional,** which means _____ .

Writing in Science

Explanation Write an introduction to a safety manual for deep-sea divers who use compressed air (scuba) tanks. Explain what air pressure is and what happens to gas molecules when air is compressed.

Video Assessment

Discovery Channel School

Solids, Liquids, and Gases

Review and Assessment

Checking Concepts

11. Describe the motion of particles in a solid.

12. Why are both liquids and gases called fluids?

13. Compare and contrast liquids with high and low viscosities.

14. How is the thermal energy of a substance related to its physical state?

15. Describe four examples of changes in state.

16. What happens to water molecules when water is heated from 90°C to 110°C?

17. What happens to the gas particles when the air in an inflated ball leaks out?

18. How does heating a gas in a rigid container change its pressure?

Thinking Critically

19. **Relating Cause and Effect** Explain why placing a dented table-tennis ball in boiling water is one way to remove the dent in the ball. (Assume the ball has no holes.)

20. **Applying Concepts** When you open a solid room air freshener, the solid slowly loses mass and volume. How do you think this happens?

21. **Interpreting Data** Use the table below that shows the volume and pressure of a gas to predict how a graph of the data would look. How can you describe the relationship between the two variables?

Volume (cm³)	Pressure (kPa)
15	222
21	159
31	108
50	67

Applying Skills

Use the table to answer Questions 22–24.

The data table tells how much mass of a compound dissolves in 100 mL of water as the temperature of the water is increased. Use the data to construct and interpret a graph.

Temperature (°C)	Mass of Compound Dissolved (g)
0	37
10	47
20	56
30	66
40	75

22. **Graphing** Label each axis of your graph with the appropriate variable, units, and range of values. Then plot the data in a line graph.

23. **Interpreting Data** What does the graph show about the effect of temperature on the amount of the compound that will dissolve in water?

24. **Predicting** Assume the amount of the compound dissolved continues to increase as the water is heated. Predict how many grams will dissolve at 50°C.

Lab zone Standards Investigation

Performance Assessment If you prepared a cartoon, read the captions to the class and discuss the illustrations. If you prepared a skit, perform the skit in front of the class. After you finish your presentation, invite the class to ask questions about your investigation. Be prepared to share the decisions you made in creating your presentation.

Choose the letter of the best answer.

1. A wet towel is hanging on a clothesline in the sun. The towel dries by the process of
   A boiling.
   B condensation.
   C evaporation.
   D sublimation.   **S 8.5.d**

2. Which of the following correctly describes a gas?
   A The particles do not move.
   B The particles are closely locked in position and can only vibrate.
   C The particles are free to move independently, colliding frequently.
   D The particles are closely packed but have enough energy to slide past one another.   **S 8.3.e**

3. Which state of matter has both definite volume and definite shape?
   A solid
   B liquid
   C gas
   D plasma   **S 8.3.e**

4. As water vapor condenses into liquid water, the relative freedom of motion of the water molecules
   A increases.
   B decreases.
   C stays the same.
   D drops to zero because the particles are no longer moving.   **S 8.3.d**

5. A gas at constant temperature is confined to a cylinder with a movable piston. The piston is slowly pushed into the cylinder, decreasing the volume of the gas. The pressure increases. What are the variables in this experiment?
   A temperature and time
   B time and volume
   C volume and pressure
   D pressure and temperature   **S 8.9.e**

The graph below shows changes in 1 kg of a crystalline solid as it absorbs energy at a constant rate. Use the graph to answer Questions 6–7.

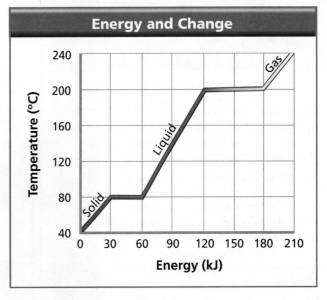

Energy and Change

6. Based on the graph, what is the total amount of energy absorbed by the substance as it changes from a solid at 40°C to a gas?
   A 30 kJ
   B 60 kJ
   C 120 kJ
   D 180 kJ   **S 8.3.d**

7. What is the melting point of the substance?
   A 0°C
   B 40°C
   C 80°C
   D 200°C   **S 8.5.d**

Apply the BIG Idea

8. Spray cans filled with gas usually have a warning printed on their labels that say, "Store in a cool place." Explain the danger in storing the can near a source of heat. Describe the motion of the gas molecules in the can when they gain thermal energy.   **S 8.5.c**

Chapter 4

Elements and the Periodic Table

Like the spices in this bazaar, elements ▶ can be organized by their properties.

Focus on the
BIG Idea

S 8.7

How is the periodic table organized?

Check What You Know

Imagine you have a piece of aluminum foil, and you cut it in half. If each of these pieces is cut in half a second, third, and fourth time, the pieces become smaller but are still aluminum. How small must a piece be so that at the next cut it will no longer be aluminum?

The images shown here represent some of the key terms in this chapter. You can use this vocabulary skill to help you understand the meaning of some key terms in this chapter.

Vocabulary Skill

Greek Word Origins

Many science words come to English from ancient Greek. For example, the word *autograph* comes from the Greek word *auto* meaning "self" and *graph* meaning "written." Therefore, an *autograph* is one's name written in one's own handwriting.

auto + **graph** = **autograph**
self   written   written in one's own handwriting

Learn these Greek origins to help you remember the key terms.

Greek Origin	Meaning	Key Words
alpha	First letter of the Greek alphabet	Alpha particle
atomos	Cannot be cut; indivisible	Atom, atomic number, atomic mass
beta	Second letter of the Greek alphabet	Beta particle
di	Two, double	Diatomic molecule
gamma	Third letter of the Greek alphabet	Gamma radiation
hals	Salt, relating to salt	Halogen

Apply It!

Review the Greek origins and meanings in the chart. What is the meaning of the prefix *di-* in *diatomic*? Predict the meaning of *diatomic molecule*. Revise your definition as needed.

Look for words with these Greek origins as you read the chapter.

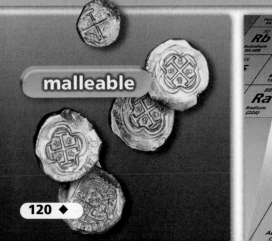

malleable

periodic table

	Potassium 39.098	Calcium 40.08	Scandium 44.956	Titanium 47.90	Vanadium 50.941	Chromium 51.996	Manganese 54.938	Iron 55.847	Cobalt 58.933	Nickel 58.71	Copper 63.546
	37 **Rb** Rubidium 85.468	38 **Sr** Strontium 87.62	39 **Y** Yttrium 88.906	40 **Zr** Zirconium 91.22	41 **Nb** Niobium 92.906	42 **Mo** Molybdenum 95.94	43 **Tc** Technetium (98)	44 **Ru** Ruthenium 101.07	45 **Rh** Rhodium 102.91	46 **Pd** Palladium 106.4	47 **Ag** Silver 107.87
55	56 **Ba** Barium 137.33	Lu 174		75 **Re** Rhenium 186.21	76 **Os** Osmium 190.2	77 **Ir** Iridium 192.22	78 **Pt** Platinum 195.09	79 **Au** Gold 196.97
	88 **Ra** Radium (226)	103 **Lr** Lawrencium (262)	104 **Rf** Rutherfordium (261)	105 **Db** Dubnium (262)	106 **Sg** Seaborgium (263)	107 **Bh** Bohrium (264)	108 **Hs** Hassium (265)	109 **Mt** Meitnerium (268)	110 **Ds** Darmstadtium (269)	111 **Rg** Roentgenium (272)

*Name not officially assigned

Lanthanides

57 **La** Lanthanum 138.91	58 **Ce** Cerium 140.12	59 **Pr** Praseodymium 140.91	60 **Nd** Neodymium 144.24	61 **Pm** Promethium (145)	62 **Sm** Samarium 150.4	63 **Eu** Europium 151.96	64 **Gd** Gadolinium 157.25

Actinides

89 **Ac** Actinium (227)	90 **Th** Thorium 232.04	91 **Pa** Protactinium 231.04	92 **U** Uranium 238.03	93 **Np** Neptunium (237)	94 **Pu** Plutonium (244)	95 **Am** Americium (243)	96 **Cm** Curium (247)

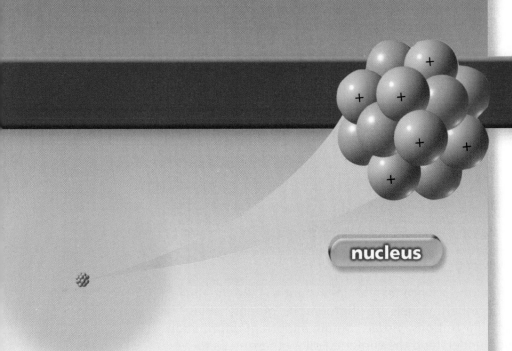

nucleus

Chapter 4 Vocabulary

Section 1 (page 124)
atom   neutron
electron   atomic
nucleus   number
proton   isotope
energy level   mass number

Section 2 (page 131)
atomic mass   group
periodic table chemical
period   symbol

Section 3 (page 138)
metal   corrosion
malleable   alkali metal
ductile   alkaline earth
thermal   metal
  conductivity transition
electrical   metal
  conductivity particle
reactivity   accelerator

Section 4 (page 148)
nonmetal   inert gas
diatomic   semimetal
  molecule   semicon-
halogen   ductor

Section 5 (page 158)
radioactive   beta particle
  decay   gamma
radioactivity   radiation
alpha particle tracer

alkali metal

nonmetal

semimetal

interactive Textbook

Build Science Vocabulary
Online
Visit: PHSchool.com
Web Code: cxj-1040

How to Read Science

Reading Skill

TARGET SKILL

Preview Visuals

Before you read the science text, it's important to take the time to preview the visuals. Visuals are photographs, graphs, tables, diagrams, and illustrations. Visuals contain important information that helps you understand the content. Follow these steps to preview visuals.

- Read the title.
- Read the labels and captions.
- Ask yourself questions about the visuals to give yourself a purpose for reading.

Preview the periodic table in Figure 14 of this chapter. Use a graphic organizer to ask questions about the table.

Figure 14: Periodic Table of the Elements

Q. Why are most of the squares in the table tinted blue?
A.
Q. Why do the symbols for some elements appear in red?
A.
Q. Why are two rows of elements listed below the main table?
A.

Apply It!

Copy the graphic organizer into your notebook. Answer the questions as you learn more about the periodic table. Preview the visuals for Sections 2 and 3, and create graphic organizers.

Standards **Investigation**

S 8.7.c

Survey Properties of Metals

Chemists have a system for organizing the elements. There are more than 100 elements, and as you will learn in this chapter, about 80 of them are classified as metals. In this investigation, you will examine more closely the physical and chemical properties of metals.

Your Goal

To survey the properties of several samples of metallic elements

To complete the investigation, you must

- interpret what the periodic table tells you about your samples
- design and conduct experiments that will allow you to test at least three properties of your metals
- compare and contrast the properties of your sample metals
- follow the safety guidelines in Appendix A

Plan It!

Study the periodic table to determine which elements are metals. Brainstorm with your classmates about the properties of metals. What properties allow you to recognize a metal? How do you think metals differ from nonmetals? Your teacher will assign samples of metals to your group. You will be observing their properties in this investigation.

Introduction to Atoms

S 8.3.a Students know the structure of the atom and know it is composed of protons, neutrons, and electrons.

S 8.7.b Students know each element has a specific number of protons in the nucleus (the atomic number) and each isotope of the element has a different but specific number of neutrons in the nucleus.

🔑 How did atomic theory develop and change?

🔑 What is the modern model of the atom?

Key Terms

- atom
- electron
- nucleus
- proton
- energy level
- neutron
- atomic number
- isotope
- mass number

Lab zone Standards Warm-Up

What's in the Box?

1. Your teacher will give you a sealed box that contains an object. Without opening the box, move the box around to find out as much as you can about the object.

2. Make a list of your observations about the object. For example, does the object slide or roll? Is it heavy or light? Is it soft or hard? Is the object round or flat?

3. Think about familiar objects that could give you clues about what's inside the box.

Think It Over

Inferring Make a sketch showing what you think the object looks like. Tell how you inferred the properties of the object from indirect observations.

Glance at the painting below and you see people enjoying an afternoon in the park. Now look closely at the circled detail of the painting. There you'll discover that the artist used thousands of small spots of color to create these images of people and the park.

Are you surprised that such a rich painting can be created from lots of small spots? Matter is like that, too. The properties of matter that you can observe result from the properties of tiny objects that you cannot see. As you learned earlier, the tiny objects that make up all matter are atoms.

FIGURE 1
Sunday Afternoon on the Island of La Grande Jatte
This painting by artist Georges Seurat, which is made from tiny dots of paint, gives you a simple model for thinking about how matter is made of atoms.

Development of Atomic Theory

If you could look into an atom, what might you see? Figuring out what atoms are made of hasn't been easy. Because atoms are so small, studying them is a bit like trying to solve the mystery of the sealed box in the Standards Warm-Up activity. Ideas about the shape and structure of atoms have changed many times.

The first people to think about the nature of matter were the ancient Greeks. Around the year 430 B.C., a Greek philosopher named Democritus proposed the idea that matter is formed of small pieces that could not be cut into smaller parts. He used the word *atomos*, which means "uncuttable," for these smallest possible pieces. In modern terms, an **atom** is the smallest particle of an element.

The ancient Greeks did not prove the existence of atoms because they did not do experiments. In science, ideas are just ideas unless they can be tested. The idea of atoms began to develop again in the 1600s. This time, however, people did do experiments. As a result, atomic theory began to take shape. ☞ **Atomic theory grew as a series of models that developed from experimental evidence. As more evidence was collected, the theory and models were revised.**

Dalton's Atomic Theory Using evidence from many experiments, John Dalton, an English chemist, inferred that atoms had certain characteristics. He began to propose an atomic theory and model for atoms. The main ideas of Dalton's theory are summarized in Figure 2. With only a few changes, Dalton's atomic theory is still accepted today.

 What is the modern definition of an atom?

For: More on atomic structure
Visit: PHSchool.com
Web Code: cgd-2011

FIGURE 2
Dalton Model
Dalton thought that atoms were like smooth, hard balls that could not be broken into smaller pieces.

Summary of Dalton's Ideas

- All elements are composed of atoms that cannot be divided.

- All atoms of the same element are exactly alike and have the same mass. Atoms of different elements are different and have different masses.

- An atom of one element cannot be changed into an atom of a different element. Atoms cannot be created or destroyed in any chemical change, only rearranged.

- Every compound is composed of atoms of different elements, combined in a specific ratio.

FIGURE 3
Thomson's Model
Thomson suggested that atoms had negatively charged electrons embedded in a positive sphere.

Thomson's Model Through a series of experiments around the start of the twentieth century, scientists discovered that atoms are made of even smaller parts. In 1897, another English scientist, J. J. Thomson, found that atoms contain negatively charged particles. Yet, scientists knew that atoms themselves had no electrical charge. So, Thomson reasoned, atoms must also contain some sort of positive charge.

Thomson proposed a model like the one in Figure 3. He described an atom that consisted of negative charges scattered throughout a ball of positive charge—something like raisins or berries in a muffin. The negatively charged particles later became known as **electrons.**

Reading Checkpoint) **Where were the electrons located in Thomson's model of an atom?**

Rutherford's Model In 1911, one of Thomson's students, Ernest Rutherford, found evidence that countered Thomson's model. In an experiment diagrammed in Figure 4, Rutherford's research team aimed a beam of positively charged particles at a thin sheet of gold foil. They predicted that, if Thomson's model were correct, the charged particles would pass right through the foil in a straight line. The gold atoms would not have enough positive charge in any one region to strongly repel the charged particles.

FIGURE 4
Rutherford's Gold Foil Experiment
Rutherford was surprised that a few particles were deflected strongly. This led him to propose an atomic model with a positively charged nucleus.

Most particles pass through the foil with little or no deflection.

A few particles are deflected strongly.

Gold foil

Gold atoms

Positive particles

Source of positively charged particles

Particle beam

Screen

Nucleus

Deflected particles

Rutherford's team observed that most of the particles passed through the foil undisturbed, as expected. But, to their surprise, a few particles were deflected strongly. Since like charges repel each other, Rutherford inferred that an atom's positive charge must be clustered in a tiny region in its center, called the **nucleus** (NOO klee us). (The plural of *nucleus* is *nuclei*.) Any particle that was deflected strongly had been repelled by a gold atom's nucleus.

Scientists knew from other experiments that electrons had almost no mass. Therefore, they reasoned that nearly all of an atom's mass must also be located in the tiny, positively charged nucleus. In Rutherford's atomic model, the atom was mostly empty space with electrons moving around the nucleus in that space. Later research suggested that the nucleus was made of one or more positively charged particles. Rutherford called the positively charged particles in an atom's nucleus **protons.**

Bohr's Model In 1913, Niels Bohr, a Danish scientist, revised the atomic model. Bohr showed that electrons could have only specific amounts of energy, leading them to move in certain orbits. The orbits in Bohr's model resemble planets orbiting the sun or the layers of an onion, as shown in Figure 6.

Cloud Model In the 1920s, the atomic model changed again. Scientists determined that electrons do not orbit the nucleus like planets. Instead, electrons can be anywhere in a cloudlike region around the nucleus. The "cloud" is a visual model. It symbolizes where electrons are likely to be found. An electron's movement is related to its **energy level,** or the specific amount of energy it has. Electrons of different energy levels are likely to be found in different places. The energy of each electron keeps it in motion around the positive nucleus to which it is attracted.

FIGURE 5
Rutherford's Model
According to Rutherford's model, an atom was mostly empty space. *Making Models* *How is a fruit with a pit at its center a simple model for Rutherford's idea?*

FIGURE 6
Later Atomic Models
Through the first part of the twentieth century, atomic models continued to change.

▼ **Bohr Model**
Niels Bohr suggested that electrons move in specific orbits around the nucleus of an atom.

◀ **Cloud Model**
According to the cloud model, electrons move rapidly in every direction around the nucleus.

FIGURE 7

Modern Model of an Atom
This model of a carbon atom consists of positively charged protons and neutral neutrons in a nucleus that is surrounded by a cloud of negatively charged electrons.
Relating Cause and Effect *What effect do the neutrons in the nucleus have on the atom's electric charge? Explain.*

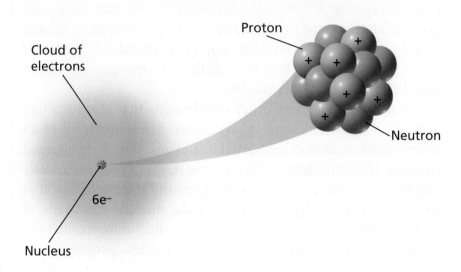

Cloud of electrons

Proton

Neutron

6e⁻

Nucleus

Try This **Activity**

How Far Away?

1. On a piece of paper, make a small circle no bigger than a dime. The circle represents the nucleus of an atom.

2. Measure the diameter of the circle in centimeters.

3. Now predict where the outer edge of this model atom would be. For example, would the outer edge be within the edges of the paper? Your desk? The classroom? The school building?

Calculating The diameter of an actual atom can be 100,000 times that of its nucleus. Calculate the diameter of your model atom. How close was your prediction in Step 3 to your calculation? (*Hint:* To understand the scale of your answer, change the units of measurement from centimeters to meters.)

The Modern Atomic Model

In 1932, English scientist James Chadwick discovered another particle in the nucleus of atoms. This new particle, called a **neutron**, was hard to detect because it has no electric charge. A neutron has nearly the same mass as a proton.

Chadwick's discovery led to an adjustment in the atomic model. This model, pictured in Figure 7, has not changed much since the 1930s. The modern atomic model describes the atom as mostly empty space. **At the center of the atom is a tiny, massive nucleus containing protons and neutrons. Surrounding the nucleus is a cloudlike region of moving electrons.** New research continues to provide data that support this model. These data also confirm many of the earlier inferences made by scientists who helped advance atomic theory.

Particle Charges Look closely at Figure 7. Protons are shown in the diagram by a plus sign (+), and electrons are shown by the symbol e⁻. If you count the number of protons, you'll see there are six—the same as the number of electrons. In an atom, the number of protons equals the number of electrons. As a result, the positive charge from the protons equals the negative charge from the electrons. The charges balance, making the atom neutral. In contrast, the number of neutrons in an atom does not have to equal the number of protons. Neutrons don't affect the charge of an atom because they have no charge.

Reading Checkpoint **Where are the electrons located in the modern model of an atom?**

Particles in an Atom				
Particle	Symbol	Charge	Relative Mass (amu)	Model
Proton	p⁺	1+	1	
Neutron	n	0	1	
Electron	e⁻	1−	$\dfrac{1}{1,836}$	

FIGURE 8
An atom is composed of positively charged protons, neutral neutrons, and negatively charged electrons. Protons and neutrons are about equal in mass. An electron has about 1/2,000 the mass of a proton or neutron.

Comparing Particle Masses Although electrons may balance protons charge-for-charge, they can't compare when it comes to mass. It takes almost 2,000 electrons to equal the mass of just one proton. A proton and a neutron are about equal in mass. Together, the protons and neutrons make up nearly all the mass of an atom.

Figure 8 compares the charges and masses of the three atomic particles. Atoms are too small to be described easily by everyday units of mass, such as grams or kilograms. Sometimes scientists use units known as atomic mass units (amu). A proton or a neutron has a mass equal to about one amu.

Scale and Size of Atoms Looking back at the modern atomic model (Figure 7), you may see that most of an atom's volume is the space in which the electrons move. In contrast, the nucleus seems tiny. But no image can be drawn in a book that would show how small the nucleus really is compared to an entire atom. To picture the scale of an atom, imagine that the nucleus were the size of an eraser on a pencil. If you put this "nucleus" on the pitcher's mound of a baseball stadium, the electrons could be as far away as the top row of seats!

Atoms are amazingly small. The tiniest visible speck of dust may contain 10 million billion atoms. Because they are so small, atoms are hard to study. Today's powerful microscopes can give a glimpse of atoms, as shown in Figure 9. But they do not show the structure of atoms. Models, such as those shown in this book, are helpful in learning more about atoms.

Atomic Number Every atom of a given element has the same number of protons. For example, the nucleus of every carbon atom has 6 protons. Every oxygen atom has 8 protons, and every iron atom has 26 protons. The number of protons in the nucleus of an atom is the **atomic number** of that atom's element. The definition of an element is based on its atomic number. Atoms with different atomic numbers are atoms of different elements. Carbon's atomic number is 6. Oxygen has an atomic number of 8. Iron has an atomic number of 26.

FIGURE 9
Imaging Atoms
This image was made by a scanning tunneling microscope. It shows a zigzag chain of cesium atoms (red) on a background of gallium and arsenic atoms (blue). The colors were added to the image.

Carbon-12
6 Neutrons

6e⁻

Carbon-13
7 Neutrons

6e⁻

Carbon-14
8 Neutrons

FIGURE 10
Isotopes
Atoms of all isotopes of carbon contain 6 protons and 6 electrons, but they differ in their number of neutrons. Carbon-12 is the most common isotope.
Interpreting Diagrams *Which isotope of carbon has the largest mass number?*

Isotopes and Mass Number Although the number of protons is fixed for a particular element, the same is not true for the number of neutrons in the nucleus. Atoms of the same element that have different numbers of neutrons are called **isotopes** (EYE suh tohps). Three carbon isotopes are illustrated in Figure 10. Each carbon atom has 6 protons and 6 electrons. But the number of neutrons is 6, 7, or 8. An isotope is identified by its **mass number,** which is the sum of the protons and neutrons in the nucleus of an atom. The most common isotope of carbon has a mass number of 12 (6 protons + 6 neutrons), and may be written as "carbon-12." Two other isotopes are carbon-13 and carbon-14. Despite their different mass numbers, all three carbon isotopes react the same way chemically.

Hydrogen also has three isotopes. All hydrogen atoms have one proton in the nucleus. The most common isotope is hydrogen-1 (1 proton + 0 neutrons). The others are hydrogen-2 (1 proton + 1 neutron) and hydrogen-3 (1 proton + 2 neutrons). Hydrogen-2 is called deuterium. Hydrogen-3 is called tritium.

Section ❶ **Assessment**

S 8.3.a, 8.7.b,
E-LA: Reading 8.1.2

Vocabulary Skill **Greek Word Origins** Use what you know about the Greek word *atomos* to explain the meaning of *atom.*

Reviewing Key Concepts

1. **a. Reviewing** Why did atomic theory change with time?
   b. Describing Describe Bohr's model of the atom. What specific information did Bohr contribute to scientists' understanding of the atom?
   c. Comparing and Contrasting How is the modern atomic model different from Bohr's model?
2. **a. Reviewing** What are the three main particles in the modern model of an atom?

   b. Explaining What is atomic number? How is it used to distinguish one element from another?
   c. Applying Concepts The atomic number of nitrogen is 7. How many protons, neutrons, and electrons make up an atom of nitrogen-15?

Lab zone **At-Home Activity**

Modeling Atoms Build a three-dimensional model of an atom using materials such as beads, cotton, and clay. Show the model to your family, and explain what makes atoms of different elements different from one another.

Organizing the Elements

CALIFORNIA
Standards Focus

S 8.7.a Students know how to identify regions corresponding to metals, nonmetals, and inert gases.

- How did Mendeleev discover the pattern that led to the periodic table?

- How are the elements organized in the modern periodic table?

Key Terms
- atomic mass
- periodic table
- period
- group
- chemical symbol

Lab zone Standards Warm-Up

Which Is Easier?

1. Make 4 sets of 10 paper squares, using a different color for each set. Number the squares in each set from 1 through 10.

2. Place all of the squares on a flat surface, numbered side up. Don't arrange them in order.

3. Ask your partner to think of a way of arranging the squares that makes it easy to find a square of a particular color and number. Have your partner describe to you how the squares should be organized.

4. Working together, arrange the squares according to the organization scheme devised by your partner.

5. Trade places with your partner and repeat Steps 2 through 4. Try to think of a different organization scheme than the one devised by your partner.

Think It Over

Drawing Conclusions Compare the different ways that you and your classmates organized the squares. Were some schemes more organized than others? Explain.

You wake up, jump out of bed, and start to get dressed for school. Then you ask yourself a question: Is there school today? To find out, you check the calendar. There's no school today because it's Saturday.

The calendar arranges the days of the month into horizontal periods called weeks and vertical groups called days of the week. This arrangement follows a repeating pattern that makes it easy to keep track of which day it is. The chemical elements can also be organized into something like a calendar. The name of the "chemists' calendar" is the periodic table.

◀ A calendar organizes the days of the week into a useful, repeating pattern.

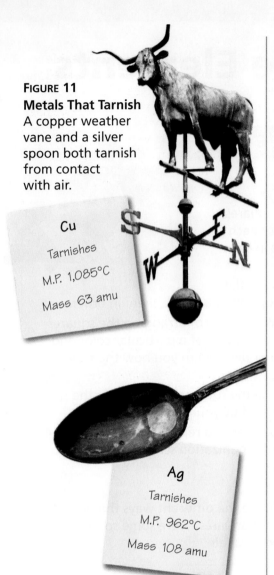

FIGURE 11
Metals That Tarnish
A copper weather vane and a silver spoon both tarnish from contact with air.

Cu
Tarnishes
M.P. 1,085°C
Mass 63 amu

Ag
Tarnishes
M.P. 962°C
Mass 108 amu

Mendeleev's Periodic Table

By 1869, a total of 63 elements had been discovered. A few were gases. Two were liquids. Most were solid metals. Some reacted explosively. Others reacted more slowly. Scientists wondered if the properties of elements followed a pattern. A Russian scientist, Dmitri Mendeleev (men duh LAY ef), discovered a set of patterns that applied to all the elements.

Patterns of Properties Mendeleev knew that some elements have similar chemical and physical properties. For example, both fluorine and chlorine are gases that irritate the lungs and form similar compounds. Silver and copper, shown in Figure 11, are both shiny metals that tarnish if exposed to air. Mendeleev thought these similarities were important clues to a hidden pattern.

To find that pattern, Mendeleev wrote each element's melting point (M.P.), density, and color on individual cards. He also included the element's atomic mass. The **atomic mass** is the average mass of all the isotopes of an element. Mendeleev then tried arranging the cards in various ways.

Mendeleev noticed that a pattern of properties appeared when he arranged the elements in order of increasing atomic mass. For example, when the 63 known elements were arranged in this order, lithium (Li) came in second, sodium (Na) came in ninth, and potassium (K) came in sixteenth. Each of these elements reacted with water in the same way. So, Mendeleev lined up the cards for these elements to form their own group. He did the same with other similar elements. Group by group, Mendeleev constructed the first periodic table. A **periodic table** is an arrangement of elements showing the repeating pattern of their properties. (The word *periodic* means "in a regular, repeated pattern.")

Reading Checkpoint What properties do silver and copper share?

FIGURE 12
Metals That React With Water
Lithium and sodium both react with water. **Interpreting Photographs** *Which metal reacts more vigorously with water?*

Na
Reacts with water
M.P. 98°C
Mass 23 amu

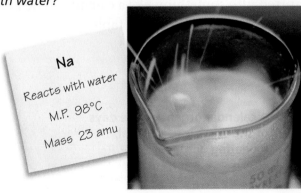

Li
Reacts with water
M.P. 180°C
Mass 7 amu

			Ti=50	Zr=90	?=180.
			V=51	Nb=94	Ta=182.
			Cr=52	Mo=96	W=186.
			Mn=55	Rh=104,4	Pt=197,4
			Fe=56	Ru=104,4	Ir=198.
		Ni=Co=59		Pl=106₆,	Os=199.
H=1			Cu=63,4	Ag=108	Hg=200.
	Be=9,4	Mg=24	Zn=65,2	Cd=112	
	B=11	Al=27,4	?=68	Ur=116	Au=197?
	C=12	Si=28	?=70	Sn=118	
	N=14	P=31	As=75	Sb=122	Bi=210
	O=16	S=32	Se=79,4	Te=128?	
	F=19	Cl=35,5	Br=80	I=127	
Li=7	Na=23	K=39	Rb=85,4	Cs=133	Tl=204
		Ca=40	Sr=57,6	Ba=137	Pb=207.
		?=45	Ce=92		
		?Er=56	La=94		
		?Yt=60	Di=95		
		?In=75,6	Th=118?		

FIGURE 13
Mendeleev's Periodic Table
When Mendeleev published his first periodic table, he left question marks in some places. Based on the properties and atomic masses of surrounding elements, he predicted that new elements with specific properties would be discovered.

Predicting New Elements Mendeleev found that arranging the known elements strictly by increasing atomic mass did not always group similar elements together. So, he moved a few of his element cards into groups where the elements did have similar properties. After arranging all 63 elements, three blank spaces were left. Mendeleev predicted that the blank spaces would be filled by elements that had not yet been discovered. He even predicted the properties of those new elements.

In 1869, Mendeleev published his periodic table. It looked something like the one shown in Figure 13. Within 16 years, chemists discovered the three missing elements—scandium, gallium, and germanium. Their properties are close to those that Mendeleev had predicted.

The Modern Periodic Table

The periodic table changed as scientists discovered new elements and learned more about atomic structure. The modern periodic table contains more than 100 elements. It is also organized differently from Mendeleev's table. In the modern periodic table, the elements are arranged in order of increasing atomic number. Recall that the atomic number of an element equals the number of protons in an atom of that element.

The modern periodic table appears on the next two pages. **The properties of an element can be predicted from its location on the periodic table.** This predictability is the reason that the periodic table is so useful to chemists.

Video Field Trip
Discovery Channel School
Elements and the Periodic Table

FIGURE 14

Periodic Table of the Elements

The modern periodic table includes over 100 elements. Many of the properties of an element can be predicted by its position in the table.

Go Online
active art

For: Periodic Table activity
Visit: PHSchool.com
Web Code: cgp-1032

Key

C	Solid
Br	Liquid
H	Gas
Tc	Not found in nature

1

1
H
Hydrogen
1.0079

Period

Symbol
One- or two-letter symbols identify most elements. Some periodic tables also list the names of the elements.

Group

2

	2		3	4	5	6	7	8	9
2	3 **Li** Lithium 6.941	4 **Be** Beryllium 9.0122							
3	11 **Na** Sodium 22.990	12 **Mg** Magnesium 24.305							
4	19 **K** Potassium 39.098	20 **Ca** Calcium 40.08	21 **Sc** Scandium 44.956	22 **Ti** Titanium 47.90	23 **V** Vanadium 50.941	24 **Cr** Chromium 51.996	25 **Mn** Manganese 54.938	26 **Fe** Iron 55.847	27 **Co** Cobalt 58.933
5	37 **Rb** Rubidium 85.468	38 **Sr** Strontium 87.62	39 **Y** Yttrium 88.906	40 **Zr** Zirconium 91.22	41 **Nb** Niobium 92.906	42 **Mo** Molybdenum 95.94	43 **Tc** Technetium (98)	44 **Ru** Ruthenium 101.07	45 **Rh** Rhodium 102.91
6	55 **Cs** Cesium 132.91	56 **Ba** Barium 137.33	71 **Lu** Lutetium 174.97	72 **Hf** Hafnium 178.49	73 **Ta** Tantalum 180.95	74 **W** Tungsten 183.85	75 **Re** Rhenium 186.21	76 **Os** Osmium 190.2	77 **Ir** Iridium 192.22
7	87 **Fr** Francium (223)	88 **Ra** Radium (226)	103 **Lr** Lawrencium (262)	104 **Rf** Rutherfordium (261)	105 **Db** Dubnium (262)	106 **Sg** Seaborgium (263)	107 **Bh** Bohrium (264)	108 **Hs** Hassium (265)	109 **Mt** Meitnerium (268)

The lanthanides and the actinides are placed off the table to save space and to make the rest of the table easier to read. Follow the blue shading to see how they fit in the table.

Lanthanides

57 **La** Lanthanum 138.91	58 **Ce** Cerium 140.12	59 **Pr** Praseodymium 140.91	60 **Nd** Neodymium 144.24	61 **Pm** Promethium (145)	62 **Sm** Samarium 150.4

Actinides

89 **Ac** Actinium (227)	90 **Th** Thorium 232.04	91 **Pa** Protactinium 231.04	92 **U** Uranium 238.03	93 **Np** Neptunium (237)	94 **Pu** Plutonium (244)

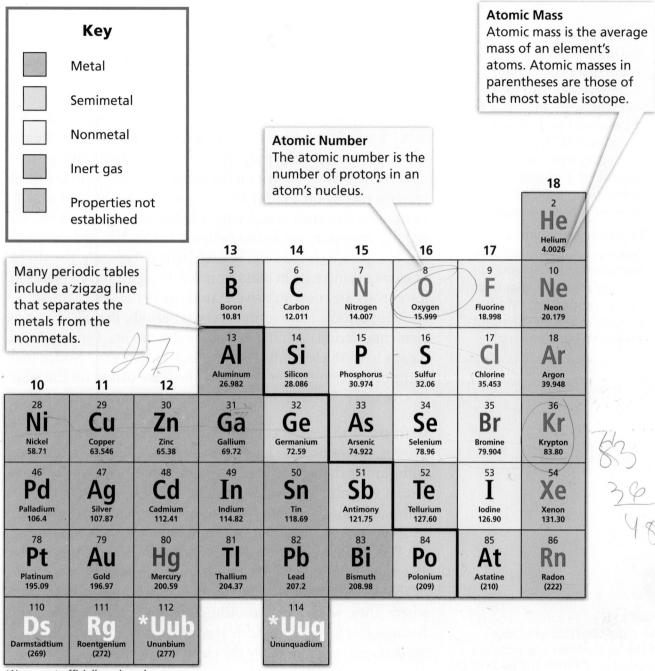

Key

- Metal
- Semimetal
- Nonmetal
- Inert gas
- Properties not established

Atomic Number
The atomic number is the number of protons in an atom's nucleus.

Atomic Mass
Atomic mass is the average mass of an element's atoms. Atomic masses in parentheses are those of the most stable isotope.

Many periodic tables include a zigzag line that separates the metals from the nonmetals.

18
2
He
Helium
4.0026

13	14	15	16	17	
5	6	7	8	9	10
B	**C**	**N**	**O**	**F**	**Ne**
Boron	Carbon	Nitrogen	Oxygen	Fluorine	Neon
10.81	12.011	14.007	15.999	18.998	20.179
13	14	15	16	17	18
Al	**Si**	**P**	**S**	**Cl**	**Ar**
Aluminum	Silicon	Phosphorus	Sulfur	Chlorine	Argon
26.982	28.086	30.974	32.06	35.453	39.948

10	11	12						
28	29	30	31	32	33	34	35	36
Ni	**Cu**	**Zn**	**Ga**	**Ge**	**As**	**Se**	**Br**	**Kr**
Nickel	Copper	Zinc	Gallium	Germanium	Arsenic	Selenium	Bromine	Krypton
58.71	63.546	65.38	69.72	72.59	74.922	78.96	79.904	83.80
46	47	48	49	50	51	52	53	54
Pd	**Ag**	**Cd**	**In**	**Sn**	**Sb**	**Te**	**I**	**Xe**
Palladium	Silver	Cadmium	Indium	Tin	Antimony	Tellurium	Iodine	Xenon
106.4	107.87	112.41	114.82	118.69	121.75	127.60	126.90	131.30
78	79	80	81	82	83	84	85	86
Pt	**Au**	**Hg**	**Tl**	**Pb**	**Bi**	**Po**	**At**	**Rn**
Platinum	Gold	Mercury	Thallium	Lead	Bismuth	Polonium	Astatine	Radon
195.09	196.97	200.59	204.37	207.2	208.98	(209)	(210)	(222)
110	111	112		114				
Ds	**Rg**	***Uub**		***Uuq**				
Darmstadtium	Roentgenium	Ununbium		Ununquadium				
(269)	(272)	(277)						

*Name not officially assigned

(Atomic masses in parentheses are those of the most stable isotope.)

63	64	65	66	67	68	69	70
Eu	**Gd**	**Tb**	**Dy**	**Ho**	**Er**	**Tm**	**Yb**
Europium	Gadolinium	Terbium	Dysprosium	Holmium	Erbium	Thulium	Ytterbium
151.96	157.25	158.93	162.50	164.93	167.26	168.93	173.04

95	96	97	98	99	100	101	102
Am	**Cm**	**Bk**	**Cf**	**Es**	**Fm**	**Md**	**No**
Americium	Curium	Berkelium	Californium	Einsteinium	Fermium	Mendelevium	Nobelium
(243)	(247)	(247)	(251)	(252)	(257)	(258)	(259)

Classifying

Choose any ten elements and assign them letters from *A* to *J*. On an index card for each element, write the letter for the element and list some of its properties. You may list properties that you learn about in this chapter or properties presented in another reference source.

Exchange cards with a classmate. Can you identify each element? Can you identify elements that have similar properties? Which properties are most helpful in identifying elements?

Classes of Elements Look at Figure 14 on the previous two pages, starting at the upper left with hydrogen (H). Notice that the atomic numbers increase from left to right. You may also notice that the table is color-coded. Each color-coded region corresponds to a different class of elements—metals, semimetals, nonmetals, and inert gases.

Periods The periodic table is organized in horizontal rows called **periods.** A period contains a series of different elements. From left to right, the properties of the elements change in a pattern. Metals are shown on the left of the table, with the most reactive metals on the far left. Nonmetals are located on the right, with the most reactive next to the inert gases on the far right. Semimetals are found between the metals and nonmetals. This pattern is repeated in each period. Typically, the atoms of elements increase in mass from left to right, and elements in lower rows are more massive than those in the upper rows.

The periodic table contains seven periods. Period 1 has two elements. Periods 2 and 3 each have 8 elements. Periods 4 and 5 each have 18 elements. Period 6 has 32 elements. Notice that some of the elements in Periods 6 and 7 are placed off the table to save space. These elements are the lanthanides and actinides.

Groups The vertical columns of the periodic table are called **groups.** A group—also known as a family—consists of elements with similar characteristics. For example, the elements in Group 1 react violently with water, while the elements in Group 2 react with water slowly or not at all. Group 17 elements react violently with Group 1 elements, but Group 18 elements rarely react at all.

The lanthanides and the actinides do not belong in the 18 groups labeled in Figure 14. Figure 15 shows a different form of the periodic table. It includes the lanthanides and actinides where they would fit, according to their atomic numbers. Because this form of the table is so wide, it is difficult to fit in a book unless you show only the elements' symbols.

FIGURE 15

An Expanded Periodic Table
If the lanthanides and actinides were placed within the body of the periodic table, they would increase the number of groups to 32.

Reading Checkpoint **How many periods does the periodic table contain?**

1	H																	He
2	Li	Be											B	C	N	O	F	Ne
3	Na	Mg											Al	Si	P	S	Cl	Ar
4	K	Ca		Sc	Ti	V	Cr	Mn	Fe	Co	Ni	Cu	Zn	Ga	Ge	As	Se	Br	Kr
5	Rb	Sr		Y	Zr	Nb	Mo	Tc	Ru	Rh	Pd	Ag	Cd	In	Sn	Sb	Te	I	Xe
6	Cs	Ba	La	Ce	Pr	Nd	Pm	Sm	Eu	Gd	Tb	Dy	Ho	Er	Tm	Yb	Lu	Hf	Ta	W	Re	Os	Ir	Pt	Au	Hg	Tl	Pb	Bi	Po	At	Rn
7	Fr	Ra	Ac	Th	Pa	U	Np	Pu	Am	Cm	Bk	Cf	Es	Fm	Md	No	Lr	Rf	Db	Sg	Bh	Hs	Mt	Ds	Rg	Uub		Uuq				

Reading The Data In the periodic table, there is one square for each element. 🔵 **In this book, each square in the periodic table lists four pieces of information: an element's atomic number, chemical symbol, name, and atomic mass.**

Iron (Fe) is the element located in Group 8, Period 4 of the periodic table. You can see the square for iron reproduced in Figure 16. The first piece of information in the square is the number 26, the atomic number of iron. An atomic number of 26 tells you that every iron atom has 26 protons in its nucleus.

Just below the atomic number are the letters Fe—the chemical symbol for iron. A **chemical symbol** is a representation of an element usually consisting of one or two letters. Often, a chemical symbol is an abbreviation of the element's English name. For example, the symbol for zinc is Zn, and the symbol for calcium is Ca. Other symbols are abbreviations of Latin names. For example, the Latin name of iron is *ferrum*, so its symbol is Fe. Still other elements have names derived from the last names of scientists. For example, Curium (Cm) is named after the French scientists Pierre and Marie Curie.

The last number in the square is the atomic mass. For iron, this value is 55.847 amu. The atomic mass is an average because most elements consist of a mixture of isotopes. For example, iron is a mixture of four isotopes. About 92 percent of iron atoms are iron-56 (having 30 neutrons). The rest are a mixture of iron-54, iron-57, and iron-58. The atomic mass of iron is determined from the combined percentages of all its isotopes.

FIGURE 16
Iron
Iron has an atomic number of 26 and an atomic mass of 55.847 amu. Bok choy, shown below, is a leafy vegetable rich in iron.
Inferring *How many protons does an iron atom contain?*

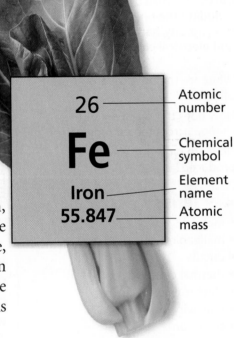

26 — Atomic number

Fe — Chemical symbol

Iron — Element name

55.847 — Atomic mass

Section ② **Assessment**

S 8.7.a, E-LA: Reading 8.2.0, Writing 8.2.4

🎯 **Target Reading Skill Preview Visuals** Review your graphic organizer for Figure 14. How did you answer your questions?

🔑 **Reviewing Key Concepts**

1. a. Reviewing In what order did Mendeleev arrange the elements in his periodic table?
   b. Explaining What pattern did Mendeleev discover when he arranged the elements?
   c. Interpreting Tables What elements did Mendeleev group with lithium in his periodic table?

2. a. Listing What information is listed in an element's square in the periodic table?

b. Comparing and Contrasting Describe two differences between Mendeleev's periodic table and the modern periodic table.

c. Interpreting Tables What element has 47 protons in its nucleus?

Writing in Science

Advertisement Write an advertisement that you could use to sell copies of Mendeleev's periodic table to chemists in 1869. Remember: chemists in 1869 have never seen such a table.

Metals

CALIFORNIA
Standards Focus

S 8.7.a Students know how to identify regions corresponding to metals, nonmetals, and inert gases.

S 8.7.c Students know substances can be classified by their properties, including their melting temperature, density, hardness, and thermal and electrical conductivity.

- What are the physical properties of metals?

- How does the reactivity of metals change across the periodic table?

- How are synthetic elements produced?

Key Terms

- metal
- malleable
- ductile
- thermal conductivity
- electrical conductivity
- reactivity
- corrosion
- alkali metal
- alkaline earth metal
- transition metal
- particle accelerator

Lab zone Standards Warm-Up

Why Use Aluminum?

1. Examine several objects made from aluminum, including a can, a disposable pie plate, heavy-duty aluminum foil, foil-covered wrapping paper, and aluminum wire.
2. Compare the shape, thickness, and general appearance of the objects.
3. Observe what happens if you try to bend and unbend each object.
4. For what purpose is each object used?

Think It Over

Inferring Use your observations to list as many properties of aluminum as you can. Based on your list of properties, infer why aluminum was used to make each object. Explain your answer.

It's hard to imagine modern life without metals. The cars you ride in are made of steel, which is mostly iron. Airplanes are covered in aluminum. A penny is coated with copper. Copper wires carry electric current to lamps, stereos, and computers.

Properties of Metals

Substances can be classified by their properties, including melting temperature, density, hardness, and thermal and electrical conductivity. **Metals** are elements that are good conductors of electric current and heat. They also tend to be shiny and bendable—like copper wire, for instance. The majority of elements in the periodic table are metals.

Physical Properties The physical properties of metals include luster, malleability, ductility, and conductivity. A **malleable** (MAL ee uh bul) material is one that can be hammered or rolled into flat sheets or other shapes. A **ductile** material is one that can be pulled out, or drawn, into a long wire. Copper is both malleable and ductile. It can be made into thin sheets or drawn into wires.

Thermal conductivity is the ability of an object to transfer heat. The ability of an object to transfer electric current is **electrical conductivity**. Most metals are good thermal conductors and electrical conductors. In addition, some metals are magnetic. For example, iron (Fe), cobalt (Co), and nickel (Ni) are attracted to magnets and can be made into magnets. Most metals are also solids at room temperature. However, one metal—mercury (Hg)—is a liquid at room temperature.

Chemical Properties The ease and speed with which a substance reacts with other substances is called its **reactivity**. Metals usually react by losing electrons to other atoms. Some metals are very reactive. For example, sodium (Na) reacts strongly when exposed to air or water. To prevent it from reacting, sodium must be stored under oil in sealed containers. By comparison, gold (Au) and platinum (Pt) are very unreactive metals.

The reactivities of other metals fall somewhere between those of sodium and gold. Iron, for example, reacts slowly with oxygen in the air, forming iron oxide, or rust. If iron is not protected by paint or plated with another metal, it will slowly turn to reddish-brown rust. The gradual wearing away of a metal due to a chemical reaction is called **corrosion.**

 **Reading Checkpoint** What are three physical properties of metals?

FIGURE 17
Properties of Metals
Metals have certain physical and chemical properties. **Classifying** *Categorize each of the properties of metals that are shown as either physical or chemical.*

Magnetism ▲
Some metals are attracted to magnets.

▼ **Malleability**
Gold can be pounded into coins.

Reactivity ▶
This iron chain is coated with rust after being exposed to air.

◀ Potassium is highly reactive with air, so it is stored in oil.

Bananas are a good source of potassium in a healthful diet. ▶

▲ The reactions of some compounds containing potassium help get fireworks off the ground.

FIGURE 18
Alkali Metals

Potassium is an alkali metal.
Making Generalizations *What characteristics do other Group 1 elements share with potassium?*

1
3 **Li** Lithium
11 **Na** Sodium
19 **K** Potassium
37 **Rb** Rubidium
55 **Cs** Cesium
87 **Fr** Francium

Metals in the Periodic Table

The metals in a group, or family, have similar properties, and these family properties change gradually as you move across the table. ⚷ **The reactivity of metals tends to decrease as you move from left to right across the periodic table.**

Alkali Metals The metals in Group 1, from lithium to francium, are called the **alkali metals.** Alkali metals, listed in Figure 18, react with other elements by losing one electron. These metals are so reactive that they are never found as uncombined elements in nature. Instead, they are found only in compounds. In the laboratory, scientists have been able to isolate alkali metals from their compounds. As pure, uncombined elements, some of the alkali metals are shiny and so soft that you can cut them with a plastic knife.

The two most important alkali metals are sodium and potassium. Sodium compounds are found in large amounts in seawater and salt beds. Your diet includes foods that contain compounds of sodium and potassium. Another alkali metal, lithium, is used in batteries and some medicines.

 Reading Checkpoint   What are the alkali metals located in the periodic table?

Alkaline Earth Metals Group 2 of the periodic table contains the **alkaline earth metals.** Each is fairly hard, gray-white, and a good conductor of electricity. Alkaline earth metals react by losing two electrons. These elements are not as reactive as the metals in Group 1, but they are more reactive than most other metals. Like the Group 1 metals, the Group 2 metals are never found uncombined in nature.

Magnesium and calcium are the most common alkaline earth metals. Mixing magnesium and a small amount of aluminum makes a strong but lightweight material used in ladders, wheel rims, and airplanes. Calcium compounds are an essential part of teeth and bones. Calcium also helps muscles work properly.

Comparing magnesium (atomic number 12) and sodium (atomic number 11) shows how just a slight change in atomic structure can result in different properties. Magnesium is a hard metal that melts at 648.8°C. Sodium is a soft metal that melts at 97.8°C.

2
4 **Be** Beryllium
12 **Mg** Magnesium
20 **Ca** Calcium
38 **Sr** Strontium
56 **Ba** Barium
88 **Ra** Radium

FIGURE 19
Alkaline Earth Metals
Calcium is one of the Group 2 elements. Without Calcium, muscles and bones cannot grow and function.

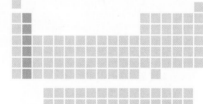

Reviewing Math: Algebra and Functions 7.1.5

Math Analyzing Data

Melting Points in a Group of Elements
The properties of elements within a single group in the periodic table often vary in a certain pattern. The following graph shows the melting points of Group 1 elements (alkali metals) from lithium to francium.

1. **Reading Graphs** As you look at Group 1 from lithium to francium, describe how the melting points of the alkali metals change.

2. **Predicting** If element number 119 were synthesized, it would fall below francium in Group 1 of the periodic table. Predict the approximate melting point of new element 119.

3. **Interpreting Data** Which of the alkali metals are liquids at 35°C?

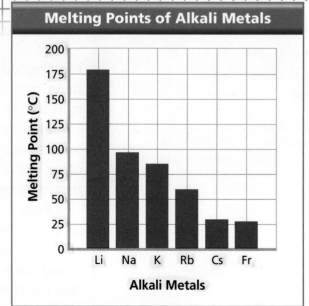

Melting Points of Alkali Metals

Melting Point (°C) vs Alkali Metals (Li, Na, K, Rb, Cs, Fr)

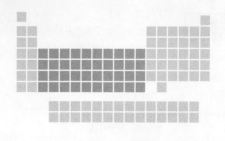

Transition Metals The elements in Groups 3 through 12 are called the **transition metals.** The transition metals include most of the familiar metals, such as iron, copper, nickel, silver, and gold. Most of the transition metals are hard and shiny. All of the transition metals are good conductors of electric current. Many of these metals form colorful compounds.

The transition metals are less reactive than the metals in Groups 1 and 2. When iron reacts with oxygen, forming rust, it sometimes takes many years to react completely. The lack of reactivity of gold is the reason ancient gold coins and jewelry are as beautiful today as they were thousands of years ago. Still, most transition metals are never found uncombined in nature. Some transition metals are important to your health. For example, iron forms the core of a large molecule called hemoglobin, which carries oxygen in your bloodstream.

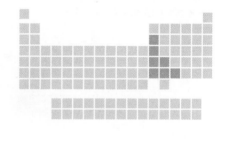

Metals in Mixed Groups Only some of the elements in Groups 13 through 15 of the periodic table are metals. These metals are never found uncombined in nature. The most familiar of these metals are aluminum, tin, and lead. Aluminum is the lightweight metal used in beverage cans and airplane bodies. A thin coating of tin protects steel from corrosion in some cans of food. Lead was once used in paints and water pipes. But lead is poisonous, so it is no longer used for these purposes. Now, its most common uses are in automobile batteries and weights for balancing tires.

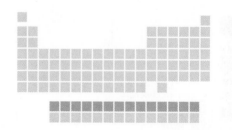

Lanthanides Two rows of elements are placed below the main part of the periodic table. This makes the table more compact. In the top row are the lanthanides (LAN thuh nydz). Lanthanides are sometimes mixed with more common metals to make alloys. An alloy is a mixture of a metal with at least one other element, usually another metal. Different lanthanides are usually found together in nature, always combined with other elements.

Two Group 3 elements—scandium (Sc) and yttrium (Y)—also show properties similar to the lanthanides. So, scientists group scandium, yttrium, and the lanthanides together as the rare earth elements. Some rare earth elements can be used to produce very strong magnets.

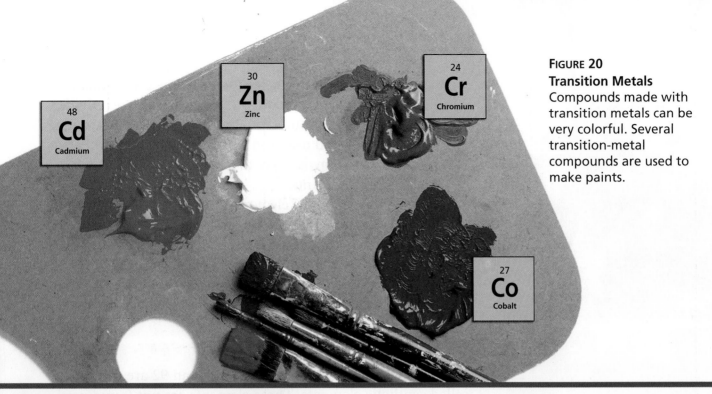

FIGURE 20
Transition Metals
Compounds made with transition metals can be very colorful. Several transition-metal compounds are used to make paints.

FIGURE 21
Metals in Groups 13, 14, and 15
Lead can be used in the borders around the glass sections in stained glass objects. Tin can be fashioned into artistic objects, such as picture frames.

FIGURE 22
Lanthanides
Neodymium is used in manufacturing the tiny speakers inside stereo headphones.

Actinides The elements below the lanthanides are called actinides (AK tuh nydz). Of the actinides, only actinium (Ac), thorium (Th), protactinium (Pa), and uranium (U) occur naturally on Earth. Uranium is used to produce energy in nuclear power plants.

All of the elements after uranium were created artificially in laboratories. The nuclei of these elements are very unstable, meaning that they break apart very quickly into smaller nuclei. In fact, many of these elements are so unstable that they last only a fraction of a second after they are made.

FIGURE 23
Actinides
Curium, one of the actinide elements, is used as a source of high-energy particles that heat and provide power for certain scientific equipment aboard the Mars Exploration Rover.
Posing Questions *Based on this information, write a question about curium.*

Synthetic Elements

Elements with atomic numbers higher than 92 are sometimes called synthetic elements. These elements are not found naturally on Earth. Instead, scientists make, or synthesize, them. ⬤ **Scientists make synthetic elements by forcing nuclear particles to crash into one another.** For example, plutonium is made by bombarding nuclei of uranium-238 with neutrons in a nuclear reactor. Americium-241 is made by bombarding plutonium nuclei with neutrons.

To make even heavier elements (with atomic numbers above 95), scientists use powerful machines called particle accelerators. **Particle accelerators** move atomic nuclei faster and faster until they have reached very high speeds. If these fast-moving nuclei crash into the nuclei of other elements with enough energy, the particles can sometimes combine into a single nucleus. Curium (Cm) was the first synthetic element to be made by colliding nuclei. In 1940, scientists in Chicago synthesized curium by colliding helium nuclei with plutonium nuclei.

In general, the difficulty of synthesizing new elements increases with atomic number. So, new elements have been synthesized only as more powerful particle accelerators have been built. For example, German scientists synthesized element 112 in 1996 by accelerating zinc nuclei and crashing them into lead. Element 112, like other elements with three-letter symbols, has been given a temporary name and symbol. In the future, scientists around the world will agree on permanent names and symbols for these elements.

Go Online
SciLINKS NSTA

For: Links on metals
Visit: www.SciLinks.org
Web Code: scn-1133

Reading Checkpoint Which elements are described as synthetic elements and why?

Americium-241 is produced in nuclear reactors. It is widely used in smoke detectors.

The heaviest synthetic elements are synthesized in particle accelerators.

FIGURE 24
Synthetic Elements
Synthetic elements are not found naturally on Earth.

Section 3 Assessment

S 8.7.a, 8.7.c,
E-LA: Reading 8.2.0

Target Reading Skill Preview Visuals Review your graphic organizer for Figure 17. How did you answer your questions?

Reviewing Key Concepts

1. a. Explaining Explain what the terms *ductility* and *thermal conductivity* mean.
   b. Classifying Give an example of how the ductility of metal can be useful.
   c. Inferring What property of metals led to the use of plastic or wood handles on many metal cooking utensils? Explain.

2. a. Identifying What family of elements in the periodic table contains the most reactive metals?
   b. Applying Concepts What area of the periodic table is the best place to look for a metal that could be used to coat another metal to protect it from corrosion?

   c. Inferring Period 4 of the periodic table contains the elements potassium, calcium, and copper. Which is the least reactive?

3. a. Describing Describe the general process by which new elements are synthesized.
   b. Applying Concepts How is plutonium made?

Lab zone At-Home **Activity**

Everyday Metals Make a survey of compounds in your home that contain metals. Look at labels on foods, cooking ingredients, dietary supplements, medicines, and cosmetics. Also look for examples of how metals are used in your home, such as in cookware and wiring. Identify for your family the ways that the properties of metals make them useful in daily life.

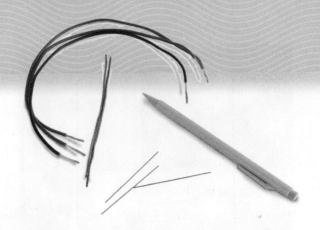

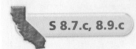

Lab zone Consumer Lab

Copper or Carbon? That Is the Question

S 8.7.c, 8.9.c

Problem

Materials scientists work to find the best materials for different products. In this lab, you will look for an answer to the following problem: How do the properties of copper and graphite determine their uses? You will compare the properties of a copper wire and a pencil lead. Pencil lead is made mostly of graphite, a form of the nonmetal element carbon.

Skills Focus

observing, classifying, controlling variables, drawing conclusions

Materials

- 1.5-V dry cell battery
- 250-mL beaker • stopwatch
- flashlight bulb and socket
- 3 lengths of insulated wire
- thin copper wire with no insulation, about 5–6 cm long
- 2 graphite samples (lead from a mechanical pencil), each about 5–6 cm long
- hot plate
- water

Procedure

1. Fill a 250-mL beaker about three-fourths full with water. Heat it slowly on a hot plate. Let the water continue to heat as you complete Part 1 and Part 2 of the investigation.

2. Compare the shininess and color of your copper and graphite samples. Record your observations.

3. Bend the copper wire as far as possible. Next, bend one of the graphite samples as far as possible. Record the results of each test.

4. Place a bulb into a lamp socket. Use a piece of insulated wire to connect one pole of a dry cell battery to the socket, as shown in the photo below.

5. Attach the end of a second piece of insulated wire to the other pole of the dry cell battery. Leave the other end of this wire free.

6. Attach the end of a third piece of insulated wire to the other pole of the lamp socket. Leave the other end of this wire free.

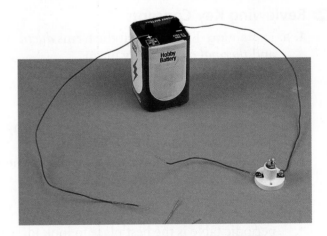

7. Touch the free ends of the insulated wire to the ends of the copper wire. Record your observations of the bulb.

8. Repeat Step 7 using a graphite sample instead of the copper wire.

PART 3 Thermal Conductivity

9. Turn off the hot plate.

10. Hold one end of a graphite sample between the fingertips of one hand. Hold one end of the copper wire between the fingertips of the other hand. **CAUTION:** *Be careful not to touch the beaker.*

11. Dip both the graphite and copper wire into the hot water at the same time. Allow only about 1 cm of each piece to reach under the water's surface. From your fingertips to the water, the lengths of both the graphite sample and the copper wire should be approximately equal.

12. Time how long it takes to feel the heat in the fingertips of each hand. Record your observations.

Analyze and Conclude

1. **Observing** Compare the physical properties of copper and graphite that you observed.

2. **Classifying** Based on the observations you made in this lab, explain why copper is classified as a metal.

3. **Controlling Variables** What parameter was controlled in Step 11 of the procedure? Explain why it was important to control this parameter.

4. **Drawing Conclusions** Which of the two materials, graphite or copper, would work better to cover the handle of a frying pan? Explain your choice.

5. **Communicating** Write a paragraph explaining why copper is better than graphite for electrical wiring. Include supporting evidence from your observations in this lab.

More to Explore

Research other uses of copper in the home and in industry. For each use, list the physical properties that make the material a good choice.

Nonmetals, Inert Gases, and Semimetals

CALIFORNIA
Standards Focus

S 8.7.a Students know how to identify regions corresponding to metals, nonmetals, and inert gases.

S 8.7.c Students know substances can be classified by their properties, including their melting temperature, density, hardness, and thermal and electrical conductivity.

- What are the properties of nonmetals and inert gases?

- How are semimetals useful?

Key Terms

- nonmetal
- diatomic molecule
- halogen
- inert gas
- semimetal
- semiconductor

Lab zone Standards **Warm-Up**

What Are the Properties of Charcoal?

1. Break off a piece of charcoal and roll it between your fingers. Record your observations.
2. Rub the charcoal on a piece of paper. Describe what happens.
3. Strike the charcoal sharply with the blunt end of a fork. Describe what happens.
4. When you are finished with your investigation, return the charcoal to your teacher and wash your hands.

Think It Over

Classifying Charcoal is a form of the element carbon. Would you classify carbon as a metal or a nonmetal? Use your observations from this activity to explain your answer.

Life on Earth depends on certain nonmetals. For example, the air you breathe contains several nonmetals, including oxygen and nitrogen. And carbon, another nonmetal, is essential to the compounds that make up all living organisms.

Metals make up the majority of the elements in the periodic table. In this section you will learn about the other classes of elements—nonmetals, inert gases, and semimetals.

These bears, the grass behind them, and all life on Earth are based on carbon, a nonmetal.

▲ Sulfur crumbles into a powder.

▲ A scuba diver's air tank contains mostly nitrogen and oxygen, which are gases at room temperature.

Nonmetals are good insulators. Carbon compounds are found in the plastic insulating these copper wires. ▶

FIGURE 25
Physical Properties of Nonmetals
Nonmetals have properties that are the opposite of metals. **Comparing and Contrasting** *Contrast the properties of these nonmetals with those of metals.*

Properties of Nonmetals

A **nonmetal** is an element that lacks most of the properties of a metal. 🔑 **Most nonmetals are poor conductors of electric current and heat. Solid nonmetals are dull and brittle.** Look at the periodic table again. All of the elements in light green-tinted boxes are nonmetals. Many of the nonmetals are common elements on Earth.

Physical Properties Four nonmetals are gases at room temperature. The air you breathe is mostly a mixture of two nonmetals, nitrogen (N) and oxygen (O). Other nonmetals, such as carbon (C), iodine (I), and sulfur (S), are solids at room temperature. Bromine (Br) is the only nonmetal that is liquid at room temperature.

Look at examples of nonmetals in Figure 25. In general, the physical properties of nonmetals are the opposite of those of the metals. Solid nonmetals are dull, meaning not shiny, and brittle, meaning not malleable or ductile. If you hit most solid nonmetals with a hammer, they break or crumble into a powder. Nonmetals are also poor conductors of heat and electric current.

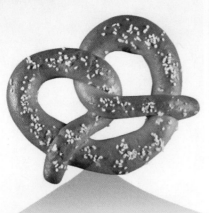

Sodium   Chlorine

e⁻

FIGURE 26
Reactions of Nonmetals
The table salt on a pretzel is mined from deposits found on Earth. The same compound can also be formed from a reaction between the metal sodium and the nonmetal chlorine.

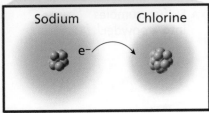

14

6
C
Carbon

14
Si
Silicon

32
Ge
Germanium

50
Sn
Tin

82
Pb
Lead

Chemical Properties Atoms of nonmetals usually gain or share electrons when they react with other atoms. When nonmetals and metals react, electrons move from the metal atoms to the nonmetal atoms, as shown by the formation of salt, shown in Figure 26. Another example is rust—a compound made of iron and oxygen (Fe_2O_3). It's the reddish, flaky coating you might see on an old piece of steel or an iron nail.

Many nonmetals can also form compounds with other nonmetals. The atoms share electrons and become bonded together into molecules.

Reading Checkpoint In which portion of the periodic table do you find nonmetals?

Families With Nonmetals

Look again at the periodic table. Notice that in Groups 14 through 17, there is a mix of nonmetals and other kinds of elements.

The Carbon Family Each element in the carbon family has atoms that can gain, lose, or share four electrons when reacting with other elements. In Group 14, only carbon is a nonmetal. What makes carbon especially important is its role in the chemistry of life. Molecules containing long chains of carbon atoms are found in all living things.

Most of the fuels that are burned to yield energy contain carbon. Coal, for example, is mostly the element carbon. Gasoline is made from crude oil, a mixture of carbon compounds with chains of 5 to 50 or more carbon atoms in their molecules.

FIGURE 27
Carbon
Charcoal is one form of carbon, the only nonmetal in Group 14.

The Nitrogen Family Group 15, the nitrogen family, contains two nonmetals, nitrogen and phosphorus. These nonmetals usually gain or share three electrons when reacting with other elements.

Earth's atmosphere is almost 80 percent nitrogen gas. Nitrogen occurs in nature as N_2, which is a diatomic molecule. A **diatomic molecule** is a molecule that consists of two atoms. In this form, nitrogen is not very reactive. Although living things need nitrogen, most of them are unable to use nitrogen from the air. However, certain kinds of bacteria can use this nitrogen to form compounds. This process is called nitrogen fixation. Plants can then take up these nitrogen compounds formed in the soil by the bacteria. Farmers also add nitrogen compounds to the soil in the form of fertilizers. Like all animals, you get the nitrogen you need from the food you eat—from plants, or from animals that ate plants.

Even though nitrogen and carbon appear next to each other on the periodic table, they have very different properties. Carbon is a solid up to very high temperatures (3,600°C). Nitrogen is a gas until it is cooled below −196°C. This illustrates how just a slight change in atomic structure can result in dramatically different properties.

Phosphorus is the other nonmetal in the nitrogen family. Phosphorus is much more reactive than nitrogen, so phosphorus in nature is always found in compounds.

15
7 **N** Nitrogen
15 **P** Phosphorus
33 **As** Arsenic
51 **Sb** Antimony
83 **Bi** Bismuth

FIGURE 28
The Nitrogen Family
Nitrogen and phosphorus are grouped in the same family of the periodic table, Group 15. **Making Generalizations** *How do atoms of both these elements change when they react?*

▼ Nitrogen is a key ingredient of fertilizers.

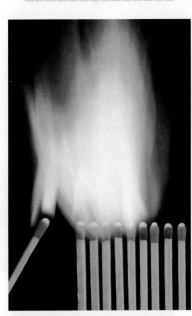

▲ Match heads contain a highly reactive phosphorus compound that ignites easily.

Show Me the Oxygen

How can you test for the presence of oxygen?

1. 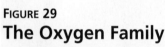 Pour about a 3-cm depth of hydrogen peroxide (H_2O_2) into a test tube.

2. Add a pea-sized amount of manganese dioxide (MnO_2) to the test tube.

3. Observe the test tube for about 1 minute.

4. When instructed by your teacher, set a wooden splint on fire.

5. Blow the splint out after 5 seconds and immediately plunge the glowing splint into the mouth of the test tube. Avoid getting the splint wet.

Observing Describe the change in matter that occurred in the test tube. What evidence indicates that oxygen was produced?

The Oxygen Family Group 16, the oxygen family, contains three nonmetals—oxygen, sulfur, and selenium. These elements usually gain or share two electrons when reacting with other elements.

You are using oxygen right now. With every breath, oxygen travels into your lungs. There, it is absorbed into your bloodstream, which distributes it all over your body. You could not live without a steady supply of oxygen. Like nitrogen, the oxygen you breathe is a diatomic molecule (O_2). In addition, oxygen sometimes forms a triatomic (three-atom) molecule, which is called ozone (O_3). Ozone collects in a layer in the upper atmosphere, where it screens out harmful radiation from the sun. However, ozone is a dangerous pollutant at ground level because it is highly reactive.

Because oxygen is highly reactive, it can combine with almost every other element. It also is the most abundant element in Earth's crust and the second-most abundant element in the atmosphere. (The first is nitrogen.)

Sulfur is the other common nonmetal in the oxygen family. If you have ever smelled the odor of a rotten egg, then you are already familiar with the smell of some sulfur compounds. Sulfur is used in the manufacture of rubber for rubber bands and automobile tires. Most sulfur is used to make sulfuric acid (H_2SO_4), one of the most important chemicals used in industry.

FIGURE 29

The Oxygen Family

The nonmetals oxygen and sulfur are the most common elements in Group 16. **Interpreting Tables** *What is the atomic number of each Group 16 element?*

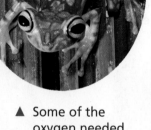

▲ Some of the oxygen needed by a frog enters through its skin.

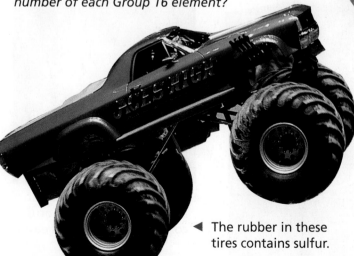

◀ The rubber in these tires contains sulfur.

16
8
O
Oxygen
16
S
Sulfur
34
Se
Selenium
52
Te
Tellurium
84
Po
Polonium

The Halogen Family Group 17 contains fluorine, chlorine, bromine, iodine, and astatine. These elements are also known as the **halogens,** which means "salt forming." All but astatine are nonmetals. A halogen atom typically gains or shares one electron when it reacts with other elements.

All of the halogens are very reactive, and the uncombined elements are dangerous to humans. Fluorine is so reactive that it reacts with almost every other known substance. Even water and powdered glass will burn in fluorine. Chlorine gas is extremely dangerous, but it is used in small amounts to kill bacteria in water supplies.

Though the halogen elements are dangerous, many of the compounds that halogens form are quite useful. Compounds of carbon and fluorine make up the nonstick coating on cookware. Small amounts of fluorine compounds that are added to water supplies help prevent tooth decay. Chlorine is one of the elements in ordinary table salt (the other is sodium). Another salt of chlorine, calcium chloride, is used to help melt ice on roads and walkways. Bromine reacts with silver to form silver bromide, which is used in photographic film.

Go Online

Sci LINKS. NSTA

For: Links on nonmetals
Visit: www.SciLinks.org
Web Code: scn-1134

FIGURE 30

The Halogens

The Group 17 elements are very reactive. Atoms of these elements easily form compounds by sharing or gaining one electron with atoms of other elements.

17
9 **F** Fluorine
17 **Cl** Chlorine
35 **Br** Bromine
53 **I** Iodine
85 **At** Astatine

◄ Bromine is highly reactive, and will burn skin on contact.

▲ Fluorine-containing compounds are found in toothpaste.

FIGURE 31
The Inert Gases
Electric current makes the Group 18 elements glow brightly inside glass tubes. **Applying Concepts** *Why are neon and the other noble gases so unreactive?*

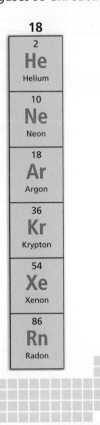

Inert Gases

The elements in Group 18 are the **inert gases.** The inert gases do not ordinarily form compounds because atoms of inert gases do not usually gain, lose, or share electrons. ⬤ **The inert gases tend to be unreactive.** Despite the name, the inert gases are not truly inert. Scientists have been able to synthesize some inert gas compounds in the laboratory. The inert gases are also known as noble gases.

All the inert gases exist in Earth's atmosphere, but only in small amounts. Because they are so unreactive, the inert gases were not discovered until the late 1800s. You have probably seen a floating balloon filled with helium, an inert gas. Inert gases are also used in glowing electric lights. These lights are commonly called neon lights, even though they are often filled with argon, xenon, or other inert gases.

Reading Checkpoint What is another name for the inert gases?

Hydrogen

Alone in the upper left corner of the periodic table is hydrogen—the element with the simplest atoms. Most hydrogen atoms have one proton and one electron. Some hydrogen atoms also have neutrons. Because the chemical properties of hydrogen differ very much from those of the other elements, it really cannot be grouped into a family. Although hydrogen makes up more than 90 percent of the atoms in the universe, it makes up only 1 percent of the mass of Earth's crust, oceans, and atmosphere. Hydrogen is rarely found on Earth as a pure element. Most hydrogen is combined with oxygen in water (H_2O).

FIGURE 32
Importance of Hydrogen
Water is a compound of hydrogen and oxygen.
Without liquid water, life on Earth would be impossible.

Semimetals

Between the metals and the nonmetals in the periodic table lie the semimetals. These elements are listed in the yellow squares in the periodic table. **Semimetals** have some properties of metals but also have properties that are typical of nonmetals. All semimetals are solids at room temperature. They are brittle, hard, and somewhat reactive.

The most common semimetal is silicon (Si). Silicon combines with oxygen to form silicon dioxide (SiO_2). Ordinary sand, which is mostly SiO_2, is the main component of glass. A compound of boron (B) and oxygen is added during the process of glassmaking to make heat-resistant glass. Compounds of boron are also used in some cleaning materials.

 **The most useful property of the semimetals is their varying ability to conduct electric current.** The electrical conductivity of a semimetal can depend on temperature, exposure to light, or the presence of impurities. Semimetals are examples of **semiconductors,** or substances that can conduct electric current under some conditions but not under other conditions. Silicon, germanium (Ge), and arsenic (As) are common semiconductor materials. Semiconductors are used to make computer chips, transistors, and lasers.

Reading Checkpoint What is the most common semimetal?

FIGURE 33
Silicon
A silicon computer chip is dwarfed by an ant, but the chip's properties as a semiconductor make it a powerful part of modern computers.

14
Si
Silicon

Section 4 Assessment

S 8.7.a, 8.7.c,
E-LA: Reading 8.1.2

Vocabulary Skill Greek Word Origins How does knowing the meaning of the Greek word *hals* help you remember the meaning of *halogen?*

Reviewing Key Concepts

1. a. **Listing** What are some properties of nonmetals?
   b. **Making Generalizations** What happens to the atoms of most nonmetals when they react with other elements?
   c. **Comparing and Contrasting** How do the physical and chemical properties of the halogens compare with those of the inert gases?

2. a. **Identifying** Where in the periodic table are the semimetals found?
   b. **Describing** What are three uses of semimetals?
   c. **Applying Concepts** What property makes semimetals useful as "switches" to turn a small electric current on and off?

Lab zone At-Home **Activity**

Halogen Hunt Identify compounds in your home that contain halogens. Look at labels on foods, cooking ingredients, cleaning materials, medicines, and cosmetics. The presence of a halogen is often indicated by the words *fluoride, chloride, bromide,* and *iodide* or the prefixes *fluoro-, chloro-, bromo-,* and *iodo-.* Show your family these examples and describe properties of the halogens.

Fx Floxxit

Q Quackzil

Do Doadeer

R Rhaatrap

Alien Periodic Table

S 8.7.a, 8.9

Problem

Imagine that inhabitants of another planet send a message to Earth that contains information about 30 elements. However, the message contains different names and symbols for these elements than those used on Earth. Which elements on the periodic table do these "alien" names represent?

Skills Focus

drawing conclusions, classifying, interpreting data, inferring

Materials

- ruler
- periodic table from text for reference

Procedure

1. Copy the blank periodic table on the next page into your notebook.

2. Listed below are data on the chemical and physical properties of the 30 elements. Place the elements in their proper position in the blank periodic table.

Alien Elements

The inert gases are **bombal (Bo)**, **wobble (Wo)**, **jeptum (J)**, and **logon (L)**. Among these gases, wobble has the greatest atomic mass and bombal the least. Logon is lighter than jeptum.

The most reactive group of metals are **xtalt (X)**, **byyou (By)**, **chow (Ch)**, and **quackzil (Q)**. Of these metals, chow has the lowest atomic mass. Quackzil is in the same period as wobble.

Apstrom (A), **vulcania (V)**, and **kratt (Kt)** are nonmetals whose atoms typically gain or share one electron. Vulcania is in the same period as quackzil and wobble.

The semimetals are **ernst (E)**, **highho (Hi)**, **terriblum (T)**, and **sississ (Ss)**. Sississ is the semimetal with the greatest atomic mass. Ernst is the semimetal with the lowest atomic mass. Highho and terriblum are in Group 14. Terriblum has more protons than highho. **Yazzer (Yz)** touches the zigzag line, but it's a metal, not a semimetal.

The lightest element of all is called **pfsst (Pf)**. The heaviest element in the group of 30 elements is **eldorado (El)**. The most chemically active nonmetal is apstrom. Kratt reacts with byyou to form table salt.

The element **doggone (D)** has only 4 protons in its atoms.

Floxxit (Fx) is important in the chemistry of life. It forms compounds made of long chains of atoms. **Rhaatrap (R)** and **doadeer (Do)** are metals in the fourth period, but rhaatrap is less reactive than doadeer.

Magnificon (M), **goldy (G)**, and sississ are all members of Group 15. Goldy has fewer electrons than magnificon.

Urrp (Up), **oz (Oz)**, and **nuutye (Nu)** all gain 2 electrons when they react. Nuutye is found as a diatomic molecule and has the same properties as a gas found in Earth's atmosphere. Oz has a lower atomic number than urrp.

The element **anatom (An)** has atoms with a total of 49 electrons. **Zapper (Z)** and **pie (Pi)** lose two electrons when they react. Zapper is used to make lightweight alloys.

Alien Periodic Table

	1			13	14	15	16	17	18
1		2							
2									
3									
4									
5									

Analyze and Conclude

1. **Drawing Conclusions** List the Earth names for the 30 alien elements in order of atomic number.

2. **Classifying** Were you able to place some elements within the periodic table with just a single clue? Explain using examples.

3. **Interpreting Data** Why did you need two or more clues to place other elements? Explain using examples.

4. **Inferring** Why could you use clues about atomic mass to place elements, even though the table is now based on atomic numbers?

5. **Communicating** Write a paragraph describing which groups of elements are not included in the alien periodic table. Explain whether or not you think it is likely that an alien planet would lack these elements.

More to Explore

Notice that Period 5 is incomplete on the alien periodic table. Create names and symbols for each of the missing elements. Then, compose a series of clues that would allow another student to identify these elements. Make your clues as precise as possible.

▼ **Radio telescopes in New Mexico**

Radioactive Elements

S 8.7.b Students know each element has a specific number of protons in the nucleus (the atomic number) and each isotope of the element has a different but specific number of neutrons in the nucleus.

How was radioactivity discovered?

What types of particles and energy can radioactive decay produce?

In what ways are radioactive isotopes useful?

Key Terms

- radioactive decay
- radioactivity
- alpha particle
- beta particle
- gamma radiation
- tracer

Lab zone Standards **Warm-Up**

What Happens When an Atom Decays?

1. Using green beads to represent protons and purple beads to represent neutrons, make a model of a beryllium-8 nucleus. Your model should contain 4 protons and 4 neutrons.

2. Beryllium-8 is an unstable isotope of the element beryllium. Its atoms can undergo decay by losing a particle made of two protons and two neutrons. Remove the appropriate number of beads from your model to represent this process.

3. Count the number of protons and neutrons left in your model.

Think It Over

Drawing Conclusions What element does your nuclear model now represent? How do you know? What is the mass number of the new model nucleus?

What if you could find a way to turn dull, cheap lead metal into valuable gold? More than a thousand years ago, many people thought it was a great idea, too. They tried everything they could think of. However, nothing worked. There is no chemical reaction that converts one element into another. Even so, elements do sometimes change into other elements. For example, atoms of carbon can become atoms of nitrogen. (But lead never changes into gold, unfortunately!) How is it possible for these changes to happen?

FIGURE 34

Trying to Make Gold From Lead
This painting from 1570 shows people trying to change lead into gold. No such chemical reaction was ever accomplished.

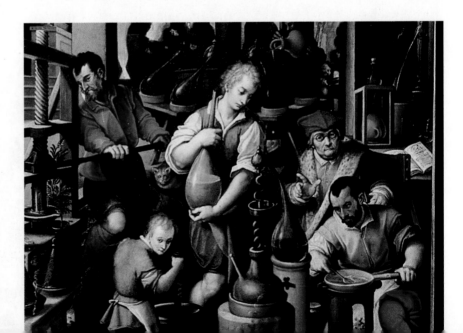

Radioactivity

Remember that atoms with the same number of protons and different numbers of neutrons are called isotopes. Some isotopes are unstable; that is, their nuclei do not hold together well. In a process called **radioactive decay,** the atomic nuclei of unstable isotopes release fast-moving particles and energy.

Discovery of Radioactivity 🔑 **In 1896, the French scientist Henri Becquerel discovered the effects of radioactive decay by accident while studying a mineral containing uranium.** He observed that with exposure to sunlight, the mineral gave off a penetrating energy that could expose film. Becquerel assumed that sunlight was necessary for the energy release. So, when the weather turned cloudy, he put away his materials in a dark desk drawer, including a sample of the mineral placed next to a photographic plate wrapped in paper.

Later, when Becquerel opened his desk to retrieve these items, he was surprised to find an image of the mineral on the photographic plate. Sunlight wasn't necessary at all. Becquerel hypothesized that uranium spontaneously gives off energy, called radiation, all the time.

Becquerel presented his findings to a young researcher, Marie Curie, and her husband, Pierre. After further study, the Curies concluded that a reaction was taking place within the uranium nuclei. The uranium showed a property of being able to spontaneously emit radiation. Marie Curie called this property **radioactivity.**

Polonium and Radium Marie Curie was surprised to find that some minerals containing uranium were even more radioactive than pure uranium. Suspecting that the minerals contained small amounts of other, highly radioactive elements, the Curies set to work. They eventually isolated two new elements, which Marie named polonium and radium.

 **Reading Checkpoint** What is radioactivity?

FIGURE 35
Radiation From Uranium
As with Becquerel's discovery, radiation from the uranium-containing mineral has exposed the photographic film.

FIGURE 36
Marie Curie
Marie Curie, her husband Pierre, and Henri Becquerel pioneered the study of radioactive elements.

FIGURE 37
Radioactive Decay

Radioactive elements give off particles and energy during radioactive decay. **Interpreting Diagrams** *Which type of radioactive decay produces a negatively charged particle?*

Alpha Decay

Radioactive nucleus

2 protons and 2 neutrons lost

Alpha particle

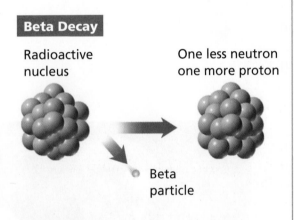

Beta Decay

Radioactive nucleus

One less neutron one more proton

Beta particle

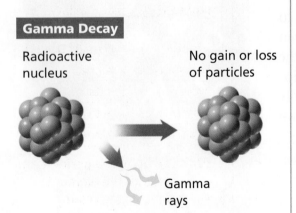

Gamma Decay

Radioactive nucleus

No gain or loss of particles

Gamma rays

Types of Radioactive Decay

There are three major forms of radiation produced during the radioactive decay of an unstable nucleus. **Radioactive decay can produce alpha particles, beta particles, and gamma rays.** The particles and energy produced during radioactive decay are forms of nuclear radiation.

Alpha Decay An **alpha particle** consists of two protons and two neutrons and is positively charged. It is the same as a helium nucleus. The release of an alpha particle by an atom decreases the atomic number by 2 and the mass number by 4. For example, a thorium-232 nucleus (atomic number 90) decays to produce an alpha particle and a radium-228 nucleus (atomic number 88).

Beta Decay Some atoms are unstable because they have too many neutrons. During beta decay, a neutron inside the nucleus of an unstable atom changes into a negatively charged beta particle and a proton. A **beta particle** is a fast-moving electron given off by a nucleus during radioactive decay. The new proton remains inside the nucleus. That means that the nucleus now has one less neutron and one more proton. Its mass number remains the same but its atomic number increases by 1. For example, a carbon-14 nucleus decays to produce a beta particle and a nitrogen-14 nucleus.

Gamma Decay Alpha and beta decay are almost always accompanied by gamma radiation. **Gamma radiation** consists of high-energy waves, similar to X-rays. Gamma radiation (also called gamma rays) has no charge and does not cause a change in either the atomic mass or the atomic number.

Effects of Nuclear Radiation Although alpha particles move very fast, they are stopped by collisions with atoms. In Figure 38, you can see that alpha particles are blocked by a sheet of paper. Alpha radiation can cause an injury to human skin that is much like a bad burn.

FIGURE 38
The Penetrating Power of Nuclear Radiation

The three types of nuclear radiation were named based on how easily each one could be blocked. Alpha, beta, and gamma are the first three letters of the Greek alphabet. Inferring *Which type of nuclear radiation is the most penetrating?*

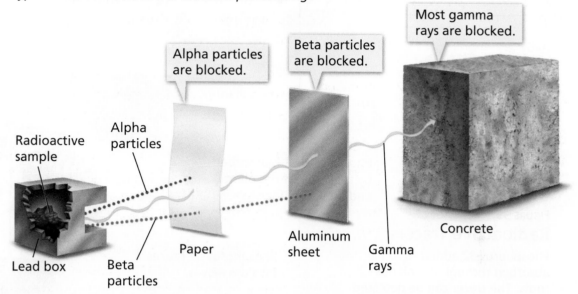

Alpha particles are blocked.

Beta particles are blocked.

Most gamma rays are blocked.

Radioactive sample

Alpha particles

Lead box

Beta particles

Paper

Aluminum sheet

Gamma rays

Concrete

Beta particles are much faster and more penetrating than alpha particles. They can pass through paper, but they are blocked by an aluminum sheet 5 millimeters thick. Beta particles can also travel into the human body and damage its cells.

Gamma rays are the most penetrating type of radiation. You would need a piece of lead several centimeters thick or a concrete wall about a meter thick to stop gamma rays. They can pass right through a human body, delivering intense energy to cells and causing severe damage.

 **Reading Checkpoint** How can alpha radiation affect the body?

Using Radioactive Isotopes

Radioactive isotopes have many uses in science and industry. In some cases, the energy released by radioactive isotopes is itself useful. Nuclear power plants, for example, harness this energy to generate electricity. In other cases, radiation is useful because it can be easily detected. **Uses of radioactive isotopes include tracing the steps of chemical reactions and industrial processes, and diagnosing and treating disease.**

Lab zone **Skills Activity**

Predicting

Look at the table of radioactive isotopes below.

Isotope	Type of Decay
Uranium-238	Alpha
Nickel-63	Beta
Iodine-131	Beta
Radium-226	Alpha

With the help of a periodic table, predict the element that forms in each case. Explain your reasoning.

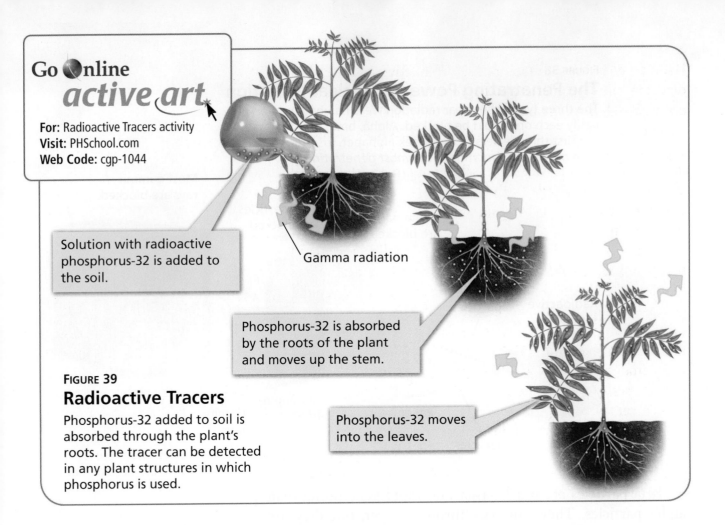

Go Online
active art

For: Radioactive Tracers activity
Visit: PHSchool.com
Web Code: cgp-1044

Solution with radioactive phosphorus-32 is added to the soil.

Gamma radiation

Phosphorus-32 is absorbed by the roots of the plant and moves up the stem.

FIGURE 39
Radioactive Tracers
Phosphorus-32 added to soil is absorbed through the plant's roots. The tracer can be detected in any plant structures in which phosphorus is used.

Phosphorus-32 moves into the leaves.

Uses in Science and Industry Like a lighthouse flashing in the night, a radioactive isotope "signals" where it is by emitting radiation that can be detected. **Tracers** are radioactive isotopes that can be followed through the steps of a chemical reaction or an industrial process. Tracers behave chemically the same way as nonradioactive forms of an element. For example, phosphorus is used by plants in small amounts for healthy growth. As shown in Figure 39, a plant will absorb radioactive phosphorus-32 added to the soil just as it does the nonradioactive form. Radiation will be present in any part of the plant that contains the isotope. In this way, biologists can learn where and how plants use phosphorus.

In industry, tracers are used to find weak spots in metal pipes, especially oil pipelines. When added to a liquid, tracers can easily be detected if they leak out of the pipes. Gamma rays can pass through metal and be detected on a photographic film. By looking at the gamma-ray images, structural engineers can detect small cracks in the metal of bridges and building frames. Without these images, a problem might not be discovered until a disaster occurs.

 **Reading Checkpoint** **What is a tracer?**

Uses in Medicine Doctors use radioactive isotopes to detect medical problems and to treat some diseases. Tracers injected into the body travel to organs and other structures where that chemical is normally used. Using equipment that detects radiation, technicians make images of the bone, blood vessel, or organ affected. For example, tracers made with technetium-99 are used to diagnose problems in the bones, liver, kidneys, and digestive system.

In a process called radiation therapy, radioactive elements are used to destroy unhealthy cells. For example, iodine-131 is given to patients with tumors of the thyroid gland—a gland in the neck that controls the rate at which nutrients are used. Because the thyroid gland uses iodine, the radioactive iodine-131 collects in the gland. Radiation from this isotope destroys unwanted cells in the gland without serious effects on other parts of the body.

Cancer tumors of different kinds often are treated from outside the body with high-energy gamma rays. Many hospitals use cobalt-60 for this purpose. When gamma radiation is directed toward a cancer tumor, it causes changes that kill the cancer cells.

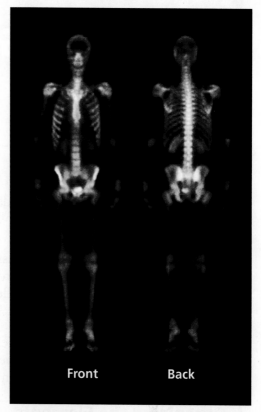

Front   Back

FIGURE 40
Radioactive Isotopes in Medicine
Front and back body scans of a healthy patient were made using a radioactive isotope.

Section 5 Assessment

S 8.7.b, E-LA: Reading 8.1.2, Writing 8.2.1

Vocabulary Skill Greek Word Origins Use what you know about the Greek words *alpha* and *beta* to explain the meanings of *alpha particle* and *beta particle*.

Reviewing Key Concepts

1. a. **Identifying** Under what circumstances did Becquerel first notice the effects of radioactivity?
   b. **Interpreting Photographs** Look at the photo in Figure 35. Explain in your own words what happened.
   c. **Applying Concepts** How did Becquerel's work lead to the discovery of two new elements?

2. a. **Listing** What are three products of radioactive decay?
   b. **Comparing and Contrasting** Contrast the penetrating power of the three major types of nuclear radiation.

   c. **Predicting** Predict the identity and mass number of the nucleus formed during the beta decay of magnesium-28.

3. a. **Explaining** How can radioactive isotopes be used as tracers?
   b. **Relating Cause and Effect** How is the use of radioactive isotopes in treating some forms of cancer related to certain properties of gamma radiation?

Writing in Science

Firsthand Account Suppose you could go back in time to interview Henri Becquerel on the day of his discovery of radioactivity. From his perspective, write an account of the discovery.

Chapter 4

Study Guide

🔑 The **BIG Idea** The organization of the periodic table is based on the properties of the elements and reflects the structure of atoms.

① Introduction to Atoms

Key Concepts S 8.3.a, 8.7.b

- Atomic theory grew as a series of models based on evidence. As more evidence was collected, the theory and models were revised.
- At the center of the atom is a tiny, massive nucleus containing protons and neutrons. It is surrounded by a cloudlike region of electrons.

Key Terms

atom	proton	atomic number
electron	energy level	isotope
nucleus	neutron	mass number

② Organizing the Elements

Key Concepts S 8.7.a

- Mendeleev noticed a pattern of properties in elements arranged by increasing atomic mass.
- The properties of an element can be predicted from its location in the periodic table.
- The periodic table lists each element's atomic number, symbol, name, and atomic mass.

Key Terms

atomic mass	group
periodic table	chemical symbol
period	

③ Metals

Key Concepts S 8.7.a, 8.7.c

- Physical properties of metals include luster, malleability, ductility, and conductivity.
- The reactivity of metals tends to decrease from left to right across the periodic table.
- Scientists make synthetic elements by forcing nuclear particles to crash into one another.

Key Terms

metal	corrosion
malleable	alkali metal
ductile	alkaline earth metal
thermal conductivity	transition metal
electrical conductivity	particle accelerator
reactivity	

④ Nonmetals Inert Gases, and Semimetals

Key Concepts S 8.7.a, 8.7.c

- Most nonmetals are poor conductors of heat and electric current. Solid nonmetals are dull and brittle.
- The inert gases tend to be unreactive.
- The most useful property of the semimetals is their varying ability to conduct electric current.

Key Terms

nonmetal	inert gas
diatomic molecule	semimetal
halogen	semiconductor

⑤ Radioactive Elements

Key Concepts S 8.7.b

- In 1896, the French scientist Henri Becquerel discovered radioactive decay quite by accident while studying a mineral containing uranium.
- Natural radioactive decay can produce alpha particles, beta particles, and gamma rays.
- Uses of radioactive isotopes include tracing the steps of chemical reactions and industrial processes, and diagnosing and treating disease.

Key Terms

radioactive decay	beta particle
radioactivity	gamma radiation
alpha particle	tracer

Radioactive nucleus

2 protons and 2 neutrons lost

Alpha particle

Review and Assessment

Target Reading Skill

Preview Visuals Complete the following graphic organizer to show that you understand Figure 37 on page 160. Add more questions and answers as needed.

Radioactive Decay

Q. What process does the art show?
A.
Q. Why are there three similar diagrams?
A.
Q. What do the arrows show?
A.

Reviewing Key Terms

Choose the letter of the best answer.

1. The atomic number of an atom is determined by the number of
   a. protons.
   b. electrons.
   c. neutrons.
   d. isotopes.

2. The horizontal rows in the periodic table are called
   a. groups.
   b. periods.
   c. nonmetals.
   d. metals.

3. Of the following, the group that contains elements that are the most reactive is the
   a. alkali metals.
   b. alkaline earth metals.
   c. carbon family.
   d. inert gases.

4. Unlike metals, solid nonmetals are
   a. good conductors of heat and electric current.
   b. malleable.
   c. dull and britttle.
   d. ductile.

5. Unstable atomic nuclei that release fast-moving particles and energy are
   a. radioactive.
   b. alloys.
   c. isotopes.
   d. alpha particles.

Complete the following sentences so that your answers clearly explain the key terms.

6. Carbon-12 and carbon-13 are examples of **isotopes,** or _____ .

7. Dmitri Mendeleev constructed the first **periodic table,** which is _____ .

8. A property of metals is high **thermal conductivity,** which means _____.

9. Germanium is an example of a **semimetal,** an element whose properties are _____ .

10. Uranium and radon share the property of **radioactivity,** which means _____ .

Writing in Science

News Report Imagine you are writing an article for a space magazine about the life cycle of a star. Which elements are produced in a star at different stages? How are these elements distributed into space?

Video Assessment

Discovery Channel School
Elements and the Periodic Table

Review and Assessment

Checking Concepts

11. What discoveries about the atom did Rutherford make from his team's experiments?

12. How do two isotopes of an element differ from one another? How are they similar?

13. Use the periodic table to find the atomic number and atomic mass of neon (Ne).

14. Use the periodic table to name two elements that have properties similar to those of chlorine (Cl).

15. Of the elements oxygen (O), zinc (Zn), and iodine (I), which one is likely to be a poor conductor of electricity and a brittle solid at room temperature?

16. What properties of radioactive isotopes make them useful?

Thinking Critically

17. Comparing and Contrasting List the three kinds of particles that make up atoms, and compare their masses and their locations in an atom.

18. Applying Concepts Below is a square taken from the periodic table. Identify the type of information given by each labeled item.

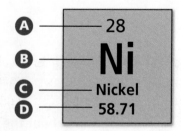

19. Relating Cause and Effect The atomic mass of iron is 55.847 amu. Why isn't this value a whole number?

20. Predicting Using the periodic table, predict which element—potassium, iron, or aluminum—is most reactive. Explain.

21. Inferring What property of the materials used in computer chips makes them useful as switches that turn electricity on and off?

Applying Skills

Use the diagram to answer Questions 22–27.

The diagram below shows the first few steps of the radioactive decay of uranium-238.

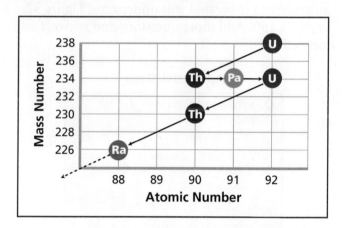

22. Reading Graphs What do the numbers on the *x*-axis and *y*-axis tell you about atomic particles in the nuclei of the isotopes?

23. Interpreting Data How many elements are in the diagram? How many different isotopes of each element are there?

24. Classifying What type of radioactive decay resulted in uranium-238 becoming thorium-234? How do you know?

25. Interpreting Diagrams Describe how thorium-234 is changed into uranium-234.

26. Inferring How do you know from the diagram that thorium-230 is radioactive?

27. Posing Questions What information would you need to have in order to extend the graph to show how radon-226 changes?

Lab zone Standards Investigation

Performance Assessment Display the chart showing the metals you studied. Be ready to discuss which properties are common to all metals. Describe other properties of metals you could not test. List all the properties that could be used to find out whether an unknown element is a metal.

Choose the letter of the best answer.

1. Why is the mass of a carbon atom greater than the total mass of its protons and electrons?
   A The mass of a proton is greater than the mass of an electron.
   B A proton is positively charged and an electron is negatively charged.
   C Most of the atom's volume is the sphere-shaped cloud of electrons.
   D One or more neutrons in the nucleus add mass to the atom. **S 8.3.a**

2. Elements that are shiny conductive solids at room temperature are likely to be classified as which of the following?
   A metals
   B nonmetals
   C inert gases
   D semimetals **S 8.7.c**

Use the diagram below to answer Question 3.

7e⁻

7 protons, 8 neutrons

3. What isotope does the diagram represent?
   A carbon-12
   B nitrogen-14
   C nitrogen-15
   D oxygen-15 **S 8.7.b**

4. Which property of aluminum makes it a suitable metal for soft drink cans?
   A It has good electrical conductivity.
   B It can be hammered into a thin sheet (malleability).
   C It can be drawn into long wires (ductility).
   D It can reflect light (shininess). **S 8.7.c**

Use the table below to answer Questions 5–7.

8	9	10
O	**F**	**Ne**
Oxygen	Fluorine	Neon
15.999	18.998	20.179
16	17	18
S	**Cl**	**Ar**
Sulfur	Chlorine	Argon
32.06	35.453	39.948

5. What element has an atomic number of 18?
   A hydrogen
   B oxygen
   C fluorine
   D argon **S 8.7.b**

6. An atom of fluorine has 10 neutrons. What is the total number of other subatomic particles in this atom?
   A 9 protons and 9 electrons
   B 9 protons and 19 electrons
   C 10 protons and 10 electrons
   D 19 protons and 19 electrons **S 8.3.a**

7. Which elements are inert gases?
   A oxygen, fluorine, and neon
   B sulfur, chlorine, and argon
   C oxygen, fluorine, and chlorine
   D neon and argon **S 8.7.a**

Apply the
BIG Idea

8. Suppose scientists synthesized a new element with the atomic number 120. Use what you know about the organization of the periodic table to predict the properties of this new element. **S 8.7**

Chemical Building Blocks
Unit 1 Review

Chapter 1
Introduction to Physical Science
The BIG Idea

Scientists investigate the natural world by posing questions, developing hypotheses, designing experiments, analyzing data, drawing conclusions, and communicating results.

🔑 What do physical scientists study?

🔑 What role do models, theories, and laws play in science?

🔑 Why do scientists use a standard system of measurement?

🔑 What should you do if a lab accident occurs?

Chapter 2
The Nature of Matter
The BIG Idea

Chemistry is the study of the properties of matter and how matter changes.

🔑 What kinds of properties are used to describe matter?

🔑 What is a physical change?

🔑 How is chemical energy related to chemical change?

Chapter 3
Solids, Liquids, and Gases
The BIG Idea

In solids, the particles vibrate in closely packed, fixed positions. In liquids, the particles are loosely connected and collide with one another. In gases, the particles are free to move independently.

🔑 How can you describe the motion of particles in a solid?

🔑 What happens to a substance during changes between liquid and gas?

🔑 How are the volume, temperature, and pressure of a gas related?

Chapter 4
Elements and the Periodic Table
The BIG Idea

The organization of the periodic table is based on the properties of the elements and reflects the structure of atoms.

🔑 How are the elements organized in the modern periodic table?

🔑 How does the reactivity of metals change across the periodic table?

🔑 What are the properties of nonmetals and inert gases?

Unit 1 Assessment

Sue and Juanita are throwing a big party for their friends. They purchase 100 2-liter bottles of seltzer (water with carbon dioxide gas in it), fill their car's trunk with all the bottles, and drive home. Since the party won't be until tomorrow, they decide to leave the seltzer in the car overnight.

The next morning, they open the car's trunk and discover that all the seltzer has frozen! They bring the bottles inside the house and let them warm up until the seltzer is liquid again.

At the party, one of the guests, Ben, asks if he can make an old-fashioned chocolate soda to drink. He fills a glass three-quarters of the way with seltzer, adds some dark brown chocolate syrup and white milk, and stirs it thoroughly. When he's done, the chocolate soda has a light brown color.

1. If the mass of all the seltzer that Sue and Juanita bought was 200 kilograms, what was the density of the seltzer? *(Chapter 1)*
   a. 1 kg/L
   b. 2 kg/L
   c. 100 kg/L
   d. 200 kg/L

2. Ben's chocolate soda is an example of a(n) *(Chapter 2)*
   a. heterogeneous mixture
   b. homogeneous mixture
   c. element
   d. compound

3. As the frozen seltzer melted into a liquid, what happened to the freedom of motion of the water molecules? *(Chapter 3)*
   a. It increased.
   b. It decreased.
   c. It stayed the same.
   d. It became zero.

4. The main component of seltzer is water. Water is a compound made up of the elements hydrogen and oxygen. Which class of elements does oxygen belong to? *(Chapter 4)*
   a. metals
   b. nonmetals
   c. semimetals
   d. inert gases

5. **Summary** Write a paragraph that summarizes the changes that the seltzer in the description above went through. Did the seltzer undergo a chemical change? Explain.

Atoms and Bonding

These models represent ▶ molecules of water (H_2O).

Focus on the BIG Idea

S 8.3.b

How do compounds form?

Check What You Know

Water is a compound made from the elements hydrogen and oxygen. How do the properties of water differ from those of the elements that it is made up of?

Build Science Vocabulary

The images shown here represent some of the key terms in this chapter. You can use this vocabulary skill to help you understand the meaning of some key terms in this chapter.

High-Use Academic Words

High-use academic words are words you are likely to meet while reading textbooks. Look for the following words in context as you read this chapter.

Word	Definition	Example Sentence
conduct (kahn DUKT) p. 199	*v.* To allow something to travel along or through it	Metal strips on a circuit board conduct electric current.
stable (STAY bul) p. 177	*adj.* Not easily or quickly changed from one state to another	Gold is a stable metal that does not rust or tarnish.
structure (STRUK chur) p. 178	*n.* The way in which parts of something are put together	The outside structure of the building is made of brick and concrete.
symbol (SIM bul) p. 187	*n.* A written sign that stands for something else	The symbol for the element oxygen is O.

Apply It!

Choose the word that best completes the sentence.

1. "H" is the _____ for hydrogen.

2. The _____ of an atom consists of a nucleus of protons and neutrons, surrounded by a cloud of moving electrons.

3. Platinum jewelry lasts a long time because the metal is very _____.

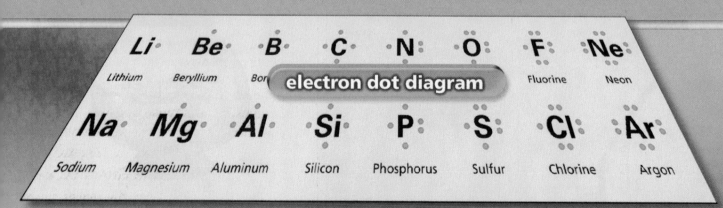

electron dot diagram

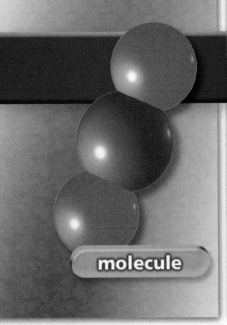

molecule

crystal

Section 1 (page 176)
valence electron
electron dot diagram
chemical bond

Section 2 (page 184)
ion
polyatomic ion
ionic bond
ionic compound
chemical formula
subscript
crystal

Section 3 (page 192)
covalent bond
molecule
double bond
triple bond
molecular compound
polar bond
nonpolar bond

Section 4 (page 198)
alloy
metallic bond

metallic bond

alloy

ᵢnteractive Textbook

Build Science Vocabulary
Online
Visit: PHSchool.com
Web Code: cxj-2050

How to Read Science

Compare and Contrast

When you compare and contrast, you examine the similarities and differences among things. You can compare and contrast by using a table.

Follow these steps to set up a compare–contrast table:

- List the items to be compared in the first column.
- List the characteristics to be compared across the top of the table.
- Complete the table by filling in information about each characteristic.

In this chapter, you will learn about chemical compounds, such as table salt (NaCl). Look at the compare–contrast table below.

Compounds and Their Component Elements

Substance	Color	State at Room Temperature
Table Salt (NaCl)	White	
Sodium (Na)	Silvery white	Solid
Chlorine (Cl)	Greenish yellow	Gas

Apply It!

After reading Section 2, copy and complete the compare–contrast table above to compare the properties of sodium chloride with those of sodium and chlorine. After reading Section 3, compare the properties of molecular compounds with those of ionic compounds.

Lab zone

Standards Investigation

S 8.3.c

Models of Compounds

In this chapter, you will learn how atoms of elements react with one another to form compounds. When they form compounds, the atoms become chemically bonded to each other. In this investigation, you will create models of chemical compounds.

Your Goal

To make models demonstrating how atoms bond in ionic compounds and in molecular compounds

To complete the investigation, you must

- select appropriate materials to make models of atoms
- indicate the number of bonds each atom forms
- use your model atoms to compare compounds that contain ionic bonds with compounds that contain covalent bonds
- follow the safety guidelines in Appendix A

Plan It!

Brainstorm with some classmates about materials you can use to represent different atoms and chemical bonds. Look ahead in the chapter to preview ionic and covalent bonding. Think about how you will show that ionic and covalent bonding are different. You may need to find some small, but highly visible, objects to represent electrons. Be ready to display your models and explain what they show.

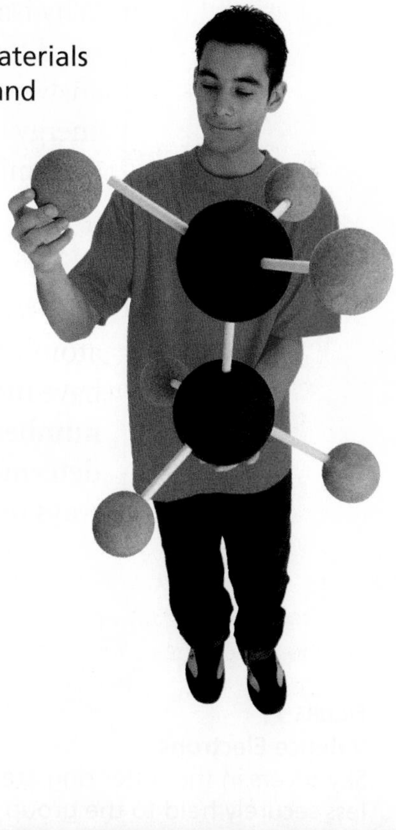

Atoms, Bonding, and the Periodic Table

CALIFORNIA
Standards Focus

S 8.3.f Students know how to use the periodic table to identify elements in simple compounds.

- How is the reactivity of elements related to valence electrons in atoms?

- What does the periodic table tell you about the atoms of elements?

Key Terms
- valence electron
- electron dot diagram
- chemical bond

Lab zone Standards **Warm-Up**

What Are the Trends in the Periodic Table?

1. Examine the periodic table of the elements that your teacher provides. Look in each square for the whole number located above the symbol of the element. As you read across a row from left to right, what trend do you see?

2. Now look at a column from top to bottom. What trend do you see in these numbers?

Think It Over
Interpreting Data Can you explain why one row ends and a new row starts? Why are certain elements in the same column?

Why isn't the world made only of elements? How do the atoms of different elements combine to form compounds? The answers to these questions are related to electrons and their energy levels. And the roadmap to understanding how electrons determine the properties of elements is the periodic table.

Valence Electrons and Bonding

You learned earlier about electrons and energy levels. An atom's **valence electrons** (VAY luns) are those electrons that have the highest energy level and are held most loosely. ⊙ **The number of valence electrons in an atom of an element determines many properties of that element, including the ways in which the atom can bond with other atoms.**

FIGURE 1
Valence Electrons
Sky divers in the outer ring are less securely held to the group than are members of the inner ring. Similarly, valence electrons are more loosely held by an atom than are electrons of lower energy levels.

Electron Dot Diagrams Each element has a specific number of valence electrons, ranging from 1 to 8. Figure 2 shows one way to depict the number of valence electrons in an element. An **electron dot diagram** includes the symbol for the element surrounded by dots. Each dot stands for one valence electron.

Chemical Bonds and Stability Atoms of most elements are more stable—that is, less likely to react—when they have eight valence electrons. For example, atoms of neon, argon, krypton, and xenon all have eight valence electrons and are very unreactive. These elements do not easily form compounds. Some small atoms, such as helium, are stable with just two valence electrons.

Atoms usually react in a way that makes each atom more stable. One of two things can happen: Either the number of valence electrons increases to eight (or two, in the case of hydrogen). Or, the atom gives up loosely held valence electrons. Atoms that react this way can become chemically combined, that is, bonded to other atoms. A **chemical bond** is the force of attraction that holds two atoms together as a result of the rearrangement of electrons between them.

Chemical Bonds and Chemical Reactions When atoms bond, electrons may be transferred from one atom to another, or they may be shared between the atoms. In either case, the change results in a chemical reaction—that is, new substances form. Later in this chapter, you will learn which elements are likely to gain electrons, which are likely to give up electrons, and which are likely to share electrons. You will also learn how the periodic table of the elements can help you predict how atoms of different elements react.

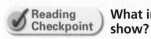
Reading Checkpoint What information does an electron dot diagram show?

FIGURE 2
Electron Dot Diagrams
An atom's valence electrons are shown as dots around the symbol of the element. Notice that oxygen atoms have six valence electrons. **Predicting** *How many more electrons are needed to make an oxygen atom stable?*

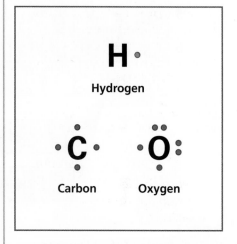

Hydrogen

Carbon   Oxygen

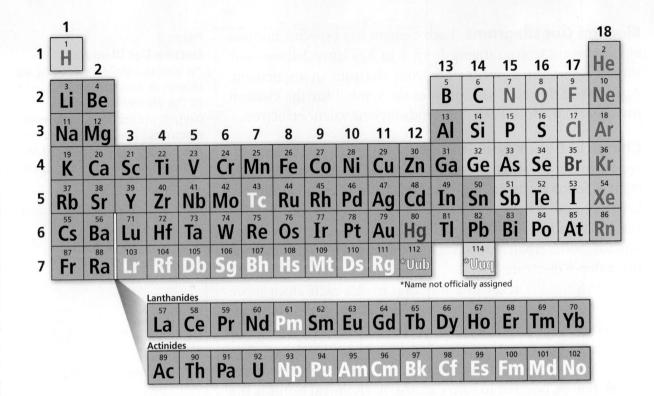

FIGURE 3
Periodic Table of the Elements
The periodic table of elements is arranged horizontally in order of increasing atomic number (number of protons) and vertically in columns of elements with similar chemical properties.

Go Online
active.art

For: Periodic Table activity
Visit: PHSchool.com
Web Code: cgp-1032

How the Periodic Table Works

The periodic table is a useful tool for identifying the elements in simple compounds. The table can also help you understand how atoms form bonds. ◆ **The periodic table reveals the underlying atomic structure of atoms, including the arrangement of the electrons.** If you know the number of valence electrons that atoms of different elements have, you have a clue as to which elements combine and how.

Relating Periods and Groups Look at Figure 3. Think about how the atoms change from left to right across a period. As the atomic number increases, the number of electrons also increases. Except for Period 1, a given period ends when the number of valence electrons reaches eight. The next period begins with atoms having valence electrons with higher energy. This repeating pattern means that the elements within a group always have the same number of valence electrons. As a result, they have similar properties.

Figure 4 compares the electron dot diagrams of elements in Periods 2 and 3. Notice that each element has one more valence electron than the element to its left. For example, Group 1 elements have one valence electron. The elements in Group 2 have two. Elements in Group 13 have three valence electrons, elements in Group 14 have four, and so on. (Elements in Groups 3 to 12 follow a slightly different pattern.)

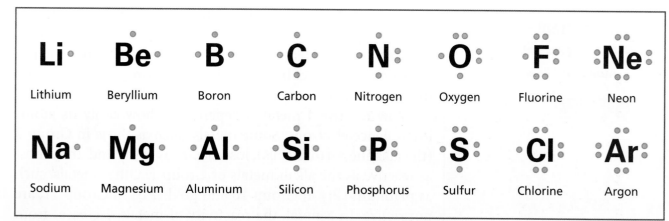

FIGURE 4
Patterns of Valence Electrons
After the number of valence electrons reaches 8, a new period begins.

Inert Gases The Group 18 elements are the inert gases. Atoms of these elements have eight valence electrons, except for helium, which has two. As you have read, atoms with eight valence electrons (or two, in the case of helium) are stable. Such atoms are unlikely to transfer electrons to other atoms or to share electrons with other atoms. As a result, inert gases do not react easily with other elements. Even so, chemists have been able to make inert gases form compounds with a few other elements.

Reactive Nonmetals and Metals Now look at the elements in the column just to the left of the inert gases. The elements in Group 17, the halogens, have atoms with seven valence electrons. A gain of just one more electron gives these atoms the stable number of eight electrons, as in the inert gases. As a result, the halogens react easily with other elements whose atoms can give up or share electrons.

At the far left side of the periodic table is Group 1, the alkali metal family. Atoms of the alkali metals have only one valence electron. Except for lithium, the next lowest energy level has a stable set of eight electrons. (Lithium atoms have a stable set of two electrons at the next lowest energy level.) Therefore, alkali metal atoms can become chemically more stable by losing their one valence electron. This property makes the alkali metals very reactive.

FIGURE 5
Reactivity of Chlorine
Chlorine is so reactive that steel wool burns when exposed to the chlorine gas in this jar.
Relating Cause and Effect *Why is chlorine so reactive?*

 **Reading Checkpoint** **How are atoms of the elements in Group 1 similar?**

Other Metals Look at the elements in Groups 2 through 12 of the periodic table. Like the Group 1 elements, these elements are metals. Most have one, two, or three valence electrons. They react by losing these electrons, especially when they combine with oxygen or one of the halogens.

How reactive a metal is depends on how easily its atoms lose valence electrons. Some metals, such as those in Group 2 (the alkaline earth metals), lose electrons easily and are almost as reactive as the alkali metals of Group 1. Other metals, such as platinum (Pt) in Group 10 and gold (Au) in Group 11, are unreactive. In general, the reactivity of metals decreases from left to right across the periodic table. Among Groups 1 and 2, reactivity increases from top to bottom.

Science and **History**

Discovery of the Elements

In 1869, Dmitri Mendeleev published the first periodic table. At that time, 63 elements were known. Since then, scientists have discovered or created about 50 new elements.

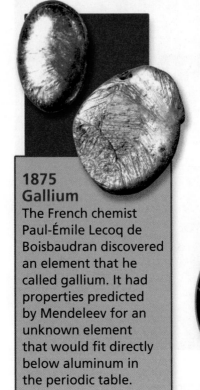

1894
Argon, Neon, Krypton, and Xenon
British chemist William Ramsay discovered an element he named argon, after the Greek word for "lazy." The name fits because argon does not react with other elements. Ramsay looked for other nonreactive gases and discovered neon, krypton, and xenon.

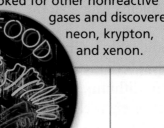

1875
Gallium
The French chemist Paul-Émile Lecoq de Boisbaudran discovered an element that he called gallium. It had properties predicted by Mendeleev for an unknown element that would fit directly below aluminum in the periodic table.

1898
Polonium and Radium
Chemists Marie Curie and her husband Pierre had to start with three tons of uranium ore to isolate a few grams of two new elements, which were named polonium and radium.

1830	1865	1900

Other Nonmetals Elements in the pale green color-coded region of the periodic table are the nonmetals. Five nonmetals are solids, four are gases, and one is a liquid. All of the nonmetals have four or more valence electrons. Like the halogens, other nonmetals become stable when they gain or share enough electrons to have a set of eight valence electrons.

The nonmetals combine with metals usually by gaining electrons. But nonmetals can also combine with other nonmetals by sharing electrons. Of the nonmetals, oxygen and the halogens are highly reactive. In fact, fluorine is the most reactive element known. It even forms compounds with some of the inert gases.

Writing in Science

Research and Write Various forms of the periodic table exist. The periodic tables used by physicists and engineers may include different information than the tables used by chemists. Use the library to find two different forms of the periodic table. Write a paragraph comparing the two tables and how scientists might use them.

1941
Plutonium
American chemist Glenn Seaborg was the first to isolate plutonium, which is found in small amounts in uranium ores. Plutonium is used as fuel in certain nuclear reactors. It has also been used to power equipment used in space exploration.

1997
Elements 101 to 109
The International Union of Pure and Applied Chemists (IUPAC) agreed on names for elements 101 to 109. Many of the names honor scientists. Seaborgium is named after Glenn Seaborg. Meitnerium is named after Lise Meitner, shown here in 1946. All the new elements are synthetic, and none is stable enough to exist in nature.

2003 to Present
Darmstadtium
Element 110, first created in the mid-1990s, is named darmstadtium. Research to produce and study new synthetic elements continues.

1939
Francium
Although Mendeleev predicted the properties of an element he called "eka-cesium," the element was not discovered until 1939. French chemist Marguerite Perey named her discovery francium, after the country France.

1935

1970

2005

◄ The quartz movement of the watch

FIGURE 6
A Semimetal at Work
This quartz-movement watch keeps time with a small quartz crystal, a compound made of the semimetal silicon and the nonmetal oxygen. The crystal vibrates at about 32,000 vibrations per second when a voltage is applied.

Semimetals Several elements known as semimetals lie along a zigzag line between the metals and nonmetals. The semimetals have from three to six valence electrons. They can either lose or share electrons when they combine with other elements. So, depending on the conditions, these elements can behave as either metals or nonmetals.

Hydrogen Notice that hydrogen is located above Group 1 in the periodic table. It is placed there because it has only one valence electron. However, hydrogen is not considered a metal. It is a reactive element, but its properties differ greatly from those of the alkali metals.

 **Reading Checkpoint** **Why is hydrogen grouped above the Group 1 elements even though it is not a metal?**

Section 1 Assessment S 8.3.f, E-LA: Reading 8.1.0

Vocabulary Skill High-Use Academic Words Use the word *stable* to explain why the halogens tend to combine easily with other elements.

Reviewing Key Concepts

1. a. **Defining** What are valence electrons?
   b. **Reviewing** What role do valence electons play in the formation of compounds from elements?
   c. **Comparing and Contrasting** Do oxygen atoms become more stable or less stable when oxygen forms compounds? Explain.

2. a. **Summarizing** Summarize how the periodic table is organized, and tell why this organization is useful.
   b. **Explaining** Why do the properties of elements change in a regular way across a period?
   c. **Relating Cause and Effect** Explain the reactivity of the inert gases in terms of valence electrons.

Lab zone **At-Home Activity**

Looking for Elements Find some examples of elements at home. Then locate the elements on the periodic table. Show your examples and the periodic table to your family. Point out the positions of the elements on the table and explain what the periodic table tells you about the elements. Include at least two nonmetals in your discussion. (*Hint:* The nonmetals may be invisible.)

Lab zone Skills Lab

Comparing Atom Sizes

S 8.3.f, 8.9.g

Problem

How is the radius of an atom related to its atomic number?

Skills Focus

making models, graphing, interpreting data

Materials

- drawing compass
- metric ruler
- calculator
- periodic table of the elements

Procedure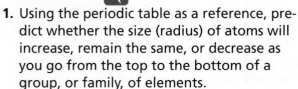

1. Using the periodic table as a reference, predict whether the size (radius) of atoms will increase, remain the same, or decrease as you go from the top to the bottom of a group, or family, of elements.

2. The data table lists the elements in Group 2 in the periodic table. The atomic radius of each element is given in picometers (pm). Copy the data table into your notebook.

3. Use the periodic table to look up the atomic numbers of the Group 2 elements. Record the values in your data table.

4. Calculate the relative radius of each atom compared to beryllium, the smallest atom listed. Do this by dividing each radius by the radius of beryllium. (*Hint:* The relative radius of magnesium would be 160 pm divided by 112 pm, or 1.4.) Record these values, rounded to the nearest tenth, in your data table.

5. Using a compass, draw a circle for each element with a radius that corresponds to the relative radius you calculated in Step 3. Use centimeters as your unit for the radius of each circle. **CAUTION:** *Do not push the sharp point of the compass against your skin.*

6. Label each model with the symbol of the element it represents.

Data Table

Element	Atomic Number	Radius (pm)*	Relative Radius
Be		112	1
Mg		160	
Ca		197	
Sr		215	
Ba		222	

*A picometer (pm) is one billionth of a millimeter.

Analyze and Conclude

1. **Making Models** Based on your models, was your prediction in Step 1 correct? Explain.

2. **Graphing** Make a graph of the data in the second and third columns of the data table. Label the horizontal axis *Atomic Number.* Mark the divisions from 0 to 60. Then label the vertical axis *Radius* and mark its divisions from 0 to 300 picometers.

3. **Interpreting Data** What trend does the graph show? Is the relationship between the variables linear or nonlinear?

4. **Predicting** Predict where you would find the largest atom in any group, or family, of elements. What evidence would you need to tell if your prediction is correct?

5. **Communicating** Write a paragraph explaining why it is useful to draw a one- to two-centimeter model of an atom that has an actual radius of 100 to 200 picometers.

More to Explore

Look up the atomic masses for the Group 2 elements. Devise a plan to model their relative atomic masses using real-world objects.

Ionic Bonds

CALIFORNIA
Standards Focus

S 8.3.b Students know that compounds are formed by combining two or more different elements and that compounds have properties that are different from their constituent elements.

S 8.3.c Students know that atoms and molecules form solids by building up repeating patterns, such as the crystal structure of NaCl or long-chain polymers.

- How do ions form bonds?
- How are the formulas and names of ionic compounds written?
- What are the properties of ionic compounds?

Key Terms

- ion
- polyatomic ion
- ionic bond
- ionic compound
- chemical formula
- subscript
- crystal

Lab zone Standards **Warm-Up**

How Do Ions Form?

1. Place three pairs of checkers (three red and three black) on your desk. The red represent electrons and the black represent protons.
2. Place nine pairs of checkers (nine red and nine black) in a separate group on your desk.
3. Move a red checker from the smaller group to the larger group.
4. Count the number of positive charges (protons) and negative charges (electrons) in each group.
5. Now sort the checkers into a group of four pairs and a group of eight pairs. Repeat Steps 3 and 4, this time moving two red checkers from the smaller group to the larger group.

Think It Over

Inferring What was the total charge on each group before you moved the red checkers (electrons)? What was the charge on each group after you moved the checkers? Based on this activity, what do you think happens to the charge on an atom when it loses electrons? When it gains electrons?

You and a friend walk past a market that sells apples for 40 cents each and pears for 50 cents each. You have 45 cents and want an apple. Your friend also has 45 cents but wants a pear. You realize that if you give your friend a nickel, she will have 50 cents and can buy a pear. You will have 40 cents left to buy an apple. Transferring the nickel gets both of you what you want. Your actions model, in a simple way, what can happen between atoms.

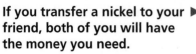

If you transfer a nickel to your ▶ friend, both of you will have the money you need.

Ions

Atoms with five, six, or seven valence electrons usually become more stable when this number increases to eight. Likewise, most atoms with one, two, or three valence electrons can lose electrons and become more stable. When these two types of atoms combine, or bond, electrons are transferred from one type of atom to the other. The transfer makes both types of atoms more stable.

How Ions Form An **ion** (EYE ahn) is an atom or group of atoms that has an electric charge. When an atom loses an electron, it loses a negative charge and becomes a positive ion. When an atom gains an electron, it gains a negative charge and becomes a negative ion. Figure 8 lists some ions you will often see in this book. Use this table as a reference while you read this section and other chapters.

Polyatomic Ions Notice in Figure 8 that some ions are made of several atoms. For example, the ammonium ion is made of nitrogen and hydrogen atoms. Ions that are made of more than one atom are called **polyatomic ions** (pahl ee uh TAHM ik). The prefix *poly* means "many," so *polyatomic* means "many atoms." You can think of a polyatomic ion as a group of atoms that reacts as a unit. Like other ions, polyatomic ions have an overall positive or negative charge.

 **Reading Checkpoint** How does an ion with a charge of 2+ form?

FIGURE 8
Ions are atoms that have lost or gained electrons. **Interpreting Tables** *How many electrons does a sulfur atom gain when it becomes a sulfide ion?*

Ions and Their Charges		
Name	**Charge**	**Symbol or Formula**
Lithium	1+	Li^+
Sodium	1+	Na^+
Potassium	1+	K^+
Ammonium	1+	NH_4^+
Calcium	2+	Ca^{2+}
Magnesium	2+	Mg^{2+}
Aluminum	3+	Al^{3+}
Fluoride	1−	F^-
Chloride	1−	Cl^-
Iodide	1−	I^-
Bicarbonate	1−	HCO_3^-
Nitrate	1−	NO_3^-
Oxide	2−	O^{2-}
Sulfide	2−	S^{2-}
Carbonate	2−	CO_3^{2-}
Sulfate	2−	SO_4^{2-}
Phosphate	3−	PO_4^{3-}

Ionic Bonds Look at Figure 9 to see how sodium atoms and chlorine atoms combine to form sodium chloride (table salt). Notice that sodium has one valence electron and chlorine has seven valence electrons. When sodium's valence electron is transferred to chlorine, both atoms become ions. The sodium atom becomes a positive ion (Na^+). The chlorine atom becomes a negative ion (Cl^-).

Because oppositely charged particles attract, the positive Na^+ ion and the negative Cl^- ion attract each other. An **ionic bond** is the attraction between two oppositely charged ions. ● **Ionic bonds form as a result of the attraction between positive and negative ions.** A compound that consists of positive and negative ions, such as sodium chloride, is called an **ionic compound.**

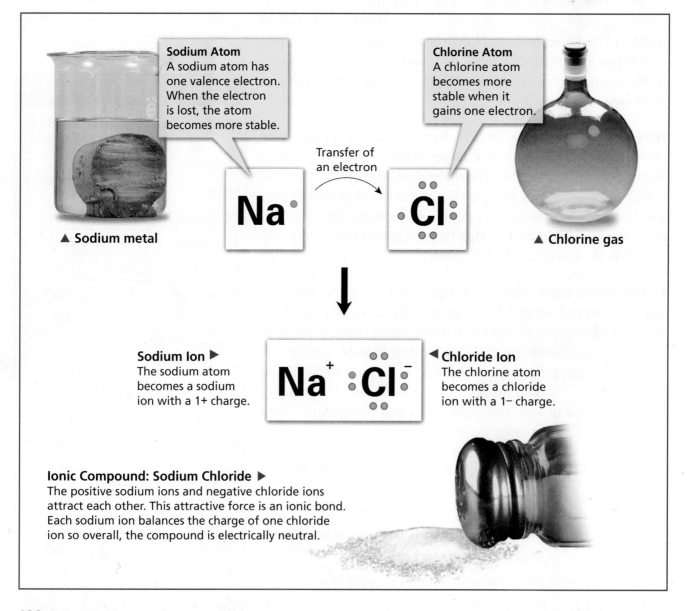

FIGURE 9

Formation of an Ionic Bond

Reactions occur easily between metals in Group 1 and nonmetals in Group 17. Follow the process below to see how an ionic bond forms between a sodium atom and a chlorine atom.

Relating Cause and Effect *Why is sodium chloride electrically neutral?*

Sodium Atom
A sodium atom has one valence electron. When the electron is lost, the atom becomes more stable.

Chlorine Atom
A chlorine atom becomes more stable when it gains one electron.

Transfer of an electron

Na·

·Cl:

▲ **Sodium metal**

▲ **Chlorine gas**

Sodium Ion ▶
The sodium atom becomes a sodium ion with a 1+ charge.

Na^+ :Cl:$^-$

◀ **Chloride Ion**
The chlorine atom becomes a chloride ion with a 1– charge.

Ionic Compound: Sodium Chloride ▶
The positive sodium ions and negative chloride ions attract each other. This attractive force is an ionic bond. Each sodium ion balances the charge of one chloride ion so overall, the compound is electrically neutral.

Chemical Formulas and Names

Compounds can be represented by chemical formulas. A **chemical formula** is a combination of symbols that shows the ratio of elements in a compound. For example, the formula for magnesium chloride is $MgCl_2$. What does the formula tell you?

Formulas of Ionic Compounds From Figure 8 you know that the charge on the magnesium ion is 2+.  **When ionic compounds form, the ions come together in a way that balances out the charges on the ions. The chemical formula for the compound reflects this balance.** Two chloride ions, each with a charge of 1– will balance the charge on the magnesium ion. That's why the formula of magnesium chloride is $MgCl_2$. The number "2" is a subscript. A **subscript** tells you the ratio of elements in the compound. For $MgCl_2$, the ratio of magnesium ions to chloride ions is 1 to 2.

If no subscript is written, the number 1 is understood. For example, the formula NaCl tells you that there is a 1 to 1 ratio of sodium ions to chloride ions. Formulas for compounds of polyatomic ions are written in a similar way. For example, calcium carbonate has the formula $CaCO_3$.

Naming Ionic Compounds Magnesium chloride, sodium bicarbonate, sodium oxide—where do these names come from?  **For an ionic compound, the name of the positive ion comes first, followed by the name of the negative ion.** The name of the positive ion is usually the name of a metal. But, a few positive polyatomic ions exist, such as the ammonium ion (NH_4^+). If the negative ion is a single element, as you've already seen with sodium chloride, the end of its name changes to -*ide*. For example, MgO is named magnesium oxide. If the negative ion is polyatomic, its name usually ends in -*ate* or -*ite*, as in Figure 8. The compound NH_4NO_3, named ammonium nitrate, is a common fertilizer for gardens and crop plants.

Reading Checkpoint What is the name of the ionic compound with the formula K_2S?

FIGURE 10

Calcium Carbonate

The white cliffs of Dover, England, are made of chalk formed from the remains of tiny sea organisms. Chalk is mostly an ionic compound, calcium carbonate.

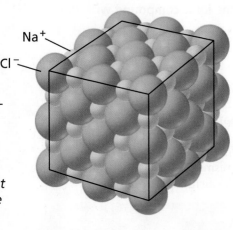
Crystal Clear

Can you grow a salt crystal?

1. Add table salt to a jar containing about 200 mL of hot tap water and stir. Keep adding salt until no more dissolves and it settles out when you stop stirring.

2. Tie a large crystal of coarse salt into the middle of a piece of thread.

3. Tie one end of the thread to the middle of a pencil.

4. Suspend the other end of the thread in the solution by laying the pencil across the mouth of the jar. Do not allow the crystal to touch the solution.

5. Place the jar in a quiet, undisturbed area. Check the size of the crystal over the next few days.

Observing Does the salt crystal change size over time? What is its shape? What do you think is happening to the ions in the solution?

Properties of Ionic Compounds

Compounds have properties that are different from their constituent elements. You have already read about the properties of metals and nonmetals. But what about the properties of ionic compounds formed when metals and nonmetals react? **In general, ionic compounds are hard, brittle solids with high melting points. When melted or dissolved in water, they conduct electric current.**

Ionic Crystals Ionic compounds form solids by building up repeating patterns of ions. Figure 11 shows a chunk of a halite, or rock salt, which is how sodium chloride occurs naturally. Pieces of halite have sharp edges, corners, flat surfaces, and a cubic shape. Equal numbers of Na^+ and Cl^- ions in solid sodium chloride are attracted in an alternating pattern, as shown in the diagram. The ions form an orderly, three-dimensional arrangement called a **crystal.**

In an ionic compound, every ion is attracted to ions of opposite charge that surround it. The pattern formed by the ions remains the same no matter what the size of the crystal. In a single grain of salt, the crystal pattern extends for millions of ions in every direction. Many crystals of ionic compounds are hard and brittle, due to the strength of their ionic bonds and the attractions among all the ions.

High Melting Points When you heat a substance such as table salt, its energy increases. When the ions have enough energy to overcome the attractive forces between them, they break away from each other. The ionic crystal melts into a liquid. Because ionic bonds are strong, a lot of energy is needed to break them. As a result, ionic compounds have high melting points. For example, the melting point of table salt is 801°C.

Na⁺
Cl⁻

FIGURE 11
Ionic Crystals
The ions in ionic compounds are arranged in specific three-dimensional shapes called crystals. Some crystals have a cube shape like these crystals of halite, or sodium chloride.
Making Generalizations *What holds the ions together in the crystal?*

FIGURE 12
Ions in Solution
A solution of sodium chloride conducts electric current across the gap between the two black rods of a conductivity tester. As a result, the bulb lights up.

Electrical Conductivity Electric current is the flow of charged particles. When ionic crystals dissolve in water, the bonds between ions are broken. As a result, the ions are free to move about, and the solution conducts current. Likewise, after an ionic compound melts, the ions are able to move freely, and the liquid conducts current. In contrast, ionic compounds in solid form do not conduct current well. The ions in the solid crystal are tightly bound to each other and cannot move from place to place. If charged particles cannot move, there is no current.

For: Links on ionic compounds
Visit: www.SciLinks.org
Web Code: scn-1213

Reading Checkpoint   **What is a crystal?**

Section 2 Assessment

S 8.3.b, 8.3.c, E-LA: Reading 8.2.0, Writing 8.2.1

Target Reading Skill Compare and Contrast
Complete your table comparing the properties of sodium, chlorine, and sodium chloride. Expand the table by adding columns for melting point and conductivity. Then compare these properties.

Reviewing Key Concepts

1. **a. Reviewing** What is an ion?
   b. Comparing and Contrasting Contrast sodium and chloride ions, including how they form. Write the symbol for each ion.
   c. Relating Cause and Effect What holds the ions together in sodium chloride? Indicate the specific charges that are involved.
2. **a. Identifying** What information is given by the formula of an ionic compound?
   b. Explaining The formula for sodium sulfide is Na_2S. Explain what this formula means.

   c. Applying Concepts Write the formula for calcium chloride. Explain how you determined this formula.
3. **a. Listing** List three properties of ionic compounds.
   b. Making Generalizations Relate each property that you listed to the characteristics of ionic bonds.

Writing in Science

Firsthand Account Pretend that you are the size of an atom, and you are observing a reaction between a potassium atom and a fluorine atom. Write an account of the formation of an ionic bond as the atoms react. Tell what happens to the valence electrons on each atom and how each atom is changed by losing or gaining electrons.

Shedding Light on Ions

 S 8.7.c, 8.9.c

Problem

What kinds of compounds produce ions in solution?

Skills Focus

controlling variables, interpreting data, inferring

Materials

- 2 dry cells, 1.5 V
- small light bulb and socket ⎫
- 4 lengths of wire with ⎬ or conductivity probe
  alligator clips on both ends ⎭
- 2 copper strips
- distilled water
- small beaker
- small plastic spoon
- sodium chloride
- graduated cylinder, 100-mL
- sucrose
- additional materials supplied by your teacher

Data Table	
Sample	Observations
Tap water	
Distilled water	
Sodium chloride	
Sodium chloride in water	

Procedure

1. Make a conductivity tester as described below or, if you are using a conductivity probe, see your teacher for instructions. Then make a data table in your notebook similar to the one above.

2. Pour about 50 mL of tap water into a small beaker. Place the copper strips in the beaker. Be sure the strips are not touching each other. Attach the alligator clip of the free end of one wire to a copper strip. Do the same with the other wire and the other copper strip. Record your observations.

3. Disconnect the wires from the copper strips. Take the strips out of the beaker, and pour out the tap water. Dry the inside of the beaker and the copper strips with a paper towel.

4. Pour 50 mL of distilled water into the beaker. Reconnect the conductivity tester and test the water as in Step 2. Keep the copper strips about the same distance apart as in Step 2. Record your observations.

Making a Conductivity Tester

A. Use wire with alligator clips to connect the positive terminal of a dry cell to a lamp socket. **CAUTION:** *The bulb is fragile and can break.*

B. Similarly connect another wire between the negative terminal of the cell and the positive terminal of the second cell.

C. Connect one end of a third wire to the negative terminal of the second dry cell.

D. Connect one end of a fourth wire to the other terminal of the lamp socket.

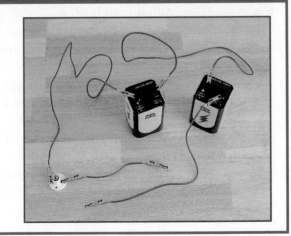

5. Use 3 spoonfuls of sodium chloride to make a small pile on a clean piece of paper. Dry off the copper strips of the conductivity tester and use it to test the conductivity of the sodium chloride. Record your observations.

6. Add 1 spoonful of sodium chloride to the distilled water in the beaker. Stir with the spoon until the salt dissolves. Repeat the conductivity test and record your observations.

7. Disconnect the conductivity tester and rinse the beaker, spoon, and copper strips with distilled water. Dry the beaker as in Step 3.

8. Test sucrose (table sugar) in the same ways that you tested sodium chloride in Steps 4 through 7. Test additional materials supplied by your teacher.
   - If the material is a solid, mix 1 spoonful of it with about 50 mL of distilled water and stir until the material dissolves. Test the resulting mixture.
   - If the substance is a liquid, simply pour about 50 mL into the beaker. Test it as you did the other mixtures.

Analyze and Conclude

1. **Designing Experiments** What were the variable parameters in your experiment? What were the controlled parameters?

2. **Controlling Variables** Why did you test both tap water and distilled water before testing the sodium chloride solution?

3. **Inferring** Could you have used tap water in your tests instead of distilled water? Explain.

4. **Drawing Conclusions** Based on your observations, add a column to your data table indicating whether each substance produced ions in solution.

5. **Inferring** How can you account for any observed differences in conductivity between dry and dissolved sodium chloride?

6. **Communicating** Based on your observations, decide whether or not you think sucrose is made up of ions. Explain your answer.

Design an Experiment

Design an experiment to test the effects of varying the spacing between the copper strips of the conductivity tester. *Obtain your teacher's permission before carrying out your investigation.*

Covalent Bonds

CALIFORNIA
Standards Focus

S 8.3.b Students know that compounds are formed by combining two or more different elements and that compounds have properties that are different from their constituent elements.

S 8.7.c Students know substances can be classified by their properties, including their melting temperature, density, hardness, and thermal and electrical conductivity.

What holds covalently bonded atoms together?

What are the properties of molecular compounds?

How does unequal sharing of electrons affect molecules?

Key Terms
- covalent bond
- molecule
- double bond
- triple bond
- molecular compound
- polar bond
- nonpolar bond

Lab zone Standards **Warm-Up**

Can Water and Oil Mix?

1. Pour water into a small jar that has a tight-fitting lid until the jar is about a third full.
2. Add an equal amount of vegetable oil to the jar. Cover the jar tightly.
3. Shake the jar vigorously for 20 seconds. Observe the contents.
4. Allow the jar to sit undisturbed for 1 minute. Observe again.
5. Remove the top and add 3 drops of liquid detergent. Cover the jar and repeat Steps 3 and 4.

Think It Over
Forming Operational Definitions Based on your observations, write an operational definition of *detergent*. How might your observations relate to chemical bonds in the detergent, oil, and water molecules?

Uh oh, you have a big project due in English class next week! You need to write a story and illustrate it with colorful posters. Art has always been your best subject, but writing takes more effort. Luckily, you're working with a partner who writes well but doesn't feel confident in art. If you each contribute your skills, together you can produce a high-quality finished project.

FIGURE 13
Sharing Skills
One student is a skilled artist, while the other is a skilled writer. By pooling their skills, the students can complete their project.

How Covalent Bonds Form

Just as you and your friend can work together by sharing your talents, atoms can become more stable by sharing electrons. The chemical bond formed when two atoms share electrons is called a **covalent bond.** Covalent bonds usually form between atoms of nonmetals. In contrast, ionic bonds usually form when a metal combines with a nonmetal.

Electron Sharing Nonmetals can bond to other nonmetals by sharing electrons. So can hydrogen. Most nonmetals can even bond with another atom of the same element. Figure 14 illustrates how two fluorine atoms can react by sharing a pair of electrons. By sharing electrons, each fluorine atom has a stable set of eight. ⬤ **The force that holds atoms together in a covalent bond is the attraction of each atom's nucleus for the shared pair of electrons.** The two bonded fluorine atoms form a molecule. A **molecule** is a neutral group of atoms joined by covalent bonds.

How Many Bonds? Look at the electron dot diagrams in Figure 15. Count the valence electrons around each atom that reacts. Hydrogen has one valence electron. Oxygen has six. Nitrogen has five. The number of covalent bonds that a non-metal atom can form equals the number of electrons needed to make a total of eight. For example, oxygen has six valence electrons, so it can form two covalent bonds. In a water molecule, oxygen forms one covalent bond with each of two hydrogen atoms. As a result, the oxygen atom has a stable set of eight valence electrons. Each hydrogen atom can form one bond because it needs only a total of two electrons to be stable.

FIGURE 14
Sharing Electrons
By sharing electrons in a covalent bond, each fluorine atom has a stable set of eight valence electrons.

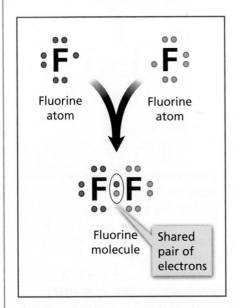

FIGURE 15
Covalent Bonds
The oxygen atom in water and the nitrogen atom in ammonia each have eight valence electrons as a result of forming covalent bonds with hydrogen atoms.
Interpreting Diagrams *How many covalent bonds can a nitrogen atom form?*

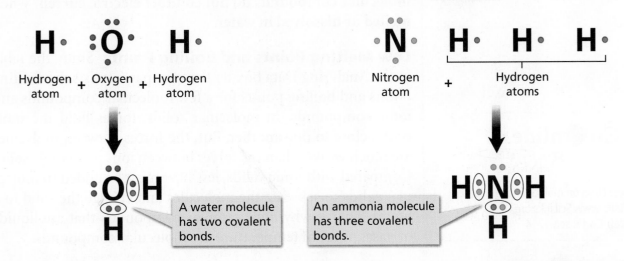

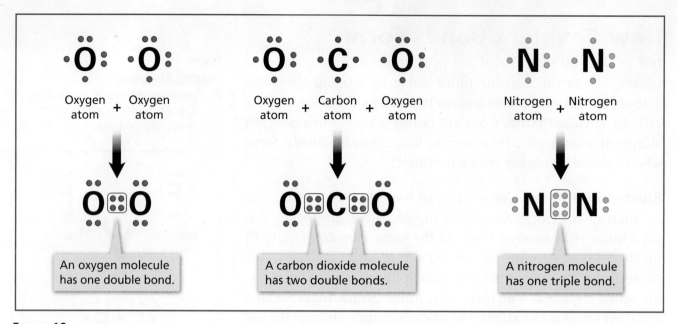

An oxygen molecule has one double bond.

A carbon dioxide molecule has two double bonds.

A nitrogen molecule has one triple bond.

FIGURE 16
Double and Triple Bonds
Double and triple bonds can form when atoms share more than one pair of electrons.
Interpreting Diagrams *In a nitrogen molecule, how many electrons does each nitrogen atom share with the other?*

Double Bonds and Triple Bonds Look at the diagram of the oxygen molecule (O_2) in Figure 16. What do you see that's different? This time the two atoms share two pairs of electrons, forming a **double bond.** In a carbon dioxide molecule (CO_2), carbon forms a double bond with each of two oxygen atoms. Elements such as nitrogen and carbon can form **triple bonds** in which their atoms share three pairs of electrons.

> **Reading Checkpoint** What is the difference between a double bond and a triple bond?

Molecular Compounds

A **molecular compound** is a compound that is composed of molecules. The molecules of a molecular compound contain atoms that are covalently bonded. ⊙ **Compared to ionic compounds, molecular compounds generally have lower melting points and boiling points. And, unlike ionic compounds, molecular compounds do not conduct electric current when melted or dissolved in water.**

Low Melting Points and Boiling Points Study the table in the Analyzing Data box on the next page. It lists the melting points and boiling points for a few molecular compounds and ionic compounds. In molecular solids, forces hold the molecules close to one another. But, the forces between molecules are much weaker than the forces between ions in an ionic solid. Compared with ionic solids, less heat must be added to molecular solids to separate the molecules and change the solid to a liquid. That is why most familiar compounds that are liquids or gases at room temperature are molecular compounds.

Math Analyzing Data

Comparing Molecular and Ionic Compounds

The table compares the melting points and boiling points of a few molecular compounds and ionic compounds. Use the table to answer the following questions.

1. **Graphing** Create a bar graph of just the melting points of these compounds. Arrange the bars in order of increasing melting point. The y-axis should start at $-200°C$ and go to $900°C$.

2. **Interpreting Data** Describe what your graph reveals about the melting points of molecular compounds compared to those of ionic compounds.

3. **Inferring** How can you account for the differences in melting points between molecular compounds and ionic compounds?

4. **Interpreting Data** How do the boiling points of the molecular and ionic compounds compare?

Melting Points and Boiling Points of Molecular and Ionic Compounds

Substance	Formula	Melting Point (°C)	Boiling Point (°C)
Methane	CH_4	−182.4	−161.5
Rubbing alcohol	C_3H_8O	−89.5	82.4
Water	H_2O	0	100
Zinc chloride	$ZnCl_2$	290	732
Magnesium chloride	$MgCl_2$	714	1,412
Sodium chloride	$NaCl$	800.7	1,465

Molecular compound   Ionic compound

5. **Predicting** Ammonia's melting point is −78°C and its boiling point is −34°C. Is ammonia a molecular compound or an ionic compound? Explain.

Poor Conductivity Most molecular compounds do not conduct electric current. No charged particles are available to move, so there is no current. Materials such as plastic and rubber are used to insulate wires because these materials are composed of molecular substances. Even as liquids, molecular compounds are poor conductors. Pure water, for example, does not conduct electric current. Neither does table sugar or alcohol when they are dissolved in pure water.

Unequal Sharing of Electrons

Have you ever played tug of war? If you have, you know that if both teams pull with equal force, the contest is a tie. But what if the teams pull with unequal forces? Then the rope moves toward the side of the stronger team. The same is true of electrons in a covalent bond. Atoms of some elements pull more strongly on shared electrons than do atoms of other elements. As a result, the electrons are shared unequally. **Unequal sharing of electrons causes the bonded atoms to have slight electrical charges.**

FIGURE 17

Nonpolar and Polar Bonds
Fluorine forms a nonpolar bond with another fluorine atom. In hydrogen fluoride, fluorine attracts electrons more strongly than hydrogen does, so the bond formed is polar.

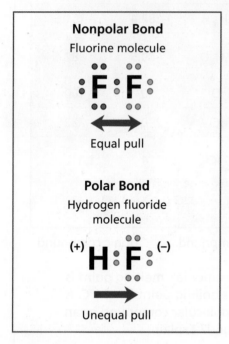

Nonpolar Bond
Fluorine molecule

Equal pull

Polar Bond
Hydrogen fluoride molecule

Unequal pull

Polar Bonds and Nonpolar Bonds The unequal sharing of electrons is enough to make the atom with the stronger pull slightly negative and the atom with the weaker pull slightly positive. A covalent bond in which electrons are shared unequally is called a **polar bond.** Of course, if two atoms pull equally on the electrons, neither atom becomes charged. A covalent bond in which electrons are shared equally is a **nonpolar bond.** Compare the bond in fluorine (F_2) with the bond in hydrogen fluoride (HF) in Figure 17.

Polar Bonds in Molecules A molecule is considered polar if it has a positively charged end opposite a negatively charged end. For example, hydrogen fluoride is a polar molecule. However, not all molecules containing polar bonds are polar. For example, in carbon dioxide, the oxygen atoms attract electrons much more strongly than carbon does. So, the bonds between the oxygen and carbon atoms are polar. But, as you can see in Figure 18, a carbon dioxide molecule has a straight-line shape. As a result, the two oxygen atoms pull with equal strength in opposite directions. The attractions cancel out, making the molecule nonpolar.

In contrast, a water molecule, with its two polar bonds, is itself polar. A water molecule has two hydrogen atoms at one end and an oxygen atom at the other end. The oxygen atom attracts electrons more strongly than do the hydrogen atoms. As a result, the oxygen end has a slight negative charge and the hydrogen end has a slight positive charge.

Attractions Among Molecules If you could shrink small enough to move among a bunch of water molecules, what would you find? The negatively charged oxygen ends of the polar water molecules attract the positively charged hydrogen ends of nearby water molecules. These attractions pull water molecules toward each other. In contrast, there is little attraction among nonpolar molecules, such as carbon dioxide molecules.

FIGURE 18
Nonpolar and Polar Molecules
A carbon dioxide molecule is a nonpolar molecule because of its straight-line shape. In contrast, a water molecule is a polar molecule because of its bent shape.
Interpreting Diagrams *What do the arrows in the diagram show?*

Nonpolar Molecule
Carbon dioxide

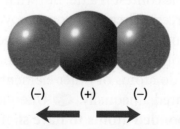

(–)   (+)   (–)

Opposite pulling cancels

Polar Molecule
Water

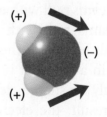

(+)

(–)

(+)

Electrons pulled toward oxygen

The properties of polar and nonpolar compounds differ because of differences in attractions between their molecules. For example, water and vegetable oil don't mix. The molecules in vegetable oil are nonpolar, and nonpolar molecules have little attraction for polar water molecules. On the other hand, the water molecules are attracted more strongly to one another than to the molecules of oil. Thus, water stays with water, and oil stays with oil.

If you did the Standards Warm-Up activity, you found that adding detergent helped oil and water to mix. This is because one end of a detergent molecule has nonpolar covalent bonds. The other end includes an ionic bond. The detergent's nonpolar end mixes easily with the oil. Meanwhile, the charged ionic end is attracted to polar water molecules, so the detergent dissolves in water.

FIGURE 19
Getting Out the Dirt
Most laundry dirt is oily or greasy. Detergents can mix with both oil and water, so when the wash water goes down the drain, the soap and dirt go with it.

 Reading Checkpoint) **Why is water (H₂O) a polar molecule but a fluorine molecule (F₂) is not?**

Section 3 **Assessment**

S 8.3.b, 8.7.c, E-LA: Reading 8.2.0, Math: 7PS1.1

Target Reading Skill Compare and Contrast
Create a table comparing the properties of molecular compounds and ionic compounds.

Reviewing Key Concepts

1. a. **Identifying** What is the attraction that holds two covalently bonded atoms together?
   b. **Inferring** A carbon atom can form four covalent bonds. How many valence electrons does it have?
   c. **Interpreting Diagrams** What is a double bond? Use Figure 16 to explain how a carbon dioxide molecule has a stable set of eight valence electrons for each atom.
2. a. **Reviewing** How are the properties of molecular compounds different from those of ionic compounds?
   b. **Relating Cause and Effect** Why are most molecular compounds poor conductors?
3. a. **Reviewing** How do some atoms in covalent bonds become slightly negative or slightly positive? What type of covalent bonds do these atoms form?

b. **Comparing and Contrasting** Both carbon dioxide molecules and water molecules have polar bonds. Why then is carbon dioxide a nonpolar molecule while water is a polar molecule?
c. **Predicting** Predict whether carbon dioxide or water would have a higher boiling point. Explain your prediction in terms of the attractions between molecules.

Lab zone At-Home **Activity**

Laundry Chemistry Demonstrate the action of soaps and detergents to your family. Pour some vegetable oil on a clean cloth and show how a detergent solution can wash the oil away better than water alone can. Explain to your family the features of soap and detergent molecules in terms of their chemical bonds.

Bonding in Metals

How do the properties of metals and alloys compare?

How do metal atoms combine?

How does metallic bonding result in useful properties of metals?

Key Terms
• alloy
• metallic bond

Lab zone Standards **Warm-Up**

Are They "Steel" the Same?

1. Wrap a stainless steel bolt, a wire nail (high-carbon steel), and a cut nail (low-carbon steel) together in a paper towel.

2. Place the towel in a plastic bag. Add about 250 mL of salt water and seal the bag.

3. After one or two days, remove the nails and bolt. Note any changes in the metals.

Think It Over

Developing Hypotheses What happened to the three types of steel? Which one changed the most, and which one changed the least? What do you think accounts for the difference?

Why would you choose metal to cover the complex shape of the building in Figure 20? You couldn't cover the building with brittle, crumbly nonmetals such as sulfur or silicon. What physical properties make metals ideal materials for making furniture, musical instruments, electrical wire, pots and pans, eating utensils, and strong beams for buildings? Why do metals have these physical properties?

FIGURE 20
Metal in Architecture
The Guggenheim Museum in Bilbao, Spain, makes dramatic use of some properties of metals. The museum's shiny outer "skin" is made of the lightweight metal titanium, which can be pressed into large, thin, flexible sheets.

Metals and Alloys

You know a piece of metal when you see it. It's usually hard, dense, and shiny. At room temperature, most metals are solids. They can be hammered or drawn out into thin wire. Electronics such as stereos, computers, and MP3 players have metal parts because metals conduct electric current.

Yet, very few of the "metals" you use every day consist of just one element. Instead, most of the metallic objects you see and use are made of alloys. An **alloy** is a mixture made of two or more elements, at least one of which is a metal. ☛ **Alloys are generally stronger and less reactive than the pure metals from which they are made**.

Physical Properties The properties of an alloy can differ greatly from those of its individual elements. But depending on how they are mixed, alloys also retain many of the physical properties of metals. For example, pure gold is shiny, but it is soft and easily bent. For that reason, gold jewelry and coins are made of an alloy of gold mixed with a harder element, such as copper or silver. These gold alloys are much harder than pure gold but still retain their beauty and shine. Even after thousands of years, objects made of gold alloys still look exactly the same as when they were first made.

Chemical Properties Iron is strong metal that you might think would be good for making tools. However, iron objects rust when they are exposed to air and water. For this reason, iron is often alloyed with one or more other elements to make steel. Tools made of steel are much stronger than iron and resist rust much better. For example, forks and spoons made of stainless steel can be washed over and over again without rusting. That's because stainless steel—an alloy of iron, carbon, nickel, and chromium—does not react with air and water as iron does.

FIGURE 22
Gold and Steel
This pipe wrench is made of steel. The necklace is made of gold alloys.

Reading Checkpoint Why is most jewelry made of gold alloys rather than pure gold?

Try This Activity

What Do Metals Do?

1. Your teacher will give you pieces of different metals. Examine each metal and try changing its shape by bending, stretching, folding, or any other action you can think of.

2. Write down the properties that are common to these metals. Write down the properties that are different.

3. What properties make each metal suitable for its intended use?

Inferring What properties must aluminum have in order to be made into foil?

Metallic Bonding

The properties of solid metals and their alloys can be explained by the structure of metal atoms and the bonding between those atoms. Recall that most metals have 1, 2, or 3 valence electrons. When metal atoms combine chemically with atoms of other elements, they usually lose valence electrons, becoming positively charged metal ions. Metals lose electrons easily because their valence electrons are not strongly held.

 **Metal atoms combine in regular patterns in which the valence electrons are free to move from atom to atom.** Most metals are crystalline solids. Within each crystal, the metal atoms exist as closely packed, positively charged ions. The valence electrons drift among the ions. Each metal ion is held in place by a **metallic bond**—an attraction between a positive metal ion and the many electrons surrounding it. Figure 23 illustrates the metallic bonds that hold together aluminum foil. The positively charged metal ions are embedded in a "sea" of valence electrons. The more valence electrons an atom can add to the "sea," the stronger the metallic bonds will be.

Reading Checkpoint What is a metallic bond?

FIGURE 23
Metallic Bonding
The type of bonding in metals is the result of loosely held electrons. **Problem Solving** *Why would nonmetals be unlikely to have the type of bonding shown here?*

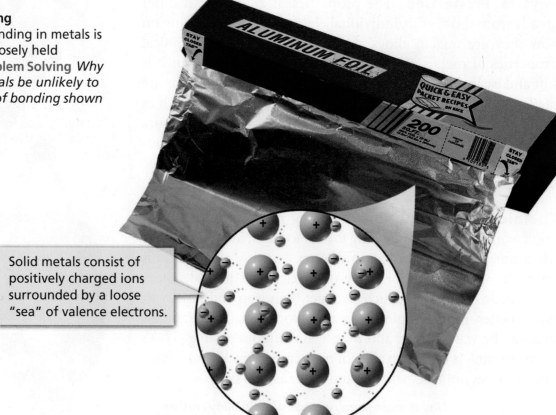

Solid metals consist of positively charged ions surrounded by a loose "sea" of valence electrons.

Metallic Properties

Suppose that you placed one hand on an unheated aluminum pan and the other hand on a wooden tabletop. The aluminum pan would feel cooler than the tabletop even though both are at the same temperature. You feel the difference because aluminum conducts heat away from your hand much faster than wood does. Metal fins called a "heat sink" are used inside many electronics to cool their insides. However, a metal's ability to conduct heat is even more useful if the metal can be bent or hammered into a useful shape.

👉 **The "sea of electrons" model of metallic bonding helps explain the malleability, ductility, luster, high electrical conductivity, and high thermal conductivity of solid metals.** Each of these properties is related to the behavior of valence electrons in metal atoms.

Malleability and Ductility Most metals are flexible and can be reshaped easily. They can be stretched, pushed, or compressed into different shapes without breaking. Metals act this way because the positive ions are attracted to the loose electrons all around them rather than to other metal ions. These ions can be made to change position, as shown in Figure 24. However, the metallic bonds between the ion and the surrounding electrons keep the metal from breaking.

Because the metal ions move easily, metals are ductile, which means that they can be bent easily and pulled into thin strands or wires. Metals are also malleable—able to be rolled into thin sheets, as in aluminum foil, or beaten into complex shapes.

Go Online
*SCi*LINKS™ NSTA

For: Links on metallic bonding
Visit: www.SciLinks.org
Web Code: scn-1215

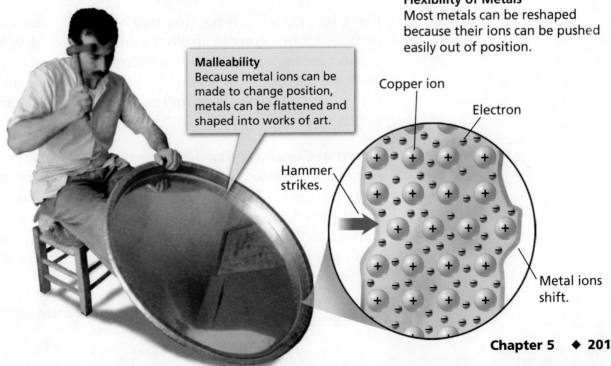

Malleability
Because metal ions can be made to change position, metals can be flattened and shaped into works of art.

Hammer strikes.

Copper ion

Electron

Metal ions shift.

FIGURE 24
Flexibility of Metals
Most metals can be reshaped because their ions can be pushed easily out of position.

FIGURE 25

Luster and Conductivity of Metals

The unique properties of metals result from the ability of their electrons to move about freely.

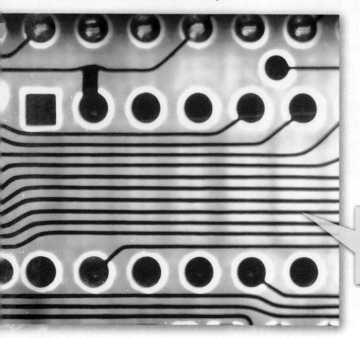

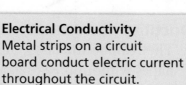

Luster
Gold in an astronaut's face shield reflects sunlight, protecting the wearer's eyes.

Electrical Conductivity
Metal strips on a circuit board conduct electric current throughout the circuit.

Luster Polished metals have a high luster—that is, they are shiny and reflective. A metal's luster is due to its valence electrons. When light strikes these electrons, they absorb the light and then give it off again. This property makes metals useful for making products as varied as mirrors, buildings, jewelry, and astronaut helmets.

Electrical Conductivity You may recall that when charged particles are free to move an electric current is possible. Metals conduct current easily because the electrons in a metal can move freely among the atoms. When connected to a device such as a battery, electric current flows into the metal at one point and out at another point.

Thermal Conductivity Recall that thermal energy flows from warmer matter to cooler matter. When this happens, the greater motion of the particles in the warmer parts of the material is passed along to the particles in the cooler parts. This transfer of thermal energy is known as heat. Metals conduct heat easily because of the valence electrons' freedom of motion within a metal or metal alloy.

 **Reading Checkpoint** Why do metals conduct electric current easily?

Thermal Conductivity
Metal fins cool a motorcycle engine by conducting heat to the outside.

Vocabulary Skill High-Use Academic Words
Use the word *conduct* in a sentence that explains one of the physical properties of metals.

Reviewing Key Concepts

1. a. **Defining** What is an alloy?
   b. **Reviewing** From what pure metals is stainless steel made?
   c. **Comparing and Contrasting** Compare and contrast the general properties of alloys and pure metals.

2. a. **Describing** What is a metallic bond?
   b. **Relating Cause and Effect** Explain how metal atoms form metallic bonds. What role do the valence electrons play?
   c. **Comparing and Contrasting** Review what you learned earlier about ionic bonds. How does a metallic bond differ from an ionic bond?

3. a. **Listing** Name four properties of metals. What accounts for these properties?
   b. **Describing** In a light bulb, a thin tungsten wire filament that is wound in a coil conducts electric current. Describe two properties of the metal tungsten that make it good material for the filament.
   c. **Applying Concepts** Why is it safer to use a nonmetal mixing spoon when cooking something on a stove?

Writing in Science

Product Label Choose a familiar metal object and create a "product label" for it. Your label should describe at least two of the metal's properties and explain why it exhibits those properties. You should include illustrations on your label as well.

Study Guide

The BIG Idea Atoms of different elements combine to form compounds by gaining, losing, or sharing electrons.

① Atoms, Bonding, and the Periodic Table

Key Concepts   S 8.3.f

- The number of valence electrons in an atom of an element determines many properties of that element, including the ways in which the atom can bond with other atoms.

- The periodic table reveals the underlying atomic structure of atoms, including the arrangement of the electrons.

Key Terms

valence electron
electron dot diagram
chemical bond

② Ionic Bonds

Key Concepts   S 8.3.b, 8.3.c

- Ionic bonds form as a result of the attraction between positive and negative ions.

- When ionic compounds form, the charges on the ions balance out.

- For an ionic compound, the name of the positive ion comes first, followed by the name of the negative ion.

- In general, ionic compounds are hard, brittle crystals that have high melting points and conduct electricity when dissolved in water.

Key Terms

ion
polyatomic ion
ionic bond
ionic compound
chemical formula
subscript
crystal

③ Covalent Bonds

Key Concepts   S 8.3.b, 8.7.c

- The force that holds atoms together in a covalent bond is the attraction of each atom's nucleus for the shared pair of electrons.

- Molecular compounds have low melting and boiling points and do not conduct electric current.

- Unequal sharing of electrons causes bonded atoms to have slight electrical charges.

Key Terms

covalent bond   molecular compound
molecule   polar bond
double bond   nonpolar bond
triple bond

④ Bonding in Metals

Key Concepts   S 8.7.c

- Alloys are generally stronger and less reactive than the pure metals from which they are made.

- Metal atoms combine in regular patterns in which the valence electrons are free to move from atom to atom.

- The "sea of electrons" model of metallic bonding helps explain the malleability, ductility, luster, high electrical conductivity, and high thermal conductivity of metals.

Key Terms

alloy
metallic bond

Review and Assessment

Go Online
PHSchool.com

For: Self-Assessment
Visit: PHSchool.com
Web Code: cxa-2050

Target Reading Skill

Compare and Contrast Complete the compare–contrast table on Types of Chemical Bonds.

Type of Chemical Bond	How Bonds Forms	Charge on Bonded Atoms	Example
Ionic bond	a. ___?___	Yes; positive and negative	b. ___?___
Polar bond	Unequal sharing of electrons	c. ___?___	d. ___?___
Nonpolar bond	e. ___?___	f. ___?___	O_2 molecule
Metallic bond	g. ___?___	yes; positive	h. ___?___

Reviewing Key Terms

Choose the letter of the best answer.

1. Valence electrons in an atom are those that are
   a. held most loosely.
   b. of the lowest energy level.
   c. always easily lost.
   d. never easily lost.

2. An electron dot diagram shows an atom's number of
   a. protons.
   b. electrons.
   c. valence electrons.
   d. chemical bonds.

3. When an atom loses or gains electrons, it becomes a(n)
   a. ion.
   b. formula.
   c. crystal.
   d. subscript.

4. A covalent bond in which electrons are shared unequally is a
   a. double bond.
   b. triple bond.
   c. polar bond.
   d. nonpolar bond.

5. The metal atoms in stainless steel are held together by
   a. ionic bonds.
   b. polar bonds.
   c. covalent bonds.
   d. metallic bonds.

Complete the following sentences so that your answers clearly explain the key terms.

6. When atoms react, they form a **chemical bond,** which is _____ .

7. **Polyatomic ions** such as ammonium ions (NH_4^-) and nitrate ions (NO_3^-) are ions that consist of _____ .

8. Magnesium chloride is an example of an **ionic compound,** which means a compound composed of _____ .

9. The formulas N_2, H_2O, and CO_2 all represent **molecules,** which are defined as _____ .

10. Pure metals tend to be weaker and more reactive than an **alloy,** which is a _____ .

Writing in Science

Comparing and Contrasting Go to your local grocery store and observe how the products on the shelves are organized. Write a paragraph comparing how foods are organized in a grocery store and how elements are organized in the periodic table.

Video Assessment

Discovery Channel School
Atoms and Bonding

Review and Assessment

Checking Concepts

11. Which element is less reactive, an element whose atoms have seven valence electrons or an element whose atoms have eight valence electrons? Explain.

12. Why do ionic compounds generally have high melting points?

13. The formula of sulfuric acid is H_2SO_4. How many atoms of hydrogen, sulfur, and oxygen are in one molecule of sulfuric acid?

14. How is the formation of an ionic bond different from the formation of a covalent bond?

15. Why is the covalent bond between two atoms of the same element a nonpolar bond?

16. Explain how metallic bonding causes metals to conduct electric current.

Thinking Critically

17. **Making Generalizations** What information does the organization of the periodic table tell you about how reactive an element may be?

18. **Classifying** Classify each molecule below as either a polar molecule or a nonpolar molecule. Explain your reasoning.

Oxygen

Carbon dioxide

19. **Relating Cause and Effect** Many molecular compounds with small molecules are gases at room temperature. Water, however, is a liquid. Use what you know about polar and nonpolar molecules to explain this difference. (*Hint:* Molecules of a gas are much farther apart than molecules of a liquid.)

20. **Applying Concepts** Why does a metal horseshoe bend but not break when a blacksmith pounds it into shape?

Applying Skills

Use the electron dot diagrams below to answer Questions 21–25.

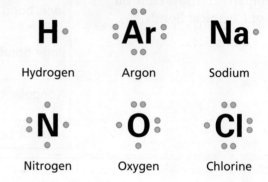

21. **Predicting** When nitrogen and hydrogen combine, what will be the ratio of hydrogen atoms to nitrogen atoms in a molecule of the resulting compound? Explain.

22. **Inferring** Which of these elements can become stable by losing one electron? Explain.

23. **Drawing Conclusions** Which of these elements is least likely to react with other elements? Explain.

24. **Interpreting Diagrams** Which of these elements would react with two atoms of sodium to form an ionic compound? Explain.

25. **Classifying** What type of bond forms when two atoms of nitrogen join to form a nitrogen molecule? When two atoms of oxygen join to form an oxygen molecule?

 ## Standards Investigation

Performance Assessment Present your models to the class, telling what the parts of each model represent. Explain why you chose particular items to model the atoms and chemical bonds. Which kind of bonds were easier to show? Why? What more would you like to know about bonding that could help improve your models?

Choose the letter of the best answer.

1. What is the atomic number of calcium?

A 6   **B** 20

C 40.08   **D** 48   **S 8.3.f**

Use the electron dot diagrams below to answer Questions 2–5.

Electron Dot Diagrams

K•   •**Ö**:   **Mg**•   •**Al**•

---

2. Which element is the most likely to lose two electrons and form an ion with a charge of 2+?

A potassium (K)

B oxygen (O)

C magnesium (Mg)

D aluminum (Al)   **S 8.3.b**

3. Oxygen has 6 valence electrons, as indicated by the 6 dots around the letter symbol "O." Based on this information, how many covalent bonds could an oxygen atom form?

A six   **B** three

C two   **D** none   **S 8.3.b**

4. If a reaction occurs between potassium (K) and oxygen (O), what will be the ratio of potassium ions to oxide ions in the resulting compound, potassium oxide?

A 1 : 1   **B** 1 : 2

C 2 : 1   **D** 2 : 2   **S 8.3.b**

5. The element boron (B) is directly above aluminum (Al) on the periodic table. Which statement about boron is true?

A Boron is in the same period as aluminum and has two valence electrons.

B Boron is in the same group as aluminum and has two valence electrons.

C Boron is in the same period as aluminum and has three valence electrons.

D Boron is in the same group as aluminum and has three valence electrons.   **S 8.3.f**

6. An ice cube (solid H_2O) and a scoop of table salt (NaCl) are left outside on a warm, sunny day. Which best explains why the ice cube melts and the salt does not?

A The attractive forces between molecules of H_2O are much weaker than those between ions in NaCl.

B NaCl can dissolve in H_2O.

C The mass of the H_2O was less than the mass of the NaCl.

D NaCl is white and H_2O is colorless.   **S 8.3.c**

The diagram below shows the crystal structure of sodium chloride. Use the diagram to answer Question 7.

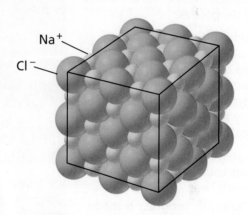

Na^+

Cl^-

7. In a crystal of sodium chloride, each sodium ion is attracted to the

A other sodium ions surrounding it.

B chloride ions surrounding it.

C neutral sodium atoms surrounding it.

D neutral chlorine atoms surrounding it.   **S 8.3.c**

Apply the
BIG Idea

8. Use the periodic table to find the number of valence electrons for potassium (K), calcium (Ca), aluminum (Al), oxygen (O), and iodine (I). Then write the formulas for the following compounds: potassium iodide, calcium oxide, aluminum iodide, and potassium oxide.   **S 8.3.b, 8.3.f**

Sparks fly as sodium metal ▶
reacts with water.

S 8.5 Chemical reactions are processes in which atoms are rearranged into different combinations of molecules. As a basis for understanding this concept:

a. Students know reactant atoms and molecules interact to form products with different chemical properties.

b. Students know the idea of atoms explains the conservation of matter. In chemical reactions the number of atoms stays the same no matter how they are arranged, so their total mass stays the same.

c. Students know chemical reactions usually liberate heat or absorb heat.

S 8.9 Scientific progress is made by asking meaningful questions and conducting careful investigations. As a basis for understanding this concept and addressing the content in the other three strands, students should develop their own questions and perform investigations. Students will:

a. Plan and conduct a scientific investigation to test a hypothesis.

b. Evaluate the accuracy and reproducibility of data.

Focus on the
BIG Idea

S 8.5

What happens during a chemical reaction?

Check What You Know

Suppose you fill a sealable bag with ice cubes, and you allow the ice to melt. How would the mass of the bag and ice before melting compare to the mass of the water and the bag after melting? Explain your answer.

The images shown here represent some of the key terms in this chapter. You can use this vocabulary skill to help you understand the meaning of some key terms in this chapter.

Identify Multiple Meanings

Some familiar words have more than one meaning. Words you use everyday may have different meanings in science.

Word	Everyday Meaning	Scientific Meaning
concentration	*n.* Close attention for a long period of time **Example:** Studying with the TV on affects her <u>concentration</u>.	*n.* The amount of a substance in a given volume **Example:** Most soft drinks contain a high <u>concentration</u> of sugar.
matter	*n.* The subject of discussion, concern, or action **Example:** The subject <u>matter</u> of the movie was space travel.	*n.* Anything that has mass and takes up space **Example:** Solids, liquids, and gases are states of <u>matter</u>.
product	*n.* Anything that is made or created **Example:** Milk and cheeses are dairy <u>products</u>.	*n.* A substance formed as a result of a chemical reaction **Example:** In a chemical reaction, substances can combine to form one or more <u>products</u>.

Apply It!

Complete the sentences below with the correct word from the list above. Then identify the terms that have scientific meanings.

1. The coach told the team to keep its _____ during the game.

2. Seawater has a high _____ of salt.

combustion

precipitate

chemical change

conservation of matter

physical property

Chapter 6
Vocabulary

Section 1 (page 214)
matter
chemistry
physical property
chemical property
physical change
chemical change
reactant
product
precipitate
endothermic reaction
exothermic reaction

Section 2 (page 224)
chemical equation
conservation of matter
open system
closed system
coefficient
synthesis
decomposition
replacement

Section 3 (page 234)
activation energy
concentration
catalyst
enzyme
inhibitor

Section 4 (page 242)
combustion
fuel

Build Science Vocabulary
Online
Visit: PHSchool.com
Web Code: cxj-2060

How to Read Science

Take Notes

Science chapters are packed with information. Each section needs to be read at least twice. After finding the main idea and important details, take notes so you have something to study.

In your notebook, create a two-column note-taking organizer.

- Label the left side "Recall Clues and Questions."
- Label the right side "Notes."
- Under "Notes," write key ideas, using phrases and abbreviations. Include a few important details.
- Use your notes to write a summary statement for each red heading.
- Under "Recall Clues and Questions," write study questions.

As you take notes, think about the key concepts and key terms in the section. Look at the example for Section 1 in this chapter.

Recall Clues & Questions	Notes
What is matter?	Matter: anything that has mass and takes up space
How can matter be described?	Properties of matter • Physical properties—melting point, boiling point, color, hardness • Chemical properties—flammability, ability to rust or tarnish Summary Statement: Matter can be described in terms of physical properties and chemical properties.

Apply It!

What are two important ideas found in the notes above? What questions in the left column help you recall the content?

Take notes as you read each section in this chapter.

Lab zone

Standards Investigation

S 8.5.b

Demonstrate Conservation of Matter

When water evaporates, it is not destroyed or lost. In fact, matter is never created or destroyed in either a physical change or a chemical reaction. In this investigation, you will design and build a closed structure in which a chemical reaction can occur. You will use the chamber to confirm that matter is not created or destroyed in a chemical reaction.

Your Goal

To design and build a closed chamber in which sugar can be broken down

Your structure must

- be made of materials that are approved by your teacher
- be built to specifications agreed upon by the class
- be a closed system so the masses of the reactants and products can be measured
- be built following the safety guidelines in Appendix A

Plan It!

Before you design your reaction chamber, find out how sugar can be broken down. Next, brainstorm with classmates to determine the safety features of your chamber. Then choose materials for your structure and sketch your design. When your teacher has approved your design, build and test your structure.

TRIPLE BEAM BALANCE

Chapter 6 ◆ 213

Observing Chemical Change

CALIFORNIA
Standards Focus

S 8.5.a Students know reactant atoms and molecules interact to form products with different chemical properties.

S 8.5.c Students know chemical reactions usually liberate heat or absorb heat.

- How can changes in matter be described?
- How can you tell when a chemical reaction occurs?

Key Terms

- matter
- chemistry
- physical property
- chemical property
- physical change
- chemical change
- reactant
- product
- precipitate
- endothermic reaction
- exothermic reaction

Lab zone Standards **Warm-Up**

How Does Matter Change?

1. Put on your safety goggles. Place 2 small spoonfuls of baking soda into a clear plastic cup.
2. Holding the cup over a large bowl or sink, add about 125 mL of vinegar. Swirl the cup gently.
3. Look at the material in the cup. What changes do you see? Feel the outside of the cup. What do you notice about the temperature?
4. Carefully fan the air above the liquid toward you. What do you smell?

Think It Over
Observing What changes did you detect using your senses of smell and touch?

Picture yourself toasting marshmallows over a campfire. You see the burning logs change from hard solids to a soft pile of ash. You hear popping and hissing sounds from the fire as the wood burns. You smell smoke. You feel the heat on your skin. Finally, you taste the results. The crisp brown surface of the toasted marshmallow tastes quite different from the soft white surface of a marshmallow just out of its bag. Firewood, skin, and marshmallows are all examples of matter. **Matter** is anything that has mass and takes up space. The study of matter and how matter changes is called **chemistry.**

Chemical change can ▶ lead to a treat.

Matter and Change

Part of chemistry is describing matter. When you describe matter, you explain its characteristics, or properties, and how it changes. Figure 1 lists some of the properties of water. Recall that matter can be described in terms of two kinds of properties—physical properties and chemical properties. 🔑 **Changes in matter can be described in terms of physical changes and chemical changes.**

Properties of Matter A **physical property** is a characteristic of a substance that can be observed without changing the substance into another substance. The temperature at which a solid melts is a physical property. For example, ice melts at a temperature of zero degrees Celsius. Color, hardness, texture, shine, and flexibility are some other physical properties of matter. The ability of a substance to dissolve in water and how well it conducts heat and electricity are examples of still more physical properties of matter.

A **chemical property** is a characteristic of a substance that describes its ability to change into other substances. To observe the chemical properties of a substance, you must change it to another substance. For example, when magnesium burns, it combines with oxygen in the air, forming a new substance called magnesium oxide. The chemical property of being able to burn in oxygen is called flammability. Other chemical properties include a material's ability to rust or tarnish.

FIGURE 1
Properties of Water
This geyser gives off hot water and water vapor, which condenses into a visible cloud in the cold air. The temperatures at which water boils and freezes are physical properties of water.
Predicting *How will the snow change when spring arrives?*

Chemical Properties of Water
- Made of hydrogen atoms and oxygen atoms in a 2 to 1 ratio
- Does not burn
- Reacts with some metals

Physical Properties of Water
- Clear, colorless liquid at room temperature
- Boils at 100°C
- Freezes at 0°C

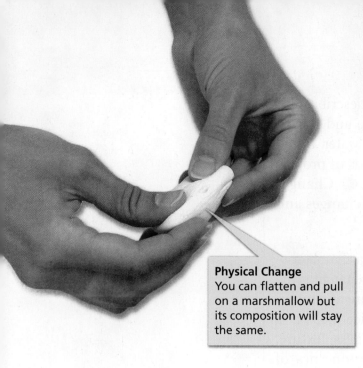

Physical Change
You can flatten and pull on a marshmallow but its composition will stay the same.

FIGURE 2
Changes in Matter
Matter can undergo both physical change and chemical change.

Chemical Change
If you toast a marshmallow, the sugars and other substances will cook or burn, producing a crust made of new substances.

Changes of Matter Like properties of matter, changes in matter can be physical or chemical. A **physical change** is any change that alters the form or appearance of a substance but does not make the substance into another substance. For example, when you squash a marshmallow, you cause a physical change. The shape of the marshmallow changes but not the taste. It's still made of the same compounds that have the same properties. In a physical change, one or more physical properties of the material are altered, but the chemical composition remains the same. Bending, crushing, breaking, and cutting are all examples of physical changes. Changes of state, such as melting, freezing, boiling, and condensing, are also physical changes.

Sometimes when matter changes, its chemical composition is changed. For example, the brown crust on a toasted marshmallow is the result of sugar changing to a mixture of different substances called caramel. A change in matter that produces one or more new substances is a **chemical change,** or chemical reaction. In a chemical change, the atoms are rearranged to form new substances with different chemical and physical properties. The substances that undergo change in a chemical reaction are called **reactants.** The new substances formed by the reaction are called **products.**

Bonding and Chemical Change ⊖ **Chemical changes occur when bonds break and new bonds form.** As a result, new substances are produced. You may recall that atoms form bonds when they share or transfer electrons. The reaction pictured in Figure 3 involves both the breaking of shared bonds and a transfer of electrons.

Oxygen gas (O_2) in the air consists of molecules made of two oxygen atoms that share electrons. These bonds are broken when oxygen reacts with magnesium (Mg). Each magnesium atom transfers two of its electrons to an oxygen atom. The oxygen atom becomes a negative ion, and the magnesium atom becomes a positive ion. Recall that oppositely charged ions attract. An ionic bond forms between the Mg^{2+} ions and the O^{2-} ions. The ionic compound magnesium oxide (MgO) is produced, and energy is released. Magnesium oxide—a white, crumbly powder—has properties that differ from those of either shiny magnesium or oxygen gas. For example, while magnesium melts at about 650°C, it takes temperatures of more than 2,800°C to melt magnesium oxide.

 What are two properties of magnesium oxide?

For: Links on chemical changes
Visit: www.SciLinks.org
Web Code: scn-1221

FIGURE 3
Bonding and Chemical Change
As magnesium burns, bonds between atoms break and new bonds form. The reaction gives off energy. *Interpreting Diagrams Why does the oxygen ion have a 2– charge?*

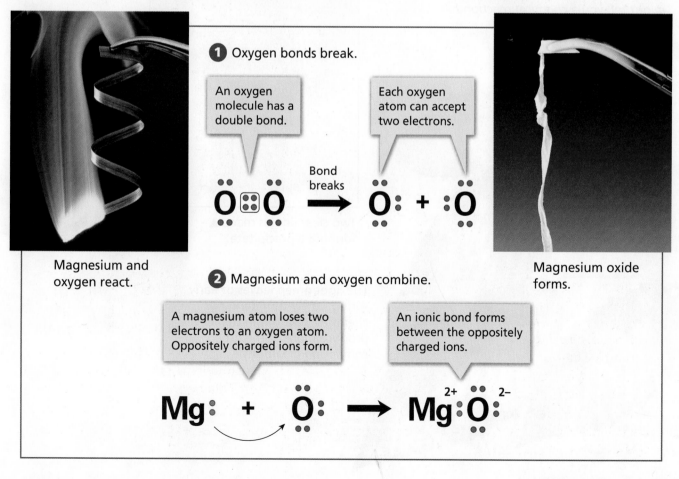

1 Oxygen bonds break.

An oxygen molecule has a double bond.

Each oxygen atom can accept two electrons.

Bond breaks

Magnesium and oxygen react.

Magnesium oxide forms.

2 Magnesium and oxygen combine.

A magnesium atom loses two electrons to an oxygen atom. Oppositely charged ions form.

An ionic bond forms between the oppositely charged ions.

Evidence for Chemical Reactions

How can you tell when a chemical reaction occurs? You need to look for clues. ⚷ **Chemical reactions involve changes in properties and changes in energy that you can observe.**

Changes in Properties One way to detect chemical reactions is to observe changes in the properties of the materials involved. Changes in properties result when new substances form. Figure 4 shows some examples. For instance, a color change may signal that a new substance has formed. Or, the mixing of two solutions may yield a precipitate. A **precipitate** (pree SIP uh tayt) is a solid that forms from solution during a chemical reaction. Another observable change is the formation of a gas from solid or liquid reactants. Physical properties such as texture and hardness may also change. For example, moist bread dough forms a dry, porous solid after baking.

Two clear liquids react, ▲ forming a precipitate.

◀ The light green leaves of early spring slowly turn darker as chemical reactions in the leaves produce more of the green compound chlorophyll.

FIGURE 4
Evidence for Chemical Reactions

Many kinds of change provide evidence that a chemical reaction has occurred.
Applying Concepts *What other evidence might tell you a chemical reaction has occurred?*

Changes in physical properties can be easy to spot as reactants change into products. But what about the chemical properties? Reactant atoms and molecules interact to form products with different chemical properties. For example, sodium (Na) and chlorine (Cl) react to form an ionic compound, sodium chloride (NaCl). Both reactants are very reactive elements. However, the product, sodium chloride, is a very stable compound.

Although you may observe a property change in matter, the change does not always indicate that a chemical reaction has taken place. Sometimes physical changes give similar results. For example, when water boils, the gas bubbles you see are made of molecules of water, just as the original liquid was. The sign of a chemical reaction is that one or more new substances are produced. For example, when an electric current is passed through water during electrolysis, two new substances are produced, hydrogen gas (H_2) and oxygen gas (O_2).

 **Reading Checkpoint** How is a precipitate evidence for a chemical reaction?

Lab zone Try This Activity

Mostly Cloudy

1. Put on your safety goggles and apron.
2. Pour about 5 mL of limewater into a plastic cup.
3. Pour an equal amount of plain water into another plastic cup.
4. Add about 5 mL of carbonated water to each of the cups.

Drawing Conclusions In which cup do you think a chemical reaction occurred? What evidence supports your conclusion?

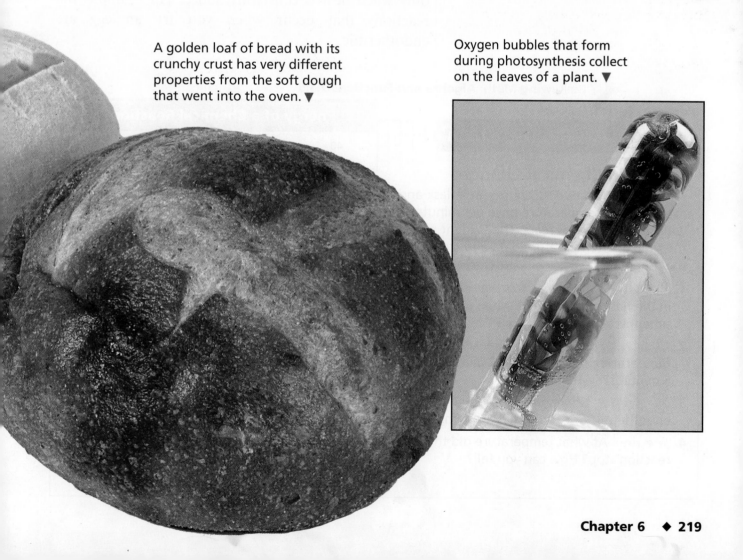

A golden loaf of bread with its crunchy crust has very different properties from the soft dough that went into the oven. ▼

Oxygen bubbles that form during photosynthesis collect on the leaves of a plant. ▼

FIGURE 5
Endothermic Reactions
When you fry an egg, it absorbs energy. The reactions that occur are endothermic. **Interpreting Photos** *What properties of the egg change as it cooks?*

Energy can change egg whites from a clear liquid into a white solid.

Changes in Energy As matter changes, it can either absorb or release energy. Chemical reactions usually absorb heat or liberate heat. One common indication of a change in energy is a change in temperature. If you did the Standards Warm-Up activity, you observed that the mixture became colder. When baking soda (sodium bicarbonate) reacts with vinegar, the reaction absorbs heat from the solution, making it feel colder.

Recall that a chemical reaction occurs when bonds break and new bonds form. Breaking bonds between atoms requires energy. Making a bond releases energy. In an **endothermic reaction** (en doh THUR mik), the total making and breaking of bonds results in a net absorption of energy. The energy is absorbed as heat from nearby matter, which cools.

The reaction of baking soda and vinegar is endothermic. During the reaction, energy is absorbed, causing the surroundings to become cooler. However, endothermic reactions do not always result in a decrease in temperature. Many endothermic reactions occur only when heat is constantly added. For example, the reactions that occur when you fry an egg are endothermic.

Reviewing Math: Algebra and Functions 7.1.5

Math Analyzing Data

Energy in Chemical Changes

A student places two substances in a flask and measures the temperature once per minute while the substances react. The student plots the time and temperature data and creates the graph at right.

1. **Reading Graphs** What was the temperature in the flask at 3 minutes? When was the first time the temperature was 6°C?

2. **Calculating** How many degrees did the temperature drop between 2 minutes and 5 minutes?

3. **Interpreting Data** Is the reaction endothermic or exothermic? Explain.

4. **Inferring** At what temperature did the reaction stop? How can you tell?

Energy of a Chemical Reaction

(Graph: Temperature (°C) vs. Time (minutes). Temperature starts near 38°C at 0 minutes, decreases to about 2°C at 9 minutes, then rises to about 14°C at 15 minutes.)

5. **Drawing Conclusions** Suppose the temperature in the flask increased instead of decreased as the reaction occurred. In terms of energy, what kind of reaction would it be? Explain.

FIGURE 6
An Exothermic Reaction
Enough energy is released by the burning of airplane fuel to keep a plane moving fast enough to fly.

In an **exothermic reaction** (ek soh THUR mik), the total making and breaking of bonds results in a net release of energy. The energy is typically released as heat into nearby matter. For example, the reaction between fuel and oxygen in an airplane engine releases energy, mostly in the form of heat. The heat causes gases in the engine to expand. The expansion and movement of the gases out of the plane exert a force that moves the plane forward.

 **Reading Checkpoint**   **What is an endothermic reaction?**

Section 1 Assessment

S 8.5.a, 8.5.c, E-LA: Reading 8.1.0, Writing 8.2.4

Vocabulary Skill **Identify Multiple Meanings**
Review the two meanings of the word *matter*. Then use the scientific meaning in a sentence.

Reviewing Key Concepts

1. **a. Explaining** What is the difference between the physical properties and the chemical properties of a substance?
   b. Posing Questions When silver coins are found in ancient shipwrecks, they are coated with a black crust. What question could you ask to help you decide whether the silver underwent a chemical change or a physical change? Explain.
   c. Making Generalizations In terms of chemical bonds and electrons, what kinds of changes occur between atoms when substances undergo chemical reactions?

2. **a. Listing** What kinds of evidence can you use to determine if a chemical reaction has occurred?
   b. Interpreting Photographs How do the properties of the cooked egg shown in Figure 5 differ from the properties of a raw egg?
   c. Comparing and Contrasting How are endothermic and exothermic reactions the same? How are they different?

Writing in Science

Persuasive Letter Imagine you have a pen pal who is studying chemistry just like you are. Your pen pal claims the change from liquid water to water vapor is a chemical change. Write a brief letter that might convince your pen pal otherwise.

Where's the Evidence?

S 8.5.a, 8.9.b

Problem

What are some signs that a chemical reaction has taken place?

Skills Focus

observing, predicting, drawing conclusions

Materials

- 4 small plastic cups
- birthday candles
- 2 plastic spoons
- sugar
- tongs
- clay
- matches
- sodium carbonate (powdered solid)
- graduated cylinder, 10 mL
- aluminum foil, about 10-cm square
- dilute hydrochloric acid in a dropper bottle
- copper sulfate solution
- sodium carbonate solution

Procedure

Preview the steps for each reaction and copy the data table into your notebook.

PART 1

1. Put a pea-sized pile of sodium carbonate into a clean plastic cup. Record in the data table the appearance of the sodium carbonate.

2. Observe a dropper containing hydrochloric acid. Record the appearance of the acid. **CAUTION:** *Hydrochloric acid can burn you or anything else it touches. Wash spills immediately with water.*

3. Make a prediction about how you think the acid and the sodium carbonate will react when mixed. Record your prediction.

4. Add about 10 drops of hydrochloric acid to the sodium carbonate. Swirl to mix the contents of the cup. Record your observations.

PART 2

5. Fold up the sides of the aluminum foil square to make a small tray.

6. Use a plastic spoon to place a pea-sized pile of sugar into the tray.

7. Carefully describe the appearance of the sugar in your data table.

Data Table

Reaction	Observations Before Reaction	Predictions	Observations During Reaction	Observations After Reaction
1. Sodium carbonate (powder) + hydrochloric acid				
2. Sugar + heat				
3. Copper sulfate + sodium carbonate solutions				

8. Secure a small candle on your desktop in a lump of clay. Carefully light the candle with a match only after being instructed to do so by your teacher. **CAUTION:** *Tie back long hair and loose clothing.*

9. Predict what you think will happen if you heat the sugar. Record your prediction.

10. Use tongs to hold the aluminum tray. Heat the sugar slowly by moving the tray gently back and forth over the flame. Make observations while the sugar is heating.

11. When you think there is no longer a chemical reaction occurring, blow out the candle.

12. Allow the tray to cool for a few seconds and set it down on your desk. Record your observations of the material left in the tray.

PART 3

13. Put about 2 mL of copper sulfate solution in one cup. **CAUTION:** *Copper sulfate is poisonous and can stain your skin and clothes. Do not touch it or get it in your mouth.* Put an equal amount of sodium carbonate solution in another cup. Record the appearance of both liquids.

14. Write a prediction of what you think will happen when the two solutions are mixed.

15. Combine the two solutions and record your observations. **CAUTION:** *Dispose of the solutions as directed by your teacher.*

16. Wash your hands when you have finished working.

Analyze and Conclude

1. **Predicting** How do the results of each reaction compare with your predictions?

2. **Observing** How did you know when the reaction in Part 1 was over?

3. **Interpreting Data** What was the evidence of a chemical reaction in Part 1? In Part 2?

4. **Observing** Was the product of the reaction in Part 3 a solid, a liquid, or a gas? How do you know?

5. **Drawing Conclusions** How do you know if new substances were formed in each reaction?

6. **Communicating** Make a table or chart briefly describing each chemical change in this lab, followed by the evidence for the chemical change.

More to Explore

Keep your data table handy as you read the rest of this chapter. As you learn more about chemical reactions, try to identify the products that formed in Parts 1, 2, and 3 of the Skills Lab. Research the physical properties of each product by using your library or the Internet. Evaluate the accuracy of your data by comparing the properties of the substances produced in the lab to the properties that you found in your research.

Describing Chemical Reactions

CALIFORNIA
Standards Focus

S 8.5.b Students know the idea of atoms explains the conservation of matter. In chemical reactions the number of atoms stays the same no matter how they are arranged, so their total mass stays the same.

- What information does a chemical equation contain?
- How is matter conserved during a chemical reaction?
- What must a balanced chemical equation show?
- What are three types of chemical reactions?

Key Terms

- chemical equation
- conservation of matter
- open system
- closed system
- coefficient
- synthesis
- decomposition
- replacement

Lab zone Standards Warm-Up

Do You Lose Anything?

1. Place about two dozen coins on a table. Sort them into stacks of pennies, nickels, dimes, and quarters.
2. Count and record the number of coins in each stack. Calculate and record the value of each stack and the total of all stacks combined.
3. Mix all the coins together and then divide them randomly into four unsorted stacks.
4. Again calculate the value of each stack and the total amount of money. Count the total number of each type of coin.
5. Repeat Steps 3 and 4.

Think It Over

Making Models What happened to the total value and types of coins when you rearranged them? Did rearranging the coins change the properties of any coin? If you think of the coins as each representing a different type of atom, what does this model tell you about chemical reactions?

You look at your cellular phone display and read the message "U wan2 gt pza 2nite?" You reply "No. MaB TPM. CUL8R." These messages are short for saying "Do you want to get some pizza tonight?" and "No. Maybe tomorrow afternoon (P.M.). See you later."

Cellular phone messages use symbols and abbreviations to express ideas in shorter form. A type of shorthand is used in chemistry too. "Hydrogen molecules react with oxygen molecules to form water molecules" is a lengthy way to describe the reaction between hydrogen and oxygen. And writing it is slow. Instead, chemists often use chemical equations in place of words.

◀ **A message on a cellular display**

What Are Chemical Equations?

A **chemical equation** is a short, easy way to show a chemical reaction, using symbols instead of words. Although chemical equations are shorter than sentences, they contain more information. 👄 **Chemical equations use chemical formulas and other symbols instead of words to summarize a reaction.**

Using Formulas All chemical equations use formulas to represent the substances involved in a reaction. You may recall that a chemical formula is a combination of symbols that represent the elements in a compound. For example, CO_2 is the formula for carbon dioxide. The formula tells you that the ratio of carbon to oxygen is 1 to 2. Carbon dioxide is a molecular compound, so it is made up of molecules. Each carbon dioxide molecule has 1 carbon atom and 2 oxygen atoms. Figure 7 lists formulas of other compounds that may be familiar to you.

Structure of an Equation All chemical equations have a common structure. A chemical equation tells you the substances you start with in a reaction and the substances you get at the end. The substances you have at the beginning are the reactants. When the reaction is complete, you have new substances called products.

The formulas for the reactants are written on the left, followed by an arrow. You read the arrow as "yields." The formulas for the products are written on the right. When there are two or more reactants, they are separated by plus signs. In a similar way, plus signs are used to separate two or more products. Below is the general plan for a chemical equation.

Reactant + Reactant $\longrightarrow$ Product + Product

The number of reactants and products can vary. Some reactions have only one reactant or product. Other reactions have two, three, or more reactants or products. In Figure 8, you can see the equation for a reaction that occurs when limestone ($CaCO_3$) is heated. Count the number of reactants and products, and familiarize yourself with the parts of the equation.

FIGURE 7
The formula of a compound identifies the elements in the compound and the ratios in which their atoms are present.

Formulas of Familiar Compounds

Compound	Formula
Water	H_2O
Carbon dioxide	CO_2
Methane	CH_4
Propane	C_3H_8
Sugar (sucrose)	$C_{12}H_{22}O_{11}$
Rubbing alcohol	C_3H_8O
Ammonia	NH_3
Sodium chloride	$NaCl$
Baking soda	$NaHCO_3$

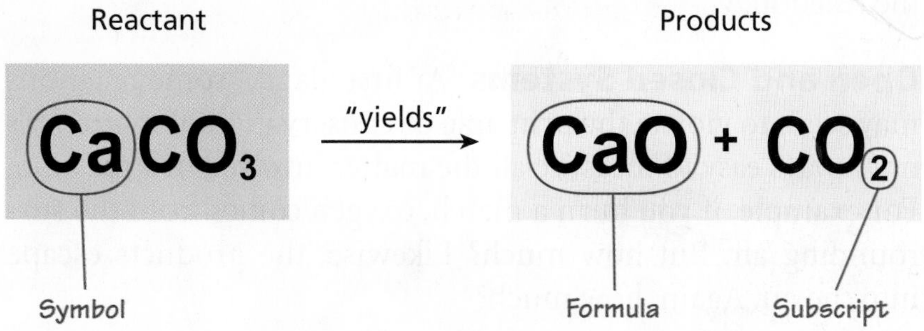

Reactant

Products

$\text{(Ca)CO}_3 \xrightarrow{\text{"yields"}} \text{(CaO)} + \text{CO}_2$

Symbol

Formula   Subscript

FIGURE 8
A Chemical Equation
Like a building, a chemical equation has a basic structure.
Interpreting Diagrams *What does the subscript 3 in the formula for calcium carbonate tell you?*

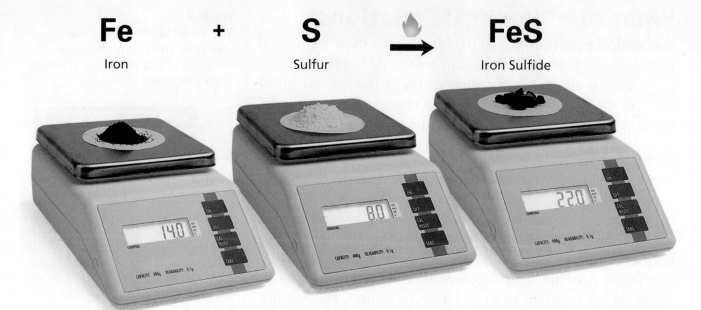

Fe + **S** → **FeS**
Iron   Sulfur   Iron Sulfide

FIGURE 9
Conservation of Matter
Matter is conserved in chemical reactions.

Lab zone Try This **Activity**

Is Matter Conserved?

1. 🫙🧍 Add water to a small, plastic sealable container until it is one-third full.

2. Measure the combined mass of the partially filled container, its screw-on cap, and one quarter of an effervescent tablet.

3. Drop the tablet into the water, and immediately screw on the cap.

4. After the fizzing stops, measure the mass of the sealed container.

5. Slowly remove the cap to release built-up pressure. Measure the combined mass of the unsealed container, its contents, and the cap.

Interpreting Data How did the mass measured in Step 2 compare to the masses measured in Steps 4 and 5? Was matter conserved?

Conservation of Matter

Look closely at the values for mass in Figure 9. Iron and sulfur can react to form iron sulfide. The photograph represents a principle first demonstrated by the French chemist Antoine Lavoisier in 1774. This principle is called **conservation of matter.** It states that, during a chemical reaction, matter is neither created nor destroyed. The total mass of the reactants must equal the total mass of the products.

Conservation of Atoms The idea of atoms explains the conservation of matter. 🗝 **In chemical reactions, the number of atoms stays the same no matter how they are arranged. So, their total mass stays the same.** Look again at Figure 9. Suppose one atom of iron reacts with one atom of sulfur. At the end of the reaction, you have one iron atom bonded to one sulfur atom in the compound FeS. All the atoms present at the start of the reaction are present at the end of the reaction. The amount of matter does not change. The total mass stays the same before and after the reaction.

Open and Closed Systems At first glance, some reactions may seem to violate the principle of conservation of matter. It's not always easy to measure all the matter involved in a reaction. For example, if you burn a match, oxygen comes from the surrounding air. But how much? Likewise, the products escape into the air. Again, how much?

A burning match is an example of an open system. In an **open system,** matter can enter from or escape to the surroundings. The burned out fire in Figure 10 is another example of an open system. If you want to measure all the matter before and after a reaction, you have to be able to contain it. In a **closed system,** matter is not allowed to enter or leave. The pear decaying under glass in Figure 10 is a closed system. So is a chemical reaction inside a sealed plastic bag.

 **Reading Checkpoint** **What is a closed system?**

FIGURE 10

Open and Closed Systems

A wood fire is an open system because gases escape into the air. A pear in a glass dome is a closed system because the reactants and products are contained inside the dome.
Problem Solving *What masses would you need to measure before and after a wood fire to show conservation of mass?*

Open System
Except for the ash, products of the wood fire have escaped up the chimney or into the room.

Closed System
The total mass of the pear and the substances produced during its decay are contained by the glass dome.

Fresh pear

Decayed pear

Go Online
active art

For: Balancing Equations activity
Visit: PHSchool.com
Web Code: cgp-2022

Balancing Chemical Equations

The principle of conservation of matter means that the total number of atoms of each element in the reactants must equal the total number of atoms of each element in the products. ⊸ **To describe a reaction accurately, a chemical equation must show the same number of each type of atom on both sides of the equation.** Chemists say an equation is balanced when it accurately represents conservation of matter. How can you write a balanced chemical equation?

❶ **Write the Equation** Suppose you want to write a balanced chemical equation for the reaction between hydrogen and oxygen that forms water. To begin, write the correct formulas for both reactants and product. Place the reactants, H_2 and O_2, on the left side of the arrow, separated by a plus sign. Then write the product, H_2O, on the right side of the arrow.

$$H_2 \quad + \quad O_2 \quad \longrightarrow \quad H_2O$$

Reactants   Products

❷ **Count the Atoms** Count the number of atoms of each element on each side of the equation. You find two atoms of oxygen in the reactants but only one atom of oxygen in the product.

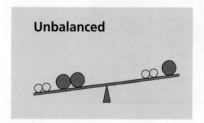

Unbalanced

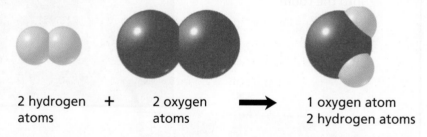

2 hydrogen atoms + 2 oxygen atoms ⟶ 1 oxygen atom 2 hydrogen atoms

How can you get the number of oxygen atoms on both sides to be the same? You cannot change the formula for water to H_2O_2 because H_2O_2 is the formula for hydrogen peroxide, a different compound. So, how can you show that mass is conserved?

❸ **Use Coefficients to Balance Atoms** To balance the equation, you can change the coefficients. A **coefficient** (koh uh FISH unt) is a number placed in front of a chemical formula in an equation. It tells you the relative amount of a reactant or a product that takes part in the reaction. In the unbalanced equation written in Step 1, the coefficients are understood to be 1.

You can balance the number of oxygen atoms by changing the coefficient of H_2O to 2. Now the right side of the equation has two water molecules, each containing an oxygen atom.

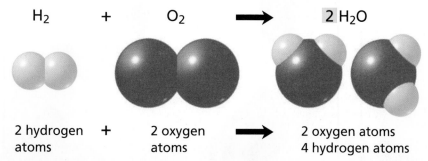

H_2 + O_2 ➡ **2** H_2O

| 2 hydrogen atoms | + | 2 oxygen atoms | ➡ | 2 oxygen atoms 4 hydrogen atoms |

By balancing the oxygen, you "unbalanced" the number of hydrogen atoms. There are now two hydrogen atoms in the reactants and four in the product. To balance the hydrogen, change the coefficient of H_2 to 2. All the atoms in the reactants are now accounted for in the products.

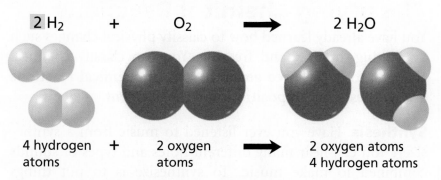

2 H_2 + O_2 ➡ 2 H_2O

| 4 hydrogen atoms | + | 2 oxygen atoms | ➡ | 2 oxygen atoms 4 hydrogen atoms |

❹ Look Back and Check The equation tells you that two hydrogen molecules react with one oxygen molecule to yield two water molecules. The total number of atoms stays the same before and after the reaction. The equation is balanced.

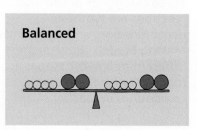

Unbalanced

Balanced

Reviewing Math: Mathematical Reasoning 7.2.6

Math ➤ Analyzing Data

Balancing Chemical Equations

Magnesium (Mg) reacts with oxygen gas (O_2), forming magnesium oxide (MgO). Write a balanced equation for this reaction by following Steps 1 through 4 described above.

1. **Balancing Chemical Equations** Balance the equation for the reaction of sodium metal (Na) with oxygen gas (O_2), forming sodium oxide (Na_2O).

2. **Balancing Chemical Equations** Balance the equation for the reaction of tin (Sn) with chlorine gas (Cl_2), forming tin chloride ($SnCl_2$).

Balancing Equations

❶ Write the Equation
$Mg + O_2 \longrightarrow MgO$

❷ Count the Atoms
$Mg + O_2 \longrightarrow MgO$
1   2   1 1

❸ Use Coefficients to Balance the Atoms
$Mg + O_2 \longrightarrow$ **2** MgO
     2   2

2 $Mg + O_2 \longrightarrow$ **2** MgO
2   2   2 2

❹ Look Back and Check

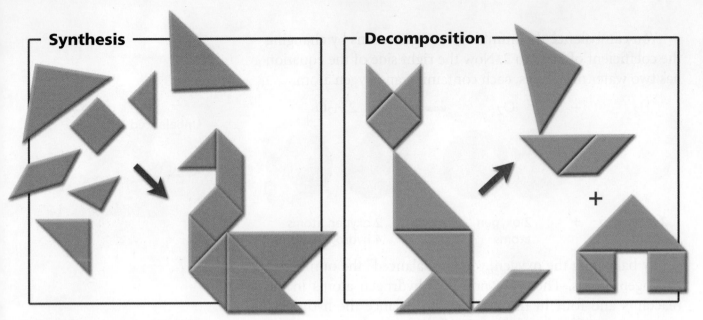

FIGURE 11

Types of Reactions

Three categories of chemical reactions are synthesis, decomposition, and replacement. **Making Models** *How do these different geometric shapes act as models for elements and compounds in reactions?*

Classifying Chemical Reactions

You have already learned how to classify physical changes such as melting, boiling, and freezing. You can classify chemical changes, too. 🔑 **Three general types of chemical reactions are synthesis, decomposition, and replacement.**

Synthesis Have you ever listened to music from a synthesizer? You can hear many different notes and types of sounds combined to make music. To synthesize is to put things together. In chemistry, when two or more elements or compounds combine to make a more complex substance, the reaction is classified as a **synthesis** (SIN thuh sis). The reaction of hydrogen and oxygen to make water is a synthesis reaction.

Decomposition In contrast to synthesis, **decomposition** occurs when compounds break down into simpler products. You may have a bottle of hydrogen peroxide (H_2O_2) in your house to clean cuts. If you keep such a bottle for a very long time, the hydrogen peroxide decomposes into water and oxygen gas.

$$2\,H_2O_2 \longrightarrow 2\,H_2O + O_2$$

Replacement When one element replaces another in a compound, or when two elements in different compounds trade places, the reaction is classified as a **replacement**. Look at this example:

$$2\,Cu_2O + C \longrightarrow 4\,Cu + CO_2$$

Copper metal can be obtained by heating copper oxide with carbon. The carbon takes the place of copper.

Replacement

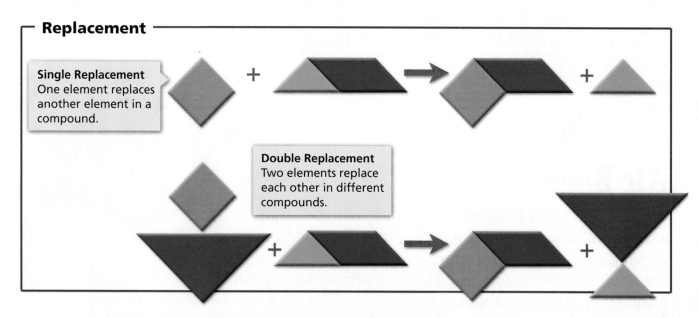

Single Replacement One element replaces another element in a compound.

Double Replacement Two elements replace each other in different compounds.

The reaction between copper oxide and carbon is called a *single* replacement reaction because one element, carbon, replaces another element, copper, in the compound. In a *double* replacement reaction, elements in one compound appear to "trade places" with elements in another compound. The following reaction is an example of a double replacement:

$$FeS + 2\ HCl \longrightarrow FeCl_2 + H_2S$$

Use Figure 11 to help you track what happens to elements in different types of chemical reactions.

Section 2 Assessment

S 8.5.b, E-LA: Reading 8.1.0, Math: 7MR2.6

Vocabulary Skill Identify Multiple Meanings Review the multiple meaning words. The substance produced in a chemical reaction is called a _____.

Reviewing Key Concepts

1. a. Identifying What do the formulas, arrow, and plus signs in a chemical equation tell you?

 b. Comparing and Contrasting How are reactants and products treated the same in a chemical reaction? How are they treated differently?

2. a. Explaining How does the idea of atoms explain the principle of conservation of matter?

 b. Applying Concepts If the total mass of the products of a reaction is 250 g, what was the total mass of the reactants?

3. a. Reviewing What are three types of chemical reactions?

 b. Inferring What is the smallest possible number of products in a decomposition reaction?

 c. Classifying Classify the following reaction:
$$P_4O_{10} + 6\ H_2O \longrightarrow 4\ H_3PO_4$$

Math Practice

Balance the following equations:

4. $Fe_2O_3 + C \longrightarrow Fe + CO_2$

5. $SO_2 + O_2 \longrightarrow SO_3$

Technology and Society

• Tech & Design •

S 8.5.a

Air Bags

What moves faster than 300 km/h, inflates in less than a second, and saves lives? An air bag, of course! When a moving car is suddenly stopped in a crash, objects inside the car keep moving forward. Death or serious injury can result when passengers hit the hard parts of the car's interior. Air bags, working with seat belts, can slow or stop a person's forward motion in a crash.

How Do Air Bags Increase Safety?

Before front air bags became a requirement in the 1990s, seat belts were the only restraints for passengers in cars. Seat belts do a great job of keeping people from flying forward in a crash, but even with seat belts, some movement takes place. Air bags were designed as a second form of protection. They provide a buffer zone between a person and the steering wheel, dashboard, or windshield.

$$2\ NaN_3 \longrightarrow 2\ Na + 3\ N_2$$

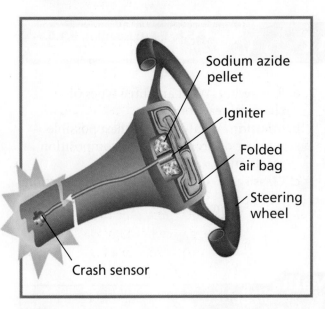

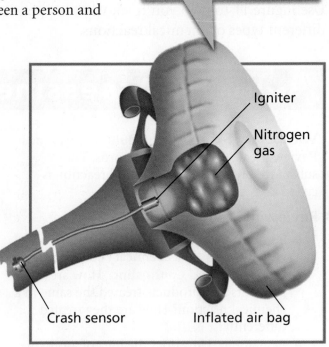

Collision Detected
The crash sensor is located toward the front of the car. The sensor detects an impact and sends a signal to the air bag igniter to start the chemical reaction.

Air Bag Inflates
Pellets of a compound called sodium azide (NaN_3) are heated, causing a rapid decomposition reaction. This reaction releases sodium metal (Na) and nitrogen gas (N_2). The nitrogen inflates the air bag in about 30 milliseconds.

During a crash test, the air bag should inflate upon impact.

Cushion or Curse?

Air bags save hundreds of lives each year. However, if your body is too close to the air bag when it inflates, the impact of the expanding bag may do more harm than good. Since 1990, more than 200 people, including 140 children, have been killed by air bags inflating close to them. Air bags are designed for adults but pose a risk to smaller, lightweight adults and children. That is why children should never ride in a front seat. They are safer in the back seat without air bags than in the front seat with air bags.

▲ Car manufacturers must test their vehicles to verify that they meet minimum government safety standards. New cars are required to have air bags on both the driver and passenger sides.

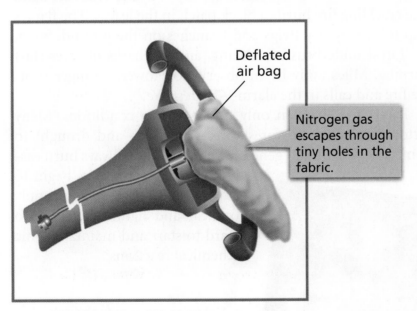

Deflated air bag

Nitrogen gas escapes through tiny holes in the fabric.

Air Bag Deflates
Tiny holes in the fabric of the air bag allow some of the nitrogen gas to escape, so the bag starts to deflate by the time a person makes contact with it. In this way, the air bag provides a deflating cushion that slows forward movement.

Weigh the Impact

1. Identify the Need
Air bags are called supplemental restraint systems. Why is it so important to restrain people in a collision?

2. Research
Use the Internet to learn how air bags are being changed, added, and redesigned to improve their safety and effectiveness.

3. Write
Choose one type of new air bag technology and summarize it in a few short paragraphs.

For: More on air bags
Visit: PHSchool.com
Web Code: cgh-2020

Controlling Chemical Reactions

CALIFORNIA
Standards Focus

S 8.5.a Students know reactant atoms and molecules interact to form products with different chemical properties.

S 8.5.c Students know chemical reactions usually liberate heat or absorb heat.

How is activation energy related to chemical reactions?

What factors affect the rate of a chemical reaction?

Key Terms
• activation energy
• concentration
• catalyst
• enzyme
• inhibitor

With a splintering crash, a bolt of lightning strikes a tree in the forest. The lightning splits the tree and sets fire to the leaves on the ground below it. The leaves are dry and crisp from drought. The crackling fire burns a black patch in the leaves. The flames leap to nearby dry twigs and branches on the ground. Soon, the forest underbrush is blazing, and the barks of trees start burning. Miles away in an observation tower, a ranger spots the fire and calls in the alarm—"Forest fire!"

Forest fires happen only under certain conditions. Many factors contribute to forest fires—lightning and drought to name just two. But, in general, wood does not always burn easily. Yet, once wood does begin to burn, it gives off a steady supply of heat and light. Why is it so hard to start and maintain some chemical reactions?

◀ **Lightning can supply enough energy to ignite a forest fire.**

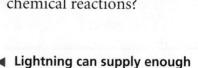

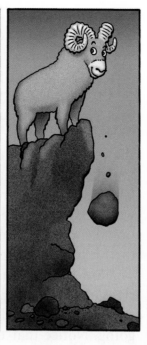

FIGURE 12
Modeling Activation Energy
The rock at the top of this hill cannot roll down the hill until a small push gets it going.
Making Models *How is this cartoon a kind of model for the role of activation energy in a chemical reaction?*

Energy and Reactions

To understand why it can be hard to start some chemical reactions, look at Figure 12. The rock at the top of the hill can fall over the cliff, releasing energy when it crashes into the rocks at the bottom. Yet it remains motionless until it's pushed over the small hump.

Activation Energy Every chemical reaction is like that rock. A reaction won't begin until the reactants have enough energy to push them "over the hump." The energy is used to break the chemical bonds of the reactants. Then, the atoms begin to form the new chemical bonds of the products. **Activation energy** is the minimum amount of energy needed to start a chemical reaction. ◯ **All chemical reactions require a certain amount of activation energy to get started.**

Consider the reaction in which hydrogen and oxygen form water. This reaction gives off a large amount of energy. But if you just mix the two gases together, they can remain unchanged for years. For the reaction to start, a tiny amount of activation energy is needed—even just an electric spark. Once a few molecules of hydrogen and oxygen react, the rest will quickly follow because the first few reactions provide activation energy for more molecules to react. Overall, the reaction releases more energy than it uses. Recall from Section 1 that this type of reaction is described as exothermic.

 **Reading Checkpoint** What is the function of a spark in a reaction between hydrogen gas and oxygen gas?

Video Field Trip
Discovery Channel School
Chemical Reactions

Exothermic and Endothermic Reactions Every chemical reaction needs activation energy to get started. Whether or not a reaction needs still more energy from the environment to keep going depends on if it is exothermic or endothermic.

Exothermic reactions follow the pattern you can see in the first diagram in Figure 13. The dotted line marks the energy of the reactants before the reaction begins. The peak in the graph shows the activation energy. Notice that at the end of the reaction, the products have less energy than the reactants. This difference results in a release of heat. The burning of fuel, such as wood, natural gas, or oil, is an example of an exothermic reaction. People can make use of the heat that is released to warm their homes and cook food.

Now look at the graph of an endothermic reaction on the right of Figure 13. Endothermic reactions also need activation energy to get started. But, in addition, they need energy to keep going. Notice that the energy of the products is higher than that of the reactants. This difference tells you that the reaction must absorb energy to continue.

When you placed baking soda in vinegar in the Standards Warm-Up in Section 1, the thermal energy already present in the solution was enough to start the reaction. The reaction continued by drawing energy from the solution, making the solution feel colder.

Reading Checkpoint In what type of reaction do the reactants have less energy than the products?

FIGURE 13
Energy Changes in Chemical Reactions
Both exothermic and endothermic reactions need energy to get started. **Reading Graphs** *What does the peak in the curve in each graph represent?*

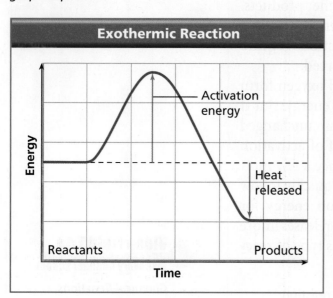

Exothermic Reaction

Energy

Activation energy

Heat released

Reactants

Products

Time

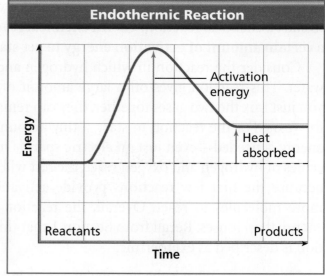

Endothermic Reaction

Energy

Activation energy

Heat absorbed

Reactants

Products

Time

Rates of Chemical Reactions

Chemical reactions don't all occur at the same rate. Some, like explosions, are very fast. Others, like the rusting of iron, are much slower. Also, a particular reaction can occur at different rates depending on the conditions.

If you want to make a chemical reaction happen faster, you need to get more reactant particles together more often and with more energy. To slow down a reaction, you need to do the opposite. ◯ **Factors that affect rates of reaction include surface area, temperature, concentration, and the presence of catalysts or inhibitors.**

Surface Area Look at Figure 14. The wreckage used to be a grain elevator. It exploded when grain dust ignited in the air above the stored grain. Although the grain itself doesn't react violently in air, the grain dust can. This difference is related to surface area. When a chunk of solid substance reacts with a liquid or gas, only the particles on the surface of the solid come into contact with the other reactant. But if you break the solid into smaller pieces, more particles are exposed and the reaction happens faster. Sometimes, speeding up a reaction this way is dangerous. Other times, increasing surface area can be useful. For example, chewing your food breaks it into smaller pieces that your body can digest more easily and quickly.

| Lab zone | Skills **Activity** |

Interpreting Data

1. Measure the length and width of a face of a gelatin cube.
2. Calculate the area of that face of the cube.
   Area = length × width
3. Repeat for each of the other five faces. Then add the six values to get the total surface area.
4. Using a plastic knife, cut the cube in half. Add the surface areas of the two pieces to get a new total.

5. How did the original total surface area compare with the total area after the cube was cut?
6. Predict the total surface area if you cut each cube in two again. If you have time, test your prediction.

FIGURE 14
Surface Area and Reaction Rate
Grain dust reacts explosively with oxygen. Minimizing grain dust in a grain elevator can help prevent an accident like the one shown here.

Temperature Another way to increase the rate of a reaction is to increase its temperature. When you heat a substance, its particles move faster. Faster-moving particles increase the reaction rate in two ways. First, the particles come in contact more often, which means there are more chances for a reaction to happen. Second, faster-moving particles have more energy. This increased energy causes more particles of the reactants to get over the activation energy "hump."

In contrast, reducing temperature slows down reaction rates. For example, milk contains bacteria, which carry out thousands of chemical reactions as they live and reproduce. At room temperature, those reactions happen faster and milk spoils more quickly. You store milk and other foods in the refrigerator because keeping foods cold slows down those reactions, so your foods stay fresh longer.

Concentration A third way to increase the rate of a chemical reaction is to increase the concentration of the reactants. **Concentration** is the amount of a substance in a given volume. For example, adding a small spoonful of sugar to a glass of lemonade will make it sweet. But adding a large spoonful of sugar makes the lemonade sweeter. The glass with more sugar has a greater concentration of sugar molecules.

Increasing the concentration of reactants supplies more particles to react. Compare the two reactions of acid and magnesium metal in Figure 15. The test tube on the left has a lower concentration of acid. This reaction is slower than the one on the right, where the acid concentration is higher. You see evidence for the increased rate of reaction in the greater amount of gas bubbles produced.

 **Reading Checkpoint** Why may an increase in temperature affect the rate of a chemical reaction?

FIGURE 15
Concentration and Reaction Rate
Bubbles of hydrogen gas form when magnesium reacts with acid. The solution heats up quickly, indicating that the reaction is exothermic.
Relating Cause and Effect *What makes the reaction faster in the test tube on the right?*

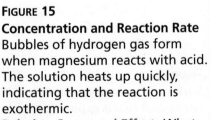

Catalysts Another way to control the rate of a reaction is to change the activation energy needed. A **catalyst** (KAT uh list) is a material that increases the rate of a reaction by lowering the activation energy. Although catalysts affect a reaction's rate, they are not permanently changed by a reaction. For this reason catalysts are not considered reactants.

Many chemical reactions happen at temperatures that would kill living things. Yet, some of these reactions are necessary for life. The cells in your body (as in all living things) contain biological catalysts called **enzymes** (EN zymz). Your body has thousands of different enzymes. Each one is specific—it affects only one chemical reaction.

As shown in Figure 16, enzymes provide a surface on which reactions can take place. By bringing reactant molecules close together, the enzyme lowers the activation energy needed. In this way, enzymes make chemical reactions that are necessary for life happen at a low temperature.

Inhibitors Sometimes a reaction is more useful when it can be slowed down rather than speeded up. A material used to decrease the rate of a reaction is an **inhibitor.** Most inhibitors work by preventing reactants from coming together. Usually they combine with one of the reactants either permanently or temporarily. Inhibitors include preservatives added to food products to prevent them from becoming stale or spoiling.

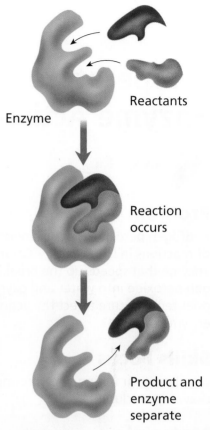

Reactants

Enzyme

Reaction occurs

Product and enzyme separate

FIGURE 16
Enzyme Action
After a reaction, an enzyme molecule is unchanged.

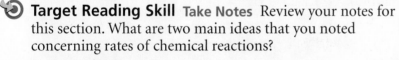

Section 3 Assessment

S 8.5.a, 8.5.c,
E-LA: Reading 8.2.4

Target Reading Skill **Take Notes** Review your notes for this section. What are two main ideas that you noted concerning rates of chemical reactions?

Reviewing Key Concepts

1. a. Defining What is activation energy?
  b. Describing What role does activation energy play in chemical reactions?
  c. Making Generalizations Look at the diagram in Figure 13, and make a generalization about activation energy in exothermic and endothermic reactions.
2. a. Identifying What are four ways that chemists can control the rates of chemical reactions?
  b. Applying Concepts Which would react more quickly in a chemical reaction: a single sugar cube or an equal mass of granulated sugar crystals? Explain.

Lab zone **At-Home Activity**

Comparing Reaction Rates Place an iron nail in a plastic cup. Add enough water to almost cover the nail. Place a small piece of fine steel wool in another cup and add the same amount of water. Ask family members to predict what will happen overnight. The next day, examine the nail and steel wool. Compare the amount of rust on each. Were your family's predictions correct? Explain how surface areas affect reaction rates.

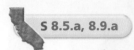

Lab zone Skills Lab

Temperature and Enzyme Activity

S 8.5.a, 8.9.a

Problem

Hydrogen peroxide is a poisonous waste product of reactions in living things. Catalase is an enzyme that speeds up the breakdown of hydrogen peroxide into water and oxygen gas. How does temperature affect the action of the enzyme catalase?

Skills Focus

calculating, graphing, interpreting data, drawing conclusions

Materials

- forceps
- stopwatch
- test tube with a one-hole stopper
- 0.1% hydrogen peroxide solution
- filter paper disks soaked in liver preparation (catalase enzyme) and kept at four different temperatures (room temperature, 0–4°C, 37°C, and 100°C)
- container to hold water (beaker or bowl)

Procedure

1. Write a hypothesis explaining how the action of the catalase enzyme is related to temperature.

Data Table		
Temperature (°C)	Time (s)	Average Time for Class (s)
0		
*		
37		
100		

*Ask your teacher for the room temperature.

2. Make a data table like the one below. Get the room temperature from your teacher.

3. Fill a container with water. Then fill a test tube with 0.1% hydrogen peroxide solution until the test tube is overflowing. Do this over a sink or the container of water.

4. Moisten the small end of a one-hole stopper with water.

5. Using forceps, remove a filter paper disk soaked in liver preparation (catalase enzyme) that has been kept at room temperature. Stick it to the moistened end of the one-hole stopper. Your partner should be ready with the stopwatch for the next step.

6. Place the stopper firmly into the test tube, hold your thumb over the hole, and quickly invert the test tube. Start the stopwatch. Put the inverted end of the test tube into the container of water, as shown in the photograph, and remove your thumb.

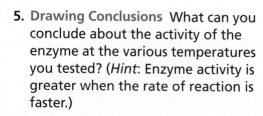

This test tube shows the vigorous reaction that occurs between hydrogen peroxide and catalase that is found in the blood. ▶

7. If the hydrogen peroxide breaks down, oxygen will be produced. Oxygen bubbles will cling to the disk and cause it to float. Record the time it takes for the disk to rise to the top. If the disk does not rise within 30 seconds, record "no reaction" and go on to Step 8.

8. Rinse the test tube and repeat the procedure with catalase enzyme disks kept at 0°C, 37°C, and 100°C. **CAUTION:** *When you remove the disk kept in the hot water bath, do not use your bare hands. Avoid spilling the hot water.*

Analyze and Conclude

1. **Calculating** Calculate the average time for each temperature based on the results of the entire class. Enter the results in your data table.

2. **Graphing** Make a line graph of the data you collected. Label the horizontal axis (*x*-axis) "Temperature" with a scale from 0°C to 100°C. Label the vertical axis (*y*-axis) "Time" with a scale from 0 to 30 seconds. Plot the class average time for each temperature.

3. **Interpreting Data** What evidence do you have that your hypothesis from Step 1 is either supported or not supported?

4. **Interpreting Data** How is the time it takes the disk to rise to the top of the inverted tube related to the rate of the reaction?

5. **Drawing Conclusions** What can you conclude about the activity of the enzyme at the various temperatures you tested? (*Hint*: Enzyme activity is greater when the rate of reaction is faster.)

6. **Predicting** Make a prediction about how active the enzyme would be at 10°C, 60°C, and 75°C. Give reasons to support your prediction.

7. **Communicating** A buildup of hydrogen peroxide in living things can damage cells. The normal human body temperature is 37°C. Write a paragraph relating your results to the body's temperature and its need to break down hydrogen peroxide.

Design an Experiment

The activity of an enzyme also depends upon the concentration of the enzyme. Design an experiment that explores the relationship between enzyme activity and enzyme concentration. (Your teacher can give you disks soaked with different enzyme concentrations.) *Obtain your teacher's permission before carrying out your investigation.*

Go Online
PHSchool.com

For: Data Sharing
Visit: PHSchool.com
Web Code: cgd-2023

Fire and Fire Safety

S 8.5.c Students know chemical reactions usually liberate heat or absorb heat.

- What are the three things necessary to maintain a fire?

- Why should you know about the causes of fire and how to prevent a fire?

Key Terms
- combustion
- fuel

Lab zone Standards Warm-Up

How Does Baking Soda Affect a Fire?

1. Put on your safety goggles.

2. Secure a small candle in a holder or a ball of clay. After instructions from your teacher, use a match to light the candle.

3. Place a beaker next to the candle. Measure 1 large spoonful of baking soda into the beaker. Add about 100 mL of water and stir. Add about 100 mL of vinegar.

4. As soon as the mixture stops foaming, tip the beaker as if you are pouring something out of it onto the flame. **CAUTION:** *Do not pour any liquid on the candle.*

5. Observe what happens to the flame.

Think It Over

Developing Hypotheses The gas produced in the beaker was carbon dioxide, CO_2. Based on the results of this experiment, develop a hypothesis to explain what you observed in Step 5.

The call comes in. Fire! A blaze has been spotted in a warehouse near gasoline storage tanks. Firefighters scramble aboard the ladder truck and the hose truck. Lights flash, sirens blare, and traffic swerves to clear a path for the trucks. The firefighters know from their training that fire is a chemical reaction that can be controlled—but only if they reach it in time.

Firefighters battle a blaze. ▼

Understanding Fire

Fire is the result of **combustion,** a rapid reaction between oxygen and a fuel. A **fuel** is a material that releases energy when it burns. Common fuels include oil, wood, gasoline, natural gas, and paper. Combustion of these types of fuel always produces carbon dioxide and water. When fuels don't burn completely, products such as smoke and poisonous gases may be produced.

The Fire Triangle Although a combustion reaction is very exothermic and fast, a fire cannot start unless conditions are right. ● **Three things necessary to start and maintain a fire are fuel, oxygen, and heat.**

You probably know that oxygen is one of the gases in air. About 20 percent of the air around you is composed of oxygen gas. If air can reach the fuel, so can oxygen. A large fire can create a strong draft that pulls air toward it. As the air around the flame is heated, it rises rapidly. Cooler air flows toward the fire, replacing the heated air and bringing a fresh supply of oxygen. If you stand in front of a fire in a fireplace, you can feel the air flow toward the fire.

Heat is a part of the "fire triangle." Fuel and oxygen can be together, but they won't react until something provides the activation energy to start combustion. This energy can come from a lighted match, an electric spark, or the heat from a stove. Once combustion starts, the heat released supplies more activation energy to keep the reaction going.

Once started, a fire can continue burning as long as all components of the fire triangle are available. Coal in abandoned mines under the town of Centralia, Pennsylvania, started burning in 1962. The coal is still burning. Many old airshafts lead into the tunnels. Because some airshafts cannot be located and sealed, air continues to flow into the mines, supporting the fire. Heat and poisonous gases coming up from the fire through cracks in the ground made living in Centralia difficult. Everyone eventually moved away. No one knows how long this fire will continue to burn.

 **Reading Checkpoint** What is heat's role in starting a fire?

FIGURE 17
The Fire Triangle
The fire triangle can be controlled in the grill below. If any point of the fire triangle is missing, a fire will not continue.
Applying Concepts *How would closing the lower air vents affect the fire?*

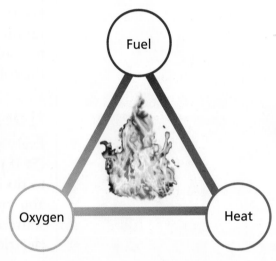

Controlling Fire Use your knowledge of chemical reactions to think of ways to control a fire. What if you remove one part of the fire triangle? For example, you can get the fuel away from the flames. You can also keep oxygen from getting to the fuel. Finally, you can cool the combustion reaction.

How do firefighters usually fight fires? They use hoses to spray huge amounts of water on the flames. Water removes two parts of the fire triangle. First, water covers the fuel, which keeps it from coming into contact with oxygen. Second, evaporation of the water uses a large amount of heat, causing the fire to cool. Without heat, there isn't enough energy to continue the combustion. Therefore, the reaction stops.

Home Fire Safety

Every year, fire claims thousands of lives in the United States. If you know how to prevent fires in your home and what to do if a fire starts, you are better prepared to take action. You may save your home or even your life! The most common sources of home fires are small heaters, cooking, and faulty electrical wiring. The fires that cause the most deaths start from carelessness with cigarettes.

Fighting Fires You can fight a small fire by using what you know about the fire triangle. For example, carbon dioxide gas can smother a fire by preventing contact between the fuel and oxygen in the air. Therefore, you can put out a small fire on the stove by throwing baking soda on it. Baking soda decomposes when heated and releases carbon dioxide gas. Or, you can use the cover of a saucepan to cut off the flow of oxygen.

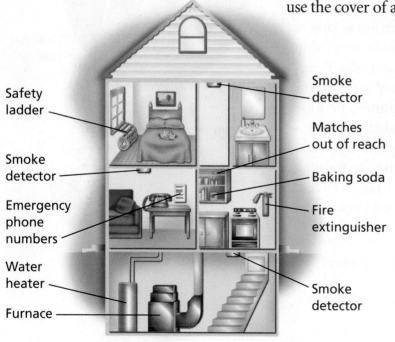

Safety ladder

Smoke detector

Emergency phone numbers

Water heater

Furnace

Smoke detector

Matches out of reach

Baking soda

Fire extinguisher

Smoke detector

FIGURE 18
A Fire-Safe House
This fire-safe house has many fire-prevention and fire safety features. **Inferring** *Why are smoke detectors located on every floor?*

244 ◆

A small fire is easy to control. You can cool a match enough to stop combustion just by blowing on it. A small fire in a trash can may be doused with a pan of water. If the fire spreads to the curtains, however, even a garden hose might not deliver enough water to put it out.

One of the most effective ways to fight a small fire is with a fire extinguisher. But a fire that is growing as you fight it is out of control. If a fire is out of control, there is only one safe thing to do—get away from the fire and call the fire department.

Preventing Trouble The best form of fire safety is prevention. Figure 18 shows some features of a fire-safe house. You can also check your home to be sure that all flammable items are stored safely away from sources of flames, such as the kitchen stove. Fires can be dangerous and deadly, but many fires can be prevented if you are careful. Understanding the chemistry of fire gives you a way to reduce risk and increase your family's safety.

 **Reading Checkpoint** How does baking soda put a fire out?

FIGURE 19
Fire-Prevention Devices
Fire extinguishers and baking soda can be used to interrupt the fire triangle. Smoke detectors can help you identify a fire and escape to safety.

Section 4 Assessment

S 8.5.c, E-LA: Reading 8.2.4

Target Reading Skill Take Notes Review your notes for this section. What important details did you include about preventing fires in your home?

Reviewing Key Concepts

1. a. Listing What three things are required for combustion?
   b. Explaining How does the fire triangle help you control fire?
   c. Applying Concepts To stop a forest fire, firefighters may remove all the trees in a strip of land that lies in the path of the fire. What part of the fire triangle is affected? Explain.

2. a. Reviewing Why is it important to know about the causes of fire and how to prevent fires?
   b. Identifying What are the three most common causes of home fires?
   c. Problem Solving Choose one common cause of home fires. Describe measures that can be taken to prevent fires of this type.

Lab zone At-Home **Activity**

Family Safety Plan Work with your family to formulate a fire safety plan. How can fires be prevented in your home? How can fires be put out if they occur? Is there a functioning smoke detector on each floor of the home, especially near the bedrooms? How can the fire department be contacted in an emergency? Design a fire escape route. Make sure all family members know the route as well as a meeting place outside.

Chapter 6

Study Guide

The BIG Idea Chemical reactions are processes in which atoms are rearranged into different combinations of molecules.

1 Observing Chemical Change

Key Concepts S 8.5.a, 8.5.c

- Changes in matter can be described in terms of physical changes and chemical changes.
- Chemical changes occur when bonds break and new bonds form.
- Chemical reactions involve changes in properties and changes in energy that you can observe.

Key Terms

matter
chemistry
physical property
chemical property
physical change
chemical change

reactant
product
precipitate
endothermic reaction
exothermic reaction

2 Describing Chemical Reactions

Key Concepts S 8.5.b

- Chemical equations use chemical formulas and other symbols instead of words to summarize a reaction.
- In chemical reactions, the number of atoms stays the same no matter how they are arranged, so their total mass stays the same.
- To describe a reaction accurately, a chemical equation must show the same number of each type of atom on both sides of the equation.
- Three general types of chemical reactions are synthesis, decomposition, and replacement.

Key Terms

chemical equation
conservation of matter
open system
closed system
coefficient
synthesis
decomposition
replacement

3 Controlling Chemical Reactions

Key Concepts S 8.5.a, 8.5.c

- All chemical reactions require a certain amount of activation energy to get started.
- Factors that affect rates of reaction include surface area, temperature, concentration, and the presence of catalysts or inhibitors.

Key Terms

activation energy
concentration
catalyst
enzyme
inhibitor

4 Fire and Fire Safety

Key Concepts S 8.5.c

- The following three things are necessary to start and maintain a fire—fuel, oxygen, and heat.
- If you know how to prevent fires in your home and what to do if a fire starts, you are better prepared to take action.

Key Terms

combustion
fuel

Review and Assessment

Target Reading Skill

Take Notes In your notebook, create a two-column note-taking organizer for Section 2: Describing Chemical Reactions. Include summary statements.

Recall Clues and Questions	Notes
What are chemical equations?	Chemical equation: an easy way to show a chemical reaction. • Chemical formulas—symbols for elements in a compound • Structure of an equation—

Reviewing Key Terms

Choose the letter of the best answer.

1. Which of the following is *not* a physical property?
   a. flexibility
   b. ability to catch fire
   c. melting point
   d. ability to conduct electricity

2. A chemical reaction that gives off heat is likely to be
   a. endothermic.　　**b.** a precipitate.
   c. a physical change.　　**d.** exothermic.

3. You can balance a chemical equation by changing the
   a. subscripts.　　**b.** coefficients.
   c. reactants.　　**d.** products.

4. A chemical reaction in which two elements combine to form a compound is called a
   a. synthesis.　　**b.** replacement.
   c. decomposition.　　**d.** precipitation.

5. The activation energy of a chemical reaction
   a. is supplied by a catalyst.
   b. is released at the end.
   c. starts the reaction.
   d. changes with time.

6. A chemical reaction in which a fuel combines rapidly with oxygen is a(n)
   a. inhibited reaction.
   b. combustion reaction.
   c. enzyme reaction.
   d. endothermic reaction.

Complete the following sentences so that your answers clearly explain the key terms.

7. A burning candle is an example of a **chemical change,** or a change in which _____ .

8. The left side of a chemical equation lists the **reactants,** or the substances that _____ .

9. By measuring the masses of the reactants and products of a reaction, you can demonstrate the principle of **conservation of matter,** which states that _____ .

10. One factor that can affect reaction rates is a reactant's **concentration,** which refers to _____ .

Writing in Science

Explanation You are a writer for a children's book about chemistry. Write a paragraph that young children would understand that explains the concept of "activation energy." Be sure to use examples, such as the burning of wood or gas.

Video Assessment

Discovery Channel School
Chemical Reactions

Review and Assessment

Checking Concepts

11. What are the two kinds of changes that occur in matter? Describe how you can tell one from the other.

12. Why can't you balance a chemical equation by changing the subscripts of the reactants or the products?

13. You find the mass of a piece of iron metal, let it rust, and measure the mass again. The mass has increased. Does this violate the principle of conservation of matter? Explain.

14. How do enzymes in your body make chemical reactions occur at safe temperatures?

15. Why does spraying water on a fire help to put the fire out?

16. How are inhibitors useful in controlling chemical reactions?

Thinking Critically

17. **Problem Solving** Steel that is exposed to water and salt rusts quickly. If you were a shipbuilder, how would you protect a new ship? Explain why your solution works.

18. **Classifying** The following are balanced equations for chemical reactions. Classify each of the equations as synthesis, decomposition, or replacement.
    a. $2 Al + Fe_2O_3 \longrightarrow 2 Fe + Al_2O_3$
    b. $2 Ag + S \longrightarrow Ag_2S$
    c. $CaCO_3 \longrightarrow CaO + CO_2$
    d. $2 NO + O_2 \longrightarrow 2 NO_2$

19. **Relating Cause and Effect** Firefighters open doors very carefully because sometimes a room will burst violently into flames when the door is opened. Based on your knowledge of the fire triangle, explain why this happens.

20. **Inferring** Some statues are made of materials that can react in acid rain and begin to dissolve. It has been observed that statues with smooth surfaces are dissolved by acid rain much slower than statues with very detailed carvings. Explain this observation.

Math Practice

Balance the chemical equations in Questions 21–24.

21. $MgO + HBr \longrightarrow MgBr_2 + H_2O$

22. $N_2 + O_2 \longrightarrow N_2O_5$

23. $C_2H_4 + O_2 \longrightarrow CO_2 + H_2O$

24. $Fe + HCl \longrightarrow FeCl_2 + H_2$

Applying Skills

Use the energy diagram to answer Questions 25–27.

The two graphs below represent the same chemical reaction under different conditions.

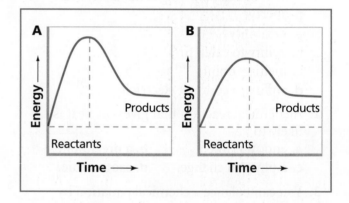

25. **Interpreting Data** How does the energy of the products compare with the energy of the reactants?

26. **Classifying** Tell whether this reaction is exothermic or endothermic.

27. **Applying Concepts** What change in condition might account for the lower "hump" in the second graph? Explain.

Standards Investigation

Performance Assessment Make a poster of your test results. Display your reaction chamber for the class. Discuss how your chamber was built to the specifications agreed upon by the class. Describe its safety features. Based on your results, rate how effectively your chamber works as a closed system.

CALIFORNIA Standards Practice

Success ⚙ Tracker™
Online at PHSchool.com

Choose the letter of the best answer.

1. Which of the following is the *best* evidence for a chemical reaction?
   A gas bubbles
   B formation of a new substance
   C change of state
   D change in temperature   S 8.5.a

2. Which statement best describes what happens to chemical bonds in a reaction?
   A Bonds are only broken, not formed
   B Bonds are only formed, not broken.
   C Bonds in the reactants are broken, and bonds in the products are formed.
   D Bonds are neither formed nor broken.
                                   S 8.5.c

3. Which shows a balanced chemical equation for the decomposition of aluminum oxide (Al_2O_3)?
   A $Al_2O_3 \longrightarrow 2\,Al + O_2$
   B $Al_2O_3 \longrightarrow 2\,Al + 3\,O_2$
   C $2\,Al_2O_3 \longrightarrow 4\,Al + O_2$
   D $2\,Al_2O_3 \longrightarrow 4\,Al + 3\,O_2$ S 8.5.b

Use the diagram below to answer Question 4.

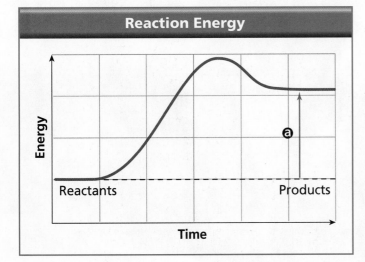

Reaction Energy

4. The quantity (a) in the diagram represents the
   A activation energy of the reaction.
   B energy absorbed by the reaction.
   C energy released by the reaction.
   D temperature of the reactants.   S 8.5.c

Base your answers to Questions 5 and 6 on the diagram below. The diagram represents molecules of two different elements that are gases. The elements react chemically to produce a third gas.

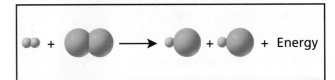

5. The diagram represents a(n)
   A endothermic reaction in which energy is released.
   B exothermic reaction in which energy is absorbed.
   C exothermic reaction in which energy is released.
   D reaction in which energy is destroyed.
                                   S 8.5.c

6. What can be inferred from the diagram?
   A Matter is not created or destroyed in a chemical reaction.
   B The rate of a reaction depends on the surface area of the reactants.
   C A gas molecule always consists of two identical atoms.
   D The product is carbon monoxide gas.
                                   S 8.5.b

Apply the BIG Idea

7. The major component of natural gas is methane (CH_4). When methane burns in oxygen gas (O_2), carbon dioxide (CO_2) and water vapor (H_2O) are produced. Write a balanced equation for this reaction. Explain why the burning of methane is a chemical change, not a physical change. Does this change absorb heat or liberate heat?   S 8.5

Acids, Bases, and Solutions

CALIFORNIA
Standards Preview

S 8.5 Chemical reactions are processes in which atoms are rearranged into different combinations of molecules. As a basis for understanding this concept:

d. Students know physical processes include freezing and boiling, in which a material changes form with no chemical reaction.

e. Students know how to determine whether a solution is acidic, basic, or neutral.

S 8.9 Scientific progress is made by asking meaningful questions and conducting careful investigations. As a basis for understanding this concept and addressing the content in the other three strands, students should develop their own questions and perform investigations. Students will:

c. Distinguish between variable and controlled parameters in a test.

Solutions containing transition metal ▶
compounds are often very colorful.

S 8.5.e

Focus on the BIG Idea

What are some characteristics of acids and bases?

Check What You Know

Suppose you dissolve a teaspoon of salt in a glass of water. Is it possible to recover the salt from the water? Explain.

Build Science Vocabulary

The images shown here represent some of the key terms in this chapter. You can use this vocabulary skill to help you understand the meaning of some key terms in this chapter.

Identify Related Word Forms

You can expand your vocabulary by learning the related forms of a word. For example, the common verb *to bake* is related to the noun *baker* and the adjective *bake*d. As you read this chapter, look for related forms of the verbs *indicate*, *saturate*, and *suspend*.

Verb	Noun	Adjective
indicate To show; to point to	**indicator** Something that shows or points to	**indicative** Serving as a sign; showing
saturate To fill up as much as is possible	**saturation** The condition of holding as much as is possible	**saturated** To be full; to hold as much as is possible
suspend To hang so as to allow free movement	**suspension** The condition of hanging or moving freely	**suspended** Hanging so as to allow free movement

Apply It!

Review the words related to *saturate.* Complete the following sentences with the correct form of the word.

1. The _____ sponge could hold no more water.
2. He continued to add water to the point of _____.

solvent

solute

solution

saturated solution

indicator

pHydrion Paper
pH2 4 6 8 10

acids

Chapter 7
Vocabulary

Section 1 (page 256)
solution
solvent
solute
colloid
suspension

Section 2 (page 262)
dilute solution
concentrated solution
solubility
saturated solution
unsaturated solution
supersaturated solution

Section 3 (page 268)
acid
corrosive
indicator
base

Section 4 (page 274)
hydrogen ion (H^+)
hydroxide ion (OH^-)
pH scale
neutral
neutralization
salt

Interactive Textbook

Build Science Vocabulary
Online
Visit: PHSchool.com
Web Code: cxj-2070

How to Read Science

Reading Skill

Create Outlines

An outline shows the relationship between main ideas and supporting ideas. An outline usually is set up like the one shown below. Roman numerals show the main topics. Capital letters show the subtopic. Use the headings, subheadings, Key Terms, and Key Concepts to help you decide what information to include in your outline. Here is a sample for the beginning of Section 1.

Title

Main topics

Understanding Solutions
I. What Is a Solution?
   A. A mixture with the same properties throughout that contains a solvent and at least one solute
      1. Solvent—the largest portion
      2. Solute—the substance dissolved in the solvent
   B. Solutions with water—the "universal solvent"
   C. Solutions without water—may contain solids, liquids, or gases
II. Colloids and Suspensions
   A. Colloids

Subheading

Key terms and definitions

Subheadings

Apply It!

1. What are the two main topics in this outline?

2. Compare the definition of *solvent* in the outline with the definition on page 256. How are they different?

In your notebook, complete the outline for Section 1. As you read Section 4, write an outline to help you understand the relationship among topics in the section.

S 8.5.e

Make Your Own Indicator

As you learn about acids and bases in this chapter, you can make your own solutions that will let you determine if something is acidic, basic, or neutral. Such solutions change color in an acid or a base and are called acid-base indicators. You can use your solutions to test for acids and bases among substances found in your home.

Your Goal

To make acid-base indicators from flowers, fruits, vegetables, or other common plant materials

To complete the investigation, you must

- make indicators that will turn colors in acids and bases
- use your indicators to test a number of substances
- compare your indicators to a standard pH scale
- rank the tested substances based on their pH values
- follow the safety guidelines in Appendix A

Plan It!

Brainstorm with your classmates about foods, spices, flowers, or other plant materials that have definite, deep colors. Think about fruits and vegetables you may find in a supermarket, These materials may make good candidates for your indicators.

Section 1

Understanding Solutions

CALIFORNIA Standards Focus

S 8.5.d Students know physical processes including freezing and boiling, in which a material changes form with no chemical reaction.

- What are the characteristics of solutions, colloids, and suspensions?
- What happens to the particles of a solute when a solution forms?
- How do solutes affect the freezing point and boiling point of a solvent?

Key Terms

- solution
- solvent
- solute
- colloid
- suspension

Lab zone Standards Warm-Up

What Makes a Mixture a Solution?

1. Put about 50 or 60 milliliters of water into a plastic cup. Add a spoonful of pepper and stir well.
2. To a similar amount of water in a second cup, add a spoonful of table salt. Stir well.
3. Compare the appearance of the two mixtures.

Think It Over

Observing What is the difference between the two mixtures? What other mixtures have you seen that are similar to pepper and water? That are similar to table salt and water?

You're really thirsty, so you drink a tall, cool glass of tap water. But exactly what is tap water? Tap water is a mixture of pure water (H_2O) and a variety of other substances, such as chloride, fluoride, and metallic ions. Gases, such as oxygen and carbon dioxide, are also dissolved in tap water. The dissolved substances give tap water its taste.

What Is a Solution?

Tap water is one example of a mixture called a solution. A **solution** is a uniform mixture that contains a solvent and at least one solute. The **solvent** is the part of a solution present in the largest amount. It dissolves the other substances. The **solute** is the substance that is present in a solution in a smaller amount and is dissolved by the solvent. **A solution has the same properties throughout. It contains solute particles (molecules or ions) that are too small to see.**

Dissolving one substance into another is an example of a physical change. In a physical change, neither substance changes into a new substance. Physical changes can often be undone to recover the original materials. Solutes and solvents have different physical properties such as boiling and melting points. You can use these different properties to recover the solute from the solvent. Suppose you dissolve salt in water. Water has a lower boiling point than salt. If you boil salt water, the water will vaporize first, leaving the salt behind.

Solutions With Water In many common solutions, the solvent is water. Sugar in water, for example, is the starting solution for flavored soda water. Adding food coloring gives the drink color. Dissolving carbon dioxide gas in the mixture produces a fizzy soda. Water dissolves so many substances that it is often called the "universal solvent." Life depends on water solutions. Nutrients used by plants are dissolved in water in the soil. Water is the solvent in blood, saliva, and tears.

Solutions Without Water Many solutions are made with solvents other than water, as you can see in Figure 1. For example, gasoline is a solution of several different liquid fuels. Some solutions, such as air or brass, don't have liquid solvents at all. A solution may be a combination of gases, liquids, or solids.

 Reading Checkpoint **What solvent is essential to living things?**

Video Field Trip
Discovery Channel School
Acids, Bases, and Solutions

Examples of Common Solutions

Solute	Solvent	Solution
Gas	Gas	Air (oxygen and other gases in nitrogen)
Gas	Liquid	Soda water (carbon dioxide in water)
Liquid	Liquid	Antifreeze (ethylene glycol in water)
Solid	Liquid	Dental filling (silver in mercury)
Solid	Liquid	Ocean water (sodium chloride and other compounds in water)
Solid	Solid	Stainless steel (chromium, nickel, and carbon in iron)

FIGURE 1
Solutions can be formed from any combination of solids, liquids, and gases.
Interpreting Photos *What are the solutes and solvent for stainless steel?*

The air in these gas bubbles is a solution of oxygen and other gases in nitrogen.

Salt water is a solution of sodium chloride and other compounds in water.

Stainless steel is a solution of chromium, nickel, and carbon in iron.

FIGURE 2

Comparing Three Mixtures
Solutions are different from colloids and suspensions.
Interpreting Photographs *In which mixture can you see the particles?*

Colloid
Fats and proteins in milk form globular particles that are big enough to scatter light, but are too small to be seen.

Suspension
Suspended particles of "snow" in water are easy to see.

Solution
In a solution of glass cleaner, particles are uniformly distributed and too small to scatter light.

Lab zone Try This Activity

Scattered Light

1. Pour 50 mL of a gelatin-and-water mixture into a small, clean glass beaker.

2. Pour 50 mL of a saltwater solution into another clean beaker that is about the same size.

3. Compare the appearance of the two liquids.

4. In a darkened room, shine a small flashlight through the side of the beaker that contains gelatin. Repeat this procedure with the saltwater solution.

5. Compare the appearance of the light inside the two beakers.

Inferring What evidence tells you that gelatin is a colloid?

Colloids and Suspensions

Not all mixtures are solutions. Colloids and suspensions are mixtures that have different properties than solutions.

Colloids Look at Figure 2. The glass cleaner is a solution. You can see through solutions because light passes through them without being scattered in all directions. Have you ever tried to look through a glass of milk? Milk is a colloid. A **colloid** is a mixture that contains small, undissolved particles that do not settle out. **A colloid contains larger particles than a solution. The particles are still too small to be seen easily, but are large enough to scatter a light beam.** Milk contains fats and proteins that form globular particles. These particles scatter light in different directions, making it impossible to see through a glass of milk.

Fog is a colloid that consists of water droplets in air. Fog scatters the headlight beams of cars, reducing visibility for drivers. Gelatin, mayonnaise, shaving cream, and whipped cream are other examples of colloids.

Suspensions If you did the Standards Warm-Up, you noticed that no matter how much you stir pepper and water, the two never really seem to "mix" completely. When you stop stirring, you can still see pepper floating on the water's surface and collecting at the bottom of the cup. Pepper and water make a suspension. A **suspension** (suh SPEN shun) is a mixture in which particles can be seen and easily separated by settling or filtration. **A suspension does not have the same properties throughout. It contains visible particles that are larger than the particles in solutions or colloids.** The snow globe in Figure 2 is another example of a suspension.

Particles in a Solution

Why does salt seem to disappear when you mix it with water? If you had a microscope powerful enough to look at the mixture's particles, what would you see? ⬤ **When a solution forms, particles of the solvent surround and separate the particles of the solute.**

Ionic and Molecular Compounds in Solution Figure 3 shows what happens when the ionic compound, salt, mixes with water. The positive and negative ions are attracted to the polar water molecules. Water molecules surround each ion as the ions leave the surface of the compound. As each layer of the compound is exposed, more ions can dissolve.

However, not every substance breaks into ions when it dissolves in water. A molecular compound, such as sugar, breaks up into individual neutral molecules. The polar water molecules attract the slightly polar sugar molecules. This causes the sugar molecules to move away from each other. The covalent bonds within the molecules remain unbroken.

Solutes and Conductivity Suppose you have a water solution, but you don't know if the solute is salt or sugar. How could you find out? Think about what you learned about the electrical conductivity of compounds. A solution of ionic compounds in water conducts electric current, but a water solution of molecular compounds normally does not. You could test the electrical conductivity of the solution. If no ions are present (as in a sugar solution), current will not flow.

 **Reading Checkpoint** **Which kind of solution conducts an electric current?**

Go **O**nline
active art

For: Salt Dissolving in Water activity
Visit: PHSchool.com
Web Code: cgp-2031

FIGURE 3
Salt Dissolving in Water
When an ionic compound —like salt—dissolves, water molecules surround and separate the positive and negative ions. Notice that the sodium ions attract the oxygen ends of the water molecules.

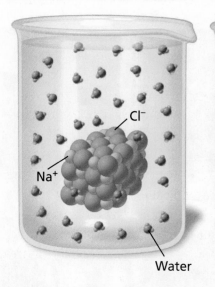

Cl⁻

Na⁺

Water

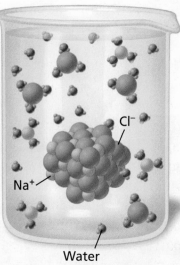

Cl⁻

Na⁺

Water

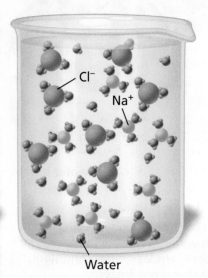

Cl⁻

Na⁺

Water

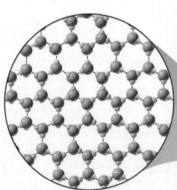
Effects of Solutes on Solvents

Ordinarily, the freezing point of pure water is 0°C, and the boiling point is 100°C. The addition of solutes to water changes these properties. ⬤ **Solutes lower the freezing point and raise the boiling point of a solvent.**

Lower Freezing Points Pure water is made only of water molecules that freeze at 0°C. When liquid water freezes, water molecules join together to form crystals of solid ice. In a salt solution, solute particles are present in the water when it freezes. The solute particles make it harder for the water molecules to form crystals. The temperature must drop lower than 0°C for the solution to freeze. The presence of a solute lowers the freezing point of water. Figure 4 illustrates the particles in pure water and in a saltwater solution.

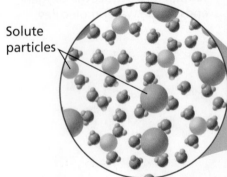

Freshwater lake ▶

Solute
particles

Saltwater bay ▶

FIGURE 4
The Effect of Salt on Freezing Point
Fresh water on the surface of a lake is frozen. Under similar conditions, salt water is not frozen.

Higher Boiling Points The directions for cooking pasta often advise adding salt to the water. Why? As the temperature of a liquid rises, the molecules gain energy and escape into the air. In pure water, all the molecules are water. But in a solution, some of the particles are water molecules and others are particles of solute. The water molecules need more energy to escape when a solute is present. The temperature must go higher than 100°C for water to boil. Solutes raise the boiling point of the solvent. Adding salt to the water decreases cooking time for the pasta because the water is hotter.

Car manufacturers make use of the effects of solutes to protect engines from heat and cold. The coolant in a car radiator is a solution of water and another liquid called antifreeze. (Often the antifreeze is ethylene glycol.) The mixture of the two liquids has a higher boiling point and lower freezing point than water alone. This solution can absorb more of the heat given off by the running engine. This reduces the risk of damage to the car from overheating. The freezing point of this solution is lower than the lowest temperature the car is likely to be exposed to. This reduces the risk of damage from freezing in very cold weather.

FIGURE 5
Calling Solutes to the Rescue?
This couple might have prevented their car from overheating by using the proper coolant in the radiator.
Relating Cause and Effect *Explain how coolant works.*

 **Reading Checkpoint** **Does salt water have a lower or higher freezing point than pure water?**

Section 1 Assessment

S 8.5.d, E-LA: Reading 8.1.0

Vocabulary Skill Identify Related Word Forms
Complete the sentence by using *solute* and *solution* correctly. A _____ is a mixture that contains at least one _____.

Reviewing Key Concepts

1. a. **Defining** What is a solution?
   b. **Comparing and Contrasting** How are solutions different from colloids and suspensions?
   c. **Inferring** Suppose you mix food coloring in water to make it blue. Have you made a solution or a suspension? Explain.
2. a. **Reviewing** What happens to the solute particles when a solution forms?
   b. **Sequencing** Describe as a series of steps how table salt in water makes a solution that can conduct electricity.
3. a. **Summarizing** What effects do solutes have on a solvent's freezing and boiling points?

b. **Relating Cause and Effect** Why is the temperature needed to freeze ocean water lower than the temperature needed to freeze the surface of a freshwater lake?
c. **Applying Concepts** Why does salt sprinkled on icy roads cause the ice to melt?

Lab zone **At-Home Activity**

Passing Through With a family member, mix together a spoonful each of sugar and pepper in about 100 mL of warm water in a plastic container. Pour the mixture through a coffee filter into a second container. Ask your family member what happened to the sugar. Let the water evaporate overnight. Describe the difference between a solution and a suspension.

Concentration and Solubility

CALIFORNIA
Standards Focus

S 8.5.d Students know physical processes including freezing and boiling, in which a material changes form with no chemical reaction.

- How is concentration measured?
- Why is solubility useful in identifying substances?
- What factors affect the solubility of a substance?

Key Terms

- dilute solution
- concentrated solution
- solubility
- saturated solution
- unsaturated solution
- supersaturated solution

Lab zone — Standards **Warm-Up**

Does It Dissolve?

1. Put half a spoonful of soap flakes into a small plastic cup. Add about 50 mL of water and stir. Observe whether the soap flakes dissolve.

2. Clean out the cup. Repeat the test for a few other solids and liquids provided by your teacher.

3. Classify the items you tested into two groups: those that dissolved easily and those that did not.

Think It Over

Drawing Conclusions Based on your observations, does the physical state (solid or liquid) of a substance affect whether or not it is able to dissolve in water? Explain.

Have you ever had syrup on your pancakes? You probably know that it's made from the sap of maple trees. Is something that sweet really made in a tree? Well, not exactly.

Concentration

You must collect approximately 43 gallons of maple sap to make one gallon of maple syrup. The sap of a maple tree and pancake syrup differ in their concentrations. That is, they differ in the amount of solute (sugar) dissolved in a certain amount of solvent (water). You make maple syrup by evaporating the water from the maple sap. By removing the water, you are left with a sweeter solution.

Making Maple Syrup ▼

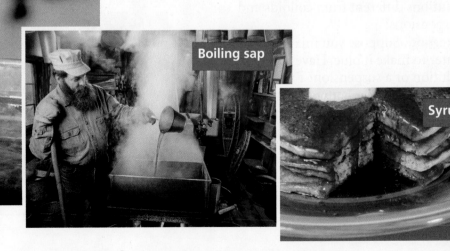
Collecting sap
Boiling sap
Syrup

Changing Concentration A **concentrated solution** has a lot of solute dissolved in a certain amount of solvent. You can make a concentrated solution by adding more solute or removing solvent. For example, fruit juices are sometimes packaged as concentrates, which are concentrated solutions. In making the concentrate, water was removed from the natural juice. A **dilute solution** has only a little solute dissolved in a certain amount of solvent. You can make a dilute solution by increasing the amount of solvent in a solution. When you make juice from concentrate, you add water, making a more dilute solution.

Measuring Concentration You know that maple syrup is more concentrated than maple sap. But how could you find the actual concentration of either solution?  **To measure concentration, you compare the amount of solute to the total amount of solution.** You might measure the mass of a solute or solvent in grams. Or you might measure the volume of a solute or solvent in milliliters or liters. You can measure concentration as the percent of solute in solution by volume or mass.

Reading Checkpoint How can you change the concentration of a solution?

Solubility

If a substance dissolves in water, you might ask, "How much can dissolve?" Suppose you add sugar to a glass of iced tea. Is there a limit to how "sweet" you can make the tea? The answer is yes. At the temperature of iced tea, several spoonfuls of sugar are about all you can add. At some point, no matter how much you stir the tea, no more sugar will dissolve. **Solubility** is a measure of how much solute can dissolve in a solvent at a given temperature.

If you can continue to dissolve more solute, you still have an **unsaturated solution.** When you've added so much solute that no more dissolves, you have a **saturated solution.** If you add more sugar to a saturated solution of iced tea, the extra sugar just settles to the bottom of the glass.

FIGURE 6
Dissolving Sugar in Tea
At some point, this boy will not be able to dissolve any more sugar in his tea.
Applying Concepts *When the boy cannot dissolve any more sugar in his tea, what term describes the solution?*

Baking Soda
6.9 g

Sugar
180 g

Solubility in 100 g of Water at 0°C	
Compound	Solubility (g)
*Carbon dioxide (CO_2)	0.335
Baking soda ($NaHCO_3$)	6.9
Table salt (NaCl)	35.7
Table sugar ($C_{12}H_{22}O_{11}$)	180

*CO_2 at 101 kPa total pressure

FIGURE 7
Each compound listed in the table dissolves in water, but in different amounts.
Interpreting Tables *Which compound is the most soluble? Which is the least soluble?*

Working With Solubility The solubility of a substance tells you how much solute you can dissolve before a solution becomes saturated. For solids, solubility is given for a particular solvent (such as water) at a particular temperature. For gases, the pressure is also given. Look at the table in Figure 7. It compares the solubility of some familiar compounds. In this case, the solvent is water and the temperature is 0°C. From the table, you can see that 100 grams of water will dissolve 6.9 grams of baking soda. But the same mass of water will dissolve 180 grams of table sugar!

Using Solubility Suppose you had a white powder. You can't tell for sure whether the white powder is table salt or sugar. How could you identify it? You could measure its solubility in water at 0°C and compare the results to the data in Figure 7. ⚬ **You can identify a substance by its solubility because it is a characteristic property of matter.**

 **Reading Checkpoint** What does the solubility of a substance tell you?

Factors Affecting Solubility

Which dissolves more sugar: iced tea or hot tea? You have already read that there is a limit to solubility. An iced tea and sugar solution becomes saturated when no more sugar will dissolve. Yet a hot, steaming cup of the same tea can dissolve much more sugar before the limit is reached. The solubilities of solutes change when conditions change. ⚬ **Factors that affect the solubility of a substance include pressure, the type of solvent, and temperature.**

Pressure Increasing the pressure increases the solubility of gases. Soda water contains dissolved carbon dioxide gas. To increase the carbon dioxide concentration in soda water, the gas is added under high pressure. Opening the bottle or can reduces the pressure. The escaping gas makes the sound you hear.

Scuba divers must be aware of the effect of pressure on gases. Air is about 80 percent nitrogen. When divers breathe from tanks of compressed air, nitrogen from the air dissolves in their blood in greater amounts as they descend. This occurs because the pressure underwater increases with depth. If divers return to the surface too quickly, nitrogen bubbles come out of solution and block blood flow. Divers double over in pain, which is why this condition is sometimes called "the bends."

Solvents Some solvents and solutes are not compatible. Have you ever tried to mix vinegar, which is mostly water, and oil to make salad dressing? If you have, you've seen how the dressing quickly separates into layers after you stop shaking it. Oil and water do not mix because water is a polar compound and oil is nonpolar. Polar compounds and nonpolar compounds do not mix very well.

For liquid solutions, the solvent affects how well a solute dissolves. The expression "like dissolves like" gives you a clue to which solutes are soluble in which solvents. Ionic and polar compounds usually dissolve in polar solvents. Nonpolar compounds do not usually dissolve in polar solvents. If you work with paints, you know that you can use soap and water to clean up water-based (latex) paints. But cleaning up oil-based paints may require a nonpolar solvent, such as turpentine.

FIGURE 8
Pressure Changes Solubility
Opening a shaken bottle of soda water may produce quite a spray as dissolved gas comes out of solution.

Just after shaking... ▶

...a little while later ▶

FIGURE 9
Solvents and Solubility
Try as she might, this girl cannot get oil and vinegar to stay mixed. Nonpolar and polar compounds don't form solutions with each other.

Math ▶ Analyzing Data

Temperature and Solubility

The solubility of the compound potassium nitrate (KNO_3) varies in water at different temperatures.

1. **Reading Graphs** At which temperature shown in the graph is KNO_3 least soluble in water?

2. **Reading Graphs** Approximately what mass of KNO_3 is needed to saturate a water solution at 40°C?

3. **Calculating** About how much more soluble is KNO_3 at 40°C than at 20°C?

4. **Interpreting Data** Does solubility increase at the same rate with every 20°C increase in temperature? Explain.

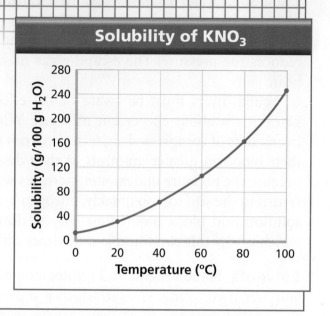

Solubility of KNO_3

y-axis: Solubility (g/100 g H_2O) — 0, 40, 80, 120, 160, 200, 240, 280

x-axis: Temperature (°C) — 0, 20, 40, 60, 80, 100

Temperature For most solids, solubility increases as the temperature increases. That is why the temperature is reported when solubilities are listed. For example, the solubility of table sugar in 100 grams of water changes from 180 grams at 0°C to 231 grams at 25°C to 487 grams at 100°C.

Cooks use the increased solubility of sugar when they make treats such as rock candy, fudge, or peanut brittle. To make peanut brittle, you start with a mixture of sugar, corn syrup, and water. At room temperature, not much sugar can dissolve in the water. The mixture must be heated until it begins to boil. Nuts and other ingredients are added while the mixture is still hot. Some recipes call for temperatures above 100°C. Because the exact temperature can affect the result, cooks use a candy thermometer to check the temperature.

Unlike most solids, gases become less soluble in a liquid when the temperature of the liquid goes up. For example, more carbon dioxide will dissolve in cold water than in hot water. Have you ever noticed that warm soda water tastes "flat"? Warm soda water contains less carbon dioxide gas. When you open a warm bottle of soda water, carbon dioxide escapes from the soda water in greater amounts than if the soda water had been chilled. So if you like soda water that's very fizzy, open it when it's cold!

FIGURE 10

Temperature Changes Solubility
Some hard candy is made by cooling a sugar water solution. **Interpreting Photographs** *Why does sugar form crystals when the solution is cooled?*

FIGURE 11
A Supersaturated Solution
Dropping a crystal of solute into a supersaturated solution (left) causes the excess solute to immediately come out of solution (center). Soon, the precipitation is complete (right).

When heated, a solution can dissolve more solute than it can at cooler temperatures. If a heated, saturated solution cools slowly, sometimes the extra solute will remain dissolved. A **supersaturated solution** has more dissolved solute than is predicted by its solubility at the given temperature. Look at Figure 11. When you drop a crystal of solute into a supersaturated solution, the extra solute will come out of the solution.

Go Online
SCI LINKS NSTA

For: Links on solubility
Visit: www.SciLinks.org
Web Code: scn-1232

✓ **Reading Checkpoint** As temperature increases, what happens to the solubility of a gas?

Section 2 Assessment

S 8.5.d; Math: 7 NS 1.3
E-LA: Reading 8.1.0

Vocabulary Skill Identify Related Word Forms Compare the meaning of the noun *solution* with the meaning of the adjective *solubility*. How are they similar? How are they different?

Reviewing Key Concepts

1. a. **Reviewing** What is concentration?
   b. **Describing** What quantities are compared when the concentration of a solution is measured?
   c. **Applying Concepts** Solution A contains 50 g of sugar. Solution B contains 100 g of sugar. Can you tell which solution has a higher sugar concentration? Explain.

2. a. **Defining** What is solubility?
   b. **Explaining** How can solubility help you identify a substance?
   c. **Calculating** Look back at the table in Figure 7. At 0°C, about how many times more soluble in water is sugar than salt?

3. a. **Listing** What are three factors that affect solubility?
   b. **Summarizing** How does temperature affect the solubility of most solids?
   c. **Relating Cause and Effect** When you heat water and add sugar, all of the sugar dissolves. When you cool the solution, some sugar comes out of solution. Explain.

Math Practice

4. **Calculating a Concentration** What is the concentration of a solution that contains 45 grams of sugar in 500 grams of solution?

5. **Calculating a Concentration** How much sugar is dissolved in 500 grams of a solution if the solution is 70 percent sugar by mass?

Section
3

Describing Acids and Bases

CALIFORNIA
Standards Focus

S 8.5.e Students know how to determine whether a solution is acidic, basic, or neutral.

What are the properties of acids and bases?

Where are acids and bases commonly used?

Key Terms
- acid
- corrosive
- indicator
- base

Lab zone Standards **Warm-Up**

What Colors Does Litmus Paper Turn?

1. Use a plastic dropper to put a drop of lemon juice on a clean piece of red litmus paper. Put another drop on a clean piece of blue litmus paper. Observe.

2. Rinse your dropper with water. Then observe other substances in the same way. You might observe orange juice, ammonia cleaner, tap water, vinegar, and solutions of soap, baking soda, and table salt. Record all your observations.

3. Wash your hands when you are finished.

Think It Over

Classifying Group the substances based on how they make the litmus paper change color. What other properties do the items in each group have in common?

Did you have an orange, an apple, or fruit juice for breakfast today? If so, an acid was part of your meal. The last time you washed your hair, did you use shampoo? If your answer is yes, then you may have used a base.

You use many products that contain acids and bases. In addition, the chemical reactions of acids and bases even keep you alive! What are acids and bases—how do they react, and what are their uses?

Properties of Acids

In order to identify an acid, you can test its properties. **Acids** are compounds whose characteristic properties include the kinds of reactions they undergo. **An acid tastes sour, reacts with metals and carbonates, and turns blue litmus paper red.** Some common acids you may have heard of are hydrochloric acid, nitric acid, sulfuric acid, carbonic acid, and acetic acid.

◀ Lemons are acidic.

Sour Taste If you've ever tasted a lemon, you've had first-hand experience with the sour taste of acids. Can you think of other foods that sometimes taste sour, or tart? Citrus fruits—lemons, grapefruits, oranges, and limes—are acidic. They all contain citric acid. Other fruits (cherries, tomatoes, apples) and many other types of foods contain acids, too.

Although sour taste is a characteristic of many acids, it is not one you should use to identify a compound as an acid. Scientists never taste chemicals in order to identify them. You should never taste a substance unless you know that it is safe to eat.

Reactions With Metals Acids react with certain metals, such as magnesium, zinc, and iron, to produce hydrogen gas. When they react, the metals seem to disappear in the solution. This observation is one reason acids are described as **corrosive,** meaning they "wear away" other materials.

The metal plate in Figure 12 is being etched with acid. Etching is one method of making printing plates that are then used to print works of art on paper. To make an etching, an artist first coats a metal plate with an acid-resistant material—often beeswax. Then the design is cut into the beeswax with a sharp tool, exposing some of the metal. When the plate is treated with acid, the acid eats away the design in the exposed metal. The metal still covered with wax remains intact. Later, ink applied to the plate collects in the grooves made by the acid. The ink is transferred to the paper when the etching is printed.

FIGURE 12
Etching With Acid
Metal etching uses the reaction of an acid with a metal. Lines are cut in a wax coating on a plate. Here, hydrochloric acid eats away at the exposed zinc metal, forming bubbles you can see in the close-up. **Applying Concepts** *What gas forms in this reaction?*

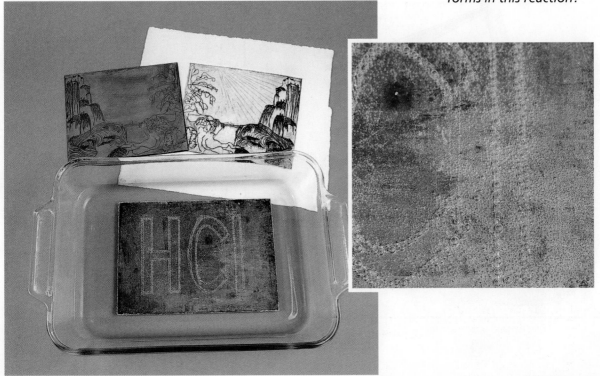

Reactions With Carbonates Acids also react with carbonate ions in a characteristic way. Recall that an ion is an atom or a group of atoms that has an electric charge. Carbonate ions contain carbon and oxygen atoms bonded together. They carry an overall negative charge (CO_3^{2-}). One product of an acid's reaction with carbonates is the gas carbon dioxide.

Geologists, scientists who study Earth, use this property of acids to identify rocks containing certain types of limestone. Limestone is a compound that contains the carbonate ion. If a geologist pours dilute hydrochloric acid on a limestone rock, bubbles of carbon dioxide appear on the rock's surface.

Reactions With Indicators If you did the Standards Warm-Up, you used litmus paper to test several substances. Litmus is an example of an **indicator,** a compound that changes color when in contact with an acid or a base. Litmus is a kind of dye derived from plants called lichens (LY kens). Litmus paper is made by coating strips of paper with litmus. Look at Figure 13 to see what happens to litmus paper as it is dipped in a solution containing acid. Acids turn blue litmus paper red. Vinegar, lemon juice, and other acids turn blue litmus paper red. Sometimes chemists use other indicators to test for acids, but litmus is one of the easiest to use.

 **Reading Checkpoint** How is litmus paper made?

FIGURE 13
The Litmus Test
Litmus paper is an easy way to identify quickly whether an unknown compound is an acid or a base. *Inferring What can you infer about a liquid that does not change the color of blue litmus paper?*

Acids turn blue litmus paper red.

Acid

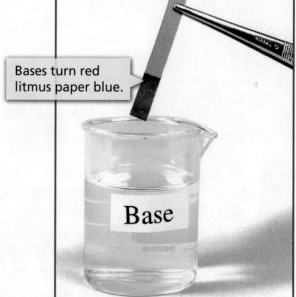

Bases turn red litmus paper blue.

Base

FIGURE 14
Bases in Soaps
If you give a dog a sudsy bath, bases in the soap could make your hands feel slippery.

Properties of Bases

Bases are another group of compounds that can be identified by their common properties. ◉ **A base tastes bitter, feels slippery, and turns red litmus paper blue.** Common bases include sodium hydroxide, calcium hydroxide, and ammonia.

Bitter Taste Bases taste bitter. The slightly bitter taste of soda water is caused by the base quinine. Soaps, some shampoos, and detergents taste bitter too, but they are not safe to taste. You should never taste a substance unless you know that it is safe to eat.

Slippery Feel Picture yourself washing a dog. As you massage the soap into the dog's fur, you notice that your hands feel slippery. This slippery feeling is another characteristic of bases. But just as you avoid tasting a substance to identify it, you wouldn't want to touch it. Strong bases can irritate or burn your skin. A safer way to identify bases is by their other properties.

Reactions With Indicators Since litmus paper can be used to test acids, it can be used to test bases, too. Look at Figure 13 to see what happens to a litmus paper as it is dipped in a basic solution. Bases turn red litmus paper blue. Like acids, bases react with other indicators. But litmus paper gives a reliable, safe test. An easy way to remember how litmus works is to remember the letter *b*. **B**ases turn litmus paper **b**lue.

Reading Checkpoint What is one safe way to identify a base?

For: Links on acids and bases
Visit: www.SciLinks.org
Web Code: scn-1233

FIGURE 15

Uses of Acids

Acids are found in vegetables and valuable products used in homes and industries.

Acids in the Home ▶
People often use dilute solutions of acids to clean brick and other surfaces. Hardware stores sell muriatic (hydrochloric) acid, which is used to clean bricks and metals.

Acids and Food ▼
Many of the vitamins in the foods you eat are acids.

Tomatoes and oranges contain ascorbic acid, or vitamin C.

Folic acid, needed for healthy cell growth, is found in green leafy vegetables.

Acids and Industry ▼
Farmers and manufacturers depend on acids for many uses.

Sulfuric acid reacts with lead and lead sulfate in a battery to produce an electric current.

Nitric acid and phosphoric acid are used to make fertilizers for crops and lawns.

Uses of Acids and Bases

Where can you find acids and bases? Almost anywhere. You already learned that acids are found in many fruits and other foods. In fact, some acids are vitamins, including ascorbic acid, or vitamin C, and folic acid. Vitamins are essential in small amounts to normal growth and functioning of the body. Many cell processes also produce acids as waste products. For example, lactic acid builds up in your muscles when you make them work hard.

Manufacturers, farmers, and builders are only some people who depend on acids and bases in their work. ⊙ **Acids and bases have many uses around the home and in industry.** Look at Figure 15 and Figure 16 to learn about a few of them. Many of the uses of bases take advantage of their ability to react with acids.

 **Reading Checkpoint** What vitamins are acids?

FIGURE 16
Uses of Bases

The reactions of bases make them valuable raw materials for a range of products.

Bases in the Home ▶
Ammonia solutions are safe to spray with bare hands, but you must wear gloves when working with drain cleaners.

Drain cleaners contain sodium hydroxide (lye).

You can't mistake the odor of household cleaning products made with ammonia.

Bases and Food ▼
Baking soda reacts with acids such as lemon juice and buttermilk to produce carbon dioxide gas in baked goods. Without these gas bubbles, breads, biscuits, cakes, and cookies would not be light and fluffy.

Bases and Industry ▲
Mortar and cement are manufactured using the bases calcium oxide and calcium hydroxide.

Section 3 Assessment

S 8.5.e, E-LA: Writing 8.2.0, Reading 8.1.0

Vocabulary Skill Identify Related Word Forms Look up the verb *corrode* in a dictionary. How does knowing the meaning of *corrode* help you understand the adjective *corrosive*?

Reviewing Key Concepts

1. a. **Listing** What are four properties of acids? Of bases?
   b. **Describing** How can you use litmus paper to distinguish an acid from a base?
   c. **Applying Concepts** How might you tell if a food contains an acid as one of its ingredients?
2. a. **Reviewing** What are three practical uses of an acid? Of a base?
   b. **Making Generalizations** Where are you most likely to find acids and bases in your own home? Explain.

c. **Making Judgments** Why is it wise to wear gloves when spreading fertilizer in a garden?

Writing in Science

Wanted Poster A bottle of acid is missing from the chemistry lab shelf! Design a wanted poster describing properties of the missing acid. Also include descriptions of tests a staff member from the chemistry lab could *safely* perform to determine if a bottle that is found actually contains acid. Add a caution on your poster that warns people *not* to touch any bottles they find. Instead, they should notify the chemistry lab.

Acids and Bases in Solution

S 8.5.e Students know how to determine whether a solution is acidic, basic, or neutral.

- What kinds of ions do acids and bases form in water?

- What does pH tell you about a solution?

- What happens in a neutralization reaction?

Key Terms

- hydrogen ion (H^+)
- hydroxide ion (OH^-)
- pH scale
- neutral
- neutralization
- salt

Lab zone Standards Warm-Up

What Can Cabbage Juice Tell You?

1. Using a dropper, put 5 drops of red cabbage juice into each of three separate plastic cups.

2. Add 10 drops of lemon juice (an acid) to one cup. Add 10 drops of ammonia cleaner (a base) to another. Keep the third cup for comparison. Record the colors you see.

3. Now add ammonia, 1 drop at a time, to the cup containing lemon juice. Keep adding ammonia until the color no longer changes. Record all color changes you see.

4. Add lemon juice a drop at a time to the ammonia until the color no longer changes. Record the changes you see.

Think It Over

Forming Operational Definitions Based on your observations, what could you add to your definitions of acids and bases?

A chemist pours hydrochloric acid into a beaker. Then she adds sodium hydroxide to the acid. The mixture looks the same, but the beaker becomes warm. If she tested the solution with litmus paper, what color would the paper turn? Would you be surprised if it did not change color at all? If exactly the right amounts and concentrations of the acid and the base were mixed, the beaker would hold nothing but salt water! How could these two harmful chemicals react to produce something harmless to the touch? In this section, you will find the answer.

Acids in Solution

What do acids have in common? Notice that each formula in the list of acids in Figure 17 begins with hydrogen. The acids you will learn about in this section all produce one or more hydrogen ions and a negative ion in solution with water. A **hydrogen ion** (H^+) is an atom of hydrogen that has lost its electron. The negative ion may be a nonmetal or a polyatomic ion. Hydrogen ions are the key to the reactions of acids.

Important Acids and Bases			
Acid	Formula	Base	Formula
Hydrochloric acid	HCl	Sodium hydroxide	NaOH
Nitric acid	HNO_3	Potassium hydroxide	KOH
Sulfuric acid	H_2SO_4	Calcium hydroxide	$Ca(OH)_2$
Carbonic acid	H_2CO_3	Aluminum hydroxide	$Al(OH)_3$
Acetic acid	$HC_2H_3O_2$	Ammonia	NH_3
Phosphoric acid	H_3PO_4	Calcium oxide	CaO

FIGURE 17
The table lists some common acids and bases.
Making Generalizations *What do all of the acid formulas in the table have in common?*

Acids in water solution separate into hydrogen ions (H^+) and negative ions. In the case of hydrochloric acid, for example, hydrogen ions and chloride ions form:

$$HCl \xrightarrow{\text{water}} H^+ + Cl^-$$

An acid produces hydrogen ions (H^+) in water. These hydrogen ions cause the properties of acids. For instance, when you add acid to certain metals, hydrogen ions interact with the metal atoms. One product of the reaction is hydrogen gas (H_2). Hydrogen ions also react with blue litmus paper, turning it red. That's why acids turn litmus paper red.

 **Reading Checkpoint** Why do acids turn litmus paper red?

Bases in Solution

Look at the table in Figure 17. Many of the bases are made of positive ions combined with hydroxide ions. The **hydroxide ion (OH^-)** is a negative ion, made of oxygen and hydrogen. When bases dissolve in water, the positive ions and hydroxide ions separate. Look at what happens to sodium hydroxide in water:

$$NaOH \xrightarrow{\text{water}} Na^+ + OH^-$$

Not all bases contain hydroxide ions. For example, the gas ammonia (NH_3) does not. But in solution, ammonia is a base that reacts with water to form hydroxide ions.

$$NH_3 + H_2O \longrightarrow NH_4^+ + OH^-$$

Notice that both reactions produce negative hydroxide ions in the product. A base produces hydroxide ions (OH^-) in water. Hydroxide ions are responsible for the bitter taste and slippery feel of bases, and turn red litmus paper blue.

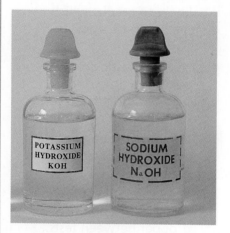

FIGURE 18
Comparing Bases
Many bases are made of positive ions combined with hydroxide ions.

FIGURE 19
Acids in Solution
Strong acids and weak acids act differently in water. Hydrochloric acid (left) is a strong acid. Acetic acid (right) is a weak acid.

**Strong Acid
(Hydrochloric Acid)**

**Weak Acid
(Acetic Acid)**

Key

Chloride ion (Cl^-)

Hydrogen ion (H^+)

Acetic acid ($HC_2H_3O_2$)

Acetate ion ($C_2H_3O_2^-$)

In a solution of a strong acid, all the acid molecules break up into ions.

In a solution of a weak acid, fewer molecules break up into ions.

Lab zone · Try This Activity

pH Predictions

1. Select materials such as fruit juices, soda water, coffee, tea, and antacids. If the sample is solid, dissolve some in a cup of water. Use a liquid as is.

2. Use what you already know to predict which materials are acidic or basic.

3. Using a plastic dropper, transfer a drop of one sample onto a fresh strip of pH paper.

4. Compare the color of the strip to the pH scale on the package.

5. Repeat for all your samples, rinsing the dropper between tests.

Interpreting Data List the samples from lowest to highest pH. Did any results surprise you?

Strength of Acids and Bases

Acids and bases may be strong or weak. Strength refers to how well an acid or a base produces ions in water. As shown in Figure 19, the molecules of a strong acid react to form ions in solution. With a weak acid, very few ions form in solution. At the same concentration, a strong acid produces more hydrogen ions (H^+) than a weak acid does. Examples of strong acids include hydrochloric acid, sulfuric acid, and nitric acid. Most other acids, such as acetic acid, are weak acids.

Strong bases react in a water solution in a similar way to strong acids. A strong base produces more hydroxide ions (OH^-) than does an equal concentration of a weak base. Ammonia is a weak base. Lye, or sodium hydroxide, is a strong base.

Measuring pH Knowing the concentration of hydrogen ions is the key to knowing how acidic or basic a solution is. To describe the concentration of ions, chemists use a numeric scale called pH. The **pH scale** is a range of values from 0 to 14. It expresses the concentration of hydrogen ions in a solution.

Figure 20 shows the pH scale and some common items. Notice that the most acidic items are at the low end of the scale. A pH lower than 7 is acidic. The most basic items are at the high end of the scale. A pH higher than 7 is basic. If the pH is 7, the solution is **neutral**. That means it's neither an acid nor a base. Pure water has a pH of 7.

A low pH indicates that the concentration of hydrogen ions is big. In contrast, a high pH indicates that the concentration of hydrogen ions is low. If you keep these ideas in mind, you can make sense of how the scale works.

You can find the pH of a solution using indicators. The student in Figure 20 is using pH paper. pH paper turns a different color for each pH value. Matching the color of the paper with the colors on the test scale indicates how acidic or basic the solution is.

You can also use an indicator solution to find the pH of a solution. Some indicator solutions will change color over the entire pH scale. Other indicator solutions only change color within a range of approximately two pH units. Knowing the pH range over which this color change occurs gives you a rough estimate of pH. Most chemistry laboratories contain a pH meter. A pH meter is an electronic device that makes rapid, accurate pH measurements.

Using Acids and Bases Safely People often say that a solution is weak when they mean it is dilute. This could be a dangerous mistake! Even a dilute solution of hydrochloric acid can eat a hole in your clothing. An equal concentration of acetic acid, however, will not. In order to handle acids and bases safely, you need to know both their strength and their concentration.

Reading Checkpoint How would a weak base differ from an equal concentration of a strong base?

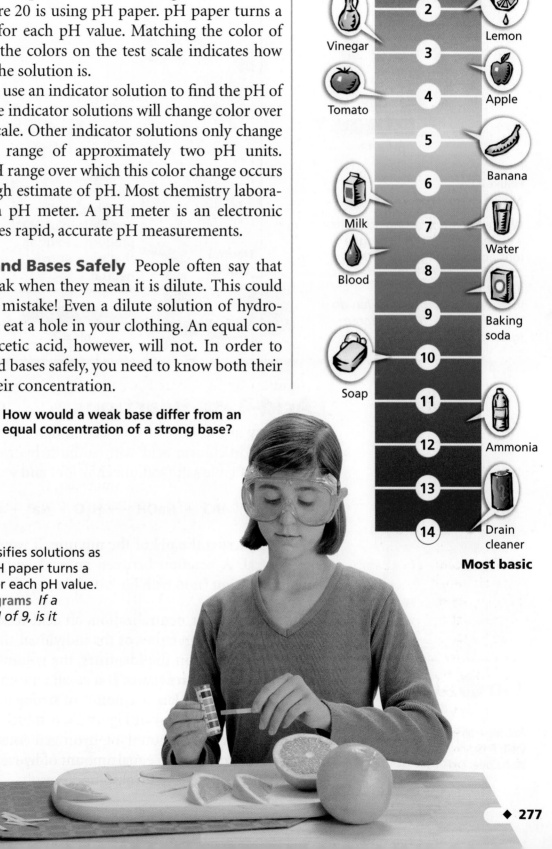

FIGURE 20
The pH Scale
The pH scale classifies solutions as acidic or basic. pH paper turns a different color for each pH value.
Interpreting Diagrams *If a solution has a pH of 9, is it acidic or basic?*

Most acidic

0
Hydrochloric acid
1
2
Lemon
Vinegar
3
4
Apple
Tomato
5
Banana
6
Milk
7
Water
Blood
8
9
Baking soda
10
Soap
11
Ammonia
12
13
14
Drain cleaner

Most basic

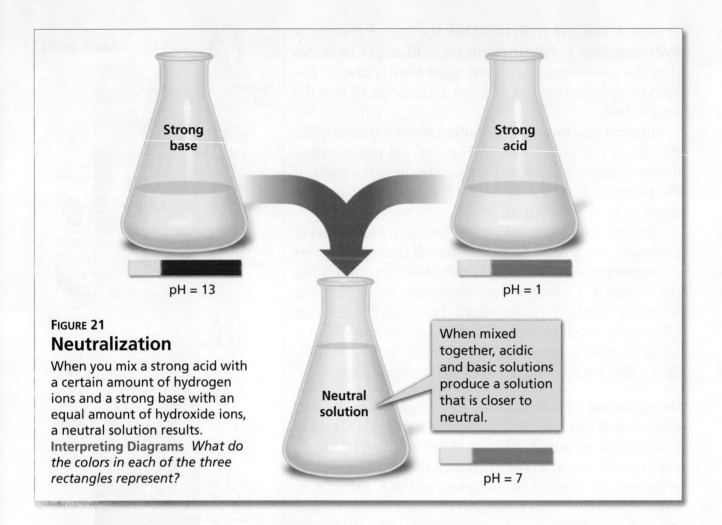

FIGURE 21
Neutralization

When you mix a strong acid with a certain amount of hydrogen ions and a strong base with an equal amount of hydroxide ions, a neutral solution results.
Interpreting Diagrams *What do the colors in each of the three rectangles represent?*

Strong base — pH = 13

Strong acid — pH = 1

Neutral solution — pH = 7

When mixed together, acidic and basic solutions produce a solution that is closer to neutral.

Go Online
PHSchool.com

For: More on pH scale
Visit: PHSchool.com
Web Code: cgd-2034

Acid-Base Reactions

The story at the start of this section describes a chemist who mixed hydrochloric acid with sodium hydroxide. She got a solution of table salt (sodium chloride) and water.

$$HCl \ + \ NaOH \longrightarrow H_2O \ + \ Na^+ + \ Cl^-$$

If you tested the pH of the mixture, it would be close to 7, or neutral. A reaction between an acid and a base is called **neutralization** (noo truh lih ZAY shun).

Reactants After neutralization, an acid-base mixture is less acidic or basic than either of the individual starting solutions. The pH depends on the identities, the volumes, and the concentrations of the reactants. If a small amount of strong base reacts with a much larger amount of strong acid, the solution will remain acidic. Look at Figure 21. A solution of strong acid contains a certain amount of hydrogen ions. A solution of strong base contains an equal amount of hydroxide ions. If you mix them together, a neutral solution results.

Products "Salt" may be the familiar name of the stuff you sprinkle on food. But to a chemist, the word refers to a specific group of compounds. A **salt** is any ionic compound that can be made from the neutralization of an acid with a base. A salt is made from the positive ion of a base and the negative ion of an acid.

Look at the equation for the reaction of nitric acid with potassium hydroxide:

$$HNO_3 + KOH \longrightarrow H_2O + K^+ + NO_3^-$$

One product of the reaction is water. The other product is potassium nitrate (KNO_3), a salt. ⬤ **In a neutralization reaction, an acid reacts with a base to produce a salt and water.** Potassium nitrate is written in the equation as separate K^+ and NO_3^- ions because it is soluble in water. Some salts, such as potassium nitrate, are soluble. Others form precipitates because they are insoluble. Look at the table in Figure 22 to see a list of some common salts and their formulas.

Common Salts	
Salt	**Uses**
Sodium chloride $NaCl$	Food flavoring; food preservative
Potassium iodide KI	Additive in "iodized" salt that prevents iodine deficiency
Calcium chloride $CaCl_2$	De-icer for roads and walkways
Potassium chloride KCl	Salt substitute in foods
Calcium carbonate $CaCO_3$	Found in limestone and seashells
Ammonium nitrate NH_4NO_3	Fertilizer; active ingredient in cold packs

FIGURE 22
Each salt listed in this table can be formed by the reaction between an acid and a base.

✓ **Reading Checkpoint** What is a salt?

Section 4 Assessment

S 8.5.e, E-LA: Reading 8.2.0

⟳ **Target Reading Skill** Create Outlines Complete your outline for Strength of Acids and Bases. Use your outline to help answer the following questions.

⬤ **Reviewing Key Concepts**

1. a. **Identifying** Which element is found in all the acids described in this section?
   b. **Describing** What kinds of ions do acids and bases form in water?
   c. **Predicting** What ions will the acid HNO_3 form when dissolved in water?

2. a. **Reviewing** What does a substance's pH tell you?
   b. **Comparing and Contrasting** If a solution has a pH of 6, would the solution contain more or fewer hydrogen ions (H^+) than an equal volume of solution with a pH of 3?
   c. **Making Generalizations** Would a dilute solution of HCl also be weak? Explain.

3. a. **Reviewing** What are the reactants of a neutralization reaction?
   b. **Explaining** What happens in a neutralization reaction?
   c. **Problem Solving** What acid reacts with KOH to produce the salt KCl?

Lab zone At-Home **Activity**

pH Lineup With a family member, search your house and refrigerator for the items found on the pH scale shown in Figure 20. Line up what you are able to find in order of increasing pH. Then ask your family member to guess why you ordered the substances in this way. Use the lineup to explain what pH means and how it is measured.

Consumer Lab

The Antacid Test

S 8.5.e, 8.9.c

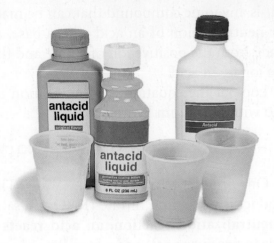

Problem

Which antacid neutralizes stomach acid with the smallest number of drops?

Skills Focus

designing experiments, interpreting data, measuring

Materials

- 3 plastic droppers • small plastic cups
- dilute hydrochloric acid (HCl), 50 mL
- methyl orange solution, 1 mL
- liquid antacid, 30 mL of each brand tested

Procedure

PART 1

1. Using a plastic dropper, put 10 drops of hydrochloric acid (HCl) into one cup.
   CAUTION: *HCl is corrosive. Rinse spills and splashes immediately with water.*

2. Use another plastic dropper to put 10 drops of liquid antacid into another cup.

3. In your notebook, make a data table like the one below. Record the colors of the HCl and the antacid.

Data Table		
Substance	Original Color	Color With Indicator
Hydrochloric Acid		
Antacid Brand A		
Antacid Brand B		

4. Add 2 drops of methyl orange solution to each cup. Record the colors you see.

5. Test each of the other antacids. Discard all the solutions and cups as directed by your teacher.

PART 2

6. Methyl orange is an indicator solution that changes color at a pH of about 4. Predict the color of the solution you expect to see when an antacid is added to a mixture of methyl orange and HCl.

7. Design a procedure for testing the reaction of each antacid with HCl. Decide how many drops of acid and methyl orange you need to use each time.

8. Devise a plan for adding the antacid so that you can detect when a change occurs. Decide how much antacid to add each time and how to mix the solutions to be sure the indicator is giving accurate results.

9. Make a second data table to record your observations.

10. Carry out your procedure and record your results.

11. Discard the solutions and cups as directed by your teacher. Rinse the plastic droppers thoroughly.

12. Wash your hands thoroughly when done.

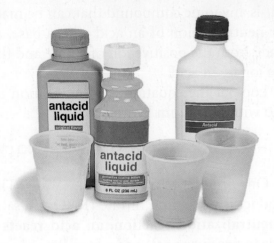

Analyze and Conclude

1. **Designing Experiments** What is the function of the methyl orange solution?

2. **Interpreting Data** Do your observations support your predictions from Step 6? Explain why or why not.

3. **Inferring** Why do you think antacids reduce stomach acid? Explain your answer, using the observations you made.

4. **Controlling Variables** What variables are controlled? Why? What are the manipulated and responding variables?

5. **Measuring** Which antacid neutralized the HCl with the smallest number of drops? Give a possible explanation for the difference.

6. **Calculating** If you have the same volume (number of drops) of each antacid, which one can neutralize the most acid?

7. **Drawing Conclusions** Did your procedure give results from which you could draw conclusions about which brand of antacid was most effective? Explain why or why not.

8. **Communicating** Write a brochure that explains to consumers what information they need to know in order to decide which brand of antacid is the best buy.

Design an Experiment

A company that sells a liquid antacid claims that its product works faster than tablets to neutralize stomach acid. Design an experiment to compare how quickly liquid antacids and chewable antacid tablets neutralize hydrochloric acid. *Obtain your teacher's permission before carrying out your investigation.*

The BIG Idea

Acids taste sour, turn blue litmus paper red, and produce hydrogen ions (H⁺) in water. Bases taste bitter, turn red litmus paper blue, and produce hydroxide ions (OH⁻) in water.

1 Understanding Solutions

Key Concepts   S 8.5.d

- A solution has the same properties throughout. It contains solute particles that are too small to see.

- A colloid contains larger particles than a solution. The particles are still too small to be seen easily, but are large enough to scatter a light beam.

- A suspension does not have the same properties throughout. It contains visible particles that are larger than the particles in solutions or colloids.

- When a solution forms, particles of the solvent surround and separate the particles of the solute.

- Solutes lower the freezing point and raise the boiling point of a solvent.

Key Terms
solution
solvent
solute
colloid
suspension

2 Concentration and Solubility

Key Concepts   S 8.5.d

- To measure concentration, you compare the amount of solute to the amount of solvent or to the total amount of solution.

- You can identify a substance by its solubility because it is a characteristic property of matter.

- Factors that affect the solubility of a substance include pressure, the type of solvent, and temperature.

Key Terms
dilute solution
concentrated solution
solubility
saturated solution
unsaturated solution
supersaturated solution

3 Describing Acids and Bases

Key Concepts   S 8.5.e

- An acid tastes sour, reacts with metals and carbonates, and turns blue litmus paper red.

- A base tastes bitter, feels slippery, and turns red litmus paper blue.

- Acids and bases have many uses around the home and in industry.

Key Terms
acid
corrosive
indicator
base

4 Acids and Bases in Solution

Key Concepts   S 8.5.e

- An acid produces hydrogen ions (H⁺) in water.

- A base produces hydroxide ions (OH⁻) in water.

- A low pH tells you that the concentration of hydrogen ions is high. In contrast, a high pH tells you that the concentration of hydrogen ions is low.

- In a neutralization reaction, an acid reacts with a base to produce a salt and water.

Key Terms
hydrogen ion (H^+)
hydroxide ion (OH^-)
pH scale
neutral
neutralization
salt

Review and Assessment

Go Online
PHSchool.com

For: Self-Assessment
Visit: PHSchool.com
Web Code: cxa-2070

Target Reading Skill

Create Outlines To help review Section 3, copy the incomplete outline for the section. Complete the outline by adding subtopics and details. Be sure to include Key Concepts and Key Terms.

Describing Acids and Bases
I. Properties of acids
A. Taste sour
B. React with metals
C.
D.
II. Properties of bases

Reviewing Key Terms

Choose the letter of the best answer.

1. Sugar water is an example of a
   a. suspension.
   b. solution.
   c. solute.
   d. colloid.

2. A solution in which more solute may be dissolved at a given temperature is a(n)
   a. neutral solution.
   b. unsaturated solution.
   c. supersaturated solution.
   d. saturated solution.

3. A compound that changes color when it contacts an acid or a base is called a(n)
   a. solute.
   b. solvent.
   c. indicator.
   d. salt.

4. A polyatomic ion made of hydrogen and oxygen is called a
   a. hydroxide ion.
   b. hydrogen ion.
   c. salt.
   d. base.

5. Ammonia is an example of a(n)
   a. acid.
   b. salt.
   c. base.
   d. antacid.

Complete the following sentences so that your answers clearly explain the Key Terms.

6. A **solution** is a mixture that contains _____ .

7. Pepper and water make a **suspension** because _____ .

8. An **acid** is a substance that tastes sour, reacts with metals and carbonates, and _____ .

9. Soap is an example of a **base** because _____ .

10. Litmus is an example of an **indicator** because _____ .

Writing in Science

Product Label Suppose you are a marketing executive for a maple syrup company. Write a description of the main ingredients of maple syrup that can be pasted on the syrup's container. Use what you've learned about concentration to explain how dilute tree sap becomes sweet, thick syrup.

Video Assessment
Discovery Channel School
Acids, Bases, and Solutions

Review and Assessment

Checking Concepts

11. Explain how you can tell the difference between a solution and a clear colloid.

12. Describe at least two differences between a dilute solution and a concentrated solution of sugar water.

13. Tomatoes are acidic. Predict two properties of tomato juice that you would be able to observe.

14. Explain how an indicator helps you distinguish between an acid and a base.

15. Give an example of a very acidic pH value.

16. What combination of acid and base can be used to make the salt sodium chloride?

Thinking Critically

17. Applying Concepts A scuba diver can be endangered by "the bends." Explain how the effects of pressure on the solubility of gases is related to this condition.

18. Relating Cause and Effect If you leave a glass of cold tap water on a table, sometime later you may see tiny bubbles of gas form in the water. Explain what causes these bubbles to appear.

19. Drawing Conclusions You have two clear liquids. One turns blue litmus paper red and one turns red litmus paper blue. If you mix them and retest with both litmus papers, no color changes occur. Describe the reaction that took place when the liquids were mixed.

20. Comparing and Contrasting Compare the types of particles formed in a water solution of an acid with those formed in a water solution of a base.

21. Problem Solving Fill in the missing salt product in the reaction below.

$$HCl + KOH \longrightarrow H_2O + \underline{\ ?\ }$$

22. Predicting What ions are formed when the base CaO is dissolved in water?

Math Practice

23. Calculating a Concentration If you have 1,000 grams of a 10-percent solution of sugar water, how much sugar is dissolved in the solution?

24. Calculating a Concentration The concentration of an alcohol and water solution is 25 percent alcohol by volume. What is the volume of alcohol in 200 mL of the solution?

Applying Skills

Use the diagram to answer Questions 25–28.

The diagram below shows the particles of an unknown acid in a water solution.

Water

Acid

25. Interpreting Diagrams How can you tell that the solution contains a weak acid?

26. Inferring Which shapes in the diagram represent ions?

27. Making Models Suppose another unknown acid is a strong acid. Make a diagram to show the particles of this acid dissolved in water.

28. Drawing Conclusions Explain how the pH of a strong acid compares with the pH of a weak acid of the same concentration.

Lab zone Standards Investigation

Performance Assessment Demonstrate the indicators you prepared. For each indicator, list the substances you tested in order from most acidic to least acidic. Would you use the same materials if you did this investigation again? Explain.

CALIFORNIA Standards Practice

Choose the letter of the best answer.

1. A scientist observes that an unknown solution turns blue litmus paper red and reacts with zinc to produce hydrogen gas. The unknown solution is most likely
  A a colloid.
  B an acid.
  C a base.
  D a suspension.   **S 8.5.e**

2. Which of the following pH values indicates a solution with the highest concentration of hydrogen ions?
  A pH = 1
  B pH = 2
  C pH = 7
  D pH = 14   **S 8.5.e**

3. A base is defined as strong if it has a pH value in the range of
  A 0-3.
  B 4-7.
  C 8-11.
  D 12-14.   **S 8.5.e**

4. Dissolving salt in water is an example of a physical change because
  A neither of the substances changes into a new substance.
  B the salt cannot be separated from the water.
  C the water cannot become saturated with salt.
  D a physical change occurs whenever a substance is mixed with water.   **S 8.5.d**

5. Which of the following things could be used to determine whether a substance is an acid or a base?
  A pH paper
  B litmus paper
  C pH meter
  D all of the above   **S 8.5.e**

Use the graph below and your knowledge of science to answer Question 6.

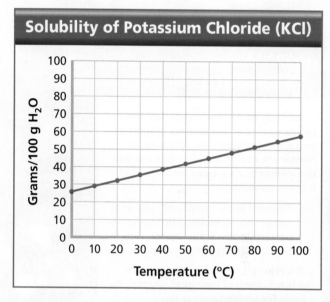

Solubility of Potassium Chloride (KCl)

6. A student makes a saturated solution of KCl and 100 g of water at 20°C. If the student leaves the solution and all of the water evaporates, how many grams of KCl will be left in the container?
  A 0 g
  B 16 g
  C 32 g
  D 40 g   **S 8.5.d**

7. Which of the following is an example of a base?
  A tomatoes
  B lemons
  C vitamin C
  D soap   **S 8.5.e**

Apply the BIG Idea

8. You have an unknown solution. You want to know whether the solution is an acid or a base. First list some of the known properties of acids and bases. Then describe a method of determining whether the solution is an acid or a base.   **S 8.5.e**

Carbon Chemistry

Butterflies, flowers, and all other living things contain carbon compounds. ▶

S 8.6.a

Focus on the
BIG Idea

Why does carbon have a central role in the chemistry of living organisms?

Check What You Know

Natural gas contains mostly methane (CH_4), a compound made of carbon and hydrogen. When methane burns, is energy absorbed or released? How do you know?

Build Science Vocabulary

The images shown here represent some of the key terms in this chapter. You can use this vocabulary skill to help you understand the meaning of some key terms in this chapter.

Use Clues to Determine Meaning

Science textbooks often contain unfamiliar words. When you are reading, use clues to figure out what these words mean. First, look for clues in the word itself. Then look at the surrounding words, sentences, and paragraphs. Look at the clues to determine the meaning of *nanotube* in the following paragraph.

Unfamiliar word → In 1991, scientists made another form of carbon— the nanotube. A **nanotube** is a form of carbon in which atoms are arranged in the shape of a long, hollow cylinder or tube. ← **Definition** Only a few nanometers wide in diameter, nanotubes are tiny, light, flexible, and extremely strong. They also are good conductors of electricity and heat.

Additional information

Apply It!

Review the clues to the meaning of *nanotube*. Then answer the following questions.

1. What is the definition of *nanotube*?
2. What additional information helps you understand nanotubes?

As you come across other unfamiliar words in the chapter, look for clues to unlock their meaning.

polymer

composite

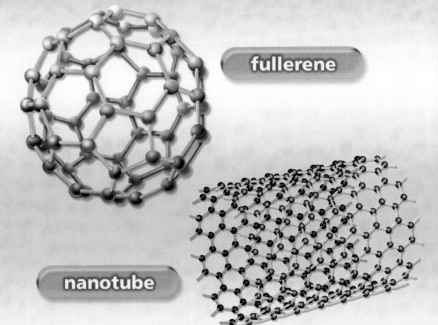

fullerene

nanotube

glucose

Section 1 (page 292)

diamond   fullerene

graphite   nanotube

. . . .

Section 2 (page 296)

organic compound

hydrocarbon

structural formula

isomer

saturated hydrocarbon

unsaturated hydrocarbon

substituted hydrocarbon

hydroxyl group

alcohol

organic acid

carboxyl group

ester

polymer

monomer

. . . .

Section 3 (page 306)

protein   plastic

amino acid   composite

. . . .

Section 4 (page 316)

carbohydrate

glucose

complex carbohydrate

starch

cellulose

lipid

fatty acid

cholesterol

nucleic acid

DNA

RNA

nucleotide

Interactive Textbook

Build Science Vocabulary
Online
Visit: PHSchool.com
Web Code: cxj-2080

How to Read Science

Reading Skill

Compare and Contrast

Science texts often make comparisons. When you compare and contrast, you examine the similarities and differences between things. When you are comparing two things, you can use a Venn diagram. Follow these steps to set up a Venn diagram.

- Draw two overlapping circles and label the two things being compared.

- Write the similarities in the center section, where the circles overlap.

- Write the differences in the outside parts of the circles.

In this chapter, you will learn about four forms of the element carbon. Look at the Venn diagram below comparing two forms—graphite and diamond.

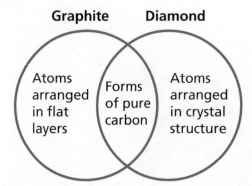

Apply It!

Review the Venn diagram and answer the following questions.

1. What things are being compared in the diagram?

2. In what way are graphite and diamond different?

In your notebook, copy and add to the Venn diagram above after you read Section 1. After you read Section 2, create a Venn diagram comparing types of hydrocarbons.

Standards **Investigation**

S 8.6.c

Check Out the Fine Print

All the foods you eat and drink contain carbon compounds. In this investigation, you will look closely at the labels on food packages to find carbon compounds.

Your Goal

To identify carbon compounds found in different foods

To complete the investigation you must

- collect at least a dozen labels with lists of ingredients and nutrition facts
- identify the carbon compounds listed, as well as substances that do not contain carbon
- interpret the nutrition facts on labels to compare amounts of substances in each food
- classify compounds in foods into the categories of polymers found in living things

Plan It!

Brainstorm with your classmates about what kinds of packaged foods you want to examine. After your teacher approves your plan, start collecting and studying food labels.

1 Properties of Carbon

S 8.6.a Students know that carbon, because of its ability to combine in many ways with itself and other elements, has a central role in the chemistry of living organisms.

- Why does carbon play a central role in the chemistry of living organisms?
- What are four forms of pure carbon?

Key Terms

- diamond
- graphite
- fullerene
- nanotube

Lab zone Standards Warm-Up

Why Do Pencils Write?

1. Tear paper into two pieces about 5 cm by 5 cm. Rub the two pieces back and forth between your fingers.
2. Now rub pencil lead (graphite) on one side of each piece of paper. Try to get as much graphite as possible on the paper.
3. Rub together the two sides covered with graphite.
4. When you are finished, wash your hands.

Think It Over

Observing Did you notice a difference between what you observed in Step 3 and what you observed in Step 1? How could the property of graphite that you observed be useful for purposes other than writing?

Open your mouth and say "aah." Uh-oh, you have a small cavity. Do you know what happens next? Your tooth needs a filling. But first the dentist's drill clears away the decayed part of your tooth.

Why is a dentist's drill hard enough and sharp enough to cut through teeth? The answer has to do with the element carbon. The tip of the drill is covered with diamond chips. Diamond is a form of carbon and the hardest substance on Earth. Because the drill tip is made of diamonds, a dentist's drill stays sharp and useful. To understand why diamond is such a hard substance, you need to take a close look at the carbon atom and the bonds it forms.

FIGURE 1
Uses of Carbon
This colorized photo shows the tip of a dentist's drill (yellow). The tip is made of diamond and is strong enough to bore into a tooth (blue).

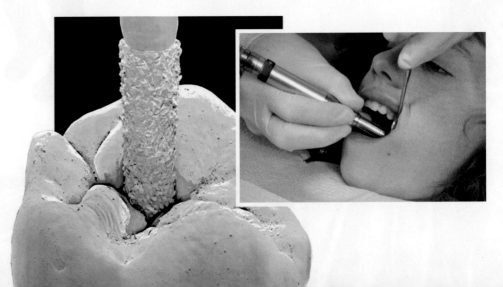

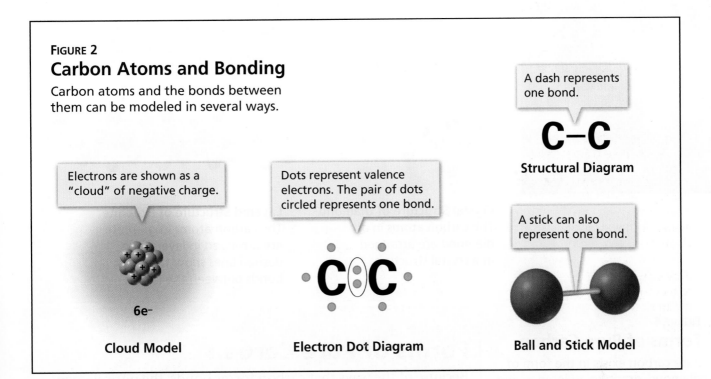

FIGURE 2
Carbon Atoms and Bonding
Carbon atoms and the bonds between them can be modeled in several ways.

Electrons are shown as a "cloud" of negative charge.

6e⁻

Cloud Model

Dots represent valence electrons. The pair of dots circled represents one bond.

Electron Dot Diagram

A dash represents one bond.

C–C

Structural Diagram

A stick can also represent one bond.

Ball and Stick Model

Carbon Atoms and Bonding

Recall that the atomic number of carbon is 6, which means that the nucleus of a carbon atom contains 6 protons. Surrounding the nucleus are 6 electrons. Of these electrons, four are valence electrons—the electrons available for bonding.

As you have learned, a chemical bond is the force that holds two atoms together. A bond between two atoms results from changes involving the atoms' valence electrons. Atoms gain, lose, or share valence electrons in a way that makes the atoms more stable. A carbon atom can share its valence electrons with other atoms, forming covalent bonds. Figure 2 shows ways that covalent bonds between atoms may be represented.

👄 **Because of its unique ability to combine in many ways with itself and other elements, carbon has a central role in the chemistry of living organisms.** With four valence electrons, each carbon atom is able to form four bonds. So, it is possible to form molecules made of thousands of carbon atoms. By comparison, hydrogen, oxygen, and nitrogen can form only one, two, or three bonds, respectively, and cannot form such long chains.

As you can see in Figure 3, it is possible to arrange the same number of carbon atoms in different ways. Carbon atoms can form straight chains, branched chains, and rings.

 **Reading Checkpoint** What happens to a carbon atom's valence electrons when it bonds to other atoms?

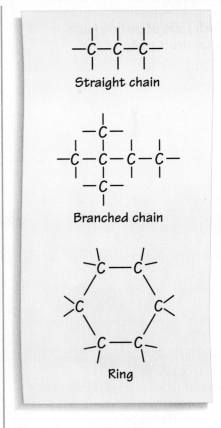

Straight chain

Branched chain

Ring

FIGURE 3
Arrangements of Carbon Atoms
Carbon chains and rings form the backbones for molecules that may contain other atoms.

Crystal Structure of Diamond
The carbon atoms in a diamond are arranged in a crystal structure.

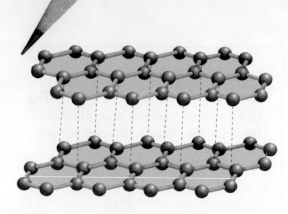

Layered Structure of Graphite
The carbon atoms in graphite are arranged in layers. The dashed lines show the weak bonds between the layers.

FIGURE 4
Forms of Pure Carbon
Pure carbon exists in the form of diamond, graphite, fullerenes, and nanotubes. The properties of each form result from the unique repeating pattern of its carbon atoms. **Interpreting Diagrams** *Which form of carbon has a crystal structure?*

Forms of Pure Carbon

Because of the ways that carbon forms bonds, the pure element can exist in different forms. **Diamond, graphite, fullerenes, and nanotubes are four forms of the element carbon.**

Diamond At very high temperatures and pressures, carbon atoms can form diamonds. **Diamond** is a crystalline form of carbon in which each carbon atom is bonded strongly to four other carbon atoms. The result is a solid that is extremely hard and nonreactive. The melting point of diamond is more than 3,500°C—as hot as the surface temperatures of some stars.

Diamonds are prized for their brilliance and clarity when cut as gems. Industrial chemists are able to make diamonds artificially, but these diamonds are not considered beautiful enough to use as gems. Both natural and artificial diamonds are used in industry. Diamonds work well in cutting tools, such as drills.

Graphite Another form of the element carbon is graphite. In **graphite**, each carbon atom is bonded tightly to three other carbon atoms in flat layers. However, the bonds between atoms in different layers are very weak, so the layers slide past one another easily.

The "lead" in a lead pencil is mostly graphite. If you run your fingers over pencil marks, you can feel how slippery graphite is. Because it is so slippery, graphite makes an excellent lubricant in machines. Graphite reduces friction between the moving parts. In your home, you might use a graphite spray to help a key work better in a sticky lock.

 **Reading Checkpoint** Why is diamond such a hard and nonreactive substance?

Spherical Structure of a Fullerene
The carbon atoms in a fullerene form a sphere that resembles a geodesic dome.

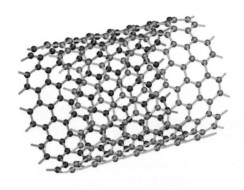

Cylindrical Structure of a Nanotube
The carbon atoms in a nanotube are arranged in a cylinder.

Fullerenes and Nanotubes In 1985, scientists made a new form of carbon. It consists of carbon atoms arranged in the shape of a hollow sphere. This form of carbon was named a **fullerene** (FUL ur een), for the architect Buckminster Fuller, who designed dome-shaped buildings called geodesic domes. One type of fullerene has been nicknamed "buckyballs."

In 1991, yet another form of carbon was made—the nanotube. In a **nanotube,** carbon atoms are arranged in the shape of a long, hollow cylinder—something like a sheet of graphite rolled into a tube. Only a few nanometers wide in diameter, nanotubes are tiny, light, flexible, and extremely strong. Nanotubes are also good conductors of electricity and heat.

Scientists are looking for ways to use the unique properties of fullerenes and nanotubes. For example, chemists are studying how fullerenes and nanotubes may be used to deliver medicine molecules into cells. Nanotubes may also be used as conductors in electronic devices and as super-strong cables.

Go Online
active art

For: Carbon Bonding activity
Visit: PHSchool.com
Web Code: cgp-2041

Section ⓵ Assessment

S 8.6.a, E-LA: Reading 8.2.0, Writing 8.2.0

↻ **Target Reading Skill** Compare and Contrast Complete your Venn diagram comparing diamond and graphite. What other differences did you add?

⚷ **Reviewing Key Concepts**

1. a. **Identifying** How many bonds can a carbon atom form?
   b. **Explaining** Why is carbon unique among the elements?
2. a. **Listing** List the four forms of pure carbon.

b. **Describing** Describe the carbon bonds in graphite.
c. **Relating Cause and Effect** How do the differences in carbon bonds explain why graphite and diamonds have different properties?

Writing in Science

Explanation Draw electron dot diagrams for a straight carbon chain and a branched chain. Then, write an explanation of what you did to show how the carbons are bonded.

Carbon Compounds

CALIFORNIA
Standards Focus

S 8.3.c Students know atoms and molecules form solids by building up repeating patterns, such as the crystal structure of NaCl or long-chain polymers.

S 8.6.a Students know that carbon, because of its ability to combine in many ways with itself and other elements, has a central role in the chemistry of living organisms.

- What are some similar properties shared by organic compounds?
- What are some properties of hydrocarbons?
- What kind of structures and bonding do hydrocarbons have?
- What are some characteristics of substituted hydrocarbons, esters, and polymers?

Key Terms
- organic compound
- hydrocarbon
- structural formula • isomer
- saturated hydrocarbon
- unsaturated hydrocarbon
- substituted hydrocarbon
- hydroxyl group • alcohol
- organic acid • carboxyl group
- ester • polymer • monomer

Lab zone Standards **Warm-Up**

What Do You Smell?
1. Your teacher will provide you with some containers. Wave your hand toward your nose over the top of each container.
2. Try to identify each of the odors.
3. After you record what you think is in each container, compare your guesses to the actual substance.

Think It Over
Developing Hypotheses Develop a hypothesis to explain the differences between the smell of one substance and another.

Imagine that you are heading out for a day of shopping. Your first purchase is a cotton shirt. Then you go to the drug store, where you buy a bottle of shampoo and a pad of writing paper. Your next stop is a hardware store. There, you buy propane fuel for your camping stove. Your final stop is the grocery store, where you buy olive oil, cereal, meat, and vegetables.

What do all of these purchases have in common? They all are made of carbon compounds. Carbon atoms act as the backbone or skeleton for the molecules of these compounds. Carbon compounds include gases (such as propane), liquids (such as olive oil), and solids (such as cotton). Mixtures of carbon compounds are found in foods, paper, and shampoo. In fact, more than 90 percent of all known compounds contain carbon.

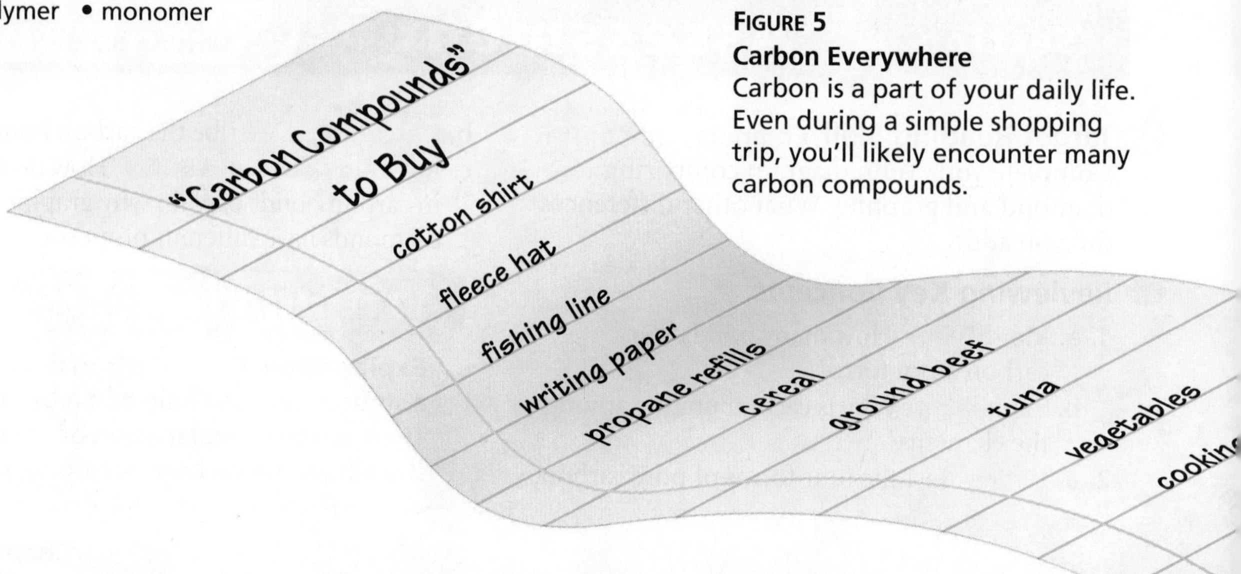

FIGURE 5
Carbon Everywhere
Carbon is a part of your daily life. Even during a simple shopping trip, you'll likely encounter many carbon compounds.

"Carbon Compounds" to Buy
cotton shirt
fleece hat
fishing line
writing paper
propane refills
cereal
ground beef
tuna
vegetables
cooking

FIGURE 6
Where Organic Compounds Are Found
These three lists represent only a few of the places where organic compounds can be found. Organic compounds are in all living things, in products from living things, and in human-made materials.

Part of Living Things
Muscle
Blood
Seeds
Leaves
Feathers
Skin

From Living Things
Wool
Cotton
Wood
Silk
Paper
Natural gas

Organic Compounds

Carbon compounds are so numerous that they are given a specific name. With some exceptions, compounds that contain carbon are called **organic compounds.** This term is used because scientists once thought that organic compounds could be produced only by living things. (The word *organic* means "of living things.") Today, however, scientists know that organic compounds also can be found in products made from living things and in materials produced artificially in laboratories and factories. Organic compounds are part of the solid matter of every organism on Earth. They are part of products that are made from organisms, such as paper made from the wood of trees. Plastics, fuels, cleaning solutions, and many other such products also contain organic compounds. The raw materials for most manufactured organic compounds come from petroleum, or crude oil.

Produced Artificially
Gasoline
Fleece
Plastics
Shampoo
Detergent
Cosmetics

🔑 **Many organic compounds have similar properties in terms of melting points, boiling points, odor, electrical conductivity, and solubility.** Many organic compounds have low melting points and low boiling points. As a result, they are liquids or gases at room temperature. Organic liquids generally have strong odors. They also do not conduct electric current. Many organic compounds do not dissolve in water. You may have seen vegetable oil, which is a mixture of organic compounds, form a separate layer in a bottle of salad dressing.

✓ **Reading Checkpoint** What is an organic compound?

ar

milk

plastic wrap

aspirin

hand cream

Hydrocarbons

Scientists classify organic compounds into different categories. The simplest organic compounds are the hydrocarbons. A **hydrocarbon** (HY droh KAHR bun) is a compound that contains only the elements carbon and hydrogen.

You might already recognize several common hydrocarbons. Methane, the main gas in natural gas, is used to heat homes. Propane is used in portable stoves and gas grills and to provide heat for hot-air balloons. Butane is the fuel in most lighters. Gasoline is a mixture of several different hydrocarbons.

Properties of Hydrocarbons Have you ever been at a gas station after a rainstorm? If so, you may have noticed a thin rainbow-colored film of gasoline or oil floating on a puddle, like the one in Figure 7. ⟐ **Like many other organic compounds, hydrocarbons mix poorly with water. Also, all hydrocarbons are flammable.** Being flammable means that they burn easily. When hydrocarbons burn, they release a great deal of energy. For this reason, they are used as fuel for stoves, heaters, cars, buses, and airplanes.

Chemical Formulas of Hydrocarbons Hydrocarbon compounds differ in the number of carbon and hydrogen atoms in each molecule. You can write a chemical formula to show how many atoms of each element makes up a molecule of a specific hydrocarbon. Recall that a chemical formula includes the chemical symbols of the elements in a compound. For molecular compounds, a chemical formula also shows the number of atoms of each element in a molecule.

FIGURE 7
Hydrocarbons
Hydrocarbons contain only the elements carbon and hydrogen. From the fuel that heats the air in hot-air balloons (above) to multicolored oil slicks (right), hydrocarbons are all around you. Making Generalizations *What properties of hydrocarbons do the hot-air balloon and oil slick demonstrate?*

The simplest hydrocarbon is methane. Its chemical formula is CH_4. The number 4 indicates the number of hydrogen atoms (H). Notice that the 4 is a subscript. Subscripts are written lower and smaller than the letter symbols of the elements. The symbol for carbon (C) in the formula is written without a subscript. This means that there is one carbon atom in the molecule.

A hydrocarbon with two carbon atoms is ethane (C_2H_6). An ethane molecule is made of two carbon atoms and six hydrogen atoms. A hydrocarbon with three carbon atoms is propane (C_3H_8).

Structure of Hydrocarbons

The properties of hydrocarbon compounds are related to the compound's structure. **The carbon chains in a hydrocarbon may be straight, branched, or ring-shaped.** If a hydrocarbon has two or more carbon atoms, the atoms can form a single line, that is, a straight chain. In hydrocarbons with four or more carbon atoms, it is possible to have branched arrangements of the carbon atoms as well as straight chains.

Structural Formulas To show how atoms are arranged in the molecules of a compound, chemists use a structural formula. A **structural formula** shows the kind, number, and arrangement of atoms in a molecule.

Figure 8 shows the structural formulas for molecules of methane, ethane, and propane. Each dash (—) represents a bond. In methane, each carbon atom is bonded to four hydrogen atoms. In ethane and propane, each carbon atom is bonded to at least one carbon atom as well as to hydrogen atoms. As you look at structural formulas, notice that every carbon atom forms four bonds. Every hydrogen atom forms one bond. There are never any dangling bonds. In other words, both ends of a dash are always connected to something.

 Reading Checkpoint **What is a structural formula?**

FIGURE 8
Structural Formulas
Each carbon atom in these structural formulas is surrounded by four dashes representing four bonds. **Interpreting Diagrams** *In propane, how many hydrogen atoms is each carbon bonded to?*

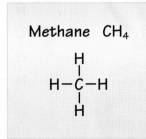

Methane CH_4

$$
\begin{array}{c}
\text{H} \\
| \\
\text{H}-\text{C}-\text{H} \\
| \\
\text{H}
\end{array}
$$

Ethane C_2H_6

$$
\begin{array}{cc}
\text{H} & \text{H} \\
| & | \\
\text{H}-\text{C}-\text{C}-\text{H} \\
| & | \\
\text{H} & \text{H}
\end{array}
$$

Propane C_3H_8

$$
\begin{array}{ccc}
\text{H} & \text{H} & \text{H} \\
| & | & | \\
\text{H}-\text{C}-\text{C}-\text{C}-\text{H} \\
| & | & | \\
\text{H} & \text{H} & \text{H}
\end{array}
$$

Math ▶ Analyzing Data

Boiling Points of Hydrocarbons

The graph shows the boiling points of several hydrocarbons. Use the graph to answer the following questions.

1. **Reading Graphs** Where is 0°C on the graph?

2. **Interpreting Data** What is the approximate boiling point of C_3H_8? C_5H_{12}? C_6H_{14}?

3. **Calculating** What is the temperature difference between the boiling points of C_3H_8 and C_5H_{12}?

4. **Drawing Conclusions** At room temperature (about 22°C), which of the hydrocarbons are gases? How can you tell?

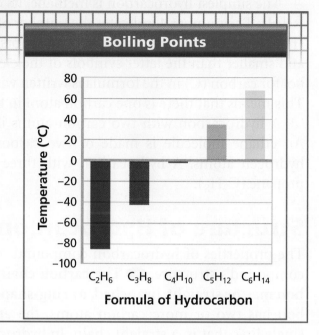

Boiling Points

Temperature (°C) vs. Formula of Hydrocarbon: C_2H_6 C_3H_8 C_4H_{10} C_5H_{12} C_6H_{14}

Isomers Consider the chemical formula of butane: C_4H_{10}. This formula does not indicate how the atoms are arranged in the molecule. In fact, there are two different ways to arrange the carbon atoms in C_4H_{10}. These two arrangements are shown in Figure 9. Compounds that have the same chemical formula but different structural formulas are called **isomers** (EYE soh murz). Each isomer is a different substance with its own characteristic properties.

Notice in Figure 9 that a molecule of one isomer, butane, is a straight chain. A molecule of the other isomer, isobutane, is a branched chain. Both molecules have 4 carbon atoms and 10 hydrogen atoms, but the atoms are arranged differently in the two molecules. And these two compounds have different properties. For example, butane and isobutane have different melting points and boiling points.

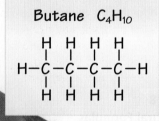

Butane C_4H_{10}

FIGURE 9
Isomers
C_4H_{10} has two isomers, butane and isobutane.
Applying Concepts *Which isomer is a branched chain?*

Isobutane C_4H_{10}

Double Bonds and Triple Bonds So far in this section, structural formulas have shown only single bonds between any two carbon atoms (C—C). A single dash means a single bond. ⊙ **In addition to forming a single bond, two carbon atoms can form a double bond or a triple bond.** A carbon atom can also form a single or double bond with an oxygen atom. Structural formulas represent a double bond with a double dash (C=C). A triple bond is indicated by a triple dash (C≡C).

Saturated and Unsaturated Hydrocarbons A hydrocarbon can be classified according to the types of bonds between its carbon atoms. If there are only single bonds, it has the maximum number of hydrogen atoms possible on its carbon chain. These hydrocarbons are called **saturated hydrocarbons**. You can think of each carbon atom as being "saturated," or filled up, with hydrogens. Hydrocarbons with double or triple bonds have fewer hydrogen atoms for each carbon atom than a saturated hydrocarbon does. They are called **unsaturated hydrocarbons**.

Notice that the names of methane, ethane, propane, and butane all end with the suffix -ane. In general, a chain hydrocarbon with a name ending in -ane is saturated, while a hydrocarbon with a name ending in -ene or -yne is unsaturated.

The simplest unsaturated hydrocarbon with one double bond is ethene (C_2H_4). Many fruits produce ethene gas. Ethene gas helps the fruit to ripen. The simplest hydrocarbon with one triple bond is ethyne (C_2H_2), which is commonly known as acetylene. Acetylene torches are used in welding.

> **Reading Checkpoint** What is the difference between saturated and unsaturated hydrocarbons?

Lab zone Skills Activity

Classifying

Determine whether each of the following hydrocarbons contains single, double, or triple bonds? (*Hint:* Remember that carbon forms four bonds and hydrogen forms one bond.)

C_2H_6	C_3H_8
C_2H_4	C_3H_4
C_2H_2	C_4H_{10}

FIGURE 10
Unsaturated Hydrocarbons
Ethene gas (C_2H_4), which causes fruits such as apples to ripen, has one double bond. Acetylene (C_2H_2), the fuel in welding torches, has one triple bond.

Ethene C_2H_4

H—C=C—H

Acetylene (Ethyne) C_2H_2

H—C≡C—H

FIGURE 11
Alcohol
Methanol is used for de-icing an airplane in cold weather.
Classifying *What makes methanol a substituted hydrocarbon?*

Substituted Hydrocarbons

Hydrocarbons contain only carbon and hydrogen. But carbon can form stable bonds with several other elements, including oxygen, nitrogen, sulfur, and members of the halogen family. **If just one atom of another element is substituted for a hydrogen atom in a hydrocarbon, a different compound is created.** In a **substituted hydrocarbon,** atoms of other elements replace one or more hydrogen atoms in a hydrocarbon. Substituted hydrocarbons include halogen-containing compounds, alcohols, and organic acids.

Compounds Containing Halogens In some substituted hydrocarbons, one or more halogen atoms replace hydrogen atoms. Recall that the halogen family includes fluorine, chlorine, bromine, and iodine.

One compound, Freon (CCl_2F_2), was widely used as a cooling liquid in refrigerators and air conditioners. When Freon was found to damage the environment, its use was banned in the United States. However, a very hazardous compound that contains halogens, trichloroethane ($C_2H_3Cl_3$), is still used in dry-cleaning solutions. It can cause severe health problems.

Alcohols The group —OH can also substitute for hydrogen atoms in a hydrocarbon. Each —OH, made of an oxygen atom and a hydrogen atom, is called a **hydroxyl group** (hy DRAHKS il). An **alcohol** is a substituted hydrocarbon that contains one or more hydroxyl groups.

Most alcohols dissolve well in water. They also have higher boiling points than hydrocarbons with a similar number of carbons. Therefore, the alcohol methanol (CH_3OH) is a liquid at room temperature, while the hydrocarbon methane (CH_4) is a gas. Methanol, which is extremely toxic, is used to make plastics and synthetic fibers. It is also used in solutions that remove ice from airplanes.

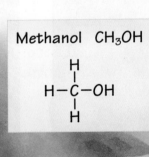

Methanol CH_3OH

$$H-\overset{\displaystyle \overset{H}{|}}{\underset{\displaystyle \underset{H}{|}}{C}}-OH$$

Formic acid   HCOOH

$$\underset{H-\overset{O}{\overset{\|}{C}}-OH}{}$$

FIGURE 12
Organic Acid
Formic acid is the simplest organic acid. It is the acid produced by ants and is responsible for the pain caused by an ant bite.

When a hydroxyl group is substituted for one hydrogen atom in ethane, the resulting alcohol is ethanol (C_2H_5OH). Ethanol is produced naturally by the action of yeast or bacteria on the sugar stored in corn, wheat, and barley. Ethanol is a good solvent for many organic compounds that do not dissolve in water. It is also added to gasoline to make a fuel for car engines called "gasohol." Ethanol is used in medicines and is found in alcoholic beverages. The ethanol used for industrial purposes is unsafe to drink. Poisonous compounds such as methanol have been added. The resulting poisonous mixture is called denatured alcohol.

Organic Acids Lemons, oranges, and grapefruits taste a little tart or sour, don't they? The sour taste of many fruits comes from citric acid, an organic acid. An **organic acid** is a substituted hydrocarbon that contains one or more carboxyl groups. A **carboxyl group** (kahr BAHKS il) is written as —COOH.

You can find organic acids in many foods. Acetic acid (CH_3COOH) is the main ingredient of vinegar. Malic acid is found in apples. Butyric acid makes butter smell rancid when it goes bad. Stinging nettle plants make formic acid (HCOOH), a compound that causes the stinging feeling. The pain from ant bites also comes from formic acid.

Esters

If you have eaten wintergreen candy, then you are familiar with the smell of an ester. An **ester** is a compound made by chemically combining an alcohol and an organic acid. ● **Many esters have pleasant, fruity smells.** Esters are responsible for the smells of pineapples, bananas, strawberries, and apples. If you did the Standards Warm-Up activity, you smelled different esters. Other esters are ingredients in medications, including aspirin and the local anesthetic used by dentists.

FIGURE 13
Esters
Strawberries contain esters, which give them a pleasant aroma and flavor.

FIGURE 14
Monomers and Polymers
This chain of plastic beads is somewhat like a polymer molecule. The individual beads are like the monomers that link together to build a polymer.
Comparing and Contrasting *How do polymers differ from monomers?*

Polymers

A very large molecule made of a chain of many smaller molecules bonded together is called a **polymer** (PAHL ih mur). The smaller molecules are called **monomers** (MAHN uh murz). The prefix *poly-* means "many," and the prefix *mono-* means "one." ⚫ **Organic compounds, such as alcohols, esters, and others, can be linked together to build polymers with thousands or even millions of atoms.**

Some polymers are made by living things. For example, sheep grow coats of wool. Cotton fibers come from the seed pods of cotton plants. And silkworms make silk. Other polymers, called synthetic polymers, are made in factories. If you are wearing clothing made from polyester or nylon, you are wearing a synthetic polymer. Any plastic item you use is most certainly made of synthetic polymers.

Reading Checkpoint What is a monomer?

Section 2 Assessment

S 8.3.c, 8.6.a,
E-LA: Reading 8.2.0

Target Reading Skill Compare and Contrast
Create a Venn diagram comparing saturated and unsaturated hydrocarbons. How are they similar? How are they different?

Reviewing Key Concepts

1. **a. Listing** List properties common to many organic compounds.
   b. Applying Concepts You are given two solid materials, one that is organic and one that is not organic. Describe three tests you could perform to help you decide which is which.
2. **a. Identifying** What are some properties of hydrocarbons?
   b. Comparing and Contrasting How are hydrocarbons similar? How are they different?
3. **a. Reviewing** What are three kinds of carbon chains found in hydrocarbons?
   b. Describing Compare the chemical and structural formulas of butane and isobutane.

c. Problem Solving Draw a structural formula for a compound called butene. In terms of bonding, how does butene differ from butane?

4. **a. Defining** What is a substituted hydrocarbon?
   b. Classifying What kinds of substituted hydrocarbons react to form an ester?
   c. Drawing Conclusions What do you think the term *polyester fabric* refers to?

Lab zone **At-Home Activity**

Mix It Up You can make a simple salad dressing to demonstrate one property of organic compounds. In a transparent container, thoroughly mix equal amounts of a vegetable oil and a fruit juice. Stop mixing, and observe the oil and juice mixture for several minutes. Explain your observations to your family.

Lab zone Skills Lab

How Many Molecules?  S 8.6.a, 8.9

Problem

In this lab you will use gumdrops to represent atoms and toothpicks to represent bonds. How many different ways can you put the same number of carbon atoms together?

Skills Focus

making models

Materials

- toothpicks • multicolored gumdrops
- other materials supplied by your teacher

Procedure

1. You will need gumdrops of one color to represent carbon atoms and gumdrops of another color to represent hydrogen atoms. When building your models, always follow these rules:
   - Each carbon atom forms four bonds.
   - Each hydrogen atom forms one bond.
   CAUTION: *Do not eat any of the food substances in this experiment.*

2. Make a model of CH_4 (methane).

3. Now make a model of C_2H_6 (ethane).

4. Make a model of C_3H_8 (propane). Is there more than one way to arrange the atoms in propane? (*Hint:* Are there any branches in the carbon chain or are all the carbon atoms in one line?)

5. Now make a model of C_4H_{10} (butane) in which all the carbon atoms are in one line.

6. Make a second model of butane with a branched chain.

7. Compare the branched-chain model with the straight-chain model of butane. Are there other ways to arrange the atoms?

8. Predict how many different structures can be formed from C_5H_{12} (pentane).

9. Test your prediction by building as many different models of pentane as you can.

Analyze and Conclude

1. **Making Models** Did any of your models have a hydrogen atom between two carbon atoms? Why or why not?

2. **Observing** How does a branched chain differ from a straight chain?

3. **Drawing Conclusions** How many different structures have the formula C_3H_8? C_4H_{10}? C_5H_{12}? Use diagrams to explain your answers.

4. **Predicting** If you bend a straight chain of carbons, do you make a different structure? Why or why not?

5. **Communicating** Compare the information you can get from models to the information you can get from formulas like C_6H_{14}. How does using models help you understand the structure of a molecule?

More to Explore

Use a third color of gumdrops to model an oxygen atom. An oxygen atom forms two bonds. Use the rules in this lab to model as many different structures for the formula $C_4H_{10}O$ as possible.

Polymers and Composites

S 8.3.c Students know atoms and molecules form solids by building up repeating patterns, such as the crystal structure of NaCl or long-chain polymers.

S 8.6.a Students know that carbon, because of its ability to combine in many ways with itself and other elements, has a central role in the chemistry of living organisms.

- How do polymers form?
- What are composites made of?
- How can you help reduce the amount of plastic waste?

Key Terms

- protein
- amino acid
- plastic
- composite

Lab zone Standards Warm-Up

What Did You Make?

1. Look at a sample of borax solution and write down the properties you observe. Do the same with white glue.
2. Put about 2 tablespoons of borax solution into a paper cup.
3. Stir the solution as you add about 1 tablespoon of white glue.
4. After 2 minutes, record the properties of the material in the cup. Wash your hands when you are finished.

Think It Over

Observing What evidence of a chemical reaction did you observe? How did the materials change? What do you think you made?

Delectable foods and many other interesting materials surround you every day. Have you ever wondered what makes up these foods and materials? You might be surprised to learn that many are partly or wholly polymers. Recall that a polymer is a large, complex molecule built from smaller molecules joined together in a repeating pattern.

The starches in pancakes and the proteins in meats and eggs are natural polymers. Many other polymers, however, are manufactured or synthetic. These synthetic polymers include plastics and polyester and nylon clothing. Whether synthetic or natural, most polymers rely on the element carbon for their fundamental structures.

FIGURE 15
Polymers
The clothing, boots, goggles, and helmet worn by this climber are all made of polymers.

Forming Polymers

Food materials, living things, and plastic have something in common. All are made of organic compounds. Organic compounds consist of molecules that contain carbon atoms bonded to each other and to other kinds of atoms. Carbon is present in several million known compounds, and more organic compounds are being discovered or invented every day.

Carbon's Chains and Rings Carbon's unique ability to form so many compounds comes from two properties. First, carbon atoms can form four covalent bonds. Second, as you have learned, carbon atoms can bond to each other in straight and branched chains and ring-shaped groups. These structures form the "backbones" to which other atoms attach.

Hydrogen is the most common element found in compounds with carbon. Other elements include oxygen, nitrogen, phosphorus, sulfur, and the halogens—especially chlorine.

Carbon Compounds and Polymers Molecules of some organic compounds can bond together, forming larger molecules, such as polymers. Recall that the smaller molecules from which polymers are built are called monomers. ⚬— **Polymers form when chemical bonds link large numbers of monomers in a repeating pattern.** A polymer may consist of hundreds or even thousands of monomers. In organic polymers, carbon, hydrogen, nitrogen, and in some cases oxygen atoms combine to form long, repetitive, stringlike molecules.

Many polymers consist of a single kind of monomer that repeats over and over again. You could think of these monomers as linked like the identical cars of a long passenger train. In other cases, two or three monomers may join in an alternating pattern. Sometimes links between monomer chains occur, forming large webs or netlike molecules. The chemical properties of a polymer depend on the monomers from which it is made.

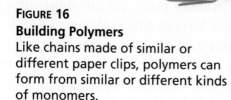

FIGURE 16
Building Polymers
Like chains made of similar or different paper clips, polymers can form from similar or different kinds of monomers.

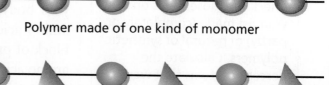

Polymer made of one kind of monomer

Polymer made of two kinds of monomers

FIGURE 17
Natural Polymers

Cellulose, the proteins in snake venom, and spider's silk are three examples of natural polymers.

▲ The cellulose in fruits and vegetables serves as dietary fiber that keeps the human digestive system healthy.

A spider's web is a silken polymer that is one of the strongest materials known. ▶

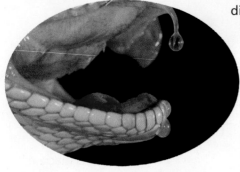

▲ Snake venom is a mixture containing approximately 90 percent proteins.

Lab zone Skills **Activity**

Calculating

Sit or stand where you have a clear view of the room you are in. Slowly sweep the room with your eyes, making a list of the objects you see. Do the same sweep of the clothes you are wearing. Check off those items on your list made (completely or partly) of natural or synthetic polymers. Calculate the percent of items that were *not* made with polymers.

Polymers and Composites

Polymers have been around as long as life on Earth. Plants, animals, and other living things produce many natural materials made of large polymer molecules.

Natural Polymers Cellulose (SEL yoo lohs) is a flexible but strong natural polymer found in the cell walls of fruits and vegetables. Cellulose is made in plants when sugar molecules are joined into long strands. Humans cannot digest cellulose. But plants also make digestible polymers called starches, formed from sugar molecules that are connected in a different way. Starches are found in pastas, breads, and many vegetables.

You can wear polymers made by animals. Silk is made from the fibers of the cocoons spun by silkworms. Wool is made from sheep's fur. These polymers can be woven into thread and cloth. Your own body makes polymers, too. For example, your fingernails and muscles are made of polymers called proteins. Within your body, **proteins** are formed from smaller molecules called amino acids. An **amino acid** is a monomer that is a building block of proteins. The properties of a protein depend on which amino acids are used and in what order. One combination builds the protein that forms your fingernails. Yet another combination forms the protein that carries oxygen in your blood.

Synthetic Polymers Many polymers you use every day are synthesized—or made—from simpler materials. The starting materials for many synthetic polymers come from coal or oil. **Plastics,** which are synthetic polymers that can be molded or shaped, are the most common products. But there are many others. Carpets, clothing, glue, and even chewing gum can be made of synthetic polymers.

Figure 18 lists just a few of the hundreds of polymers people use. Although the names seem like tongue twisters, see how many you recognize. You may be able to identify some polymers by their initials printed on the bottoms of plastic bottles.

Compare the uses of polymers shown in the figure with their characteristics. Notice that many products require materials that are flexible, yet strong. Others must be hard or lightweight. When chemical engineers develop a new product, they have to think about how it will be used. Then they synthesize a polymer with properties to match.

 **Reading Checkpoint** What are plastics?

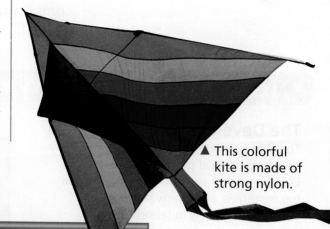

▲ This colorful kite is made of strong nylon.

Some Synthetic Polymers You Use		
Name	**Properties**	**Uses**
Low-density polyethylene (LDPE)	Flexible, soft, melts easily	Plastic bags, squeeze bottles, electric wire insulation
High-density polyethylene (HDPE)	Stronger than LDPE; higher melting temperatures	Detergent bottles, gas cans, toys, milk jugs
Polypropylene (PP)	Hard, keeps its shape	Toys, car parts, bottle caps
Polyvinyl chloride (PVC)	Tough, flexible	Garden hoses, imitation leather, plumbing pipes
Polystyrene (PS)	Lightweight, can be made into foam	Foam drinking cups, insulation, furniture, "peanut" packing material
Nylon	Strong, can be drawn into flexible thread	Stockings, parachutes, fishing line, fabric
Teflon (polytetrafluoroethylene)	Nonreactive, low friction	Nonstick coating for cooking pans

FIGURE 18
The properties of synthetic polymers make them ideal starting materials for many common objects.
Applying Concepts
Which synthetic polymer would you use to make a cover for a picnic table?

Comparing Polymers Synthetic polymers are often used in place of natural materials that are too expensive or wear out too quickly. Polyester and nylon fabrics, for example, are frequently used instead of wool, silk, and cotton to make clothes. Laminated countertops and vinyl floors replace wood in many kitchens. Other synthetic polymers have uses for which there is no suitable natural material. Compact discs, computer parts, artificial heart valves, and even bicycle tires couldn't exist without synthetic polymers.

Composites Every substance has its desirable and undesirable properties. What would happen if you could take the best properties of two substances and put them together? A **composite** combines two or more substances in a new material with different properties.

• Tech & Design in History •

The Development of Polymers
The first synthetic polymers were made by changing natural polymers in some way. Later, crude oil and coal became the starting materials. Now, new polymers are designed regularly in laboratories.

**1869
Celluloid**
Made using cellulose, celluloid became a substitute for ivory in billiard balls and combs and brushes. It was later used to make movie film. Because celluloid is very flammable, other materials have replaced it for almost all purposes.

**1839
Synthetic
Rubber**
Charles Goodyear invented a process that turned natural rubber into a hard, stretchable polymer. It did not get sticky and soft when heated or become brittle when cold, as natural rubber does. Bicycle tires were an early use.

**1909
Bakelite**
Bakelite was the first commercial polymer made from compounds in coal tar. Bakelite doesn't get soft when heated, and it doesn't conduct electricity. These properties made it useful for handles of pots and pans, for telephones, and for parts in electrical outlets.

1800   **1850**   **1900**

By combining the useful properties of two or more substances in a composite, chemists can make a new material that works better than either one alone. ◯➤ **Many composites include one or more polymers.** The idea of putting two different materials together to get the advantages of both was inspired by the natural world. Many synthetic composites are designed to imitate a common natural composite—wood.

Wood is made of long fibers of cellulose, held together by another plant polymer called lignin. Cellulose fibers are flexible and can't support much weight. Lignin is brittle and would crack under the weight of the tree branches. But the combination of the two polymers makes a strong tree trunk.

Reading Checkpoint Why is wood a composite?

Writing in Science

Research and Write Find out more about the invention of one of these polymers. Write a newspaper headline announcing the invention. Then write the first paragraph of the news report telling how the invention will change people's lives.

**1934
Nylon**
A giant breakthrough came with a synthetic fiber that imitates silk. Nylon replaced expensive silk in women's stockings and fabric for parachutes and clothing. It can also be molded to make objects like buttons, gears, and zippers.

**1971
Kevlar**
Kevlar is five times stronger than steel. Kevlar is tough enough to substitute for steel ropes and cables in offshore oil rigs but light enough to use in spacecraft parts. It is also used in protective clothing for firefighters and police officers.

**2002
Light-Emitting Polymers**
Discovered accidentally in 1990, light-emitting polymers (LEPs) are used commercially in products such as MP3 audio players and electric shavers with display screens. LEPs give off light when exposed to low-voltage electricity. Newer, more colorful LEPs may be useful as flexible monitors for computers, TV screens, and watch-sized phones.

1950   **2000**   **2050**

FIGURE 19
Synthetic Composites
The composites in the fishing rod above make it flexible so that it will not break when reeling in a fish. Fiberglass makes the snowboard at right both lightweight and strong.

Uses of Composites The idea of combining the properties of two substances to make a more useful one has led to many new products. Fiberglass composites are one example. Strands of glass fiber are woven together and strengthened with a liquid plastic that sets like glue. The combination makes a strong, hard solid that can be molded around a form to give it shape. These composites are lightweight but strong enough to be used as a boat hull or car body. Also, fiberglass will not rust as metal does.

Many other useful composites are made from strong polymers combined with lightweight ones. Bicycles, automobiles, and airplanes built from such composites are much lighter than the same vehicles built from steel or aluminum. Some composites are used to make fishing rods, tennis rackets, and other sports equipment that needs to be flexible but strong.

 **Reading Checkpoint** **What are two examples of composites?**

Recycling Plastics

You can hardly look around without seeing something made of synthetic polymers. They have replaced many natural materials for several reasons. Synthetic polymers are inexpensive to make, strong, and last a long time.

But synthetic polymers have caused some problems, too. Many of the disadvantages of using plastics come from the same properties that make them so useful. For example, it is often cheaper to throw plastics away and make new ones than it is to reuse them. As a result, plastics increase the volume of trash.

One of the reasons that plastics last so long is that most plastics don't react very easily with other substances. As a result, plastics don't break down—or degrade—into simpler materials in the environment. In contrast, natural polymers do. Some plastics are expected to last thousands of years. How do you get rid of something that lasts that long?

👈 **You can help reduce the amount of plastic waste by recycling.** When you recycle, you collect waste plastics that can be used as raw material for making new plastic products. Recycling has led to industries that create new products from discarded plastics. Bottles, fabrics for clothing, and parts for new cars are just some of the many items that can come from waste plastics. A pile of empty soda bottles can even be turned into synthetic wood. Look around your neighborhood. You may see park benches or "wooden" fences made from recycled plastics. Through recycling, the disposal problem is eased and new, useful items are created.

FIGURE 20
Recycling Plastics
Plastics can be recycled to make many useful products. This boardwalk, for example, is made of recycled plastics. *Making Judgments What advantages or disadvantages does this material have compared to wood?*

Section 3 Assessment

S 8.3.c, 8.6.a, E-LA: Reading 8.1.3, Writing 8.2.0

Vocabulary Skill Use Clues to Determine Meaning Reread the paragraphs that follow the heading Composites. What clues help you understand the meaning of the word *composite*?

🔑 Reviewing Key Concepts

1. a. **Defining** What are polymers made of?
   b. **Identifying** What properties enable carbon atoms to form polymers and so many other compounds?
   c. **Interpreting Diagrams** How do the two kinds of polymers modeled in Figure 16 differ?

2. a. **Reviewing** Distinguish between natural polymers, synthetic polymers, and composites.
   b. **Classifying** Make a list of polymers you can find in your home. Classify them as natural or synthetic.
   c. **Drawing Conclusions** Why are composites often more useful than the individual materials from which they are made?

3. a. **Listing** List two benefits and two problems associated with the use of synthetic polymers.
   b. **Explaining** What happens to waste plastics when they are recycled?
   c. **Making Judgments** Think of something plastic that you have used today. Is there some other material that would be better than plastic for this use?

Writing in Science

Advertisement You are a chemist. You invent a polymer that can be a substitute for a natural material such as wood, cotton, or leather. Write an advertisement for your polymer, explaining why you think it is a good replacement for the natural material.

S 8.3.c

Polyester Fleece

Would you go hiking in the freezing Antarctic wearing a bunch of plastic beverage bottles? If you are like most serious hikers, you would. Polyester fleece is a lightweight, warm fabric made from plastic, including recycled soda bottles. The warmth of the fabric is due to its ability to trap and hold air. Polyester fleece is easy to wash and requires less energy to dry than wool or goose down.

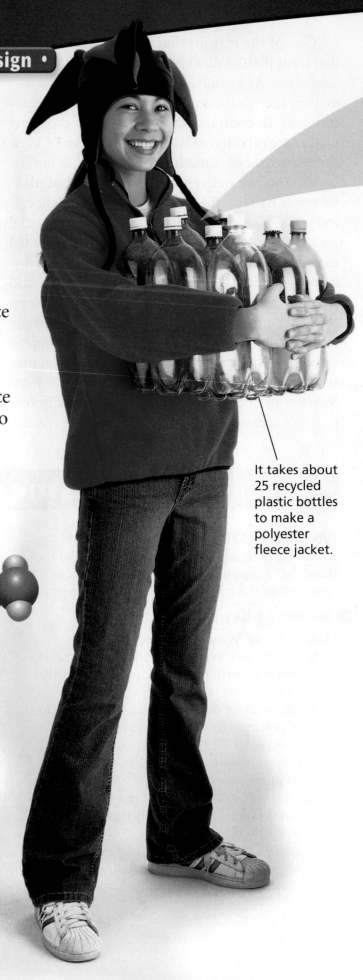

It takes about 25 recycled plastic bottles to make a polyester fleece jacket.

Molecular Model
A simplified molecular model of the polymer used to create polyester fleece is shown here. The molecules form long, straight chains.

Making Polyester Fleece

Polyethylene terephthalate, or PET, is the polymer that is used to make polyester fleece. The first step in the process is creating the polyester fiber or thread. It can be made from raw materials or recycled PET plastic. The thread is then knit into fabric, which can be dyed or printed. It is then dried and "napped." In the napping process, the fibers are first raised and then clipped to an even height. This process increases the amount of air the fabric can hold, which helps keep you warm in cold weather.

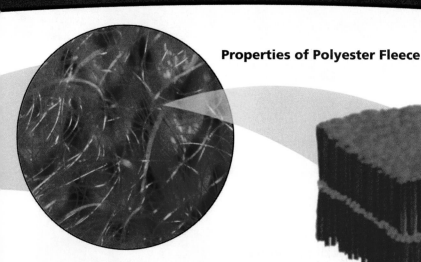

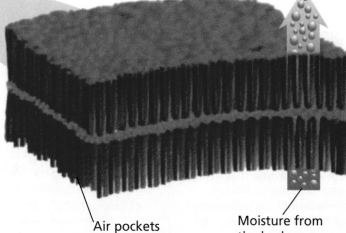

▲ **Fleece Fabric**
Similar to yarn in a sweater, fleece fibers are knit together to create a stretchy, dense fabric that is soft, lightweight, and durable.

Air pockets between fibers trap body heat.

Moisture from the body passes through the fabric.

Polyester Fleece and the Environment

Making polyester fleece fabric uses water and energy, like other fabric-making processes. Using recycled materials to create polyester fleece saves energy and reduces wastes. One trade-off involves the safety of workers in the fleece factories. The clipping process creates dust particles in the air that workers then breathe. Some companies that produce fleece are developing technology that should reduce dust in the workplace, as well as technologies that conserve and reuse energy and water.

Plastic Bottle Granules
PET plastic bottles are chipped to create granules like those shown here. The granules can be used in making polyester fleece.▼

Weigh the Impact

1. Identify the Need
What are some benefits of using polyester fleece to make clothing and blankets?

2. Research
Use the Internet to find companies that make or sell polyester fleece made from recycled plastic. Identify ways in which this form of recycling helps the environment.

3. Write
Create a pamphlet to encourage your classmates to recycle plastics. Describe how PET plastic can be used to create polyester fleece.

For: More on polyester fleece
Visit: PHSchool.com
Web Code: cgh-1040

Life With Carbon

S 8.6.b Students know that living organisms are made of molecules consisting largely of carbon, hydrogen, nitrogen, oxygen, phosphorus, and sulfur.

S 8.6.c Students know that living organisms have many different kinds of molecules, including small ones, such as water and salt, and very large ones, such as carbohydrates, fats, proteins, and DNA.

🔑 What are four classes of organic compounds required by living things, and how are they used in the body?

🔑 Why do organisms need water, vitamins, minerals, and salts?

Key Terms
- carbohydrate
- glucose
- complex carbohydrate
- starch
- cellulose
- lipid
- fatty acid
- cholesterol
- nucleic acid
- DNA
- RNA
- nucleotide

A bowl of soup contains a variety of nutrients. ▼

Lab zone Standards **Warm-Up**

What Is in Milk?

1. Pour 30 mL of milk into a plastic cup.
2. Pour another 30 mL of milk into a second plastic cup. Rinse the graduated cylinder. Measure 15 mL of vinegar and add it to the second cup. Swirl the two liquids together and let the mixture sit for a minute.
3. Set up two funnels with filter paper, each supported in a narrow plastic cup.
4. Filter the milk through the first funnel. Filter the milk and vinegar through the second funnel.
5. What is left in each filter paper? Examine the liquid that passed through each filter paper.

Think It Over

Observing Where did you see evidence of solids? What do you think was the source of these solids?

Have you ever been told to eat all the organic compounds on your plate? Have you heard how eating a variety of polymers and monomers contributes to good health? What? No one has ever said those things to you? Well, maybe what you really heard was something about eating all the vegetables on your plate, or eating a variety of foods to give you a healthy balance of carbohydrates, proteins, fats, and other nutrients. All these nutrients are organic compounds, which are the building blocks of all living things.

Foods provide organic compounds, which the cells of living things use, change, or store. ⊙ **The four classes of organic compounds required by living things are carbohydrates, proteins, lipids, and nucleic acids.** Carbohydrates, proteins, and lipids are nutrients. Nutrients (NOO tree unts) are substances that provide the energy and raw materials the body needs to grow, repair worn parts, and function properly.

Carbohydrates

A **carbohydrate** (kahr boh HY drayt) is an energy-rich organic compound made of the elements carbon, hydrogen, and oxygen. The word *carbohydrate* is made of two parts: *carbo-* and *-hydrate*. *Carbo-* means "carbon" and *-hydrate* means "combined with water." If you remember that water is made up of the elements hydrogen and oxygen, then you should be able to remember the three elements in carbohydrates.

Simple Carbohydrates The simplest carbohydrates are sugars. You may be surprised to learn that there are many different kinds of sugars. The sugar listed in baking recipes, which you can buy in bags or boxes at the grocery store, is only one kind. Other sugars are found naturally in fruits, milk, and some vegetables.

One of the most important sugars in your body is **glucose.** Its chemical formula is $C_6H_{12}O_6$. Glucose is sometimes called "blood sugar" because the body circulates glucose to all body parts through blood. The structural formula for a glucose molecule is shown in Figure 21.

The white sugar that sweetens cookies, candies, and many soft drinks is called sucrose. Sucrose is a more complex molecule than glucose and has a chemical formula of $C_{12}H_{22}O_{11}$.

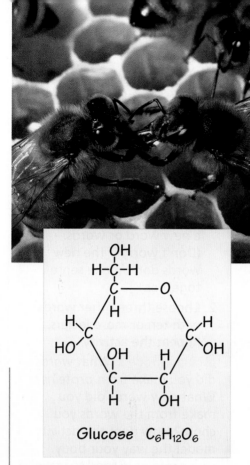

Glucose $C_6H_{12}O_6$

FIGURE 21
Carbohydrates
The honey made by honeybees contains glucose, a simple carbohydrate. **Applying Concepts** *What are some other examples of foods that contain carbohydrates?*

Try This **Activity**

Alphabet Soup
Here's how you can model the rearrangement of amino acids in your body.

1. Rearrange the letters of the word *proteins* to make a new word or words. (Don't worry if the new words don't make sense together.)
2. Choose three other words with ten or more letters. Repeat the activity.

Making Models What words did you make from *proteins*? What new words did you make from the words you chose? How does this activity model the way your body uses proteins in food to make new proteins?

FIGURE 22
Cellulose
Cellulose, found in celery and other vegetables, is a carbohydrate your body needs.

Complex Carbohydrates When you eat plants or food products made from plants, you are often eating complex carbohydrates. Each molecule of a simple carbohydrate, or sugar, is relatively small compared to a molecule of a complex carbohydrate. A **complex carbohydrate** is a polymer made of smaller molecules that are simple carbohydrates bonded to one another. As a result, just one molecule of a complex carbohydrate may have hundreds of carbon atoms.

Two of the complex carbohydrates assembled from glucose molecules are starch and cellulose. Starch and cellulose are both polymers built from glucose, but the glucose molecules are arranged differently in each case. Having different arrangements means that starch and cellulose are different compounds. They serve different functions in the plants that make them. Your body also uses starch very differently from the way it uses cellulose.

Starch Plants store energy in the form of the complex carbohydrate **starch.** You can find starches in food products such as bread, cereal, pasta, rice, and potatoes.

The process of breaking large molecules, such as starch, into smaller ones involves chemical reactions that occur during digestion. The body digests the large starch molecules from these foods into individual glucose molecules. The body then breaks apart the glucose molecules, releasing energy in the process. **The energy released by breaking down starch allows the body to carry out its life functions.**

Cellulose Plants build strong stems and roots with the complex carbohydrate **cellulose** and other polymers. Most fruits and vegetables are high in cellulose. So are foods made from whole grains. Even though the body can break down starch, it cannot break down cellulose into individual glucose molecules. Therefore the body cannot use cellulose as an energy source. In fact, when you eat foods with cellulose, the molecules pass through you undigested. However, this undigested cellulose helps keep your digestive tract active and healthy. Cellulose is sometimes called fiber.

 What foods are high in cellulose?

318 ◆

Proteins

If the proteins in your body suddenly disappeared, you would not have much of a body left! Your muscles, hair, skin, and fingernails are all made of proteins. A bird's feathers, a spider's web, a fish's scales, and the horns of a rhinoceros are also made of proteins.

Chains of Amino Acids As you have learned, proteins are polymers formed from combinations of monomers called amino acids. There are 20 kinds of amino acids found in living things. Different proteins are made when different sequences of amino acids are linked into long chains. Since proteins can be made of combinations of amino acids in any order and number, a huge variety of proteins is possible.

The structure of an amino acid is shown in Figure 23. Each amino acid molecule has a carboxyl group (—COOH). The *acid* in the term *amino acid* comes from this part of the molecule. An amino group, with the structure —NH$_2$, is the source of the *amino* half of the name. The remaining part of the molecule differs for each kind of amino acid.

Food Proteins Become Your Proteins Some of the best sources of protein include meat, fish, eggs, and milk or milk products. If you did the Discover activity, you used vinegar to separate proteins from milk. Some plant products, such as beans, are good sources of protein as well.

👄 **The body uses proteins from food to build and repair body parts and to regulate cell activities.** But first the proteins must be digested. Just as starch is broken down into glucose molecules, proteins are broken down into amino acids. Then the body reassembles those amino acids into thousands of different proteins that can be used by cells.

 **Reading Checkpoint** What are good sources of dietary protein?

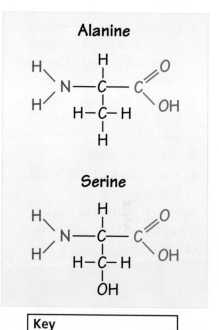

FIGURE 23
Amino Acids
Alanine and serine are two of the 20 amino acids in living things. Each amino acid has a carboxyl group (—COOH) and an amino group (—NH$_2$).

Alanine

Serine

Key

Amino group

Carboxyl group

FIGURE 24
Proteins
Your body needs proteins, which are available in fish and meat. **Drawing Conclusions** *How are amino acids related to proteins?*

Lab zone Try This **Activity**

Like Oil or Water?

Oils mix poorly with water. They also do not evaporate very quickly when exposed to air.

1. Obtain a piece of brown paper and some samples of liquids provided by your teacher.
2. Using a dropper, place one drop of liquid from each sample on the paper.
3. Wait 5 minutes.
4. Note which of the liquids leaves a spot.

Inferring Which of the liquids is a fat or oil? How can you tell?

FIGURE 25
Fats and Oils
Foods that contain fats and oils include peanut butter, butter, cheese, corn, and olives.

Lipids

The third class of organic compounds in living things is lipids. Like carbohydrates, **lipids** are energy-rich compounds made of carbon, oxygen, and hydrogen. Lipids include fats, oils, waxes, and cholesterol. **Gram for gram, lipids release twice as much energy in your body as do carbohydrates.** Like hydrocarbons, lipids mix poorly with water.

Fats and Oils Have you ever gotten grease on your clothes from foods that contain fats or oils? Fats are found in foods such as meat, butter, and cheese. Oils are found in foods such as corn, sunflower seeds, peanuts, and olives.

Fats and oils have the same basic structure. Each fat or oil is made from three **fatty acids** and one alcohol named glycerol. There is one main difference between fats and oils, however. Fats are usually solid at room temperature, whereas oils are liquid. The temperature at which a fat or an oil becomes a liquid depends on the chemical structure of its fatty acid molecules.

You may hear fats and oils described as "saturated" or "unsaturated." Like saturated hydrocarbons, the fatty acids of saturated fats have no double bonds between carbon atoms. Unsaturated fatty acids are found in oils. Monounsaturated oils have fatty acids with one double bond. Polyunsaturated oils have fatty acids with many double bonds. Saturated fats tend to have higher melting points than unsaturated oils have.

Cholesterol Another important lipid is **cholesterol** (kuh LES tuh rawl), a waxy substance found in all animal cells. The body needs cholesterol to build cell structures and to form compounds that serve as chemical messengers. Unlike other lipids, cholesterol is not a source of energy. The body produces the cholesterol it needs from other nutrients. Foods that come from animals—cheese, eggs, and meat—also provide cholesterol. Plants do not produce cholesterol.

Although cholesterol is often found in the same foods as saturated fats, they are different compounds. An excess level of cholesterol in the blood can contribute to heart disease. So can saturated fats. And saturated fats can affect the level of cholesterol in the blood. For this reason it is wise to limit your intake of both nutrients.

 Reading Checkpoint **What are sources of cholesterol in the diet?**

FIGURE 26

The Molecules of Life

Complex carbohydrates, proteins, lipids, and nucleic acids are all large organic molecules. They are built of smaller molecules linked in different patterns. Applying Concepts *What are the building blocks of proteins?*

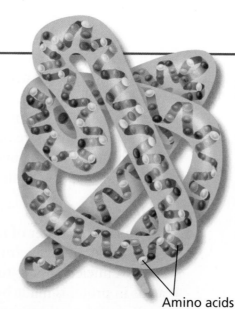

Proteins
The building blocks of proteins are amino acids. Although protein chains are never branched, each chain can twist and bend, forming complex three-dimensional shapes.

Amino acids

Starch

Cellulose

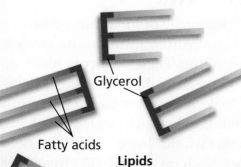

Glucose

Complex Carbohydrates
Complex carbohydrates are polymers of simple carbohydrates. Starch and cellulose, both made of glucose, differ in how their molecules are arranged.

Nucleic Acids
DNA is made from four different kinds of nucleotides. In each DNA molecule, two strands are twisted in a spiral ladder shape.

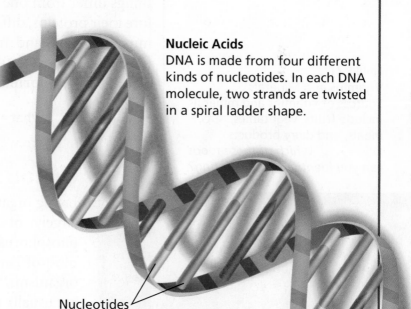

Glycerol

Fatty acids

Lipids
Each fat or oil molecule is made from one short glycerol molecule and three long fatty acids.

Nucleotides

Nucleic Acids

The fourth class of organic compounds in living things is nucleic acids. **Nucleic acids** (noo KLEE ik) are very large organic molecules made up of carbon, oxygen, hydrogen, nitrogen, and phosphorus. There are two types of nucleic acids—DNA and RNA. You have probably heard of **DNA,** or deoxyribonucleic acid (dee ahk see ry boh noo KLEE ik). **RNA** stands for ribonucleic acid (ry boh noo KLEE ik).

Video Field Trip
Discovery Channel School
Carbon Chemistry

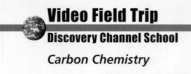

Nucleotides DNA and RNA are made of different kinds of small molecules connected in a pattern. The building blocks of nucleic acids are called **nucleotides** (NOO klee oh tydz). In even the simplest living things, the DNA contains billions of nucleotides! There are only four kinds of nucleotides in DNA. RNA is also built of only four kinds of nucleotides, but the nucleotides in RNA differ from those in DNA.

DNA and Proteins The differences among living things depend on the order of nucleotides in their DNA. The order of DNA nucleotides determines a related order in RNA. The order of RNA nucleotides, in turn, determines the sequence of amino acids in proteins made by a living cell.

Remember that proteins regulate cell activities. Living things differ from one another because their DNA, and therefore their proteins, differ from one another. The cells in a hummingbird grow and function differently from the cells in a flower or in you. **When living things reproduce, they pass DNA and the information it carries to the next generation.**

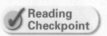

Reading Checkpoint **What are the building blocks of nucleic acids?**

FIGURE 27
Vitamins and Minerals
Sources of vitamins and minerals include fruits, vegetables, nuts, meats, and dairy products.
Observing *Which of these foods can you identify in the painting?*

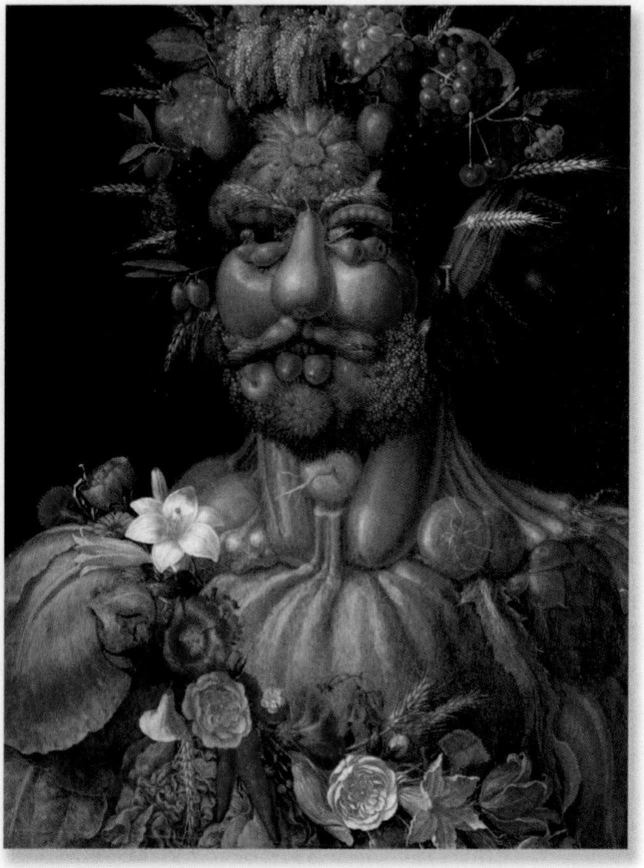

Other Nutrients

Living organisms are made of molecules consisting largely of carbon, hydrogen, nitrogen, oxygen, phosphorus, and sulfur. These elements make up most of Earth's biomass, or the total mass of living organisms. The molecules that make up organisms are usually large molecules, such as DNA, proteins, carbohydrates, and fats. But living things also need simple molecules such as water. **Organisms require water, vitamins, minerals, and salts to support the functioning of large molecules.**

Water Your body needs water to survive. Water makes up most of your body's fluids, including about 90 percent of the liquid part of your blood. Nutrients and other important substances are dissolved in the watery part of the blood and carried throughout the body. Many chemical reactions, such as the breakdown of nutrients, take place in water. Wastes from cells dissolve in the blood and are carried away.

Vitamins Vitamins are organic compounds that serve as helper molecules in a variety of chemical reactions in your body. For example, vitamin C, or ascorbic acid, is important for keeping your skin and gums healthy. Vitamin D helps your bones and teeth develop and keeps them strong.

Minerals Minerals are elements in the form of ions needed by your body. Unlike the other nutrients discussed in this chapter, minerals are not organic compounds. Minerals include calcium, iron, iodine, sodium, and potassium. They are important in many body processes.

Salts Salts are ionic compounds found in your body as dissolved ions. One important salt is sodium chloride. It supplies sodium ions, which help in the contraction of muscles and in the transmission of messages through nerves. Other salts are vital to such functions as the healthy growth of bones and teeth or keeping blood pH balanced. If you eat a variety of foods, you are more likely to get the vitamins, minerals, and salts you need. A balanced diet of fruits, vegetables, and sources of protein and calcium contains the nutrients your body uses.

Go Online
SciLINKS NSTA

For: Links on organic compounds
Visit: www.SciLinks.org
Web Code: scn-1243

Reading Checkpoint What is a vitamin?

Section 4 Assessment

S 8.6.b, 8.6.c, E-LA: Reading 8.1.3, Writing 8.2.0

Vocabulary Skill Use Clues to Determine Meaning Reread the paragraph on cholesterol under the heading Lipids. What clues help you understand the meaning of the word *cholesterol*?

Reviewing Key Concepts

1. a. **Naming** What are the four main classes of organic compounds required by living things?
   b. **Classifying** To what class of organic compounds does each of the following belong: glucose, RNA, cholesterol, cellulose, and oil?
   c. **Making Generalizations** How is each class of organic compounds used by the body?
   d. **Comparing and Contrasting** Compare the building blocks found in complex carbohydrates with those found in proteins.

2. a. **Identifying** What nutrients help support the functioning of large molecules in organisms?

b. **Explaining** Why does your body need water to survive?
c. **Comparing and Contrasting** How do vitamins and salts differ?

Writing in Science

Advertisement Collect several food advertisements from magazines and watch some TV commercials. What do the ads say about nutrients? What do they emphasize? What do they downplay? Choose one ad and rewrite it to reflect the nutritional value of the product.

Consumer **Lab**

Are You Getting Your Vitamins?

 S 8.6.c, 8.9.c

Problem

Fruit juices contain vitamin C, an important nutrient. Which juice should you drink to obtain the most vitamin C?

Skills Focus

controlling variables, interpreting data, inferring

Materials

- 6 small cups • 6 plastic droppers
- starch solution • iodine solution
- vitamin C solution
- samples of beverages (orange juice, apple juice, sports drink, fruit-flavored drink)

Procedure

PART 1 Vitamin C Test

1. Using a plastic dropper, place 25 drops of tap water into one of the small cups. Add 2 drops of starch solution.

2. Add 1 drop of iodine solution to the cup. **CAUTION:** *Iodine solution can stain skin or clothing.* Observe the color of the mixture. Save this cup to use for comparison in Step 4.

3. Using a fresh dropper, place 25 drops of vitamin C solution into another cup. Add 2 drops of starch solution.

4. Add 1 drop of iodine solution to the cup and swirl. Continue adding iodine a drop at a time, swirling after each drop, until you get a dark blue color similar to the color obtained in Step 2. Record the number of iodine drops.

5. Save the cup from Step 4 and use it for comparison during Part 2.

PART 2 Comparison Test

6. Make a data table in your notebook similar to the one on the next page.

7. Which beverage sample do you think has the most vitamin C? Which do you think has the least? Rank your beverage samples according to your predictions.

Data Table			
Test Sample	Drops of Iodine	Predicted Rank	Actual Rank
Vitamin C			
Orange juice			
Apple juice			
Sports drink			
Fruit-flavored drink			

8. Adapt the procedure from Part 1 so you can compare the amount of vitamin C in your beverage samples to the vitamin C solution.

9. Carry out your procedure after your teacher approves.

Analyze and Conclude

1. **Controlling Variables** What was the purpose for the test of the mixture of starch and water in Step 2?

2. **Controlling Variables** What was the purpose for the test of the starch, water, and vitamin C in Step 4?

3. **Drawing Conclusions** What do you think caused differences between your data from Step 2 and Step 4?

4. **Controlling Variables** Why did you have to add the same amount of starch to each of the beverages?

5. **Predicting** What would happen if someone forgot to add the starch to the beverage before they began adding iodine?

6. **Measuring** Of the four drinks you tested, which took the most drops of iodine before changing color? Which took the fewest?

7. **Interpreting Data** Which beverage had the most vitamin C? Which had the least? How do you know?

8. **Inferring** When you tested orange juice, the color of the first few drops of the iodine faded away. What do you think happened to the iodine?

9. **Communicating** If a beverage scored low in your test for vitamin C, does that mean it isn't good for you? Write a paragraph in which you explain what other factors might make a beverage nutritious or take away from its nutrient value.

Design an Experiment

Foods are often labeled with expiration dates. Labels often also say to "refrigerate after opening." Design an experiment to find out if the vitamin C content of orange juice changes over time at different temperatures. *Obtain your teacher's permission before carrying out your investigation.*

The BIG Idea

Because of its ability to combine in many ways with itself and with other elements, carbon has a central role in the chemistry of living organisms.

1 Properties of Carbon

Key Concepts
S 8.6.a

- Because of its ability to combine in many ways with itself and other elements, carbon has a central role in the chemistry of organisms.
- Diamond, graphite, fullerenes, and nanotubes are four forms of the element carbon.

Key Terms

diamond
graphite
fullerene
nanotube

2 Carbon Compounds

Key Concepts
S 8.3.c, 8.6.a

- Many organic compounds have similar properties in terms of melting points, boiling points, odor, electrical conductivity, and solubility.
- Hydrocarbons mix poorly with water. Also, all hydrocarbons are flammable.
- The carbon chains in a hydrocarbon ring may be straight, branched, or ring-shaped. In addition to forming a single bond, two carbon atoms can form a double bond or a triple bond.
- If just one atom of another element is substituted for a hydrogen atom in a hydrocarbon, a different compound is created.
- Many esters have pleasant, fruity smells.
- Organic compounds can be linked together to build polymers with thousands or even millions of atoms.

Key Terms

organic compound
hydrocarbon
structural formula
isomer
saturated
  hydrocarbon
unsaturated
  hydrocarbon

substituted
  hydrocarbon
hydroxyl group
alcohol
organic acid
carboxyl group
ester
polymer
monomer

3 Polymers and Composites

Key Concepts
S 8.3.c, 8.6.a

- Polymers form when chemical bonds link large numbers of monomers in a repeating pattern.
- Many composites include one or more polymers.
- You can help reduce the amount of plastic waste by recycling.

Key Terms

protein
amino acid
plastic
composite

4 Life With Carbon

Key Concepts
S 8.6.b, 8.6.c

- The four classes of organic compounds required by living things are carbohydrates, proteins, lipids, and nucleic acids.
- The energy released by breaking down starch allows the body to carry out its life functions.
- The body uses proteins from food to build and repair body parts and to regulate cell activities.
- Gram for gram, lipids release twice as much energy in your body as do carbohydrates.
- When living things reproduce, they pass DNA and the information it carries to the next generation.
- Organisms require water, vitamins, minerals, and salts to help support the functioning of large molecules.

Key Terms

carbohydrate
glucose
complex carbohydrate
starch
cellulose
lipid

fatty acid
cholesterol
nucleic acid
DNA
RNA
nucleotide

Review and Assessment

Target Reading Skill

Compare and Contrast In your notebook, copy the Venn diagram comparing proteins and nucleic acids. Complete the diagram and add a title.

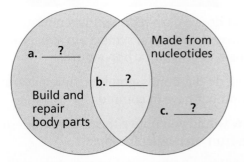

a. ___?___

Made from nucleotides

b. ___?___

Build and repair body parts

c. ___?___

Reviewing Key Terms

Choose the letter of the best answer.

1. A form of carbon in which the carbon bonds are arranged in a repeating pattern similar to a geodesic dome is
   a. a fullerene.
   b. graphite.
   c. diamond.
   d. a nanotube.

2. A compound that contains only hydrogen and carbon is defined as
   a. a monomer.
   b. an isomer.
   c. a hydrocarbon.
   d. a polymer.

3. Fiberglass is a type of
   a. polymer.
   b. alloy.
   c. ceramic.
   d. composite.

4. The smaller molecules from which cellulose is made are
   a. glucose.
   b. amino acids.
   c. nucleotides.
   d. fatty acids.

5. Cholesterol is a type of
   a. nucleic acid.
   b. carbohydrate.
   c. lipid.
   d. cellulose.

Complete the following sentences so that your answers clearly explain the key terms.

6. Methane and acetic acid are examples of **organic compounds,** which are defined as _____ .

7. Butane and isobutane are **isomers,** or compounds that _____ .

8. Fingernails and muscles are made of **proteins,** which are polymers of _____ .

9. Sucrose and starch are examples of **carbohydrates,** which are defined as _____ .

10. Glucose is considered a **monomer** because _____ .

Writing in Science

Web Site You are writing a feature article on carbon for a chemistry Web site. In your article, describe four forms of the element carbon. Include in your descriptions how the carbon atoms are arranged and how the bonds between the carbon atoms affect the properties of the substance. Include any helpful illustrations.

Video Assessment

Discovery Channel School
Carbon Chemistry

Review and Assessment

Checking Concepts

11. What does a dash represent when written between two carbon symbols in a diagram of a chain or ring of carbon atoms?

12. What do diamonds, graphite, fullerenes, and nanotubes have in common?

13. How would you notice the presence of esters in a fruit such as a pineapple?

14. Name some polymers that are produced in nature. Tell where they come from.

15. Starch and cellulose are both complex carbohydrates. How does your body treat these compounds differently?

16. Compare and contrast the fatty acids in fats that are solid at room temperature with fatty acids in oils that are liquids.

Thinking Critically

17. Relating Cause and Effect What features of the element carbon allow it to form the "backbone" of such a varied array of different compounds?

18. Applying Concepts Which of the diagrams below represents a saturated hydrocarbon? Which represents an unsaturated hydrocarbon? Explain your answer.

19. Making Judgments The plastic rings that hold beverage cans together are sometimes hazardous to living things in the ocean. Do you think companies that make soft drinks should be allowed to continue using plastic rings? Consider what could replace them.

20. Posing Questions Glucose and fructose are both simple carbohydrates with the formula $C_6H_{12}O_6$. What else do you need to know about glucose and fructose to decide if they should be considered different compounds?

Applying Skills

Use the following structural formulas to answer Questions 21–25.

21. Classifying Which type of substituted hydrocarbons are compounds A and B? What information in the structural formulas did you use to decide your answer?

22. Observing What is the correct subscript for the carbon atoms (C) in the chemical formula that corresponds to each structural formula?

23. Inferring Are compounds A and B isomers? How can you tell?

24. Predicting Would you expect these two compounds to have identical properties or different properties? Explain.

25. Problem Solving What kind of compound would result if an organic acid were chemically combined with compound A? What properties would you expect the new compound to have?

Lab zone Standards Investigation

Performance Assessment Display your data table classifying compounds in foods, along with the labels from which you collected your data. Point out the nutrients that are found in almost all foods and the nutrients found in only a few.

Choose the letter of the best answer.

1. What kind of molecule is made of a chain of many smaller molecules bonded together?
   A monomer
   B polymer
   C carboxyl group
   D amino acid   S 8.3.c

2. Living organisms are made of molecules consisting largely of the elements hydrogen, nitrogen, oxygen, phosphorus, sulfur, and
   A calcium.
   B sodium.
   C carbon.
   D iron.   S 8.6.b

3. The formula $C_5H_{11}OH$ represents an
   A amino acid.
   B organic acid.
   C alcohol.
   D ester.   S 8.6.c

4. Material X is an organic compound that mixes poorly with water and is highly flammable. Of the following choices, material X is most likely a(n)
   A carbohydrate.
   B ester.
   C alcohol.
   D hydrocarbon.   S 8.6.c

5. Which of the following is an example of a synthetic polymer?
   A cellulose
   B protein
   C nylon
   D starch   S 8.3.c

6. The smaller molecules that make up complex carbohydrates are called
   A sugars.
   B amino acids.
   C fatty acids.
   D nucleotides.   S 8.6.c

Use the structural diagrams below and your knowledge of science to answer Questions 7–9.

7. Isomers are organic compounds having the same chemical formula, but different structural formulas. Which pair of compounds are isomers?
   A 1 and 2   **B** 1 and 3
   C 2 and 3   **D** 2 and 4   S 8.6.a

8. Which structural diagram represents an unsaturated hydrocarbon?
   A 1   **B** 2
   C 3   **D** 4   S 8.6.a

9. What is the ratio of carbon atoms to hydrogen atoms in the compound represented by 1?
   A 1 to 9
   B 9 to 1
   C 3 to 6
   D 6 to 3   S 8.6.a

Apply the BIG Idea

10. Explain why carbohydrates, lipids, and proteins are important parts of a well-balanced diet.   S 8.6.c

Chemical Interactions

Unit 2 Review

Chapter 5
Atoms and Bonding
🔑 The **BIG Idea**

Atoms of different elements combine to form compounds by gaining, losing, or sharing electrons.

- 🔑 How is the reactivity of elements related to valence electrons?
- 🔑 How do ions form bonds?
- 🔑 What holds covalently bonded atoms together?
- 🔑 How do metal atoms combine?

Chapter 6
Chemical Reactions
🔑 The **BIG Idea**

Chemical reactions are processes in which atoms are rearranged into different combinations of molecules.

- 🔑 How can you tell when a chemical reaction occurs?
- 🔑 How is matter conserved during chemical reactions?
- 🔑 What factors affect the rate of a chemical reaction?
- 🔑 What are the three things necessary to maintain a fire?

Chapter 7
Solutions, Acids, and Bases
🔑 The **BIG Idea**

Acids taste sour, turn blue litmus paper red, and produce hydrogen ions (H^+) in water. Bases taste bitter, turn red litmus paper blue, and produce hydroxide ions (OH^-) in water.

- 🔑 What are the characteristics of solutions, colloids, and suspensions?
- 🔑 Why is solubility useful in identifying substances?
- 🔑 What are the properties of acids and bases?
- 🔑 What does pH tell you about a solution?

Chapter 8
Carbon Chemistry
🔑 The **BIG Idea**

Because of its ability to combine in many ways with itself and with other elements, carbon has a central role in the chemistry of living organisms.

- 🔑 What are four forms of pure carbon?
- 🔑 What are some properties shared by organic compounds?
- 🔑 What organic compounds are required by living things?

Unit 2 Assessment

Bob and Ted are cooking a meal to share with friends. For the side dish, they decide to make a potato dish using a recipe they found in a cookbook. The main ingredients for the recipe are potatoes, vinegar, and sea salt.

As Bob places the potatoes into a pot of cold water, Ted goes to the pantry and takes out the salt. Another name for salt is sodium chloride, because it is a compound made up of sodium ions and chlorine ions. Ted pours the salt into the pot and turns on the stove so that the potatoes can simmer. When raw potatoes are boiled, they become softer because the boiling breaks down the cell membranes, allowing water and carbohydrates to leave. The breaking down of the cell membranes is a chemical reaction.

After thirty minutes, Ted drains the potatoes and puts them in a bowl, while Bob gets the vinegar out of the pantry. Vinegar contains acetic acid, which gives it its sour taste. They add the vinegar and the rest of the salt to the potatoes and stir.

The last ingredient they add is olive oil. Although the oil mixes with the rest of the ingredients, no chemical reaction takes place when it is added.

1. How many valence electrons does a sodium atom have? *(Chapter 5)*
   a. 1   b. 2
   c. 7   d. 8

2. Which of the following is not a chemical reaction? *(Chapter 6)*
   a. synthesis   b. decomposition
   c. replacement   d. conservation of matter

3. Which of the following pH values would be closest to that of vinegar? *(Chapter 7)*
   a. 3   b. 7
   c. 11   d. 14

4. Which of the following is a polymer that humans can digest? *(Chapter 8)*
   a. cellulose   b. polyester
   c. starch   d. nylon

5. Summary Write a paragraph summarizing the changes that take place while the potato recipe is prepared. Which changes are chemical, and which are physical? Explain.

Motion and Energy

S 8.1 The velocity of an object is the rate of change of its position. As a basis for understanding this concept:

a. Students know position is defined in relation to some choice of a standard reference point and a set of reference directions.

b. Students know that average speed is the total distance traveled divided by the total time elapsed and that the speed of an object along the path traveled can vary.

c. Students know how to solve problems involving distance, time, and average speed.

d. Students know the velocity of an object must be described by specifying both the direction and the speed of the object.

e. Students know changes in velocity may be due to changes in speed, direction, or both.

f. Students know how to interpret graphs of position versus time and graphs of speed versus time for motion in a single direction.

S 8.9 Scientific progress is made by asking meaningful questions and conducting careful investigations. As a basis for understanding this concept and addressing the content in the other three strands, students should develop their own questions and perform investigations. Students will:

d. Recognize the slope of the linear graph as the constant in the relationship $y = kx$ and apply this principle in interpreting graphs constructed from data.

g. Distinguish between linear and nonlinear relationships on a graph of data.

The wild horses running across this ▶ meadow are in motion.

Focus on the BIG Idea

S 8.1

How can you describe an object's motion?

Check What You Know

You are in a stationary car and another car passes you. How would you describe the motion of the other car?

The images shown here represent some of the Key Terms in this chapter. You can use this vocabulary skill to help you understand the meaning of some Key Terms in this chapter.

High-Use Academic Words

Knowing these academic words will help you become a better reader in all subject areas. Look for these words in context as you read this chapter.

Word	Definition	Example Sentence
conclude (kun KLOOD) p. 339	*v.* to decide by reasoning	After investigating the evidence, they <u>concluded</u> that everyone should wear a bicycle helmet.
formula (FAWR myoo luh) p. 343	*n.* a series of numbers and symbols that represents a mathematical rule	The <u>formula</u> for the area of a circle is $A = \pi r^2$.
potential (poh TEN shul) p. 360	*adj.* the possibility that something will develop in a certain way	The student who is studying chemistry is a <u>potential</u> chemist.

Apply It!

Choose the word from the table that best completes the sentence.

1. The _____ for finding the area of a rectangle is $A = \ell \times w$.

2. After waiting for 20 minutes, he _____ that his friend was not coming.

3. The heavy rains and rising river are a _____ problem for people who live beside the river.

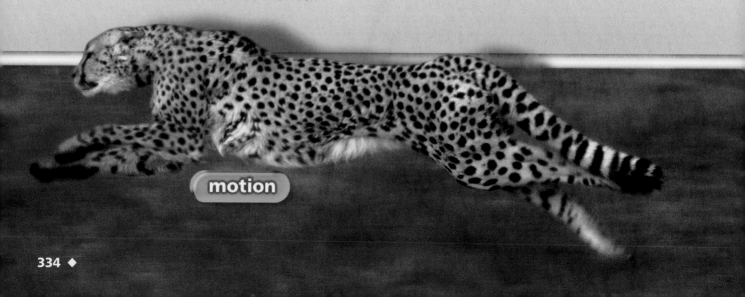

motion

acceleration

elastic potential energy

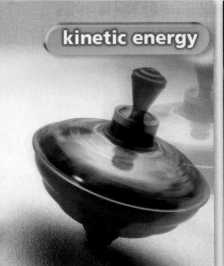

kinetic energy

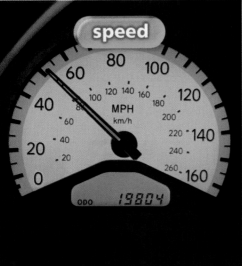

speed

Chapter 9
Vocabulary

Section 1 (page 338)
motion
reference point
distance
displacement
vector

Section 2 (page 342)
speed
average speed
instantaneous speed
velocity
slope

Section 3 (page 350)
acceleration

Section 4 (page 358)
work
energy
kinetic energy
potential energy
gravitational potential energy
elastic potential energy
mechanical energy
law of conservation of energy

interactive Textbook

Build Science Vocabulary
Online
Visit: PHSchool.com
Web Code: cxj-3090

How to Read Science

 Reading Skill

Identify Main Ideas

The main idea is the most important point in a passage of text. Sometimes the main idea is stated directly at the beginning or end of a passage. The main idea is supported by details and examples.

Here are some tips to help you identify the main idea.

- Note the details in the passage.
- Look for the connections among the supporting details.
- Then look for a sentence that pulls all the details together.

Read the paragraph below and identify the main idea and supporting details.

> A measurement of distance can tell you how far an object travels. A cyclist, for example, might travel 30 kilometers. A sprinter runs 100 meters. An ant might walk 2 centimeters.

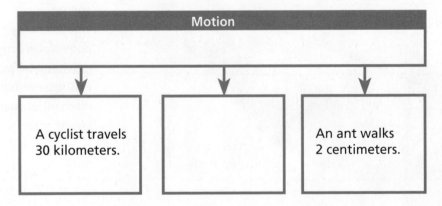

Motion

A cyclist travels 30 kilometers.

An ant walks 2 centimeters.

Apply It!

Draw a graphic organizer like the one shown. Fill in the main idea and details. Then answer the following questions.

1. What is the main idea in the paragraph?
2. What is a good title for this graphic organizer?

Complete a graphic organizer like the one above for the headings Calculating Speed in Section 2, Changing Velocity in Section 3, and Potential Energy in Section 4.

S 8.1.b, 8.1.c

Show Some Motion

You are constantly surrounded by objects in motion. Cars, trains, buses, and airplanes carry people from one place to another. Baseballs, animals, and even the planets in the sky also move. How can you measure the motion you see?

Your Goal

In this investigation, you will identify the motion of several common objects and calculate how fast each one moves.

To complete this investigation, you must

- measure distance and time accurately
- calculate the average speed of each object using your data
- prepare display cards of your data, diagrams, and calculations
- follow the safety guidelines in Appendix A

Plan It!

With your classmates, brainstorm several examples of objects in motion, such as a feather falling, your friend riding a bicycle, or the minute hand moving on a clock. Choose your examples and have your teacher approve them. Create a data table for each example and record your measurements. For accuracy, repeat your measurements. Then calculate the average speed of each object. Make display cards for each example that show data, diagrams, and calculations.

Describing Motion

CALIFORNIA
Standards Focus

S 8.1.a Students know position is defined in relation to some choice of a standard reference point and a set of reference directions.

🔑 When is an object in motion?

🔑 What is the difference between distance and displacement?

Key Terms

- motion
- reference point
- distance
- displacement
- vector

Lab zone Standards **Warm-Up**

How Fast and How Far?

1. Using a stopwatch, find out how long it takes you to walk 5 meters at a normal pace. Record your time.

2. Now choose a starting point and find out how far you can walk in 5 seconds at a normal pace. Record your distance.

3. Repeat Steps 1 and 2, walking slower than your normal pace. Then repeat Steps 1 and 2 walking faster than your normal pace.

Think It Over

Inferring What is the relationship between the distance you walk, the time it takes you to walk, and your walking speed?

How do you know if you are moving? If you've ever traveled on a train, you know you cannot always tell if you are in motion. Looking at a building outside the window helps you decide. Although the building seems to move past the train, it's you and the train that are moving.

However, sometimes you may see another train that appears to be moving. Is the other train really moving, or is your train moving? How do you tell?

Motion

How do you decide if an object is moving? You are probably sitting in a chair as you read this book. Are you moving? Your eyes blink and your chest moves up and down. But you would probably say that you are not moving. An object is in **motion** if its distance from another object is changing. Because your distance from your chair is not changing, you conclude you are not in motion.

Reference Points To decide if you are moving, you use your chair as a reference point. A **reference point** is a place or object used for comparison to determine if something is in motion. ⊶ **An object is in motion if it changes position relative to a reference point.**

Objects that we call stationary—such as a tree, a flagpole, or a building—make good reference points. From the point of view of the train passenger in Figure 1, such objects are not in motion. If the passenger is moving relative to a tree, he can conclude that the train is in motion.

Once you have selected your reference point, you can indicate a change in position by using a plus (+) or minus (−) sign. The signs stand for any pair of opposing directions from the reference point, such as to the right and left, up and down, away from and toward, or in front of and behind. If you make the passenger on the train your reference point, then three seats in front of him could be shown as +3. A distance of −5 would mean 5 seats behind him.

 **What is a reference point?**

FIGURE 1
Reference Points
The passenger can use a tree as a reference point to decide if the train is moving. A tree makes a good reference point because it is stationary from the passenger's point of view.
Applying Concepts *Why is it important to choose a stationary object as a reference point?*

FIGURE 2
Relative Motion Whether or not an object is in motion depends on the reference point.
Comparing and Contrasting *Are the skydivers moving relative to the airplane from which they jumped? Are they moving relative to the ground?*

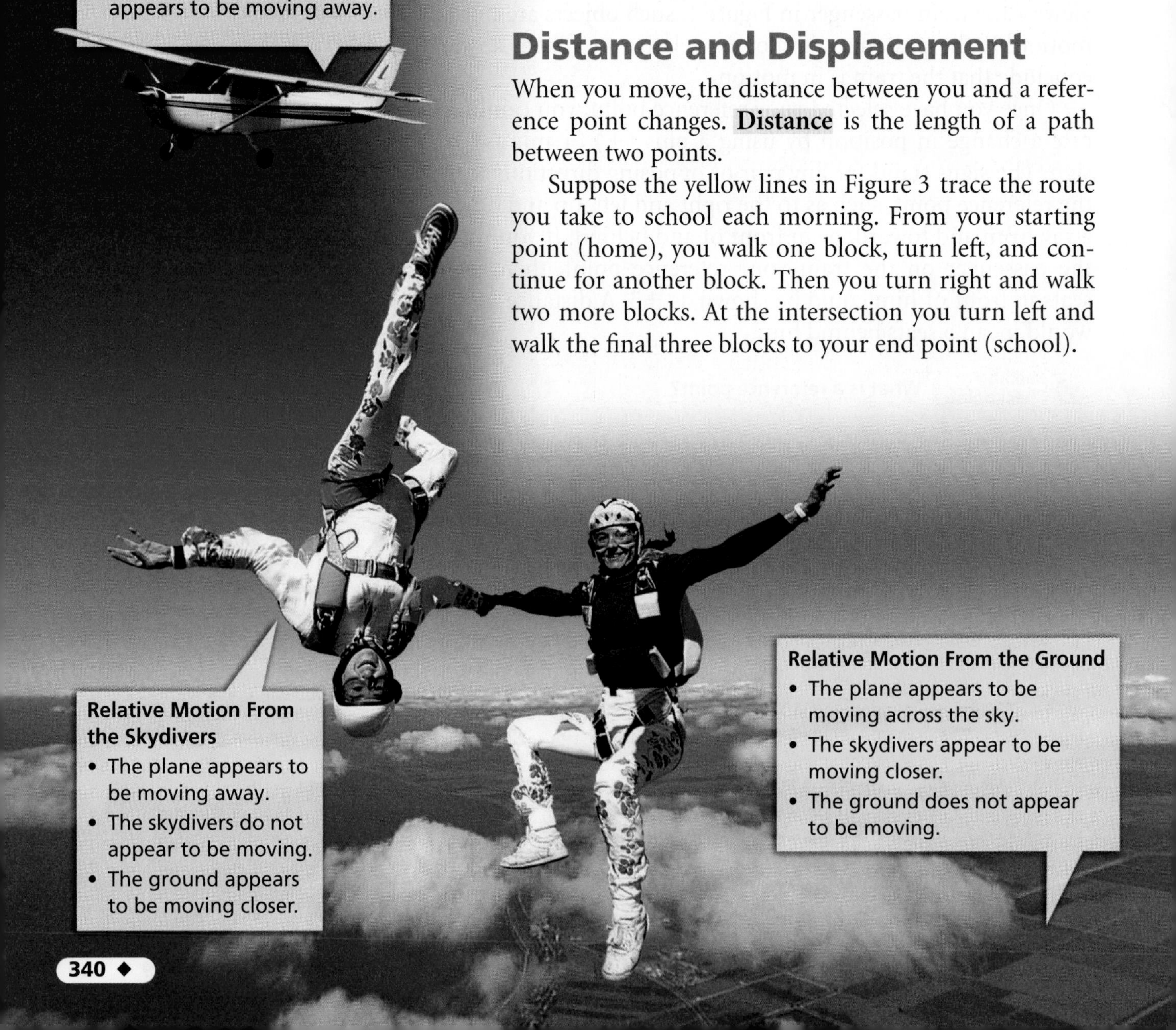

Relative Motion From the Plane
- The plane does not appear to be moving.
- The skydivers appear to be moving away.
- A point on the ground appears to be moving away.

Relative Motion From the Skydivers
- The plane appears to be moving away.
- The skydivers do not appear to be moving.
- The ground appears to be moving closer.

Relative Motion From the Ground
- The plane appears to be moving across the sky.
- The skydivers appear to be moving closer.
- The ground does not appear to be moving.

Relative Motion Are you moving as you read this book? The answer depends on your reference point. When your chair is your reference point, you are not moving. But if you choose another reference point, you may be moving.

Suppose you choose the sun as a reference point instead of your chair. If you compare yourself to the sun, you are moving quite rapidly. This is because you and your chair are on Earth, which moves around the sun. Earth moves about 30 kilometers every second. So you, your chair, this book, and everything else on Earth move that quickly as well. Going that fast, you could travel from New York City to Los Angeles in about 2 minutes! Relative to the sun, both you and your chair are in motion. But because you are moving with Earth, you do not seem to be moving.

Distance and Displacement

When you move, the distance between you and a reference point changes. **Distance** is the length of a path between two points.

Suppose the yellow lines in Figure 3 trace the route you take to school each morning. From your starting point (home), you walk one block, turn left, and continue for another block. Then you turn right and walk two more blocks. At the intersection you turn left and walk the final three blocks to your end point (school).

How many blocks did you walk in all? The lengths of the segments of your walk are 1 block, 1 block, 2 blocks, and 3 blocks. Therefore, your walk from home to school is a total distance of 7 blocks.

Now look at the red arrow in Figure 3. It shows the displacement from the starting point. **Displacement** is the length and direction that an object has moved from its starting point.

◉ **Distance is the total length of the actual path between two points. Displacement is the length and direction of a straight line between starting and ending points.** According to Figure 3, you walked a *distance* (yellow lines) of 7 blocks, but your *displacement* (red arrow) was 5 blocks northeast.

As you learn about motion, you will find other measurements that also have a magnitude, or size, and a direction. A quantity that consists of both a magnitude and a direction is called a **vector.** Displacement is a vector, but distance is not. Other examples of vectors include velocity, acceleration, and force. You will learn about these vectors later in this book.

Vectors are shown graphically by using an arrow. The length of the arrow represents the vector's magnitude. The direction of the arrow indicates the direction of the vector.

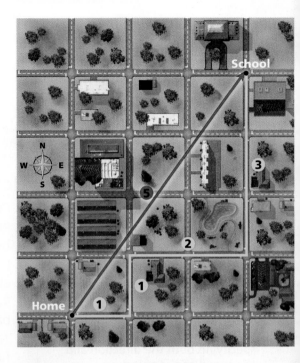

FIGURE 3
Distance and Displacement
The yellow lines show the distance between home and school along a particular path. The red arrow shows the displacement between the same two points.

 **Reading Checkpoint** What is displacement?

Section ① **Assessment**   S 8.1.a, E-LA: Reading 8.1.0

Vocabulary Skill High-Use Academic Words
Describe a situation in which you have used a reference point to determine your relative motion. Use the word *conclude* in your explanation.

◉ **Reviewing Key Concepts**

1. a. **Reviewing** How do you know if an object is moving?
   b. **Explaining** Why is it important to know if your reference point is moving?
   c. **Applying Concepts** Suppose you are riding in a car. Describe your motion relative to the car, the road, and the sun.
2. a. **Defining** What is displacement?
   b. **Comparing and Contrasting** How are distance and displacement similar? How are they different?

c. **Applying Concepts** An object moves 3 cm to the right, then 6 cm to the left, then 8 cm to the right. What is the object's final displacement from its origin?

Lab zone **At-Home Activity**

Walkabout Place a penny or other marker on the floor or ground to show your starting point. Then walk a few steps in one direction and a few more in another. Use a ruler to estimate the distance that you walked and your displacement from the starting point. How do these values compare?

Speed and Velocity

CALIFORNIA
Standards Focus

S 8.1.b Students know that average speed is the total distance traveled divided by the total time elapsed and that the speed of an object along the path traveled can vary.

S 8.1.c Students know how to solve problems involving distance, time, and average speed.

S 8.1.d Students know the velocity of an object must be described by specifying both the direction and the speed of the object.

- How do you calculate speed?
- How can you describe changes in velocity?
- How can you interpret graphs of distance versus time?

Key Terms
- speed
- average speed
- instantaneous speed
- velocity
- slope

Lab zone Standards **Warm-Up**

How Slow Can It Flow?

1. Put a spoonful of honey on a plate.
2. Place a piece of tape 4 cm from the bottom edge of the honey.
3. Lift one side of the plate just high enough that the honey starts to flow.
4. Reduce the plate's angle until the honey barely moves. Prop up the plate at this angle.
5. Time how long the honey takes to reach the tape. Predict how far the honey would move in twice the time.

Think It Over

Forming Operational Definitions When an object doesn't appear to be moving at first glance, how can you tell if it is?

A measurement of distance can tell you how far an object travels. A cyclist, for example, might travel 30 kilometers. An ant might travel 2 centimeters. If you know the distance an object travels in a certain amount of time, you can calculate the speed of the object. Speed is a type of rate. A rate tells you the amount of something that occurs or changes in one unit of time. The **speed** of an object is the distance the object travels per unit of time.

Calculating Speed

To calculate the speed of an object, divide the distance the object travels by the amount of time it takes to travel that distance. This relationship can be written as an equation.

$$\text{Speed} = \frac{\text{Distance}}{\text{Time}}$$

The speed equation consists of a unit of distance divided by a unit of time. If you measure distance in meters and time in seconds, you express speed in meters per second, or m/s. (The slash is read as "per.") If you measure distance in kilometers and time in hours, you express speed in kilometers per hour, or km/h. For example, a cyclist who travels 30 kilometers in 1 hour has a speed of 30 km/h. An ant that moves 2 centimeters in 1 second is moving at a speed of 2 centimeters per second, or 2 cm/s.

Average Speed The speed of most moving objects is not constant. The cyclists shown in Figure 4, for example, change their speeds many times during the race. They might ride at a constant speed along flat ground but move more slowly as they climb hills. Then they might move more quickly as they come down hills. Occasionally, they may stop to fix their bikes.

Although a cyclist does not have a constant speed, the cyclist does have an average speed throughout a race. To calculate **average speed** (v), divide the total distance traveled (d) by the total time (t).

For example, suppose a cyclist travels 32 kilometers during the first 2 hours. Then the cyclist travels 13 kilometers during the next hour. The average speed of the cyclist is the total distance divided by the total time.

Total distance (d) = 32 km + 13 km = 45 km

Total time (t) = 2 h + 1 h = 3 h

Average speed (v) = $\dfrac{d}{t}$ = $\dfrac{45 \text{ km}}{3 \text{ h}}$ = 15 km/h

The cyclist's average speed is 15 kilometers per hour. You can write the formula for speed $v = d/t$ as $d = vt$ or $t = d/v$. So, if you know any two of these quantities, you can calculate the third.

Instantaneous Speed Calculating the average speed of a cyclist during a race is important. However, it is also useful to know the cyclist's instantaneous speed. **Instantaneous speed** is the rate at which an object is moving at a given instant in time.

 **Reading Checkpoint** How do you calculate average speed?

FIGURE 4
Measuring Speed
Cyclists use an electronic device known as a cyclometer to track their speed over the course of their travel. A cyclometer can calculate both average and instantaneous speed.
Comparing and Contrasting *Explain why the instantaneous speed and the average speed shown below are different.*

INST. SPEED
22 km/h
AVG. SPEED
15 km/h

Velocity

Suppose you hear that a thunderstorm is traveling at a speed of 25 km/h. Should you prepare for the storm? That depends on the direction of the storm's motion.

Velocity (*v*) is speed in a given direction. Like displacement, velocity is a vector. It has both a magnitude (speed) and a direction. For example, the velocity of a storm can be described as moving 25 km/h to the east. As with all vectors, the magnitude and direction of velocity are shown by the length and the direction of an arrow. Like speed, velocity may change over time. **Changes in velocity may be due to changes in speed, changes in direction, or both.** Thus, if the storm continued to move at the same speed but changed direction, this would be a change in its velocity.

• Tech & Design in History •

The Speed of Transportation
The speed with which people can travel from one place to another has increased over the years.

1818
National Road Constructed
The speed of transportation has been limited largely by the quality of roadways. The U.S. government paid for the construction of a highway named the Cumberland Road. It ran from Cumberland, Maryland, to Wheeling, in present-day West Virginia. Travel by horse and carriage on the roadway was at a speed of about 11 km/h.

1885
Benz Tricycle Car Introduced
This odd-looking vehicle was the first internal combustion (gasoline-powered) automobile sold to the public. Although it is an ancestor of the modern automobile, its top speed was only about 15 km/h—not much faster than a horse-drawn carriage.

1908
Ford Model T Mass-Produced
Between 1908 and 1927, over 15 million of these automobiles were sold. The Model T had a top speed of 65 km/h.

1800	1850	1900

In some situations, describing the velocity of moving objects can be very important. For example, air traffic controllers must keep close track of the velocities of the aircraft under their control. These velocities continually change as airplanes move overhead and on the runways. An error in determining a velocity, either in speed or in direction, could lead to a collision.

Velocity is also important to airplane pilots. For example, stunt pilots make spectacular use of their control over the velocity of their aircrafts. To avoid colliding with other aircraft, these skilled pilots must have precise control of both their speed and direction. Stunt pilots use this control to stay in close formation while flying graceful maneuvers at high speed.

 **Reading Checkpoint** **What is velocity?**

Writing in Science

Research and Write What styles of automobile were most popular during the 1950s, 1960s, and 1970s? Were sedans, convertibles, station wagons, or sports cars the bestsellers? Choose an era and research automobiles of that time. Then write an advertisement for one particular style of car. Be sure to include information from your research.

1934 Zephyr Introduced
The first diesel passenger train in the United States was the *Zephyr*. The *Zephyr* set a long-distance record, traveling from Denver to Chicago at an average speed of 125 km/h for more than 1,600 km.

1956 Interstate Highway System Established
The passage of the Federal-Aid Highway Act established the Highway Trust Fund. This act allowed the construction of the Interstate and Defense Highways. Nonstop transcontinental auto travel became possible. Speed limits in many parts of the system were more than 100 km/h.

2003 Maglev in Motion
The first commercial application of high-speed maglev (magnetic levitation) was unveiled in Shanghai, China. During the 30-km trip from Pudong International Airport to Shanghai's financial district, the train operates at a top speed of 430 km/h, reducing commuting time from 45 minutes to just 8 minutes.

1950   2000   2050

FIGURE 5
Graphing Motion

You can use distance-versus-time graphs to interpret motion. On the jogger's first day of training, her speed is the same at every point. On the second day of training, her speed varies. **Reading Graphs** *On the first day, how far does the jogger run in 5 minutes?*

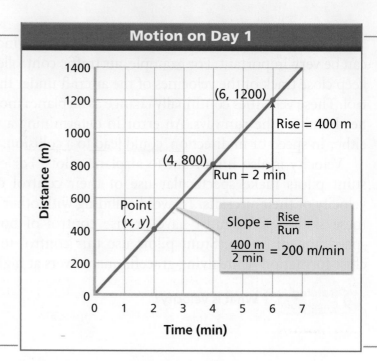

Motion on Day 1

Graphing Speed

You can show the motion of an object on a line graph in which you plot distance versus time. The graphs you see in Figure 5 are distance-versus-time graphs. Time is shown on the horizontal axis, or x-axis. Distance, or position, is shown on the vertical axis, or y-axis. A point on the line represents the distance an object has traveled from the origin or a reference point at a particular time. The x-value of the point is time, and the y-value is distance.

The steepness of a line on a graph is called **slope.** The slope tells you how fast one variable changes in relation to the other variable in the graph. In other words, slope tells you the rate of change. **The slope of a distance-versus-time graph represents speed, that is, the rate that distance changes in relation to time.** The steeper the slope is, the greater the speed. A constant slope represents motion at constant speed.

Calculating Slope You can calculate the slope of a line by dividing the rise by the run. The rise is the vertical difference between any two points on the line. The run is the horizontal difference between the same two points.

$$\text{Slope} = \frac{\text{Rise}}{\text{Run}}$$

In Figure 5, using the points shown, the rise is 400 meters and the run is 2 minutes. To find the slope, you divide 400 meters by 2 minutes. The slope is 200 meters per minute.

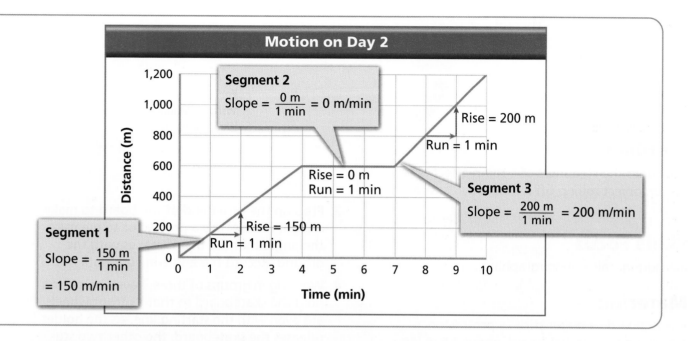

Motion on Day 2

Segment 2
Slope = $\frac{0 \text{ m}}{1 \text{ min}}$ = 0 m/min

Rise = 200 m
Run = 1 min

Rise = 0 m
Run = 1 min

Segment 3
Slope = $\frac{200 \text{ m}}{1 \text{ min}}$ = 200 m/min

Rise = 150 m
Run = 1 min

Segment 1
Slope = $\frac{150 \text{ m}}{1 \text{ min}}$
= 150 m/min

Distance (m)

Time (min)

Different Slopes Most moving objects do not travel at a constant speed. The graph above shows a jogger's motion on her second day. The line is divided into three segments. The slope of each segment is different. From the steepness of the slopes you can tell that the jogger ran the fastest during the third segment. The horizontal line in the second segment shows that the jogger's distance did not change at all.

Section 2 Assessment

S 8.1.b, 8.1.c, 8.1.d, E-LA: Reading 8.2.4, Writing 8.2.0

Target Reading Skill Identify Main Ideas
Reread the first two paragraphs under *Calculating Speed* on page 342. Draw a graphic organizer showing the main idea and supporting details. The boldfaced sentence is the main idea.

Reviewing Key Concepts

1. a. **Defining** What is speed?
   b. **Calculating** What is the average speed of a car that travels 160 km in 2 hours?
   c. **Calculating** If you walked at an average speed of 1.2 m/s, how long would it take to cross a road that is 16-m wide?

2. a. **Defining** What is velocity?
   b. **Describing** Describe the two ways in which velocity can change.
   c. **Applying Concepts** Your car's speedometer reads a constant 35 mi/hr. Can you say your velocity is constant? Explain.

3. a. **Identifying** What does the slope of a distance-versus-time graph show you about the motion of an object?
   b. **Calculating** The rise of a line on a distance-versus-time graph is 600 m and the run is 3 minutes. What is the slope of the line?

Writing in Science

Explanation Think about a recent trip that you have taken. What was the approximate total distance that you traveled and the total time it took? Calculate your average speed from this information. Then explain how your instantaneous speed varied over the course of the trip.

Lab zone Skills Lab

Inclined to Roll

S 8.1.b, S 8.9.e

For: Data sharing
Visit: PHSchool.com
Web Code: cgd-3012

Problem

How does the steepness of a ramp affect how fast an object rolling off it moves across the floor?

Skills Focus

measuring, calculating, graphing

Materials

• skateboard • meter stick • protractor
• masking tape • flat board, about 1.5 m long
• small piece of sturdy cardboard
• supports to prop up the board (books, boxes)
• two stopwatches

Procedure

1. In your notebook, make a data table like the one below. Include space for five angles.

2. Lay the board flat on the floor. Using masking tape, mark a starting line in the middle of the board. Mark a finish line on the floor 1.5 m beyond one end of the board. Place a barrier after the finish line.

3. Prop up the other end of the board to make a slight incline. Use a protractor to measure the angle that the board makes with the ground. Record the angle in your data table.

4. Working in groups of three, have one person hold the skateboard so that its front wheels are even with the starting line. As the holder releases the skateboard, the other two students should start their stopwatches.

5. One timer should stop his or her stopwatch when the front wheels of the skateboard reach the end of the incline.

6. The second timer should stop his or her stopwatch when the front wheels reach the finish line. Record the times in your data table in the columns labeled Time 1 and Time 2.

7. Repeat Steps 4–6 two more times. If your results for the three times aren't within 0.2 second of one another, carry out more trials.

Data Table							
Angle (degrees)	Trial Number	Time 1 (to bottom) (s)	Time 2 (to finish) (s)	Avg Time 1 (s)	Avg Time 2 (s)	Avg Time 2 – Avg Time 1 (s)	Avg Speed (m/s)
	1						
	2						
	3						
	1						
	2						
	3						
	1						
	2						

8. Repeat Steps 3–7 four more times, making the ramp gradually steeper each time.

9. For each angle of the incline, complete the following calculations and record them in your data table.
   a. Find the average time the skateboard takes to get to the bottom of the ramp (Time 1).
   b. Find the average time the skateboard takes to get to the finish line (Time 2).
   c. Subtract the average of Time 1 from the average of Time 2.

Analyze and Conclude

1. **Calculating** How can you find the average speed of the skateboard across the floor for each angle of the incline? Determine the average speed for each angle and record it in your data table.

2. **Classifying** Which is your manipulated variable and which is your responding variable in this experiment? Explain. (For a discussion of manipulated and responding variables, see the Skills Handbook.)

3. **Graphing** On a graph, plot the average speed of the skateboard (on the y-axis) against the angle of the ramp (on the x-axis).

4. **Drawing Conclusions** What does your graph show about the relationship between the skateboard's speed and the angle of the ramp?

5. **Measuring** If your measurements for distance, time, or angle were inaccurate, how would your results have been affected?

6. **Communicating** Do you think your method of timing was accurate? Did the timers start and stop their stopwatches exactly at the appropriate points? How could the accuracy of the timing be improved? Write a brief procedure for your method.

Design an Experiment

A truck driver transporting new cars needs to roll the cars off the truck. You offer to design a ramp to help with the task. What measurements would you make that might be useful? Design an experiment to test your ideas. Obtain your teacher's permission before carrying out your investigation.

Acceleration

CALIFORNIA
Standards Focus

S 8.1.e Students know changes in velocity may be due to changes in speed, direction, or both.

S 8.1.f Students know how to interpret graphs of position versus time and graphs of speed versus time for motion in a single direction.

- What kind of motion does acceleration refer to?
- How do you calculate acceleration?
- What graphs can be used to analyze the motion of an accelerating object?

Key Term
- acceleration

Lab zone Standards **Warm-Up**

Will You Hurry Up?

1. Measure 10 meters in an open area. Mark the distance with masking tape.
2. Walk the 10 meters in such a way that you keep moving faster throughout the entire distance. Have a partner time you.
3. Repeat Step 2, walking the 10 meters in less time than you did before. Then try it again, this time walking the distance in twice the time as the first. Remember to keep speeding up throughout the entire 10 meters.

Think It Over

Inferring How is the change in your speed related to the time in which you walk the 10-meter course?

The pitcher throws. The ball speeds toward the batter. Off the bat it goes. It's going, going, gone! A home run!

Before landing, the ball went through several changes in motion. It sped up in the pitcher's hand, and lost speed as it traveled toward the batter. The ball stopped when it hit the bat, changed direction, sped up again, and eventually slowed down. Most examples of motion involve similar changes.

Changing Velocity

Suppose you are a passenger in a car stopped at a red light. When the light changes to green, the driver steps on the accelerator. As a result, the car speeds up, or accelerates. In everyday language, *acceleration* means "the process of speeding up."

Acceleration has a more specific definition in science. Scientists define **acceleration** as the rate at which velocity changes with time. Recall that velocity describes both the speed and direction of an object. A change in velocity can involve a change in either speed or direction—or both. **In science, acceleration refers to increasing speed, decreasing speed, or changing direction.** Like displacement and velocity, acceleration is a vector with a magnitude and a direction.

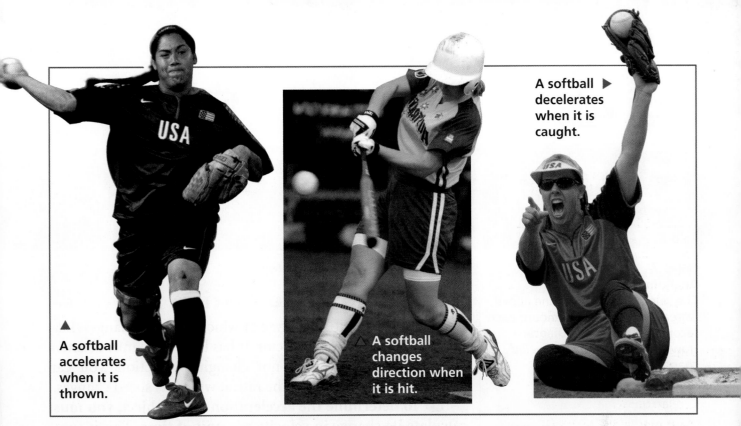

▲ A softball accelerates when it is thrown.

△ A softball changes direction when it is hit.

▶ A softball decelerates when it is caught.

FIGURE 6
Acceleration
A softball accelerates when it is thrown, caught, or hit.
Classifying *What change in motion occurs in each example?*

Increasing Speed Whenever an object's speed increases, the object accelerates. A softball accelerates when the pitcher throws it, and again when a bat hits it. A car that begins to move from a stopped position or speeds up to pass another car is accelerating. People can accelerate too. For example, you accelerate when you coast down a hill on your bike.

Decreasing Speed Just as objects can speed up, they can also slow down. This change in speed is sometimes called deceleration, or negative acceleration. For example, a softball decelerates when it lands in a fielder's mitt. A car decelerates when it stops at a red light.

Changing Direction Even an object that is traveling at a constant speed can be accelerating. Recall that acceleration can be a change in direction. Therefore, a car accelerates as it follows a curve in the road, even if its speed remains constant. Runners accelerate as they round the curve in a track. A softball accelerates when it changes direction as it is hit. Thus acceleration may be due to changes in speed, direction, or both.

Many objects continuously change direction without changing speed. The simplest example of this type of motion is circular motion, or motion along a circular path. For example, the seats on a Ferris wheel accelerate because they move in a circle.

 **Reading Checkpoint** How can a car be accelerating if its speed is constant at 65 km/h?

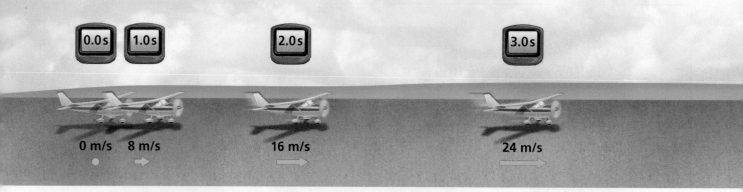

FIGURE 7
Analyzing Acceleration
The velocity of the airplane above increases by the same amount each second. **Interpreting Diagrams** *How does the distance traveled change in each second?*

Calculating Acceleration

Acceleration describes the rate at which velocity changes. Like velocity, acceleration is a vector. It has both a magnitude and a direction. If an object is not changing direction, you can describe its acceleration as the rate at which its speed changes.

To determine the acceleration of an object, you must calculate its change in velocity per unit of time. This is summarized by the following formula.

$$\text{Acceleration} = \frac{\text{Final velocity} - \text{Initial velocity}}{\text{Time}}$$

If velocity is measured in meters per second (m/s) and time is measured in seconds, the SI unit of acceleration is meters per second per second, or m/s^2. Suppose velocity is measured in kilometers per hour and time is measured in hours. Then the unit for acceleration is kilometers per hour per hour, or km/h^2.

To understand acceleration, imagine a small airplane moving down a runway in a straight line. Figure 7 shows the airplane's motion after each of the first five seconds of its acceleration. To calculate the acceleration of the airplane, you must first subtract the initial velocity of 0 m/s from the final velocity of 40 m/s. Then divide the change in velocity by the time, 5 seconds.

$$\text{Acceleration} = \frac{40 \text{ m/s} - 0 \text{ m/s}}{5 \text{ s}}$$

$$\text{Acceleration} = 8 \text{ m/s}^2$$

The airplane accelerates to the right at a rate of 8 m/s^2. This means that the airplane's velocity increases by 8 m/s every second. Notice in Figure 7 that, after each second of travel, the airplane's velocity is 8 m/s greater than it was the previous second.

Go Online
SCI LINKS NSTA

For: Links on acceleration
Visit: www.SciLinks.org
Web Code: scn-1313

 **Reading Checkpoint** What must you know about an object to calculate its acceleration?

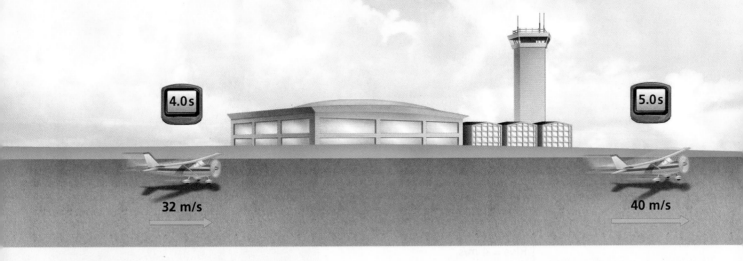

4.0 s

5.0 s

32 m/s

40 m/s

Math: Algebra I, 15.0

Math Sample Problem

Calculating Acceleration

As a roller coaster car starts down a slope, its velocity is 4 m/s. But 3 seconds later, its velocity is 22 m/s in the same direction. What is its acceleration?

1 Read and Understand
What information are you given?

    Initial velocity = 4 m/s

    Final velocity = 22 m/s

    Time = 3 s

2 Plan and Solve
What quantity are you trying to calculate?

    The acceleration of the roller coaster car = ■

What formula contains the given quantities and the unknown quantity?

$$\text{Acceleration} = \frac{\text{Final velocity} - \text{Initial velocity}}{\text{Time}}$$

Perform the calculation.

$$\text{Acceleration} = \frac{22 \text{ m/s} - 4 \text{ m/s}}{3 \text{ s}}$$

$$\text{Acceleration} = \frac{18 \text{ m/s}}{3 \text{ s}}$$

$$\text{Acceleration} = 6 \text{ m/s}^2$$

The acceleration is 6 m/s^2 down the slope.

3 Look Back and Check
Does your answer make sense?

    The answer is reasonable. If the car's velocity increases by 6 m/s each second, its velocity will be 10 m/s after 1 second, 16 m/s after 2 seconds, and 22 m/s after 3 seconds.

Math Practice

1. **Calculating Acceleration** A falling raindrop accelerates from 10 m/s to 30 m/s in 2 seconds. What is the raindrop's acceleration?

2. **Calculating Acceleration** A certain car can accelerate from rest to 27 m/s in 9 seconds. Find the car's acceleration.

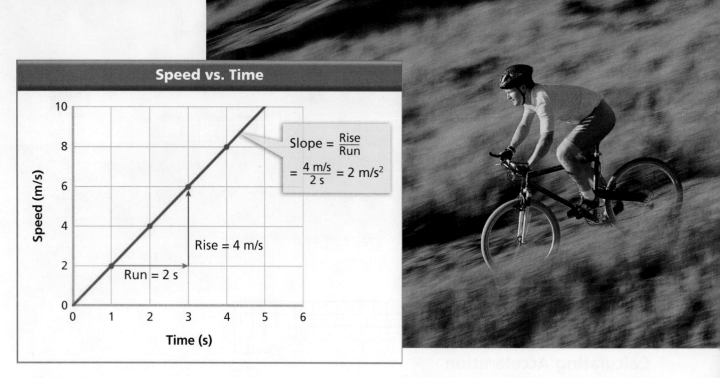

Speed vs. Time

Speed (m/s) vs. Time (s)

Slope = $\dfrac{\text{Rise}}{\text{Run}}$

= $\dfrac{4 \text{ m/s}}{2 \text{ s}}$ = 2 m/s²

Rise = 4 m/s

Run = 2 s

FIGURE 8

Speed-Versus-Time Graph
The slanted, straight line on this speed-versus-time graph tells you that the cyclist is accelerating at a constant rate. The slope of a speed-versus-time graph tells you the object's acceleration.
Predicting *How would the slope of the graph change if the cyclist were accelerating at a greater rate? At a lesser rate?*

Graphing Acceleration

Suppose you ride your bicycle down a long, steep hill. At the top of the hill your speed is 0 m/s. As you start down the hill, your speed increases. Each second, you move at a greater speed and travel a greater distance than the second before. During the five seconds it takes you to reach the bottom of the hill, you are an accelerating object. **You can use both a speed-versus-time graph and a distance-versus-time graph to analyze the motion of an accelerating object.**

Speed-Versus-Time Graph Figure 8 shows a speed-versus-time graph for your bicycle ride down the hill. What can you learn by analyzing this graph? Since the line slants upward, the graph shows that your speed was increasing. Next, since the line is straight, you can tell that your acceleration was constant. A slanted, straight line on a speed-versus-time graph means that the object is accelerating at a constant rate. This is an example of a linear graph. In a linear graph, the displayed data form a straight line. A horizontal line on a speed-versus-time graph means that the object is moving at a constant speed. The slope of a line on a speed-versus-time graph represents acceleration. To calculate the slope, choose any two points on the line. Then, divide the rise by the run.

$$\text{Slope} = \frac{\text{Rise}}{\text{Run}} = \frac{8 \text{ m/s} - 4 \text{ m/s}}{4 \text{ s} - 2 \text{ s}} = \frac{4 \text{ m/s}}{2 \text{ s}} = 2 \text{ m/s}^2$$

You accelerated down the hill at a constant rate of 2 m/s².

Distance-Versus-Time Graph You can also show the motion of an accelerating object with a distance-versus-time graph. Figure 9 shows a distance-versus-time graph for your bike ride. On this type of graph, a curved line means that the object is accelerating. The graph shown in Figure 9 is nonlinear. In a nonlinear graph, the data form a curved line when plotted.

The curved line in Figure 9 tells you that during each second, you traveled a greater distance than the second before. For example, you traveled a greater distance during the third second than you did during the first second.

The curved line in Figure 9 also tells you that during each second your speed is greater than the second before. Recall that the slope of a distance-versus-time graph is the speed of an object. From second to second, the slope of the line in Figure 9 gets steeper and steeper. Since the slope is increasing, you can conclude that the speed is also increasing. You are accelerating.

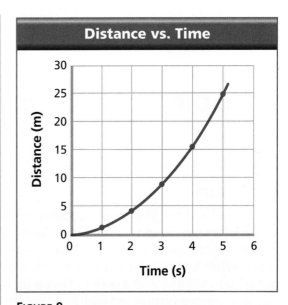

FIGURE 9
Distance-Versus-Time Graph
The curved line on this distance-versus-time graph tells you that the cyclist is accelerating.

 **Reading Checkpoint** What does a curved line on a distance-versus-time graph tell you?

Section 3 Assessment

S 8.1.e, 8.1.f, E-LA: Reading 8.2.4, Math: Algebra I, 8.15.0

Target Reading Skill Identify Main Ideas Reread the text under *Changing Velocity* on pages 350–351. Draw a graphic organizer for this topic. Use the boldfaced sentence as the main idea.

Reviewing Key Concepts

1. a. **Describing** What are the three ways that an object can accelerate?
   b. **Summarizing** Describe how a baseball player accelerates as he runs around the bases after hitting a home run.
   c. **Applying Concepts** An ice skater glides around a rink at a constant speed of 2 m/s. Is the skater accelerating? Explain your answer.
2. a. **Identifying** What formula do you use to calculate the acceleration of an object moving in a straight line?
   b. **Calculating** The velocity of a cyclist moving in a straight line changes from 0 m/s to 15 m/s in 10 seconds. What is the cyclist's acceleration?

3. a. **Naming** What types of graphs can you use to analyze the acceleration of an object?
   b. **Describing** Describe the motion of an object if its speed-versus-time graph is a horizontal line.
   c. **Predicting** What would a distance-versus-time graph look like for the moving object in part (b)?

Math Practice

4. **Calculating Acceleration** A downhill skier reaches the steepest part of a trail. Her velocity increases from 9 m/s to 18 m/s in 3 seconds. What is her acceleration?

5. **Calculating Acceleration** What is a race car's acceleration if its velocity changes from 0 m/s to 40 m/s in 4 seconds?

Skills Lab

Stopping on a Dime

S 8.1.c, S 8.9.f

Problem

The school will put in a new basketball court in a small area between two buildings. Safety is an important consideration in the design of the court. What is the distance needed between an out-of-bounds line and a wall so that a player can stop before hitting the wall?

Skills Focus

calculating, interpreting data

Materials

- wooden meter stick • tape measure
- 2 stopwatches or watches with second hands

Procedure

PART 1   Reaction Time

1. Have your partner suspend a wooden meter stick, zero end down, between your thumb and index finger, as shown. Your thumb and index finger should be about 3 cm apart.

2. Your partner will drop the meter stick without giving you any warning. Try to grab it with your thumb and index finger.

3. Note the level at which you grabbed the meter stick and use the chart shown to determine your reaction time. Record the time in the class data table.

4. Reverse roles with your partner and repeat Steps 1–3.

PART 2   Stopping Distance

5. On the school field or in the gymnasium, mark off a distance of 25 m. **CAUTION:** *Be sure to remove any obstacles from the course.*

6. Have your partner time how long it takes you to run the course at full speed. After you pass the 25-m mark, come to a stop as quickly as possible and remain standing. You must not slow down before the mark.

7. Have your partner measure the distance from the 25-m mark to your final position. This is the distance you need to come to a complete stop. Enter your time and distance into the class data table.

8. Reverse roles with your partner. Enter your partner's time and distance into the class data table.

Reaction Time			
Distance (cm)	Time (s)	Distance (cm)	Time (s)
15	0.175	25	0.226
16	0.181	26	0.230
17	0.186	27	0.235
18	0.192	28	0.239
19	0.197	29	0.243
20	0.202	30	0.247
21	0.207	31	0.252
22	0.212	32	0.256
23	0.217	33	0.260
24	0.221	34	0.263

Class Data Table			
Student Name	Reaction Time (s)	Running Time (s)	Stopping Distance (m)

Analyze and Conclude

1. **Calculating** Calculate the average speed of the student who ran the 25-m course the fastest.

2. **Interpreting Data** Multiply the speed of the fastest student (calculated in Question 1) by the slowest reaction time listed in the class data table. Why would you be interested in this product?

3. **Interpreting Data** Add the distance calculated in Question 2 to the longest stopping distance in the class data table. What does this total distance represent?

4. **Drawing Conclusions** Explain why it is important to use the fastest speed, the slowest reaction time, and the longest stopping distance in your calculations.

5. **Controlling Variables** What other factors should you take into account to get results that apply to a real basketball court?

6. **Communicating** Suppose you calculate that the distance from the out-of-bounds line to the wall of the basketball court is too short for safety. Write a proposal to the school that describes the problem. In your proposal, suggest a strategy for making the court safer.

More to Explore

Visit a local playground and examine it from the viewpoint of safety. Use what you learned about stopping distance as one of your guidelines, but also try to identify other potentially unsafe conditions. Write a letter to the Department of Parks or to the officials of your town informing them of your findings.

CALIFORNIA
Standards Focus

S 8 Framework Students should begin to grasp four concepts that help to unify physical sciences: force and energy; the laws of conservation; . . .

- What factors affect an object's kinetic energy and potential energy?

- How can kinetic energy and potential energy be transformed?

- What is the law of conservation of energy?

Key Terms
- work
- energy
- kinetic energy
- potential energy
- gravitational potential energy
- elastic potential energy
- mechanical energy
- law of conservation of energy

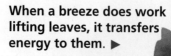

When a breeze does work lifting leaves, it transfers energy to them. ▶

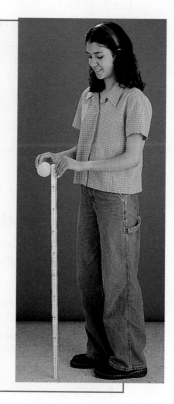

Lab zone **Standards Warm-Up**

How High Does a Ball Bounce?

1. Hold a meter stick vertically, with the zero end on the ground.

2. Drop a tennis ball from 50 cm. Record the height to which it bounces.

3. Drop the tennis ball from the 100-cm mark and record the height to which it bounces.

4. Predict how high the ball will bounce if dropped from the 75-cm mark. Test your prediction.

Think It Over

Observing How does the height from which you drop the ball relate to the height to which the ball bounces?

When a breeze blows a leaf through the air, it causes a change. In this case, the change is in the position of the leaf. A scientist would describe the wind as doing work on the leaf. **Work** is done when an object is caused to move a certain distance. The ability to do work or cause change is called **energy.** So, the wind has energy.

When an object or living thing does work on another object, some of its energy is transferred to that second object. You can think of work, then, as the transfer of energy. When energy is transferred, the object upon which work is done gains energy. The SI unit for both work and energy is the joule.

Kinetic Energy

A moving object, such as the wind, can do work when it strikes another object and moves it some distance. Because the moving object does work, it has energy. The energy an object has due to its motion is called **kinetic energy**. The word *kinetic* comes from the Greek word *kinetos*, which means "moving."

 The kinetic energy of an object depends on both its mass and its speed. Kinetic energy increases as mass increases. For example, the left lane in Figure 10 shows a bowling ball and a golf ball rolling down a bowling lane at the same speed. The bowling ball has more mass, so you must use more energy to roll it. The bowling ball is more likely to knock down the pins because it has more kinetic energy than the golf ball.

Kinetic energy also increases when speed increases. For example, suppose you have two identical bowling balls and you roll one ball so it moves at a greater speed than the other. You must throw the ball harder to give it the greater speed. In other words, you transfer more energy to it. Therefore, the faster ball has more kinetic energy. There is a mathematical relationship between kinetic energy, mass, and speed.

$$\text{Kinetic energy} = \frac{1}{2} \times \text{Mass} \times \text{Speed}^2$$

Note that changing the speed of an object will have a greater effect on its kinetic energy than changing its mass by the same factor. This is because speed is squared in the kinetic energy equation. For instance, doubling the mass of an object will double its kinetic energy. But doubling its speed will quadruple its kinetic energy.

Reading Checkpoint What is kinetic energy?

FIGURE 10
Kinetic Energy
Kinetic energy increases as mass and speed increase.
Predicting *In each example, which object will transfer more energy to the pins? Why?*

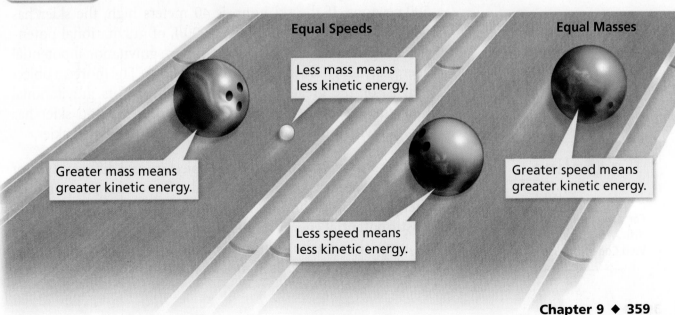

Equal Speeds

Less mass means less kinetic energy.

Greater mass means greater kinetic energy.

Less speed means less kinetic energy.

Equal Masses

Greater speed means greater kinetic energy.

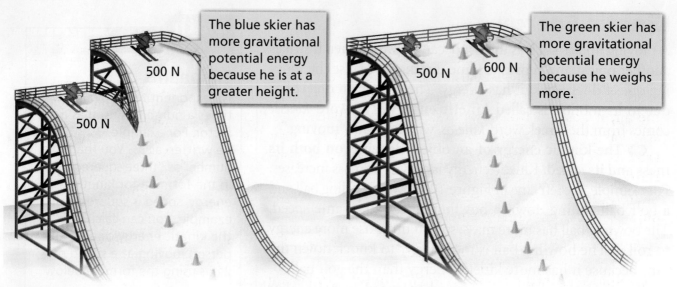

The blue skier has more gravitational potential energy because he is at a greater height.

500 N

500 N

The green skier has more gravitational potential energy because he weighs more.

500 N

600 N

FIGURE 11
Gravitational Potential Energy
Gravitational potential energy increases as weight and height increase. **Interpreting Diagrams** *Does the red skier have more gravitational potential energy on the higher ski jump or the lower one? Why?*

Go Online

SCiLINKS NSTA

For: Links on energy
Visit: www.SciLinks.org
Web Code: scn-1351

Potential Energy

Some objects have stored energy as a result of their positions or shapes. When you lift a book up from the floor or compress a spring, you transfer energy to it. The energy is stored. It might be used later when the book falls to the floor or the spring is released. Stored energy that results from the position or shape of an object is called **potential energy**. This type of energy has the potential to do work.

Gravitational Potential Energy Potential energy related to an object's height is called **gravitational potential energy**. An object's gravitational potential energy depends on its weight and on its height relative to a reference point.

> **Gravitational potential energy = Weight × Height**

For example, the red skier on the left in Figure 11 weighs 500 newtons. If the ski jump is 40 meters high, the skier has 500 newtons × 40 meters, or 20,000 J, of gravitational potential energy. A 500-newton skier has more gravitational potential energy on a high ski jump than on a low one. The more an object weighs, or the greater its height, the greater its gravitational potential energy. At the same height, a 600-newton skier has more gravitational potential energy than a 500-newton skier.

Elastic Potential Energy An object gains a different type of potential energy when it is stretched or squeezed. The potential energy of objects that can be stretched or compressed is called **elastic potential energy**. For example, an archer pulling back on an arrow changes the shape of the bow. The bow now has potential energy that can be used to send the arrow flying to its target.

Energy Transformation and Conservation

Look at Figure 12. The quarterback transfers energy to the football as he throws it to the receiver. As the ball sails through the air, it has kinetic energy because it is moving. The ball also has potential energy because of its position above the ground. An object's combined kinetic energy and potential energy is called **mechanical energy**.

You can find an object's mechanical energy by adding the object's kinetic energy and potential energy.

> **Mechanical energy = Kinetic energy + Potential energy**

You can use this formula to find the mechanical energy of the football in Figure 12. Suppose a football has a weight of 4 newtons and a mass of 0.4 kg. If the football is moving at a speed of 14 m/s, it has a kinetic energy of $1/2 \times 0.4$ kg $\times (14 \text{ m/s})^2 = 39$ J. If the football is 3 meters above the ground, it has a gravitational potential energy of $4 \text{ N} \times 3 \text{ m} = 12$ J due to its position. The total mechanical energy of the football at that point is 39 joules + 12 joules, or 51 joules.

 **Reading Checkpoint** **What two forms of energy combine to make mechanical energy?**

Go Online
SciLINKS NSTA

For: Links on forms of energy
Visit: www.SciLinks.org
Web Code: scn-1352

FIGURE 12
Mechanical Energy
To find the football's mechanical energy, add its kinetic energy to its potential energy. **Observing** *Why does the football have potential energy?*

Mechanical energy = 39 J + 12 J = 51 J

Gravitational potential energy = 12 J

Kinetic energy = 39 J

Transformations Between Potential and Kinetic Energy One of the most common energy transformations is the transformation between potential energy and kinetic energy. In waterfalls such as Yosemite Falls, potential energy is transformed to kinetic energy. The water at the top of the falls has gravitational potential energy. As the water plunges, its speed increases. Its potential energy becomes kinetic energy.

🔑 **Any object that rises or falls experiences a change in its kinetic and gravitational potential energy.** Look at the orange in Figure 13. When it moves, the orange has kinetic energy. As it rises, it slows down. Its potential energy increases as its kinetic energy decreases. At the highest point in its path, the orange stops moving for an instant. Since there is no motion, the orange no longer has kinetic energy. But it has potential energy. As the orange falls, kinetic energy increases while potential energy decreases.

In a pendulum, a continuous transformation between kinetic and potential energy takes place. At the highest point in its swing, the pendulum in Figure 14 comes to a stop, so it has only gravitational potential energy. As the pendulum swings downward, it speeds up. Its potential energy is transformed to kinetic energy. The pendulum is at its greatest speed at the bottom of its swing. There, all its energy is kinetic energy.

As the pendulum swings to the other side, its height increases. The pendulum regains gravitational potential energy and loses kinetic energy. At the top of its swing, it comes to a stop again. The pattern of energy transformation continues.

FIGURE 13
Juggling
The kinetic energy of an orange thrown into the air becomes gravitational potential energy. Its potential energy becomes kinetic energy as it falls.

Go Online
active art

For: Energy Transformations activity
Visit: PHSchool.com
Web Code: cgp-3053

FIGURE 14
Pendulum
A pendulum continuously transforms energy from kinetic to potential energy and back.
Interpreting Diagrams *At what two points is the pendulum's potential energy greatest?*

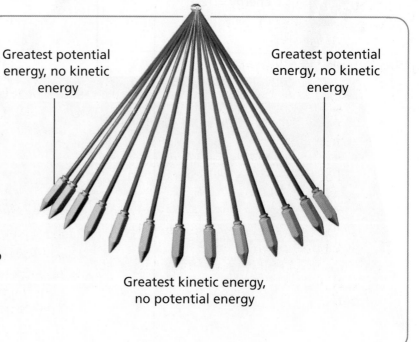

Greatest potential energy, no kinetic energy

Greatest potential energy, no kinetic energy

Greatest kinetic energy, no potential energy

Conservation of Energy If you set a spinning top in motion, will the top remain in motion forever? No, it will not. Then what happens to its energy? Is the energy destroyed? Again, the answer is no. The **law of conservation of energy** states that when one form of energy is transformed to another, no energy is destroyed in the process. **⊙ According to the law of conservation of energy, energy cannot be created or destroyed.** So the total amount of energy is the same before and after any transformation. If you add up all the new forms of energy after a transformation, all of the original energy will be accounted for.

So what happens to the energy of the top in Figure 15? As the top spins, it rubs against the floor and encounters air resistance. As a result, some of its kinetic energy is transformed into thermal energy. So, the mechanical energy of the spinning top is transformed to thermal energy. The top slows and eventually falls on its side, but its energy is not destroyed—it is transformed.

 **Reading Checkpoint** What causes a top to stop spinning?

FIGURE 15
Conservation of Energy
A spinning top's kinetic energy is not lost. It is transformed into thermal energy through friction. **Applying Concepts** *How much of the top's kinetic energy becomes thermal energy?*

Section ❹ **Assessment**

S 8 Framework, E-LA: Reading 8.1.0 Reviewing Math: NS 7.2.3

⊙ Vocabulary Skill High-Use Academic Words What is the meaning of the word *potential* in the term *potential energy*?

⊙ Reviewing Key Concepts

1. a. **Identifying** What is kinetic energy? In what unit is it measured?
   b. **Explaining** What factors affect an object's kinetic energy?
   c. **Calculating** A 1,500-kg car is moving at a speed of 10 m/s. What is the car's kinetic energy?

2. a. **Identifying** What is potential energy?
   b. **Explaining** What factors affect an object's gravitational potential energy?
   c. **Calculating** What is the potential energy of a 500-N pole-vaulter when she is 4 m above the ground?

3. a. **Summarizing** State the law of conservation of energy in your own words.
   b. **Describing** Describe the energy transformations that occur when you bounce a ball.
   c. **Applying Concepts** Suppose a ball had a potential energy of 5 J when you dropped it. What would be its kinetic energy just as it hit the ground? (Ignore the effect of air resistance.)

Math Practice

4. **Exponents** What is the kinetic energy of a 1.0-kg ball moving at 3.0 m/s?

5. **Exponents** How would the kinetic energy of the ball in Question 4 change if its mass were doubled? If its speed were doubled?

Study Guide

The BIG Idea You can describe the motion of an object by its position, speed, direction, and acceleration.

1 Describing Motion

Key Concepts S 8.1.a

- An object is in motion if it changes position relative to a reference point.
- Distance is the total length of the actual path between two points. Displacement is the length and direction of a straight line between starting and ending points.

Key Terms

motion
reference point
distance

displacement
vector

2 Speed and Velocity

Key Concepts S 8.1.b, 8.1.c, 8.1.d

- To calculate the speed of the object, divide the distance the object travels by the time it takes to travel that distance.
- $\text{Speed} = \dfrac{\text{Distance}}{\text{Time}}$
- Changes in velocity may be due to changes in speed, changes in direction, or both.
- The slope of a distance-versus-time graph represents speed, that is, the rate that distance changes in relation to time.
- $\text{Slope} = \dfrac{\text{Rise}}{\text{Run}}$

Key Terms

speed
average speed
instantaneous speed

velocity
slope

3 Acceleration

Key Concepts S 8.1.e, 8.1.f

- In science, acceleration refers to increasing speed, decreasing speed, or changing direction.
- To determine the acceleration of an object, you must calculate its change in velocity per unit of time.
- $\text{Acceleration} = \dfrac{\text{Final velocity} - \text{Initial velocity}}{\text{Time}}$
- You can use both a speed-versus-time graph and a distance-versus-time graph to analyze the motion of an accelerating object.

Key Term

acceleration

4 Energy

Key Concepts S 8 Framework

- The kinetic energy of an object depends on both its mass and its speed.
- $\text{Kinetic Energy} = \dfrac{1}{2} \times \text{Mass} \times \text{Speed}^2$
- An object's gravitational potential energy depends on its weight and on its height relative to a reference point.
- Gravitational potential energy = Weight × Height
- Mechanical energy = Potential energy + Kinetic energy
- Any object that rises or falls experiences a change in its kinetic and gravitational potential energy.
- According to the law of conservation of energy, energy cannot be created or destroyed.

Key Terms

work
energy
kinetic energy
potential energy
gravitational potential
  energy

elastic potential
  energy
mechanical energy
law of conservation of
  energy

Review and Assessment

Go Online
PHSchool.com

For: Self-Assessment
Visit: PHSchool.com
Web Code: cxa-3090

Target Reading Skill

Identifying Main Ideas
Reread the first paragraph under *Potential Energy*. Then complete the following graphic organizer.

Potential Energy

| |
| Some objects have stored energy. | | |

Reviewing Key Terms

Choose the letter of the best answer.

1. A change in position with respect to a reference point is called
   a. acceleration.
   b. velocity.
   c. direction.
   d. motion.

2. If you know a car travels 30 km in 20 minutes, you can find its
   a. acceleration.
   b. average speed.
   c. direction.
   d. instantaneous speed.

3. You do not know an object's velocity until you know its
   a. speed and distance.
   b. displacement.
   c. speed and direction.
   d. acceleration.

4. The rate at which velocity changes is called
   a. acceleration.
   b. constant speed.
   c. average speed.
   d. displacement.

5. The energy that an object has due to its motion is called
   a. gravitational potential energy.
   b. elastic potential energy.
   c. kinetic energy.
   d. thermal energy.

Complete the following sentences so that your answers clearly explain the key terms.

6. **Displacement** is different from distance because _____ .

7. Both velocity and acceleration are **vectors** because _____ .

8. You can calculate the **average speed** of an object by _____ .

9. An object moving in a circle at a constant speed is undergoing **acceleration** because _____ .

10. The **law of conservation of energy** states that _____ .

Writing in Science

News Report Two trucks have competed in a race. Write an article describing the race and who won. Explain the role the average speed of the trucks played. Tell how average speed can be calculated.

Video Assessment
Discovery Channel School
Motion

Review and Assessment

Checking Concepts

11. A passenger walks toward the rear of a moving train. Describe her motion as seen from a reference point on the train. Then describe it from a reference point on the ground.

12. Which has a greater speed, a heron that travels 600 m in 60 seconds or a duck that travels 60 m in 5 seconds? Explain.

13. An insect lands on a compact disc that is put into a player. If the insect spins with the disc, is the insect accelerating? Why or why not?

14. An eagle flies from its perch in a tree to the ground. Describe its energy transformations.

Thinking Critically

15. Inferring How can you tell if an object is moving when its motion is too slow to see?

16. Interpreting Graphs The graph below shows the motion of a remote-control car. Calculate the car's average speed over the time intervals 0-4 s, 4-8 s, 8-12 s, and over the entire time shown. During which interval is the car moving the fastest? The slowest?

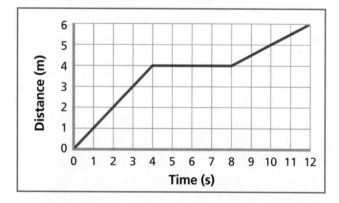

17. Applying Concepts A family takes a car trip. They travel for an hour at 80 km/h and then for 2 hours at 40 km/h. Find their average speed during the trip.

18. Problem Solving A 380-N girl walks down a flight of stairs so that she is 2.5 m below her starting level. What is the change in the girl's gravitational potential energy?

Math Practice

19. Calculating Acceleration During a slap shot, a hockey puck takes 0.5 second to reach the goal. It started from rest and reached a final velocity of 35 m/s. What is the puck's acceleration?

20. Exponents What is the value of 12^2?

21. Exponents What is the kinetic energy of a 1,350 kg car travelling at 12 m/s?

Applying Skills

Use the illustration of the motion of a ladybug to answer Questions 22–24.

22. Measuring Measure the distance from the starting line to line B, and from line B to the finish line. Measure to the nearest tenth of a centimeter.

23. Calculating Starting at rest, the ladybug accelerated to line B and then moved at a constant speed until it reached the finish line. If the ladybug took 2.5 seconds to move from line B to the finish line, calculate its constant speed during that time.

24. Interpreting Data The speed you calculated in Question 23 is also the speed the ladybug had at the end of its acceleration at line B. If it took 2 seconds for the ladybug to accelerate from the start line to line B, what is its acceleration during that time?

Lab zone Standards Investigation

Performance Assessment Organize your display cards so that they are easy to follow. Remember to put a title on each card stating the speed that you measured. Place the cards in order from the slowest speed to the fastest. Then display them. Compare your results with those of other students.

Choose the letter of the best answer.

1. Suppose you moved 8 meters forward and then 3 meters backward. What is your displacement from your original position?

A 5 m forward   **B** 8 m forward

C 11 m backward   **D** 24 m backward

S 8.1.a

2. Your father is driving to the beach. He drives at one speed for two hours. He drives at a different speed for another two hours and a third speed for the final hour. How would you find his average speed for all five hours?

A Divide total time by total distance.

B Multiply total time by total distance.

C Divide total distance by total time.

D Subtract total time from total distance.

S 8.1.b

3. A car travels at a constant speed of 60 km/h for 3 hours. What is the total distance that the car traveled?

A 20 km   **B** 57 km

C 63 km   **D** 180 km   **S 8.1.c**

Use the graph below to answer Question 4.

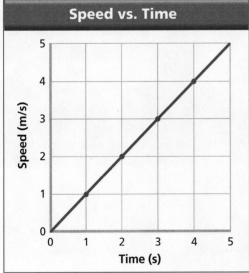

4. According to the graph of a cyclist's motion above, the cyclist is

A moving at a constant speed.

B accelerating at a constant rate.

C slowing down at a constant rate.

D moving a constant distance per second.

S 8.1.f

5. Which of the following is NOT a vector?

A displacement

B speed

C velocity

D acceleration   **S 8.1.d**

6. Two objects traveling at the same speed have different velocities if they

A start at different times.

B travel different distances.

C have different masses.

D move in different directions.   **S 8.1.e**

Use the graph below to answer Question 7.

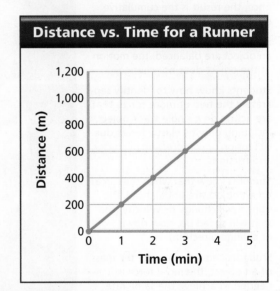

7. The graph shows distance versus time for a runner moving at a constant speed. What is the runner's speed?

A 100 m/min

B 200 m/min

C 400 m/min

D 1,000 m/min   **S 8.1.f**

Apply the BIG Idea

8. Write a paragraph that describes the similarities and differences among speed, velocity, and acceleration.   **S 8.1.e**

Chapter

10

Forces

CALIFORNIA
Standards Preview

S 8.2 Unbalanced forces cause changes in velocity. As a basis for understanding this concept:

a. Students know a force has both direction and magnitude.

b. Students know when an object is subject to two or more forces at once, the result is the cumulative effect of all the forces.

c. Students know when the forces on an object are balanced, the motion of the object does not change.

d. Students know how to identify separately the two or more forces that are acting on a single static object, including gravity, elastic forces due to tension or compression in matter, and friction.

e. Students know that when the forces on an object are unbalanced, the object will change its velocity (that is, it will speed up, slow down, or change direction).

f. Students know the greater the mass of an object, the more force is needed to achieve the same rate of change in motion.

S 8.9 Scientific progress is made by asking meaningful questions and conducting careful investigations. As a basis for understanding this concept and addressing the content in the other three strands, students should develop their own questions and perform investigations. Students will:

c. Distinguish between variable and controlled parameters in a test.

e. Construct appropriate graphs from data and develop quantitative statements about the relationships between variables.

A softball player exerts a force on ▶ the softball.

Focus on the BIG Idea

S 8.2

What causes an object's velocity to change?

Check What You Know

You drop a tennis ball and a baseball at the same time. Why do the balls fall to the floor?

Build Science Vocabulary

The images shown here represent some of the key terms in this chapter. You can use this vocabulary skill to help you understand the meaning of some key terms in this chapter.

Latin Word Origins

Many science words come to English from Latin. In this chapter you will learn the word *compress*. *Compress* comes from the Latin words *com* meaning "together" and *premere* meaning "to press." *Compress* means "to press together."

com	**+ premere**	**= compress**
together	press	to press together

Learn these Latin words to help you remember the key terms.

Latin Origin	Meaning	Key Term
centri-	Center	Centripetal force
com-	Together, with	Compression
jacere	Throw	Projectile
premere	Press	Compression
pro-	Forward, before	Projectile
tensus	Stretch	Tension

Apply It!

Look at *pro-* and *jacere* and predict the meaning of *projectile*. Revise your definition as needed as you read the chapter.

Look for words with these Latin origins as you read the chapter.

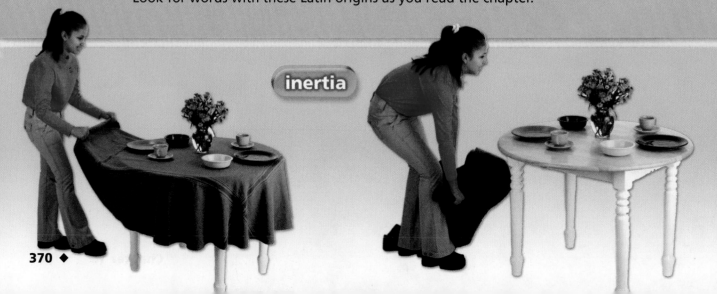

inertia

projectile

momentum

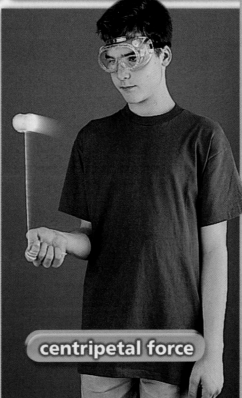

force

centripetal force

air resistance

Chapter 10 Vocabulary

Section 1 (page 374)
force
newton
net force
unbalanced forces
balanced forces

Section 2 (page 380)
friction
static friction
sliding friction
rolling friction
fluid friction
gravity
mass
weight
free fall
air resistance
projectile
compression
tension

Section 3 (page 389)
inertia

Section 4 (page 393)
momentum
law of conservation
of momentum

Section 5 (page 402)
satellite
centripetal force

interactive Textbook
Build Science Vocabulary
Online
Visit: PHSchool.com
Web Code: cxj-3100

How to Read Science

Take Notes

Science chapters are packed with information. Each section needs to be read at least twice. After finding the main idea and important details in a section, take notes so you have something to study. In your notebook, create a two-column note-taking organizer.

- Label the left side "Recall Clues and Questions."
- Label the right side "Notes."
- Under "Notes," write key ideas, using phrases and abbreviations; include a few important details.
- Under "Recall Clues and Questions," write review and study questions.
- Write a summary statement for each red heading.

Look at the following example for Section 1 in this chapter.

Recall Clues & Questions	Notes
What is force?	Force—a push or pull • A vector quantity • Describes magnitude and direction • Arrows show direction and strength of force
What are the SI units for force?	SI unit called newton (N) Summary Statement: A force is described by its magnitude and by the direction in which it acts.

Apply It!

What are two important ideas found in the notes? What questions in the left column help you recall the content?

Take notes as you read each section in this chapter.

S 8.2.a, 8.2.e

Newton Scooters

Have you ever wondered what force pushes a rocket upward? As you will learn in this chapter, an object will accelerate only when a net force acts on it. The rocket accelerates upward because it is acted on by a net force from the gases it pushes outward. This is an example of Newton's third law. In this investigation, you will use Newton's third law to design a vehicle.

Your Goal

To design and build a vehicle that moves without the use of gravity, electricity, or a person pushing or pulling it.

Your vehicle must

- move forward by pushing back on something
- travel a minimum distance of 1.5 meters
- be built following the safety guidelines in Appendix A

Plan It!

Preview the chapter to find out about Newton's third law of motion. Determine factors that will affect the acceleration of your vehicle. Brainstorm possible designs for your vehicle, but be careful not to lock yourself into a single idea. Remember that a car with wheels is only one type of vehicle.

Think of ways to use household materials to build your vehicle. Draw a diagram of your proposed design and identify the force that will propel your vehicle. Have your teacher approve your design. Then build your vehicle and see if it works!

Section

1

The Nature of Force

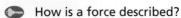
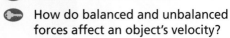
CALIFORNIA
Standards Focus

S 8.2.a Students know a force has both direction and magnitude.

S 8.2.c Students know when the forces on an object are balanced, the motion of the object does not change.

How is a force described?

How do balanced and unbalanced forces affect an object's velocity?

Key Terms

- force
- newton
- net force
- unbalanced forces
- balanced forces

Lab zone Standards Warm-Up

Is the Force With You?

1. Attach a spring scale to each end of a skateboard. Place the skateboard upright.

2. Gently pull on one spring scale with a force of 4 N, while your partner pulls on the other with the same force. Observe the motion of the skateboard.

3. Now try to keep your partner's spring scale reading at 2 N while you pull with a force of 4 N. Observe the motion of the skateboard.

Think It Over

Observing Describe the motion of the skateboard when you and your partner pulled with the same force. How was the motion of the skateboard affected when you pulled with more force than your partner?

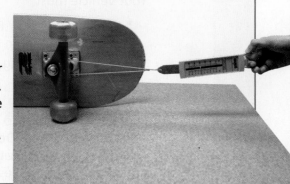

A hard kick sends a soccer ball shooting down the field toward the goal. Just in time, the goalie leaps forward, stops the ball, and quickly kicks it in the opposite direction. In a soccer game, the ball is rarely still. Its motion is constantly changing. What causes an object to start moving, stop moving, or change direction? The answer is force.

What Is a Force?

In science, the word *force* has a simple and specific meaning. A **force** is a push or a pull. You use a force to open a door, to stretch a rubber band, and to carry your backpack. When one object pushes or pulls another object, you say that the first object exerts a force on the second object.

Like velocity and acceleration, force is a vector quantity. **A force is described by its magnitude and by the direction in which it acts.** If you push on a door, you exert a force in a different direction than if you pull on the door.

FIGURE 1
Force and Motion
The force of the kick changes the direction of the soccer ball.

You can use an arrow to represent the direction and strength of a force. The arrow points in the direction of a force. The length of the arrow tells you the strength of a force—the longer the arrow, the greater the force.

The SI unit for the magnitude, or strength, of a force is the **newton** (N). This unit is named after the English scientist and mathematician Isaac Newton. You exert about one newton of force when you lift a small apple.

 **Reading Checkpoint** What SI unit is used to measure the strength of a force?

Combining Forces

Often, more than a single force acts on an object at one time. When an object is subject to two or more forces at once, the result is the combination, or cumulative effect, of all the forces. The combination of all forces acting on an object is called the **net force.** The net force determines whether an object moves and also in which direction it moves.

When two or more forces act in the same direction, the net force is found by adding the strengths of the individual forces. In Figure 2, the lengths of the two arrows, are added together to find the net force. The net force acts in the same direction as the individual forces.

When two or more forces act in opposite directions, the net force is also found by adding the strengths of the forces. However, you must note the direction of each force. Adding a force acting in one direction to a force acting in the opposite direction is the same as adding a positive number to a negative number. The net force always acts in the direction of the greater force. If the opposing forces are of equal strength, there is no net force.

FIGURE 2
Combining Force Vectors
The strength and direction of the individual forces determine the net force. Calculating *How do you find the net force when two forces act in opposite directions?*

5 N	5 N	10 N

Two forces acting in the same direction produce a larger net force than either original force.

5 N	−7 N	−2 N

Two unequal forces acting in opposite directions produce a net force in the direction of the larger force.

10 N	−10 N	= 0

Equal but opposite forces may cancel each other and produce no net force.

Individual forces

200 N

100 N

Net force

300 N

Individual forces

200 N -100 N

Net force

100 N

Unbalanced Forces in the Same Direction
When two forces act in the same direction, the net force is the sum of the two individual forces. The box moves to the right.

Unbalanced Forces in the Opposite Direction
When two forces act in opposite directions, the net force is the difference between the two individual forces. The box moves to the right.

Unbalanced Forces Whenever there is a net force acting on an object, the forces are unbalanced. **Unbalanced forces** will cause the velocity of an object to change. The object can speed up, slow down, or change direction. 🔑 **Unbalanced forces acting on an object result in a net force and cause a change in the object's velocity.**

Figure 3 shows two people exerting forces on a box. When they both push a box to the right, their individual forces add together to produce a net force in that direction. Since unbalanced forces act on the box, there is a net force and the box moves to the right.

When the two people push the box in opposite directions, the net force on the box is the difference between their individual forces. Because the boy pushes with a greater force than the girl, their forces are unbalanced and a net force acts on the box to the right. As a result, the box moves to the right.

✓ **Reading Checkpoint** What is the result of unbalanced forces acting on an object?

Balanced Forces In a tug-of-war between two people, each person pulls on opposite ends of the rope. If each person pulls with equal force, neither the rope nor the people will move. Equal forces acting on one object in opposite directions are called **balanced forces.**

Individual forces

200 N   −200 N

No net force

Balanced Forces in Opposite Directions
When two equal forces act in opposite directions,
they cancel each other out. The box doesn't move.

FIGURE 3
Unbalanced and Balanced Forces
When the forces acting on an object are
unbalanced, a net force acts on the object.
The object will move. When balanced forces act
on an object, no net force acts on the object.
The object's motion remains unchanged.
*Predicting If both girls pushed the box on the
same side, would the motion of the box change?
Why or why not?*

When equal forces are exerted in opposite directions, there
is no net force. 🔑 **Balanced forces acting on an object do not
change the object's velocity.** In Figure 3, when two people
push on the box with equal force in opposite directions, the
forces are balanced. The box does not move.

Section 1 Assessment

S 8.2.a, S 8.2.c
E-LA: Reading 8.2.4

🎯 **Target Reading Skill** **Take Notes** Review your
notes for this section. What are two important
ideas that you noted under Combining Forces?

🔑 **Reviewing Key Concepts**

1. a. **Defining** What is a force?
   b. **Explaining** How is a force described?
   c. **Interpreting Diagrams** In a diagram, one
   force arrow is longer than the other arrow.
   What can you tell about the forces?
2. a. **Reviewing** How can you find the net force
   if two forces act in opposite directions?
   b. **Comparing and Contrasting** How do
   balanced forces acting on an object affect its
   motion? How do unbalanced forces acting
   on an object affect its motion?

c. **Calculating** You exert a force of 120 N on a
desk. Your friend exerts a force of 150 N in
the same direction. What net force do you
and your friend exert on the desk?

Lab zone At-Home **Activity**

House of Cards Carefully set two playing
cards upright on a flat surface so that their top
edges lean on each other. In terms of balanced
forces, explain to a family member why the
cards are able to stand by themselves. Then push
one of the cards. Explain to a family member the
role of unbalanced forces in what happens.

Consumer Lab

Sticky Sneakers

 S 8.2.a, 8.9.c

Problem

Friction is a force that opposes an object's motion. Friction can be useful. For example, friction between sneakers and the ground can help an athlete to start and stop running. How does the amount of friction between a sneaker and a surface compare for different brands of sneakers?

Skills Focus

controlling variables, interpreting data

Materials

- three or more different brands of sneakers
- 2 spring scales, 5-N and 20-N, or force sensors
- mass set(s) • tape • 3 large paper clips
- balance

Procedure

1. Sneakers are designed to deal with various friction forces, including these:
   - starting friction, which occurs when you start from a stopped position
   - forward-stopping friction, which occurs when you come to a forward stop
   - sideways-stopping friction, which occurs when you come to a sideways stop

2. Prepare a data table in which you can record each type of friction for each sneaker.

3. Place each sneaker on a balance. Put masses in each sneaker so that the total mass of the sneaker plus the masses is 1,000 g. Spread the masses out evenly inside the sneaker.

4. Tape a paper clip to each sneaker and attach a spring scale to the paper clip. (If you are using force sensors, see your teacher for instructions.)
   To measure
   - starting friction, attach the paper clip to the back of the sneaker
   - forward-stopping friction, attach the paper clip to the front of the sneaker
   - sideways-stopping friction, attach the paper clip to the side of the sneaker

Data Table			
Sneaker	Starting Friction (N)	Sideways-Stopping Friction (N)	Forward-Stopping Friction (N)
A			
B			

5. The force necessary to make the sneaker start moving is equal to the starting friction force. To measure starting friction, pull the sneaker backward until it starts to move. Use the 20-N spring scale first. If the reading is less than 5 N, use a 5-N scale. Record the starting friction force in your data table.

6. To measure either sideways or forward stopping friction, use the spring scale to pull each sneaker at a slow, constant speed. Record the stopping friction force in your data table.

7. Repeat Steps 4–6 for the remaining sneakers.

Analyze and Conclude

1. **Controlling Variables** What variables are controlled? Explain your answers. What are the manipulated and responding variables? Explain your answers. (See the Skills Handbook to read about experimental variables.)

2. **Applying Concepts** Why is the reading on the spring scale equal to the friction force in each case?

3. **Interpreting Data** Which sneaker had the most starting friction? Which had the most forward-stopping friction? Which had the most sideways-stopping friction?

4. **Drawing Conclusions** Do you think that using a sneaker with a small amount of mass in it is a fair test of the friction of the sneakers? Why or why not? (*Hint*: Consider that sneakers are used with people's feet inside them.)

5. **Inferring** Why did you pull the sneaker at a slow speed to test for stopping friction? Why did you pull a sneaker that wasn't moving to test starting friction?

6. **Drawing Conclusions** Can you identify a relationship between the brand of sneaker and the amount of friction you observed? If so, describe the relationship. What do you observe that might cause one sneaker to grip the floor better than another?

7. **Communicating** Choose one of the brands of sneakers that you tested. In a paragraph, explain why this sneaker is the best one to wear while playing a particular sport or activity. Be sure to include the results of this lab in your explanation.

Design an Experiment

The strength of the friction force is determined by both the design of the sneaker and the type of surface it presses against. Design an experiment to find out how various types of surfaces affect the force of friction acting upon the sneaker. *Obtain your teacher's permission before carrying out your investigation.*

Friction, Gravity, and Elastic Forces

CALIFORNIA
Standards Focus

S 8.2.b Students know when an object is subject to two or more forces at once, the result is the cumulative effect of all the forces.

S 8.2.d Students know how to identify separately the two or more forces that are acting on a single static object, including gravity, elastic forces due to tension or compression in matter, and friction.

- What factors determine the strength of the friction force between two surfaces?

- What factors affect the gravitational force between two objects?

- Why do objects accelerate during free fall?

- When is matter considered to be elastic?

Key Terms

- friction
- static friction
- sliding friction
- rolling friction
- fluid friction
- gravity
- mass
- weight
- free fall
- air resistance
- projectile
- compression
- tension

Lab zone Standards Warm-Up

The Flexible Meter Stick

1. Place a meter stick across two desks so that it spans the gap between the desks.
2. Rest a book on top of the meter stick. Using another ruler, measure how much the meter stick sags under the book's weight.
3. Place another book on top of the first book. Measure how much the meter stick sags under the weight of two books.

Think It Over

Observing Did the meter stick sag more with two books resting on it? Why? Why doesn't the meter stick break?

Have you ever pulled your little sister in a sled up the side of a snow-covered hill and then watched as she raced down it? Have you ever thought about some of the forces at work? The tension in the rope allows you to apply the force necessary to pull the sled up the hill. Gravity causes the sled to accelerate down the hill. Friction ultimately brings the sled to a stop at the bottom of the hill. All the while the snow is compressing under the sled's weight. You will learn about friction, gravity, compression, and tension forces in this chapter.

◀ **Friction and gravity act on the sled.**

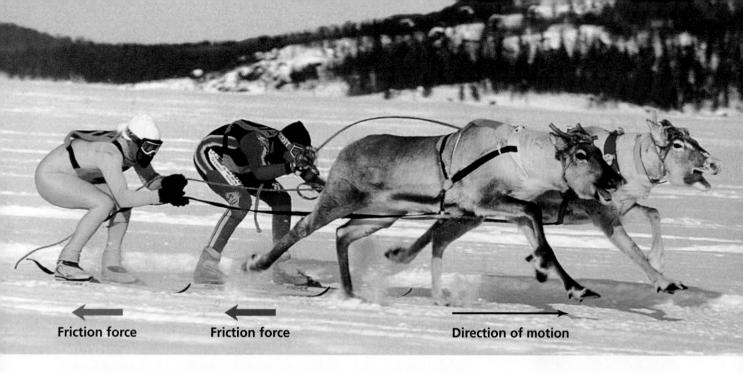

Friction force   Friction force   Direction of motion

FIGURE 4
Friction and Smooth Surfaces The smooth surfaces of
the skis make for a fast ride for these Finnish skiers.
Relating Diagrams and Photos *How does the direction
of friction compare to the direction of motion?*

Friction

A classmate is sitting at the end of a long table and asks to see
your book. You slide it toward her, but it slows down and stops
before it reaches her. Why does it stop sliding? A force called
friction acts in a direction opposite to the motion of objects.
Friction is a force that two surfaces exert on each other when
they rub against each other. Without friction or another unbalanced force, a moving object will not stop until it strikes
another object.

The Causes of Friction In general, smooth surfaces produce less friction than rough surfaces. A piece of metal may
seem quite smooth. But, as you can see in Figure 5, even the
smoothest objects have irregular, bumpy surfaces. When the
irregularities of one surface come into contact with those of
another surface, friction occurs.

 **The strength of the force of friction depends on the
types of surfaces involved and on how hard the surfaces push
together.** The skiers in Figure 4 get a fast ride because there is
very little friction between their skis and the snow. The reindeer
would not be able to pull them easily over a rough surface such
as sand. Friction also increases if surfaces push hard against
each other. If you rub your hands together forcefully, there is
more friction than if you rub your hands together lightly.

FIGURE 5
A Smooth Surface?
If you look at the polished surface
of an aluminum alloy under a
powerful microscope, you'll find
that it is actually quite rough.

Static Friction Four types of friction are shown in Figure 6. The friction that acts on objects that are not moving is called **static friction.** Because of static friction, you must use extra force to start the motion of stationary objects. For example, think about what happens when you try to push a heavy desk across a floor. If you push on the desk with a force less than the force of static friction between the desk and the floor, the desk will not move. To make the desk move, you must exert a force greater than the force of static friction. Once the desk is moving, there is no longer any static friction. However, there is another type of friction—sliding friction.

Sliding Friction Sliding friction occurs when two solid surfaces slide over each other. When an object is pulled at a constant velocity across a level surface, the pulling force equals the sliding friction. This is another example of balanced forces. Sliding friction can be useful. For example, you can spread sand on an icy path to improve your footing. Ballet dancers apply a sticky powder to the soles of their ballet slippers so they won't slip on the dance floor. And when you stop a bicycle with hand brakes, rubber pads push against the metal rim of the wheel, causing the wheels to slow and eventually stop.

Rolling Friction When an object rolls across a surface, rolling friction occurs. Rolling friction is less than sliding friction for similar materials. This type of friction is important to engineers who design skates, skateboards, and bicycles which need wheels that move freely. Engineers use ball bearings to reduce the friction between the wheels and the rest of the product. These ball bearings are small, smooth steel balls that reduce friction by rolling between moving parts.

Fluid Friction Fluids, such as water, oil, or air, are materials that flow easily. **Fluid friction** occurs when a solid object moves through a fluid. Fluid friction is usually less than sliding friction. This is why the parts of machines that must slide over each other are often bathed in oil. In this way, the solid parts move through the fluid instead of sliding against each other. When you ride a bike, fluid friction occurs between you and the air. Cyclists often wear streamlined helmets and specially designed clothing to reduce fluid friction.

 **Reading Checkpoint** What are two ways in which friction can be useful?

FIGURE 6

Types of Friction

Types of friction include static, sliding, rolling, and fluid friction. **Making Generalizations** *In what direction does friction act compared to an object's motion?*

Static Friction ▼
To make the sled move, the athlete first has to overcome the force of static friction. Static friction acts in the opposite direction to the intended motion.

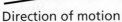

Sliding friction

Direction of motion

Sliding Friction ▲
Once the sled is moving, it slides over the floor. Sliding friction acts between the sled and the floor in the opposite direction to the sled's motion.

Static friction

Intended direction of motion

Rolling Friction ▼
Rolling friction occurs when an object rolls over a surface. For the skateboarder, rolling friction acts in the direction opposite to the skateboard's motion.

Direction of motion

Fluid friction

Fluid Friction ▲
When an object pushes fluid aside, friction occurs. The surfer must overcome the fluid friction of the water.

Direction of motion   Rolling friction

Gravity

When you drop a ball, it falls down. Have you ever thought about why it falls down and not up? One person who thought about it was Isaac Newton. He concluded that a force acts to pull objects straight down toward the center of Earth. This force is called gravity. **Gravity** is a force that pulls objects toward each other.

Newton realized that gravity acts everywhere in the universe, not just on Earth. It is also the force that keeps the moon orbiting around Earth. It is the force that keeps all the planets in our solar system orbiting around the sun.

What Newton realized is now called the Universal Law of Gravitation. The Universal Law of Gravitation states that the force of gravity acts between all objects in the universe. This means that any two objects in the universe, without exception, attract each other. You are attracted not only to Earth but also to all the other objects around you. Earth and the objects around you are attracted to you as well. However, you do not notice the attraction among objects because these forces are small compared to the force of Earth's attraction.

Mass and Distance ⬩ **The force of gravity between objects increases with greater mass and decreases with greater distance.** The measure of the amount of matter in an object is its **mass**. The SI unit of mass is the kilogram. One kilogram is the mass of about 400 modern pennies.

Look at Figure 8. The more mass an object has, the greater its gravitational force. Because the sun's mass is so great, it exerts a large gravitational force on the planets. This causes the planets to orbit the sun.

FIGURE 7
Gravity and Earth
The diver falls into the pool because gravity is pulling her toward the center of Earth.

FIGURE 8
Gravity Between Objects
Gravity increases with mass and decreases with distance. **Inferring** *What happens to the force of gravity between two objects if the distance between them decreases?*

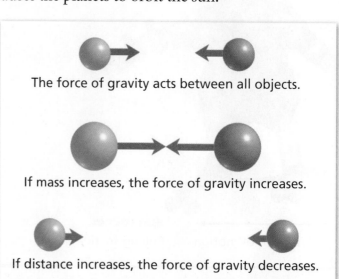

The force of gravity acts between all objects.

If mass increases, the force of gravity increases.

If distance increases, the force of gravity decreases.

In addition to mass, gravitational force depends on the distance between the objects. The farther apart two objects are, the lesser the gravitational force between them. For a spacecraft traveling toward Mars, Earth's gravitational pull decreases as the spacecraft's distance from Earth increases. Eventually the gravitational pull of Mars becomes greater than Earth's, and the spacecraft is more attracted toward Mars.

Gravity and Weight The gravitational force exerted on a person or object at the surface of a planet is known as **weight.** When you step on a bathroom scale, you are determining the gravitational force Earth is exerting on you. Objects that have a greater mass will have a greater weight. You can calculate the weight of an object by using a formula.

Weight = Mass × Acceleration due to gravity

Weight is measured in newtons and mass in kilograms. The acceleration due to gravity is 9.8 m/s^2 at Earth's surface. For example, a 50-kg person weighs 50 kg × 9.8 m/s^2 = 490 N.

Unlike mass, weight varies with the strength of the gravitational force. The strength of the gravitational force exerted on an object or a person by the moon is one sixth of the force exerted by Earth. Suppose you weighed yourself on Earth to be 450 newtons. Then you traveled to the moon and weighed yourself again. You would weigh only about 75 newtons or one sixth your weight on Earth. You weigh less on the moon because the moon's mass is only a fraction of Earth's.

 **Reading Checkpoint** What is the difference between weight and mass?

FIGURE 9

Mass and Weight This astronaut jumps easily on the moon.
Comparing and Contrasting *How do his mass and weight on the moon compare to his mass and weight on Earth?*

Astronaut in Spacesuit	
Weight on Moon =	270 N
Weight on Earth =	1,617 N
Mass on Moon =	165 kg
Mass on Earth =	165 kg

Gravity and Motion

If you drop a ball, it falls straight down. If you throw a ball outward, it travels out while it falls down. An acorn drops steadily to the ground while a leaf flutters slowly. Gravity and air resistance are the two forces responsible for these motions.

Free Fall When the only force acting on an object is gravity, the object is said to be in **free fall.** An object in free fall is accelerating. Do you know why? 🔑 **In free fall, the force of gravity alone causes an object to accelerate in the downward direction.**

How much do objects accelerate as they fall? Near the surface of Earth, the acceleration due to gravity is 9.8 m/s^2. This means that for every second an object is falling, its velocity increases by 9.8 m/s. For example, suppose an object is dropped from the top of a building. Its starting velocity is 0 m/s. After one second, its velocity has increased to 9.8 m/s. After two seconds, its velocity is 19.6 m/s (9.8 m/s + 9.8 m/s). The velocity continues to increase by 9.8 m/s each second as the object falls.

All objects in free fall accelerate at the same rate regardless of their masses. This means that two objects dropped at the same time will strike the ground at the same time. Look at Figure 10. The ball on the right has more mass than the ball on the left, yet the balls remain side by side as they fall.

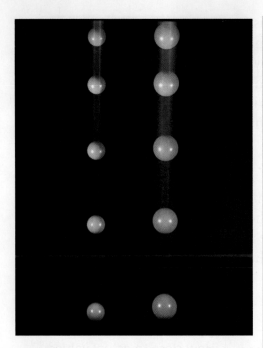

FIGURE 10
Free Fall
When gravity is the only force present, two objects with different masses fall at exactly the same rate.

Reviewing Math: Algebra and Functions 7.3.3

Math ▶ Analyzing Data

Free Fall

The graph shows how the speed of an object in free fall changes with time. Use the graph to answer the following questions.

1. **Interpreting Graphs** What is the speed of the object at 1 second? At 3 seconds?

2. **Calculating** Calculate the slope of the graph. What does this number represent?

3. **Predicting** Use the slope that you calculated in Step 2 to predict the object's speed at 6 seconds.

4. **Drawing Conclusions** The graph has a constant slope. What does the slope tell you about the object's motion?

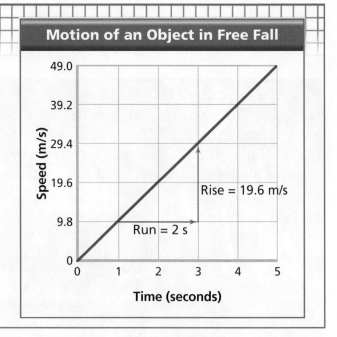

Motion of an Object in Free Fall

Rise = 19.6 m/s
Run = 2 s

Speed (m/s) — Time (seconds)

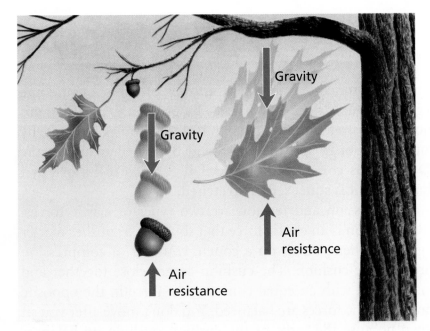

FIGURE 11
Air Resistance
Falling objects with a greater surface area experience more air resistance. If the leaf and the acorn fall from the tree at the same time, the acorn will hit first. **Comparing and Contrasting** *If the objects fall in a vacuum, which one will hit first? Why?*

Air Resistance In a vacuum, where there is no air, all objects fall with exactly the same rate of acceleration. So why does an oak leaf flutter slowly to the ground, while an acorn drops straight down? A type of fluid friction called **air resistance** acts on objects falling through air. Remember that friction acts in the direction opposite to motion. Air resistance is an upward force exerted on falling objects. Objects with a greater surface area experience more air resistance as they fall. A leaf falls more slowly than an acorn because the leaf has a larger surface area.

You can see the effect of air resistance if you drop a flat piece of paper and a crumpled piece of paper at the same time. Even though the two pieces of paper have the same mass, the flat piece has a greater surface area, so it experiences greater air resistance and falls more slowly. In a vacuum, both pieces of paper would fall at the same rate.

Projectile Motion Rather than dropping a ball straight down, what happens if you throw it horizontally? An object that is thrown is called a **projectile** (pro JEK tul). Will a projectile that is thrown horizontally land on the ground at the same time as an object that is dropped?

Look at Figure 12. The yellow ball was given a horizontal push at the same time as the red ball was dropped. Even though the yellow ball moves horizontally, gravity continues to act on it in the same way it acts on the red ball. The yellow ball falls at the same rate as the red ball. Thus, both balls will hit the ground at exactly the same time.

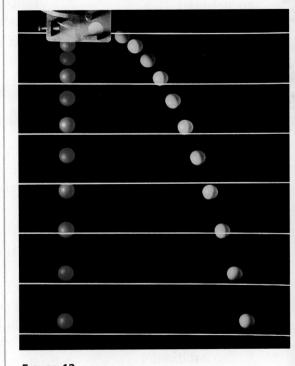

FIGURE 12
Projectile Motion
One ball is dropped vertically and a second ball is thrown horizontally at the same time.
Making Generalizations *Does the horizontal velocity of the ball affect how fast it falls? Why?*

 **Reading Checkpoint** | **How does gravity affect objects that are moving horizontally?**

FIGURE 13
Tension
Tension on the fishing line acts in opposite directions. The shoe does not fall because the forces are balanced.
Interpreting Photos What force causes the downward tension on the line?

Elastic Forces

When you squeeze a sponge, the sides of the sponge come together, but it does not break. To pull on a pair of gym shorts, you stretch the waistband. It doesn't break either. Why don't the sponge and the waistband break? They are elastic. ◉ **Matter is considered elastic if it returns to its original shape after it is squeezed or stretched.**

Compression and tension are two types of elastic forces. **Compression** is an elastic force that squeezes or pushes matter together. When you sit on a couch, you exert a compression force on the cushion. The cushion comes close together and pushes back with an equal compression force in the opposite direction. The forces are balanced. You don't move after you sit down because the force of the cushion pushing up balances your weight pushing down.

An elastic force that stretches or pulls matter is called **tension.** Look at Figure 13. A shoe hanging from the line on a fishing pole exerts a downward tension force on the line. At the same time, the fishing pole exerts an equal upward tension force on the line. The line is pulled in both directions. The shoe does not move up or down because the upward force of tension balances the shoe's weight. Other examples of tension are the strings on a guitar and the cables holding up a suspension bridge.

Section 2 Assessment

S 8.2.b, 8.2.d E-LA: Reading 8.1.2, Writing 8.2.0

Vocabulary Skill Latin Word Origins Review the word origins of *compression* and *tension*. How do the word origins help you tell the difference between the two words?

◉ **Reviewing Key Concepts**

1. **a. Summarizing** What factors affect the friction force between two surfaces?
   b. Listing What are the four types of friction?
   c. Classifying What types of friction occur when you ride a bike through a puddle?

2. **a. Identifying** What is the law of universal gravitation?
   b. Explaining How do mass and distance affect the force of gravity between objects?
   c. Predicting How would your weight change on the surface of an Earth-sized planet whose mass was greater than Earth's? Why?

3. **a. Reviewing** Why does an object accelerate when it falls toward Earth's surface?

   b. Describing How does the mass of an object affect its acceleration during free fall?
   c. Applying Concepts What force changes when a sky diver's parachute opens? What force stays the same?

4. **a. Listing** What are two types of elastic forces?
   b. Applying Concepts Describe the forces on a rope that support a tire swing when a child sits on the tire.

Writing in Science

Relating Cause-and-Effect Suppose Earth's gravitational force were decreased by half. How would this change affect a game of basketball? Write a paragraph explaining how the motion of the players and the ball would be different.

Newton's First and Second Laws

S 8.2.e Students know that when the forces on an object are unbalanced, the object will change its velocity (that is, it will speed up, slow down, or change direction).

S 8.2.f Students know the greater the mass of an object, the more force is needed to achieve the same rate of change in motion.

- What is Newton's first law of motion?
- What is Newton's second law of motion?

Key Term
- inertia

Standards **Warm-Up**

Lab zone

What Changes Motion?

1. Stack several metal washers on top of a toy car.
2. Place a heavy book on the floor near the car.
3. Predict what will happen to both the car and the washers if you roll the car into the book. Test your prediction.

Think It Over

Observing What happened to the car when it hit the book? What happened to the washers? What force(s) could account for any difference between the motions of the car and the washers?

How and why objects move as they do has fascinated scientists for thousands of years. In the early 1600s, the Italian astronomer Galileo Galilei suggested that, once an object is in motion, force is needed only to change the motion of an object. A force is not necessary to keep it moving. Galileo's ideas paved the way for Isaac Newton. Newton proposed the three basic laws of motion in the late 1600s.

The First Law of Motion

Newton's first law restates Galileo's ideas about force and motion. **Newton's first law of motion states that an object will remain at rest or moving at a constant velocity unless it is acted upon by an unbalanced force.** An unbalanced force will cause an object to speed up, slow down, or change direction.

If an object is not moving, it will not move until a force acts on it. The clothes on the floor of your room will stay there unless you pick them up. You provide the force to move your clothes. A tennis ball flies through the air once you hit it with a racket. A moving object, such as the tennis ball, will move at a constant velocity until a force acts to change its speed or direction. On Earth, gravity and air resistance are forces that will change the tennis ball's velocity as it flies through the air.

Isaac Newton

FIGURE 14
Inertia The inertia of the objects on the table keeps them from moving.
Inferring Why should the girl use a slippery tablecloth?

Inertia Whether an object is moving or not, it resists any change to its motion. Galileo's concept of the resistance to a change in motion is called inertia. **Inertia** (in UR shuh) is the tendency of an object to resist a change in motion. Newton's first law of motion is also called the law of inertia.

Inertia explains many common events, such as why you move forward in your seat when a car stops suddenly. When a car stops, inertia keeps you moving forward. A force, such as the pull of a seat belt, is required to change your motion.

Inertia Depends on Mass Suppose you need to move an empty aquarium and an aquarium full of water. Obviously, the full aquarium is harder to move than the empty one, because it has more mass. The greater the mass of an object is, the greater its inertia, and the greater the force required to change its motion. The full aquarium is more difficult to move because it has more inertia than the empty aquarium.

Reading Checkpoint　How is mass related to inertia?

The Second Law of Motion

Suppose you are baby-sitting two children who love wagon rides. Their favorite part is when you accelerate quickly. Recall that acceleration is the rate at which velocity changes. When you get tired and sit in the wagon, one of the children pulls you. He soon finds he cannot accelerate the wagon nearly as fast as you can. How is the wagon's acceleration related to the force pulling it? How is the acceleration related to the wagon's mass?

Lab zone **Try This Activity**

Around and Around

An object moving in a circle has inertia.

1. Tape one end of a length of thread (about 1 m) to a table tennis ball.
2. Suspend the ball in front of you and swing it in a horizontal circle, keeping it 2–3 cm above the floor.
3. Let go of the thread and observe how the ball rolls.

Observing Describe how the ball moves when you let go of the thread. Explain why it moves in this way.

Changes in Force and Mass How do you get a wagon to speed up, slow down, or turn a corner? You apply a force to it. What if you want the wagon to speed up, slow down, or turn a corner at a faster rate? You apply even more force. An increase in force results in an increase in acceleration.

Another way to increase acceleration is to change the mass. Suppose your friend gets into the wagon with you. The wagon now has more mass. If the child pulls with the same force as before, the wagon will move very slowly, if at all. For a constant force, an increase in the mass will result in a decrease in the acceleration.

Determining Acceleration Newton's second law of motion states that acceleration depends on the net force acting on the object and on the object's mass. This relationship can be written as a formula.

$$\text{Acceleration} = \frac{\text{Net force}}{\text{Mass}}$$

Acceleration is measured in meters per second per second (m/s^2), net force is measured in newtons (N), and mass is measured in kilograms (kg). You can also write this formula as Net force $= \text{Mass} \times \text{Acceleration}$. You can think of 1 newton as the force required to give a 1-kg mass an acceleration of 1 m/s^2.

 What does the acceleration of an object depend upon?

For: More on Newton's laws
Visit: PHSchool.com
Web Code: cgd-3023

FIGURE 15
Force and Mass
The force of the boy's pull and the mass of the wagon determine the wagon's acceleration.
Predicting *If more mass is added to the wagon and if the boy pulls with the same force, how will its acceleration change?*

Math ▸ Sample Problem

Calculating Force

A speedboat pulls a 55-kg water-skier. The skier accelerates at 2.0 m/s². Calculate the net force that causes this acceleration.

1 Read and Understand
What information are you given?

Mass of the water-skier (m) = **55 kg**
Acceleration of the water-skier (a) = **2.0 m/s²**

2 Plan and Solve
What quantity are you trying to calculate?

The net force (F_{net}) = ▪

What formula contains the given quantities and the unknown quantity?

$$a = \frac{F_{net}}{m} \quad \text{or} \quad F_{net} = m \times a$$

Perform the calculation.

$F_{net} = m \times a = 55 \text{ kg} \times 2.0 \text{ m/s}^2$
$F = 110 \text{ kg} \cdot \text{m/s}^2$
$F = 110 \text{ N}$

3 Look Back and Check
Does your answer make sense?

A net force of 110 N is required. This does not include the force that overcomes friction.

Math ▸ Practice

1. **Calculating Force** What is the net force on a 1,000-kg object accelerating at 3 m/s²?

2. **Calculating Force** What net force is needed to accelerate a 25-kg cart at 14 m/s²?

Section 3 Assessment

S 8.2.e, 8.2.f, E-LA: Reading 8.1.2

Vocabulary Skill **Latin Word Origins** The word *inertia* comes from two Latin words—*in* meaning "not" and *ars* meaning "moving" or "active." How does the word origin help you remember the term *inertia*?

Reviewing Key Concepts

1. **a. Reviewing** What is Newton's first law of motion?
   b. Explaining Why is Newton's first law of motion sometimes called the law of inertia?
   c. Inferring Use inertia to explain why you feel pressed back into the seat of a car when it accelerates.
2. **a. Defining** State Newton's second law of motion.
   b. Problem Solving How could you keep an object's acceleration the same if the force acting on the object were doubled?

c. Applying Concepts Explain why a car with a large mass might use more fuel than a car with a smaller mass. Assume both cars drive the same distance.

Math ▸ Practice

3. **Calculating Force** What is the net force acting on a 0.15-kg hockey puck accelerating at a rate of 12 m/s²?

4. **Calculating Acceleration** Find the acceleration of an 800-kg car that has a net force of 4,000 N acting upon it.

Newton's Third Law

CALIFORNIA
Standards Focus

S 8.2.e Students know that when the forces on an object are unbalanced, the object will change its velocity (that is, it will speed up, slow down, or change direction).

🔑 What is Newton's third law of motion?

🔑 How can you calculate the momentum of an object?

🔑 What is the law of conservation of momentum?

Key Terms
- momentum
- law of conservation of momentum

Lab zone Standards **Warm-Up**

How Pushy Is a Straw?

1. Stretch a rubber band around the middle of the front cover of a medium-size hardcover book.
2. Place four marbles in a small square on a table. Place the book on the marbles face up so that the cover with the rubber band is on top.
3. Hold the book steady by placing one index finger on the spine. Then, as shown, push a straw against the rubber band with your other index finger.
4. Push the straw until the rubber band stretches about 10 cm. Then let go of both the book and the straw at the same time.

Think It Over
Developing Hypotheses What did you observe about the motion of the book and the straw? Write a hypothesis to explain what happened in terms of the forces on the book and the straw.

Have you ever tried to teach a friend how to roller-skate? It's hard if you are both wearing skates. When your friend pushes against you to get started, you move too. And when your friend runs into you to stop, you both end up moving! To understand why this happens you need to know about Newton's third law of motion and the law of conservation of momentum.

Newton's Third Law of Motion

Newton proposed that whenever one object exerts a force on a second object, the second object exerts a force back on the first object. The force exerted by the second object is equal in strength and opposite in direction to the first force. Think of one force as the "action" and the other force as the "reaction." 🔑 **Newton's third law of motion states that if one object exerts a force on another object, then the second object exerts a force of equal strength in the opposite direction on the first object.** Another way to state Newton's third law is that for every action there is an equal but opposite reaction.

Action force

Reaction force

When the gymnast does a flip, he pushes down on the vaulting horse. The reaction force of the vaulting horse pushes him up to complete the flip.

Action force   Reaction force

The kayaker's paddle pulls on the water. The reaction force of the water pushes back on the paddle, causing the kayak to move.

Action force

Reaction force

When the dog leaps, it pushes down on the ground. The reaction force of the ground pushes the dog into the air.

FIGURE 16
Action-Reaction Pairs
Action-reaction pairs explain how a gymnast can flip over a vaulting horse, how a kayaker can move through the water, and how a dog can leap off the ground. **Interpreting Photos** *Describe how the velocities of the gymnast, the kayaker, and the dog change as a result of reaction forces.*

Action-Reaction Pairs You're probably familiar with many examples of Newton's third law. Pairs of action and reaction forces are all around you. When you jump, you push on the ground with your feet. This is an action force. The ground pushes back on your feet with an equal and opposite force. This is the reaction force. You speed up and move in an upward direction when you jump because the ground is pushing you! In a similar way, the kayaker speeds up by exerting an action force on the water with a paddle. The water pushes back on the paddle with an equal reaction force that propels the kayak forward.

Now you can understand what happens when you teach your friend to roller-skate. Your friend exerts an action force when he pushes against you to start. You exert a reaction force in the opposite direction. As a result, both of you speed up in opposite directions.

Detecting Motion Can you always detect motion when paired forces are in action? The answer is no. For example, when Earth's gravity pulls on an object, you cannot detect the equal and opposite reaction of Earth. Suppose you drop your pencil. Gravity pulls the pencil downward. At the same time, the pencil pulls Earth upward with an equal and opposite reaction force. You don't see Earth accelerate toward the pencil because Earth's inertia is so great that its acceleration is too small to notice.

Do Action-Reaction Forces Cancel? Earlier you learned that if two equal forces act in opposite directions on an object, the forces are balanced. Because the two forces add up to zero, they cancel each other out and produce no change in velocity. Why then don't the action and reaction forces in Newton's third law of motion cancel out as well? After all, they are equal and opposite.

The action and reaction forces do not cancel out because they are acting on different objects. Look at the volleyball player on the left in Figure 17. She exerts an upward action force on the ball. In return, the ball exerts an equal but opposite downward reaction force back on her wrists. The action and reaction forces act on different objects.

On the other hand, the volleyball players on the right are both exerting a force on the *same* object—the volleyball. When they hit the ball from opposite directions, each of their hands exerts a force on the ball equal in strength but opposite in direction. The forces on the volleyball are balanced and the ball does not move either to the left or to the right.

 Reading Checkpoint) **Why don't action and reaction forces cancel each other?**

FIGURE 17
Action-Reaction Forces
In the photo on the left, the player's wrists exert the action force. In the photo below, the ball exerts reaction forces on both players.
Interpreting Diagrams *In the photo below, will the volleyball's velocity change? Why?*

Force on wrists

Force on ball

Forces on hands

Force on ball

Force on ball

Momentum

All moving objects have what Newton called a "quantity of motion." Another name for this quantity is momentum. **Momentum** (moh MEN tum) is a characteristic of a moving object that depends on both the mass and the velocity of the object. ⬤ **You can calculate the momentum of a moving object by multiplying the object's mass and velocity.**

Momentum = Mass × Velocity

Since mass is measured in kilograms and velocity is measured in meters per second, the unit for momentum is kilogram-meters per second (kg·m/s). Like velocity, acceleration, and force, momentum is described by its direction as well as its quantity. The momentum of an object is in the same direction as its velocity.

Math Sample Problem

Reviewing Math: Measurement and Geometry 7.1.3

Calculating Momentum

Which has more momentum: a 3.0-kg sledgehammer swung at 1.5 m/s, or a 4.0-kg sledgehammer swung at 0.9 m/s?

1 Read and Understand
What information are you given?

Mass of smaller sledgehammer = 3.0 kg
Velocity of smaller sledgehammer = 1.5 m/s
Mass of larger sledgehammer = 4.0 kg
Velocity of larger sledgehammer = 0.9 m/s

2 Plan and Solve
What quantities are you trying to calculate?

The momentum of each sledgehammer = ■

What formula contains the given quantities and the unknown quantity?

Momentum = Mass × Velocity

Perform the calculations.

Smaller sledgehammer: 3.0 kg × 1.5 m/s = **4.5 kg·m/s**
Larger sledgehammer: 4.0 kg × 0.9 m/s = **3.6 kg·m/s**

3 Look Back and Check
Does your answer make sense?

It is possible for the 3.0-kg hammer to have more momentum than the 4.0-kg one because it has a greater velocity.

Math Practice

1. **Calculating Momentum**
A golf ball travels at 16 m/s, while a baseball moves at 7 m/s. The mass of the golf ball is 0.045 kg and the mass of the baseball is 0.14 kg. Which has greater momentum?

2. **Calculating Momentum**
What is the momentum of a bird with a mass of 0.018 kg flying at 15 m/s?

FIGURE 18
Momentum
An object's momentum is the product of the object's mass and velocity.
Problem Solving *If both dogs have the same velocity, which one has the greater momentum?*

The more momentum a moving object has, the harder it is to change its velocity. For example, it is easier to change the velocity of a baseball moving at 20 m/s than it is to change the velocity of a car moving at 20 m/s. The car has more momentum because it has a greater mass. It is however harder to change the velocity of a baseball moving at 20 m/s than it is to change the velocity of a baseball moving at 5 m/s. The baseball moving at 20 m/s has more momentum because it has a greater velocity.

 **Reading Checkpoint** **What must you know to determine an object's momentum?**

Conservation of Momentum

In everyday language, conservation means saving resources. You might conserve water or fossil fuels, for example. In physical science, the word *conservation* has a more specific meaning. It refers to the conditions before and after some event. An amount that is conserved is the same amount after an event as it was before.

The total amount of momentum objects have is conserved when they collide. Momentum may be transferred from one object to another as the velocity of the objects change, but none is lost. This is called the law of conservation of momentum.

The **law of conservation of momentum** states that, in the absence of outside forces, the total momentum of objects that interact does not change. The amount of momentum is the same before and after they interact. ⬬ **The total momentum of any group of objects remains the same, or is conserved, unless outside forces act on the objects.** Friction is an example of an outside force.

FIGURE 19

Conservation of Momentum

In the absence of friction, momentum is conserved when two train cars collide. **Interpreting Diagrams** *In which diagram is all of the momentum transferred from the blue car to the green car?*

A Two Moving Objects

Before

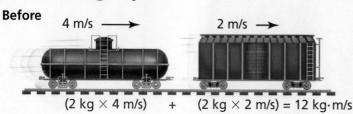

Before the collision, the blue car moves faster than the green car. Afterward, the green car moves faster. The total momentum stays the same.

$$(2 \text{ kg} \times 4 \text{ m/s}) + (2 \text{ kg} \times 2 \text{ m/s}) = 12 \text{ kg·m/s}$$

After

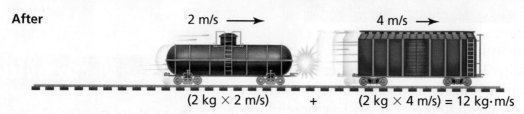

$$(2 \text{ kg} \times 2 \text{ m/s}) + (2 \text{ kg} \times 4 \text{ m/s}) = 12 \text{ kg·m/s}$$

B One Moving Object

When the green car is at rest before the collision, all of the blue car's momentum is transferred to it. Momentum is conserved.

Before

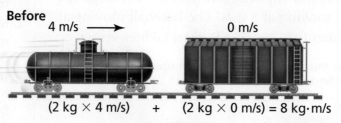

$$(2 \text{ kg} \times 4 \text{ m/s}) + (2 \text{ kg} \times 0 \text{ m/s}) = 8 \text{ kg·m/s}$$

After

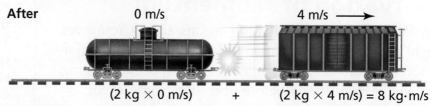

$$(2 \text{ kg} \times 0 \text{ m/s}) + (2 \text{ kg} \times 4 \text{ m/s}) = 8 \text{ kg·m/s}$$

C Two Connected Objects

Before

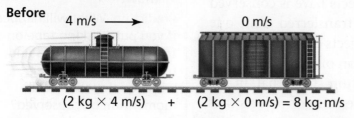

If the two cars couple together, momentum is still conserved. Together, the cars move slower than the blue car did before the collision.

$$(2 \text{ kg} \times 4 \text{ m/s}) + (2 \text{ kg} \times 0 \text{ m/s}) = 8 \text{ kg·m/s}$$

After

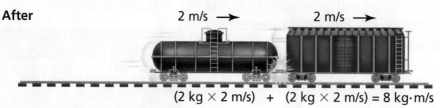

$$(2 \text{ kg} \times 2 \text{ m/s}) + (2 \text{ kg} \times 2 \text{ m/s}) = 8 \text{ kg·m/s}$$

Collisions With Two Moving Objects In Figure 19A, the blue train car travels at 4 m/s down the same track as the green train car traveling at only 2 m/s. The two train cars have equal masses. The blue car catches up with the green car and bumps into it. During the collision, the speed of each car changes. The blue car slows down to 2 m/s, and the green car speeds up to 4 m/s. Momentum is conserved—the momentum of one train car decreases while the momentum of the other increases.

Collisions With One Moving Object In Figure 19B, the blue car travels at 4 m/s but the green car is not moving. Eventually the blue car hits the green car. After the collision, the blue car is no longer moving, but the green car travels at 4 m/s. Even though the situation has changed, momentum is conserved. All of the momentum has been transferred from the blue car to the green car.

Collisions With Connected Objects Suppose that, instead of bouncing off each other, the two train cars couple together when they hit. Is momentum still conserved in Figure 19C? After the collision, the coupled train cars make one object with twice the mass. The velocity of the coupled trains is 2 m/s—half the initial velocity of the blue car. Since the mass is doubled and the velocity is divided in half, the total momentum remains the same.

Section 4 Assessment

S 8.2.e, Math: 7 MG 1.3
E-LA: Reading 8.2.4

Target Reading Skill Take Notes Review your notes for this section. What three important ideas did you include about Newton's Third Law of Motion?

Reviewing Key Concepts

1. a. **Reviewing** State Newton's third law of motion.
   b. **Summarizing** According to Newton's third law of motion, how are action and reaction forces related?
   c. **Applying Concepts** A boy catches a ball while standing on roller skates. What happens to the boy's velocity and the ball's velocity?
2. a. **Defining** What is momentum?
   b. **Predicting** What is the momentum of a parked car?
   c. **Relating Cause and Effect** Why is it important for drivers to allow more distance between their cars when they travel at faster speeds?

3. a. **Identifying** What is meant by "conservation of momentum"?
   b. **Inferring** The total momentum of two marbles before a collision is 0.06 kg·m/s. No outside forces act on the marbles. What is the total momentum of the marbles after the collision?

Math Practice

4. **Calculating Momentum** What is the momentum of a 920-kg car moving at a speed of 25 m/s?
5. **Calculating Momentum** Which has more momentum: a 250-kg dolphin swimming at 4 m/s, or a 350-kg manatee swimming at 2 m/s?

Forced to Accelerate

S 8.2.f, 8.9.e

Problem

How is the acceleration of a skateboard related to the force that is pulling it?

Skills Focus

calculating, graphing, interpreting data

Materials

- skateboard • meter stick • string
- stopwatch • masking tape
- spring scale, 5-N
- several bricks or other large mass(es)

Procedure

1. Attach a loop of string to a skateboard. Place the bricks on the skateboard.

2. Using masking tape, mark off a one-meter distance on a level floor. Label one end "Start" and the other "Finish."

3. Attach a spring scale to the loop of string. Pull it so that you maintain a force of 2.0 N. Be sure to pull with the scale straight out in front. Practice applying a steady force to the skateboard as it moves.

4. Copy the data table into your notebook.

5. Find the smallest force needed to pull the skateboard at a slow, constant speed. Do not accelerate the skateboard. Record this force on the first line of the table.

6. Add 0.5 N to the force in Step 5. This will be enough to accelerate the skateboard. Record this force on the second line of the table.

7. Have one of your partners hold the front edge of the skateboard at the starting line. Then pull on the spring scale with the force you found in Step 6.

8. When your partner says "Go" and releases the skateboard, maintain a constant force until the skateboard reaches the finish line. A third partner should time how many seconds it takes the skateboard to go from start to finish. Record the time in the column labeled Trial 1.

9. Repeat Steps 7 and 8 twice more. Record your results in the columns labeled Trial 2 and Trial 3.

10. Repeat Steps 7, 8, and 9 using a force 1.0 N greater than the force you found in Step 5.

11. Repeat Steps 7, 8, and 9 twice more. Use forces that are 1.5 N and 2.0 N greater than the force you found in Step 5.

Data Table							
Force (N)	Trial 1 Time (s)	Trial 2 Time (s)	Trial 3 Time (s)	Average Time (s)	Average Speed (m/s)	Final Speed (m/s)	Acceleration (m/s²)

Analyze and Conclude

1. **Calculating** For each force, find the average of the three times that you measured. Record the average time in your data table.

2. **Calculating** For each force, find the average speed of the skateboard. Use this formula:

   Average speed = 1 m ÷ Average time

   Record this value for each force.

3. **Calculating** To obtain the final speed of the skateboard, multiply each average speed by 2. Record the result in your data table.

4. **Calculating** To obtain the acceleration, divide each final speed you found by the average time. Record the acceleration in your data table.

5. **Graphing** Make a line graph. Show the force on the *x*-axis and the acceleration on the *y*-axis. The *x*-axis should go from 0 N to 3.0 N. The *y*-axis scale should go from 0 m/s^2 to about 1 m/s^2. If your data points seem to form a straight line, draw a line through them.

6. **Interpreting Data** Your first data point is the pulling force required for an acceleration of zero. If the acceleration is zero, what is the net force on the skateboard? Explain.

7. **Interpreting Data** According to your graph, how is the acceleration of the skateboard related to the pulling force?

8. **Communicating** Write a paragraph in which you identify the manipulated variable and the responding variable in this experiment. Explain why the mass of the skateboard is kept constant. (See the Skills Handbook to read about experimental variables.)

Design an Experiment

Design an experiment to test how the acceleration of the loaded skateboard depends on its mass. Think about how you would vary the mass of the skateboard. What quantity would you need to measure that you did not measure in this experiment? What quantity would you keep constant? Do you have the equipment to make that measurement? If not, what other equipment would you need? *Obtain your teacher's permission before carrying out your investigation.*

Rockets and Satellites

S 8.2.e Students know that when the forces on an object are unbalanced, the object will change its velocity (that is, it will speed up, slow down, or change direction).

- How does a rocket lift off the ground?

- What keeps a satellite in orbit?

Key Terms

- satellite
- centripetal force

Lab zone Standards **Warm-Up**

What Makes an Object Move in a Circle?

1. Tie a small mass, such as an empty thread spool, to the end of a string no more than one meter long.

2. Swing the object around in a circle that is perpendicular to the floor. Make sure no one is near the swinging object, and don't let it go!

Think It Over

Observing Is there a net force acting on the object? How do you know?

In October 1957, 14-year-old Homer Hickam looked upward and saw a speck of light move across the sky. It was the Russian satellite *Sputnik*, the first artificial satellite. It was propelled into space by a powerful rocket. This sight inspired Homer and his friends. They spent the next three years designing, building, and launching rockets in their hometown of Coalwood, West Virginia. Many of their first attempts failed, but they did not give up. Eventually, they built a rocket that soared to a height of almost ten kilometers. Their hard work paid off. In 1960, they won first place in the National Science Fair. Since then, rocket launches have become more familiar, but they are still an awesome sight.

◄ Homer Hickam holds a rocket that he and his friends designed.

How Do Rockets Lift Off?

A space shuttle like the one in Figure 20 has a mass of more than 2 million kilograms when loaded with fuel. An incredible amount of force is required to get the shuttle to overcome Earth's gravity and rise into space. Rockets and space shuttles lift into space using Newton's third law of motion. They burn fuel and push the exhaust gases downward at a high velocity as they lift off. In turn, the gases push upward on the rocket. 👁 **A rocket can rise into the air because the gases it expels with a downward action force exert an equal but opposite reaction force on the rocket.** As long as this upward force, called thrust, is greater than the downward pull of gravity, there is an unbalanced force in the upward direction that causes a change in the rocket's velocity. As a result, the rocket accelerates upward into space.

What Is a Satellite?

Rockets are often used to carry satellites into space. A **satellite** is any object that orbits another object in space. The moon is a satellite because it orbits Earth. An artificial satellite is a device that is launched into orbit. Artificial satellites are designed for many purposes, such as communications, military intelligence, weather analysis, and geographical surveys.

Circular Motion Artificial satellites travel around Earth in an almost circular path. An object traveling in a circle is constantly changing direction so it is accelerating. If an object is accelerating, an unbalanced force must be acting on it. Any force that causes an object to move in a circular path is a **centripetal force** (sen TRIP ih tul). The word *centripetal* means "center-seeking." The centripetal force acts in a direction perpendicular to the direction the object is moving at any given point.

In the Standards Warm-Up, the string supplies the centripetal force. The string pulls the object toward the center, and thereby keeps it moving in a circular path. For a satellite, the centripetal force that pulls the satellite toward the center of Earth is gravity.

 **Reading Checkpoint** What type of force causes an object to move in a circular path?

Action force

Reaction force

FIGURE 20
A Rocket Launch
The action force pushes the rocket's exhaust gases downward. The reaction force of the gases sends the rocket into space. **Predicting** *As the rocket ascends, how will its mass change?*

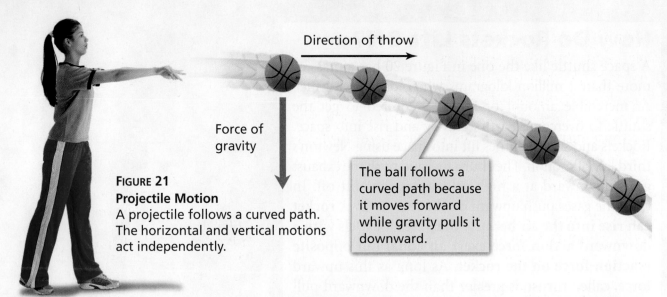

Direction of throw

Force of gravity

FIGURE 21
Projectile Motion
A projectile follows a curved path. The horizontal and vertical motions act independently.

The ball follows a curved path because it moves forward while gravity pulls it downward.

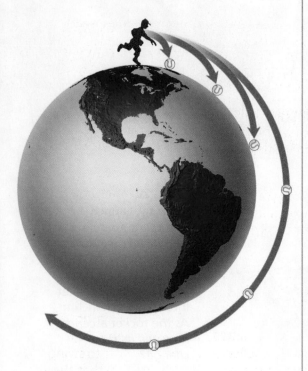

FIGURE 22
Satellite Motion
The faster a projectile is thrown, the farther it travels before it hits the ground. A projectile with enough velocity moves in a circular orbit. **Interpreting Diagrams** *How does the direction of gravity compare to the direction of the orbiting projectile's motion at any point?*

Satellite Motion Gravity pulls satellites toward Earth. So why don't satellites fall to the ground, as a ball thrown through the air would? The answer is that satellites have a greater horizontal velocity than a ball would have. Instead of falling to Earth, satellites fall around Earth.

If you throw a ball horizontally, as shown in Figure 21, the ball will move away from you at the same time that the unbalanced force, gravity, causes a change in direction. The horizontal and vertical motions act independently, and the ball follows a curved path toward the ground. If you throw the ball faster, it will land even farther in front of you. The faster you throw a projectile, the farther it travels before it lands.

Now suppose, as Isaac Newton did, what would happen if you were on a high mountain and could throw a ball as fast as you wanted. The faster you threw it, the farther away it would land. But, at a certain speed, the path of the ball would match the curve of Earth. Although the ball would keep falling due to gravity, Earth's surface would curve away from the ball at the same rate. Thus the ball would fall around Earth in a circle, as shown in Figure 22.

Satellites in orbit around Earth continuously fall toward Earth, but because Earth is curved they travel around it. In other words, a satellite is a falling projectile that keeps missing the ground! It falls around Earth rather than into it. A satellite does not need fuel because it continues to move ahead due to its inertia. At the same time, the unbalanced force, gravity, continuously changes the satellite's direction. The speed with which an object must be thrown in order to orbit Earth turns out to be about 7,900 m/s!

Satellite Location Some satellites, such as mapping and observation satellites, are put into low orbits of less than 1,000 kilometers. In a low orbit, satellites complete a trip around Earth in less than two hours. Other satellites are sent into higher orbits. At those distances, a satellite travels more slowly, taking longer to circle Earth. For example, communications satellites travel about 36,000 kilometers above Earth's surface. At that height, they circle Earth once every 24 hours. Because Earth rotates once every 24 hours, a satellite above the equator always stays at the same point above Earth as it orbits.

 **Reading Checkpoint** How does gravity help keep satellites in orbit?

FIGURE 23
Satellite Locations
Depending on their uses, artificial satellites orbit at different heights.

Communications satellite
35,800 km

Global Positioning System
20,000 km

Research satellite
6,000 km

Space shuttle
400 km

Section 5 Assessment

S 8.2.e, E-LA: Reading 8.1.2

Vocabulary Skill Latin Word Origins How does knowing the meaning of the word origin of *centr-* help you remember the meaning of *centripetal*?

Reviewing Key Concepts

1. a. **Identifying** Which of Newton's three laws of motion explains how a rocket lifts off?
   b. **Explaining** How do action-reaction pairs explain how a rocket lifts off?
   c. **Applying Concepts** As a rocket travels upward from Earth, air resistance decreases along with the force of gravity. The rocket's mass also decreases as its fuel is used up. If thrust remains the same, how do these factors affect the rocket's acceleration?

2. a. **Defining** What is a satellite?
   b. **Relating Cause and Effect** What causes satellites to stay in orbit rather than falling toward Earth?

c. **Inferring** In Figure 22, a projectile is thrown with enough velocity to orbit Earth. What would happen if the projectile were thrown with a greater velocity?

Lab zone At-Home **Activity**

Swing the Bucket Fill a small plastic bucket halfway with water and take it outdoors. Challenge a family member to swing the bucket in a vertical circle. Explain that the water won't fall out at the top if the bucket is moving fast enough. Tell your family member that if the bucket falls as fast as the water, the water will stay in the bucket. Relate this activity to a satellite that also falls due to the unbalanced force of gravity, yet remains in orbit.

The BIG Idea
An unbalanced force will cause a change in an object's velocity.

1 The Nature of Force

Key Concepts   S 8.2.a, 8.2.c

- A force is described by its magnitude and by the direction in which it acts.
- Unbalanced forces on an object result in a net force and change an object's velocity.
- Balanced forces acting on an object do not change the object's velocity.

Key Terms
- force • newton • net force
- unbalanced forces • balanced forces

2 Friction, Gravity, and Elastic Forces

Key Concepts   S 8.2.b, 8.2.d

- The strength of the force of friction depends on the types of surfaces involved and on how hard the surfaces are pushed together.
- Gravity between objects increases with greater mass and decreases with greater distance.
- In free fall, the force of gravity alone causes an object to accelerate in the downward direction.
- Matter is considered elastic if it returns to its original shape after it is squeezed or stretched.

Key Terms
- friction • static friction • sliding friction
- rolling friction • fluid friction • gravity
- mass • weight • free fall • air resistance
- projectile • compression • tension

3 Newton's First and Second Laws

Key Concepts   S 8.2.e, 8.2.f

- Newton's first law of motion states that an object will remain at rest or moving at a constant velocity unless it is acted upon by an unbalanced force.
- Newton's second law of motion states that acceleration depends on the net force acting on the object and on the object's mass.

$$\text{Acceleration} = \frac{\text{Net force}}{\text{Mass}}$$

Key Term
inertia

4 Newton's Third Law

Key Concepts   S 8.2.e

- Newton's third law of motion states that if one object exerts a force on another object, then the second object exerts a force of equal strength in the opposite direction on the first object.
- You can calculate the momentum of a moving object by multiplying the object's mass and velocity.

$$\text{Momentum} = \text{Mass} \times \text{Velocity}$$

- The total momentum of any group of objects remains the same, or is conserved, unless outside forces act on the objects.

Key Terms
momentum
law of conservation of momentum

5 Rockets and Satellites

Key Concepts   S 8.2.e

- A rocket can rise into the air because the gases it expels with a downward action force exert an equal but opposite reaction force on the rocket.
- Satellites in orbit around Earth continuously fall toward Earth, but because Earth is curved they travel around it.

Key Terms
satellite   centripetal force

Review and Assessment

Target Reading Skill

Take Notes In your notebook, create a two-column note-taking organizer for Section 4. Include summary statements.

Recall Clues & Questions	Notes
What is friction?	Friction—a force that two surfaces exert on each other
	Strength depends on • types of surfaces • how hard they are pushed together

Reviewing Key Terms

Choose the letter of the best answer.

1. When an unbalanced force acts on an object, the force
   a. changes the motion of the object.
   b. is canceled by another force.
   c. does not change the motion of the object.
   d. is equal to the weight of the object.

2. Which of the following is an elastic force?
   a. friction
   b. gravity
   c. tension
   d. air resistance

3. Which of the following is not a projectile?
   a. a satellite
   b. a thrown ball
   c. a ball on the ground
   d. a soaring arrow

4. The resistance of an object to any change in its motion is called
   a. inertia.
   b. friction.
   c. gravity.
   d. weight.

5. The product of an object's mass and its acceleration is called the
   a. net force.
   b. weight.
   c. momentum.
   d. gravitation.

Complete the following sentences so that your answers clearly explain the key terms.

6. When two people push on a box and the box does not move, this is an example of **balanced forces,** which are _____ .

7. **Friction** depends upon how hard the surfaces are pushed together and _____ .

8. A force that pulls objects toward each other is called **gravity,** which depends upon _____ .

9. The force of **air resistance** is greater on a leaf than an acorn because _____ .

10. The **momentum** of an object depends on ___ .

Writing in Science

Descriptive Paragraph Suppose you have been asked to design a new amusement park ride. Write a description of how you will design it. Explain the role that friction and gravity will play in the ride's design.

Video Assessment

Discovery Channel School

Forces

Review and Assessment

Checking Concepts

11. Four children pull on the same toy at the same time, yet there is no net force on the toy. How is that possible?

12. Why are parts of machines that slide over each other often bathed in oil?

13. A yo-yo is hanging motionless from a string. Identify and describe the forces exerted on the string.

14. Explain how force, mass, and acceleration are related by Newton's second law of motion.

15. Suppose you are an astronaut making a space walk outside your space station when your jet pack runs out of fuel. How can you use your empty jet pack to get you back to the station?

16. Draw a diagram showing the motion of a satellite around Earth. Draw the force vectors acting on the satellite. Is the satellite accelerating?

Thinking Critically

17. Classifying What is the name of the force you exert on a sponge when you squeeze it?

18. Applying Concepts You are moving fast on a skateboard when your wheel gets stuck in a crack on the sidewalk. Using the term *inertia*, explain what happens.

19. Problem Solving Look at the diagram below of two students pulling a bag of volleyball equipment. The friction force between the bag and the floor is 15 N. What is the net force acting on the bag? What is the acceleration of the bag?

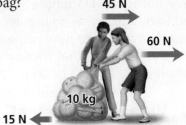

45 N

60 N

10 kg

15 N

20. Relating Cause and Effect If you push a book across a table at a constant velocity, is the friction force less than, equal to, or more than your pushing force? How do you know?

Math Practice

21. Calculating Force A 7.3-kg bowling ball accelerates at a rate of 3.7 m/s². What force acts on the bowling ball?

22. Calculating Momentum A 240-kg snowmobile travels at 16 m/s. The mass of the driver is 75 kg. What is the momentum of the snowmobile and driver?

Applying Skills

Use the illustration showing a collision between two balls to answer Questions 23–25.

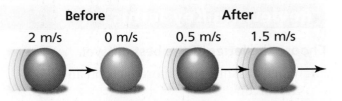

Before		After	
2 m/s	0 m/s	0.5 m/s	1.5 m/s

23. Calculating Use the formula for momentum to find the momentum of each ball before and after the collision. Assume the mass of each ball is 0.4 kg.

24. Inferring Find the total momentum before and after collision. Is the law of conservation of momentum satisfied in this collision? Explain.

25. Designing Experiments Design an experiment in which you could show that momentum is not conserved between the balls when friction is strong.

Lab zone Standards Investigation

Performance Assessment Test your vehicle to make sure it will work on the type of floor in your classroom. Will the vehicle stay within the bounds set by your teacher? Identify all the forces acting on the vehicle. What was the most significant source of friction for your vehicle? List at least three features you included in the design of the vehicle that led to an improvement in its performance. For example, did you give it a smooth shape for low air resistance?

CALIFORNIA
Standards Practice

Choose the letter of the best answer.

1. Which of the following is determined by the force of gravity?
   A weight
   B momentum
   C mass
   D distance   S 8.2.d

2. When an object is pulled across a level surface at a constant velocity, what force is the pulling force equal to?
   A gravity
   B friction
   C inertia
   D an unbalanced force   S 8.2.e

3. What force makes it less likely for a person to slip on a dry sidewalk as opposed to an icy sidewalk?
   A air resistance
   B friction
   C inertia
   D momentum   S 8.2.e

Use the diagram below to answer questions 4 and 5.

Force Force   Motion

4. What conclusion can you draw by looking at the diagram?
   A Air resistance in front of the balloon pushes it backward.
   B Gravity forces air out of the balloon's open end.
   C The force of the air leaving the balloon causes it to accelerate forward.
   D Friction causes the balloon's acceleration to decrease.   S 8.2.a

5. In the diagram above, why don't the two forces cancel each other out?
   A They are not equal.
   B They both act on the air.
   C They both act on the balloon.
   D They act on different objects.   S 8.2.e

6. The table below shows the mass of and net force on four objects. Which object has the greatest acceleration?

Calculating Acceleration		
Object	Net Force (N)	Mass (kg)
Boulder	1,000	100
Suitcase	20	20
Shopping cart	25	50
Book	2	1

   A boulder
   B suitcase
   C shopping cart
   D book   S 8.2.f

7. In a game of tug-of-war, you pull on the rope with a force of 100 N to the right and your friend pulls on the rope with a force of 100 N to the left. What is the net force on the rope?
   A 200 N to the right
   B 200 N to the left
   C 0 N
   D 100 N to the right   S 8.2.c

Apply the
BIG Idea

8. Two dogs are pulling on opposite ends of a bone. One dog pulls to the right with a force of 50 N while the other pulls to the left with a force of 40 N. Are the forces on the bone balanced or unbalanced? How do you know? What is the net force on the bone? Would the bone's velocity change? Why?

                                    S 8.2.b, S 8.2.f

The force of air pushing on a hang glider's ▶ wing helps to keep the glider aloft.

Focus on the
BIG Idea

 S 8.8.d

How can you predict if an object will sink or float in a fluid?

Check What You Know

You dive into a pool wearing a life vest. Wearing the vest makes you bigger and makes you weigh more. So why do you float?

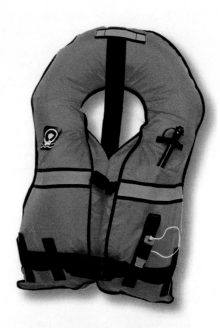

Build Science Vocabulary

The images shown here represent some of the Key Terms in this chapter. You can use this vocabulary skill to help you understand the meaning of some Key Terms in this chapter.

Identify Multiple Meanings

Some familiar words have more than one meaning. Words you use every day may have different meanings in science. Look at the different meanings of the words below.

Word	Everyday Meaning	Scientific Meaning
fluid	*n.* A liquid **Example:** It's good for your health to drink plenty of <u>fluids</u> every day.	*n.* A substance that can easily flow; a gas or a liquid **Example:** Like water, air is a <u>fluid</u>.
force	*v.* To use power to make someone do something **Example:** She had to <u>force</u> herself to get up early.	*n.* A push or a pull exerted on an object **Example:** You exert <u>force</u> when you open and close a door.
pressure	*n.* A feeling of being pushed to do things **Example:** Students may feel <u>pressure</u> from adults to do well on tests.	*n.* The force exerted on a surface divided by the total area over which the force is exerted **Example:** When air leaks from a tire, the <u>pressure</u> is reduced and the tire becomes soft.

Apply It!

Read the sentences below. Then identify the term that has a scientific meaning.

1. When a gas is heated, the *pressure* of the gas increases.

2. Her parents are putting *pressure* on her to find a job.

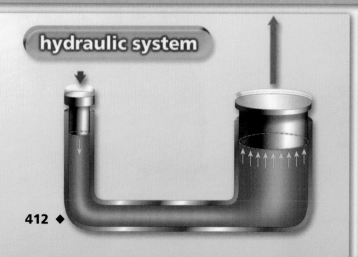

hydraulic system

barometer

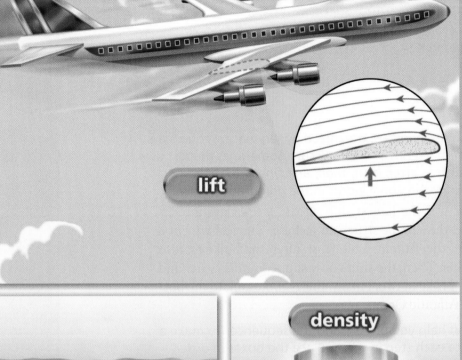

lift

buoyant force

density

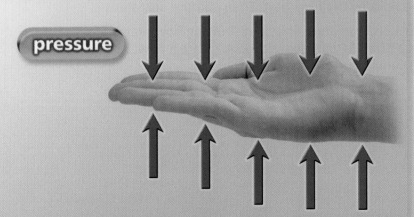

pressure

Chapter 11 Vocabulary

Section 1 (page 416)
pressure
pascal
fluid
barometer

Section 2 (page 424)
density
buoyant force
Archimedes' principle

Section 3 (page 432)
Pascal's principle
hydraulic system

Section 4 (page 437)
Bernoulli's principle
lift

Interactive Textbook

Build Science Vocabulary
Online
Visit: PHSchool.com
Web Code: cxj-3110

Chapter 11 ◆ **413**

How to Read Science

Sequence

Many parts of a textbook are organized by sequence. Sequence is the order in which a series of events occurs. Sometimes the text uses signal words, such as *after, next, then,* and *finally* to show sequence. Look for the signal words in the paragraph below.

> The *Titanic* was the largest ship afloat. A few days into its first voyage, the *Titanic* struck an iceberg. The iceberg cut a long hole in the *Titanic's* hull. <u>Soon after,</u> the hull began to fill with water. <u>Then,</u> the ship's bow slipped under water and the *Titanic* broke in two. <u>Finally,</u> the *Titanic* sank to the bottom of the Atlantic Ocean.

A flowchart can help you understand the sequence. To make a flowchart, write each step in a box. Place the boxes in order.

The *Titanic*

The *Titanic* struck an iceberg.

↓

The iceberg cut a long hole in the *Titanic's* hull.

↓

The hull began to fill with water.

↓

Apply It!

In your notebook, copy the flowchart. Then add the next steps.

As you read Section 3, create a flowchart showing how pressure is transmitted in a fluid. As you read Section 4, create a flowchart on how an atomizer works.

S 8.8.d

Staying Afloat

Why doesn't a heavy boat sink? In this investigation, you will design and build a boat that can float in water and carry cargo. You will find out what forces in fluids make an object sink or float.

Your Goal

To construct a boat that can float in water and carry cargo

Your boat must

- be made of metal only
- support a cargo of 50 pennies without allowing any water to enter for at least 10 seconds
- travel at least 1.5 meters
- be built following the safety guidelines in Appendix A

Plan It!

Before you design your boat, think about the shape of real ships. Preview the chapter to find out what makes an object float. Then look for simple metal objects that you can form into a boat. Compare different materials and designs to build the boat that best fits the goals listed above. After your teacher approves your design, build your boat and test it.

Pressure

CALIFORNIA
Standards Focus

S 8.8.d Students know how to predict whether an object will float or sink.

S 8.9.f Apply simple mathematical relationships to determine a missing quantity in a mathematic expression, given the two remaining terms (including speed = distance/time, density = mass/volume, force = pressure × area, volume = area × height).

- What does pressure depend on?
- How do fluids exert pressure?
- How does fluid pressure change with elevation and depth?

Key Terms

- pressure
- pascal
- fluid
- barometer

Lab zone Standards **Warm-Up**

Does Water Push Back?

1. Fill a large sink with water. Drop a deflated balloon into the water and note what happens.

2. Now fill the balloon with air and push the balloon into the water. Note what happens when you let go of the balloon.

Think It Over

Drawing Conclusions Compare your observations in Steps 1 and 2. Why did an air-filled balloon act differently from the deflated one?

Outside, deep snow covers the ground. You put on your sneakers and head out, shovel in hand. When you step outside, your foot sinks deep into the snow. It's nearly up to your knees! Nearby, a sparrow hops across the surface of the snow. Unlike you, the bird does not sink. In fact, it barely leaves a mark! Why do you sink into the snow while the sparrow rests on the surface? The answer has to do with pressure.

What Is Pressure?

The word *pressure* is related to the word *press*. You may recall that Earth's gravity pulls you downward with a force equal to your weight. Due to gravity, your feet exert a force on the surface of Earth over an area the size of your feet. In other words, your feet exert pressure on the ground.

Exerting pressure on snow ▶

Area = 250 cm²

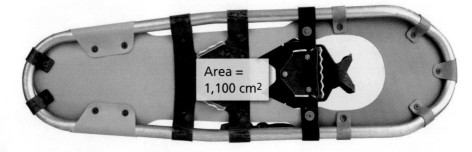
Area = 1,100 cm²

FIGURE 1
Pressure and Area
The amount of pressure depends on the area over which
a force is distributed. **Inferring** *Which type of shoe*
would you use to keep from sinking into deep snow?

Pressure and Area  **The amount of pressure you exert
depends on the area over which you exert a force.** The larger
the area over which the force is distributed, the less pressure
is exerted.

In order to stand on snow without sinking, you can change
the area over which you exert the force of your weight. Figure 1
shows that if you wear sneakers, your weight is distributed over
the soles of both shoes. You'll exert pressure over an area of only
about 250 cm² × 2, or 500 cm², and sink into the snow. But if
you wear snowshoes, your weight is distributed over a much
greater area—about 1,100 cm² × 2, or 2,200 cm². Because your
weight is distributed over a greater area, the pressure exerted on
the snow is much less. Like a sparrow, you can stand on the
snow without sinking!

Calculating Pressure Pressure is equal to the force exerted
on a surface divided by the total area over which the force is
exerted. You can calculate pressure using the formula below.

$$\text{Pressure} = \frac{\text{Force}}{\text{Area}}$$

Force is measured in newtons (N). Area is measured in
square meters (m²). Since force is divided by area, the SI unit of
pressure is the newton per square meter (N/m²). This unit of
pressure is also called the **pascal** (Pa): $1 \text{ N/m}^2 = 1 \text{ Pa}$. It is
named for the French mathematician Blaise Pascal.

Reading Checkpoint What is the SI unit of pressure called?

Math Skills

Area
The area of a surface is the
number of square units that
it covers. To find the area
of a rectangle, multiply its
length by its width. The area
of the rectangle below is
2 cm × 3 cm, or 6 cm².

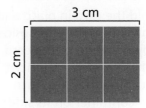
3 cm
2 cm

Practice Problem Which has
a greater area: a rectangle
that is 4 cm × 20 cm, or a
square that is 10 cm × 10 cm?

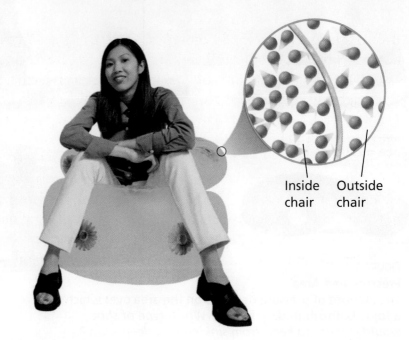

FIGURE 2
Fluid Particles
The particles that make up a fluid move constantly in all directions. When a particle collides with a surface, it exerts a force on the surface.
Relating Cause and Effect *What will happen to the force exerted by the particles in the chair when you add more air to the chair?*

Inside   Outside
chair   chair

Fluid Pressure

Solids such as sneakers are not the only materials that exert pressure. Fluids also exert pressure. A **fluid** is a material that can easily flow. As a result, a fluid can change shape. Liquids such as water and oil and gases such as air and helium are examples of fluids. Understanding pressure in fluids will help you to predict whether an object will float or sink.

What Causes Fluid Pressure? Think about the tiny particles that make up a fluid. Particles in a fluid constantly move in all directions, as shown in Figure 2. As they move, the particles collide with each other and with any surface that they meet.

As each particle of a fluid collides with a surface, it exerts a force on the surface. **In a fluid, all of the forces exerted by the individual particles combine to make up the pressure exerted by the fluid.** Because the number of particles is large, you can consider the fluid as a whole. So, the pressure exerted by a fluid is the total force exerted by the fluid divided by the area over which the force is exerted.

Air Pressure Did you know that you live at the bottom of 100 kilometers of fluid? This fluid, called air, is the mixture of gases that makes up Earth's atmosphere. These gases press down on everything on Earth's surface, all the time. Air exerts pressure because it has mass. Each cubic meter of air around you has a mass of about 1 kilogram. Because the force of gravity pulls down on this mass of air, the air has weight. The weight of the air is the force that produces air pressure, or atmospheric pressure.

Lab zone Try This **Activity**

Card Trick

1. Fill a small plastic cup to the brim with water. Gently place an index card over the top of the cup.

2. Hold the card in place and slowly turn the cup upside down. Let go of the card. What happens? Without touching the card, turn the container on its side.

Inferring Why does the water stay in the cup when you turn the cup upside down?

Balanced Pressure Hold out your hand, palm up. You are holding up air. At sea level, atmospheric pressure is about 101,300 Pa. The surface area of your hand is about 100 cm². So, the weight supported by the surface area of your hand is about 1,000 newtons, or about the same weight as that of a large washing machine!

How could your hand possibly support that weight and not feel it? In a stationary fluid, pressure at a given point is exerted equally in all directions. The weight of the atmosphere does not just press down on your hand. It presses on your hand from every direction. The pressures balance each other.

Balanced pressures also explain why the tremendous air pressure pushing on you from all sides does not crush you. Your body contains fluids that exert outward pressure. For example, your lungs and sinus cavities contain air. Your cells and blood vessels contain liquids. Pressure from fluids inside your body balances the air pressure outside your body.

What happens when air pressure becomes unbalanced? Look at Figure 4. When the can is full of air, the air pressure inside the can balances the atmospheric pressure outside the can. When air is removed from the can, the unbalanced force of the outside air pressure crushes the can.

 **How is the pressure on your hand balanced?**

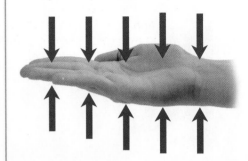

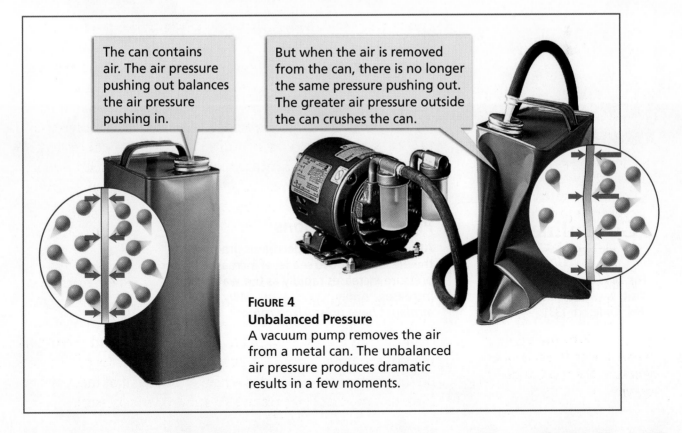

The can contains air. The air pressure pushing out balances the air pressure pushing in.

But when the air is removed from the can, there is no longer the same pressure pushing out. The greater air pressure outside the can crushes the can.

FIGURE 4
Unbalanced Pressure
A vacuum pump removes the air from a metal can. The unbalanced air pressure produces dramatic results in a few moments.

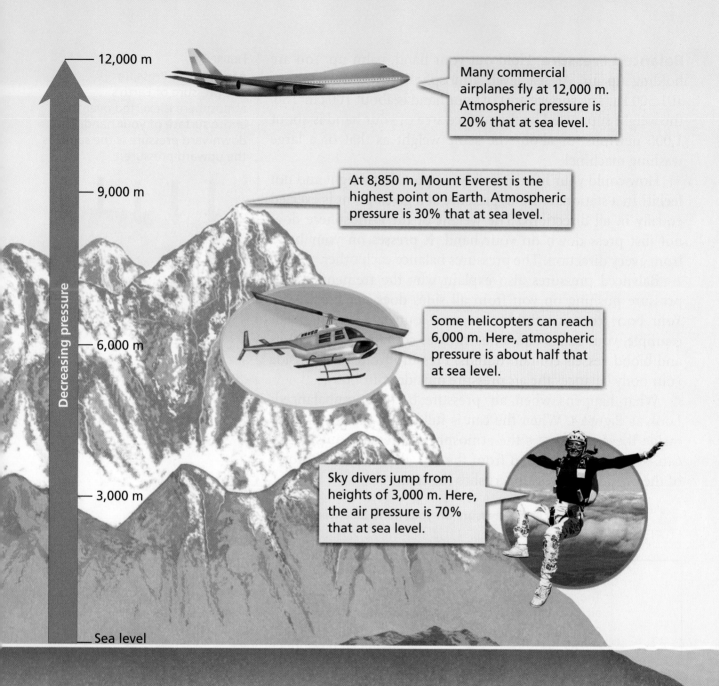

12,000 m — Many commercial airplanes fly at 12,000 m. Atmospheric pressure is 20% that at sea level.

9,000 m — At 8,850 m, Mount Everest is the highest point on Earth. Atmospheric pressure is 30% that at sea level.

6,000 m — Some helicopters can reach 6,000 m. Here, atmospheric pressure is about half that at sea level.

3,000 m — Sky divers jump from heights of 3,000 m. Here, the air pressure is 70% that at sea level.

Sea level

Decreasing pressure

FIGURE 5
Pressure Variations
Atmospheric pressure decreases gradually as the elevation above sea level increases. Water pressure increases rapidly as the water depth increases. **Applying Concepts** *Why do airplanes have pressurized cabins?*

Variations in Fluid Pressure

Have you ever felt your ears "pop" as you rode up in an elevator? What happens to pressure as you climb to a higher elevation or sink to a lower depth within a fluid? Figure 5 shows how pressure changes depending on where you are.

Atmospheric Pressure and Elevation The "popping" in your ears is caused by changing air pressure. At higher elevations, there is less air above you and therefore less air pressure. **Atmospheric pressure decreases as your elevation increases.**

When the air pressure outside your body decreases, the air pressure inside also decreases, but more slowly. So, for a moment, the air pressure behind your eardrums is greater than it is in the air outside. Your body releases this pressure with a "pop," balancing the pressures.

Water Pressure and Depth You experience a different type of presssure change if you dive underwater. **Water pressure increases as depth increases.** So if you dive into a body of water, pressure becomes greater as you descend. The deeper you swim, the greater the pressure you feel.

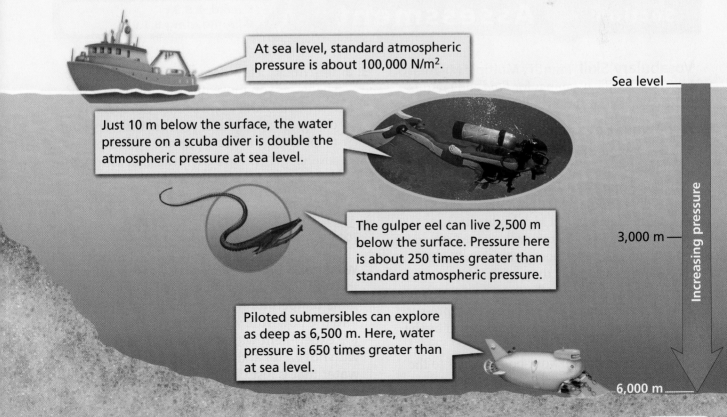

At sea level, standard atmospheric pressure is about 100,000 N/m².

Just 10 m below the surface, the water pressure on a scuba diver is double the atmospheric pressure at sea level.

The gulper eel can live 2,500 m below the surface. Pressure here is about 250 times greater than standard atmospheric pressure.

Piloted submersibles can explore as deep as 6,500 m. Here, water pressure is 650 times greater than at sea level.

Sea level

Increasing pressure

3,000 m

6,000 m

FIGURE 6

Aneroid Barometer

An aneroid barometer measures atmospheric pressure.

Interpreting Photographs What type of weather might be coming when atmospheric pressure decreases?

Water pressure is a result of the weight of the water above a particular point. At greater depths, there is more water above that point and therefore more weight to support. In addition, air in the atmosphere pushes down on the water. Therefore, the total pressure at a given point beneath the water results from the weight of the water plus the weight of the air above it. In the deepest parts of the ocean, the pressure is more than 1,000 times the air pressure you experience every day.

Measuring Pressure You can measure atmospheric pressure with an instrument called a **barometer.** Weather forecasters use the pressure reading from a barometer to help forecast the weather. Rapidly decreasing atmospheric pressure usually means a storm is on its way. Increasing pressure is often a sign of fair weather.

The barometer you usually see hanging on a wall is an aneroid barometer. Forecasters will often express the pressure in units of millimeters of mercury or inches of mercury. Those units are based on the original type of barometer, which measured how far the atmosphere pushed liquid mercury up a tube. Standard atmospheric pressure at sea level may be reported as 760 millimeters of mercury, which is about the same as 101,300 Pa.

Reading Checkpoint What instrument measures atmospheric pressure?

Section 1 Assessment

S 8.8.d, S 8.9.f
E-LA: Reading 8.1.0

Vocabulary Skill Identify Multiple Meanings Use the scientific meanings for *fluid* and *pressure* to help you define the term *fluid pressure.*

Reviewing Key Concepts

1. **a. Reviewing** What two factors does pressure depend on?
   b. Comparing and Contrasting Who exerts more pressure on the ground—a 500-N woman standing in high heels with a total area of 0.005 m^2, or the same woman standing in work boots with a total area of 0.05 m^2? Calculate the pressure she exerts on the ground in both cases.
2. **a. Summarizing** How do fluids exert pressure?
   b. Explaining Why aren't you crushed by the weight of the atmosphere?
   c. Inferring How is your body similar to the can containing air shown in Figure 4?

3. **a. Describing** How does atmospheric pressure change as you move up away from sea level?
   b. Comparing and Contrasting Compare the change in atmospheric pressure with elevation to the change in water pressure with depth.
   c. Applying Concepts Why must an astronaut wear a pressurized suit in space?

Lab zone At-Home Activity

Water and Weight Fill a pot with water from the sink. Fill a sandwich bag with water at the same temperature. Seal the bag and drop it into the pot. Note what happens. Then repeat the experiment with a sandwich bag filled with hot water and a sandwich bag filled with water that is just slightly above the freezing point. Describe your observations.

Spinning Sprinklers

Problem

What factors affect the speed of rotation of a lawn sprinkler?

Skills Focus

designing experiments, controlling variables

Materials

• empty soda can
• fishing line, 30 cm
• waterproof marker
• wide-mouth jar or beaker
• stopwatch
• nails of various sizes
• large basin

Procedure

PART 1 Making a Sprinkler

1. Fill the jar with enough water to completely cover a soda can. Place the jar in the basin.

2. Bend up the tab of a can and tie the end of a length of fishing line to it. **CAUTION:** *The edge of the can opening can be sharp.*

3. Place a mark on the can to help you keep track of how many times the can spins.

4. Using the small nail, make a hole in the side of the can about 1 cm up from the bottom. Poke the nail straight in. Then twist the nail until it makes a right angle with the radius of the can as shown in the figure above. **CAUTION:** *Nails are sharp and should be used only to puncture the cans.*

5. Submerge the can in the jar and fill the can to the top with water.

6. Quickly lift the can with the fishing line so that it is 1–2 cm above the water level in the jar. Practice counting how many spins the can completes in 15 seconds.

PART 2 What Factors Affect Spin?

7. How does the size of the hole affect the number of spins made by the can? Propose a hypothesis and then design an experiment to test the hypothesis. Obtain your teacher's approval before carrying out your experiment. Record all your data.

8. How does the number of holes affect the number of spins made by the can? Propose a hypothesis and then design an experiment to test the hypothesis. Obtain your teacher's approval before carrying out your experiment. Record all your data.

Analyze and Conclude

1. **Designing Experiments** How does the size of the hole affect the rate of spin of the can? How does the number of holes affect the rate of spin of the can?

2. **Controlling Variables** What controlled parameters did you leave unchanged in this experiment? What other parameters might affect the number of spins made by the can?

3. **Interpreting Data** Explain the motion of the can in terms of unbalanced forces.

4. **Classifying** Which of Newton's three laws of motion could you use to explain the motion of the can? Explain.

5. **Communicating** Use the results of your experiment to write a paragraph that explains why a spinning lawn sprinkler spins.

More to Explore

Some sprinkler systems use water pressure to spin. Examine one of these sprinklers to see the size, direction of spin, and number of holes. What would happen if you connected a second sprinkler to the first with another length of hose? If possible, try it.

Floating and Sinking

CALIFORNIA
Standards Focus

S 8.8.c Students know the buoyant force on an object in a fluid is an upward force equal to the weight of the fluid the object has displaced.

S 8.8.d Students know how to predict whether an object will float or sink.

🔑 How can you predict whether an object will float or sink in a fluid?

🔑 What is the effect of the buoyant force?

Key Terms
- density
- buoyant force
- Archimedes' principle

Lab zone Standards **Warm-Up**

What Can You Measure With a Pencil? 🦺 👤

1. Carefully stick a metal thumbtack in the eraser of an unsharpened wooden pencil. You have built a device called a hydrometer.
2. Place the pencil in a glass of water with the eraser and tack pointing down. Note how far the pencil sinks in the water by marking the edge of the pencil at the water's surface line with a waterproof marker.
3. Remove the pencil from the water. Measure the length the pencil sunk in centimeters.
4. Dissolve 10 spoonfuls of sugar into the glass of water. Try out your hydrometer in this liquid. Again mark how far the pencil sinks. Then remove the pencil from the water and once again measure the length the pencil sunk in centimeters.

Think It Over
Predicting Compare your observations in Steps 3 and 4. Predict what will happen if you use 20 spoonfuls of sugar in a glass of water. Test your prediction.

In April 1912, the *Titanic* departed from England on its first and only voyage. At the time, it was the largest ship afloat—nearly three football fields long. The *Titanic* was also the most technologically advanced ship in existence. Its hull was divided into compartments, and it was considered to be unsinkable.

Yet a few days into the voyage, the *Titanic* struck an iceberg. One compartment after another filled with water. Less than three hours later, the bow of the great ship slipped under the waves. As the stern rose high into the air, the ship broke in two. Both pieces sank to the bottom of the Atlantic Ocean. More than a thousand people died.

◀ **The bow section of the Titanic resting on the ocean floor**

Density

The Titanic sank because of a change in its density. Recall that the **density** of a substance is its mass per unit volume.

$$\text{Density} = \frac{\text{Mass}}{\text{Volume}}$$

For example, one cubic centimeter (cm³) of copper has a mass of 8.8 grams, so its density is 8.8 g/cm³. One cubic centimeter of plastic has a mass of only about 0.93 gram. So the density of plastic is about 0.93 g/cm³. Copper is more dense than plastic. The density of water is 1.0 g/cm³. So water is less dense than copper but more dense than plastic.

Comparing Densities of Substances Figure 7 shows several substances and their densities. Each substance has its own density. Some liquids float on top of other liquids. The substances with the greatest densities are near the bottom.

 **By comparing densities, you can predict whether an object will float or sink in a fluid.** An object that is more dense than the fluid it is in sinks. An object that is less dense than the fluid floats on the surface. An object with a density equal to that of the fluid floats at a constant depth.

> **Reading Checkpoint** When will an object float on a fluid's surface?

Math Skills

Calculating Density

The density of a substance is its mass per unit of volume.

$$\text{Density} = \frac{\text{Mass}}{\text{Volume}}$$

For example, a sample of liquid has a mass of 24 g and a volume of 16 mL. What is its density?

$$\text{Density} = \frac{24 \text{ g}}{16 \text{ mL}}$$
$$= 1.5 \text{ g/mL}$$

Practice Problem A piece of metal has a mass of 43.5 g and a volume of 15 cm³. What is its density?

Substance	Density (g/cm³)
Wood	0.7
Corn oil	0.925
Plastic	0.93
Water	1.00
Tar ball	1.02
Glycerin	1.26
Rubber washer	1.34
Corn syrup	1.38
Copper wire	8.8
Mercury	13.6

FIGURE 7
Densities of Substances
You can use density to predict whether an object will sink or float when placed in a liquid.
Predicting *Will a rubber washer sink or float in corn oil?*

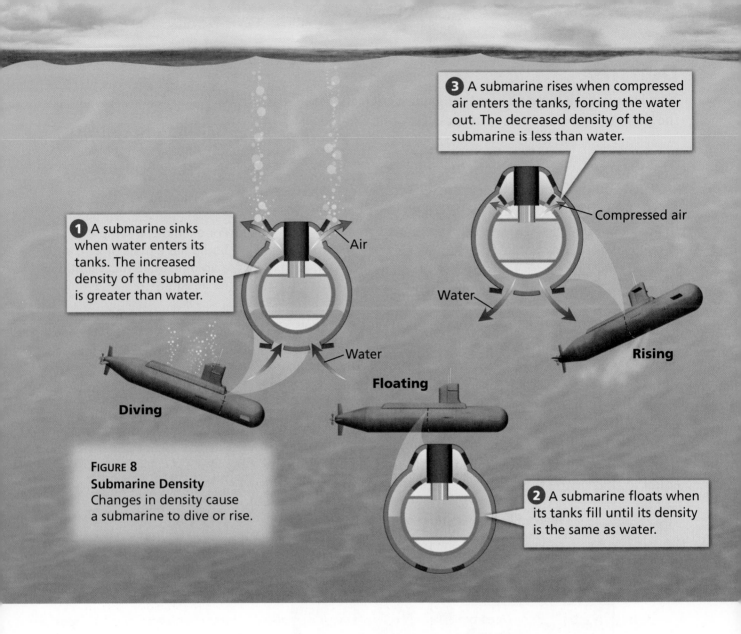

❸ A submarine rises when compressed air enters the tanks, forcing the water out. The decreased density of the submarine is less than water.

Compressed air

❶ A submarine sinks when water enters its tanks. The increased density of the submarine is greater than water.

Air

Water

Water

Rising

Diving

Floating

FIGURE 8
Submarine Density
Changes in density cause a submarine to dive or rise.

❷ A submarine floats when its tanks fill until its density is the same as water.

Changing Density Changing density can explain why an object floats or sinks. For example, you can change the density of water by freezing it into ice. Since water expands when it freezes, the ice occupies more space than the water. That's why ice is less dense than water. But it's just a bit less dense! So most of an ice cube floating on the surface is below the water's surface.

You can make an object sink or float in a fluid by changing its density. Look at Figure 8 to see how this happens to a submarine. The density of a submarine increases when water fills its flotation tanks. This happens because the overall mass of the submarine increases, but its volume remains the same. So the submarine will sink. To make the submarine rise in the water, the engineer pumps water out of the flotation tanks, decreasing the submarine's mass. Its density decreases, and it rises.

 Reading Checkpoint **When will a submarine rise?**

Buoyancy

Ships are designed to have buoyancy—the ability to float. How is it possible that a huge ship can float easily on the surface of water under certain conditions, and then in a few hours become a sunken wreck? To answer this question, you need to understand the buoyant force.

Gravity and the Buoyant Force If you have ever picked up an object under water, you know that it seems much lighter in water than in air. Water and other fluids exert an upward force called the **buoyant force** that acts on a submerged object. ☞ **The buoyant force acts in the direction opposite to the force of gravity, so it makes an object feel lighter.** The less dense the object is, the greater the buoyant force it experiences.

As you can see in Figure 9, a fluid exerts pressure on all surfaces of a submerged object. Since the pressure in a fluid increases with depth, the upward pressure on the bottom of the object is greater than the downward pressure on the top. The result is a net force acting upward on the submerged object. This is the buoyant force.

Remember that the weight of a submerged object is a downward force. If an object's weight is greater than the buoyant force, a net force acts downward on the object. The object will sink. If the weight of an object is equal to the buoyant force, no net force acts on the object. The object will not sink. A submerged object whose weight is equal to the buoyant force also has no net force acting on it. The object will not sink.

Remember that you can also use density to explain why objects float or sink. In Figure 10, the density of the jellyfish is less than that of water, while the turtle's density is equal to that of water. The jellyfish and the turtle float. The density of the lobster is greater than water. The lobster sinks.

FIGURE 9
Buoyant Force
The pressure on the bottom of a submerged object is greater than the pressure on the top. The result is a net force in the upward direction.

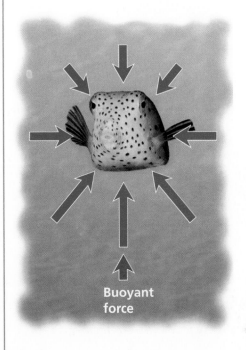

Buoyant force

FIGURE 10
Buoyant Force and Weight
The buoyant force works opposite the weight of an object. The forces acting on the jellyfish and turtle are balanced, so they float in place. The forces on the lobster are unbalanced.
Comparing and Contrasting *Why does the lobster sink?*

Weight

Buoyant force

Weight

Buoyant force

Weight

Buoyant force

◆ 427

Floating
When the film can is empty, it floats. The volume of displaced fluid is equal to the volume of the submerged portion of the can.

Film can

Displaced fluid

Displaced fluid

Sinking
When the film can has film in it, it sinks. The volume of fluid displaced by the can is equal to the volume of the can.

FIGURE 11
Archimedes' Principle
Archimedes' principle applies to sinking and floating objects.
Predicting *If you press down on the floating film can, what will happen to the volume of the displaced fluid in the small beaker?*

Video Field Trip
Discovery Channel School
Forces in Fluids

Archimedes' Principle

All objects take up space. A submerged object displaces, or takes the place of, a volume of fluid equal to its own volume. A partly submerged object displaces a volume of fluid equal to the volume of its submerged portion only. You can see this in Figure 11.

Archimedes, a mathematician of ancient Greece, discovered a connection between the weight of a fluid displaced by an object and the buoyant force acting on it. **Archimedes' principle** states that the buoyant force acting on a submerged object is equal to the weight of the volume of fluid displaced by the object. Suppose your body displaces 50 liters of water in a swimming pool. The buoyant force on you will be equal to the weight of 50 liters of water, or about 500 N.

Submarines How can a submarine dive and float? Since the buoyant force is equal to the weight of the displaced fluid, the buoyant force on the submerged submarine stays the same. Changing the water level in the flotation tanks changes the weight of the submarine. The submarine sinks when its weight is greater than the buoyant force. It rises when its weight is less than the buoyant force.

Balloons Air is a fluid. A balloon filled with air is denser than the surrounding air because the air inside it is under pressure. The denser air inside makes it fall to the ground. But if the air inside the balloon is heated, it becomes less dense, and the balloon rises. You can also fill a balloon with helium. A helium balloon rises because helium is less dense than air.

 **Reading Checkpoint** Why does a helium balloon float in air?

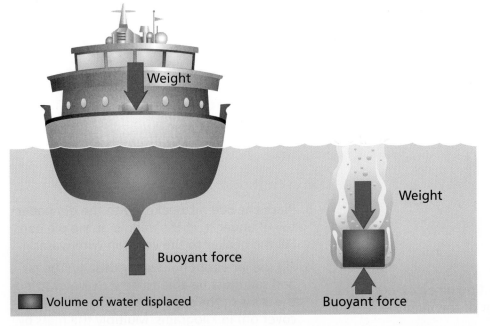

Weight

Buoyant force

Volume of water displaced

Weight

Buoyant force

Ships You can use Archimedes' principle to explain why a ship floats on the surface. Since the buoyant force equals the weight of the displaced fluid, the buoyant force will increase if more fluid is displaced. A large object displaces more fluid than a small object. A greater buoyant force acts on the larger object even if the large object has the same weight as the small object.

Look at Figure 12. The ship's hull has the same mass as the solid block of steel, but its shape causes the ship to displace a greater volume of water. According to Archimedes' principle, the buoyant force is equal to the weight of the displaced water. Since a ship displaces more water than a block of steel, a greater buoyant force acts on the ship. The buoyant force acting on it is equal to its weight, and the ship floats on the surface.

Section 2 Assessment

S 8.8.c, 8.8.d E-LA: Reading 8.1.0

Vocabulary Skill Identify Multiple Meanings
Use the scientific meaning of *force* to define the key term *buoyant force*.

Reviewing Key Concepts

1. **a. Defining** What is density?
   b. Explaining How can you use the density of an object to predict whether it will float or sink in water?
   c. Applying Concepts Some canoes have compartments on either end that are hollow and watertight. These canoes won't sink, even when they capsize. Explain why.

2. **a. Explaining** How does the buoyant force affect a submerged object?
   b. Summarizing How does Archimedes' principle relate the buoyant force acting on an object to the fluid displaced by the object?

   c. Calculating An object that weighs 340 N floats on a lake. What is the weight of the displaced water? What is the buoyant force?

Lab zone At-Home Activity

Changing Balloon Density Attach paper clips to the string of a helium balloon. Ask a family member to predict how many paper clips you will need to attach to make the balloon sink to the floor. How many paper clips can you attach and still keep the helium balloon suspended in the air? Explain how adding paper clips changes the overall density of the balloon.

Sink and Spill

S 8.8.c, 8.9.a

Problem

How is the buoyant force acting on an object in a fluid related to the weight of the fluid the object displaces?

Skills Focus

controlling variables, interpreting data, drawing conclusions

Materials

- paper towels • pie pan
- triple-beam balance • beaker, 600-mL
- jar with watertight lid, about 30-mL
- table salt

Procedure

1. Preview the procedure and copy the data table into your notebook. Predict the relationship you will find between the buoyant force and the weight of the displaced water.

2. Find the mass, in kilograms, of a dry paper towel and the pie pan together. To convert grams to kilograms, divide the mass in grams by 1,000. Multiply the mass by 9.8 m/s^2. This gives you the weight in newtons. Record it in your data table.

3. Place the 600-mL beaker, with the dry paper towel under it, in the middle of the pie pan. Fill the beaker to the very top with water.

4. Fill the jar about halfway with salt. (The jar and salt must be able to float in water.) Find the mass of the salt and the dry jar (with its cover on) in kilograms. Multiply the mass by 9.8 m/s^2. Record this weight in your data table.

5. Gently lower the jar into the 600-mL beaker. (If the jar sinks, take it out and remove some salt. Repeat Steps 2, 3, and 4.) Estimate the fraction of the jar that is underwater, and record it.

6. Once all of the displaced water has been spilled, find the total mass of the paper towel and pie pan containing the water in kilograms. Multiply the mass by 9.8 m/s^2 and record the result in your data table.

7. Empty the pie pan. Dry off the pan and jar.

8. Repeat Steps 3 through 7 several more times. Each time fill the jar with a different amount of salt, but make sure the jar still floats.

9. Record the buoyant force for each trial in your data table. (*Hint:* When an object floats, the buoyant force is equal to the weight of the object.)

10. Calculate the weight of the displaced water in each case. Record it in your data table.

Data Table						
Jar	Weight of Empty Pie Pan and Dry Paper Towel (N)	Weight of Jar, Salt, and Cover (N)	Weight of Pie Pan With Displaced Water and Paper Towel (N)	Fraction of Jar Submerged in Water	Buoyant Force (N)	Weight of Displaced Water (N)
1						
2						
3						

Analyze and Conclude

1. **Controlling Variables** In each trial, the jar had a different weight. How did this affect the way that the jar floated?

2. **Interpreting Data** The jar had the same volume in every trial. Why did the volume of displaced water vary?

3. **Drawing Conclusions** What can you conclude about the relationship between the buoyant force acting on an object and the weight of the water it displaces?

4. **Drawing Conclusions** If you put too much salt in the jar, it will sink. What can you conclude about the buoyant force in this case? How can you determine the buoyant force for an object that sinks?

5. **Communicating** Write a paragraph suggesting changes to the experiment that would improve the accuracy of your results.

Design an Experiment

How do you think your results would change if you used a liquid that is more dense or less dense than water? Design an experiment to test your hypothesis. What liquids will you use? Will you need equipment other than what you used for this experiment? If so, what will you need? *Obtain your teacher's permission before carrying out your investigation.*

Pascal's Principle

S 8.8.c Students know the buoyant force on an object in a fluid is an upward force equal to the weight of the fluid the object has displaced.

- What does Pascal's principle say about change in fluid pressure?

- How does a hydraulic system work?

Key Terms

- Pascal's principle
- hydraulic system

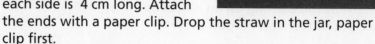

Lab zone Standards **Warm-Up**

Why Does the Cartesian Diver Sink?

1. Fill a plastic jar or bottle almost completely with water.

2. Make a Cartesian diver by bending a plastic straw into a U shape. Cut the ends so that each side is 4 cm long. Attach the ends with a paper clip. Drop the straw in the jar, paper clip first.

3. Attach more paper clips to the first one until the straw floats with its top about 0.5 cm above the surface. This is the diver.

4. Put the lid on the jar. Observe what happens when you slowly squeeze and release the jar several times.

Think It Over

Observing Describe the behavior of the Cartesian diver.

At first, you hesitate, but then you hold out your hand. The aquarium attendant places the sea star in your palm. You can feel motion on your skin. The many tiny "feet" on the animal's underside look something like suction cups, and they tickle just a bit! The attendant explains that the sea star has a system of tubes containing water in its body. As the water moves around in the tubes, it creates changes in fluid pressure that allows the sea star to move.

◀ A sea star uses fluid ▶ pressure to move.

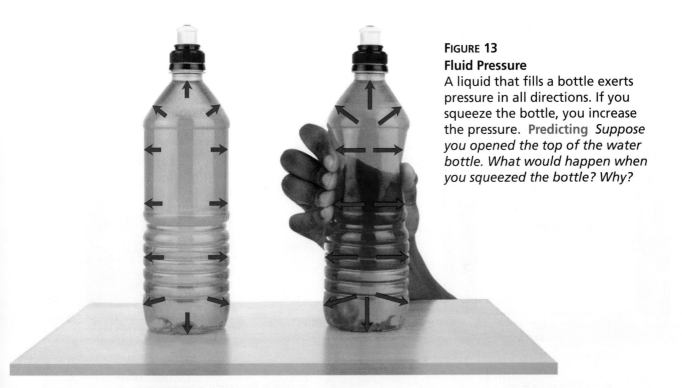

FIGURE 13
Fluid Pressure
A liquid that fills a bottle exerts pressure in all directions. If you squeeze the bottle, you increase the pressure. **Predicting** *Suppose you opened the top of the water bottle. What would happen when you squeezed the bottle? Why?*

Transmitting Pressure in a Fluid

If you did the Standards Warm-Up, you may be wondering why the buoyancy of the Cartesian diver changes. Squeezing the bottle made the diver sink because you increased the pressure on the water inside the bottle. The water pushed into the straw, reducing the size of the pocket of air and increasing the diver's density. This happened no matter where you squeezed the bottle. By changing the fluid pressure at any spot in the closed container, you transmitted pressure throughout the container.

Pascal's Principle In the 1600s, Blaise Pascal developed a principle to explain how pressure is transmitted in a fluid. As you know, fluid exerts pressure on any surface it touches. For example, the colored water in each bottle shown in Figure 13 exerts pressure on the entire surface of the bottle—up, down, and sideways.

What happens if you squeeze the bottle when its top is closed? The water has nowhere to go, so it presses harder on the inside surface of the bottle. The water pressure increases everywhere in the bottle. This is shown by the increased length of the arrows on the right in Figure 13.

Pascal's principle states that pressure increases by the same amount throughout an enclosed or confined fluid. ⊙ **When force is applied to a confined fluid, the change in pressure is transmitted equally to all parts of the fluid.**

 **Reading Checkpoint** What is Pascal's principle?

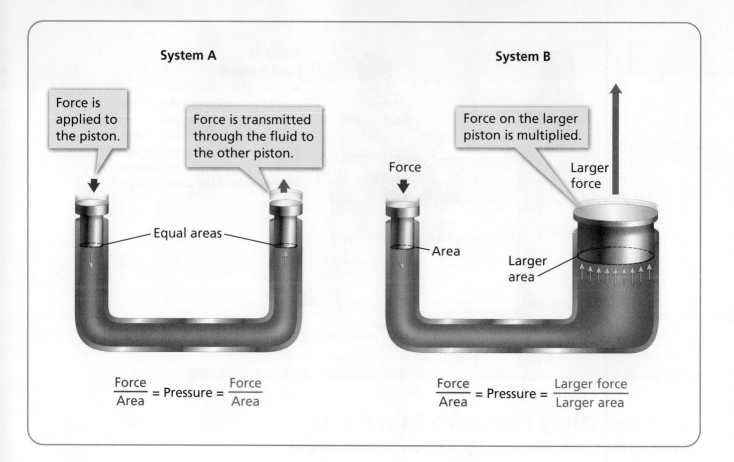

System A

Force is applied to the piston.

Force is transmitted through the fluid to the other piston.

Equal areas

$$\frac{Force}{Area} = Pressure = \frac{Force}{Area}$$

System B

Force on the larger piston is multiplied.

Force

Larger force

Area

Larger area

$$\frac{Force}{Area} = Pressure = \frac{Larger\ force}{Larger\ area}$$

FIGURE 14
Hydraulic Devices
In a hydraulic device, a force applied to one piston increases the fluid pressure equally throughout the fluid. By changing the area of the pistons, the force can be multiplied.
Problem Solving *To multiply the force applied to the left piston four times, how much larger must the area of the right piston be compared to the left piston?*

For: Hydraulic Systems activity
Visit: PHSchool.com
Web Code: cgp-3033

Pascal's Principle at Work You can see Pascal's principle at work in Figure 14. A hydraulic device consists of two pistons, one at each end of a U-shaped tube. A piston is like a stopper that slides up and down in a tube.

Suppose you fill System A with water and then push down on the left piston. The increase in fluid pressure will be transmitted to the right piston. According to Pascal's principle, both pistons experience the same fluid pressure. Because both pistons have the same surface area, they will experience the same force.

Now look at System B. The right piston has a greater surface area than the left piston. Suppose the area of the small piston is 1 square centimeter and the area of the large piston is 9 square centimeters. The right piston has an area nine times greater than the area of the left piston. If you push down on the left piston, pressure is transmitted equally to the right piston. The force you exert on the left piston is multiplied nine times when it reaches the right piston. By changing the area of the pistons, you can multiply force by almost any amount you wish.

 **Reading Checkpoint** How is force multiplied in System B?

Hydraulic Systems

Have you ever wondered how a person can stop a large car by pressing down on a little pedal? Or how mechanics are able to raise cars off the ground so they can repair them? In both cases, hydraulic systems using Pascal's principle are at work. A **hydraulic system** uses liquids to transmit pressure and multiply force in a confined fluid.  **A hydraulic system multiplies force by applying the force to a small surface area. The increase in pressure is then transmitted to another part of the confined fluid, which pushes on a larger surface area.** Because they use fluids to transmit pressure, hydraulic systems have few moving parts that can jam, break, or wear down.

Hydraulic Lifts Hydraulic lift systems are used to raise cars off the ground so mechanics can repair them with ease. They are also used to lift the heavy ladder on a fire truck to reach the upper windows of a burning building. In addition, hydraulic lifts are used to operate many pieces of heavy construction equipment such as dump trucks, backhoes, snowplows, and cranes. Next time you see a construction vehicle at work, see if you can spot the hydraulic pistons in action.

Math > Analyzing Data

Reviewing Math: Algebra and Functions 7.3.3

Comparing Hydraulic Lifts

The graph shows the relationship between the applied force and the lifting force for two hydraulic lifts.

1. **Reading Graphs** Suppose a force of 1,000 N is applied to both lifts. Use the graph to determine the lifting force of each lift.

2. **Reading Graphs** For Lift A, how much force must be applied to lift a 12,000-N object?

3. **Interpreting Data** By how much is the applied force multiplied for Lift A? Lift B?

4. **Interpreting Data** What does the slope of each line represent?

5. **Drawing Conclusions** Which lift would you choose if you wanted to lift a weight of 4,000 N? Explain.

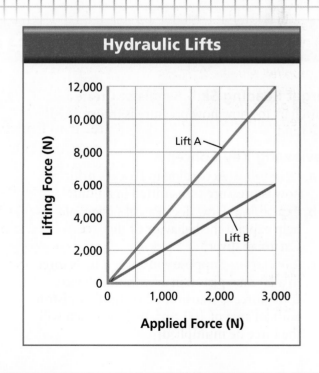

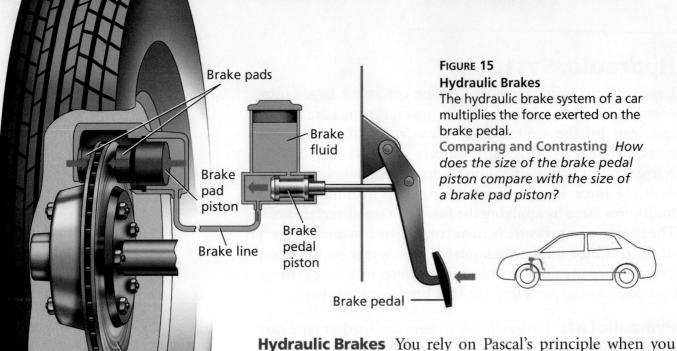

Brake pads

Brake fluid

Brake pad piston

Brake line

Brake pedal piston

Disc

Tire

Brake pedal

FIGURE 15
Hydraulic Brakes
The hydraulic brake system of a car multiplies the force exerted on the brake pedal.
Comparing and Contrasting *How does the size of the brake pedal piston compare with the size of a brake pad piston?*

Hydraulic Brakes You rely on Pascal's principle when you ride in a car. The brake system of a car is a hydraulic system. Figure 15 shows a simplified brake system with disc brakes. When a driver pushes down on the brake pedal, he or she pushes a small piston. The piston exerts pressure on the brake fluid. The increased pressure is transmitted through the fluid in the brake lines to larger pistons within the wheels of the car. Each of these pistons pushes on a brake pad. The brake pads rub against the brake disc, and the wheel's motion is slowed down by the force of friction. Because the brake system multiplies force, a person can stop a large car with only a light push on the brake pedal.

Section 3 Assessment

S 8.8.c, E-LA: Reading 8.2.0

Target Reading Skill Sequence Create a flowchart to show how pressure is transmitted in a fluid.

Reviewing Key Concepts

1. **a. Reviewing** According to Pascal's principle, how is pressure transmitted in a fluid?
   b. Explaining How does Pascal's principle help explain the behavior of the Cartesian diver?
   c. Calculating Suppose you apply a 10-N force to a 10-cm² piston in a hydraulic device. If the force is transmitted to another piston with an area of 100 cm², by how much will the force be multiplied?

2. **a. Defining** What is a hydraulic system?
   b. Explaining How does a hydraulic system work?
   c. Sequencing Describe what happens in the brake system of a car from the time a driver steps on the brake pedal to the time the car stops.

Writing in Science

Cause-and-Effect Letter You are a mechanic who fixes hydraulic brakes. A customer asks you why his brakes do not work. When you examine the car, you notice a leak in the brake line and repair it. Write a letter to the customer explaining why a leak in the brake line caused his brakes to fail.

Bernoulli's Principle

S 8.2.e Students know that when the forces on an object are unbalanced, the object will change its velocity (that is, it will speed up, slow down, or change direction).

🔑 How is fluid presssure related to the motion of a fluid?

🔑 What are some applications of Bernoulli's principle?

Key Terms
• Bernoulli's principle
• lift

Lab zone Standards **Warm-Up**

Does the Movement of Air Create Unbalanced Forces?

1. Use your thumb and forefinger to hold a sheet of paper by the corners.
2. Hold the paper just below your mouth, so that its edge is horizontal and the paper hangs down.
3. Blow across the top of the paper.
4. Repeat this several times, blowing harder each time.

Think It Over

Inferring On what side of the paper is the force greater? How do you know?

In December 1903, Wilbur and Orville Wright brought an odd-looking vehicle to a deserted beach in Kitty Hawk, North Carolina. People had flown in balloons for more than a hundred years, but the Wright brothers' goal was something no one had ever done before. They flew a plane that was heavier (denser) than air! They had spent years experimenting with different wing shapes and surfaces, and they had carefully studied the flight of birds. Their first flight at Kitty Hawk lasted just 12 seconds. The plane flew more than 36 meters and made history.

What did the Wright brothers know about flying that allowed them to construct the first airplane? And how can the principles they used explain how a jet can fly across the country? The answer has to do with fluid pressure and how a moving fluid can create an unbalanced force.

◄ **On December 17, 1903, the Wright brothers' plane *Flyer* flew for the first time.**

Try This Activity

Faucet Force

1. Hold a plastic spoon loosely by the edges of its handle so it swings freely between your fingers.
2. Turn on a faucet to produce a steady stream of water. Predict what will happen if you touch the bottom of the spoon to the stream of water.
3. Test your prediction. Repeat the test several times.

Developing Hypotheses Use your observations to develop a hypothesis explaining why the spoon moved as it did.

Pressure and Moving Fluids

So far in this chapter, you have learned about fluids that are not moving. What makes a fluid flow? And what happens to fluid pressure when a fluid moves?

Fluid Motion A fluid tends to flow from an area of high pressure to an area of low pressure. This happens, for example, when you sip a drink from a straw. When you start to sip, you remove the air from the straw. This creates an area of low pressure in the straw. The higher air pressure pushing down on the surface of your drink forces the drink up into the straw.

Bernoulli's Principle In the 1700s, Swiss scientist Daniel Bernoulli (bur NOO lee) discovered that the pressure of a moving fluid is different than the pressure of a fluid at rest. **Bernoulli's principle** states that the faster a fluid moves, the less pressure the fluid exerts.

If you did the Standards Warm-Up, you saw that air moving over the paper caused the paper to rise. Bernoulli's principle explains the behavior of the paper. 🔑 **Bernoulli's principle states that as the speed of a moving fluid increases, the pressure exerted by the fluid decreases.** The air above the paper moves, but the air below the paper does not. The moving air exerts less pressure than the still air. As a result, the still air exerts greater pressure on the bottom of the paper, creating an unbalanced force which pushes the paper up.

Reading Checkpoint What is Bernoulli's principle?

FIGURE 16
Making Air Move
Blowing air quickly between two cans lowers the air pressure between them. Higher pressure exerted by the still air to either side pushes the cans toward each other.

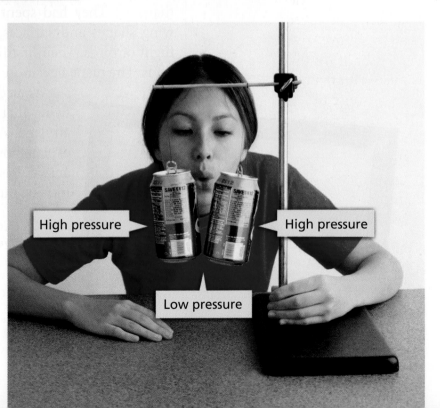

High pressure
High pressure
Low pressure

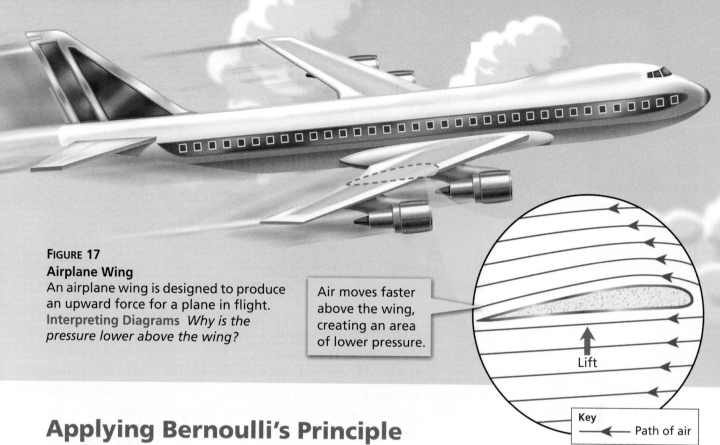

FIGURE 17
Airplane Wing
An airplane wing is designed to produce an upward force for a plane in flight. *Interpreting Diagrams Why is the pressure lower above the wing?*

Air moves faster above the wing, creating an area of lower pressure.

Lift

Key
Path of air

Applying Bernoulli's Principle

The Wright brothers understood Bernoulli's principle. They used it when they built their plane. **Bernoulli's principle helps explain how planes fly. It also helps explain how an atomizer works, why smoke rises up a chimney, and how a flying disk glides through the air.**

Objects in Flight Bernoulli's principle is one factor that helps explain flight—from a small kite to a huge airplane. Objects can be designed so that their shapes cause air to move at different speeds above and below them. If the air moves faster above the object, fluid pressure pushes the object upward. If the air moves faster below the object, fluid pressure pushes it downward.

Because of its design, the wing of an airplane produces **lift,** or an upward force. Look at Figure 17 to see the design of a wing. Both the slant and the shape of the wing are sources of lift. Because the wing is slanted, the wing forces the air downward as the plane moves. The air exerts an equal and opposite force on the wing and pushes it upward. This unbalanced upward force helps an airplane to take off.

The curved shape of a wing also gives an airplane lift. Because the top of the wing is curved, air moving over the top has a greater speed than air moving under the bottom. As a result, the air moving over the top exerts less pressure than the air below. The difference in air pressure above and below the wing creates lift.

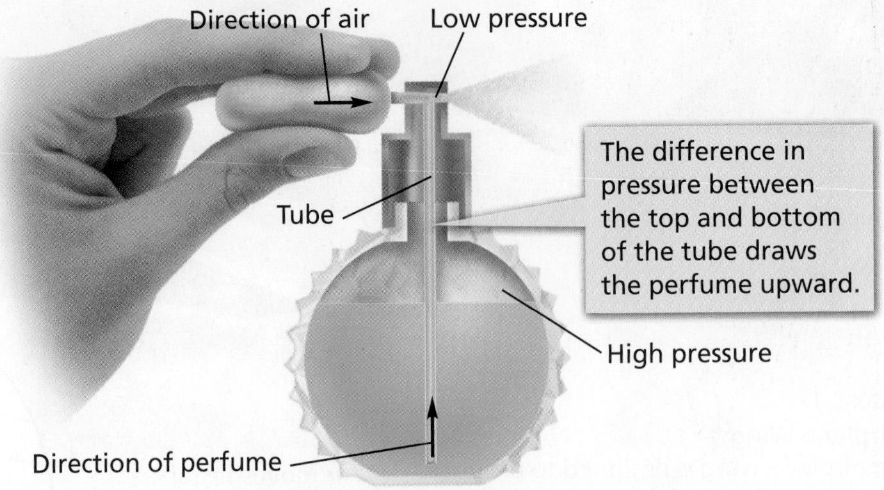

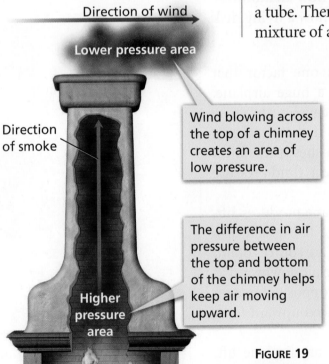

FIGURE 18
Perfume Atomizer
An atomizer is an application of Bernoulli's principle.
Applying Concepts *Why is the perfume pushed up and out of the flask?*

Direction of air   Low pressure

The difference in pressure between the top and bottom of the tube draws the perfume upward.

Tube

High pressure

Direction of perfume

Atomizers Bernoulli's principle can help you understand how the perfume atomizer shown in Figure 18 works. When you squeeze the rubber bulb, air moves quickly past the top of the tube. The moving air lowers the pressure at the top of the tube. The greater pressure in the flask pushes the liquid up into the tube. The air stream breaks the liquid into small drops, and the liquid comes out as a fine mist. In a similar way, pressure differences in the carburetors of older gasoline engines push gasoline up a tube. There, the gasoline combines with air to create the mixture of air and fuel that runs the engine.

Chimneys You can sit next to a fireplace enjoying a cozy fire thanks in part to Bernoulli's principle. Smoke rises up the chimney partly because hot air rises, and partly because it is pushed. Wind blowing across the top of a chimney lowers the air pressure there. The higher pressure at the bottom pushes air and smoke up the chimney. Smoke will rise faster in a chimney on a windy day than on a calm day.

Direction of wind

Lower pressure area

Direction of smoke

Wind blowing across the top of a chimney creates an area of low pressure.

The difference in air pressure between the top and bottom of the chimney helps keep air moving upward.

Higher pressure area

 **Reading Checkpoint** How does an atomizer work?

FIGURE 19
Chimney
Thanks in part to Bernoulli's principle, you can enjoy an evening by a warm fireplace without the room filling up with smoke.
Making Generalizations *Why does the smoke rise up the chimney?*

Flying Disks Did you ever wonder what allows a flying disk to glide through the air? The upper surface of a flying disk is curved like an airplane wing. Bernoulli's principle explains that the faster-moving air following the disk's curved upper surface exerts less pressure than the slower-moving air beneath it. A net force acts upward on the flying disk, creating lift. Tilting the disk slightly toward you as you throw it also helps to keep it in the air. A tilted disk pushes air down. The air exerts an equal and opposite force on the disk, pushing it up. The spinning motion of a flying disk keeps it stable as it flies.

FIGURE 20
Flying Disk
Like an airplane wing, a flying disk uses a curved upper surface to create lift. **Comparing and Contrasting** *How does a flying disk differ from an airplane wing?*

Section 4 Assessment

S 8.2.e, E-LA: Reading 8.2.0

Target Reading Skill Sequence Create a flowchart to explain how an atomizer works.

Reviewing Key Concepts

1. a. **Reviewing** How can you make fluid flow up a straw?
   b. **Summarizing** What does Bernoulli's principle say about the pressure exerted by a moving fluid?
   c. **Applying Concepts** You are riding in a car on a highway when a large truck speeds by you. Explain why your car is pushed toward the truck.

2. a. **Listing** List four applications of Bernoulli's principle.
   b. **Explaining** Why does the air pressure above an airplane wing differ from the pressure below it? How is this pressure difference involved in flight?
   c. **Relating Cause and Effect** How could strong winds from a hurricane blow the roof off a house?

Lab zone At-Home Activity

Paper Chimney With a family member, see how a chimney works by using a paper cup and a hair dryer. Cut up several small pieces of tissue and place them in the bottom of a paper cup. Hold on to the paper cup with one hand. With your other hand, use the hair dryer to blow cool air across the top of the cup. Explain to your family member how Bernoulli's principle explains how the chimney works.

Helicopters

S 8.2.e

Most aircraft are like eagles—they take off majestically, glide among the clouds, and land with ease. But helicopters are the hummingbirds of aircraft. They can fly forward, backward, sideways, and up and down. They can stop abruptly and hover in midair. In fact, helicopters can fly circles around other types of aircraft.

Science in Action

On the top of a helicopter are large blades that turn rapidly. These blades are curved on top like the wings of an airplane. Air flowing over the curved blades helps cause lift—the upward force for the helicopter—just as air flowing over wings helps cause lift for most airplanes. Action and reaction forces as described by Newton's third law of motion also play a role in causing lift. As the tilted blades push down on the air, the air pushes up on the blade.

Main Rotor
The main rotor turns the blades and controls their angle.

Blades
Air flows over the curved, rotating blades. Along with action and reaction forces, this helps to give the helicopter lift.

As the main rotor spins, the reaction force pushes the helicopter's body in the opposite direction. If not for the tail rotor, the body would spin too.

Hand Controls and Foot Pedals
These controls are connected to the main rotor. The collective control guides the helicopter up or down. The cyclic control guides the helicopter forward, backward, or sideways. The foot pedals allow the helicopter to rotate in tight circles.

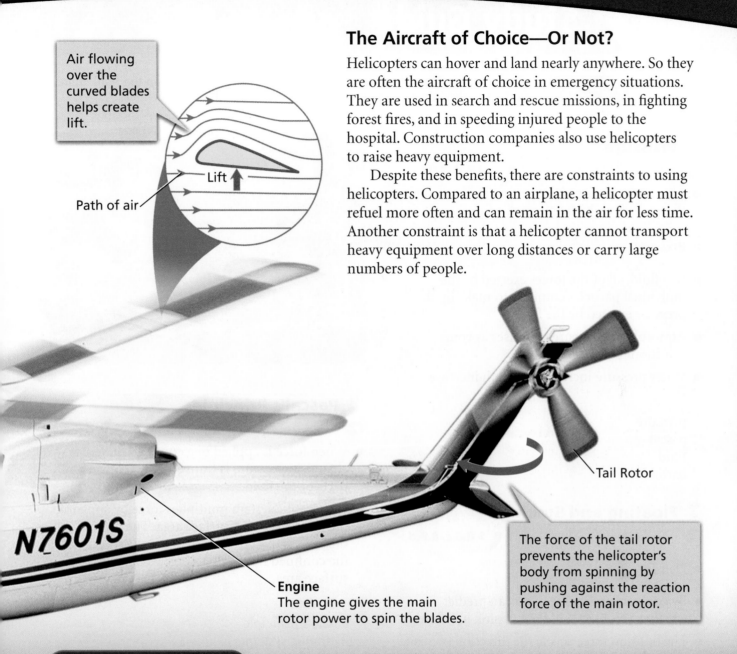

Air flowing over the curved blades helps create lift.

Path of air

Lift

The Aircraft of Choice—Or Not?

Helicopters can hover and land nearly anywhere. So they are often the aircraft of choice in emergency situations. They are used in search and rescue missions, in fighting forest fires, and in speeding injured people to the hospital. Construction companies also use helicopters to raise heavy equipment.

Despite these benefits, there are constraints to using helicopters. Compared to an airplane, a helicopter must refuel more often and can remain in the air for less time. Another constraint is that a helicopter cannot transport heavy equipment over long distances or carry large numbers of people.

N7601S

Tail Rotor

The force of the tail rotor prevents the helicopter's body from spinning by pushing against the reaction force of the main rotor.

Engine
The engine gives the main rotor power to spin the blades.

Weigh the Impact

1. Identify the Need
What advantages do helicopters have over airplanes?

2. Research
Using the Internet, research how helicopters are used in national parks, such as Yellowstone National Park. Choose one helicopter mission. Make notes on the mission's difficulty level, purpose, location, procedures, and outcome.

3. Write
Suppose you are a park ranger. Use your notes to write a report to your supervisor explaining why a helicopter was or was not the best technology to use for this mission.

Go Online
PHSchool.com

For: More on helicopters
Visit: PHSchool.com
Web Code: cgh-3030

Study Guide

① Pressure

Key Concepts S 8.8.d, 8.9.f

- The amount of pressure you exert depends on the area over which you exert a force.

- $\text{Pressure} = \dfrac{\text{Force}}{\text{Area}}$

- In a fluid, all of the forces exerted by the individual particles combine to make up the pressure exerted by the fluid.

- Atmospheric pressure decreases as your elevation increases.

- Water pressure increases as depth increases.

Key Terms

pressure
pascal
fluid
barometer

② Floating and Sinking

Key Concepts S 8.8.c, 8.8.d

- $\text{Density} = \dfrac{\text{Mass}}{\text{Volume}}$

- By comparing densities, you can predict whether an object will float or sink in a fluid.

- The buoyant force acts in the direction opposite to the force of gravity, so it makes an object feel lighter.

Key Terms

density
buoyant force
Archimedes' principle

③ Pascal's Principle

Key Concepts S 8.8.c

- When force is applied to a confined fluid, the change in pressure is transmitted equally to all parts of the fluid.

- A hydraulic system multiplies force by applying the force to a small surface area. The increase in pressure is then transmitted to another part of the confined fluid, which pushes on a larger surface area.

Key Terms

Pascal's principle
hydraulic system

④ Bernoulli's Principle

Key Concepts S 8.2.e

- Bernoulli's principle states that as the speed of a moving fluid increases, the pressure exerted by the fluid decreases.

- Bernoulli's principle helps explain how planes fly. It also helps explain how an atomizer works, why smoke rises up a chimney, and how a flying disk glides through the air.

Key Terms

Bernoulli's principle
lift

Review and Assessment

Go Online
PHSchool.com

For: Self-Assessment
Visit: PHSchool.com
Web Code: cxa-3110

Target Reading Skill

Sequence Create a flowchart that shows how a hydraulic device multiplies force.

How a Hydraulic Device Works

Force applied to small piston

↓

a. _____?_____

↓

b. _____?_____

↓

c. _____?_____

↓

d. _____?_____

Reviewing Key Terms

Choose the letter of the best answer.

1. If you divide the force exerted on a surface by the total area of the surface, you will know
   a. density. **b.** pressure.
   c. lift. **d.** buoyant force.

2. If you divide the mass of an object by its volume, you also know the object's
   a. mass. **b.** weight.
   c. density. **d.** pressure.

3. The weight of an object that floats has the same value as the
   a. object's density. **b.** object's mass.
   c. object's volume. **d.** buoyant force.

4. The concept that an increase in pressure on a confined fluid is transmitted equally to all parts of the fluid is known as
   a. Pascal's principle.
   b. Bernoulli's principle.
   c. Archimedes' principle.
   d. Newton's third law.

5. The concept that the pressure in a fluid decreases as the speed of the fluid increases is known as
   a. Pascal's principle.
   b. Bernoulli's principle.
   c. Archimedes' principle.
   d. Newton's first law.

Complete the following sentences so that your answers clearly explain the key terms.

6. If you stand on one foot, you increase the **pressure** you exert on the ground, because _____.

7. Whether an object will float or sink in a fluid depends on its **density**, which is defined as _____.

8. A submerged object is easier to lift due to the **buoyant force**, which is _____.

9. A ship is able to float on the surface of the ocean because of **Archimedes' principle**, which states that _____.

10. An airplane is able to fly partly due to **Bernoulli's principle**, which states that _____.

Writing in Science

News Report Suppose that you are a newspaper journalist on the day after the Titanic sank. Write a news report that tells what happened. Explain how the buoyancy of a ship is affected when it fills with water. Include information about the various fluid forces involved.

Video Assessment
Discovery Channel School
Forces in Fluids

Review and Assessment

Checking Concepts

11. How does the amount of pressure you exert on the floor when you are lying down compare with the amount of pressure you exert when you are standing up?

12. Why aren't people crushed by the air pressure they experience?

13. Why do you seem to weigh more in air than you do in water?

14. In a hydraulic system, why is the force exerted on a small piston multiplied when it acts on a larger piston?

15. Name two hydraulic systems that an auto mechanic would know well.

16. Why is air pressure at the top of a chimney less than air pressure at the bottom?

Thinking Critically

17. **Making Generalizations** How does the water pressure change at each level in the jug below? How can you tell?

18. **Problem Solving** You have two fluids of unknown density. Suggest a method to determine which is denser, without mixing the two fluids.

19. **Developing Hypotheses** A sphere made of steel is put in water and, surprisingly, it floats. Develop a possible explanation for this observation.

20. **Applying Concepts** One method of raising a sunken ship to the surface is to inflate large bags or balloons inside its hull. Explain why this procedure could work.

Math Practice

21. **Area** The cover of your textbook measures about 28 cm × 22 cm. Find its area.

22. **Area** A dollar bill measures about 15.9 cm × 6.7 cm. The Chinese yuan note measures 14.5 cm × 7.0 cm. Which currency uses a larger bill?

Applying Skills

The illustration shows an object supported by a spring scale, both in and out of water. Use the illustration to answer Questions 23–25.

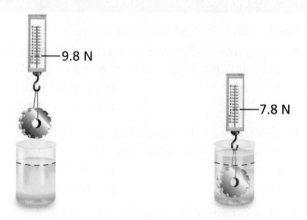

23. **Inferring** Why is there a difference between the weight of the object in air and its measured weight in water?

24. **Calculating** What is the buoyant force acting on the object?

25. **Drawing Conclusions** What can you conclude about the water above the dotted line?

Lab zone Standards Investigation

Performance Assessment Test your boat to make sure it does not leak. Display the diagrams of different designs you tried and the observations and data you recorded for each design. Then demonstrate for the class how the boat floats. Point out to your classmates the features you used in your final design.

Choose the letter of the best answer.

1. You place a block of wood into a beaker of water and it floats. What can you say about the buoyant force on the block?
   A It is equal to the block's weight.
   B It is less than the block's weight.
   C It is greater than the block's weight.
   D It is equal to the weight of the surrounding water. **S 8.8.c**

2. You carefully drop a stone into a beaker full of water. The stone sinks to the bottom and water spills out. What can you say about the weight of the displaced water?
   A It is greater than the weight of the stone.
   B It is equal to the weight of the stone.
   C It is less than the weight of the stone.
   D It is equal to the weight of the water still in the beaker. **S 8.8.c**

Use the photos below to answer Question 3.

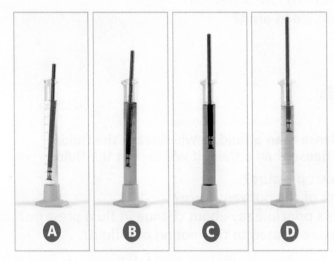

3. You place a pencil hydrometer into four different unknown liquids, labeled A, B, C, and D. The hydrometer floats at different levels in the four liquids. Which liquid is the most dense?
   A Liquid A
   B Liquid B
   C Liquid C
   D Liquid D **S 8.8.d**

4. Why does an airplane rise in the air?
   A It experiences a buoyant force because it is less dense than the air.
   B The moving air above and below the wings creates an unbalanced force that pushes the airplane up.
   C The air pressure above the wings is greater than the air pressure below the wings.
   D The airplane's cabin is pressurized. **S 8.2.e**

5. You observe that a chunk of tar sinks in puddles of rainwater but floats on the ocean. An experiment to explain the behavior of the tar should measure
   A the difference between atmospheric pressure and water pressure.
   B the densities of fresh water, salt water, and tar.
   C the height from which the chunk of tar is dropped.
   D the depth of each type of water. **S 8.8.d**

6. A helium balloon rises because the helium
   A is hotter than the surrounding air.
   B is colder than the surrounding air.
   C is less dense than the surrounding air.
   D is more dense than the surrounding air.
   S 8.8.d

Apply the BIG Idea

7. Explain why objects experience a buoyant force when immersed in a fluid. How can you find the value of the buoyant force? How can knowing the density of an object and a fluid help you predict if the object will float or sink in the fluid? **S 8.8**

Motion, Forces, and Energy
Unit 3 Review

Chapter 9
Motion and Energy
The BIG Idea

You can describe the motion of an object by its position, speed, direction, and acceleration.

- When is an object in motion?
- How do you calculate speed?
- How do you calculate acceleration?
- What affects an object's kinetic energy and potential energy?

Chapter 10
Forces
The BIG Idea

An unbalanced force will cause a change in an object's velocity.

- How do balanced and unbalanced forces affect velocity?
- Why do objects accelerate during free fall?
- What is Newton's second law of motion?
- What is Newton's third law of motion?
- What keeps a satellite in orbit?

Chapter 11
Forces in Fluids
The BIG Idea

If an object is less dense than a fluid, it will float in the fluid.
If an object is more dense than a fluid, it will sink in the fluid.

- How do fluids exert pressure?
- What is the effect of the buoyant force?
- What does Pascal's principle say about change in fluid pressure?
- How is fluid pressure related to the motion of a fluid?

Unit 3 Assessment

Welcome to the Summer Triathlon. Do you have what it takes to compete in all three athletic events?

Today's triathlon will begin with a 750-m swim. We've set up buoys floating in the water so you can follow the path of the race properly. Don't swim too far away from these floating markers, or you'll go off course and have to get back on track!

Next you will cycle 20 km. When you get to the finish line, remember to brake as quickly as possible so you can start the last leg of the event.

Finally, you will have to run 5 km along the edge of the lake. The view is beautiful, but don't forget to keep your eye on the prize. You'll have to turn around at the halfway mark and change direction because the race finishes at the same bridge where it begins.

Remember to pace yourself! And at the end, we have a special surprise for you. All athletes who complete the triathlon win a medal!

1. It took you half an hour to run the final 5 km of the triathlon. Using that information, what can you find? *(Chapter 9)*
   a. average speed **b.** instantaneous speed
   c. acceleration **d.** direction

2. At the end of the bicycle race, what kind of friction do you rely on when you use your hand brakes to come to a stop? *(Chapter 10)*
   a. static friction **b.** sliding friction
   c. rolling friction **d.** fluid friction

3. Which of the following is a possible density for the buoys floating in the lake?
   (Chapter 11)
   a. 0.9 g/cm³ **b.** 9 g/cm³
   c. 90 g/cm³ **d.** 900 g/cm³

4. **Summary** Write a paragraph that describes the different forces you experienced while running in the triathlon. Did these forces cause changes in your motion? Explain.

S. 8.2.c

Bridges—
From Vines to Steel

Have you ever

- balanced on a branch or log to cross a brook?
- jumped from rock to rock in a streambed?
- swung on a vine or rope over a river?

Vine Footbridge
A girl crosses over the Hunza River in northern Pakistan.

Then you have used the same ways that early people used to get over obstacles. Fallen trees, twisted vines, and natural stones formed the first bridges.

Bridges provide easy ways of getting over difficult obstacles. For thousands of years, bridges have also served as forts for defense, scenes of great battles, and homes for shops and churches. They have also been sites of mystery, love, and intrigue. They span history—linking cities, nations, and empires and encouraging trade and travel.

But bridges have not always been as elaborate as they are today. The earliest ones were made of materials that were free and plentiful. In deep forests, people used beams made from small trees. In tropical regions where vegetation was thick, people wove together vines and grasses, then hung them to make walkways over rivers and gorges.

No matter what the structures or materials, bridges reflect the people who built them. The ancient civilizations of China, Egypt, Greece, and Rome all designed strong, graceful bridges to connect and control their empires.

Roman Arch Bridge
Ponte Sant'Angelo is in Rome.

The Balance of Forces

What keeps a bridge from falling down? How does it support its own weight and the weight of people and traffic on it? Builders found the answers by considering the various forces that act on a bridge.

The weight of the bridge and the traffic on it are called the *load*. When a heavy truck crosses a beam bridge, the weight of the load forces the beam to curve downward. This creates tension forces that stretch the bottom of the beam. At the same time, the load also creates compression forces at the top of the beam.

Since the bridge doesn't collapse under the load, there must be upward forces to balance the downward forces. In simple beam bridges, builders anchor the beam to the ground or to end supports called abutments. To cross longer spans or distances, they construct piers under the middle span. Piers and abutments are structures that act as upward forces—reaction forces.

Another type of bridge, the arch bridge, supports its load by compression. A heavy load on a stone arch bridge squeezes or pushes the stones together, creating compression throughout the structure. Weight on the arch bridge pushes down to the ends of the arch. The side walls and abutments act as reaction forces.

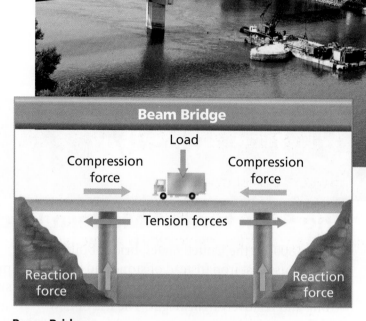

Beam Bridge
A beam bridge spans the Rhone River in France (top).

Early engineers discovered that arch bridges made of stone could span wider distances than simple beam bridges. Arch bridges are also stronger and more durable. Although the Romans were not the first to build arch bridges, they perfected the form in their massive, elegant structures. Early Roman arch bridges were built without mortar, or "glue." The arch held together because the stones were skillfully shaped to work in compression. After nearly 2,000 years, some of these Roman arch bridges are still standing.

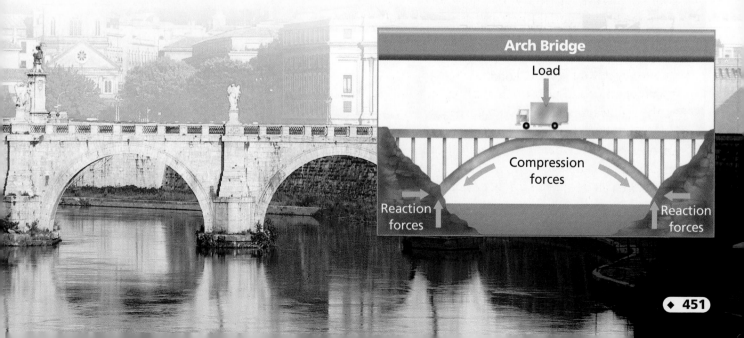

The Structure of Modern Bridges

By the 1800s in the United States, bridge builders began to use cast iron instead of stone and wood. By the late 1800s, they were using steel, which was strong and relatively lightweight. The use of new building materials was not the only change. Engineers began designing different types of bridges as well. They found that they could build longer, larger bridges by using a suspension structure.

Suspension bridges are modern versions of long, narrow, woven bridges found in tropical regions. These simple, woven suspension bridges can span long distances. Crossing one of these natural structures is like walking a tightrope. The weight of people and animals traveling over the bridge pushes down on the ropes, stretching them and creating tension forces.

Modern suspension bridges follow the same principles of tension as do woven bridges. A suspension bridge is strong in tension. In suspension bridges, parallel cables are stretched the entire length of the bridge—over giant towers. The cables are anchored at each end of the bridge. The roadway hangs from the cables, attached by wire suspenders. The weight of the bridge and the load on it act to pull apart or stretch the cables. This pulling apart creates tension forces.

The towers of a suspension bridge act as supports for the bridge cables. The abutments that anchor the cables exert reaction forces as well. So forces in balance keep a suspension bridge from collapsing.

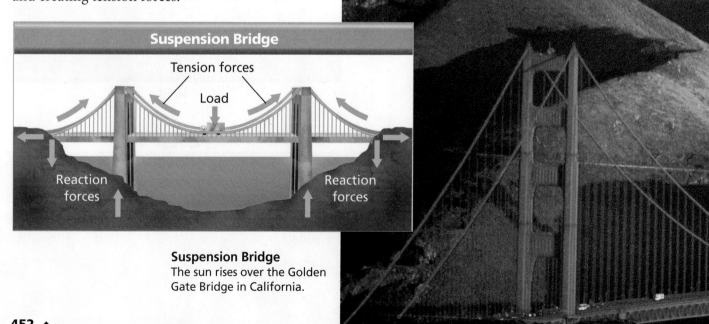

Suspension Bridge
The sun rises over the Golden Gate Bridge in California.

Cable-Stayed Bridge
The Sunshine Skyway Bridge spans a broad section of Tampa Bay in Florida. The cables, attached to the center of the roadway, enable travelers to have a clear view.

Science Activity

Work in groups to make a suspension bridge, using two chairs, a wooden plank, rope, and some books.

- Place two chairs back-to-back and stretch 2 ropes over the backs of the chairs. Hold the ropes at both ends.

- Tie three pieces of rope to the longer ropes. Place the plank through the loops.

- With a partner, hold the ropes tightly at each end. Load books on top of the plank to see how much it will hold.

Why is it important to anchor the ropes tightly at each end?

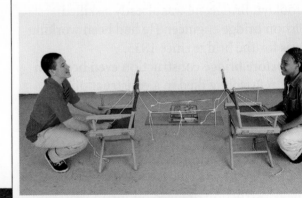

When the Brooklyn Bridge opened in New York City in 1883, it was the longest suspension bridge in the world. The Golden Gate Bridge in San Francisco, which was opened in 1937, was another great engineering feat.

Recently, engineers have developed a new bridge design called the cable-stayed bridge. It looks similar to a suspension bridge because both are built with towers and cables. But the two bridges are quite different. The cables on the cable-stayed bridge attach to the towers, so the towers bear the weight of the bridge and the load on it. In contrast, the cables on a suspension bridge ride over the towers and anchor at the abutments. So on a suspension bridge, both the towers and abutments bear the load.

Brooklyn Bridge
This bridge connects Brooklyn and Manhattan (above).
It took 14 years for workers to complete the bridge (left).

Against All Odds

When John Roebling was hired in 1868 to build the Brooklyn Bridge, he was already a skilled suspension bridge engineer. He had been working on plans for the bridge since 1855.

But before bridge construction even began in 1869, John Roebling died in a construction accident. Fortunately, he had worked out his bridge design to the last detail. His son, Colonel Washington Roebling, who was also a skilled engineer, dedicated himself to carrying out his father's plans.

The construction dragged on for 14 years and cost nearly 30 lives. Colonel Roebling himself became so disabled that he was forced to direct construction from his home. Using a telescope, Colonel Roebling followed every detail. His remarkable, energetic wife, Emily Warren Roebling, learned enough engineering principles to deliver and explain his orders to the workers.

As soon as the giant towers were up, workers unrolled the steel wire back and forth across the towers to weave the cables. The next step was to twist the wires together. But the workmen were terrified of hanging so high on the bridge and refused to work.

Finally, Frank Farrington, the chief mechanic, crossed the river on a small chair dangling from a wheel that ran across an overhead line. Farrington completed his journey to the roar of the crowd. Somewhat reassured, the builders returned to work. But it took two more years to string the cables. The bridge was one of the greatest engineering achievements of its time.

In the end, the Brooklyn Bridge project succeeded only because of the determination and sacrifices of the Roebling family. It became the model for hundreds of other suspension bridges.

Social Studies Activity

How do you think the Brooklyn Bridge changed the lives of New Yorkers? In groups, research the history of another famous bridge. Present your findings to your class along with drawings and photos. Find out

- when and why the bridge was built
- what type of bridge it is
- what effects the bridge has on people's lives—on trade, travel, and population
- how landforms affected the bridge building
- about events connected to the bridge

TWO GREAT CITIES UNITED

MAY 25, 1883—The Brooklyn Bridge was successfully opened yesterday. The pleasant weather brought visitors by the thousands from all around. Spectators were packed in masses through which it was almost impossible to pass, and those who had tickets to attend the ceremonies had hard work to reach the bridge. Every available house-top and window was filled, and an adventurous party occupied a tall telegraph pole. It required the utmost efforts of the police to keep clear the necessary space.

After the exercises at the bridge were completed the Brooklyn procession was immediately re-formed and the march was taken up to Col. Roebling's residence. From the back study on the second floor of his house Col. Roebling had watched through his telescope the procession as it proceeded along from the New York side until the Brooklyn tower was reached. Mrs. Roebling received at her husband's side and accepted her share of the honors of the bridge.

For blocks and blocks on either side of the bridge there was scarcely a foot of room to spare. Many persons crossed and re-crossed the river on the ferry boats, and in that way watched the display. Almost every ship along the river front was converted into a grand stand.

The final ceremonies of the opening of the great bridge began at eight o'clock, when the first rocket was sent from the center of the great structure, and ended at nine o'clock, when a flight of 500 rockets illuminated the sky. The river-front was one blaze of light, and on the yachts and smaller vessels blue fires were burning and illuminating dark waters around them.

————Excerpted with permission from
The New York Times

Brooklyn Bridge
This historic painting shows fireworks at the opening of the bridge in 1883.

THE GRAND DISPLAY OF FIREWORKS AND ILLUMINATIONS

Language Arts Activity

A reporter's goal is to inform and entertain the reader. Using a catchy opening line draws interest. Then the reader wants to know the facts—who, what, where, when, why, and how (5 W's and H).

You are a school reporter. Write about the opening of a bridge in your area. It could be a highway overpass or a bridge over water, a valley, or railroad tracks.

- Include some of the 5 W's and H.
- Add interesting details and descriptions.

Bridge Geometry

As railroad traffic increased in the late 1800s, truss bridges became popular. Designed with thin vertical and diagonal supports to add strength, truss bridges were actually reinforced beam bridge structures. Many of the early wood truss bridges couldn't support the trains that rumbled over them. Cast iron and steel trusses soon replaced wood trusses.

Using basic triangular structures, engineers went to work on more scientific truss bridge designs. The accuracy of the design is crucial to handling the stress from heavy train loads and constant vibrations. As in all bridge structures, each steel piece has to be measured and fitted accurately—including widths, lengths, angles, and points of intersection and attachment.

Geometric Angles and Figures
Engineers use various geometric figures in drawing bridge plans. Figures that have right angles are squares, rectangles, and right triangles. Figures that have acute angles and obtuse angles can be triangles and parallelograms.

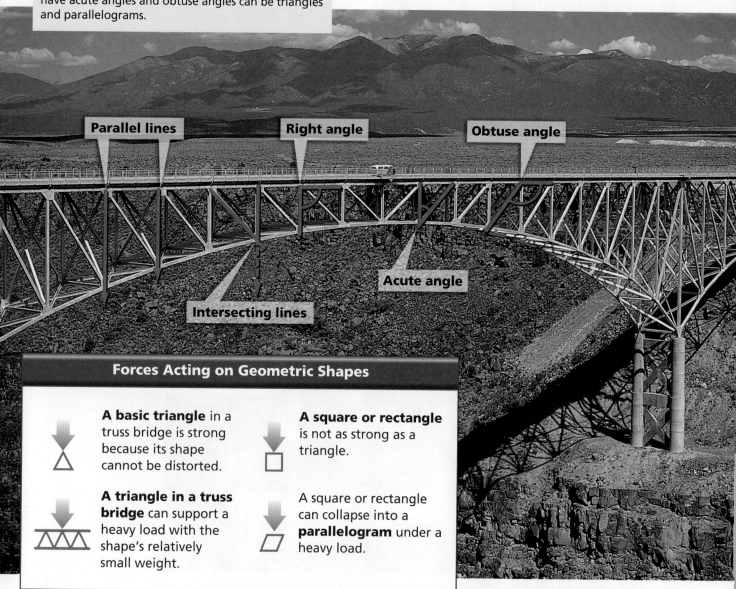

Parallel lines

Right angle

Obtuse angle

Acute angle

Intersecting lines

Forces Acting on Geometric Shapes

A basic triangle in a truss bridge is strong because its shape cannot be distorted.

A square or rectangle is not as strong as a triangle.

A triangle in a truss bridge can support a heavy load with the shape's relatively small weight.

A square or rectangle can collapse into a **parallelogram** under a heavy load.

Math Activity

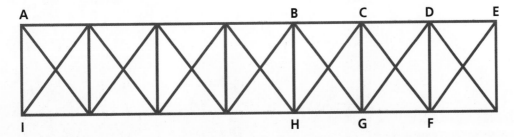

The chief building engineer has asked you to draw up exact plans for a new truss bridge. How well will you do as an assistant? Review the captions and labels on the previous page. Then answer these questions:

1. Which lines are parallel?

2. Which lines intersect?

3. What kind of figure is formed by *ABHI*?

4. What kind of figure is formed by *HCF*?

5. What kind of angle is *BGF*—obtuse or right?

6. What kind of angle is *CHG*?

7. What kind of triangle is *BHG*? What makes it this kind of triangle?

8. Why is a triangle stronger than a square?

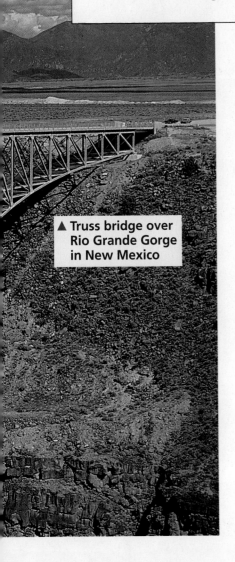

▲ **Truss bridge over Rio Grande Gorge in New Mexico**

Tie It Together

Work in small groups to build a model of a bridge out of a box of spaghetti and a roll of masking tape. Meet as a group to choose the type of bridge you will build. Each bridge should be strong enough to hold a brick. You can build

- a beam bridge

- a truss bridge

- an arch bridge

- a suspension bridge (This one is challenging.)

After drawing a sketch of the bridge design, assign jobs for each team member. Then

- decide how long the bridge span will be

- measure and cut the materials

- build the roadway first for beam, truss, and suspension bridges

- build the arch first in an arch bridge

When your bridge is complete, display it in the classroom. Test the strength of each bridge by placing a brick on the roadway. Discuss the difference in bridge structures. Determine which bridge design is the strongest.

Earth, Moon, and Sun

This time lapse photo shows an eclipse ▶ of the moon as it rises over the Golden Gate Bridge in San Francisco.

Focus on the BIG Idea

S 8.4.e

What events are caused by the motion of Earth and the moon?

Check What You Know

Imagine that you are looking up at a full moon in the sky. Why is the moon so bright? Does the moon produce its own light, like a flashlight, or does its light come from somewhere else? Explain your reasoning.

Build Science Vocabulary

The images shown here represent some of the key terms in this chapter. You can use this vocabulary skill to help you understand the meaning of some key terms in this chapter.

Latin Word Origins

Many science words come to English from Latin. For example, the adjective *solar*, which means "of the sun," comes from the Latin word *solaris*, or "sun."

Use the Latin words in the table below to help you remember the Key Terms.

Latin Word	Meaning	Key Terms
aequalis	equal	equinox
crater	large mixing bowl	crater
gravitas	weight, heaviness	gravity, gravitation
luna	moon	lunar eclipse, lunar highlands
mare	sea	mare, maria
solaris	sun	solar eclipse
umbra	shade, shadow	umbra, penumbra

Apply It!

Review the Latin words and meanings in the chart. Look at the meaning of *crater*. Predict what a *crater* might be if it were seen on the surface of the moon. Revise your definition as needed.

solar eclipse

rotation

crater

astronomy

Chapter 12 Vocabulary

Section 1 (page 464)
astronomy
axis
rotation
revolution
orbit
calendar
solstice
equinox

Section 2 (page 474)
force
gravity
Universal Law of Gravitation
mass
weight
inertia
Newton's first law of motion

Section 3 (page 478)
phase
eclipse
solar eclipse
umbra
penumbra
lunar eclipse
tide
spring tide
neap tide

Section 4 (page 488)
telescope
maria
crater
meteoroid

Interactive Textbook

Build Science Vocabulary
Online
Visit: PHSchool.com
Web Code: cxj-4120

How to Read Science

Sequence

Some processes in science occur as part of a cycle. A cycle is a continuous process or sequence of events that does not have an end. When the final event is over, the first event begins again. The changing seasons on Earth are an example of a cycle.

Use a cycle diagram to show a cycle. Write the first event in a circle at the top of the page. Then, write each event in sequence, moving clockwise. Draw arrows to connect each event to the one that occurs next.

Seasons of the Year

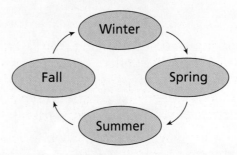

Apply It!

Review the diagram. Why is using a cycle diagram a good way to explain the seasons?

1. After you read about the seasons in Section 1, create your own cycle diagram of the seasons. Include information about the tilt of Earth's axis and how the tilt affects the seasons in the Northern and Southern Hemispheres.

2. As you read Section 3, prepare a cycle diagram showing four major phases of the moon.

S 8.4.e, 8.9.e

Track the Moon

How does the moon move across the sky? How does its appearance change over the course of a month? In this investigation, you will observe how the position and apparent shape of the moon change over time.

Your Goal

To observe the shape of the moon and its position in the sky every day for one month

To complete this project, you must

- observe the compass direction in which you see the moon, its phase, and its height above the horizon
- use your observations to explain the phases of the moon
- develop rules you can use to predict when and where you might see the moon each day

Plan It!

Begin by preparing an observation log. You will record the date and time of each observation, the direction and height of the moon, a sketch of its shape, and notes about cloud cover and other conditions. Observe the moon every clear night, looking for patterns.

Make a map of your observation site on which you will plot the direction of the moon. You can measure the moon's height in degrees above the horizon by making a fist and holding it at arm's length. One fist above the horizon is 10°, two fists are 20°, and so on. On at least one day, compare your observations of the moon an hour or two apart.

Once your observations are complete, prepare a presentation of your results. Your presentation should include a set of graphs and a discussion of any patterns that you noticed.

Earth in Space

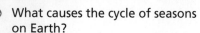
S 8.4.e Students know the appearance, general composition, relative position and size, and motion of objects in the solar system, including planets, planetary satellites, comets, and asteroids.

🔑 How does Earth move in space?

🔑 What causes the cycle of seasons on Earth?

Key Terms

- astronomy
- axis
- rotation
- revolution
- orbit
- calendar
- solstice
- equinox

Lab zone Standards **Warm-Up**

What Causes Day and Night?

1. Place a lamp with a bare bulb on a table to represent the sun. Put a globe at the end of the table about 1 meter away to represent Earth.

2. Turn the lamp on and darken the room. Which parts of the globe have light shining on them? Which parts are in shadow?

3. Find your location on the globe. Turn the globe once. Notice when it is lit—day—at your location and when it is dark—night.

Think It Over

Making Models What does one complete turn of the globe represent? In this model, how many seconds represent one day? How could you use the globe and bulb to represent a year?

Each year, ancient Egyptian farmers eagerly awaited the flood of the Nile River. For thousands of years, their planting was ruled by it. As soon as the Nile's floodwaters withdrew, the farmers had to be ready to plow and plant their fields along the river. Therefore, the Egyptians wanted to predict when the flood would occur. Around 3000 B.C., people noticed that the bright star Sirius first became visible in the early morning sky every year shortly before the flood began. The Egyptians used this knowledge to predict each year's flood. The ancient Egyptians were among the first people to study the stars. The study of the moon, stars, and other objects in space is called **astronomy.**

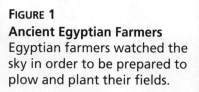

FIGURE 1
Ancient Egyptian Farmers
Egyptian farmers watched the sky in order to be prepared to plow and plant their fields.

How Earth Moves

Ancient astronomers studied the movements of the sun and the moon as they appeared to travel across the sky. It seemed to them as though Earth was standing still and the sun and moon were moving. Actually, the sun and moon seem to move across the sky each day because Earth is rotating on its axis. Earth also moves around the sun. **Earth moves through space in two major ways: rotation and revolution.**

Rotation Look at Figure 2. The imaginary line that passes through Earth's center and the North and South poles is Earth's **axis.** The spinning of Earth on its axis is called **rotation.**

Earth's rotation causes day and night. As Earth rotates eastward, the sun appears to move westward across the sky. It is day on the side of Earth facing the sun. As Earth continues to turn to the east, the sun appears to set in the west. Sunlight can't reach the side of Earth facing away from the sun, so it is night there. It takes Earth about 24 hours to rotate once. As you know, each 24-hour cycle of day and night is called a day.

Revolution In addition to rotating on its axis, Earth travels around the sun. As shown in Figure 3, a **revolution** is the movement of one object around another. One complete revolution of Earth around the sun is called a year. Earth follows a path, or **orbit,** as it revolves around the sun. Earth's orbit is not quite circular. It is a slightly elongated circle, or ellipse.

FIGURE 2
Rotation
The rotation of Earth on its axis is similar to the movement of the figure skater as she spins.

Axis— N

S Earth

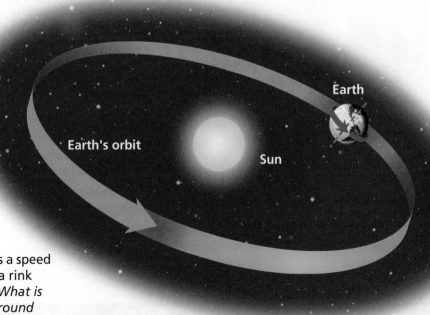

Earth's orbit

Sun

Earth

FIGURE 3
Revolution
Earth revolves around the sun just as a speed skater travels around the center of a rink during a race. **Applying Concepts** *What is one complete revolution of Earth around the sun called?*

Calendars People of many different cultures have struggled to establish calendars based on the length of time that Earth takes to revolve around the sun. A **calendar** is a system of organizing time that defines the beginning, length, and divisions of a year.

The ancient Egyptians created one of the first calendars. Egyptian astronomers counted the number of days between each first appearance of the star Sirius in the morning. In this way, they found that there are about 365 days in a year.

Dividing the year into smaller parts was also difficult. Early people used moon cycles to divide the year. The time from one full moon to the next is about $29\frac{1}{2}$ days. A year of 12 of these "moonths" adds up to only 354 days. The ancient Egyptian calendar had 12 months of 30 days each, with an extra 5 days at the end.

Science and **History**

Tracking the Cycle of the Year
For thousands of years, people have used observations of the sky to keep track of the time of year.

1500 B.C. British Isles
Ancient peoples complete Stonehenge, a monument with giant stones that mark the directions in which the sun rises and sets on the shortest and longest days of the year.

1300 B.C. China
Chinese astronomers make detailed observations of the sun, planets, and other objects they see in the night sky. Chinese astronomers calculated that the length of a year is $365\frac{1}{4}$ days.

80 B.C. Greece
Astronomers in Greece develop an instrument called the Antikythera Calculator. This instrument used a system of gears to show the movement of the sun, moon, planets, and stars.

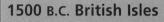

| 1500 B.C. | 1000 B.C. | 500 B.C. |

The Romans borrowed the Egyptian calendar of 365 days. But in fact, Earth orbits the sun in about $365\frac{1}{4}$ days. The Romans adjusted the Egyptian calendar by adding one day every four years. You know this fourth year as "leap year." In a leap year, February is given 29 days instead of its usual 28. Using a system of leap years helps to ensure that annual events, such as the beginning of summer, occur on about the same date each year.

The Roman calendar was off by a little more than 11 minutes a year. Over the centuries, these minutes added up. By the 1500s, the beginning of spring was about ten days too early. To straighten things out, Pope Gregory XIII dropped ten days from the year 1582. He also made some other minor changes to the Roman system to form the calendar that we use today.

 Reading Checkpoint **What is a leap year?**

Writing in Science

Writing Dialogue Research one of the accomplishments discussed in the timeline. Write a conversation, or dialogue, in which two people from the time and culture that made the discovery or structure discuss its importance in their lives. Examples might include their work or the timing of their celebrations.

A.D. 900 Mexico
The Mayas study the movement of the sun, the moon, and the planet Venus. They had two different calendars, one with 365 days for everyday use and the other with 260 days for religious uses.

A.D. 1600 Turkey
Astronomers use a variety of astronomical instruments, including astrolabes, at an observatory in Istanbul. Astrolabes were used to predict the positions of stars and planets.

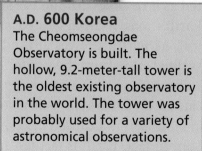

A.D. 600 Korea
The Cheomseongdae Observatory is built. The hollow, 9.2-meter-tall tower is the oldest existing observatory in the world. The tower was probably used for a variety of astronomical observations.

A.D. 500	A.D. 1000	A.D. 1500

FIGURE 4

Sunlight Striking Earth's Surface
Near the equator, sunlight strikes
Earth's surface more directly and is
less spread out than near the poles.
*Relating Cause and Effect Why is it
usually colder near the poles than
near the equator?*

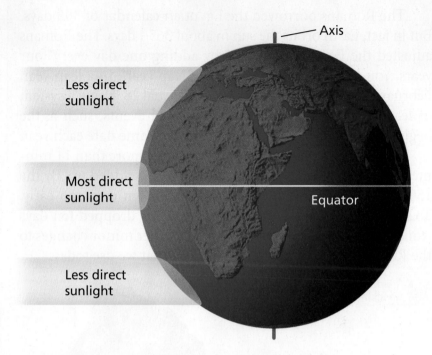

Axis

Less direct
sunlight

Most direct
sunlight

Equator

Less direct
sunlight

 **Try This Activity**

Sun Shadows

The sun's shadow changes
predictably through the day.

1. On a sunny day, stand
   outside in the sun and use
   a compass to find north.

2. Have your partner place a
   craft stick about one meter
   to the north of where you
   are standing. Repeat for
   east, south, and west.

3. Insert a meter stick in the
   ground at the center of the
   craft sticks. Make sure the
   stick is straight up.

4. Predict how the sun's
   shadow will move
   throughout the day.

5. Record the direction and
   length of the sun's shadow
   at noon and at regular
   intervals during the day.

Predicting How did the
actual movement of the sun's
shadow compare with your
prediction? How do you think
the direction and length of
the sun's shadow at these
same times would change
over the next six months?

The Seasons on Earth

Most places outside the tropics and polar regions have four distinct seasons: winter, spring, summer, and autumn. But there are great differences in temperature from place to place. For instance, it is generally warmer near the equator than near the poles. Why is this so?

How Sunlight Hits Earth Figure 4 shows how sunlight strikes Earth's surface. Notice that sunlight hits Earth's surface most directly near the equator. Near the poles, sunlight arrives at a steep angle. As a result, it is spread out over a greater area. That is why it is warmer near the equator than near the poles.

Earth's Tilted Axis If Earth's axis were straight up and down relative to its orbit, temperatures would remain fairly constant year-round. There would be no seasons. **Earth has seasons because its axis is tilted as it revolves around the sun.**

Notice in Figure 5 that Earth's axis is always tilted at an angle of 23.5° from the vertical. As Earth revolves around the sun, the north end of its axis is tilted away from the sun for part of the year and toward the sun for part of the year.

Summer and winter are caused by Earth's tilt as it revolves around the sun. The change in seasons is not caused by changes in Earth's distance from the sun. In fact, Earth is farthest from the sun when it is summer in the Northern Hemisphere.

Reading Checkpoint When is Earth farthest from the sun?

FIGURE 5
The Seasons

The yearly cycle of the seasons is caused by the tilt of Earth's axis as it revolves around the sun.

Go Online
active art

For: Seasons activity
Visit: PHSchool.com
Web Code: cfp-5012

June Solstice
The north end of Earth's axis is tilted toward the sun. It is summer in the Northern Hemisphere and winter in the Southern Hemisphere.

March Equinox

June Solstice

December Solstice

March and September Equinoxes
Neither end of Earth's axis is tilted toward the sun. Both hemispheres receive the same amount of energy.

September Equinox

December Solstice
The south end of Earth's axis is tilted toward the sun. It is summer in the Southern Hemisphere and winter in the Northern Hemisphere.

The height of the sun above the horizon varies with the season.
Interpreting Graphics *When is the sun at its maximum height in the Northern Hemisphere?*

June Solstice

March and September Equinoxes

December Solstice

January in the Southern Hemisphere

January in the Northern Hemisphere

FIGURE 6
Solstices and Equinoxes

Summer in the Southern Hemisphere (left) occurs at the same time as winter in the Northern Hemisphere (right). Similarly, when it is spring in the Southern Hemisphere, it is fall in the Northern Hemisphere. *Interpreting Photographs In which direction was Earth's axis pointing at the time that each of the photographs was taken?*

Earth in June In June, the north end of Earth's axis is tilted toward the sun. In the Northern Hemisphere, the noon sun is high in the sky and there are more hours of daylight than darkness. The combination of direct rays and more hours of sunlight heats the surface more in June than at any other time of the year. It is summer in the Northern Hemisphere.

At the same time south of the equator, the sun's rays are less direct. The sun is low in the sky and days are shorter than nights. The combination of less direct rays and fewer hours of sunlight heats Earth's surface less than at any other time of the year. It is winter in the Southern Hemisphere.

Earth in December In December, people in the Southern Hemisphere receive the most direct sunlight, so it is summer there. At the same time, the sun's rays in the Northern Hemisphere are more slanted and there are fewer hours of daylight. So it is winter in the Northern Hemisphere.

Solstices The sun reaches its farthest position north or south of the equator twice each year. Each of these days, when the sun is farthest north or south of the equator, is known as a **solstice** (SOHL stis). The day when the sun is farthest north of the equator is the summer solstice in the Northern Hemisphere. It is also the winter solstice in the Southern Hemisphere. This solstice occurs around June 21 each year. It is the longest day of the year in the Northern Hemisphere and the shortest day of the year in the Southern Hemisphere.

Similarly, around December 21, the sun is farthest south of the equator. This is the winter solstice in the Northern Hemisphere and the summer solstice in the Southern Hemisphere.

October in the Southern Hemisphere

October in the Northern Hemisphere

Equinoxes Halfway between the solstices, neither hemisphere is tilted toward or away from the sun. This occurs twice a year, when the noon sun is directly overhead at the equator. Each of these days is known as an **equinox,** which means "equal night." During an equinox, day and night are each about 12 hours long everywhere on Earth. The vernal (spring) equinox occurs around March 21 and marks the beginning of spring in the Northern Hemisphere. The autumnal equinox occurs around September 22. It marks the beginning of fall in the Northern Hemisphere.

 **Reading Checkpoint** **What is an equinox?**

Section 1 Assessment

S 8.4.e, E-LA: Writing 8.2.0, Reading 8.2.0

Target Reading Skill Sequence Use your cycle diagram of the seasons to help answer the following questions.

Reviewing Key Concepts

1. a. **Identifying** What are the two major motions of Earth as it travels through space?
   b. **Explaining** Which motion causes day and night?
2. a. **Relating Cause and Effect** What causes the seasons?
   b. **Comparing and Contrasting** What are solstices and equinoxes? How are they related to the seasons?
   c. **Predicting** How would the seasons be different if Earth were not tilted on its axis?

Writing in Science

Descriptive Paragraph What seasons occur where you live? Write a detailed paragraph describing the changes that take place each season in your region. Explain how seasonal changes in temperature and hours of daylight relate to changes in Earth's position as it moves around the sun.

Reasons for the Seasons

S 8.4.e, S 8.9

Problem

How does the tilt of Earth's axis affect the light received by Earth as it revolves around the sun?

Skills Focus

making models, observing, inferring, predicting

Materials (per pair of students)

- books
- flashlight
- paper
- pencil
- protractor
- toothpick
- acetate sheet with thick grid lines drawn on it
- plastic foam ball marked with poles and equator

Procedure

1. Make a pile of books about 15 cm high.

2. Tape the acetate sheet to the head of the flashlight. Place the flashlight on the pile of books.

3. Carefully push a pencil into the South Pole of the plastic foam ball, which represents Earth.

4. Use the protractor to measure a 23.5° tilt of the axis of your Earth away from your "flashlight sun," as shown in the top diagram. This position represents winter in the Northern Hemisphere.

5. Hold the pencil so that Earth is steady at this 23.5° angle and about 15 cm from the flashlight head. Turn the flashlight on. Dim the room lights.

6. The squares on the acetate should show up on your model Earth. Move the ball closer if necessary or dim the room lights more. Observe and record the shape of the squares at the equator and at the poles.

7. Carefully stick the toothpick straight into your model Earth about halfway between the equator and the North Pole. Observe and record the length of the shadow.

8. Without changing the tilt, turn the pencil to rotate the model Earth once on its axis. Observe and record how the shadow of the toothpick changes.

9. Tilt your model Earth 23.5° toward the flashlight, as shown in the bottom diagram. This is summer in the Northern Hemisphere. Observe and record the shape of the squares at the equator and at the poles. Observe how the toothpick's shadow changes.

10. Rotate the model Earth and note the shadow pattern.

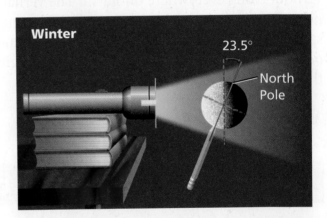

Winter   23.5°   North Pole

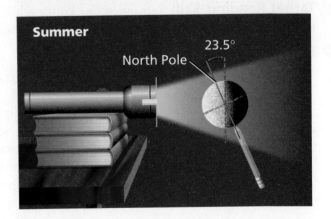

Summer   North Pole   23.5°

Analyze and Conclude

1. **Observing** When it is winter in the Northern Hemisphere, which areas on Earth get the most concentrated light? Which areas get the most concentrated light when it is summer in the Northern Hemisphere?

2. **Observing** Compare your observations of how the light hits the area halfway between the equator and the North Pole during winter (Step 6) and during summer (Step 9).

3. **Inferring** If the squares projected on the ball from the acetate become larger, what can you infer about the amount of heat distributed in each square?

4. **Inferring** According to your observations, which areas on Earth are consistently coolest? Which areas are consistently warmest? Why?

5. **Predicting** What time of year will the toothpick's shadow be longest? When will the shadow be shortest?

6. **Drawing Conclusions** How are the amounts of heat and light received in a square related to the angle of the sun's rays?

7. **Communicating** Use your observations of an Earth-sun model to write an explanation of what causes the seasons.

More to Explore

You can measure how directly light from the sun hits Earth's surface by making a shadow stick. You will need a stick or pole about 1 m long. With the help of your teacher, push the stick partway into the ground where it will not be disturbed. Make sure the stick stays vertical. At noon on the first day of every month, measure the length of the stick's shadow. The shorter the shadow, the higher the sun is in the sky and the more directly the sun's rays are hitting Earth. At what time of the year are the shadows longest? Shortest? How do your observations help explain the seasons?

Gravity and Motion

S 8.2.g Students know the role of gravity in forming and maintaining the shapes of planets, stars, and the solar system.

🔑 What determines the strength of the force of gravity between two objects?

🔑 What two factors combine to keep the moon and Earth in orbit?

Key Terms

- force
- gravity
- Universal Law of Gravitation
- mass
- weight
- inertia
- Newton's first law of motion

Lab zone ## Standards **Warm-Up**

Can You Remove the Bottom Penny?

1. Place 25 or so pennies in a stack on a table.
2. Write down your prediction of what will happen if you attempt to knock the bottom penny out of the stack.
3. Quickly slide a ruler along the surface of the table and strike the bottom penny. Observe what happens to the stack of pennies.
4. Repeat Step 3 several times, knocking more pennies from the bottom of the stack.

Think It Over

Developing Hypotheses Explain what happened to the stack of pennies as the bottom penny was knocked out of the stack.

Earth revolves around the sun in a nearly circular orbit. The moon orbits Earth in the same way. But what keeps Earth and the moon in orbit? Why don't they just fly off into space?

The first person to answer these questions was the English scientist Isaac Newton. Late in his life, Newton told a story of how watching an apple fall from a tree in 1666 had made him think about the moon's orbit. Newton realized that there must be a force acting between Earth and the moon that kept the moon in orbit. Recall that a **force** is a push or a pull. Most everyday forces require objects to be in contact. Newton realized that the force that holds the moon in orbit is different in that it acts over long distances between objects that are not in contact.

Gravity

Newton hypothesized that the force that pulls an apple to the ground also pulls the moon toward Earth, keeping it in orbit. This force, called **gravity,** attracts all objects toward each other. In Newton's day, most scientists thought that forces on Earth were different from those elsewhere in the universe. Although Newton did not discover gravity, he was the first person to realize that gravity occurs everywhere. Newton's **Universal Law of Gravitation** states that every object in the universe attracts every other object.

The force of gravity is measured in units called newtons, named after Isaac Newton.  **The strength of the force of gravity between two objects depends on two factors: the masses of the objects and the distance between them.**

Gravity, Mass, and Weight According to the law of universal gravitation, all of the objects around you, including Earth and even this book, are pulling on you, just as you are pulling on them. Why don't you notice a pull between you and the book? Because the strength of gravity depends in part on the masses of each of the objects. As you have learned, **mass** is the amount of matter in an object.

Because Earth is so massive, it exerts a much greater force on you than this book does. Similarly, Earth exerts a gravitational force on the moon, large enough to keep the moon in orbit. The moon also exerts a gravitational force on Earth, as you will learn later in this chapter when you study the tides.

The force of gravity on an object is the object's **weight**. Unlike mass, which doesn't change, an object's weight can change depending on its location. For example, on the moon you would weigh about one sixth of your weight on Earth. This is because the moon is much less massive than Earth, so the pull of the moon's gravity on you would be far less than that of Earth's gravity.

Gravity and Distance The strength of gravity is affected by the distance between two objects as well as their masses. The force of gravity decreases rapidly as distance increases. For example, if the distance between two objects were doubled, the force of gravity between them would decrease to one fourth of its original value.

✓ **Reading Checkpoint** What is an object's weight?

FIGURE 7
Gravity, Mass, and Distance
The strength of the force of gravity between two objects depends on their masses and the distance between them. *Inferring How would the force of gravity change if the distance between the objects decreased?*

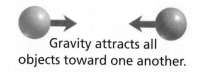
Gravity attracts all objects toward one another.

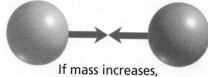
If mass increases, force also increases.

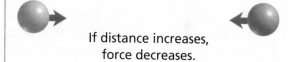
If distance increases, force decreases.

FIGURE 8
Earth Over the Moon
The force of gravity holds Earth and the moon together.

Math Analyzing Data

Gravity Versus Distance

As a rocket leaves a planet's surface, the force of gravity between the rocket and the planet changes. Use the graph at the right to answer the questions below.

1. **Reading Graphs** What is the force of gravity on the rocket at the planet's surface?

2. **Reading Graphs** What is the force of gravity on the rocket at a distance of two units (twice the planet's radius from its center)?

3. **Making Generalizations** According to the graph, is the relationship between gravity and distance linear or nonlinear? Explain.

4. **Drawing Conclusions** In general, how does the force of gravity pulling on the rocket change as the distance between it and the planet increases?

5. **Predicting** Estimate the force of gravity on the rocket at a distance of five units.

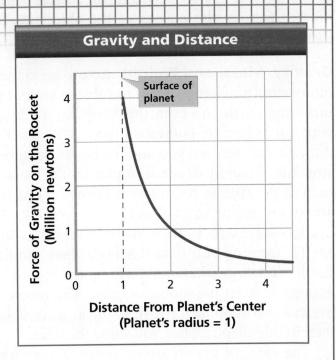

Gravity and Distance

Surface of planet

Force of Gravity on the Rocket (Million newtons)

Distance From Planet's Center (Planet's radius = 1)

Go Online

SciLINKS NSTA

For: Links on gravity
Visit: www.SciLinks.org
Web Code: scn-0612

Inertia and Orbital Motion

If the sun and Earth are constantly pulling on one another because of gravity, why doesn't Earth fall into the sun? Similarly, why doesn't the moon crash into Earth? The fact that such collisions have not occurred shows that there must be another factor at work. That factor is called inertia.

Inertia The tendency of an object to resist a change in motion is **inertia.** You feel the effects of inertia every day. When you are riding in a car and it stops suddenly, you keep moving forward. If you didn't have a seat belt on, your inertia could cause you to bump into the car's windshield or the seat in front of you. The more mass an object has, the greater its inertia. An object with greater inertia is more difficult to start or stop.

Isaac Newton stated his ideas about inertia as a scientific law. **Newton's first law of motion** says that an object at rest will stay at rest and an object in motion will stay in motion with a constant speed and direction unless acted on by an unbalanced force.

 **Reading Checkpoint** What is inertia?

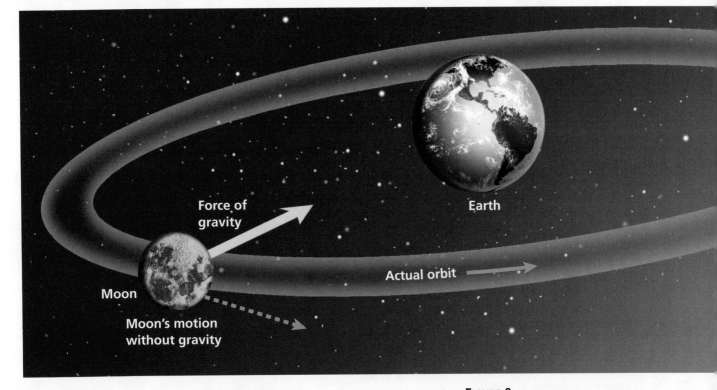

Force of gravity

Earth

Actual orbit

Moon

Moon's motion without gravity

Orbital Motion Why do Earth and the moon remain in their orbits? 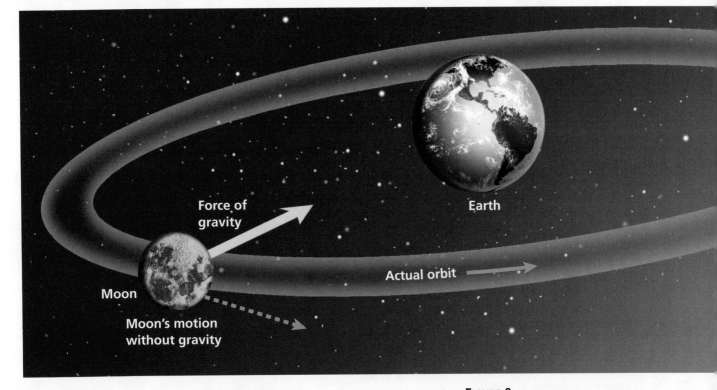 **Newton concluded that two factors—inertia and gravity—combine to keep Earth in orbit around the sun and the moon in orbit around Earth.**

As shown in Figure 9, Earth's gravity keeps pulling the moon toward it, preventing the moon from moving in a straight line. At the same time, the moon keeps moving ahead because of its inertia. If not for Earth's gravity, inertia would cause the moon to move off through space in a straight line. In the same way, Earth revolves around the sun because the sun's gravity pulls on it while Earth's inertia keeps it moving ahead.

FIGURE 9
Gravity and Inertia
A combination of gravity and inertia keeps the moon in orbit around Earth. If there were no gravity, inertia would cause the moon to travel in a straight line. **Interpreting Diagrams** *What would happen to the moon if it were not moving in orbit?*

Section 2 Assessment

S 8.2.g, E-LA: Writing 8.2.0, Reading 8.1.2

Vocabulary Skill Latin Word Origins How does the Latin word origin of *gravity* help you to remember its meaning?

Reviewing Key Concepts

1. a. **Summarizing** What is the law of universal gravitation?
   b. **Reviewing** What two factors determine the force of gravity between two objects?
   c. **Predicting** Suppose the moon were closer to Earth. How would the force of gravity between Earth and the moon be different?

2. a. **Identifying** What two factors act together to keep Earth in orbit around the sun?

   b. **Applying Concepts** Why doesn't Earth simply fall into the sun?
   c. **Predicting** How would Earth move if the sun (including its gravity) suddenly disappeared? Explain your answer.

Writing in Science

Cause and Effect Paragraph Suppose you took a trip to the moon. Write a paragraph describing how and why your weight would change. Would your mass change too?

CALIFORNIA
Standards Focus

S 8.2.g Students know the role of gravity in forming and maintaining the shapes of planets, stars, and the solar system.

S 8.4.d Students know that stars are the source of light for all bright objects in outer space and that the Moon and planets shine by reflected sunlight, not by their own light.

- What causes the phases of the moon?
- What are solar and lunar eclipses?
- What causes the tides?

Key Terms

- phase
- eclipse
- solar eclipse
- umbra
- penumbra
- lunar eclipse
- tide
- spring tide
- neap tide

Lab zone Standards Warm-Up

How Does the Moon Move?

1. Place a quarter flat on your desk to represent Earth. Put a penny flat on your desk to represent the moon.
2. One side of the moon always faces Earth. Move the moon through one revolution around Earth, keeping Lincoln's face always looking at Earth. How many times did the penny make one complete rotation?

Think It Over

Inferring From the point of view of someone on Earth, does the moon seem to rotate? Explain your answer.

When you look up at the moon, you may see what looks like a face. Some people call this "the man in the moon." What you are really seeing is a pattern of light-colored and dark-colored areas on the moon's surface that just happens to look like a face. Oddly, this pattern never seems to move. That is, the same side of the moon, the "near side," always faces Earth. The "far side" of the moon always faces away from Earth. The reason has to do with how the moon moves in space.

Motions of the Moon

Like Earth, the moon moves through space in two ways. The moon revolves around Earth and also rotates on its own axis.

As the moon revolves around Earth, the relative positions of the moon, Earth, and sun change. **The changing relative positions of the moon, Earth, and sun cause the phases of the moon, eclipses, and tides.**

The moon rotates once on its axis in the same amount of time as it revolves around Earth. Thus, a "day" and a "year" on the moon are the same length. For this reason, the same side of the moon always faces Earth. The length of the moon's day is somewhat shorter than the 29.5 days between consecutive full moons. This is because as the moon revolves around Earth, Earth revolves around the sun. Thus, the moon has to travel a little farther than one complete orbit between each full moon.

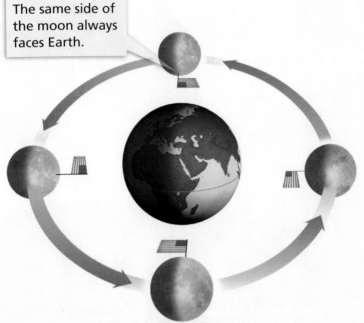

The same side of the moon always faces Earth.

FIGURE 10
The Moon in Motion
The moon rotates on its axis and revolves around Earth in the same amount of time. As a result, the near side of the moon (shown with a flag) always faces Earth. **Interpreting Diagrams** *Would Earth ever appear to set below the horizon for someone standing next to the flag on the moon? Explain.*

Phases of the Moon

On a clear night when the moon is full, the bright moonlight can keep you awake. But the moon does not produce the light you see. Instead, it reflects light from the sun. Imagine taking a flashlight into a dark room. If you were to shine the flashlight on a chair, you would see the chair because the light from your flashlight would bounce, or reflect, off the chair. In the same way that the chair wouldn't shine by itself, the moon doesn't give off light by itself. You can see the moon because it reflects the light of the sun.

When you see the moon in the sky, sometimes it appears round. Other times you see only a thin sliver, or crescent. The different shapes of the moon you see from Earth are called **phases.** The moon goes through its whole set of phases each time it makes a complete revolution around Earth.

Phases are caused by changes in the relative positions of the moon, Earth, and the sun. Because the sun lights the moon, half the moon is almost always in sunlight. However, since the moon revolves around Earth, you see the moon from different angles. The half of the moon that faces Earth is not always the half that is sunlit. ☞ **The phase of the moon you see depends on how much of the sunlit side of the moon faces Earth.**

1 New Moon
The sunlit side faces away from Earth.

2 Waxing Crescent
The portion of the moon you can see is waxing, or growing, into a crescent shape.

3 First Quarter
You can see half of the sunlit side of the moon.

4 Waxing Gibbous
The moon continues to wax. The visible shape of the moon is called gibbous.

FIGURE 11

Phases of the Moon

The photos at the top of the page show how the phases of the moon appear when you look up at the moon from Earth's surface. The circular diagram at the right shows how the Earth and moon would appear to an observer in space as the moon revolves around Earth.

Interpreting Diagrams *During what phases are the moon, Earth, and sun aligned in a straight line?*

Go Online
active art

For: Moon Phases and Eclipses activity
Visit: PHSchool.com
Web Code: cfp-5013

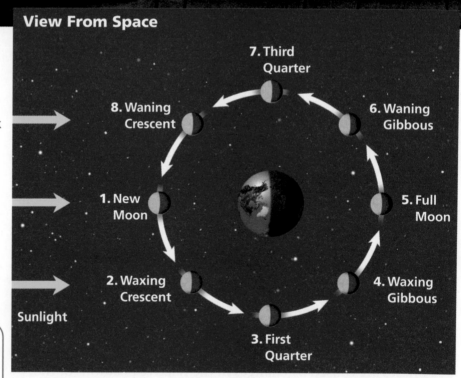

View From Space

7. Third Quarter

8. Waning Crescent

6. Waning Gibbous

1. New Moon

5. Full Moon

2. Waxing Crescent

4. Waxing Gibbous

Sunlight

3. First Quarter

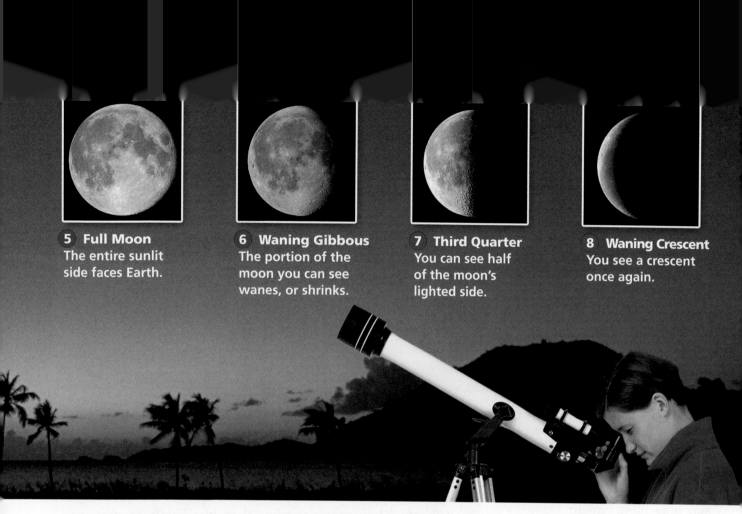

5 Full Moon
The entire sunlit side faces Earth.

6 Waning Gibbous
The portion of the moon you can see wanes, or shrinks.

7 Third Quarter
You can see half of the moon's lighted side.

8 Waning Crescent
You see a crescent once again.

To understand the phases of the moon, study Figure 11. During the new moon, the lit side of the moon faces completely away from Earth. As the moon revolves around Earth, you see more and more of the lighted side of the moon every day, until the side of the moon you see is fully lit. As the moon continues in its orbit, you see less and less of the lighted side. About 29.5 days after the last new moon, the cycle is complete, and a new moon occurs again.

 **Reading Checkpoint** What is a new moon?

Eclipses

As Figure 12 shows, the moon's orbit around Earth is slightly tilted with respect to Earth's orbit around the sun. As a result, in most months the moon revolves around Earth without moving into Earth's shadow or the moon's shadow hitting Earth. **When the moon's shadow hits Earth or Earth's shadow hits the moon, an eclipse occurs.** When an object in space comes between the sun and a third object, it casts a shadow on that object, causing an **eclipse** (ih KLIPS) to take place. There are two types of eclipses: solar eclipses and lunar eclipses. (The words *solar* and *lunar* come from the Latin words for "sun" and "moon.")

FIGURE 12
The Moon's Orbit
The moon's orbit is tilted about 5 degrees relative to Earth's orbit around the sun.

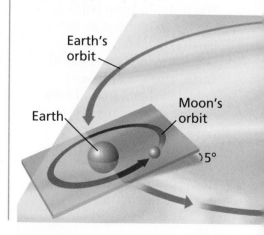

Earth's orbit

Earth

Moon's orbit

5°

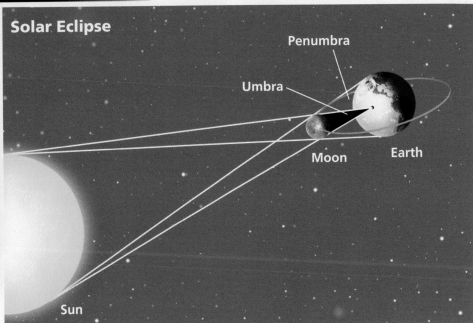

Solar Eclipse

Penumbra

Umbra

Moon

Earth

Sun

FIGURE 13
The outer layer of the sun's atmosphere, the solar corona, is visible surrounding the dark disk of the moon during a solar eclipse. During a solar eclipse, the moon blocks light from the sun, preventing sunlight from reaching parts of Earth's surface.

Lab zone Skills Activity

Making Models

Here is how you can draw a scale model of a solar eclipse. The moon's diameter is about one fourth Earth's diameter. The distance from Earth to the moon is about 30 times Earth's diameter. Make a scale drawing of the moon, Earth, and the distance between them. (*Hint:* Draw Earth 1 cm in diameter in one corner of the paper.) From the edges of the moon, draw and shade in a triangle just touching Earth to show the moon's umbra.

When Do Solar Eclipses Occur? During a new moon, the moon lies between Earth and the sun. But most months, as you have seen, the moon travels a little above or below the sun in the sky. ● **A solar eclipse occurs when the moon passes directly between Earth and the sun, blocking sunlight from Earth.** The moon's shadow then hits Earth, as shown in Figure 13. So a **solar eclipse** occurs when a new moon blocks your view of the sun.

Total Solar Eclipses The very darkest part of the moon's shadow, the **umbra** (UM bruh), is cone-shaped. From any point in the umbra, light from the sun is completely blocked by the moon. The moon's umbra happens to be long enough so that the point of the cone can just reach a small part of Earth's surface. Only the people within the umbra experience a total solar eclipse. During the short period of a total solar eclipse, the sky grows as dark as night, even in the middle of a clear day. The air gets cool and the sky becomes an eerie color. You can see the stars and the solar corona, which is the faint outer atmosphere of the sun.

Partial Solar Eclipses In Figure 13, you can see that the moon casts another part of its shadow that is less dark than the umbra. This larger part of the shadow is called the **penumbra** (peh NUM bruh). In the penumbra, part of the sun is visible from Earth. During a solar eclipse, people in the penumbra see only a partial eclipse. Since an extremely bright part of the sun still remains visible, it is not safe to look directly at the sun during a partial solar eclipse (just as you wouldn't look directly at the sun during a normal day).

482 ◆

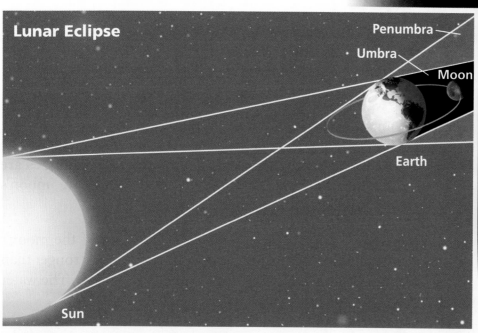

Lunar Eclipse

Penumbra

Umbra

Moon

Earth

Sun

When Do Lunar Eclipses Occur? During most months, the moon moves near Earth's shadow but not quite into it. A **lunar eclipse** occurs at a full moon when Earth is directly between the moon and the sun. You can see a lunar eclipse in Figure 14. **During a lunar eclipse, Earth blocks sunlight from reaching the moon.** The moon is then in Earth's shadow and looks dim from Earth. Lunar eclipses occur only when there is a full moon because the moon is closest to Earth's shadow at that time.

Total Lunar Eclipses Like the moon's shadow in a solar eclipse, Earth's shadow has an umbra and a penumbra. When the entire moon is in Earth's umbra, you see a total lunar eclipse. You can see the edge of Earth's shadow on the moon before and after a total lunar eclipse.

Unlike a total solar eclipse, a total lunar eclipse can be seen anywhere on Earth that the moon is visible. So you are more likely to see a total lunar eclipse than a total solar eclipse.

Partial Lunar Eclipses For most lunar eclipses, Earth, the moon, and the sun are not quite in line, and only a partial lunar eclipse results. A partial lunar eclipse occurs when the moon passes partly into the umbra of Earth's shadow. The edge of the umbra appears blurry, and you can watch it pass across the moon for two or three hours.

FIGURE 14
During a lunar eclipse, Earth blocks sunlight from reaching the moon's surface. The photo of the moon above was taken during a total lunar eclipse. The moon's reddish tint occurs because Earth's atmosphere bends some sunlight toward the moon.
Interpreting Diagrams *What is the difference between the umbra and the penumbra?*

Go Online
active art

For: Moon Phases and Eclipses activity
Visit: PHSchool.com
Web Code: cfp-5013

 **During which phase of the moon can lunar eclipses occur?**

FIGURE 15
High and Low Tides
In some locations, such as along this beach in Australia, there can be dramatic differences between the height of high and low tides.

Tides

Have you ever built a sand castle on an ocean beach? Was it washed away by rising water? This is an example of **tides,** the rise and fall of ocean water that occurs every 12.5 hours or so. The water rises for about six hours, then falls for about six hours, in a regular cycle.

The force of gravity pulls the moon and Earth (including the water on Earth's surface) toward each other. ◐ **The tides are caused mainly by differences in how much the moon's gravity pulls on different parts of Earth.**

The Tide Cycle Look at Figure 16. The force of the moon's gravity at point A, which is closer to the moon, is stronger than the force of the moon's gravity on Earth as a whole. The water flows toward point A, and a high tide forms.

The force of the moon's gravity at point C, which is on the far side of Earth from the moon, is weaker than the force of the moon's gravity on Earth as a whole. Earth is pulled toward the moon more strongly than the water at point C, so the water is "left behind." Water flows toward point C, and a high tide occurs there too. Between points A and C, water flows away from points B and D, causing low tides.

At any one time there are two places with high tides and two places with low tides on Earth. As Earth rotates, one high tide stays on the side of Earth facing the moon. The second high tide stays on the opposite side of Earth. Each location on Earth sweeps through those two high tides and two low tides every 25 hours or so.

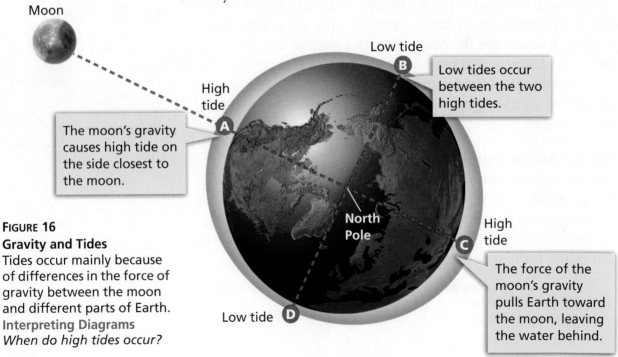

FIGURE 16
Gravity and Tides
Tides occur mainly because of differences in the force of gravity between the moon and different parts of Earth.
Interpreting Diagrams
When do high tides occur?

Spring Tides The sun's gravity also pulls on Earth's waters. As shown in the top diagram of Figure 17, the sun, moon, and Earth are nearly in a line during a new moon. The gravity of the sun and the moon pull in the same direction. Their combined forces produce a tide with the greatest difference between consecutive low and high tides, called a **spring tide**.

At full moon, the moon and the sun are on opposite sides of Earth. Since there are high tides on both sides of Earth, a spring tide is also produced. It doesn't matter in which order the sun, Earth, and moon line up. Spring tides occur twice a month, at new moon and at full moon.

Neap Tides During the moon's first-quarter and third-quarter phases, the line between Earth and the sun is at right angles to the line between Earth and the moon. The sun's pull is at right angles to the moon's pull. This arrangement produces a **neap tide**, a tide with the least difference between consecutive low and high tides. Neap tides occur twice a month.

 **Reading Checkpoint** What is a neap tide?

FIGURE 17
Spring and Neap Tides
When Earth, the sun, and the moon are in a straight line (top), a spring tide occurs. When the moon is at a right angle to the sun (bottom), a neap tide occurs.

Spring Tide

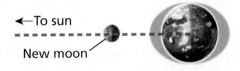

←To sun

New moon

Neap Tide

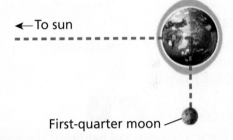

←To sun

First-quarter moon

Section 3 Assessment

S 8.2.g, 8.4.d,
E-LA: Reading 8.2.0

Target Reading Skill **Sequence** Create a cycle diagram with four phases of the moon: new moon, first quarter, full moon, and third quarter. For each phase, include a sketch of how the moon looks from Earth.

Reviewing Key Concepts

1. a. **Explaining** What causes the moon to shine?
   b. **Relating Cause and Effect** Why does the moon appear to change shape during the course of a month?
   c. **Interpreting Diagrams** Use Figure 11 to explain why you can't see the moon at the time of a new moon.
2. a. **Explaining** What is an eclipse?
   b. **Comparing and Contrasting** How is a solar eclipse different from a lunar eclipse?
   c. **Relating Cause and Effect** Why isn't there a solar eclipse and a lunar eclipse each month?
3. a. **Summarizing** What causes the tides?
   b. **Explaining** Explain why most coastal regions have two high tides and two low tides each day.
   c. **Comparing and Contrasting** Compare the size of high and low tides in a spring tide and a neap tide. What causes the difference?

Lab zone **At-Home Activity**

Tracking the Tides Use a daily newspaper or the Internet to track the height of high and low tides at a location of your choice for at least two weeks. Make a graph of your data, with the date as the x-axis and tide height as the y-axis. Also find the dates of the new moon and full moon and add them to your graph. Show your completed graph to a relative and explain what the graph shows.

A "Moonth" of Phases

S 8.4.d, 8.4.e

Problem

What causes the phases of the moon?

Skills Focus

making models, observing, drawing conclusions

Materials

- floor lamp with 150-watt bulb
- pencils
- plastic foam balls

Procedure

1. Place a lamp in the center of the room. Remove the lampshade.

2. Close the doors and shades to darken the room, and switch on the lamp.

3. Carefully stick the point of a pencil into the plastic foam ball so that the pencil can be used as a "handle."

4. Draw 8 circles on a sheet of paper. Number them 1–8.

5. Have your partner hold the plastic foam ball at arm's length in front and slightly above his or her head so that the ball is between him or her and the lamp. **CAUTION:** *Do not look directly at the bulb.*

6. The ball should be about 1 to 1.5 m away from the lamp. Adjust the distance between the ball and the lamp so that the light shines brightly on the ball.

7. Stand directly behind your partner and observe what part of the ball facing you is lit by the lamp. If light is visible on the ball, draw the shape of the lighted part of the ball in the first circle.

8. Have your partner turn 45° to the left while keeping the ball in front and at arm's length.

9. Repeat Step 7. Be sure you are standing directly behind your partner.

10. Repeat Steps 8 and 9 six more times until your partner is facing the lamp again. See the photograph for the 8 positions.

11. Change places and repeat Steps 4–10.

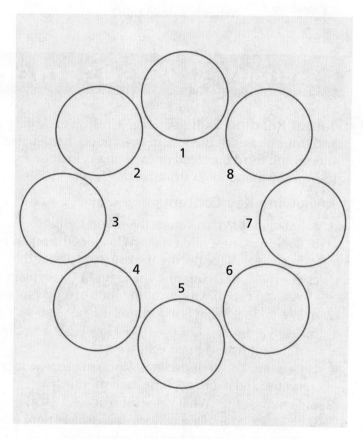

Analyze and Conclude

1. **Making Models** In your model, what represents Earth? The sun? The moon?

2. **Observing** Refer back to your 8 circles. How much of the lighted part of the ball did you see when facing the lamp?

3. **Classifying** Label your drawings with the names of the phases of the moon. Which drawing represents a full moon? A new moon? Which represents a waxing crescent? A waning crescent?

4. **Observing** How much of the lighted part of the ball did you see after each turn?

5. **Drawing Conclusions** Whether you could see it or not, how much of the ball's surface was always lit by the lamp? Was the darkness of the new moon caused by an eclipse? Explain your answer.

6. **Communicating** Write a brief analysis of this lab. How well did making a model help you understand the phases of the moon? What are some disadvantages of using models? What is another way to make a model to represent the various phases of the moon?

More to Explore

Design a model to show a lunar eclipse and a solar eclipse. What objects would you use for Earth, the sun, and the moon? Use the model to demonstrate why there isn't an eclipse every full moon and new moon.

45°

Earth's Moon

CALIFORNIA
Standards Focus

S 8.4.e Students know the appearance, general composition, relative position and size, and motion of objects in the solar system, including planets, planetary satellites, comets, and asteroids.

- What features are found on the moon's surface?

- What are some characteristics of the moon?

- How did the moon form?

Key Terms
- telescope
- maria
- crater
- meteoroid

Lab zone Standards **Warm-Up**

Why Do Craters Look Different From Each Other?

The moon's surface has pits in it, called craters.

1. Put on your goggles. Fill a large plastic basin to a depth of 2 cm with sand.

2. Drop marbles of different masses from about 20 cm high. Take the marbles out and view the craters they created.

3. Predict what will happen if you drop marbles from a higher point. Smooth out the sand. Now drop marbles of different masses from about 50 cm high.

4. Take the marbles out and view the craters they left.

Think It Over

Developing Hypotheses In which step do you think the marbles were moving faster when they hit the sand? If objects hitting the moon caused craters, how did the speeds of the objects affect the sizes of the craters? How did the masses of the objects affect the sizes of the craters?

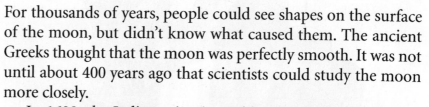

For thousands of years, people could see shapes on the surface of the moon, but didn't know what caused them. The ancient Greeks thought that the moon was perfectly smooth. It was not until about 400 years ago that scientists could study the moon more closely.

In 1609, the Italian scientist Galileo Galilei heard about a **telescope,** a device built to observe distant objects by making them appear closer. Galileo soon made his own telescope by putting two lenses in a wooden tube. The lenses focused the light coming through the tube, making distant objects seem closer. When Galileo pointed his telescope at the moon, he was able to see much more detail than anyone had ever seen before. What Galileo saw astounded him. Instead of the perfect sphere imagined by the Greeks, he saw that the moon has an irregular surface with a variety of remarkable features.

◄ Galileo used a telescope to help make this drawing of the moon.

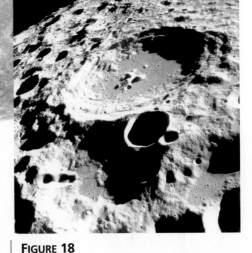

The dark, flat areas on the moon's surface are called maria.

The light-colored features that cover much of the moon's surface are highlands.

The Moon's Surface

Recent photos of the moon show much more detail than Galileo could see with his telescope. ☞ **Features on the moon's surface include maria, craters, and highlands.**

Maria The moon's surface has dark, flat areas, which Galileo called **maria** (MAH ree uh), the Latin word for "seas." Galileo incorrectly thought that the maria were oceans. The maria are actually hardened rock formed from huge lava flows that occurred between 3 and 4 billion years ago.

Craters Galileo saw that the moon's surface is marked by large round pits called **craters.** Some craters are hundreds of kilometers across. For a long time, many scientists mistakenly thought that these craters had been made by volcanoes. Scientists now know that these craters were caused by the impacts of **meteoroids,** chunks of rock or dust from space.

The maria have few craters compared to surrounding areas. This means that most of the moon's craters formed from impacts early in its history, before the maria formed. On Earth, such ancient craters have disappeared. They were worn away over time by water, wind, and other forces. But since the moon has no liquid water or atmosphere, its surface has changed little for billions of years.

Highlands Galileo correctly inferred that some of the light-colored features he saw on the moon's surface were highlands, or mountains. The peaks of the lunar highlands and the rims of the craters cast dark shadows, which Galileo could see. The rugged lunar highlands cover much of the moon's surface.

FIGURE 18
The Moon's Surface
The moon's surface is covered by craters, maria, and highlands. Craters on the moon formed from the impact of meteoroids. Most large craters are named after famous scientists or philosophers. **Observing** *What are the light regions in the top photograph called?*

For: Links on Earth's moon
Visit: www.SciLinks.org
Web Code: scn-0614

 **Reading Checkpoint** **What are meteoroids?**

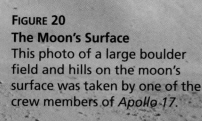

FIGURE 19
The Moon's Size
The diameter of the moon is a little less than the distance across the contiguous United States.
Calculating *What is the ratio of the moon's diameter to the distance between Earth and the moon?*

Characteristics of the Moon

Would you want to take a vacation on the moon? At an average distance of about 384,000 kilometers (about 30 times Earth's diameter), the moon is Earth's closest neighbor in space. Despite its proximity, the moon is very different from Earth. **The moon is dry and airless. Compared to Earth, the moon is small and has large variations in its surface temperature.** If you visited the moon, you would need to wear a bulky space suit to provide air to breathe, protect against sunburn, and to keep you at a comfortable temperature.

Size and Density The moon is 3,476 kilometers in diameter, a little less than the distance across the United States. This is about one-fourth Earth's diameter. However, the moon has only one-eightieth as much mass as Earth. Though Earth has a very dense core, its outer layers are less dense. The moon's average density is similar to the density of Earth's outer layers.

Temperature and Atmosphere On the moon's surface, temperatures range from a torrid 130°C in direct sunlight to a frigid −180°C at night. Temperatures on the moon vary so much because it has no atmosphere. The moon's surface gravity is so weak that gases can easily escape into space.

Water The moon has no liquid water. However, there is evidence that there may be large patches of ice near the moon's poles. Some areas are shielded from sunlight by crater walls. Temperatures in these regions are so low that ice there would remain frozen. If a colony were built on the moon in the future, any such water would be very valuable. It would be very expensive to transport large amounts of water to the moon from Earth.

FIGURE 20
The Moon's Surface
This photo of a large boulder field and hills on the moon's surface was taken by one of the crew members of *Apollo 17*.

 **Reading Checkpoint** **Where on the moon is there evidence of the existence of ice?**

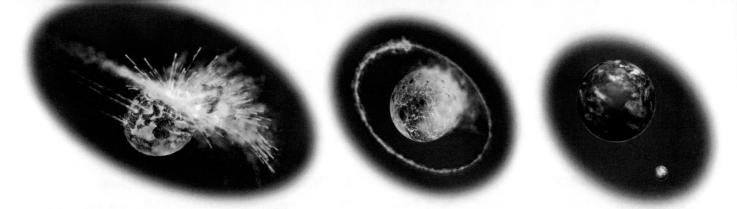

The Origin of the Moon

People have long wondered how the moon formed. Scientists have suggested many possible hypotheses. For example, was the moon formed elsewhere in the solar system and captured by Earth's gravity as it came near? Was the moon formed near Earth at the same time that Earth formed? Scientists have found reasons to reject these ideas.

The theory of the moon's origin that seems to best fit the evidence is called the collision-ring theory. It is illustrated in Figure 21. About 4.5 billion years ago, when Earth was very young, the solar system was full of rocky debris. Some of this debris was the size of small planets. ⬭ **Scientists theorize that a planet-sized object collided with Earth to form the moon.** Material from the object and Earth's outer layers was ejected into orbit around Earth, where it formed a ring. Gravity caused this material to combine to form the moon.

FIGURE 21
Formation of the Moon
According to the collision-ring theory, the moon formed early in Earth's history when a planet-sized object struck Earth. The resulting debris formed the moon.

Video Field Trip
Discovery Channel School
Earth, Moon, and Sun

Section 4 Assessment

S 8.4.e, E-LA: Reading 8.1.2

Vocabulary Skill Latin Word Origins What are maria? Why did Galileo select the word *maria* for this feature of the moon? Does the Latin origin of this word accurately describe what scientists today know about the moon? Why or why not?

⬭ **Reviewing Key Concepts**

1. a. **Identifying** Name three major features of the moon's surface.
   b. **Explaining** How did the moon's craters form?
   c. **Relating Cause and Effect** Why is the moon's surface much more heavily cratered than Earth's surface?
2. a. **Describing** Describe the range of temperatures on the moon.
   b. **Comparing and Contrasting** Compare Earth and the moon in terms of size and surface gravity.

c. **Relating Cause and Effect** What is the relationship between the moon's surface gravity, lack of an atmosphere, and temperature range?

3. a. **Identifying** What theory best describes the moon's origin?
   b. **Describing** What was the solar system like when the moon formed?
   c. **Sequencing** Explain the various stages in the formation of the moon.

Lab zone At-Home **Activity**

Moonwatching With an adult, observe the moon a few days after the first-quarter phase. Make a sketch of the features you see. Label the maria, craters, and highlands.

🔑 The **BIG Idea**   The motions of Earth and the moon and their position relative to the sun result in day and night, the seasons, phases of the moon, eclipses, and tides.

1 Earth in Space

🔑 **Key Concepts**   🔬 S 8.4.e

- Earth moves through space in two major ways: rotation and revolution.
- Earth has seasons because its axis is tilted as it revolves around the sun.

Key Terms

astronomy	axis
rotation	revolution
orbit	calendar
solstice	equinox

2 Gravity and Motion

🔑 **Key Concepts**   🔬 S 8.2.g

- The strength of the force of gravity between two objects depends on two factors: the masses of the objects and the distance between them.
- Newton concluded that two factors—inertia and gravity—combine to keep Earth in orbit around the sun and the moon in orbit around Earth.

Key Terms

force
gravity
Universal Law of Gravitation
mass
weight
inertia
Newton's first law of motion

3 Phases, Eclipses, and Tides

🔑 **Key Concepts**   🔬 S 8.2.g, 8.4.d

- The changing relative positions of the moon, Earth, and sun cause the phases of the moon, eclipses, and tides.
- The phase of the moon you see depends on how much of the sunlit side of the moon faces Earth.
- When the moon's shadow hits Earth or Earth's shadow hits the moon, an eclipse occurs.
- A solar eclipse occurs when the moon passes directly between Earth and the sun, blocking sunlight from Earth.
- During a lunar eclipse, Earth blocks sunlight from reaching the moon.
- The tides are caused mainly by differences in how much the moon's gravity pulls on different parts of Earth.

Key Terms

phase	eclipse
solar eclipse	umbra
penumbra	lunar eclipse
tide	spring tide
neap tide	

4 Earth's Moon

🔑 **Key Concepts**   🔬 S 8.4.e

- Features on the moon's surface include maria, craters, and highlands.
- The moon is dry and airless. Compared to Earth, the moon is small and has large variations in its surface temperature.
- Scientists theorize that a planet-sized object collided with Earth to form the moon.

Key Terms

telescope
maria
crater
meteoroid

Review and Assessment

Go Online
PHSchool.com
For: Self-Assessment
Visit: PHSchool.com
Web Code: cxa-4120

Target Reading Skill

Sequence Draw a cycle diagram for the phases of the moon. Label the phases in which a solar eclipse and a lunar eclipse could occur.

Phases of the Moon

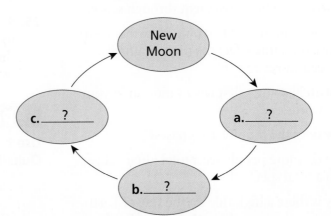

New Moon

c. ___?___

a. ___?___

b. ___?___

Reviewing Key Terms

Choose the letter of the best answer.

1. The movement of Earth around the sun once a year is called Earth's
   a. inertia.
   b. rotation.
   c. revolution.
   d. axis.

2. A day when the sun reaches its farthest position north or south of the equator is called a(an)
   a. umbra.
   b. penumbra.
   c. equinox.
   d. solstice.

3. The tendency of an object to resist a change in motion is called
   a. gravity.
   b. inertia.
   c. force.
   d. the Universal Law of Gravitation.

4. When Earth's shadow falls on the moon, the shadow causes a
   a. new moon.
   b. solar eclipse.
   c. full moon.
   d. lunar eclipse.

5. The craters on the moon were caused by
   a. tides.
   b. volcanoes.
   c. meteoroids.
   d. maria.

Complete the following sentences so that your answers clearly explain the key terms.

6. Earth completes one **revolution,** or _____, in about 365 1/4 days.

7. Newton's **Universal Law of Gravitation** states that _____ .

8. A **solar eclipse** occurs when _____ .

9. The gravitational effects of the moon and sun combine to influence the height of the **tides,** which are _____ .

10. The moon's surface is marked by **craters** because _____ .

Writing in Science

News Report Imagine that you are a reporter asked to write a story about the origin of the moon. Write an article explaining how the moon formed.

Video Assessment
Discovery Channel School
Earth, Moon, and Sun

Review and Assessment

Checking Concepts

11. Explain how the length of the day and year are related to Earth's movement through space.

12. Suppose you moved two objects farther apart. How would this affect the force of gravity between those objects?

13. Explain Newton's first law of motion in your own words.

14. Why does the moon have phases?

15. Why do more people see a total lunar eclipse than a total solar eclipse?

16. Why is there a high tide on the side of Earth closest to the moon? On the side of Earth farthest from the moon?

17. Does the diagram below show a spring tide or a neap tide? How do you know?

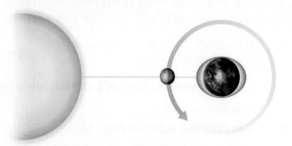

18. How did the invention of the telescope contribute to our knowledge of the moon's surface?

19. Why do temperatures vary so much on the moon?

20. Explain how scientists think the moon originated.

Thinking Critically

21. **Inferring** Mars's axis is tilted at about the same angle as Earth's axis. Do you think Mars has seasons? Explain your answer.

22. **Comparing and Contrasting** How are mass and weight different?

23. **Calculating** Suppose a person weighs 450 newtons (about 100 pounds) on Earth. How much would she weigh on the moon?

24. **Applying Concepts** At about what time does the full moon rise? Is it visible in the eastern sky or the western sky?

25. **Posing Questions** Suppose you were assigned to design a spacesuit for astronauts to wear on the moon. What characteristics of the moon would be important to consider in your design?

Applying Skills

Use the illustration below to answer Questions 26–28.

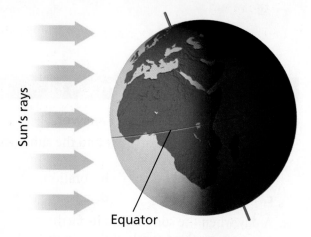

Equator

26. **Interpreting Diagrams** On which hemisphere are the sun's rays falling most directly?

27. **Inferring** In the Northern Hemisphere, is it the summer solstice, winter solstice, or one of the equinoxes? How do you know?

28. **Predicting** Six months after this illustration, Earth will have revolved halfway around the sun. Draw a diagram that shows which end of Earth's axis will be tilted toward the sun.

Lab zone Standards Investigation

Performance Assessment Present your observation log, map, and drawings of the moon. Some ways to graph your data include time of moonrise for each date; how often you saw the moon in each direction; or how often you saw the moon at a specific time. Display your graphs. Discuss any patterns that you discovered.

Choose the letter of the best answer.

1. You observe a thin crescent moon in the western sky during the early evening. About two weeks later, a full moon is visible in the eastern sky during the early evening. Which conclusion is best supported by these observations?
   A The moon revolves around Earth.
   B The moon rotates on its axis.
   C Earth revolves around the sun.
   D Earth's axis is tilted relative to the moon. **S 8.4.e**

2. Only one side of the moon is visible from Earth because
   A the moon does not rotate on its axis.
   B the moon does not revolve around Earth.
   C the moon rotates faster than it revolves.
   D the moon revolves once and rotates once in the same period of time. **S 8.4.e**

3. What type of eclipse occurs when Earth's umbra covers the moon?
   A a partial solar eclipse
   B a total solar eclipse
   C a partial lunar eclipse
   D a total lunar eclipse **S 8.4.d**

4. The force of gravity depends on
   A mass and weight.
   B speed and distance.
   C mass and distance.
   D weight and speed. **S 8.2.g**

5. The craters on the moon were caused by
   A tides.
   B volcanoes.
   C meteoroids.
   D maria. **S 8.4.e**

6. You can see the moon at night because
   A the moon produces its own light.
   B the moon reflects light from the sun.
   C the moon reflects light produced on Earth.
   D the near side of the moon always faces the sun. **S 8.4.d**

The diagram below shows the relative positions of the sun, moon, and Earth. The numbers indicate specific locations of the moon in its orbit. Use the diagram to answer Questions 7–9.

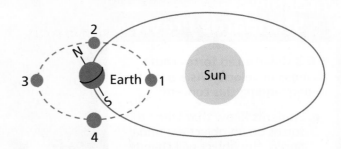

7. Which of the following can occur when the moon is at location 1?
   A only a lunar eclipse
   B only a solar eclipse
   C both a solar and a lunar eclipse
   D neither a solar nor a lunar eclipse **S 8.4.d**

8. When the moon is at location 2, at most coastal locations there would be
   A only one high tide each day.
   B only one low tide each day.
   C two high tides and two low tides each day, with the most difference between high and low tide.
   D two high tides and two low tides each day, with the least difference between high and low tide. **S 8.2.g**

9. When the moon is in location 3, a person standing on Earth at night would see
   A a full moon.
   B a crescent moon.
   C a quarter moon.
   D a new moon. **S 8.4.d**

Apply the BIG Idea

10. In what ways do Earth and the moon move through space? How do these motions produce such phenomena as day and night, the seasons, phases of the moon, and eclipses? **S 8.4.e**

An astronaut working on the International ▶ Space Station in orbit around Earth

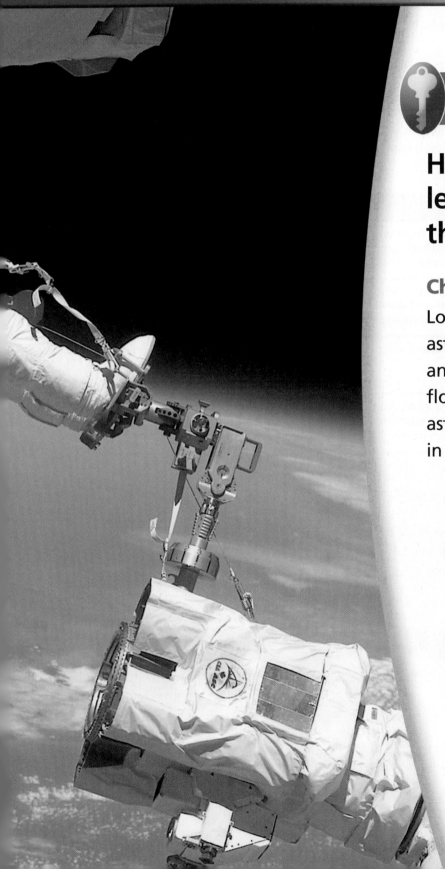

S 8.4.d

Focus on the
BIG Idea

How do scientists learn more about the solar system?

Check What You Know

Look at the photo of an astronaut below. The astronaut and other objects seem to be floating. Why do you think astronauts appear to float when in orbit?

The images shown here represent some of the key terms in this chapter. You can use this vocabulary skill to help you understand the meaning of some key terms in this chapter.

Vocabulary Skill

High-Use Academic Words

Knowing these academic words will help you read and write in many different subjects. Look for these words in context as you read the chapter.

Word	Definition	Example Sentence
source (sawrs) p. 517	*n.* That from which something comes into existence	Gasoline is the <u>source</u> of power for most cars.
consumer (kun SOOM ur) p. 522	*n.* A person who buys goods and services for personal needs	People who buy food, clothing, and TVs are <u>consumers</u>.
benefit (BEN uh fit) p. 523	*v.* To bring help; aid	Daily exercise <u>benefits</u> nearly everyone.
technology (tek NAHL uh jee) p. 523	*n.* A way of changing the natural world to meet human needs	The <u>technology</u> of personal computers has changed the way people communicate.

Apply It!

From the list above, choose the word that best completes the sentence.

1. When you buy new clothes, you are a _____ .

2. DVD players are an example of a new _____.

3. Medicines _____ people who are sick.

microgravity

space station

rocket

satellite

Chapter 13
Vocabulary

Section 1 (page 502)
rocket
thrust
velocity
orbital velocity
escape velocity

· ·

Section 2 (page 510)
satellite

· ·

Section 3 (page 515)
space shuttle
space station
space probe
rover

· ·

Section 4 (page 520)
vacuum
microgravity
space spinoff
remote sensing
geostationary orbit

interactive Textbook

Build Science Vocabulary
Online
Visit: PHSchool.com
Web Code: cxj-4130

How to Read Science

Relate Cause and Effect

Many passages in science textbooks describe cause-and-effect relationships. A cause makes something happen. An effect is what happens. As you read a passage, look for words that signal cause and effect. Signal words and phrases include *because, due to, for this reason, result of, so that,* and *therefore*.

Read the following paragraph, noting the words that signal cause and effect.

> The moon's orbit is *the result of* two factors—inertia and gravity. The moon keeps moving ahead *because* of inertia. At the same time, gravity keeps pulling the moon toward Earth. *For this reason*, the moon does not travel in a straight line. The combined effects of inertia and gravity cause the moon to revolve around Earth.

The cause-and-effect relationships in this passage can be illustrated with a graphic organizer like the one below.

Causes

| Inertia causes the moon to keep moving forward. |

Effect

| The moon revolves around Earth |

| |

Apply It!

Complete the cause-and-effect graphic organizer above. Then complete the following sentence in your own words.

The moon revolves around Earth because _____.

Create cause-and-effect graphic organizers for Sections 1 and 2.

Design and Build a Space Exploration Vehicle

How do scientists study the other planets in our solar system? One way is to send a remotely operated vehicle to explore the surface, as was done recently by two Mars rovers. Such a vehicle must be designed to meet specific requirements, such as communicating with scientists on Earth and being able to operate in a variety of environments.

Your Goal

To design, build, and test a vehicle for exploring the surface of a planet

You will

- identify the geological features that are found on the planets and moons of the solar system
- select a planet or moon, and brainstorm ways to build a vehicle that can move around its surface
- design and sketch a model of the vehicle
- build and test a model vehicle, and present your vehicle to the class
- follow the safety guidelines in Appendix A

Plan It!

Begin by identifying the different types of planetary surfaces found in the solar system. Next, brainstorm how a vehicle could move over some of these surfaces. You may want to think about how all-terrain vehicles on Earth are designed. Consider how you would build a model of the vehicle, and what materials you will need. Then build and test your vehicle.

The Science of Rockets

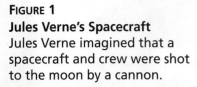
CALIFORNIA
Standards Focus

S 8.2.e Students know that when the forces on an object are unbalanced, the object will change its velocity (that is, it will speed up, slow down, or change direction).

- How were rockets developed?
- How does a rocket work?
- What is the main advantage of a multistage rocket?

Key Terms
- rocket
- thrust
- velocity
- orbital velocity
- escape velocity

Lab zone Standards **Warm-Up**

What Force Moves a Balloon?
1. Put on your goggles. Blow up a balloon and hold its neck closed with your fingers.
2. Point the far end of the balloon in a direction where there are no people. Put your free hand behind the balloon's neck, so you will be able to feel the force of the air from the balloon on your hand. Let go of the balloon. Observe what happens.
3. Repeat Steps 1 and 2 without your free hand behind the neck of the balloon.

Think It Over
Inferring What happened when you let go of the balloon? Which direction did the balloon move in comparison to the direction the air moved out of the balloon? What do you think caused the balloon to move in that direction? Did the position of your free hand affect the balloon's movement?

People have dreamed of traveling through space for centuries. Although the moons and planets of our solar system are much closer than the stars, they are still very far away. How could someone travel such great distances through space?

FIGURE 1
Jules Verne's Spacecraft
Jules Verne imagined that a spacecraft and crew were shot to the moon by a cannon.

In the 1860s, the science fiction writer Jules Verne envisioned a spacecraft shot to the moon out of a huge cannon. When people finally did travel to the moon, though, they used rockets rather than cannons. Although Verne was wrong about how humans would reach the moon, he did anticipate many aspects of the space program. By the late 1900s, rocket-powered spacecraft were able to travel to the moon and to many other places in the solar system.

A History of Rockets

You've probably seen rockets at fireworks displays. As the rockets moved skyward, you may have noticed a fiery gas rushing out of the back. A **rocket** is a device that expels gas in one direction to move in the opposite direction. **Rocket technology originated in China hundreds of years ago and gradually spread to other parts of the world.** Rockets were developed for military use as well as for fireworks.

Origins of Rockets The first rockets were made in China in the 1100s. These early rockets were very simple—they were arrows coated with a flammable powder that were lighted and shot with bows. By about 1200, the Chinese were using gunpowder inside their rockets.

The British greatly improved rocketry in the early 1800s. British ships used rockets against American troops in the War of 1812. The *Star-Spangled Banner* contains the words "the rockets' red glare, the bombs bursting in air." These words describe a British rocket attack on Fort McHenry in Baltimore, Maryland.

Development of Modern Rockets Modern rockets were first developed in the early 1900s. They owe much of their development to a few scientists. One was the Russian physicist Konstantin Tsiolkovsky. In the early 1900s, Tsiolkovsky described in scientific terms how rockets work and proposed designs for advanced rockets. The American physicist Robert Goddard also designed rockets. Beginning around 1915, Goddard went a step further and built rockets to test his designs.

Rocket design made major advances during World War II. Military rockets were used to carry explosives. The Germans used a rocket called the V2 to destroy both military and civilian targets. The V2 was a large rocket that could travel about 300 kilometers. The designer of the V2, Wernher von Braun, came to the United States after the war was over. Von Braun used his experience to direct the development of many rockets used in the United States space program.

FIGURE 2
Chinese Rockets
According to a Chinese legend, around 1500 an official named Wan-Hoo tried to fly to the moon by tying a number of rockets to his chair. The rockets exploded with a tremendous roar. Once the smoke cleared, there was no trace of Wan-Hoo or his chair.

 **Reading Checkpoint** Name three scientists who contributed to the development of modern rockets.

Be a Rocket Scientist
You can build a rocket.

1. Use a plastic or paper cup as the rocket body. Cut out a paper nose cone. Tape it to the bottom of the cup.

2. Obtain an empty film canister with a lid that snaps on inside the canister. Go outside to do Steps 3–5.

3. Fill the canister about one-quarter full with water.

4. 🥽 Put on your goggles. Now add half of a fizzing antacid tablet to the film canister and quickly snap on the lid.

5. Place the canister on the ground with the lid down. Place your rocket over the canister and stand back.

Observing
What action happened inside the film canister? What was the reaction of the rocket?

How Do Rockets Work?

A rocket can be as small as your finger or as large as a sky-scraper. An essential feature of any rocket, though, is that it expels gas in one direction. ⬭ **A rocket moves forward when gases shooting out the back of the rocket push it in the opposite direction.**

A rocket works in much the same way as a balloon that is pro-pelled through the air by releasing gas. In most rockets, fuel is burned to make hot gas. The gas pushes outward in every direc-tion, but it can leave the rocket only through openings at the back. The movement of gas out of these openings moves the rocket forward. Figure 3 shows how rockets move.

Action and Reaction Forces The movement of a rocket demonstrates Newton's third law of motion: For every force, or action, there is an equal and opposite force, or reaction. The force of the air moving out of a balloon is an action force. An equal force—the reaction force—pushes the balloon forward.

The reaction force that propels a rocket forward is called **thrust.** The amount of thrust depends on several factors, including the mass and speed of the gases propelled out of the rocket. The greater the thrust, the greater a rocket's velocity. Recall that **velocity** is speed in a given direction.

Orbital and Escape Velocity In order to lift off the ground, a rocket must have more upward thrust than the downward force of gravity. Once a rocket is off the ground, it must reach a certain velocity in order to go into orbit. **Orbital velocity** is the velocity a rocket must achieve to establish an orbit around Earth. If the rocket moves slower than orbital velocity, Earth's gravity will cause it to fall back to the surface.

FIGURE 3
Rocket Action and Reaction
The force of gas propelled out of the back of a rocket (action) produces an opposing force (reaction) that propels the rocket forward.
Interpreting Diagrams *How can a rocket rise from the ground into space?*

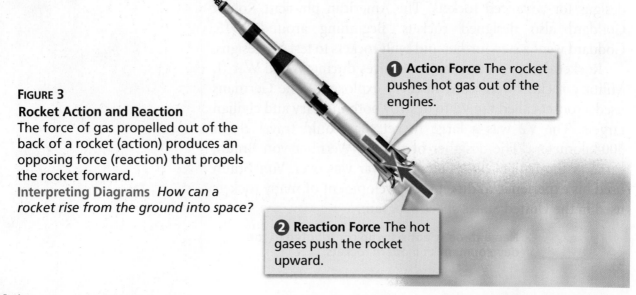

❶ Action Force The rocket pushes hot gas out of the engines.

❷ Reaction Force The hot gases push the rocket upward.

Rocket Altitude

A rocket's altitude is how high it is above the ground. Use the graph at the right to answer the following questions about how a model rocket's altitude changes over time.

1. **Reading Graphs** What two variables are being graphed? In what unit is each measured?

2. **Reading Graphs** What was the rocket's altitude after 2 seconds? After 4 seconds?

3. **Reading Graphs** At what time did the rocket reach its greatest altitude?

4. **Inferring** Why do you think the rocket continued to rise after it ran out of fuel?

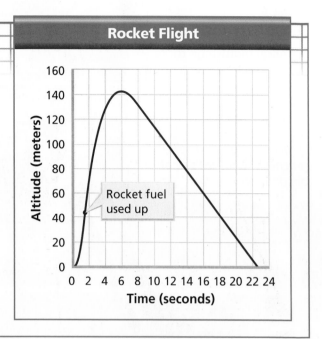

Rocket Flight

Graph: Altitude (meters) vs. Time (seconds)

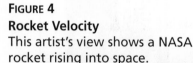

Rocket fuel used up

Reviewing Math:
Algebra and Functions 7.1.5

If the rocket has an even greater velocity, it can fly off into space. **Escape velocity** is the velocity a rocket must reach to fly beyond a planet's gravitational pull. The escape velocity a rocket needs to leave Earth is about 40,200 kilometers per hour. That's more than 11 kilometers every second!

Rocket Fuels Rockets create thrust by ejecting gas. Three types of fuel are used to power modern spacecraft: solid fuel, liquid fuel, and electrically charged particles of gas (ions). Solid-fuel and liquid-fuel rockets carry oxygen that allows the fuel to burn.

In a solid-fuel rocket, oxygen is mixed with the fuel, which is a dry explosive chemical. A fireworks rocket is a good example of a solid-fuel rocket. For such a simple rocket, a match can be used to ignite the fuel. Large solid-fuel rockets have a device called an igniter that can be triggered from a distance. Once a solid-fuel rocket is ignited, it burns until all the fuel is gone.

In a liquid-fuel rocket, both the oxygen and the fuel are in liquid form. They are stored in separate compartments. When the rocket fires, the fuel and oxygen are pumped into the same chamber and ignited. An advantage of liquid-fuel rockets is that the burning of fuel can be controlled by regulating how much liquid fuel and oxygen are mixed together.

Ion rockets do not burn chemical fuels. Rather, they expel gas ions out of their engines at very high speeds. Ion rockets generally create less thrust than solid-fuel or liquid-fuel rockets. But they are very fuel efficient.

FIGURE 4
Rocket Velocity
This artist's view shows a NASA rocket rising into space.

 Reading Checkpoint **What are the three types of rocket fuel?**

FIGURE 5

A Multistage Rocket

A typical multistage rocket
~~has three stages. Each of the~~
fuel and then drops off. The
next stage then takes over.
Interpreting Diagrams
*Which part of the rocket
reaches the rocket's final
destination?*

4 Second stage
separates and falls
to Earth.

3 Second stage ignites
and continues with
third stage.

2 First stage
separates and
falls to Earth.

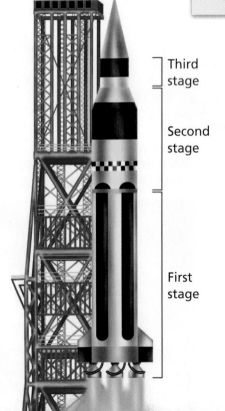

Third
stage

Second
stage

First
stage

1 Heavy first stage
provides thrust
for launch.

Multistage Rockets

A rocket can carry only so much fuel. As the
fuel in a rocket burns, its fuel chambers begin
to empty. Even though much of the rocket is
empty, the whole rocket must still be pushed
upward by the remaining fuel. But what if the
empty part of the rocket could be thrown off?
Then the remaining fuel wouldn't have to
push a partially empty rocket. This is the idea
behind multistage rockets.

Konstantin Tsiolkovsky proposed the
idea of multistage rockets in 1903. ☛ **The
main advantage of a multistage rocket is
that the total weight of the rocket is greatly
reduced as the rocket rises.**

In a multistage rocket, smaller rockets, or
stages, are placed one on top of the other and
then fired in succession. Figure 5 shows how
a multistage rocket works. As each stage of the
rocket uses up its fuel, the empty fuel container falls away. The next stage then ignites
and continues powering the rocket toward its
destination. At the end, only the very top of
the rocket is left.

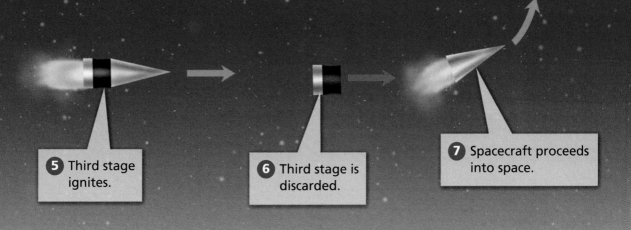

5 Third stage ignites.

6 Third stage is discarded.

7 Spacecraft proceeds into space.

Go **Online**
active art

For: Multistage Rocket activity
Visit: PHSchool.com
Web Code: cfp-5021

In the 1960s, the development of powerful multistage rockets such as the Saturn V made it possible to send spacecraft to the moon and the solar system beyond. The mighty Saturn V rocket stood 111 meters tall—higher than the length of a football field. It was by far the most powerful rocket ever built. Today, multistage rockets are used to launch a wide variety of satellites and space probes.

Reading Checkpoint) **What is a multistage rocket?**

Section **1** **Assessment**

S 8.2.e, E-LA: Reading 8.2.0
Writing 8.2.0

Target Reading Skill **Relate Cause and Effect** Reread *A History of Rockets* on page 503. Create a cause-and-effect graphic organizer that shows the development of modern rockets. Include the contributions of the Chinese, Tsiolkovsky, Goddard, and von Braun.

Reviewing Key Concepts

1. a. **Defining** What is a rocket?
   b. **Reviewing** Where and when were rockets first developed?
   c. **Summarizing** For what purposes were rockets initially developed?
2. a. **Explaining** What is thrust?
   b. **Explaining** How do rockets create thrust?
   c. **Interpreting Diagrams** Use Figure 3 to explain how a rocket moves forward.
3. a. **Describing** Describe how a multistage rocket works.

b. **Comparing and Contrasting** What is the main advantage of a multistage rocket compared to a single-stage rocket?
c. **Relating Cause and Effect** Why can the third stage of a multistage rocket go faster than the first stage of the rocket, even though it has less fuel?

Writing in Science

Interview Suppose you were able to interview one of the scientists who helped to develop modern rockets. Choose one of the scientists identified in the section and write a series of questions that you would like to ask this person. Then use what you've learned to construct likely answers to these questions.

Design and Build a Water Rocket

S8.2.e, 8.9

Problem

Can you design and build a rocket propelled by water and compressed air?

Design Skills

observing, evaluating the design, redesigning

Materials

- large round balloon • tap water
- graduated cylinder • modeling clay
- 50 paper clips in a plastic bag
- empty 2-liter soda bottle • poster board
- scissors • hot glue gun or tape
- bucket, 5 gallon • stopwatch
- rocket launcher and tire pump (one per class)

Procedure 🌀 👔 ✂️ ⚠️

PART 1 Research and Investigate

1. Copy the data table onto a separate sheet of paper.

Data Table	
Volume of Water (mL)	Motion of Balloon
No water	

2. In an outdoor area approved by your teacher, blow up a large round balloon. Hold the balloon so the opening is pointing down. Release the balloon and observe what occurs. **CAUTION:** *If you are allergic to latex, do not handle the balloon.*

3. Measure 50 mL of water with a graduated cylinder. Pour the water into the balloon. Blow it up to about the same size as the balloon in Step 2. Hold the opening down and release the balloon. Observe what happens.

4. Repeat Step 3 twice, varying the amount of water each time. Record your observations in the data table.

PART 2 Design and Build

5. You and a partner will design and build a water rocket using the materials provided or approved by your teacher. Your rocket must
   - be made from an empty 2-liter soda bottle
   - have fins and a removable nosecone
   - carry a load of 50 paper clips
   - use air only or a mixture of air and water as a propulsion system
   - be launched on the class rocket launcher
   - remain in the air for at least 5 seconds

6. Begin by thinking about how your rocket will work and how you would like it to look. Sketch your design and make a list of materials that you will need.

7. Rockets often have a set of fins to stabilize them in flight. Consider the best shape for fins, and decide how many fins your rocket needs. Use poster board to make your fins.

8. Decide how to safely and securely carry a load of 50 paper clips in your rocket.

9. Based on what you learned in Part 1, decide how much, if any, water to pour into your rocket.

10. After you obtain your teacher's approval, build your rocket.

◀ Rocket launcher

PART 3 Evaluate and Redesign

11. Test your rocket by launching it on the rocket launcher provided by your teacher.
CAUTION: *Make sure that the rocket is launched vertically in a safe, open area that is at least 30 m across. All observers should wear goggles and stay at least 8–10 m away from the rocket launcher. The rocket should be pumped to a pressure of no more than 50 pounds per square inch.*

12. Use a stopwatch to determine your rocket's flight time (how long it stays in the air.)

13. Record in a data table the results of your own launch and your classmates' launches.

14. Compare your design and results with those of your classmates.

Analyze and Conclude

1. **Observing** What did you observe about the motion of the balloon as more and more water was added?

2. **Drawing Conclusions** What purpose did adding water to the balloon serve?

3. **Designing a Solution** How did your results in Part 1 affect your decision about how much water, if any, to add to your rocket?

4. **Evaluating the Design** Did your rocket meet all the criteria listed in Step 5? Explain.

5. **Evaluating the Design** How did your rocket design compare to the rockets built by your classmates? Which rocket had the greatest flight time? What design features resulted in the most successful launches?

6. **Redesigning** Based on your launch results and your response to Question 5, explain how you could improve your rocket. How do you think these changes would help your rocket's performance?

7. **Evaluating the Impact on Society** Explain how an understanding of rocket propulsion has made space travel possible.

Communicate

Write a paragraph that describes how you designed and built your rocket. Explain how it worked. Include a labeled sketch of your design.

For: Data sharing
Visit: PHSchool.com
Web Code: cfd-5021

CALIFORNIA
Standards Focus

S 8.4.d Framework Various types of exploratory missions have yielded much information about the reflectivity, structure, and composition of the Moon and the planets. Those missions have included spacecraft flying by and orbiting those bodies, the soft landing of spacecraft fitted with instruments, and, of course, the visits of astronauts to the Moon.

🔑 What was the space race?

🔑 What were the major events in human exploration of the moon?

Key Term
• satellite

Lab zone Standards Warm-Up

Where on the Moon Did Astronauts Land?

1. Use a large map of the moon to find these locations: Sea of Tranquility, Ocean of Storms, Fra Mauro, Apennine Mountains, Descartes Highlands, and Valley of Taurus-Littrow.

2. American astronauts landed on and explored each of the locations you found. Using what you know about the moon and what you can see on the map, describe what you think astronauts saw at each place.

Think It Over

Inferring Did the names of the moon locations seem to fit with what you could see? Do you think the astronauts had to use boats to explore the Sea of Tranquility and the Ocean of Storms?

Sometimes competition results in great achievements. Maybe you've been motivated to try harder in a foot race when someone passed you by. Perhaps watching a friend accomplish a feat made you determined to do it, too. Competition resulted in one of the greatest achievements in history: In 1969 the first human set foot on the moon. This competition, though, was not between friends, but between the two most powerful nations in the world, the United States and the Soviet Union. Their rivalry in the exploration of space was called the "space race."

The Race for Space

The space race began in the 1950s. At that time, the Soviet Union was the greatest rival to the United States in politics and military power. The tensions between the two countries were so high that they were said to be in a "cold war." These tensions increased when the Soviets launched a satellite into space. 🔑 **The space race began in 1957 when the Soviets launched the satellite *Sputnik I* into orbit. The United States responded by speeding up its own space program.**

◀ The first living creature sent into space was a dog named Laika. She orbited Earth aboard the Soviet spacecraft *Sputnik II* in November 1957.

FIGURE 6
John Glenn
Friendship 7 lifted off from Cape Canaveral, Florida, in February 1962. It carried astronaut John Glenn, the first American to orbit Earth. The closeup photo shows Glenn climbing into the *Friendship 7* space capsule.
Observing *Where on the rocket was the space capsule located?*

The First Artificial Satellites A satellite is an object that revolves around another object in space. The moon is a natural satellite of Earth. A spacecraft orbiting Earth is an artificial satellite. *Sputnik I* was the first artificial satellite. This success by the Soviets caused great alarm in the United States.

The United States responded in early 1958 by launching its own satellite, *Explorer 1,* into orbit. Over the next few years, both the United States and the Soviet Union placed many more satellites into orbit around Earth.

Later in 1958, the United States established a government agency in charge of its space program, called the National Aeronautics and Space Administration (NASA). NASA brought together the talents of many scientists and engineers who worked together to solve the many difficult technical problems of space flight.

Humans in Space In 1961 the space race heated up even more when the Soviets launched the first human into space. Yuri Gagarin flew one orbit around Earth aboard *Vostok 1.* Less than a month later, astronaut Alan Shepard became the first American in space. His tiny spacecraft, called *Freedom 7,* was part of the U.S. Mercury space program. Other Soviet cosmonauts and American astronauts soon followed into space.

The first American to orbit Earth was John Glenn, who was launched into space in 1962 aboard *Friendship 7.* The spacecraft he traveled in was called a space capsule because it was like a small cap on the end of the rocket. The tiny capsule orbited Earth three times before returning to the surface.

 **Reading Checkpoint** Who was the first American in space?

Calculating

If you went to the moon, your weight would be about one sixth of your weight on Earth. Recall that in SI, weight is measured in newtons (1 lb ≈ 4.5 N). To find the approximate weight of an object on the moon, divide its weight on Earth by six.

An astronaut weighs 667 N on Earth. She wears a spacesuit and equipment that weigh 636 N on Earth. What is the astronaut's total weight on the moon?

Missions to the Moon

"I believe that this nation should commit itself to achieving the goal, before the decade is out, of landing a man on the moon and returning him safely to Earth." With these words from a May 1961 speech, President John F. Kennedy launched an enormous program of space exploration and scientific research. ⟳ **The American effort to land astronauts on the moon was named the Apollo program.**

Exploring the Moon Between 1964 and 1972, the United States and the Soviet Union sent many unpiloted spacecraft to explore the moon. When a U.S. spacecraft called *Surveyor* landed on the moon, it didn't sink into the surface. This proved that the moon had a solid surface. Next, scientists searched for a suitable place to land humans on the moon.

The Moon Landings In July 1969, three American astronauts circled the moon aboard *Apollo 11*. Once in orbit, Neil Armstrong and Buzz Aldrin entered a tiny spacecraft called *Eagle*. On July 20, the *Eagle* descended toward a flat area on the moon's surface called the Sea of Tranquility. When Armstrong radioed that the *Eagle* had landed, cheers rang out at the NASA Space Center in Houston. A few hours later, Armstrong and Aldrin left the *Eagle* to explore the moon. When Armstrong first set foot on the surface, he said, "That's one small step for man, one giant leap for mankind." Armstrong meant to say, "That's one small step for *a* man," meaning himself, but in his excitement he never said the "a."

FIGURE 7
Apollo 11
On July 20, 1969, *Apollo 11* astronaut Neil Armstrong became the first person to walk on the moon. He took this photograph of Buzz Aldrin. The inset photo shows Armstrong's footprint on the lunar soil.

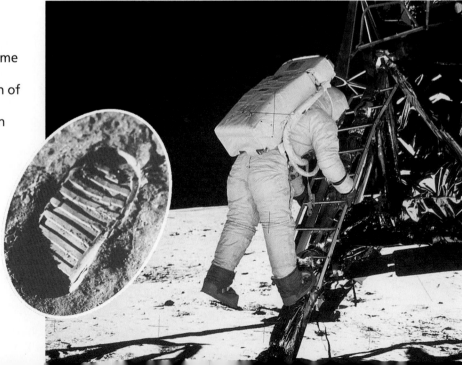

On the Moon's Surface Everything that the *Apollo 11* astronauts found was new and exciting. For about two hours, Armstrong and Aldrin explored the moon's surface, collecting samples to take back to Earth. They also planted an American flag.

Over the next three years, five more Apollo missions landed on the moon. In these later missions, astronauts were able to stay on the moon for days instead of hours. As shown in Figure 8, some astronauts even used a lunar rover, or buggy, to explore larger areas of the moon.

Moon Rocks and Moonquakes The astronauts collected nearly 400 kilograms of lunar samples, commonly called "moon rocks." When scientists analyzed these samples, they learned a great deal about the moon. For instance, they learned that the minerals that make up moon rocks are the same minerals that are found on Earth. However, in some moon rocks these minerals combine to form kinds of rocks that are not found on Earth. Scientists were also able to calculate the ages of the moon rocks. With that information, they could better estimate when different parts of the moon's surface formed.

One way that Apollo astronauts explored the structure of the moon was to purposely crash equipment onto the moon's surface. Instruments they left behind measured the "moonquake" waves that resulted. Using data collected from these artificial moonquakes, scientists determined that the moon may have a small core of molten rock at its center.

 **What did scientists learn from analyzing moon rocks?**

FIGURE 8
Lunar Buggy
Astronauts on the later Apollo missions had a lunar buggy. *Inferring How could a lunar buggy help the astronauts to explore the moon's surface?*

Go Online
PHSchool.com

For: More on lunar exploration
Visit: PHSchool.com
Web Code: cfd-5022

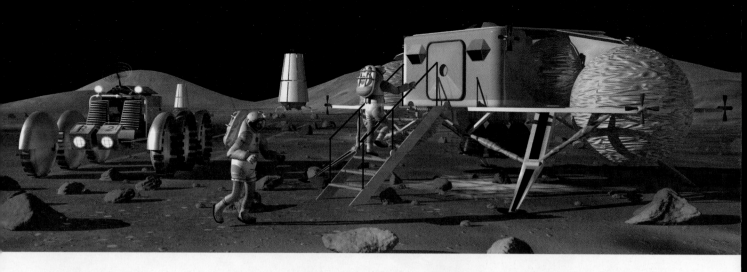

FIGURE 9
Lunar Base
A possible future base on the moon is shown in this painting.
Predicting *How might a lunar base be useful for the future human exploration of Mars?*

New Missions to the Moon The Apollo missions were a tremendous achievement. They yielded fascinating information and memorable images. Yet, the cost of those missions was high, and there were few immediate benefits beyond the knowledge gained about the moon. NASA moved on to other projects. For decades, the moon was largely ignored.

Recently, however, interest in the moon has revived. In 2003, the European Space Agency launched an unpiloted spacecraft to orbit the moon. Its main purpose was to collect data for a detailed map of the moon. Private businesses have funded similar research spacecraft.

Soon, humans may walk again on the moon. In 2004, the United States announced a plan to establish a permanent colony of people on the moon. From such a base, missions could be launched to carry people to Mars.

Section 2 Assessment

S 8.4.d, E-LA: 8.2.0

Target Reading Skill Relate Cause and Effect Create a cause-and-effect graphic organizer that shows the causes of the space race. Use your graphic organizer to answer Question 1.

Reviewing Key Concepts

1. a. **Summarizing** What was the "space race"?
   b. **Identifying** What event began the space race?
   c. **Relating Cause and Effect** What role did competition play in the space race? Who were the competitors?
2. a. **Identifying** What was the Apollo program?
   b. **Sequencing** Place these events in the correct sequence: first humans on the moon, *Sputnik I*, first American in space, John Glenn orbits Earth, NASA formed, Yuri Gagarin orbits Earth.
   c. **Drawing Conclusions** Was the Apollo program successful in meeting President Kennedy's challenge?

Lab zone At-Home Activity

Landmarks in Space Flight Interview someone who remembers the early space programs. Prepare your questions in advance, such as: What did you think when you heard that *Sputnik* was in orbit? How did you feel when the first Americans went into space? Did you watch any of the space flights on TV? You may want to record your interview and then write it out later.

Exploring Space Today

CALIFORNIA
Standards Focus

S 8.4.d Framework Various types of exploratory missions have yielded much information about the reflectivity, structure, and composition of the Moon and the planets. Those missions have included spacecraft flying by and orbiting those bodies, the soft landing of spacecraft fitted with instruments, and, of course, the visits of astronauts to the Moon.

- What are the roles of space shuttles and space stations?

- What features do space probes have in common?

Key Terms
- space shuttle
- space station
- space probe
- rover

Lab zone Standards **Warm-Up**

What Do You Need to Survive in Space?

1. Make a list of everything that would be essential to your well-being if you were placed in a spacecraft in orbit around Earth.
2. Cross out everything on the list that you wouldn't be able to find while in orbit.
3. For each of the items you crossed out, suggest a way you could provide yourself with that essential item while in space.

Think It Over

Drawing Conclusions Is there anything necessary to your well-being that you wouldn't have to take with you into space? How hard would it be to provide everything you need for a journey into space?

Can you imagine living in space? When you're in orbit, you feel weightless, so there is no up or down. Astronaut Janet Kavandi knows how it feels. She spent eleven days aboard the Russian space station *Mir*. As she floated inside the central cabin, she could look into modules that extended outward in every direction.

"It was very amusing to look into one module and see people standing on the wall, working on an experiment. In the adjacent module, someone might be jogging on a treadmill on the ceiling. Beneath your feet, you might see someone having a meal. Above your head, you'd hear the thumping of a body coming toward you, and you'd have to move aside to let him pass."

Janet Kavandi aboard ▶ the space shuttle

FIGURE 10
The Space Shuttle
The Space Shuttle *Discovery* is launched into space by liquid–fuel powered engines as well as by a pair of reusable solid-fuel booster rockets.
Inferring What is one advantage of a reusable space vehicle?

External fuel tank

Solid fuel rocket booster

Shuttle orbiter

Working in Space

After the great success of the moon landings, the question for space exploration was, "What comes next?" Scientists and public officials decided that one goal should be to build space shuttles and space stations where astronauts can live and work.

Space Shuttles Before 1983, spacecraft could be used only once. In contrast, a space shuttle is like an airplane—it can fly, land, and then fly again. A **space shuttle** is a spacecraft that can carry a crew into orbit, return to Earth, and then be reused for the same purpose. A space shuttle includes large rockets that launch it into orbit and then fall away. At the end of a mission, a shuttle returns to Earth by landing like an airplane. **NASA has used space shuttles to perform many important tasks. These include taking satellites into orbit, repairing damaged satellites, and carrying astronauts and equipment to and from space stations.**

During a shuttle mission, astronauts live in a pressurized crew cabin at the front of the shuttle. There, they can wear regular clothes and breathe without an oxygen tank. Behind the crew cabin is a large, open area called the payload bay. The payload bay is like the trailer end of a large truck that carries supplies to stores and factories. A shuttle payload bay might carry a satellite to be released into orbit or a scientific laboratory in which astronauts can perform experiments.

NASA has built six shuttles. Tragically, two—*Challenger* and *Columbia*—were destroyed during flights. After the *Columbia* disaster in 2003, there was much debate about whether to continue the shuttle program. One reason to keep flying space shuttles is to deliver astronauts and supplies to the International Space Station. NASA currently plans to retire the shuttle by 2010 and replace it with a new reusable spacecraft.

FIGURE 11
International Space Station

The International Space Station is a cooperative project involving 16 countries, including the United States, Russia, Japan, and Canada. This is an artist's view of how the station will look when completed.

Space Stations A space station is a large artificial satellite on which people can live and work for long periods. ⬤ A **space station provides a place where long-term observations and experiments can be carried out in space.** In the 1970s and 1980s, both the United States and the Soviet Union placed space stations in orbit. The Soviet space station *Mir* stayed in orbit for 15 years before it fell to Earth in 2001. Astronauts from many countries, including Janet Kavandi and other Americans, spent time aboard *Mir*.

In the 1980s, the United States and 15 other countries began planning the construction of the International Space Station. The first module, or section, of the station was placed into orbit in 1998. Since then, many other modules have been added. On board, astronauts and scientists from many countries are already carrying out experiments in various fields of science. They are also learning more about how humans adapt to space. Figure 11 shows how the space station will look when completed. It will be longer than a football field, and the living space will be about as large as the inside of the largest passenger jet.

The International Space Station has large batteries to guarantee that it always has power. Its main source of power, though, is its eight large arrays of solar panels. Together, the solar panels contain more than 250,000 solar cells, each capable of converting sunlight into electricity. At full power, the solar panels produce enough electricity to power about 55 houses on Earth.

 **Reading Checkpoint** What is a space station?

Video Field Trip
Discovery Channel School
Exploring Space

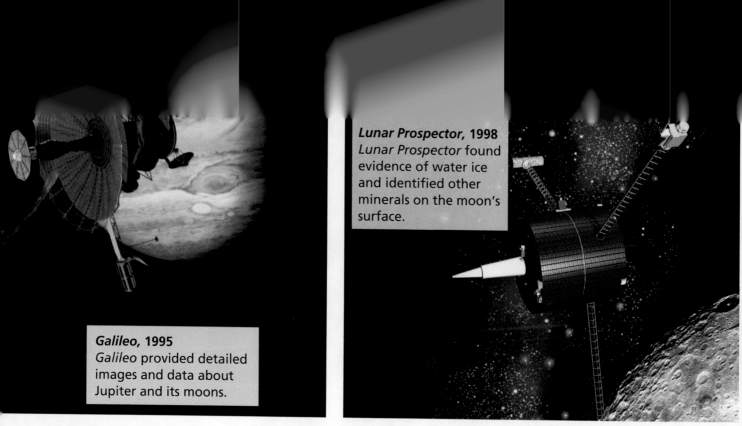

Lunar Prospector, 1998
Lunar Prospector found evidence of water ice and identified other minerals on the moon's surface.

Galileo, 1995
Galileo provided detailed images and data about Jupiter and its moons.

FIGURE 12
Space Probes

These are artist's views of the *Galileo, Lunar Prospector, Mars Exploration Rover,* and *Cassini* space probes.
Comparing and Contrasting *What advantage does a rover have compared to a probe that remains in orbit?*

Go Online

SCi **NSTA**
LINKS™

For: Links on space exploration
Visit: www.SciLinks.org
Web Code: scn-0623

Space Probes

Since space exploration began in the 1950s, only 24 people have traveled as far as the moon—and no one has traveled farther. Yet, during this period space scientists have gathered great amounts of information about other parts of the solar system. This data was collected by space probes. A **space probe** is a spacecraft that carries scientific instruments that can collect data, but has no human crew.

How Do Probes Work? Each space probe is designed for a specific mission. Some probes are designed to land on a certain planet. Other probes collect information about a planet from orbit. Still other probes are designed to fly by and collect data about more than one planet or moon. Thus, each probe is unique. Still, all probes have some features in common. **Each space probe has a power system to produce electricity, a communication system to send and receive signals, and scientific instruments to collect data and perform experiments.**

The scientific instruments that a probe contains depend on the probe's mission. Some probes are equipped to photograph and analyze the atmosphere of a planet. Other probes are equipped to land on a planet and analyze the materials on its surface. Some probes have small robots called **rovers** that move around on the surface. A rover typically has instruments that collect and analyze soil and rock samples.

Mars Exploration Rovers, 2004–2006
Two rovers, *Opportunity* and *Spirit*, explored Mars's surface and found evidence of ancient water.

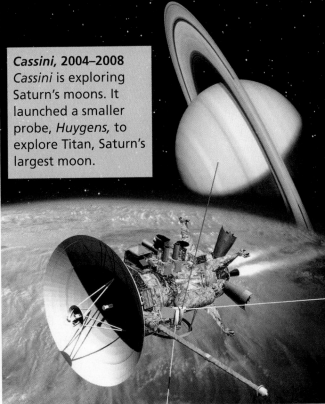

Cassini, 2004–2008
Cassini is exploring Saturn's moons. It launched a smaller probe, *Huygens,* to explore Titan, Saturn's largest moon.

Exploring With Space Probes Probes have now visited or passed near to all of the planets. They have also explored many moons, asteroids, and comets. The information gathered by probes has given scientists tremendous new insights about the environments on the different planets. These probes have helped to solve many of the mysteries of the solar system.

 **Reading Checkpoint** What is a rover?

Section 3 Assessment

S 8.4.d, E-LA: Reading 8.1.0, Writing 8.2.0

Vocabulary Skill High-Use Academic Words In a complete sentence, identify the main *source* of power of the International Space Station.

🔑 Reviewing Key Concepts

1. a. **Describing** What is the space shuttle? What is its main advantage?
   b. **Defining** What is a space station?
   c. **Comparing and Contrasting** What are the roles of space shuttles and space stations in the space program?
2. a. **Summarizing** What is a space probe?
   b. **Listing** List three features that are common to all space probes.
   c. **Making Judgments** What do you think are some advantages and disadvantages of a space probe compared to a piloted spacecraft?

Writing in Science

News Report As a newspaper reporter, you are covering the launch of a new space probe. Write a brief news story, including details on the probe's mission and how the probe works. What planet will it explore? What question will it try to answer?

Using Space Science on Earth

CALIFORNIA
Standards Focus

S 8.7.c Students know substances can be classified by their properties, including their melting temperature, density, hardness, and thermal and electrical conductivity.

🔑 How are the conditions in space different from those on Earth?

🔑 How has space technology benefited modern society?

🔑 What are some uses of satellites orbiting Earth?

Key Terms

- vacuum
- microgravity
- space spinoff
- remote sensing
- geostationary orbit

Lab zone **Standards Warm-Up**

Which Tool Would Be More Useful in Space?

1. Observe your teacher using two types of drills.
2. Pick up each drill and examine how it works.
3. Repeat Step 2 for a space pen and a regular pen.

Think It Over

Drawing Conclusions What is the main difference between the two drills? The pens? Which drill would be more useful to have while constructing the International Space Station? Why? How would a space pen be useful in space?

You've probably used a joystick to play a video game. A joystick is a great way to control images on a screen. It's easy to use because it is designed to fit the hand just right. Joystick controllers have many uses besides video games. They're so well engineered that people with disabilities can use them to operate a wheelchair.

The joystick was invented for controlling airplanes. It was later improved by NASA for the space program. Apollo astronauts used a joystick to operate a lunar rover on the moon. From the surface of the moon to video games on Earth—it's not such a stretch. Many materials and devices have made a similar transition from use in space to everyday use by people on Earth.

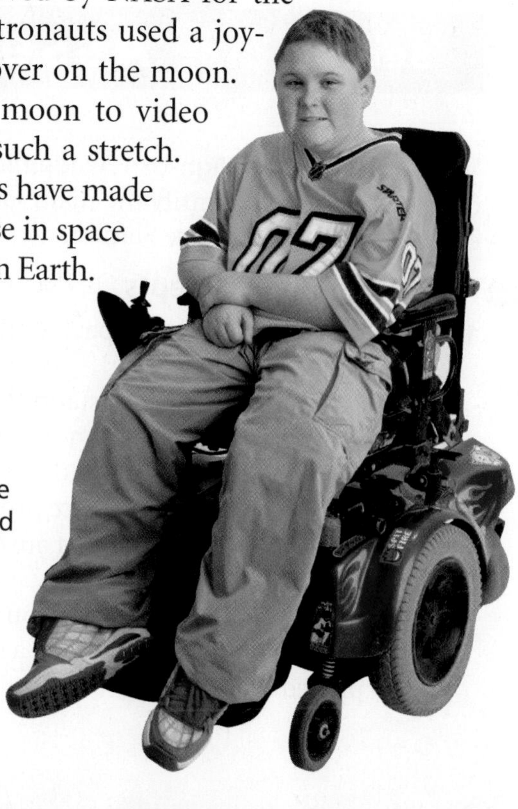

FIGURE 13
Joystick Controls
The joysticks used for some wheelchairs were improved for the space program.

The Challenges of Space

Astronauts who travel into space face conditions that are quite different from those on Earth. ⌨ **Conditions in space that differ from those on Earth include near vacuum, extreme temperatures, and microgravity.** Many types of engineers and scientists have worked together to respond to the challenges of space.

Vacuum Space is nearly a vacuum. A **vacuum** is a place that is empty of all matter. Except for a few stray atoms and molecules, most of space is empty. Since there is no air in space, there is no oxygen for astronauts to breathe. To protect astronauts, spacecraft must be airtight.

Because there is no air in space, there is nothing to hold the sun's heat. In direct sunlight, the surface of a spacecraft heats up to high temperatures. But in shadow, temperatures fall to very low levels. Spacecraft must be well insulated to protect astronauts against the extreme temperatures outside.

Microgravity Astronauts in orbit experience a feeling of weightlessness, or **microgravity**. Their mass is the same as it was on Earth, but on a scale their weight would register as zero. Although they are in microgravity, they are still under the influence of Earth's gravity. In fact, Earth's gravity is holding them in orbit. Astronauts in orbit feel weightless because they are falling through space with their spacecraft. They don't fall to Earth because their inertia keeps them moving forward.

Space engineers must create systems and devices that are capable of working in microgravity. For example, drink containers must be designed so that their contents do not simply float away. Long periods in microgravity can cause health problems. Scientists are trying to discover how to reduce the effects of microgravity on people.

Reading Checkpoint What is microgravity?

FIGURE 14
Microgravity
This astronaut appears to be floating in space, but he is actually falling through space at the same rate as the nearby spacecraft.
Inferring Why doesn't the astronaut fall directly down toward Earth?

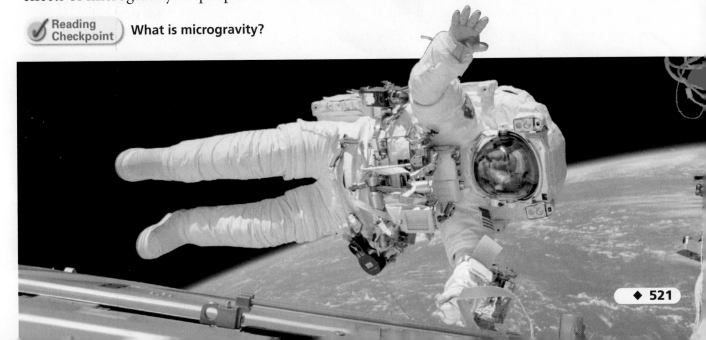

For: Links on satellite technology
Visit: www.SciLinks.org
Web Code: scn-0624

Space Spinoffs

The scientists and engineers who have worked on the space program have developed thousands of new materials and devices for use in space. Many of these items have proved useful on Earth as well. An item that has uses on Earth but was originally developed for use in space is called a **space spinoff.** Often such spinoffs are modified somewhat for use on Earth.

🗝 **The space program has developed thousands of products that affect many aspects of modern society, including consumer products, new materials, medical devices, and communications satellites.** Figure 15 shows a few familiar examples.

Consumer Products Space spinoffs include many devices that are used in consumer products. The joystick controller is one example. The bar codes on every product you buy at a grocery store are another space spinoff. Similar bar codes were developed by NASA to keep an accurate inventory of the many parts used in spacecraft.

Cordless power tools were also originally developed for astronauts. There's no place to "plug in" a tool when repairing a satellite in space. Cordless, rechargeable tools met the need for work in space. Now they're very popular here on Earth. Other examples of consumer product spinoffs from the space program include scratch-resistant lenses, freeze-dried foods, shock-absorbing helmets, and smoke detectors.

FIGURE 15
Spinoffs From the Space Program

Many technologies that were developed for the space program have proved useful on Earth as well. A few of these technologies are shown here.
Applying Concepts *What advantage is there to fog-free vision in space? On Earth?*

▲ Miniature parts developed for space have been adapted for use on Earth. Artificial limbs have been made with controls as small as coins.

▼ A metal alloy of nickel and titanium used in dental braces was originally developed for space equipment such as antennas.

New Materials A variety of materials were first developed by chemists and engineers for use in spacecraft. These materials have specific physical properties—such as low density, high strength, or low thermal conductivity—that make them useful for certain products in space or on Earth. For example, flexible metal eyeglass frames are made with metals that "remember" their former shapes when bent. The composite materials used in modern tennis rackets were developed to make spacecraft components lightweight yet strong. Some athletic shoes contain a shock-absorbing material developed for moon boots.

Highly efficient insulating materials were developed to protect spacecraft against radiation and the extreme temperatures of space. These insulating materials are now being used in houses, cars, and trucks. Fire-resistant material developed for spacesuits is used in fireproof clothing and firefighter's suits.

Medical Devices Medical science has benefited greatly from the technology of the space program. Medical spinoffs include devices that use lasers to clean clogged arteries and pacemakers for hearts. These pacemakers use longer-life batteries originally developed for space power systems. Most hospitals use computer-aided imaging techniques developed for use on the moon during the Apollo program.

 **Reading Checkpoint** Why did NASA develop cordless power tools?

▼ Fire-resistant material developed for spacesuits is used in fireproof clothing such as suits worn by race-car drivers and firefighters.

◄ Many bicyclists use a lightweight, aerodynamic helmet with cooling vents that was developed with NASA's help.

◄ The design of the Apollo helmet, which gave the astronauts fog-free sight, has been adapted for use in ski goggles.

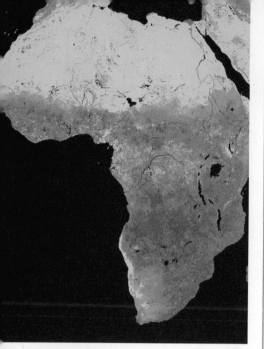

FIGURE 16
Remote Sensing
This satellite image shows patterns of vegetation in Africa. It is a false-color image, meaning that the colors have been adjusted to make certain features more obvious.
Inferring What do you think the yellow areas in the image represent?

Satellites

When a World Cup soccer final is played, almost everyone around the world can watch! Today, hundreds of satellites are in orbit around Earth, relaying television signals from one part of the planet to another. Satellites also relay telephone signals and computer data. **Satellites are used for communications and for collecting weather data and other scientific data.**

Observation satellites are used for many purposes, including tracking weather systems, mapping Earth's surface, and observing changes in Earth's environment. Observation satellites collect data using **remote sensing,** which is the collection of information about Earth and other objects in space without being in direct contact. Modern computers take the data collected by satellites and produce images for various purposes. For example, Figure 16 shows vegetation patterns in Africa. Satellite data might also be used to analyze the amount of rainfall over a wide area, or they might be used to discover where oil deposits lie underground.

Satellites are placed in different orbits depending on their purpose. Most communications satellites are placed in a geostationary orbit. In a **geostationary orbit,** a satellite orbits Earth above the equator at the same rate as Earth rotates and thus stays over the same place on Earth all the time. Read the *Technology and Society* feature on pages 526–527 to learn more about communications satellites.

Reading Checkpoint What is remote sensing?

Section 4 Assessment

S 8.7.c, E-LA: Reading 8.1.0

Vocabulary Skill High-Use Academic Words
In a complete sentence, identify two ways that new *technology* was developed for use in space.

Reviewing Key Concepts

1. a. Listing Name three ways that conditions in space are different from conditions on Earth.
   b. Relating Cause and Effect How have engineers designed spacecraft to operate in the special conditions of space?

2. a. Defining What is a space spinoff?
   b. Summarizing How has medical science benefited from the space program?
   c. Comparing and Contrasting Choose one space spinoff and compare how it is used in space and on Earth.

3. a. Listing Name three uses of satellites that affect everyday life.
   b. Inferring What advantage would there be to placing a satellite in geostationary orbit?
   c. Designing Experiments How could a scientist use satellites to determine whether a rain forest was becoming smaller over time?

Lab zone **At-Home Activity**

Spinoffs at Home Look back at the various space spinoffs discussed in the chapter. Then, with a family member, make a list of space spinoffs in your home.

Space Spinoffs  S 8.7.c, 8.9.c

Problem

Which blanket protects better against heat loss?

Skills Focus

graphing, drawing conclusions

Materials

- 1 foil blanket piece • 1 cloth blanket piece
- 3 thermometers • 1 beaker, 600 mL • ice
- 3 identical small test tubes • hot water
- 3 identical large test tubes • cotton balls
- cellophane tape or rubber bands • tap water

Procedure

1. On a separate sheet of paper, copy the data table below to record your observations.

2. Wrap the outside of one small test tube with the foil blanket piece. Wrap a second small test tube with the cloth blanket piece. Use tape or rubber bands to secure the blankets. Leave the third small test tube unwrapped.

3. Fill each of the three small test tubes half full with hot water. Be sure to use the same volume of water in each test tube. Insert a thermometer into each small test tube. Use cotton to "seal" the top of the small test tube and to hold the thermometer in place. Then, insert each small test tube into a large test tube.

4. Put ice in the beaker and fill the beaker two-thirds of the way with water.

5. Put the large test tubes into the ice water. Do not let water enter the test tubes. Record the starting temperatures of all three thermometers.

6. Allow the test tubes to sit in the ice water bath for about 10 minutes. Every minute note the temperature of each thermometer and record the results in your data table.

Analyze and Conclude

1. **Graphing** Graph the temperature over time for each of the thermometers.

2. **Calculating** Calculate the difference between the starting and ending temperatures of each thermometer. Which thermometer was best protected against heat loss?

3. **Controlling Variables** What was the purpose of the third, unwrapped small test tube?

4. **Drawing Conclusions** Which type of blanket protects better against heat loss? Explain.

5. **Communicating** Write an advertisement for the blanket that proved to be the best insulator. In the ad, describe the test procedures you used to justify your claim. Also explain why this blanket would benefit consumers.

Design an Experiment

The activity you just completed tested how well different materials protected against the loss of heat. Design an experiment that would test how well the same blankets would protect against an increase in heat. Obtain your teacher's approval before conducting your experiment.

Data Table			
Time (minutes)	Temperature (°C)		
	Foil-Wrapped Thermometer	Cloth-Wrapped Thermometer	Unwrapped Thermometer
0			
1			

Communications Satellites

What do watching TV, talking on a cellular phone, and sending e-mails have in common? Satellites orbiting Earth make these types of communication possible. Using microwaves, communications satellites receive and transmit radio, telephone, TV, computer data, and other signals. This technology has changed the way people around the globe communicate.

Orbiting Satellites

Communications satellites orbit Earth at different speeds and different altitudes. One type—geostationary satellites—are especially useful for long-distance communication because they orbit Earth at the same rate as Earth rotates. As a result, these satellites remain over fixed points on Earth. Geostationary satellites orbit at an altitude of about 35,880 km. Today there are more than 150 geostationary satellites located in a band around the Equator.

Bus
The bus is the satellite framework. It holds and protects the computer, the engine, and other equipment. Batteries in the bus store the energy that's used to power the satellite.

Kick Motor
The kick motor maintains the orbit of the satellite.

Receiving Antenna
This antenna receives signals sent from Earth and converts them to messages that the onboard computer understands.

Ground Station
These stations receive and transmit signals.

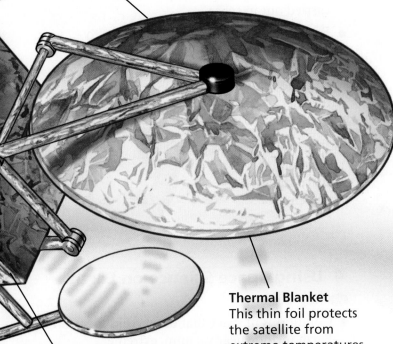

Solar Panels
Solar cells in the solar panels convert sunlight into electricity. Batteries store the energy that's used to power the satellite.

Transmitting Antenna
This antenna changes data into signals that can be sent to Earth.

Thermal Blanket
This thin foil protects the satellite from extreme temperatures.

Onboard Computer
A computer controls and monitors all parts of the satellite.

Ground Station

The Cost of Going Global

Communications satellites can relay signals, allowing the immediate exchange of information worldwide. Like all technology, though, there are trade-offs to using satellites. Earth's atmosphere can interfere with signals, causing problems such as static and time delays. Satellites cost hundreds of millions of dollars to build and even more to launch into space. When they are no longer useful, many burn up in space or become space junk.

Cellular phone signals are sent by communications satellites.

Weigh the Impact

1. Identify the Need
How have communications satellites changed people's lives?

2. Research
Research the uses of communications satellites over the last 20 years. List their influences on society.

3. Write
In several paragraphs, describe ways in which you and your family use this satellite technology in your daily lives.

Go Online
PHSchool.com

For: More on communications satellites
Visit: PHSchool.com
Web Code: cfh-5020

🔑 The **BIG Idea** Scientists have learned much about the solar system through various types of space missions.

① The Science of Rockets

🔑 **Key Concepts**   S 8.2.e

- Rocket technology originated in China hundreds of years ago and gradually spread to other parts of the world.
- A rocket moves forward when gases shooting out the back of the rocket push it in the opposite direction.
- The main advantage of a multistage rocket is that the total weight of the rocket is greatly reduced as the rocket rises.

Key Terms
rocket
thrust
velocity
orbital velocity
escape velocity

② The Space Program

🔑 **Key Concepts**   S 8.4.d Framework

- The space race began in 1957 when the Soviets launched the satellite *Sputnik I* into orbit. The United States responded by speeding up its own space program.
- The American effort to land astronauts on the moon was named the Apollo program.

Key Term
satellite

③ Exploring Space Today

🔑 **Key Concepts**   S 8.4.d Framework

- NASA has used space shuttles to perform many important tasks. These include taking satellites into orbit, repairing damaged satellites, and carrying astronauts and equipment to and from space stations.
- A space station provides a place where long-term observations and experiments can be carried out in space.
- Each space probe has a power system to produce electricity, a communication system to send and receive signals, and scientific instruments to collect data and perform experiments.

Key Terms
space shuttle
space station
space probe
rover

④ Using Space Science on Earth

🔑 **Key Concepts**   S 8.7.c

- Conditions in space that differ from those on Earth include near vacuum, extreme temperatures, and microgravity.
- The space program has developed thousands of products that affect many aspects of modern society, including consumer products, new materials, medical devices, and communications satellites.
- Satellites are used for communications and for collecting weather data and other scientific data.

Key Terms
vacuum
microgravity
space spinoff
remote sensing
geostationary orbit

Review and Assessment

Target Reading Skill

Relate Cause and Effect
The work of the many scientists who participated in the space program has resulted in many benefits to society. Create a cause-and-effect graphic organizer that shows at least three benefits of the space program.

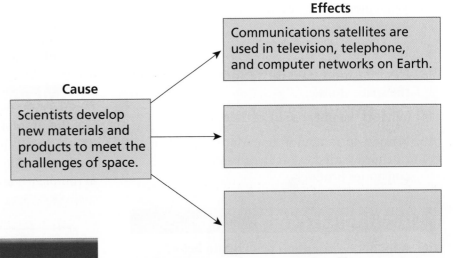

Cause

Scientists develop new materials and products to meet the challenges of space.

Effects

Communications satellites are used in television, telephone, and computer networks on Earth.

Reviewing Key Terms

Choose the letter of the best answer.

1. A device that expels gas in one direction to move in the opposite direction is a
   a. rocket.   **b.** space probe.
   c. space station.   **d.** rover.

2. To fly beyond a planet's gravitational pull, a spacecraft must reach
   a. velocity.
   b. orbital velocity.
   c. escape velocity.
   d. geostationary orbit.

3. Any object that revolves around another object in space is called a
   a. vacuum.   **b.** space station.
   c. satellite.   **d.** rocket.

4. A spacecraft that can carry a crew into space, return to Earth, and then be reused for the same purpose is a
   a. rover.
   b. space shuttle.
   c. space station.
   d. space probe.

5. Acquiring information about Earth and other objects in space without being in direct contact with these worlds is called
   a. microgravity.
   b. spinoff.
   c. thrust.
   d. remote sensing.

Complete the following sentences so that your answers clearly explain the key terms.

6. In order to move, a rocket must generate **thrust,** which is _____ .

7. **Space probes,** which are _____ , are often used to gather data about distant planets.

8. Astronauts in orbit experience **microgravity,** which is _____ .

9. *Mir* is an example of a **space station,** which is _____ .

10. Observation satellites collect data using **remote sensing,** which is _____ .

Writing in Science

Descriptive Paragraph Imagine that you are a scientist planning the first human expedition to Mars. In a detailed paragraph, list some of the major challenges that such a mission would face and provide possible solutions. Think about the physical stresses of space travel and how the crew's basic needs will be met.

Video Assessment
Discovery Channel School
Exploring Space

Review and Assessment

Checking Concepts

11. What are three types of rocket fuels?

12. What did Neil Armstrong say when he first set foot on the moon?

13. Describe some tasks carried out by the crew of the space shuttle.

14. What is the purpose of a space station?

15. Name a space spinoff in each of the following categories: medical devices, materials, and consumer products.

Thinking Critically

16. **Applying Concepts** The diagram below shows a rocket lifting off. What does each of the arrows represent?

17. **Classifying** A jet airplane usually uses liquid fuel that is burned with oxygen from the atmosphere. A jet engine expels hot gases to the rear, and the airplane moves forward. Is a jet a type of rocket? Explain.

18. **Relating Cause and Effect** When the Soviet Union launched *Sputnik I* into orbit in 1957, educators in the United States decided to improve math and science education in U.S. schools. Why do you think educators made that decision?

19. **Making Judgments** Do you think that the benefits of the Apollo program outweighed the program's costs? Explain.

20. **Comparing and Contrasting** How is orbital velocity different from escape velocity?

21. **Making Generalizations** How could the International Space Station help with further exploration of the solar system?

Applying Skills

Use the graph below to answer Questions 22–24.

The graph shows the amounts of time needed for satellites at different altitudes above Earth's surface to complete one orbit.

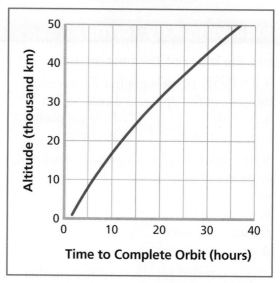

22. **Interpreting Diagrams** How long will a satellite orbiting at an altitude of 50,000 km take to complete one orbit?

23. **Applying Concepts** A geostationary satellite orbits Earth once every 24 hours. At what altitude does such a satellite orbit?

24. **Making Generalizations** What is the relationship between satellite altitude and the time needed to complete one orbit?

Lab zone Standards Investigation

Performance Assessment Before testing your vehicle, list your design goals and criteria. Describe some of the challenges you faced. What could you change to improve your model?

Choose the letter of the best answer.

1. Which of the following developments was most directly responsible for the creation of rockets that were capable to going to the moon?
   A gunpowder
   B explosives
   C single-stage rockets
   D multistage rockets   **S 8.4.d Framework**

2. What force must a rocket overcome to be launched into space?
   A thrust   B gravity
   C orbital velocity   D escape velocity
                         S 8.2.e, S 8.2.g

The diagram below shows a rocket and the direction of four forces. Use the diagram and your knowledge of rockets to answer Question 3.

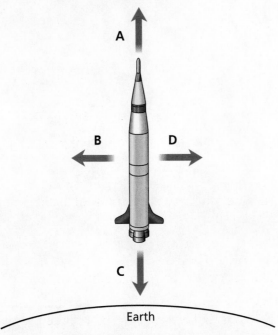

Earth

3. Which of the lettered forces shown in the diagram represents an equal and opposite force to the thrust of the rocket?
   A Force A
   B Force B
   C Force C
   D Force D   **S 8.2.e**

4. Space shuttles have been used to perform all of the following tasks except
   A placing satellites in orbit.
   B landing on the moon.
   C carrying astronauts and equipment to and from space stations.
   D repairing damaged satellites.
                         S 8.4.d Framework

5. A satellite in geostationary orbit revolves around Earth once each
   A hour.   B week.
   C month.   D day.
                         S 8.4.d Framework

6. Spacecraft fitted with instruments but lacking a human crew are called
   A space probes.
   B space shuttles.
   C space stations.
   D space spinoffs.   **S 8.4.d Framework**

7. During the space race, the former Soviet Union was the first to accomplish all of the following except
   A launching the first satellite into orbit.
   B sending the first living creature into space.
   C sending the first human into space.
   D landing the first human on the moon.
                         S 8.4.d Framework

8. In order to collect soil and rock samples on Mars, scientists would probably use a
   A space station.
   B rover.
   C vacuum.
   D satellite in geostationary orbit.
                         S 8.4.d Framework

Apply the
BIG Idea

9. Space probes have been used to explore all the planets, but not yet Pluto. Describe three types of information that a probe orbiting Pluto could gather about it.
                         S 8.4.d Framework, S 8.4.e

Chapter 14

The Solar System

CALIFORNIA Standards Preview

S 8.2 Unbalanced forces cause changes in velocity. As a basis for understanding this concept:

g. Students know the role of gravity in forming and maintaining the shapes of planets, stars, and the solar system.

S 8.4 The structure and composition of the universe can be learned from studying stars and galaxies and their evolution. As a basis for understanding this concept:

b. Students know that the Sun is one of many stars in the Milky Way galaxy and that stars may differ in size, temperature, and color.

c. Students know how to use astronomical units and light years as measures of distance between the Sun, stars, and Earth.

d. Students know that stars are the source of light for all bright objects in outer space and that the Moon and planets shine by reflected sunlight, not by their own light.

e. Students know the appearance, general composition, relative position and size, and motion of objects in the solar system, including planets, planetary satellites, comets, and asteroids.

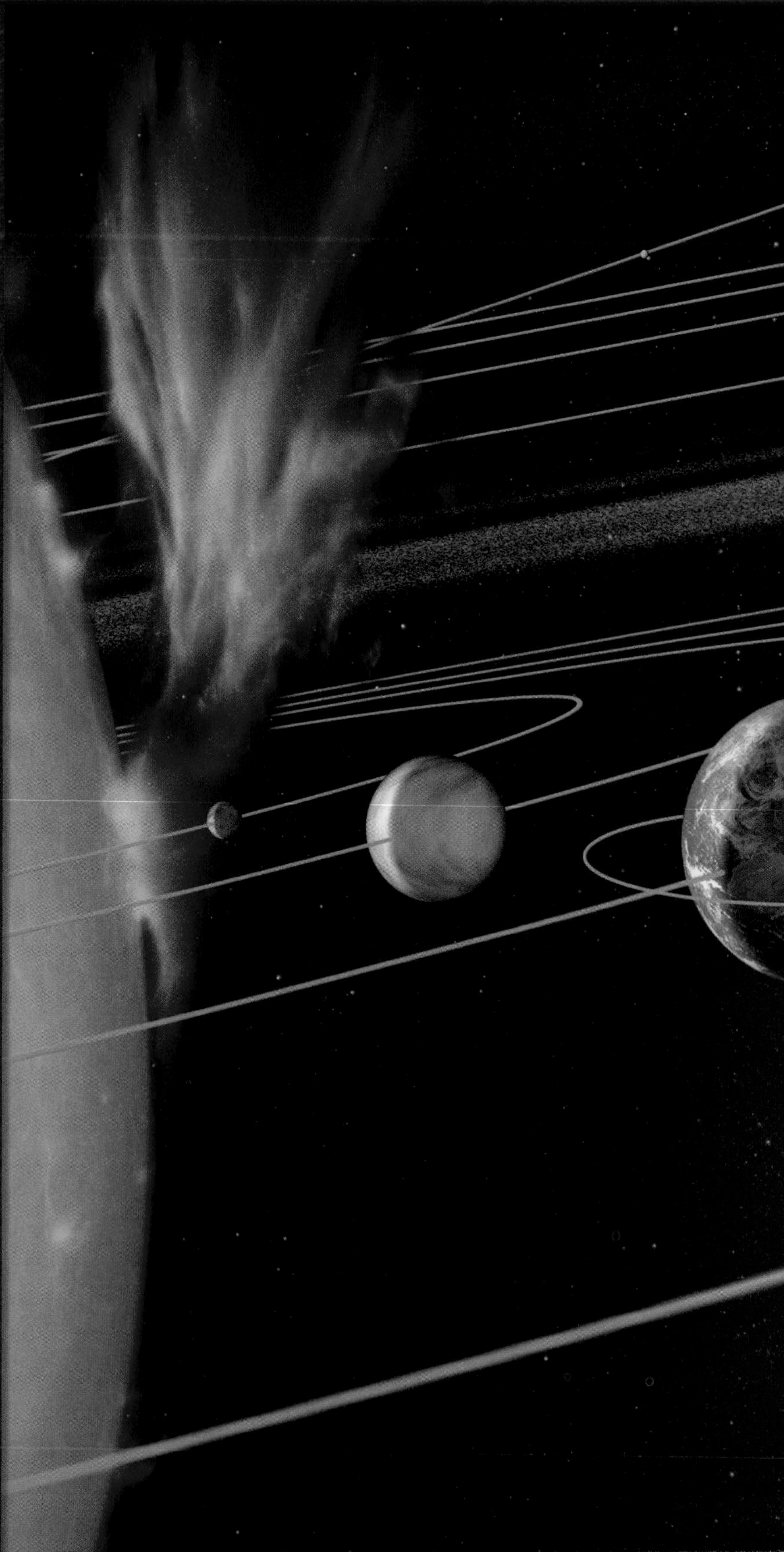

This illustration shows several planets in orbit around the sun. ▶

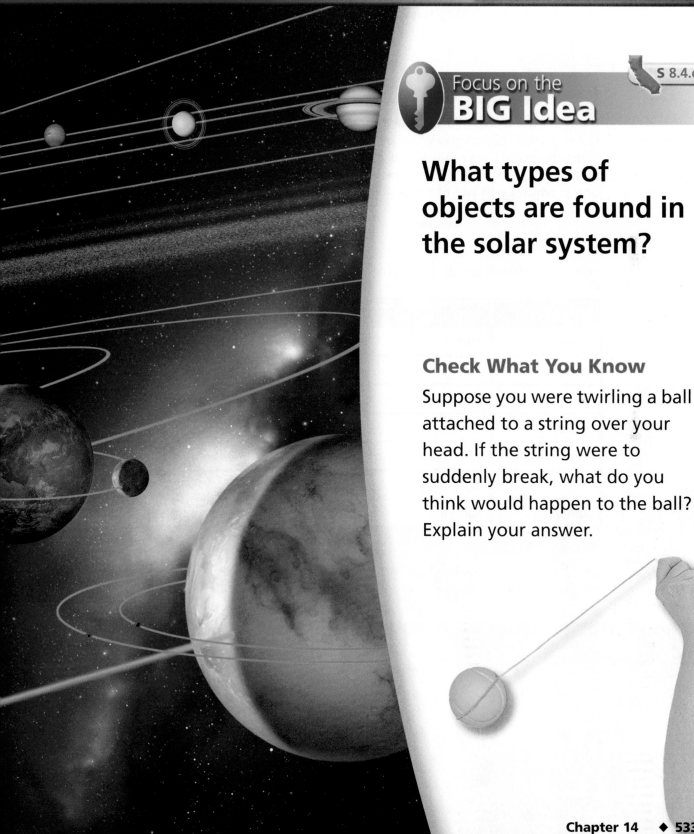

S 8.4.e

Focus on the
BIG Idea

What types of objects are found in the solar system?

Check What You Know

Suppose you were twirling a ball attached to a string over your head. If the string were to suddenly break, what do you think would happen to the ball? Explain your answer.

Build Science Vocabulary

The images shown here represent some of the key terms in this chapter. You can use this vocabulary skill to help you understand the meaning of some key terms in this chapter.

Vocabulary Skill

Greek Word Origins

Many science words related to astronomy come from ancient Greek. In this chapter you will learn the word *geocentric,* which comes from the Greek words *geo,* meaning "Earth" and *kentron,* meaning "center." Early Greeks believed in a *geocentric* universe, one in which <u>Earth</u> was at the <u>center</u>.

geo	+	kentron	=	geocentric
Earth		center		Earth-centered

Learn these Greek words to help remember key terms.

Greek Word	Meaning	Key Terms
astron	star	astronomy, asteroid
chróma	color	chromosphere
geo	Earth	geocentric
helios	sun	heliocentric
kentron	near the center, central	geocentric, heliocentric
photo	light	photosphere
sphaira	sphere	photosphere, chromosphere

Apply It!

Use what you have learned about *geocentric* to predict what *heliocentric* means. Revise your definition as you read Section 1.

terrestrial planets

comet

moons

sunspot

extraterrestrial life

ring

Chapter 14 Vocabulary

Section 1 (page 538)
geocentric
heliocentric
ellipse
moon
astronomical unit

Section 2 (page 545)
nuclear fusion
core
radiation zone
convection zone
photosphere
chromosphere
corona
solar wind
sunspot
prominence
solar flare

Section 3 (page 552)
terrestrial planets
greenhouse effect

Section 4 (page 562)
gas giant
ring

Section 5 (page 572)
comet
coma
nucleus
Kuiper belt
Oort cloud
asteroid
asteroid belt
meteroid
meteor
meteorite

Section 6 (page 576)
extraterrestrial life

Build Science Vocabulary
Online
Visit: PHSchool.com
Web Code: cxj-4140

How to Read Science

Reading Skill

Create Outlines

You have learned to identify main ideas and supporting details as you read this textbook. An outline shows the relationship between main ideas and supporting details. An outline has a formal structure as in the example shown below. Roman numerals show the main topics. Capital letters show subtopics. Numbers show supporting details, including key terms.

Preview Section 1 and then look at the outline below.

> **Title**
>
> **Observing the Solar System**
> I. Earth at the Center
>   A. Greek Observations
>   1. Geocentric—Earth-Centered
>   2. Geocentric system—Earth at the center of planets and stars
>   B. Ptolemy's Model
>   1. Planets on small circles that move on bigger circles
>   2. Model was incorrect, but accepted for 1,500 years
> II. Sun at the Center
>   A.

Subtopic

Key Term

Key Concept

Main topics

Supporting details

Apply It!

Answer each of the following questions in a complete sentence.

1. What are the most important topics in this outline?

2. Where in this outline can you find the definition of the key kerm *geocentric?*

3. Make outlines for the other sections of this chapter.

Standards **Investigation**

Build a Model of the Solar System

The solar system is a vast region containing the sun, planets, and many other objects. To help you understand the huge distances involved, you will design three different scale models of the solar system.

Your Goal

To design scale models of the solar system

To complete this investigation, you will

- design a model to show the planets' distances from the sun
- design a model to show the planets' sizes compared to the sun
- test different scales to see if you can use the same scale for both size and distance in one model

Plan It!

Begin by previewing Figures 13 and 20 in this chapter and Appendix D on pages 654 and 655. With a group of classmates, brainstorm how to build your models.

Then design two models—one to show distances and one to show diameters. Next, design a third model that uses the same scale for both size and distance. Try several different scales to find which works best.

Prepare a data table to record your calculations. You will present your scale models and graphs at the end of the chapter.

Observing the Solar System

CALIFORNIA
Standards Focus

S 8.4.c Students know how to use astronomical units and light years as measures of distance between the Sun, stars, and Earth.

S 8.4.d Students know that stars are the source of light for all bright objects in outer space and that the Moon and planets shine by reflected sunlight, not by their own light.

- What are the geocentric and heliocentric systems?
- How did Copernicus, Galileo, and Kepler contribute to our knowledge of the solar system?
- What objects make up the solar system?

Key Terms

- geocentric
- heliocentric
- ellipse
- moon
- astronomical unit

Lab zone Standards Warm-Up

What Is at the Center?

1. Stand about 2 meters from a partner who is holding a flashlight. Have your partner shine the flashlight in your direction. Tell your partner not to move the flashlight.
2. Continue facing your partner, but move sideways in a circle, staying about 2 meters away from your partner.
3. Record your observations about your ability to see the light.
4. Repeat the activity, but this time remain stationary and continually face one direction. Have your partner continue to hold the flashlight toward you and move sideways around you, remaining about 2 meters from you.
5. Record your observations about your ability to see the light.

Think It Over

Drawing Conclusions Compare your two sets of observations. If you represent Earth and your partner represents the sun, is it possible, just from your observations, to tell whether Earth or the sun is in the center of the solar system?

Have you ever gazed up at the sky on a starry night? If you watch for several hours, the stars seem to move across the sky. The sky seems to be rotating right over your head. In fact, from the Northern Hemisphere, the sky appears to rotate completely around the North Star once every 24 hours.

Now think about what you see every day. During the day, the sun appears to move across the sky. From here on Earth, it seems as if Earth is stationary and that the sun, moon, and stars are moving around Earth. But is the sky really moving above you? Centuries ago, before there were space shuttles or even telescopes, there was no easy way to find out.

FIGURE 1
Star Trails
This photo was made by exposing the camera film for several hours. Each star trails along a circle, and all the stars seem to revolve around the North Star.

Earth at the Center

When the ancient Greeks watched the stars move across the sky, they noticed that the patterns of the stars didn't change. Although the stars seemed to move, they stayed in the same position relative to one another. These patterns of stars, called constellations, kept the same shapes from night to night and from year to year.

Greek Observations As the Greeks observed the sky, they noticed something surprising. Several points of light seemed to wander slowly among the stars. The Greeks called these objects *planets,* from the Greek word meaning "wanderers." The Greeks made careful observations of the motions of the planets that they could see. You know these planets by the names the ancient Romans later gave them: Mercury, Venus, Mars, Jupiter, and Saturn.

Most early Greek astronomers believed the universe to be perfect, with Earth at the center. The Greeks thought that Earth is inside a rotating dome they called the celestial sphere. Since *geo* is Greek for "Earth," an Earth-centered model is known as a **geocentric** (jee oh SEN trik) system. ⬤ **In a geocentric system, Earth is at the center of the revolving planets and stars.**

Ptolemy's Model About A.D. 140, the Greek astronomer Ptolemy (TAHL uh mee) further developed the geocentric model. Like the earlier Greeks, Ptolemy thought that Earth is at the center of a system of planets and stars. In Ptolemy's model, however, the planets move on small circles that move on bigger circles.

Even though Ptolemy's geocentric model was incorrect, it explained the motions observed in the sky fairly accurately. As a result, the geocentric model of the universe was widely accepted for nearly 1,500 years after Ptolemy.

✔ **Reading Checkpoint** What is a geocentric system?

FIGURE 2
Geocentric System
In a geocentric system, the planets and stars are thought to revolve around a stationary Earth. In the 1500s, an astronomy book published the illustration of Ptolemy's geocentric system shown below.
Interpreting Diagrams *Where is Earth located in each illustration?*

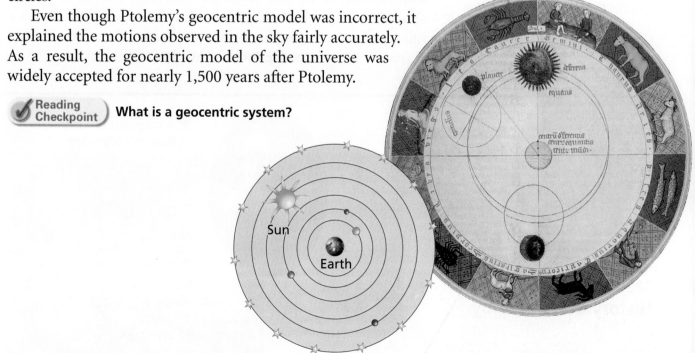

Sun at the Center

Not everybody believed in the geocentric system. An ancient Greek scientist developed another explanation for the motion of the planets. This sun-centered model is called a **heliocentric** (hee lee oh SEN trik) system. 🔑 **In a heliocentric system, Earth and the other planets revolve around the sun.** This model was not well received in ancient times, however, because people could not accept that Earth is not at the center of the universe.

The Copernican Revolution In 1543, the Polish astronomer Nicolaus Copernicus further developed the heliocentric model. 🔑 **Copernicus worked out the arrangement of the known planets and how they move around the sun.** Copernicus's theory would eventually revolutionize the science of astronomy. But at first, many people were unwilling to accept his theory. In the 1500s and early 1600s, most people still believed in the geocentric model. However, evidence collected by the Italian scientist Galileo Galilei eventually proved that the heliocentric model was correct.

Galileo's Evidence 🔑 **Galileo used the newly invented telescope to make discoveries that supported the heliocentric model.** For example, in 1610, Galileo used a telescope to discover four moons revolving around Jupiter. This proved that not every body in space revolves around Earth.

Galileo's observations of Venus also supported the heliocentric system. Galileo knew that Venus is always seen near the sun. He discovered that Venus goes through a series of phases similar to those of Earth's moon. But Venus would not have a full set of phases if it circled around Earth. Therefore, Galileo reasoned, the geocentric model must be incorrect.

FIGURE 3
Heliocentric System
In a heliocentric system, Earth and the other planets revolve around the sun. The illustration by Andreas Cellarius (top) was made in the 1660s.
Interpreting Diagrams *In a heliocentric model, what revolves around Earth?*

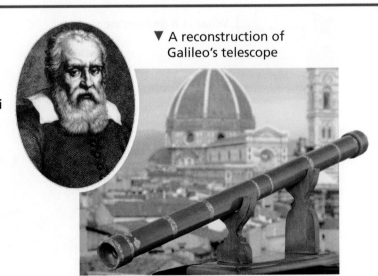

Nicolaus Copernicus
1473–1543

Galileo Galilei
1564–1642

▼ A reconstruction of Galileo's telescope

FIGURE 4
Major Figures in the History of Astronomy

540 ◆

Motions of the Planets

Copernicus correctly placed the sun at the center of the planets. But he incorrectly assumed that the planets travel in orbits that are perfect circles. Copernicus had based his ideas on observations made by the ancient Greeks.

Tycho Brahe's Observations In the late 1500s, the Danish astronomer Tycho Brahe (TEE koh BRAH uh) and his assistants made much more accurate observations. For more than 20 years, they carefully observed and recorded the positions of the planets. Surprisingly, these observations were made without using a telescope. Telescopes had not yet been invented!

Kepler's First Law Tycho Brahe died in 1601. His assistant, Johannes Kepler, went to work analyzing the observations. **Kepler used Tycho Brahe's data to develop three laws that describe the motions of the planets.**

Kepler began by trying to figure out the shape of Mars's orbit. At first, he assumed that the orbit was a perfect circle. But his calculations did not fit the observations. Kepler eventually found out that Mars's orbit was a slightly flattened circle, or ellipse. An **ellipse** is an oval shape, which may be elongated or nearly circular.

After years of detailed calculations, Kepler reached a remarkable conclusion about the motion of the planets. Kepler found that the orbit of each planet is an ellipse. This is now known as Kepler's first law of motion. Kepler had used the evidence gathered by Tycho Brahe to disprove the long-held belief that the planets move in perfect circles.

 **Reading Checkpoint** What is the heliocentric system?

Tycho Brahe
1546–1601

Johannes Kepler
1571–1630

◀ Brahe's observatory on an island between Denmark and Sweden

Mercury 58,000,000 km, 0.39 AU
Venus 108,000,000 km, 0.72 AU
Earth 150,000,000 km, 1.0 AU
Mars 228,000,000 km, 1.5 AU

Jupiter
779,000,000 km
5.2 AU

Saturn
1,434,000,000 km
9.6 AU

FIGURE 5
The Sun and Planets
This illustration shows the average distances of the planets from the sun. The solar system also includes smaller objects, such as Pluto. These distances are drawn to scale, but the sizes of the planets are not drawn to the same scale.
Observing *Which planet is closest to the sun?*

Kepler's Second Law Kepler also discovered how the speed of a given planet changes as it revolves around the sun. Kepler found that each planet moves faster when it is closer to the sun and slower when it is farther away from the sun. This is Kepler's second law of motion.

Kepler's Third Law Kepler also found that the time that it takes a planet to orbit the sun and its average distance from the sun are related. He found planets that are closer to the sun orbit the sun faster than planets that are farther from the sun. You can use Kepler's third law of motion to calculate a planet's average distance from the sun if you know how long it takes for the planet to complete one orbit.

Reviewing Math: Algebra
and Functions 7.1.5

Math ▸ Analyzing Data

Planet Speed Versus Distance
Use the graph to help discover what Kepler learned about the relationship between the speed of a planet and its distance from the sun.

1. **Reading Graphs** According to the graph, what is Earth's average speed?

2. **Interpreting Data** Which is closer to the sun, Mercury or Mars? Which moves faster?

3. **Drawing Conclusions** What is the general relationship between a planet's speed and its average distance from the sun?

4. **Predicting** The planet Uranus is about 2,900 million km from the sun. Predict whether its speed is greater or less than Jupiter's speed. Explain your answer.

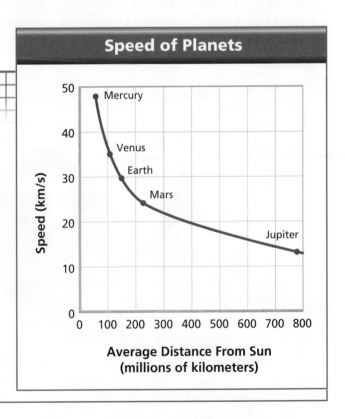

Speed of Planets

Uranus	Neptune	Pluto
2,873,000,000 km	4,495,000,000 km	5,870,000,000 km
19.2 AU	30.0 AU	39.2 AU

Modern View of the Solar System

Today, people talk about the "solar system" rather than the "Earth system." This shows that people accept the idea that Earth and the other planets revolve around the sun.

Components of the Solar System Since Galileo's time, our knowledge of the solar system has increased dramatically. Galileo knew the same planets that the ancient Greeks had known—Mercury, Venus, Earth, Mars, Jupiter, and Saturn. Since Galileo's time, astronomers have discovered two more planets—Uranus and Neptune, as well as Pluto, which is no longer considered to be a planet.

The planets vary greatly in size and appearance. They also differ in terms of mass, composition, distance from the sun, tilt of their axis, and other characteristics. Appendix D provides detailed data for each of the planets. All of the planets except Mercury and Venus have moons. A **moon** is a natural satellite that revolves around a planet. Astronomers have also identified many other objects in the solar system, such as comets and asteroids. ⬤ **Today we know that the solar system consists of the sun, the planets and their moons, and several kinds of smaller objects that revolve around the sun.**

Measuring Distances in the Solar System The distances between the sun and the planets are very large compared to distances that are typically used on Earth. As a result, astronomers commonly describe distances within the solar system using astronomical units. One **astronomical unit,** or 1 AU, equals Earth's average distance from the sun (about 150 million kilometers). In Figure 5, you can see that Saturn's distance from the sun is 9.6 AU. This means that, on average, Saturn is 9.6 times farther from the sun than Earth.

 Reading Checkpoint **What is an astronomical unit?**

Go Online
active art

For: Solar System activity
Visit: PHSchool.com
Web Code: cfp-5031

Lab zone Skills **Activity**

Calculating

If you know an object's distance from the sun in AU, you can convert this distance to kilometers by multiplying it by 150,000,000. (Recall that 1 AU ≈ 150 million km.)

For example, Ceres is the largest of a group of objects called asteroids. Ceres orbits the sun at an average distance of 2.77 AU. How far is Ceres from the sun in kilometers? Between the orbits of which two planets does Ceres' orbit lie? How far is Ceres' orbit from Earth's orbit in both AU and kilometers?

Exploring the Solar System Galileo used a telescope to observe distant parts of the solar system from Earth's surface. Astronomers today still use telescopes located on Earth, but they have also placed telescopes in space to gain a better view of the universe beyond Earth.

The sun is the source of visible light in the solar system. You learned in the last chapter that the moon does not produce its own light. Rather, you can see the moon because its surface reflects sunlight. Similarly, the other planets and moons of the solar system don't produce their own light, although they do give off radiation in the form of heat. The planets and moons are visible because sunlight reflects from their surfaces.

In addition to observations made with telescopes, scientists have sent astronauts to the moon and launched numerous space probes to explore the far reaches of the solar system. Our understanding of the solar system continues to grow every day. Who knows what new discoveries will be made in your lifetime!

FIGURE 6
Saturn
This false-color image of Saturn and its rings was taken by the Cassini spacecraft, which is currently exploring Saturn and its moons.

Section 1 Assessment

S 8.4.c, 8.4.d, ELA: Reading 8.1.2

Vocabulary Skill Greek Word Origins How does knowing Greek word origins help you remember the terms *geocentric* and *heliocentric*?

Reviewing Key Concepts

1. **a. Explaining** What are the geocentric and heliocentric systems?
   b. Comparing and Contrasting How was Copernicus's model of the universe different from Ptolemy's model?
   c. Drawing Conclusions What discoveries by Galileo support the heliocentric model?
   d. Applying Concepts People often say the sun rises in the east, crosses the sky, and sets in the west. Is this literally true? Explain.
2. **a. Interpreting Data** How did Kepler use Tycho Brahe's data?
   b. Describing What did Kepler discover about the shapes of the planets' orbits?
   c. Inferring How did Tycho Brahe and Kepler employ the scientific method?

3. **a. Describing** What objects make up the solar system?
   b. Listing What are the planets, in order of increasing distance from the sun?
   c. Interpreting Diagrams Use Figure 5 to find the planet with the closest orbit to Earth.

Writing in Science

Dialogue Write an imaginary conversation between Ptolemy and Galileo about the merits of the geocentric and heliocentric systems. Which system would each scientist favor? What evidence could each offer to support his view? Do you think that one scientist could convince the other to change his mind? Use quotation marks around the comments of each scientist.

The Sun

CALIFORNIA
Standards Focus

S 8.2.g Students know the role of gravity in forming and maintaining the shapes of planets, stars, and the solar system.

S 8.4.b Students know that the Sun is one of many stars in the Milky Way galaxy and that stars may differ in size, temperature, and color.

🔑 How does the sun produce energy?

🔑 What are the layers of the sun's interior and the sun's atmosphere?

🔑 What features form on or above the sun's surface?

Key Terms

- nuclear fusion
- core
- radiation zone
- convection zone
- photosphere
- chromosphere
- corona
- solar wind
- sunspot
- prominence
- solar flare

Lab zone Standards **Warm-Up**

How Can You Safely Observe the Sun?

1. Clamp a pair of binoculars to a ring stand as shown in the photo.

2. Cut a hole in a 20-cm by 28-cm sheet of thin cardboard so that it will fit over the binoculars, as shown in the photo. The cardboard should cover one lens, but allow light through the other lens. Tape the cardboard on securely.

3. Use the binoculars to project an image of the sun onto a sheet of white paper. The cardboard will shade the white paper. Change the focus and move the paper back and forth until you get a sharp image. **CAUTION:** *Never look directly at the sun. You will hurt your eyes if you do. Do not look up through the binoculars.*

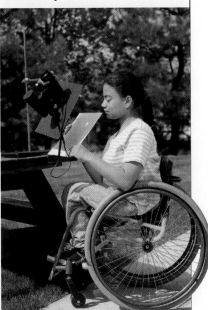

Think It Over

Observing Draw what you see on the paper. What do you see on the surface of the sun?

Suppose you are aboard a spaceship approaching the solar system from afar. Your first impression of the solar system might be that it consists of a single star, the sun, with a few tiny objects orbiting around it.

Your first impression wouldn't be that far off. In fact, the sun accounts for 99.8 percent of the solar system's total mass. As a result of its huge mass, the sun exerts a powerful gravitational force throughout the solar system. Although this force decreases rapidly with distance, it is strong enough to hold all the planets and many other distant objects in orbit.

Go Online
PLANET DIARY

For: More on the sun
Visit: PHSchool.com
Web Code: cfd-5032

Energy from the Sun

Unlike Earth, the sun does not have a solid surface. Rather, the sun is a huge ball of ionized gas, or plasma, throughout. About three-quarters of the sun's mass is hydrogen. About one-quarter of the sun's mass is helium. There are also small amounts of other elements.

Nuclear Fusion The sun shines brightly, providing energy needed for life on Earth. But how is this energy produced? Early scientists hypothesized that the sun produced its energy through a chemical reaction, such as burning fuel. However, if this were the case, the sun would have lasted for just a few thousand years before its fuel ran out. Since the sun is actually about 4.6 billion years old, this hypothesis is clearly wrong.

In the early 1900s, scientists discovered the real source of the sun's energy. 🔑 **The sun produces energy through nuclear fusion.** As shown in Figure 7, in the process of **nuclear fusion,** two atomic nuclei combine, forming a larger, more massive nucleus and releasing energy. Within the sun, hydrogen atoms join together to form helium.

Nuclear fusion can occur only under conditions of extremely high pressure and temperature. Such conditions exist in the sun's **core,** or central region. The temperature within the core reaches about 15 million degrees Celsius, high enough for nuclear fusion to take place.

The total mass of the helium produced by nuclear fusion is slightly less than the total mass of the hydrogen that goes into it. The missing mass is changed into energy. It moves slowly outward from the core, eventually escaping into space. Some of this energy reaches Earth, where you experience it as light and heat.

FIGURE 7
Nuclear Fusion
During nuclear fusion, two atomic nuclei collide and fuse.

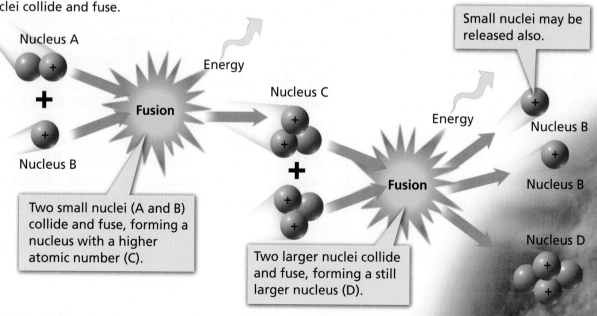

Forces in Balance Nuclear fusion in the sun's core produces an incredible amount of energy. This energy causes gas ions within the sun to move very fast, generating a tremendous pressure pushing outward from the core. This pressure would cause the sun to explode if it weren't balanced by an equal and opposite force. This opposing force is the sun's own gravity, which pulls matter inward. The weight of matter pressing inward and the outward pushing pressure are balanced throughout the sun. As a result, the sun is stable. The sun will remain stable as long as there is a steady energy source within it. Astronomers estimate that the sun will be stable for another 5 billion years or so.

The Sun's Interior

Like Earth, the sun has an interior and an atmosphere. 🔑 **The sun's interior consists of the core, the radiation zone, and the convection zone.**

The Core As you have learned, the sun's energy is produced in its central core. Here, the temperature and pressure are so high that nuclear fusion can take place. The sun's core has a diameter of about 400,000 km, more than 30 times Earth's diameter.

The Radiation Zone The energy produced in the sun's core moves outward through the middle layer of the sun's interior, the radiation zone. The **radiation zone** is a region of very tightly packed gas where energy is transferred mainly in the form of electromagnetic radiation. Because the radiation zone is so dense, energy can take more than 100,000 years to move through it.

The Convection Zone The **convection zone** is the outermost layer of the sun's interior. Hot gases rise from the bottom of the convection zone and gradually cool as they approach the top. Cooler gases sink, forming loops of gas that move energy toward the sun's surface.

 **Reading Checkpoint** What is the convection zone?

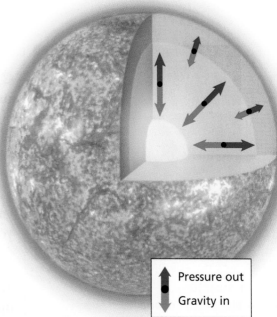

⬆	Pressure out
⬇	Gravity in

FIGURE 8
Forces Within the Sun
Gravity and outward pressure are balanced throughout the sun. These forces combine to produce the sun's spherical shape.
Interpreting Diagrams *In which region of the sun's interior is the force of gravity strongest?*

FIGURE 9
Active Sun
The sun is a huge, hot ball of glowing gas.

FIGURE 10
The Sun's Corona
During a total solar eclipse, you can see light from the corona, the outer layer of the sun's atmosphere, around the dark disk of the moon.

Lab zone Try This **Activity**

Viewing Sunspots
You can observe changes in the number of sunspots.

1. Make a data table to record the number of sunspots you see each day.

2. Decide on a time to study sunspots each day.

3. View the sun's image in the way described in the Discover activity in this section. **CAUTION:** *Never look directly at the sun. You will hurt your eyes if you do.*

4. Make and record your observations.

Interpreting Data How much did the number of sunspots change from day to day?

The Sun's Atmosphere

 **The sun's atmosphere includes the photosphere, the chromosphere, and the corona.** Each layer has unique properties.

The Photosphere The inner layer of the sun's atmosphere is called the **photosphere** (FOH tuh sfeer). The Greek word *photos* means "light," so *photosphere* means the sphere that gives off visible light. The sun does not have a solid surface, but the gases of the photosphere are thick enough to be visible. When you look at a typical image of the sun, you are looking at the photosphere. It is considered to be the sun's surface layer.

The Chromosphere During a total solar eclipse, the moon blocks light from the photosphere. The photosphere no longer produces the glare that keeps you from seeing the sun's faint, outer layers. At the start and end of a total eclipse, a reddish glow is visible just around the photosphere. This glow comes from the middle layer of the sun's atmosphere, the **chromosphere** (KROH muh sfeer). The Greek word *chroma* means "color," so the chromosphere is the "color sphere."

The Corona During a total solar eclipse an even fainter layer of the sun becomes visible, as you can see in Figure 10. This outer layer, which looks like a white halo around the sun, is called the **corona,** which means "crown" in Latin. The corona extends into space for millions of kilometers. It gradually thins into streams of electrically charged particles called the **solar wind.**

Reading Checkpoint During what event could you see the sun's corona?

Features on the Sun

For hundreds of years, scientists have used telescopes to study the sun. They have spotted a variety of features on the sun's surface. **Features on or just above the sun's surface include sunspots, prominences, and solar flares.**

Sunspots Early observers noticed dark spots on the sun's surface. These became known as sunspots. Sunspots look small. But in fact, they can be larger than Earth. **Sunspots** are areas of gas on the sun's surface that are cooler than the gases around them. Cooler gases don't give off as much light as hotter gases, which is why sunspots look darker than the rest of the photosphere. Sunspots seem to move across the sun's surface, showing that the sun rotates on its axis, just as Earth does. The number of sunspots on the sun varies over a period of about 11 years.

FIGURE 11

The Layers of the Sun

The sun has an interior and an atmosphere, each of which consists of several layers. The diameter of the sun (not including the chromosphere and the corona) is about 1.4 million kilometers.
Interpreting Diagrams *Name the layers of the sun's interior, beginning at its center.*

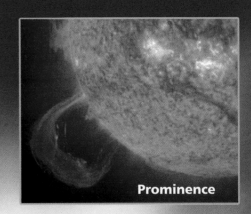

Prominence

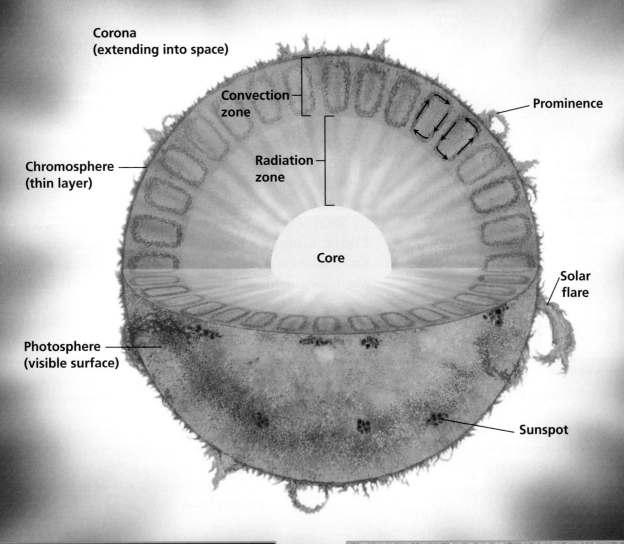

Corona
(extending into space)

Convection
zone

Prominence

Chromosphere
(thin layer)

Radiation
zone

Core

Solar
flare

Photosphere
(visible surface)

Sunspot

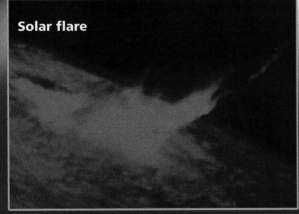

Solar flare

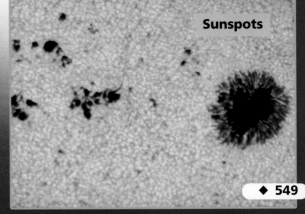

Sunspots

Prominences Sunspots usually occur in groups. Huge, reddish loops of gas called **prominences** often link different parts of sunspot regions. When a group of sunspots is near the edge of the sun as seen from Earth, these loops can be seen extending over the edge of the sun.

Solar Flares Sometimes the loops in sunspot regions suddenly connect, converting large amounts of magnetic energy into thermal energy. The energy heats gas on the sun to millions of degrees Celsius, causing the gas to erupt into space. These eruptions are called **solar flares.**

Solar Wind Solar flares can greatly increase the solar wind from the corona, resulting in an increase in the number of particles reaching Earth's upper atmosphere. Normally, Earth's atmosphere and magnetic field block these particles. However, near the North and South poles, the particles can enter Earth's atmosphere, where they create powerful electric currents that cause gas molecules in the atmosphere to glow. The result is rippling sheets of light in the sky called auroras.

Solar wind particles can also affect Earth's magnetic field, causing magnetic storms. Magnetic storms sometimes disrupt radio, telephone, and television signals. Magnetic storms can also cause electrical power problems.

FIGURE 12
Auroras
Auroras such as this can occur near Earth's poles when particles of the solar wind strike gas molecules in Earth's upper atmosphere.

Reading Checkpoint **What is a prominence?**

Section 2 **Assessment**

S 8.2.g, 8.4.b,
E-LA: Reading 8.1.2

Vocabulary Skill Greek Word Origins Use Greek word origins to explain the difference between *photosphere* and *chromosphere*.

Reviewing Key Concepts

1. **a. Defining** What is nuclear fusion?
   b. Explaining Where is the sun's energy produced?
   c. Sequencing Describe the steps involved in the process of nuclear fusion within the sun.
2. **a. Listing** List the layers of the sun's interior and atmosphere, starting from the center.
   b. Identifying Which of the sun's layers produces its visible light?
   c. Relating Cause and Effect Why is it usually impossible to see the sun's corona from Earth?

3. **a. Describing** Describe three features found on or just above the sun's surface.
   b. Relating Cause and Effect Why do sunspots look darker than the rest of the sun's photosphere?

Lab zone **At-Home Activity**

Sun Symbols As the source of heat and light, the sun is an important symbol in many cultures. With family members, look around your home and neighborhood for illustrations of the sun on signs, flags, clothing, and in artwork. Which parts of the sun's atmosphere do the illustrations show?

Stormy Sunspots

S 8.4, 8.9.e

Problem

How are magnetic storms on Earth related to sunspot activity?

Skills Focus

graphing, interpreting data

Materials

- graph paper
- ruler

Procedure

1. Use the data in the table of Annual Sunspot Numbers to make a line graph of sunspot activity between 1972 and 2002.

2. On the graph, label the x-axis "Year." Use a scale with 2-year intervals, from 1972 to 2002.

3. Label the y-axis "Sunspot Number." Use a scale of 0 through 160 in intervals of 10.

4. Graph a point for the Sunspot Number for each year.

5. Complete your graph by drawing lines to connect the points.

Analyze and Conclude

1. **Graphing** Based on your graph, which years had the highest Sunspot Number? The lowest Sunspot Number?

2. **Interpreting Data** How often does the cycle of maximum and minimum activity repeat?

3. **Interpreting Data** When was the most recent maximum sunspot activity? The most recent minimum sunspot activity?

4. **Inferring** Compare your sunspot graph with the magnetic storms graph. What relationship can you infer between periods of high sunspot activity and magnetic storms? Explain.

Annual Sunspot Numbers			
Year	Sunspot Number	Year	Sunspot Number
1972	68.9	1988	100.2
1974	34.5	1990	142.6
1976	12.6	1992	94.3
1978	92.5	1994	29.9
1980	154.6	1996	8.6
1982	115.9	1998	64.3
1984	45.9	2000	119.6
1986	13.4	2002	104.0

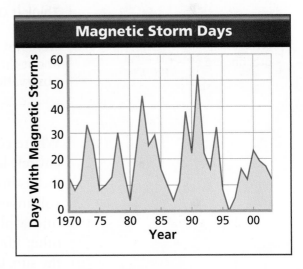

5. **Communicating** Suppose you are an engineer working for an electric power company. Write a brief summary of your analysis of sunspot data. Explain the relationship between sunspot number and electrical disturbances on Earth.

More to Explore

Using the pattern of sunspot activity you found, predict the number of peaks you would expect in the next 30 years. Around which years would you expect the peaks to occur?

The Inner Planets

CALIFORNIA
Standards Focus

S 8.4.e Students know the appearance, general composition, relative position and size, and motion of objects in the solar system, including planets, planetary satellites, comets, and asteroids.

- What characteristics do the inner planets have in common?

- What are the main characteristics that distinguish each of the inner planets?

Key Terms

- terrestrial planets
- greenhouse effect

Lab zone **Standards Warm-Up**

How Does Mars Look From Earth?

1. Work in pairs. On a sheet of paper, draw a circle 20 cm across to represent Mars. Draw about 100 small lines, each about 1 cm long, at random places inside the circle.

2. Have your partner look at your drawing of Mars from the other side of the room. Your partner should draw what he or she sees.

3. Compare your original drawing with what your partner drew. Then look at your own drawing from across the room.

Think It Over

Observing Did your partner draw any connecting lines that were not actually on your drawing? What can you conclude about the accuracy of descriptions of other planets based on observations from Earth?

Where could you find a planet whose atmosphere has almost entirely leaked away into space? How about a planet whose surface is hot enough to melt lead? And how about a planet with volcanoes higher than any on Earth? Finally, where could you find a planet with oceans of water brimming with fish and other life? These are descriptions of the four planets closest to the sun, known as the inner planets.

Earth and the three other inner planets—Mercury, Venus, and Mars—are more similar to each other than they are to the five outer planets. **The four inner planets are small and dense and have rocky surfaces.** The inner planets are often called the **terrestrial planets,** from the Latin word *terra,* which means "Earth." Figure 13 summarizes data about the inner planets.

Earth

As you can see in Figure 14, Earth has three main layers—a crust, a mantle, and a core. The crust includes the solid, rocky surface. Under the crust is the mantle, a layer of hot molten rock. When volcanoes erupt, this hot material rises to the surface. Earth has a dense core made of mainly iron and nickel. The outer core is liquid, but the inner core is solid.

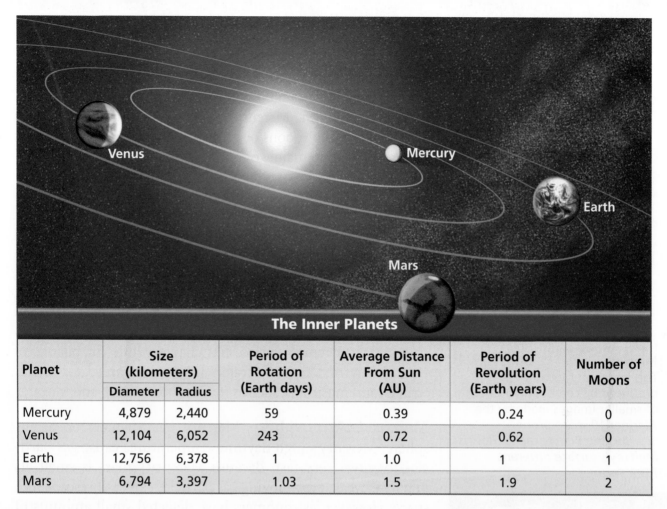

The Inner Planets

Planet	Size (kilometers)		Period of Rotation (Earth days)	Average Distance From Sun (AU)	Period of Revolution (Earth years)	Number of Moons
	Diameter	Radius				
Mercury	4,879	2,440	59	0.39	0.24	0
Venus	12,104	6,052	243	0.72	0.62	0
Earth	12,756	6,378	1	1.0	1	1
Mars	6,794	3,397	1.03	1.5	1.9	2

Water 🌐 **Earth is unique in our solar system in having liquid water at its surface.** In fact, most of Earth's surface, about 70 percent, is covered with water. Perhaps our planet should be called "Water" instead of "Earth"! Earth has a suitable temperature range for water to exist as a liquid, gas, or solid. Water is important in shaping Earth's surface, wearing it down and changing its appearance over time.

Atmosphere Earth has enough gravity to hold on to most gases. These gases make up Earth's atmosphere, which extends more than 100 kilometers above its surface. Other planets in the solar system have atmospheres too, but only Earth has an atmosphere that is rich in oxygen. The oxygen you need to live makes up about 20 percent of Earth's atmosphere. Nearly all the rest is nitrogen, with small amounts of other gases such as argon and carbon dioxide. The atmosphere also includes varying amounts of water in the form of a gas. Water in a gaseous form is called water vapor.

 **Reading Checkpoint** What two gases make up most of Earth's atmosphere?

FIGURE 13
The inner planets take up only a small part of the solar system. Note that sizes and distances are not drawn to scale.

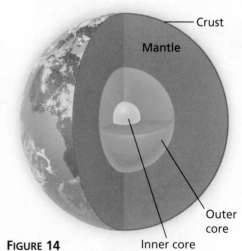

FIGURE 14
Earth's Layers
Earth has a solid, rocky surface.
Interpreting Diagrams *What are Earth's three main layers?*

Size of Mercury
compared to Earth

Mercury

Mercury is the smallest terrestrial planet and the planet closest to the sun. Mercury is not much larger than Earth's moon and has no moons of its own. The interior of Mercury is probably made up mainly of the dense metal iron.

Exploring Mercury Because Mercury is so close to the sun, it is hard to see from Earth. Much of what astronomers know about Mercury's surface came from a single probe, *Mariner 10*. It flew by Mercury three times in 1974 and 1975. Two new missions to Mercury are planned. The first of these, called *MESSENGER*, is scheduled to go into orbit around Mercury in 2011.

Mariner 10's photographs show that Mercury has many flat plains and craters on its surface. The large number of craters shows that Mercury's surface has changed little for billions of years. Many of Mercury's craters have been named for artists, writers, and musicians, such as the composers Bach and Mozart.

Mercury's Atmosphere Mercury has virtually no atmosphere. Mercury's high daytime temperatures cause gas particles to move very fast. Because Mercury's mass is small, its gravity is weak. Fast-moving gas particles can easily escape into space. However, astronomers have detected small amounts of sodium and other gases around Mercury.

Mercury is a planet of extremes, with a greater temperature range than any other planet in the solar system. It is so close to the sun that during the day, the side facing the sun reaches temperatures of 430°C. Because Mercury has almost no atmosphere, at night its heat escapes into space. Then its temperature drops below −170°C.

 **Reading Checkpoint** Compare daytime and nighttime temperatures on Mercury.

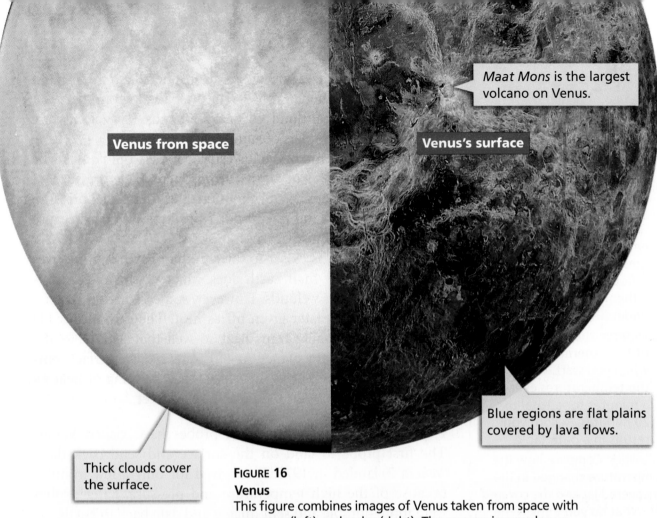

Maat Mons is the largest volcano on Venus.

Venus from space

Venus's surface

Blue regions are flat plains covered by lava flows.

Thick clouds cover the surface.

FIGURE 16
Venus
This figure combines images of Venus taken from space with a camera (left) and radar (right). The camera image shows Venus's thick atmosphere. Radar is able to penetrate Venus's clouds to reveal the surface. Both images are false color.

Venus

You can sometimes see Venus in the west just after sunset. When Venus is visible in that part of the sky, it is known as the "evening star," though of course it really isn't a star at all. At other times, Venus rises in the east before the sun in the morning. Then it is known as the "morning star."

Venus is so similar in size and mass to Earth that it is sometimes called "Earth's twin." ☁ **Venus's density and internal structure are similar to Earth's. But, in other ways, Venus and Earth are very different.**

Venus's Rotation Venus takes about 7.5 Earth months to revolve around the sun. It takes about 8 months for Venus to rotate once on its axis. Thus, Venus rotates so slowly that its day is longer than its year! Oddly, Venus rotates from east to west, the opposite direction from most other planets and moons. Astronomers hypothesize that this unusual rotation was caused by a very large object that struck Venus billions of years ago. Such a collision could have caused Venus to change its direction of rotation. Another hypothesis is that Venus's thick atmosphere could have somehow altered its rotation.

Size of Venus compared to Earth

Go Online

SCLINKS NSTA

For: Links on the planets
Visit: www.SciLinks.org
Web Code: scn-0633

Venus's Atmosphere Venus's atmosphere is so thick that it is always cloudy there. From Earth or space, astronomers can see only a smooth cloud cover over Venus. The clouds are made mostly of droplets of sulfuric acid.

If you could stand on Venus's surface, you would quickly be crushed by the weight of its atmosphere. The pressure of Venus's atmosphere is 90 times greater than the pressure of Earth's atmosphere. You couldn't breathe on Venus because its atmosphere is mostly carbon dioxide.

Because Venus is closer to the sun than Earth is, it receives more solar energy than Earth does. Much of this radiation is reflected by Venus's clouds. However, some radiation reaches the surface and is later given off as heat. The carbon dioxide in Venus's atmosphere traps heat so well that Venus has the hottest surface of any planet. At 460°C, its average surface temperature is hot enough to melt lead. This trapping of heat by the atmosphere is called the **greenhouse effect**.

Exploring Venus Many space probes have visited Venus. The first probe to land on the surface and send back data, *Venera 7*, landed in 1970. It survived for only a few minutes because of the high temperature and pressure. Later probes were more durable and sent images and data back to Earth.

The *Magellan* probe reached Venus in 1990, carrying radar instruments. Radar works through clouds, so *Magellan* was able to map nearly the entire surface. The *Magellan* data confirmed that Venus is covered with rock. Venus's surface has many volcanoes and broad plains formed by lava flows.

✓ Reading Checkpoint What are Venus's clouds made of?

FIGURE 17
Maat Mons
Scientists used radar data to develop this computer image of the giant volcano *Maat Mons*. The heights of the mountains are exaggerated to make them stand out.

Mars

Mars is called the "red planet." When you see it in the sky, it has a slightly reddish tinge. This reddish color is due to the breakdown of iron-rich rocks, which creates a rusty dust that covers much of Mars's surface.

Mars's Atmosphere The atmosphere of Mars is more than 95 percent carbon dioxide. It is similar in composition to Venus's atmosphere, but much thinner. You could walk around on Mars, but you would have to wear an airtight suit and carry your own oxygen, like a scuba diver. Mars has few clouds, and they are very thin compared to clouds on Earth. Mars's transparent atmosphere allows people on Earth to view its surface with a telescope. Temperatures on the surface range from −140°C to 20°C.

Water on Mars In 1877, an Italian astronomer named Giovanni Schiaparelli (sky ah puh REL ee) announced that he had seen long, straight lines on Mars. He called them *canale*, or channels. In the 1890s and early 1900s, Percival Lowell, an American astronomer, convinced many people that these lines were canals that had been built by intelligent Martians to carry water. Astronomers now know that Lowell was mistaken. There are no canals on Mars.

Images of Mars taken from space do show a variety of features that look as if they were made by ancient streams, lakes, or floods. There are huge canyons and features that look like the remains of ancient coastlines. 🌐 **Scientists think that a large amount of liquid water flowed on Mars's surface in the distant past.** Scientists infer that Mars must have been much warmer and had a thicker atmosphere at that time.

At present, liquid water cannot exist for long on Mars's surface. Mars's atmosphere is so thin that any liquid water would quickly turn into a gas. So where is Mars's water now? Some of it is located in the planet's two polar ice caps, which contain frozen water and carbon dioxide. A small amount also exists as water vapor in Mars's atmosphere. Some water vapor has probably escaped into space. But scientists think that a large amount of water may still be frozen underground.

Size of Mars compared to Earth

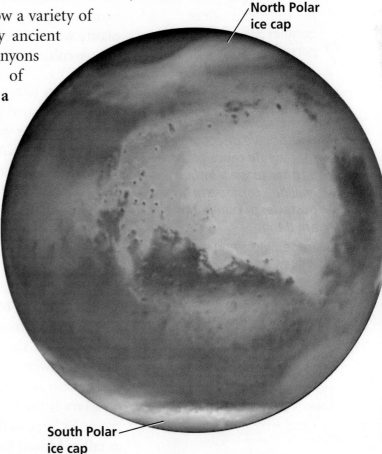

FIGURE 18
Mars
Because of its thin atmosphere and its distance from the sun, Mars is quite cold. Mars has ice caps at both poles. **Inferring** *Why is it easy to see Mars's surface from space?*

North Polar ice cap

South Polar ice cap

Remote Control

How hard is it to explore another planet by remote control?

1. Tape a piece of paper over the front of a pair of goggles. Have your partner put them on.

2. 🖐 Walk behind your partner and direct him or her to another part of the room. **CAUTION:** *Do not give directions that would cause your partner to walk into a wall or a corner, trip on an obstacle, or bump into anything.*

3. Trade places and repeat Steps 1 and 2.

Drawing Conclusions Which verbal directions worked best? How quickly could you move? How is this activity similar to the way engineers have moved rovers on Mars? How fast do you think such a rover could move?

Seasons on Mars Because Mars has a tilted axis, it has seasons just as Earth does. During the Martian winter, an ice cap grows larger as a layer of frozen carbon dioxide covers it. Because the northern and southern hemispheres have opposite seasons, one ice cap grows while the other one shrinks.

As the seasons change on the dusty surface of Mars, windstorms arise and blow the dust around. Since the dust is blown off some regions, these regions look darker. A hundred years ago, some people thought these regions looked darker because plants were growing there. Astronomers now realize that the darker color is often just the result of windstorms.

Exploring Mars Many space probes have visited Mars. The first ones seemed to show that Mars is barren and covered with craters like the moon. Recently, two new probes landed on Mars's surface. NASA's *Spirit* and *Opportunity* rovers explored opposite sides of the planet. They examined a variety of rocks and soil samples. At both locations, the rovers found strong evidence that liquid water was once present. The European Space Agency's *Mars Express* probe orbited overhead, finding clear evidence of frozen water (ice). However, the *Mars Express* lander failed.

Volcanoes on Mars Some regions of Mars have giant volcanoes. Astronomers see signs that lava flowed from the volcanoes in the past, but the volcanoes are not currently active. However, volcanic eruptions may have occurred in some areas within the past few million years. *Olympus Mons* on Mars is the largest volcano in the solar system. It covers a region as large as the state of Missouri and is nearly three times as tall as Mount Everest, the tallest mountain on Earth!

FIGURE 19
Mars's Surface
As the large photo shows, the surface of Mars is rugged and rocky. Mars has many large volcanoes. The volcano *Olympus Mons* (inset) rises about 27 km from the surface. It is the largest volcano in the solar system.

Mars's Moons Mars has two very small, oddly-shaped moons. Phobos, the larger moon, is only 27 kilometers in diameter, about the distance a car can travel on the highway in 20 minutes. Deimos is even smaller, only 15 kilometers in diameter. Like Earth's moon, Phobos and Deimos are covered with craters. Phobos, which is much closer to Mars than Deimos is, is slowly spiraling down toward Mars. Astronomers predict that Phobos will smash into Mars in about 40 million years.

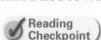 **Reading Checkpoint** **How many moons does Mars have? What are their names?**

Section 3 Assessment

S 8.4.e, ELA: Writing 8.2.0, Reading 8.2.0

Target Reading Skill Create Outlines Use your outline of this section to help answer the following questions.

Reviewing Key Concepts

1. a. **Listing** List the four inner planets in order of size, from smallest to largest.
   b. **Comparing and Contrasting** How are the four inner planets similar to one another?
2. a. **Describing** Describe an important characteristic of each inner planet.
   b. **Comparing and Contrasting** Compare the atmospheres of the four inner planets.
   c. **Relating Cause and Effect** Venus is much farther from the sun than Mercury is. Yet average temperatures on Venus's surface are much higher than those on Mercury. Explain why.

Writing in Science

Travel Brochure Select one of the inner planets other than Earth. Design a travel brochure for your selected planet, including basic facts and descriptions of places of interest. Also include a few sketches or photos to go along with your text.

Space Exploration— Is It Worth the Cost?

Imagine that your spacecraft has just landed on the moon or on Mars. You've spent years planning for this moment. Canyons, craters, plains, and distant mountains stretch out before you. Perhaps a group of scientists has already begun construction of a permanent outpost. You check your spacesuit and prepare to step out onto the rocky surface.

Is such a trip likely? Would it be worthwhile? How much is space flight really worth to human society? Scientists and public officials have already started to debate such questions. Space exploration can help us learn more about the universe. But exploration can be risky and expensive. Sending people into space costs billions of dollars and risks the lives of astronauts. How can we balance the costs and benefits of space exploration?

▼ **Moon Landing**
A rocket is preparing to dock with a lander on the moon's surface in this imaginative artwork.

The Issues

Should Humans Travel Into Space?

Many Americans think that Neil Armstrong's walk on the moon in 1969 was one of the great moments in history. Learning how to keep people alive in space has led to improvements in everyday life. Safer equipment for firefighters, easier ways to package frozen food, and effective heart monitors have all come from space program research.

What Are the Alternatives?

Space exploration can involve a project to establish a colony on the moon or Mars. It also can involve a more limited use of scientific instruments near Earth, such as the Hubble Space Telescope. Instead of sending people, we could send space probes like *Cassini* to other planets.

◄ Lunar Outpost
A mining operation on the moon is shown in this imaginative artwork. Such a facility may someday harvest oxygen from the moon's soil.

◄ Lunar Module
This artwork shows a futuristic vehicle that may one day be used to explore the moon and Mars. The vehicle serves as a combination lander, rover, and habitat for astronauts.

Is Human Space Exploration Worth the Cost?

Scientists who favor human travel into space say that only people can collect certain kinds of information. They argue that the technologies developed for human space exploration will have many applications on Earth. But no one knows if research in space really provides information more quickly than research that can be done on Earth. Many critics of human space exploration think that other needs are more important. One United States senator said, "Every time you put money into the space station, there is a dime that won't be available for our children's education or for medical research."

You Decide

1. Identify the Problem
In your own words, list the various costs and benefits of space exploration.

2. Analyze the Options
Make a chart of three different approaches to space exploration: sending humans to the moon or another planet, doing only Earth-based research, and one other option. What are the benefits and drawbacks of each of these approaches?

3. Find a Solution
Imagine that you are a member of Congress who has to vote on a new budget. There is a fixed amount of money to spend, so you have to decide which needs are most important. Make a list of your top ten priorities. Explain your decisions.

For: More on space exploration
Visit: PHSchool.com
Web Code: cfh-5030

The Outer Planets

CALIFORNIA
Standards Focus

S 8.4.e Students know the appearance, general composition, relative position and size, and motion of objects in the solar system, including planets, planetary satellites, comets, and asteroids.

- What characteristics do the gas giants have in common?

- What characteristics distinguish each of the outer planets?

Key Terms
- gas giant
- ring

Lab zone Standards **Warm-Up**

How Big Are the Planets?

The table shows the diameters of the outer planets compared to Earth. For example, Jupiter's diameter is about 11 times Earth's diameter.

Planet	Diameter (Earth = 1)
Earth	1.0
Jupiter	11.2
Saturn	9.4
Uranus	4.0
Neptune	3.9

1. Measure the diameter of a quarter in millimeters. Trace the quarter to represent Earth.

2. If Earth were the size of a quarter, calculate how large Jupiter would be. Now draw a circle to represent Jupiter.

3. Repeat Step 2 for each of the other planets in the table.

Think It Over

Classifying List the outer planets in order from largest to smallest. What is the largest outer planet?

Imagine you are in a spaceship approaching Jupiter. You'll quickly discover that Jupiter is very different from the terrestrial planets. The most obvious difference is Jupiter's great size. Jupiter is so large that more than 1,300 Earths could fit within it!

As your spaceship enters Jupiter's atmosphere, you encounter thick, colorful bands of clouds. Next, you sink into a denser and denser mixture of hydrogen and helium gas. Eventually, if the enormous pressure of the atmosphere does not crush your ship, you'll reach an incredibly deep "ocean" of liquid hydrogen and helium. But where exactly is Jupiter's surface? Surprisingly, there isn't a solid surface. Like the other giant planets, Jupiter has no real surface, just a core buried deep within the planet.

◄ An illustration of the space probe *Galileo* approaching the cloud-covered atmosphere of Jupiter.

The Outer Planets and Pluto

Planet or Dwarf Planet	Size (kilometers)		Period of Rotation (Earth days)	Average Distance From Sun (AU)	Period of Revolution (Earth years)	Number of Moons
	Diameter	Radius				
Jupiter	143,000	71,490	0.41	5.2	12	63+
Saturn	120,500	60,270	0.45	9.6	29	47+
Uranus	51,120	25,560	0.72	19.2	84	27+
Neptune	49,530	24,760	0.67	30.0	164	13+
Pluto	2,390	1,200	6.4	39.2	248	3

Gas Giants and Pluto

Jupiter and the other planets farthest from the sun are called the outer planets. 🔊 **The four outer planets—Jupiter, Saturn, Uranus, and Neptune—are much larger and more massive than Earth, and they do not have solid surfaces.** Because these four planets are all so large, they are often called the **gas giants.** Figure 20 provides information about these planets. It also includes Pluto, which is now classified as a dwarf planet.

Like the sun, the gas giants have atmospheres composed mainly of hydrogen and helium. Because they are so massive, the gas giants exert a much stronger gravitational force than the terrestrial planets. Gravity keeps the giant planets' gases from escaping, so they have thick atmospheres. Despite the name "gas giant," much of the hydrogen and helium is actually in liquid form because of the enormous pressure inside the planets. The outer layers are extremely cold because of their great distance from the sun. Temperatures increase greatly within the planets.

All the gas giants have many moons. In addition, each of the gas giants is surrounded by a set of rings. A **ring** is a thin disk of small particles of ice and rock.

FIGURE 20
The outer planets are much farther apart than the inner planets. Pluto is now considered to be a dwarf planet. Note that planet sizes and distances are not drawn to scale. *Observing Which outer planet has the most moons?*

For: More on the planets
Visit: PHSchool.com
Web Code: ced-5034

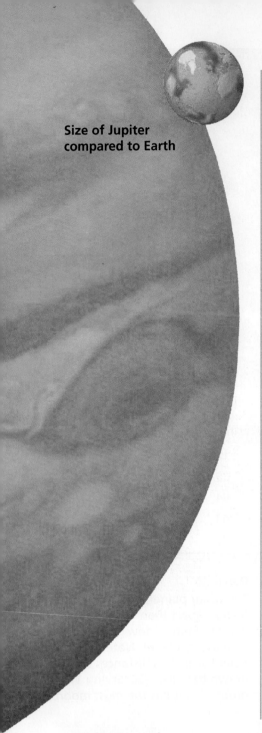

Size of Jupiter compared to Earth

Jupiter

Jupiter is the largest and most massive planet. Jupiter's enormous mass dwarfs the other planets. In fact, its mass is about $2\frac{1}{2}$ times that of all the other planets combined!

Jupiter's Atmosphere Like all of the gas giants, Jupiter has a thick atmosphere made up mainly of hydrogen and helium. An especially interesting feature of Jupiter's atmosphere is its Great Red Spot, a storm that is larger than Earth! The storm's swirling winds blow hundreds of kilometers per hour, similar to a hurricane. But hurricanes on Earth weaken quickly as they pass over land. On Jupiter, there is no land to weaken the huge storm. The Great Red Spot, which was first observed in the mid-1600s, shows no signs of going away soon.

Jupiter's Structure Astronomers think that Jupiter, like the other giant planets, may have a dense core of rock and iron at its center. As shown in Figure 21, a thick mantle of liquid hydrogen and helium surrounds this core. Because of the crushing weight of Jupiter's atmosphere, the pressure at Jupiter's core is estimated to be about 30 million times greater than the pressure at Earth's surface.

Jupiter's Moons Recall that Galileo discovered Jupiter's four largest moons. These moons, which are highlighted in Figure 22, are named Io (EYE oh), Europa, Ganymede, and Callisto. All four are larger than Earth's own moon. However, they are very different from one another. Since Galileo's time, astronomers have discovered dozens of additional moons orbiting Jupiter. Many of these are small moons that have been found in the last few years thanks to improved technology.

 **Reading Checkpoint** What is Jupiter's atmosphere composed of?

Hydrogen and helium gas

Liquid hydrogen and helium

Liquid "ices" such as water and methane

Rocky core

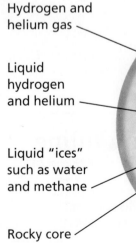

FIGURE 21
Jupiter's Structure
Jupiter is composed mainly of the elements hydrogen and helium. Although Jupiter is often called a "gas giant," much of it is actually liquid. **Comparing and Contrasting** *How does the structure of Jupiter differ from that of a terrestrial planet?*

FIGURE 22
Jupiter's Moons
The astronomer Galileo discovered Jupiter's four largest moons. These images are not shown to scale.
Interpreting Photographs *Which is the largest of Jupiter's moons?*

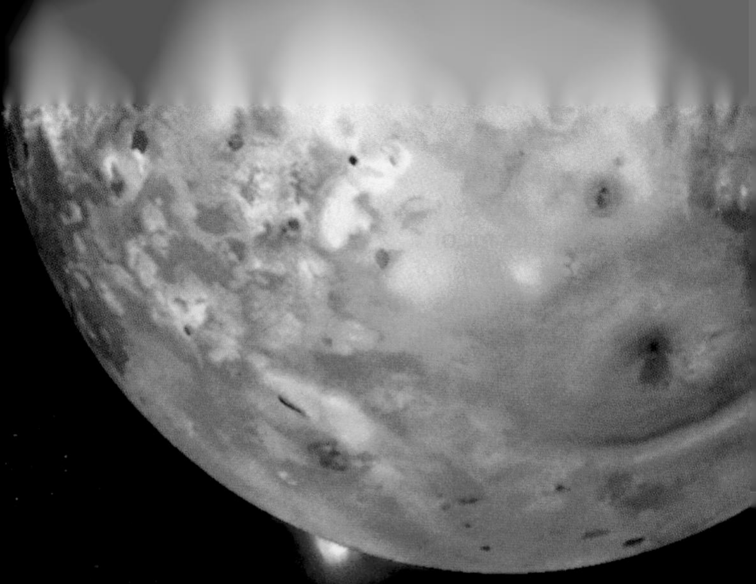

Callisto's surface is icy and covered with craters. ▼

▲ Io's surface is covered with large, active volcanoes. An eruption of sulfur lava can be seen near the bottom of this photo. Sulfur gives Io its unusual colors.

Ganymede is the largest moon in the solar system. It is larger than either Mercury or Pluto. ▼

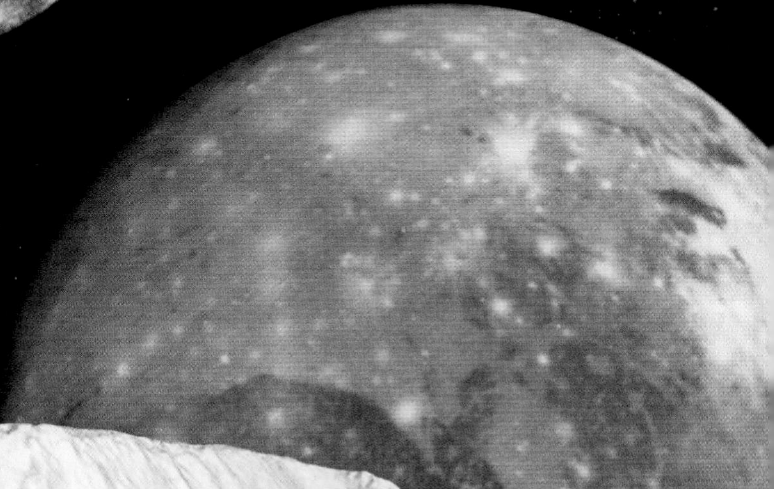

Europa ▼

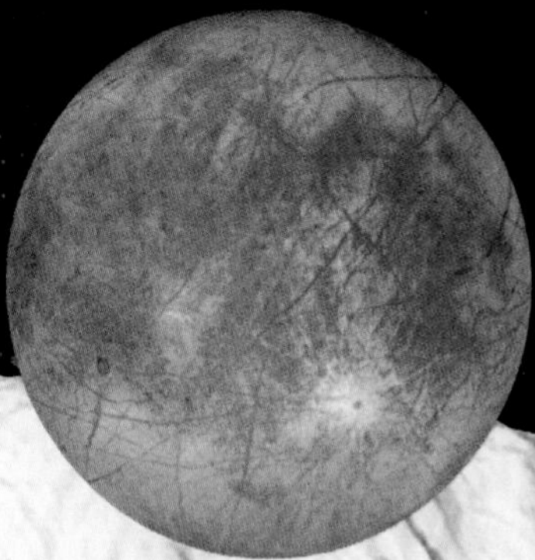

Astronomers suspect that Europa's icy crust covers an ocean of liquid water underneath. This illustration shows Europa's icy surface.

FIGURE 23
Exploring Saturn
The *Cassini* probe is exploring Saturn and its moons.
Observing *Why might it be hard to see Saturn's rings when their edges are facing Earth?*

Size of Saturn compared to Earth

Saturn

The second-largest planet in the solar system is Saturn. The *Voyager* probes showed that Saturn, like Jupiter, has a thick atmosphere made up mainly of hydrogen and helium. Saturn's atmosphere also contains clouds and storms, but they are less dramatic than those on Jupiter. Saturn is the only planet whose average density is less than that of water.

Saturn's Rings When Galileo first looked at Saturn with a telescope, he could see something sticking out on the sides. But he didn't know what it was. A few decades later, an astronomer using a better telescope discovered that Saturn had rings around it. These rings are not solid. They are made of chunks of ice and rock, each traveling in its own orbit around Saturn.

Saturn has the most spectacular rings of any planet. From Earth, it looks as though Saturn has only a few rings and that they are divided from each other by narrow, dark regions. The *Voyager* spacecraft discovered that each of these obvious rings is divided into many thinner rings. Saturn's rings are broad and thin, like a compact disc.

Saturn's Moons Saturn's largest moon, Titan, is larger than the planet Mercury. Titan was discovered in 1665 but was known only as a point of light until the *Voyager* probes flew by. The probes showed that Titan has an atmosphere so thick that little light can pass through it. Four other moons of Saturn are each over 1,000 kilometers in diameter.

 **Reading Checkpoint** What are Saturn's rings made of?

Lab zone **Skills Activity**

Making Models

1. Use a plastic foam sphere 8 cm in diameter to represent Saturn.

2. Use an overhead transparency to represent Saturn's rings. Cut a circle 18 cm in diameter out of the transparency. Cut a hole 9 cm in diameter out of the center of the circle.

3. Stick five toothpicks into Saturn, spaced equally around its equator. Put the transparency on the toothpicks and tape it to them. Sprinkle baking soda on the transparency.

4. Use a peppercorn to represent Titan. Place the peppercorn 72 cm away from Saturn on the same plane as the rings.

5. What do the particles of baking soda represent?

Size of Uranus
compared to Earth

Uranus

Although the gas giant Uranus (YOOR uh nus) is about four times the diameter of Earth, it is still much smaller than Jupiter and Saturn. Uranus is twice as far from the sun as Saturn, so it is much colder. Uranus looks blue-green because of traces of methane in its atmosphere. Like the other gas giants, Uranus is surrounded by a group of thin, flat rings, although they are much darker than Saturn's rings.

Discovery of Uranus In 1781, Uranus became the first new planet discovered since ancient times. Astronomer William Herschel, in England, found a fuzzy object in the sky that did not look like a star. At first he thought it might be a comet, but it soon proved to be a planet beyond Saturn. The discovery made Herschel famous and started an era of active solar system study.

Exploring Uranus About 200 years after Herschel's discovery, *Voyager 2* arrived at Uranus and sent back close-up views of that planet. Images from *Voyager 2* show only a few clouds on Uranus's surface. But even these few clouds allowed astronomers to calculate that Uranus rotates in about 17 hours.

 Uranus's axis of rotation is tilted at an angle of about 90 degrees from the vertical. Viewed from Earth, Uranus is rotating from top to bottom instead of from side to side, the way most of the other planets do. Uranus's rings and moons rotate around this tilted axis. Astronomers think that billions of years ago Uranus was hit by an object that knocked it on its side.

Uranus's Moons Photographs from *Voyager 2* show that Uranus's five largest moons have icy, cratered surfaces. The craters show that rocks from space have hit the moons. Uranus's moons also have lava flows on their surfaces, suggesting that material has erupted from inside each moon. *Voyager 2* images revealed 10 moons that had never been seen before. Recently, astronomers discovered several more moons, for a total of at least 27.

 **Reading Checkpoint** Who discovered Uranus?

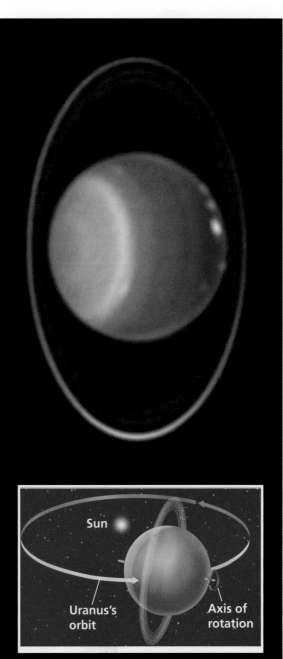

Sun

Uranus's orbit

Axis of rotation

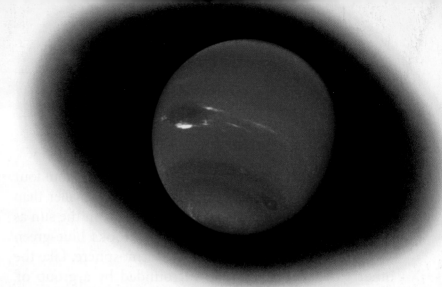

FIGURE 25
Neptune
The Great Dark Spot was a giant storm in Neptune's atmosphere. White clouds, probably made of methane ice crystals, can also be seen in the photo.

Size of Neptune compared to Earth

Circumference

To calculate the circumference of a circle, use this formula:

$$C = 2\pi r$$

In the formula, $\pi \approx 3.14$, and r is the circle's radius, which is the distance from the center of the circle to its edge. The same formula can be used to calculate the circumference of planets, which are nearly spherical.

Neptune's radius at its equator is about 24,760 km. Calculate its circumference.

$C = 2\pi r$

$= 2.00 \times 3.14 \times 24,760$ km

$= 156,000$ km

Practice Problem Saturn's radius is about 60,270 km. What is its circumference?

Neptune

Neptune is even farther from the sun than Uranus. In some ways, the two planets look like twins. They are similar in size and color. **Neptune is a cold, blue planet. Its atmosphere contains visible clouds.** Scientists think that Neptune, shown in Figure 25, is slowly shrinking, causing its interior to heat up. As this energy rises toward Neptune's surface, it produces clouds and storms in the planet's atmosphere.

Discovery of Neptune Neptune was discovered as a result of a mathematical prediction. Astronomers noted that Uranus was not quite following the orbit predicted for it. They hypothesized that the gravity of an unseen planet was affecting Uranus's orbit. By 1846, mathematicians in England and France had calculated the orbit of this unseen planet. Shortly thereafter, an observer saw an unknown object in the predicted area of the sky. It was the new planet, now called Neptune.

Exploring Neptune In 1989, *Voyager 2* flew by Neptune and photographed a Great Dark Spot about the size of Earth. Like the Great Red Spot on Jupiter, the Great Dark Spot was probably a giant storm. But the storm didn't last long. Images taken five years later showed that the Great Dark Spot was gone. Other, smaller spots and regions of clouds on Neptune also seem to come and go.

Neptune's Moons Astronomers have discovered at least 13 moons orbiting Neptune. The largest moon is Triton, which has a thin atmosphere. The *Voyager* images show that the region near Triton's south pole is covered by nitrogen ice.

 Before they could see Neptune, what evidence led scientists to conclude that it existed?

Size of Pluto compared to Earth

Pluto

Pluto is very different from the gas giants. ✏ **Pluto has a solid surface and is much smaller and denser than the outer planets.** In fact, Pluto is smaller than Earth's moon. Pluto is probably made of a mixture of rock and ice.

Pluto has three known moons. The largest of these, Charon, is more than half of Pluto's size.

Pluto's Orbit Pluto is so far from the sun that it revolves around the sun only once every 248 Earth years. Pluto's orbit is very elliptical, bringing it closer to the sun than Neptune on part of its orbit.

Dwarf Planets Until recently, Pluto was considered to be the ninth planet in our solar system. Pluto was always thought to be something of an oddball because of its small size and unusual orbit. Then, in recent years, astronomers discovered many icy objects beyond Neptune's orbit. Some of these were fairly similar to Pluto in size and makeup. Following the discovery of a body that is even larger and farther from the sun than Pluto, astronomers decided to create a new class of objects called "dwarf planets." A dwarf planet, like a planet, is round and orbits the sun. But unlike a planet, a dwarf planet has not cleared out the neighborhood around its orbit. Astronomers classified Pluto and two other bodies as dwarf planets.

FIGURE 26
Pluto and Charon
The illustration above shows Pluto (lower right) and its moon Charon. Charon is more than half the size of Pluto.

Section 4 Assessment

S 8.4.e, E-LA: Reading 8.2.0, Reviewing Math: 6MG1.1

🔖 **Target Reading Skill** **Create Outlines** Review your outline for this section. What three details did you include under *Gas Giants and Pluto*?

🔑 **Reviewing Key Concepts**

1. a. **Describing** How are the gas giants similar to one another?
   b. **Explaining** Why do all of the gas giants have thick atmospheres?
   c. **Listing** List the outer planets in order of size, from smallest to largest.
   d. **Comparing and Contrasting** Compare the structure of a typical terrestrial planet with that of a gas giant.

2. a. **Describing** Describe an important characteristic of each outer planet that helps to distinguish it from the other outer planets.
   b. **Comparing and Contrasting** How is Pluto different from the gas giants?
   c. **Classifying** Why did astronomers reclassify Pluto as a dwarf planet?

Math **Practice**

3. **Circumference** Jupiter's radius is about 71,490 km. What is its circumference?

Speeding Around the Sun

S 8.4.e, 8.9.a

Problem

How does a planet's distance from the sun affect its period of revolution?

Skills Focus

making models, developing hypotheses, designing experiments

Materials

- string, 1.5 m
- plastic tube, 6 cm
- meter stick
- weight or several washers
- one-hole rubber stopper
- stopwatch or watch with second hand

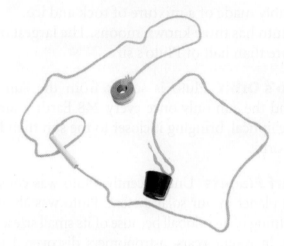

Procedure

PART 1   Modeling Planetary Revolution

1. Copy the data table onto a sheet of paper.

Data Table				
Distance (cm)	Period of Revolution			
	Trial 1	Trial 2	Trial 3	Average
20				
40				
60				

2. Make a model of a planet orbiting the sun by threading the string through the rubber stopper hole. Tie the end of the string to the main part of the string. Pull tightly to make sure that the knot will not become untied.

3. Thread the other end of the string through the plastic tube and tie a weight to that end. Have your teacher check both knots.

4. Pull the string so the stopper is 20 cm away from the plastic tube. Hold the plastic tube in your hand above your head. Keeping the length of string constant, swing the rubber stopper in a circle above your head just fast enough to keep the stopper moving. The circle represents a planet's orbit, and the length of string from the rubber stopper to the plastic tube represents the distance from the sun. **CAUTION:** *Stand away from other students. Make sure the swinging stopper will not hit students or objects. Do not let go of the string.*

5. Have your lab partner time how long it takes for the rubber stopper to make ten complete revolutions. Determine the period for one revolution by dividing the measured time by ten. Record the time in the data table.

6. Repeat Step 5 two more times. Be sure to record each trial in a data table. After the third trial, calculate and record the average period of revolution.

PART 2 **Designing an Experiment**

7. Write your hypothesis for how a planet's period of revolution would be affected by changing its distance from the sun.

8. Design an experiment that will enable you to test your hypothesis. Write the steps you plan to follow to carry out your experiment. As you design your experiment, consider the following factors:
   • What different distances will you test?
   • What variables are involved in your experiment and how will you control them?
   • How many trials will you run for each distance?

9. Have your teacher review your step-by-step plan. After your teacher approves your plan, carry out your experiment.

Analyze and Conclude

1. **Making Models** In your experiment, what represents the planet and what represents the sun?

2. **Making Models** What force does the pull on the string represent?

3. **Interpreting Data** What happened to the period of revolution when you changed the distance in Part 2? Did your experiment prove or disprove your hypothesis?

4. **Drawing Conclusions** Which planets take less time to revolve around the sun—those closer to the sun or those farther away? Use the model to support your answer.

5. **Designing Experiments** As you were designing your experiment, which variable was the most difficult to control? How did you design your procedure to control that variable?

6. **Drawing Conclusions** Did you obtain the same results in all three trials? What do your results indicate about the accuracy of your data?

7. **Communicating** Write a brief summary of your experiment for a science magazine. Describe your hypothesis, procedure, and results in one or two paragraphs.

More to Explore

Develop a hypothesis for how a planet's mass might affect its period of revolution. Then, using a stopper with a different mass, modify the activity to test your hypothesis. Before you swing your stopper, have your teacher check your knots.

5 Comets, Asteroids, and Meteors

S 8.4.e Students know the appearance, general composition, relative position and size, and motion of objects in the solar system, including planets, planetary satellites, comets, and asteroids.

- What are the characteristics of comets?

- Where are most asteroids found?

- What are meteoroids and how do they form?

Key Terms

- comet
- coma
- nucleus
- Kuiper belt
- Oort cloud
- asteroid
- asteroid belt
- meteoroid
- meteor
- meteorite

Standards **Warm-Up**

Which Way Do Comet Tails Point?

1. Form a small ball out of modeling clay to represent a comet.

2. Using a pencil point, push three 10-cm lengths of string into the ball. The strings represent the comet's tail. Stick the ball onto the pencil point, as shown.

3. Hold the ball about 1 m in front of a fan. The air from the fan represents the solar wind. Move the ball toward the fan, away from the fan, and from side to side.
CAUTION: *Keep your fingers away from the fan blades.*

Think It Over
Inferring How does moving the ball affect the direction in which the strings point? What determines which way the tail of a comet points?

Imagine watching a cosmic collision! That's exactly what happened in July 1994. The year before, Eugene and Carolyn Shoemaker and David Levy discovered a comet that had previously broken into pieces near Jupiter. When the comet's orbit passed near Jupiter again, the fragments crashed into Jupiter. On Earth, many people were fascinated to view images of the huge explosions—some were as large as Earth!

As this example shows, the sun, planets, and moons aren't the only objects in the solar system. There are also many smaller objects moving through the solar system. These objects are classified as comets, asteroids, or meteoroids.

FIGURE 27

Structure of a Comet
The main parts of a comet are the nucleus, the coma, and the tail. The nucleus is deep within the coma. Most comets have two tails—a bluish gas tail and a white dust tail.

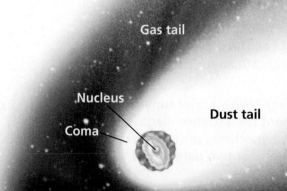

Gas tail

Nucleus

Coma

Dust tail

Comets

One of the most glorious things you can see in the night sky is a comet. But what exactly is a comet? You can think of a **comet** as a "dirty snowball" about the size of a mountain. ⬭ **Comets are loose collections of ice, dust, and small rocky particles whose orbits are usually very long, narrow ellipses.**

A Comet's Head When a comet gets close enough to the sun, the energy in the sunlight turns the ice into gas, releasing gas and dust. Clouds of gas and dust form a fuzzy outer layer called a **coma.** Figure 27 shows the coma and the **nucleus,** the solid inner core of a comet. The brightest part of a comet, the comet's head, is made up of the nucleus and coma.

A Comet's Tail As a comet approaches the sun and heats up, some of its gas and dust stream outward, forming a tail. The name *comet* means "long-haired star" in Greek. Comets often have two tails—a gas tail and a dust tail. The gas tail always points directly away from the sun, as shown in Figure 28.

A comet's tail can be more than 100 million kilometers long and stretch across most of the sky. The material is stretched out very thinly, however, so there is little mass in a comet's tail.

Origin of Comets Most comets originate from one of two distant regions of the solar system: the Kuiper belt and the Oort cloud. The **Kuiper belt** is a doughnut-shaped region that extends from beyond Neptune's orbit to about 100 times Earth's distance from the sun. The **Oort cloud** is a spherical region of comets that surrounds the solar system from about 1,000 to 10,000 times the distance between Pluto and the sun.

 **Reading Checkpoint** What is the Oort cloud?

Go Online
SCi LINKS NSTA

For: Links on comets, asteroids, and meteors
Visit: www.SciLinks.org
Web Code: scn-0635

FIGURE 28
Comet Orbits
Most comets revolve around the sun in very long, narrow orbits. Gas and dust tails form as the comet approaches the sun. **Observing** *What shape is a comet's orbit?*

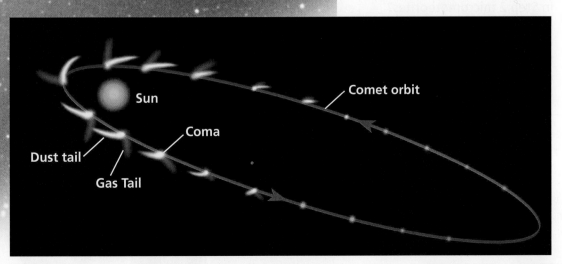

Sun
Comet orbit
Coma
Dust tail
Gas Tail

Micrometeorites

An estimated 300 tons of material from space fall on Earth each day. Much of this is micrometeorites, tiny, dust-sized meteorites.

1. To gather magnetic micrometeorites, tie a string to a small, round magnet and place the magnet in a plastic freezer bag. Lower the magnet close to the ground as you walk along sidewalk cracks, drain spouts, or a parking lot.

2. To gather nonmagnetic and magnetic micrometeorites, cover one side of a few microscope slides with petroleum jelly. Leave the slides outside for several days in a place where they won't be disturbed.

3. Use a microscope to examine the materials you have gathered. Any small round spheres you see are micrometeorites.

Estimating Which technique allows you to gather a more complete sample of micro-meteorites? Were all the particles that were gathered in Step 2 micrometeorites? How could you use the method described in Step 2 to estimate the total number of micrometeorites that land on Earth each day?

Asteroids

Between 1801 and 1807, astronomers discovered four small objects between the orbits of Mars and Jupiter. They named the objects Ceres, Pallas, Juno, and Vesta. Over the next 80 years, astronomers found 300 more. These rocky objects, called **asteroids,** are too small and too numerous to be considered full-fledged planets. ⬤ **Most asteroids revolve around the sun in fairly circular orbits between the orbits of Mars and Jupiter.** This region of the solar system, shown in Figure 29, is called the **asteroid belt.**

Astronomers have discovered more than 100,000 asteroids, and they are constantly finding more. Most asteroids are small—less than a kilometer in diameter. Only Ceres, Pallas, Vesta, and Hygiea are more than 300 kilometers across. The largest asteroid, Ceres, was recently classified as a dwarf planet. At one time, scientists thought that asteroids were the remains of a shattered planet. However, the combined mass of all the asteroids is too small to support this idea. Scientists now hypothesize that the asteroids are leftover pieces of the early solar system that never came together to form a planet.

Some asteroids have very elliptical orbits that bring them closer to the sun than Earth's orbit. Someday, one of these asteroids could hit Earth. One or more large asteroids did hit Earth about 65 million years ago, filling the atmosphere with dust and smoke and blocking out sunlight around the world. Scientists hypothesize that many species of organisms, including the dinosaurs, became extinct as a result.

 Reading Checkpoint **Name the four largest asteroids.**

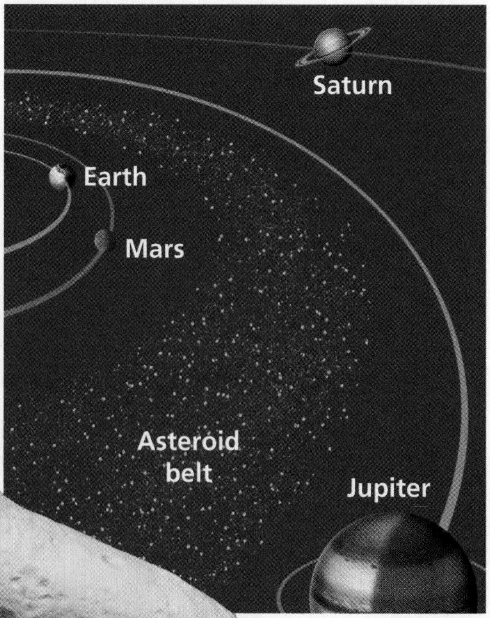

FIGURE 29
Asteroids
The asteroid belt (right) lies between Mars and Jupiter. Asteroids come in many sizes and shapes. The photo below shows the oddly shaped asteroid Eros.

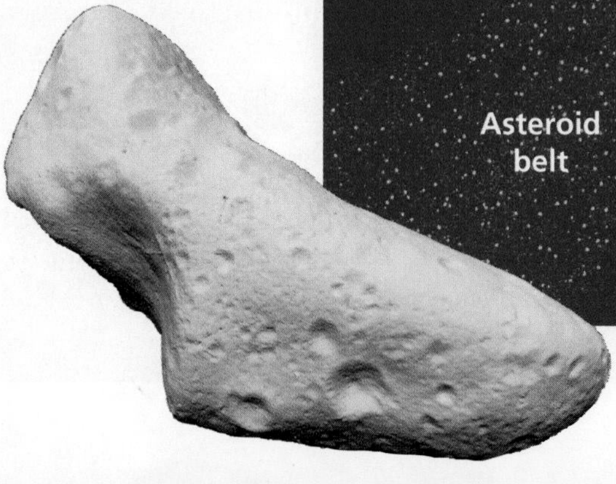

Saturn

Earth

Mars

Asteroid belt

Jupiter

Meteors

It's a perfect night for stargazing—dark and clear. Suddenly, a streak of light flashes across the sky. For an hour or so, you see a streak at least once a minute. You are watching a meteor shower. Meteor showers happen regularly, several times a year.

Even when there is no meteor shower, you often can see meteors if you are far from city lights and the sky is not cloudy. On average, a meteor streaks overhead every 10 minutes.

A **meteoroid** is a chunk of rock or dust in space. **Meteoroids come from comets or asteroids.** Some meteoroids form when asteroids collide in space. Others form when a comet breaks up and creates a cloud of dust that continues to move through the solar system. When Earth passes through one of these dust clouds, bits of dust enter Earth's atmosphere.

When a meteoroid enters Earth's atmosphere, friction with the air creates heat and produces a streak of light in the sky—a **meteor.** If the meteoroid is large enough, it may not disintegrate completely. Meteoroids that pass through the atmosphere and strike Earth's surface are called **meteorites.** The craters on the moon were formed by meteoroids.

FIGURE 30
Meteors
Meteoroids make streaks of light called meteors, like the one above, as they enter the atmosphere.

Reading Checkpoint What is a meteorite?

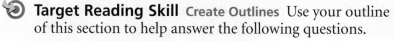
Section 5 Assessment   S 8.4.e, E-LA: Reading 8.2.0

Target Reading Skill Create Outlines Use your outline of this section to help answer the following questions.

Reviewing Key Concepts

1. **a. Defining** What is a comet?
   b. Listing What are the different parts of a comet?
   c. Relating Cause and Effect How does a comet's appearance change as it approaches the sun? Why do these changes occur?
2. **a. Describing** What is an asteroid?
   b. Explaining Where are most asteroids found?
   c. Summarizing How did the asteroids form?
3. **a. Describing** What is a meteoroid?
   b. Explaining What are the main sources of meteoroids?
   c. Comparing and Contrasting What are the differences between meteoroids, meteors, and meteorites?

Lab zone At-Home Activity

Observing Meteors Meteor showers occur regularly on specific dates. (The Perseid meteor shower, for example, occurs around August 12 each year.) Look in the newspaper, on the Internet, or in an almanac for information about the next meteor shower. With adult family members, go outside on that night and look for meteors. Explain to your family what causes the display.

Section 6

Integrating Life Science

Is There Life Beyond Earth?

CALIFORNIA Standards Focus

S 8.4.e Students know the appearance, general composition, relative position and size, and motion of objects in the solar system, including planets, planetary satellites, comets, and asteroids.

S 8.6.c Students know that living organisms have many different kinds of molecules, including small ones, such as water and salt, and very large ones, such as carbohydrates, fats, proteins, and DNA.

- What conditions do living things need to exist on Earth?
- Why do scientists think Mars and Europa are good places to look for signs of life?

Key Term

- extraterrestrial life

Lab zone Standards Warm-Up

Is Yeast Alive or Not?

1. Open a package of yeast and pour it into a bowl.
2. Look at the yeast carefully. Make a list of your observations.
3. Fill the bowl about halfway with warm water (about 20°C). Add a spoonful of sugar. Stir the mixture with the spoon. Wait 5 minutes.
4. Now look at the yeast again and make a list of your observations.

Think It Over

Forming Operational Definitions Which of your observations suggest that yeast is not alive? Which observations suggest that yeast is alive? How can you tell if something is alive?

Most of Antarctica is covered with snow and ice. You would not expect to see rocks lying on top of the whiteness. But surprisingly, people have found rocks lying on Antarctica's ice. When scientists examined the rocks, they found that many were meteorites. A few of these meteorites came from Mars. Astronomers think that meteoroids hitting the surface of Mars blasted chunks of rock into space. Some of these rocks eventually entered Earth's atmosphere and landed on its surface.

In 1996, a team of scientists announced that a meteorite from Mars found in Antarctica has tiny shapes that look like fossils—the remains of ancient life preserved in rock—though much smaller. Most scientists now doubt that the shapes really are fossils. But if they are, it would be a sign that microscopic lifeforms similar to bacteria once existed on Mars. Life other than that on Earth would be called **extraterrestrial life.**

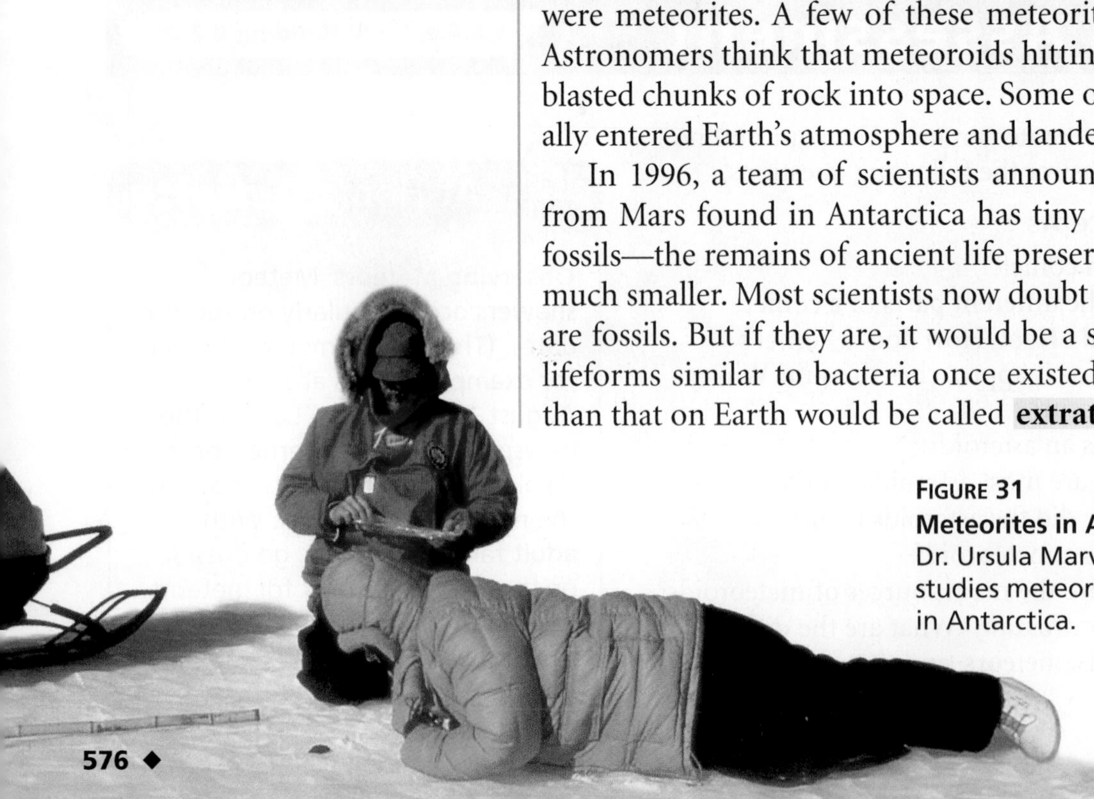

FIGURE 31
Meteorites in Antarctica
Dr. Ursula Marvin (lying down) studies meteorites like this one in Antarctica.

Life on Earth

Sometimes it can be hard to tell whether something is alive or not. But all living things on Earth have several characteristics in common. Living things are made up of one or more cells. Living things take in energy and use it to grow and develop. They reproduce, producing new living things of the same type. Living things also give off waste.

The "Goldilocks" Conditions No one knows whether life exists anywhere other than Earth. Scientists often talk about the conditions needed by "life as we know it." **Earth has liquid water and a suitable temperature range and atmosphere for living things to survive.** Scientists sometimes call these favorable conditions the "Goldilocks" conditions. That is, the temperature is not too hot and not too cold. It is just right. If Earth were much hotter, water would always be a gas—water vapor. If Earth were much colder, water would always be solid ice.

Are these the conditions necessary for life? Or are they just the conditions that Earth's living things happen to need? Scientists have only one example to study: life on Earth. Unless scientists find evidence of life somewhere else, there is no way to answer these questions for certain.

Extreme Conditions Recently, scientists have discovered living things in places where it was once believed that life could not exist. Giant tubeworms have been found under the extremely high pressures at the bottom of the ocean. Single-celled organisms have been found in the near-boiling temperatures of hot springs. Tiny life-forms have been discovered deep inside solid rock. Scientists have even found animals that do not require the energy of sunlight, but instead get their energy from chemicals.

These astounding discoveries show that the range of conditions in which life can exist is much greater than scientists once thought. Could there be life-forms in the solar system that do not need the "Goldilocks" conditions?

 **Reading Checkpoint** What are some characteristics of all living things?

FIGURE 32
Hot Spring
Bacteria that thrive in near-boiling water help to produce the striking colors of Grand Prismatic Spring in Wyoming. **Inferring** *How does studying unusual organisms on Earth help scientists predict what extraterrestrial life might be like?*

Lab zone Skills **Activity**

Communicating You are writing a letter to a friend who lives on another planet. Your friend has never been to Earth and has no idea what the planet is like. Explain in your letter why the conditions on Earth make it an ideal place for living things.

Life Elsewhere in the Solar System?

Recall that Mars is the planet most similar to Earth. That makes Mars the most obvious place to look for living things.

Life on Mars? Spacecraft have found regions on the surface of Mars that look like streambeds with crisscrossing paths of water. Shapes like those shown in Figure 33 were almost certainly formed by flowing water. ⬤ **Since life as we know it requires water, scientists hypothesize that Mars may have once had the conditions needed for life to exist.**

In 1976 twin *Viking* spacecraft reached Mars. Each of the *Viking* landers carried a small laboratory meant to search for life forms. These laboratories tested Mars's air and soil for signs of life. None of these tests showed evidence of life.

More recently, the *Spirit* and *Opportunity* rovers found rocks and other surface features on Mars that were certainly formed by liquid water. However, the rovers were not equipped to search for past or present life.

Interest in life on Mars was increased by a report in 1996 about a meteorite from Mars that may contain fossils. The scientists' report started a huge debate. What were the tube-shaped things in the meteorite? Some scientists have suggested that the tiny shapes found in the meteorite are too small to be the remains of life forms. The shapes may have come from natural processes on Mars.

The most effective way to answer these questions is to send more probes to Mars. Future Mars missions should be able to bring samples of rocks and soil back to Earth for detailed analysis. Scientists may not yet have evidence of life on Mars, but hope is growing that we can soon learn the truth.

 **Reading Checkpoint** What did the *Spirit* and *Opportunity* rovers discover on Mars?

FIGURE 33
Liquid Water on Mars
The river-like patterns on the surface of Mars indicate that liquid water once flowed there.
Applying Concepts *Why does this evidence make it more likely that there may once have been life on Mars?*

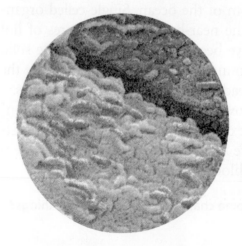

FIGURE 34
Martian Fossils?
This false-color electron microscope image shows tiny fossil-like shapes found in a meteorite from Mars. These structures are less than one-hundredth the width of a human hair.

Life on Europa? Many scientists think that Europa, one of Jupiter's moons, may have the conditions necessary for life to develop. Europa has a smooth, icy crust with giant cracks. Close-up views from the *Galileo* space probe show that Europa's ice has broken up and re-formed, resulting in large twisted blocks of ice. Similar patterns occur in the ice crust over Earth's Arctic Ocean. Scientists hypothesize that there is a liquid ocean under Europa's ice. The water in the ocean could be kept liquid by heat coming from inside Europa. 🔑 **If there is liquid water on Europa, there might also be life.**

How could scientists study conditions under Europa's ice sheet? Perhaps a future space probe might be able to use radar to "see" through Europa's icy crust. After that, robotic probes could be sent to drill through the ice to search for life in the water below.

FIGURE 35
Exploring Europa
Scientists have discussed sending a robotic probe to search for life in the ocean below Europa's icy crust.

Section 6 Assessment

S 8.4.e, 8.6.c,
E-LA: Reading 8.2.0

Target Reading Skill Create Outlines Review your outline. What are two of the main ideas being discussed in this section?

Reviewing Key Concepts

1. **a. Relating Cause and Effect** What conditions does life on Earth need to survive?
   b. Summarizing Why is Earth said to have the "Goldilocks" conditions?
   c. Applying Concepts Do you think there could be life as we know it on Neptune? Explain. (*Hint*: Review Section 4.)

2. **a. Explaining** Why do astronomers think there could be life on Europa?
   b. Identifying Scientists think that in the past Mars may have had the conditions needed for life to exist. What are these conditions? Do they still exist?

   c. Making Generalizations What characteristic do Mars and Europa share with Earth that makes them candidates to support extraterrestrial life?

Lab zone At-Home **Activity**

Make a Message Imagine that scientists have found intelligent extraterrestrial life. With family members, make up a message to send to the extraterrestrials. Remember that they will not understand English, so you should use only symbols and drawings in your message.

🔑 Apply the **BIG Idea** The solar system includes the sun, the planets and their moons, and smaller objects such as comets, asteroids, and meteoroids.

1 Observing the Solar System

🔑 **Key Concepts**   S 8.4.c, 8.4.d

- In a geocentric system, Earth is at the center. In a heliocentric system, Earth and the other planets revolve around the sun.
- Galileo's discoveries supported the heliocentric model. Kepler developed three laws that describe the motions of the planets.
- The solar system consists of the sun, the planets and their moons, and a series of smaller objects that revolve around the sun.

Key Terms
- geocentric • heliocentric • ellipse
- moon • astronomical unit

2 The Sun

🔑 **Key Concepts**   S 8.2.g, 8.4.b

- The sun produces energy through fusion.
- The sun's interior consists of the core, radiation zone, and convection zone. The sun's atmosphere consists of the photosphere, chromosphere, and corona.
- Features on or just above the sun's surface include sunspots, prominences, and solar flares.

Key Terms
- nuclear fusion • core • radiation zone
- convection zone • photosphere
- chromosphere • corona • solar wind
- sunspot • prominence • solar flare

3 The Inner Planets

🔑 **Key Concepts**   S 8.4.e

- The four inner planets are small and dense.
- Earth is unique in our solar system in having liquid water at its surface.
- Mercury is the smallest terrestrial planet.
- Venus's internal structure is similar to Earth's.
- Liquid water flowed on Mars in the distant past.

Key Terms
- terrestrial planets • greenhouse effect

4 The Outer Planets

🔑 **Key Concepts**   S 8.4.e

- Jupiter, Saturn, Uranus, and Neptune are much larger and more massive than Earth, and they do not have solid surfaces.
- Jupiter is the largest and most massive planet in the solar system.
- Saturn has spectacular rings.
- Uranus's axis of rotation is tilted at an angle of about 90 degrees from the vertical.
- Neptune is a cold, blue planet. Its atmosphere contains visible clouds.
- Pluto has a solid surface and is much smaller and denser than the outer planets.

Key Terms
- gas giant • ring

5 Comets, Asteroids, and Meteors

🔑 **Key Concepts**   S 8.4.e

- Comets are loose collections of ice, dust, and small rocky particles whose orbits are usually very long, narrow ellipses.
- Most asteroids revolve around the sun between the orbits of Mars and Jupiter.
- Meteoroids come from comets or asteroids.

Key Terms
- comet • coma • nucleus • Kuiper belt
- Oort cloud • asteroid • asteroid belt
- meteoroid • meteor • meteorite

6 Is There Life Beyond Earth?

🔑 **Key Concepts**   S 8.4.e, 8.6.c

- Earth has liquid water and a suitable temperature range and atmosphere for life.
- Scientists hypothesize that Mars may have once had the conditions for life to exist.
- If there is liquid water on Europa, there might also be life.

Key Term
- extraterrestrial life

Review and Assessment

Target Reading Skill

Create Outlines In your notebook, complete your outline for Section 1 on *Observing the Solar System.*

Observing the Solar System

I. Earth at the Center
   A. Greek Observations
      1. Geocentric—Earth-centered
      2. Geocentric system—Earth at the center of revolving planets and stars
   B. Ptolemy's Model
      1. Planets on small circles that move on bigger circles
      2. Model was incorrect, but accepted for 1,500 years
II. Sun at the Center
   A.

Reviewing Key Terms

Choose the letter of the best answer.

1. Copernicus thought that the solar system was
   a. an ellipse.
   b. a constellation.
   c. geocentric.
   d. heliocentric.

2. The part of the sun where nuclear fusion occurs is the
   a. photosphere.
   b. core.
   c. chromosphere.
   d. corona.

3. Pluto is a(n)
   a. inner planet.
   b. terrestrial planet.
   c. dwarf planet.
   d. gas giant.

4. The region between Mars and Jupiter where many rocky objects are found is the
   a. asteroid belt.
   b. Oort cloud.
   c. convection zone.
   d. Kuiper belt.

5. A meteoroid that reaches Earth's surface is called a(n)
   a. comet.   c. meteor.
   b. meteorite.   d. asteroid.

Complete the following sentences so that your answers clearly explain the key terms.

6. Each planet moves around the sun in an **ellipse,** which is _____ .

7. The **photosphere** is the layer of the sun that _____ .

8. Venus has the hottest surface of any planet because of the **greenhouse effect,** which is _____ .

9. Like the other **gas giants,** Jupiter's characteristics include _____ .

10. Mars and Europa are possible locations where **extraterrestrial life,** which is _____ , might be found.

Writing in Science

News Report Imagine you are on a mission to explore the solar system. Write a brief news report telling the story of your trip from Earth to another terrestrial planet and to a gas giant. Include a description of each planet.

Video Assessment
Discovery Channel School
The Solar System

Review and Assessment

Checking Concepts

11. Describe the contributions Tycho Brahe and Johannes Kepler made to modern astronomy.

12. What is the solar wind?

13. Why does Mercury have very little atmosphere?

14. Why can astronomers see the surface of Mars clearly but not the surface of Venus?

15. What evidence do astronomers have that water once flowed on Mars?

Math Practice

16. Circumference Mars has a radius of 3,397 km at its equator. Find its circumference.

17. Circumference Jupiter has a circumference of about 449,000 km at its equator. Calculate its radius.

Thinking Critically

18. Applying Concepts Explain why Venus is hotter than it would be if it had no atmosphere.

19. Predicting Do you think astronomers have found all of the moons of the outer planets? Explain.

20. Comparing and Contrasting Compare and contrast comets, asteroids, and meteoroids.

21. Classifying Look at the diagram below. Do you think it represents the structure of a terrestrial planet or a gas giant? Explain.

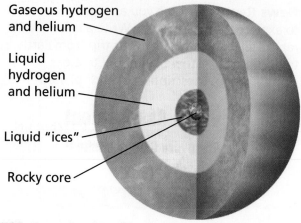

Gaseous hydrogen and helium

Liquid hydrogen and helium

Liquid "ices"

Rocky core

22. Making Generalizations Why would the discovery of liquid water on another planet be important?

Applying Skills

Use the diagram of an imaginary, newly discovered planetary system around Star X to answer Questions 23–25.

The periods of revolution of planets A, B, and C are 75 Earth days, 200 Earth days, and 300 Earth days.

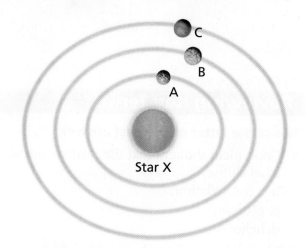

Star X

23. Interpreting Data Which planet in this new planetary system revolves around Star X in the shortest amount of time?

24. Making Models In 150 days, how far will each planet have revolved around Star X? Copy the diagram and sketch the positions of the three planets to find out. How far will each planet have revolved around Star X in 400 days? Sketch their positions.

25. Drawing Conclusions Can Planet C ever be closer to Planet A than to Planet B? Study your drawings to figure this out.

Lab zone Standards Investigation

Performance Assessment Present your scale models of the solar system. Display your data tables showing how you did the calculations and how you checked them for accuracy.

Choose the letter of the best answer.

1. What characteristic do all of the inner planets share?
   A They are larger and more massive than the sun.
   B They have thick atmospheres of hydrogen and helium.
   C They have rocky surfaces.
   D They each have many moons.   **S 8.4.e**

2. Mercury has a daytime temperature of about 430°C and a nighttime temperature below −170°C. What is the best explanation?
   A Mercury has a greenhouse effect.
   B Global warming is occurring on Mercury.
   C Mercury is the closest planet to the sun.
   D Mercury has no real atmosphere.   **S 8.4.e**

3. The process by which the sun produces energy is called
   A combustion.
   B a chemical reaction.
   C nuclear fusion.
   D nuclear fission.   **S 8.4.b**

4. You can see the planets at night because
   A they produce their own light.
   B sunlight reflects from their surfaces.
   C nuclear fusion takes place in their cores.
   D their surfaces are brighter than those of the stars.   **S 8.4.d**

5. The sun remains stable as a result of a balance between the
   A outward pressure of nuclear fission and the inward pull of nuclear fusion.
   B outward pressure of nuclear fusion and the inward pull of gravity.
   C outward pressure of gravity and the inward pull of nuclear fusion.
   D outward pressure of the greenhouse effect and the inward pull of gravity.   **S 8.2.g**

The table below shows data for five planets in our solar system. Use the table and your knowledge of science to answer Questions 6–8.

Planet	Period of Rotation (Earth days)	Period of Revolution (Earth years)	Average Distance From the Sun (AU)
Mars	1.03	1.9	1.5
Jupiter	0.41	12	5.2
Saturn	0.45	29	9.6
Uranus	0.72	84	19.2
Neptune	0.67	164	30.0

6. Which planet has a "day" that is most similar in length to a day on Earth?
   A Mars   B Jupiter
   C Uranus   D Neptune   **S 8.4.e**

7. Light takes about 8 minutes and 20 seconds to travel from the sun to Earth, 1 AU away. About how long does it take light to travel from the sun to Jupiter?
   A 10 minutes   B 25 minutes
   C 43 minutes   D 112 minutes **S 8.4.c**

8. Which of the following conclusions about planets is supported by information in the table?
   A As distance from the sun increases, period of rotation increases.
   B As distance from the sun increases, period of revolution increases.
   C As distance from the sun increases, period of revolution decreases.
   D There is no relationship between distance from the sun and period of revolution.
                                          S 8.4.e

Apply the
BIG Idea

9. Describe three major differences between the terrestrial planets and the gas giants.   **S 8.4.b**

Chapter

15

Stars, Galaxies, and the Universe

The dark Horsehead Nebula is visible ▶ against red-glowing hydrogen gas.

Focus on the
BIG Idea

S 8.4.b

What is the structure and composition of the universe?

Check What You Know

Suppose you shine the beam of a flashlight against the wall of a darkened room. You then measure the size of the circle made by the beam on the room. What do you think would happen to the size and brightness of the circle if you moved closer to the wall? Farther from the wall? Explain your answer.

Build Science Vocabulary

The images shown here represent some of the key terms in this chapter. You can use this vocabulary skill to help you understand the meaning of some key terms in this chapter.

Suffixes

A suffix is a letter or group of letters added to the end of a word to change its meaning and often its part of speech. For example, the suffix *-ory* means "a place for." The suffix *-ory* added to the verb *observe* forms the noun *observatory*. An *observatory* is a place used to *observe* stars and planets through a telescope.

In this chapter, you will learn key terms that have the suffixes *-al*, *-ic*, *-ness*, and *-ory*.

Suffix	Meaning	Part of Speech	Key Terms
-al	relating to	adjective	optical, elliptical
-ic	relating to	adjective	electromagnetic, scientific
-ness	state or quality of	noun	brightness
-ory	a place for	noun	observatory

Apply It!

Complete the sentence below with the correct form of the word (*science/scientific*).

A theory in _____ is a well-tested concept that is based on _____ evidence.

When you come across an unfamiliar word, look at the suffix to help you determine its meaning. Then check the definition in the glossary or a dictionary.

galaxy

constellation

planetary nebula

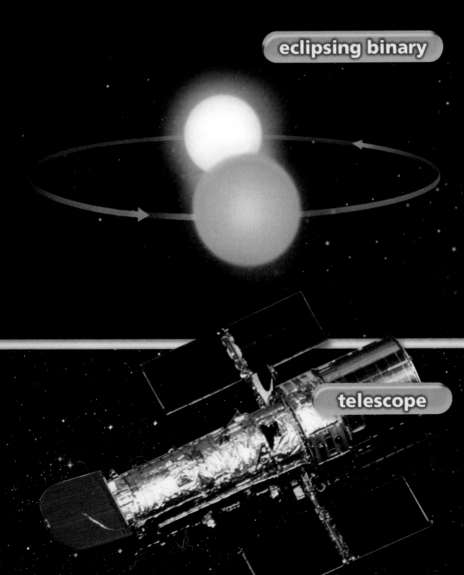
eclipsing binary

telescope

Section 1 (page 590)

electromagnetic radiation
visible light
wavelength
spectrum
optical telescope

refracting telescope
convex lens
reflecting telescope
radio telescope
observatory

Section 2 (page 598)

constellation
spectrograph
apparent brightness
absolute brightness

light-year
parallax
Hertzsprung-Russell diagram
main sequence

Section 3 (page 608)

nebula
protostar
planetary nebula
white dwarf

supernova
neutron star
pulsar
black hole

Section 4 (page 614)

binary star
eclipsing binary
open cluster
globular cluster
galaxy
quasar

spiral galaxy
elliptical galaxy
irregular galaxy
universe
scientific notation

Section 5 (page 622)

big bang
Hubble's law
cosmic background radiation

solar nebula
planetesimal
dark matter
dark energy

interactive Textbook

Build Science Vocabulary
Online
Visit: PHSchool.com
Web Code: cxj-4150

How to Read Science

 TARGET SKILL

Identify Supporting Evidence

Science textbooks often describe the scientific evidence that supports a theory or hypothesis. Remember that scientific evidence includes data and facts that have been confirmed by observation or experiments.

You can use a graphic organizer like the one below to help you understand how supporting evidence is related to a theory. When you draw a graphic organizer, include

- a title
- supporting evidence on the left
- the hypothesis or theory on the right

This chapter discusses the theory of how the universe was formed.

Evidence

All distant galaxies are moving away from us and from each other.

Theory

The universe formed in an instant in an enormous explosion.

Apply It!

1. What is a good title for this graphic organizer?

2. What kind of information would you include in the ovals on the left?

As you read Section 5, complete the graphic organizer explaining the big bang theory.

S 8.4.b, 8.4.d

Star Stories

Many years ago, people created stories to explain the patterns of stars they saw in the sky. In your investigation, you'll learn how the names of these constellations reflect the cultures of the people who named them.

Your Goal

To complete this investigation you will

- learn the star patterns of at least three constellations
- research the myths that gave one constellation its name
- create your own star myth

Plan It!

Begin by making a list of constellations that you have heard about. Then use the star charts in Appendix E on pages 656 and 657 to locate constellations in the night sky. The constellations that are visible change from season to season and over the course of a night. So read the instructions in the appendix carefully to learn how to use the star charts. Once you are familiar with the charts, find a safe, unobstructed area to view the stars. Make a sketch of the constellations that you locate.

Choose one constellation, and research the myths that gave it its name. Draw a new picture for the star pattern in your constellation, and choose a name for it. Finally, write a story about your constellation. At the end of the chapter, you will present your constellation and a story that explains its name.

Telescopes

CALIFORNIA
Standards Focus

S 8.4.d Students know that stars are the source of light for all bright objects in outer space and that the Moon and planets shine by reflected sunlight, not by their own light.

- What are the regions of the electromagnetic spectrum?
- What are telescopes and how do they work?
- Where are most large telescopes located?

Key Terms

- electromagnetic radiation
- visible light
- wavelength
- spectrum
- optical telescope
- refracting telescope
- convex lens
- reflecting telescope
- radio telescope
- observatory

Lab zone Standards **Warm-Up**

How Does Distance Affect an Image?

1. Hold a plastic hand lens about 7 cm away from your eye and about 5 cm away from a printed letter on a page. Move the lens slowly back and forth until the letter is in clear focus.

2. Keep the letter about 5 cm from the lens as you move your eye back to about 20 cm from the lens. Then, keeping the distance between your eye and the lens constant, slowly move the object away from the lens.

Think It Over

Observing What did the letter look like through the lens in Step 1 compared with how it looked without the lens? How did the image change in Step 2?

Galileo's ▶ telescope

Ancient peoples often gazed up in wonder at the many points of light in the night sky. But they could see few details with their eyes alone. It was not until the invention of the telescope in 1608 that people could observe objects in the sky more closely. Recall that a telescope is a device that makes distant objects appear to be closer. The telescope revolutionized astronomy. Scientists now had a tool that allowed them to see many objects in space for the first time.

Although Galileo was not the first person to use a telescope, he soon made it famous as he turned his homemade instrument to the sky. With his telescope, Galileo saw things that no one had even dreamed of. He was the first to see sunspots, Saturn's rings, and the four large moons of Jupiter. Galileo could see fine details, such as mountains on the moon, which cannot be seen clearly by the unaided eye.

Since Galileo's time, astronomers have built ever larger and more powerful telescopes. These telescopes have opened up a whole universe of wonders that would have amazed even Galileo.

Electromagnetic Radiation

To understand how telescopes work, it's useful to understand the nature of electromagnetic radiation. Light is a form of **electromagnetic radiation,** or energy that can travel through space in the form of waves. Stars produce such radiation during the process of nuclear fusion. You can see stars when the light that they produce reaches your eyes.

Forms of Radiation All the colors that you can see are **visible light.** Visible light is just one of many types of electromagnetic radiation. Many objects give off radiation that you can't see. For example, in addition to their reddish light, the glowing coils of an electric heater give off infrared radiation, which you feel as heat. Radio transmitters produce radio waves that carry signals to radios and televisions. Objects in space give off all types of electromagnetic radiation.

The Electromagnetic Spectrum As shown in Figure 1, the distance between the crest of one wave and the crest of the next wave is called a **wavelength.** Visible light has very short wavelengths, less than one millionth of a meter. Some electromagnetic waves have even shorter wavelengths. Other waves have much longer wavelengths, even several meters long.

If you shine white light through a prism, the light spreads out to make a range of different colors with different wavelengths, called a **spectrum.** The spectrum of visible light is made of the colors red, orange, yellow, green, blue, indigo, and violet. ☛ The electromagnetic spectrum includes the entire range of radio waves, infrared radiation, visible light, ultraviolet radiation, X-rays, and gamma rays.

Reading Checkpoint What is electromagnetic radiation?

Go Online
Sci LINKS™ NSTA

For: Links on telescopes
Visit: www.SciLinks.org
Web Code: scn-0641

FIGURE 1
The Electromagnetic Spectrum
The electromagnetic spectrum ranges from long-wavelength radio waves through short-wavelength gamma rays.
Interpreting Diagrams *Are infrared waves longer or shorter than ultraviolet waves?*

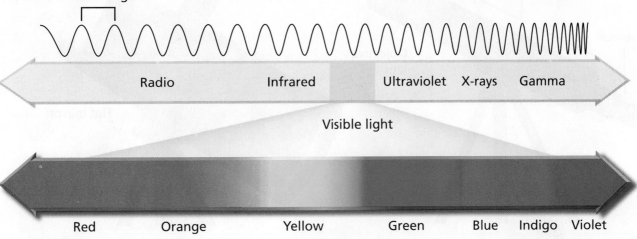

Wavelength

Radio   Infrared   Ultraviolet   X-rays   Gamma

Visible light

Red   Orange   Yellow   Green   Blue   Indigo   Violet

Types of Telescopes

On a clear night, your eyes can see at most a few thousand stars. But with a telescope, you can see many millions. Why? The light from stars spreads out as it moves through space, and your eyes are too small to gather much light.

👉 **Telescopes are instruments that collect and focus light and other forms of electromagnetic radiation.** Telescopes make distant objects appear larger and brighter. A telescope that uses lenses or mirrors to collect and focus visible light is called an **optical telescope.** The two major types of optical telescopes are refracting telescopes and reflecting telescopes.

Modern astronomy is based on the detection of forms of electromagnetic radiation besides visible light. Non-optical telescopes collect and focus different types of electromagnetic radiation, just as optical telescopes collect visible light.

Refracting Telescopes A **refracting telescope** uses a convex lens to gather and focus light. A **convex lens** is a piece of transparent glass, curved so that the middle is thicker than the edges.

Figure 2 shows a simple refracting telescope. This telescope has two convex lenses, one at each end of a long tube. Light enters the telescope through the large objective lens at the top. The objective lens focuses the light at a certain distance from the lens. This distance is the focal length of the lens. The larger the objective lens, the more light the telescope can collect. This makes it easier for astronomers to see faint objects.

The smaller lens at the lower end of a refracting telescope is called the eyepiece. The eyepiece magnifies the image produced by the objective lens.

FIGURE 2
Refracting and Reflecting Telescopes
A refracting telescope uses a convex lens to focus light. A reflecting telescope has a curved mirror in place of an objective lens.

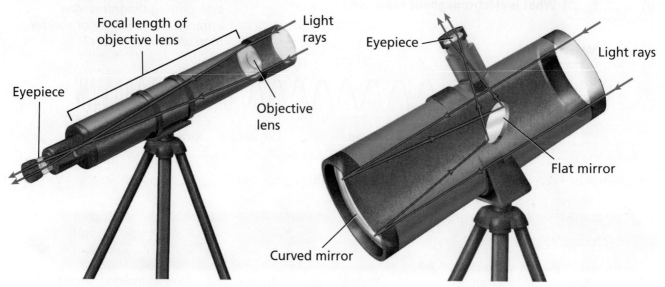

Refracting Telescope
Focal length of objective lens
Light rays
Eyepiece
Objective lens

Reflecting Telescope
Eyepiece
Light rays
Flat mirror
Curved mirror

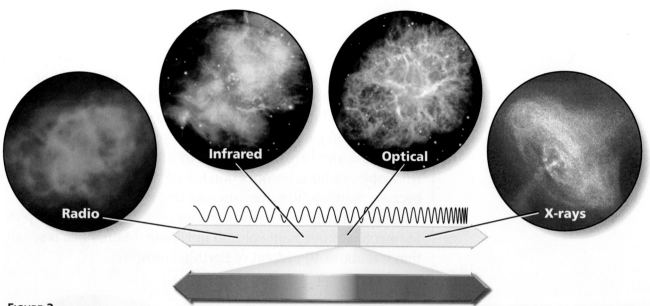

FIGURE 3
Four Views of the Crab Nebula
Different types of telescopes collect electromagnetic radiation at different wavelengths. Astronomers are able to learn a great deal about the Crab Nebula by examining these different images. The images are shown at different scales.

Reflecting Telescopes In 1668, Isaac Newton built the first reflecting telescope. A **reflecting telescope** uses a curved mirror to collect and focus light. Like the objective lens in a refracting telescope, the curved mirror in a reflecting telescope focuses a large amount of light onto a small area. The larger the mirror, the more light the telescope can collect. The largest optical telescopes today are all reflecting telescopes.

Radio Telescopes Devices used to detect radio waves from objects in space are called **radio telescopes.** Most radio telescopes have curved, reflecting surfaces—up to 305 meters in diameter. These surfaces focus radio waves the way the mirror in a reflecting telescope focuses light waves. The surfaces concentrate the faint radio waves from space onto small antennas like those on radios. As with optical telescopes, the larger a radio telescope is, the more radio waves it can collect.

Other Telescopes Some telescopes detect infrared radiation, which has longer wavelengths than visible light but shorter wavelengths than radio waves. There are also telescopes that detect the shortest wavelengths—ultraviolet radiation, X-rays, and gamma rays.

 **Reading Checkpoint** Who built the first reflecting telescope?

Lab zone Try This **Activity**

Locating Radio Waves
You can use an umbrella to focus radio waves.

1. Line the inside of an open umbrella with aluminum foil.

2. Turn on a small radio and tune it to a station.

3. Move the radio up and down along the umbrella handle. Find the position where the station is clearest. Radio waves reflecting off the foil focus at this point. Tape the radio to the handle.

4. Hold the umbrella at different angles. At which angle is the station the clearest?

Inferring In which direction do you think the radio station's transmitter is located? Explain.

Observatories

In general, an **observatory** is a building that contains one or more telescopes. But some observatories are located in space. 👁 **Many large observatories are located on mountaintops or in space.** Why? Earth's atmosphere makes objects in space look blurry. The sky on some mountaintops is clearer than at sea level and is not brightened much by city lights. Unlike optical telescopes, radio telescopes don't need to be on mountaintops because many radio waves can pass through the atmosphere.

One of the best observatory sites on Earth is on the top of Mauna Kea, a dormant volcano in Hawaii. Mauna Kea is so tall that it is above 40 percent of Earth's atmosphere.

• Tech & Design in History •

Development of Modern Telescopes
During the last century, astronomers have built larger telescopes, which can collect more visible light and other types of radiation. Today's astronomers use tools that could not have been imagined 100 years ago.

1897 Yerkes Telescope
The 1-meter-diameter telescope at Yerkes Observatory in Wisconsin is the largest refracting telescope ever built. Because its main lens is so large, the Yerkes telescope can collect more light than any other refracting telescope.

1931 Beginning of Radio Astronomy
Karl Jansky, an American engineer, was trying to find the source of static that was interfering with radio communications. Using a large antenna, he discovered that the static was radio waves given off by objects in space. Jansky's accidental discovery led to the beginning of radio astronomy.

1963 Arecibo Radio Telescope
This radio telescope in Puerto Rico was built in a natural bowl in the ground. It is 305 meters in diameter, the largest radio telescope in existence.

1900   1940   1960

Advanced Telescopes Today, many large optical telescopes are equipped with systems that significantly improve the quality of their images. Optical telescopes on Earth equipped with such systems are able to produce images of small regions of the sky that rival those of optical telescopes based in space.

Some new telescopes are equipped with computer systems that correct images for problems such as telescope movement and changes in air temperature or mirror shape. Other advanced telescopes use lasers to monitor conditions in the atmosphere. The shape of the telescope's mirror is automatically adjusted thousands of times each second in response to changes in the atmosphere.

Writing in Science

Research and Write
Research one of these telescopes or another large telescope. Create a publicity brochure in which you describe the telescope's features, when and where it was built, and what types of research it is used for.

1980 Very Large Array
The Very Large Array is a set of 27 radio telescopes in New Mexico. The telescopes can be moved close together or far apart. The telescopes are linked, so they can be used as if they were one giant radio telescope 25 kilometers in diameter.

1990 Hubble Space Telescope
The Hubble Space Telescope views objects in space from high above the atmosphere. As a result, it can produce extremely sharp images.

2003 Spitzer Space Telescope
The Spitzer Space Telescope is a powerful 0.85-meter diameter telescope that surveys the sky in the infrared range of the spectrum.

1980	2000	2020

FIGURE 4
Repairing Hubble
Astronauts have repaired and upgraded the Hubble Space Telescope on several occasions.

Telescopes in Space X-rays, gamma rays, and most ultraviolet radiation are blocked by Earth's atmosphere. To detect these wavelengths, astronomers have placed telescopes in space. Some space telescopes are designed to detect visible light or infrared radiation, since Earth's atmosphere also interferes with the transmission of these forms of radiation.

The Hubble Space Telescope is a reflecting telescope with a mirror 2.4 meters in diameter. Because the Hubble telescope orbits Earth above the atmosphere, it can produce very detailed images in visible light. It also collects ultraviolet and infrared radiation. The spectacular Hubble telescope images have changed how astronomers view the universe.

The hottest objects in space give off X-rays. The Chandra X-ray Observatory produces images in the X-ray portion of the spectrum. Chandra's X-ray images are much more detailed than those of earlier X-ray telescopes.

The most recent addition to NASA's lineup of telescopes in space is the Spitzer Space Telescope. Launched in 2003, the Spitzer telescope produces images in the infrared portion of the spectrum.

 **Reading Checkpoint** **What is an observatory?**

Section 1 Assessment

S 8.4.d, E-LA: Reading 8.1.0 Writing 8.2.6

Vocabulary Skill **Suffixes** What suffix do you see in the word *electromagnetic?* What part of speech does it indicate? Define *electromagnetic radiation.*

Reviewing Key Concepts

1. **a. Sequencing** List the main types of electromagnetic waves, from longest wavelength to shortest.
   b. Applying Concepts Why are images from the Hubble Space Telescope clearer than images from telescopes on Earth?
2. **a. Identifying** What are the two major types of optical telescope?
   b. Explaining How does a refracting telescope work?
   c. Comparing and Contrasting Use Figure 2 to explain the major differences between reflecting and refracting telescopes.

3. **a. Summarizing** How does the atmosphere affect electromagnetic radiation?
   b. Explaining Why are many large optical telescopes located on mountaintops?
   c. Applying Concepts Would it make sense to place an X-ray or gamma ray telescope on a mountaintop? Explain why or why not.

Writing in Science

Writing Technical Instructions List the sequence of steps needed to build and operate a reflecting telescope for a booklet to be included in a model telescope kit. Be sure to describe the shape and position of each of the lenses or mirrors. You may include drawings.

Technology Lab
· Tech & Design ·

Design and Build a Telescope

S 8.4.d

Eyepiece Foam holder Paper towel tubes

Objective lens (tape to the end of tube)

Problem

Can you design and build a telescope?

Skills Focus

evaluating the design, redesigning

Materials

- 2 paper towel tubes of slightly different diameters • several plastic objective lenses
- several plastic eyepiece lenses • meter stick
- foam holder for eyepiece • transparent tape

Procedure

1. Fit one of the paper towel tubes inside the other. Make sure you can move the tubes but that they will not slide on their own.

2. Place the large objective lens flat against the end of the outer tube. Tape the lens in place.

3. Insert the small eyepiece lens into the opening in the foam holder.

4. Place the foam eyepiece lens holder into the inner tube at the end of the telescope opposite to the objective lens.

5. Tape a meter stick to the wall. Look through the eyepiece at the meter stick from 5 m away. Slide the tubes in and out to focus your telescope so that you can clearly read the numbers on the meter stick. Draw your telescope. On the drawing, mark the tube position that allows you to read the numbers most clearly.

6. Use your telescope to look at other objects at different distances, both in your classroom and through the window. For each object you view, draw your telescope, marking the tube position at which you see the object most clearly. **CAUTION:** *Do not look at the sun. You will damage your eyes.*

7. Design and build a better telescope. Your new telescope should make objects appear larger than your first model from the same observing distance. It should have markings on the inner tube to enable you to pre-focus the telescope for a given observing distance.

8. Draw a design for your new telescope. List the materials you'll need. Obtain your teacher's approval. Then build your new model.

Analyze and Conclude

1. **Inferring** Why do you need two tubes?

2. **Observing** If you focus on a nearby object and then focus on something farther away, do you have to move the tubes together or apart?

3. **Evaluating the Design** How could you improve on the design of your new telescope? What effects would different lenses or tubes have on its performance?

4. **Redesigning** Describe the most important factors in redesigning your telescope.

Communicate

Write a product brochure for your new telescope. Be sure to describe in detail why your new telescope is better than the first telescope.

Characteristics of Stars

S 8.4.b Students know that the Sun is one of many stars in the Milky Way galaxy and that stars may differ in size, temperature, and color.

S 8.4.c Students know how to use astronomical units and light years as measures of distance between the Sun, stars, and Earth.

- How are stars classified?
- How do astronomers measure distances to the stars?
- What is an H-R diagram and how do astronomers use it?

Key Terms

- constellation
- spectrograph
- apparent brightness
- absolute brightness
- light-year
- parallax
- Hertzsprung-Russell diagram
- main sequence

Lab zone Standards **Warm-Up**

How Does Your Thumb Move?

1. Stand facing a wall, at least an arm's length away. Stretch your arm out with your thumb up and your fingers curled.
2. Close your right eye and look at your thumb with your left eye. Line your thumb up with something on the wall.
3. Now close your left eye and open your right eye. How does your thumb appear to move along the wall?
4. Bring your thumb closer to your eye, about half the distance as before. Repeat Steps 2 and 3.

Think It Over

Observing How does your thumb appear to move in Step 4 compared to Step 3? How are these observations related to how far away your thumb is at each step? How could you use this method to estimate distances?

When ancient observers around the world looked up at the night sky, they imagined that groups of stars formed pictures of people or animals. Today, we call these imaginary patterns of stars **constellations.**

Different cultures gave different names to the constellations. For example, a large constellation in the winter sky is named Orion, the Hunter, after a Greek myth. In this constellation, Orion is seen with a sword in his belt and an upraised arm. On the other hand, the ancient Sumerians thought that the stars in Orion formed the outline of a sheep. In ancient China, this group of stars was called "three," probably because of the three bright stars in Orion's belt.

Astronomers use the patterns of the constellations to locate objects in the night sky. But although the stars in a constellation look as if they are close to one another, they generally are not. They just happen to lie in the same part of the sky as seen from Earth.

Illustration of Orion ▶

Classifying Stars

Like the sun, all stars are huge spheres of glowing gas. They are made up mostly of hydrogen, and they produce energy through the process of nuclear fusion. This energy makes stars shine brightly. Astronomers classify stars according to their physical characteristics. **Characteristics used to classify stars include color, temperature, size, composition, and brightness.**

Color and Temperature If you look at the night sky, you can see slight differences in the colors of the stars. For example, Betelgeuse (BAY tul jooz), the bright star in Orion's shoulder, looks reddish. Rigel, the star in Orion's heel, is blue-white.

Like hot objects on Earth, a star's color reveals its surface temperature. If you watch a toaster heat up, you can see the wires glow red-hot. The wires inside a light bulb are even hotter and glow white. Similarly, the coolest stars—with a surface temperatures of about 3,200 degrees Celsius—appear reddish. With a surface temperature of about 5,500 degrees Celsius, the sun appears yellow. The hottest stars in the sky, with surface temperatures of over 20,000 degrees Celsius, appear bluish.

Size When you look at stars in the sky, they all appear to be points of light of the same size. Many stars are actually about the size of the sun, which is a medium-sized star. However, some stars are much larger than the sun. Very large stars are called giant stars or supergiant stars. If the supergiant star Betelgeuse were located where our sun is, it would be large enough to fill the solar system as far out as Jupiter.

Most stars are much smaller than the sun. White dwarf stars are about the size of Earth. Neutron stars are even smaller, only about 20 kilometers in diameter.

Go Online
PHSchool.com

For: More on types of stars
Visit: PHSchool.com
Web Code: cfd-5042

FIGURE 5
Star Size
Stars vary greatly in size. Giant stars are typically 10 to 100 times larger than the sun and more than 1,000 times the size of a white dwarf. **Calculating** *Betelgeuse has a diameter of 420 million kilometers. How many times larger is this than the sun, which has a diameter of 1.4 million kilometers?*

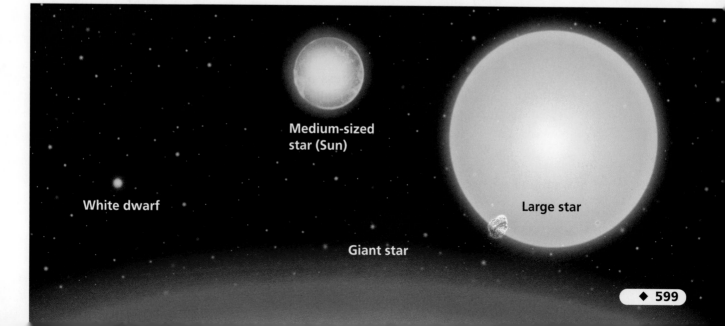

Medium-sized star (Sun)

White dwarf

Large star

Giant star

FIGURE 6

Spectrums of Four Stars
Astronomers can use line spectrums to identify the chemical elements in a star. Each element produces a characteristic pattern of spectral lines.

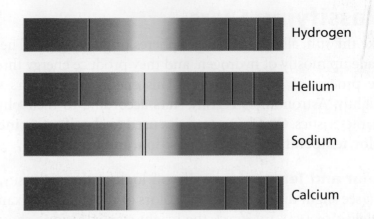

Hydrogen

Helium

Sodium

Calcium

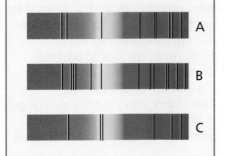

Lab zone Skills Activity

Inferring

The lines on the spectrums below are from three different stars. Each of these star spectrums is made up of an overlap of spectrums from the individual elements shown in Figure 6. In star A, which elements can you detect? Which can you find in star B? In star C?

A

B

C

Chemical Composition Stars vary in their chemical composition. The chemical composition of most stars is about 73 percent hydrogen, 25 percent helium, and 2 percent other elements by mass. This is similar to the composition of the sun.

Astronomers use spectrographs to determine the elements found in stars. A **spectrograph** (SPEK truh graf) is a device that breaks light into colors and produces an image of the resulting spectrum. Most large telescopes have spectrographs.

The gases in a star's atmosphere absorb some wavelengths of light produced within the star. When the star's light is seen through a spectrograph, each absorbed wavelength is shown as a dark line on a spectrum. Each chemical element absorbs light at particular wavelengths. Just as each person has a unique set of fingerprints, each element has a unique set of lines for a given temperature. Figure 6 shows the spectral lines of four elements. By comparing a star's spectrum with the spectrums of known elements, astronomers can infer how much of each element is found in the star.

✓ Reading Checkpoint   **What is a spectrograph?**

Brightness of Stars

Stars also differ in brightness, the amount of light they give off. ☛ **The brightness of a star depends upon both its size and temperature.** Recall that the photosphere is the visible surface of a star. Betelgeuse is fairly cool, so a square meter of its photosphere doesn't give off much light compared to hotter stars. But Betelgeuse is very large, so it shines brightly.

Rigel, on the other hand, is very hot, so each square meter of Rigel's photosphere gives off a lot of light. Even though it is smaller than Betelgeuse, Rigel shines more brightly.

How bright a star looks from Earth depends on both its distance from Earth and how bright the star truly is. Because of these two factors, the brightness of a star can be described in two ways: apparent brightness and absolute brightness.

Apparent Brightness A star's **apparent brightness** is its brightness as seen from Earth. Astronomers can measure apparent brightness fairly easily using electronic devices. However, astronomers can't tell how much light a star gives off just from the star's apparent brightness. Just as a flashlight looks brighter the closer it is to you, a star looks brighter the closer it is to Earth. For example, the sun looks very bright. This does not mean that the sun gives off more light than all other stars. The sun looks so bright simply because it is so close. In reality, the sun is a star of only average brightness.

Absolute Brightness A star's **absolute brightness,** or luminosity, is the brightness the star would have if it were at a standard distance from Earth. Finding a star's absolute brightness is more complex than finding its apparent brightness. An astronomer must first find out both the star's apparent brightness and its distance from Earth. The astronomer can then calculate the star's absolute brightness.

Astronomers have found that the absolute brightness of stars can vary tremendously. The brightest stars are more than a billion times brighter than the dimmest stars!

 **Reading Checkpoint** What is a star's absolute brightness?

FIGURE 7
Absolute Brightness
The streetlights in this photo all give off about the same amount of light, and so have about the same absolute brightness.
Applying Concepts *Why do the closer streetlights appear brighter than the more distant lights?*

Measuring Distances to Stars

Imagine that you could travel to the stars at the speed of light. To travel from Earth to the sun would take about 8 minutes, not very much time for such a long trip. The next nearest star, Proxima Centauri, is much farther away. A trip to Proxima Centauri at the speed of light would take 4.2 years!

The Light-Year Distances on Earth's surface are often measured in kilometers. However, distances to the stars are so large that kilometers are not very practical units. 👁 **Astronomers typically use a unit called the light-year to measure distances between the stars.** In space, light travels at a speed of about 300,000 kilometers per second. A **light-year** is the distance that light travels in one year, about 9.5 million million kilometers.

Note that the light-year is a unit of distance, not time. To help you understand this, consider an everyday example. If you bicycle at 10 kilometers per hour, it would take you 1 hour to go to a mall 10 kilometers away. You could say that the mall is "1 bicycle-hour" away.

Parallax Standing on Earth looking up at the sky, it may seem as if there is no way to tell how far away the stars are. However, astronomers have found ways to measure those distances. 👁 **Astronomers often use parallax to measure distances to nearby stars.**

Parallax is the apparent change in position of an object when you look at it from different places. For example, imagine that you and a friend have gone to a movie. A woman with a large hat sits down in front of you, as shown in Figure 8. Because you and your friend are sitting in different places, the woman's hat blocks different parts of the screen. If you are sitting on her left, the woman's hat appears to be in front of the large dinosaur. But to your friend on the right, she appears to be in front of the bird.

Have the woman and her hat moved? No. But because you are looking from different places, she appears to have moved. This apparent movement when you look from two different positions is parallax.

FIGURE 8
Parallax at the Movies
You and your friend are sitting behind a woman with a large hat. Applying Concepts *Why is your view of the screen different from your friend's view?*

Your View

Your friend's view

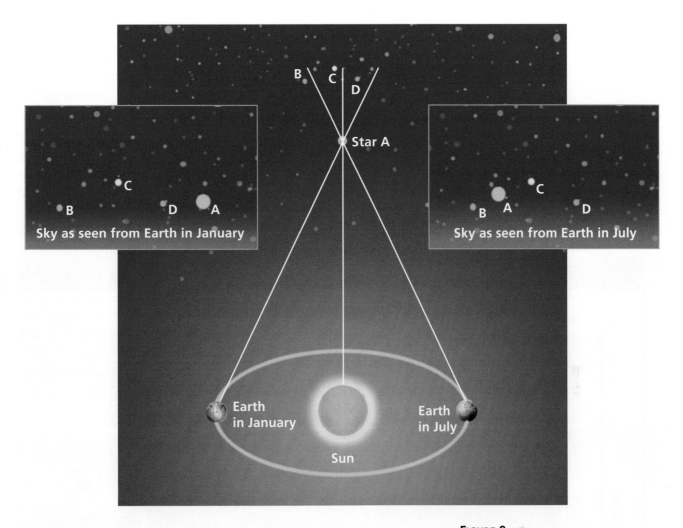

Sky as seen from Earth in January

Sky as seen from Earth in July

Star A

Earth in January

Earth in July

Sun

Parallax in Astronomy Astronomers are able to measure the parallax of nearby stars to determine their distances. As shown in Figure 9, astronomers look at a nearby star when Earth is on one side of the sun. Then they look at the same star again six months later, when Earth is on the opposite side of the sun. Astronomers measure how much the nearby star appears to move against a background of stars that are much farther away. They can then use this measurement to calculate the distance to the nearby star. The less the nearby star appears to move, the farther away it is.

Astronomers can use parallax to measure distances up to a few hundred light-years from Earth. The parallax of any star that is farther away is too small to measure accurately with existing technology.

 **How is parallax useful in astronomy?**

FIGURE 9
Parallax of Stars
The apparent movement of a star when seen from a different position is called parallax. Astronomers use parallax to calculate the distance to nearby stars. Note that the diagram is not to scale.
Interpreting Diagrams *Why do nearby stars appear to change position between January and July?*

The Hertzsprung-Russell Diagram

About 100 years ago, two scientists working independently made the same discovery. Both Ejnar Hertzsprung (EYE nahr HURT sprung) in Denmark and Henry Norris Russell in the United States made graphs to find out if the temperature and the absolute brightness of stars are related. They plotted the surface temperatures of stars on the *x*-axis and their absolute brightness on the *y*-axis. The points formed a pattern. The graph they made is still used by astronomers today. It is called the **Hertzsprung-Russell diagram,** or H-R diagram.

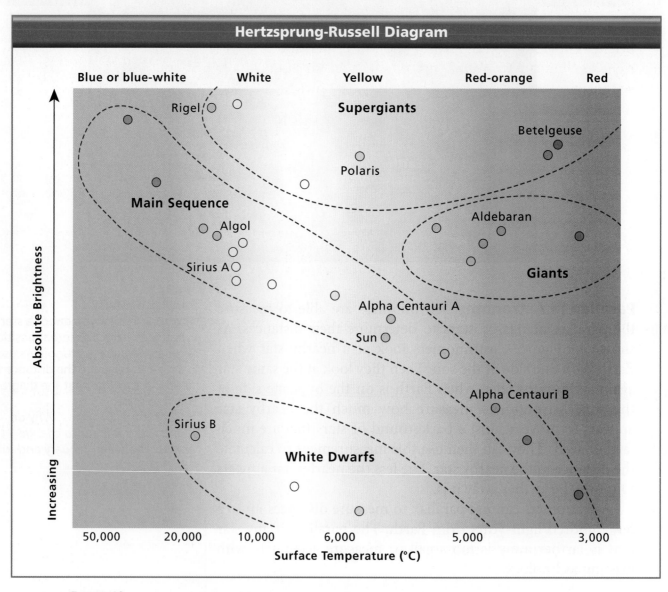

Hertzsprung-Russell Diagram

FIGURE 10
The Hertzsprung-Russell diagram shows the relationship between the surface temperature and absolute brightness of stars.
Interpreting Diagrams *Which star has a hotter surface: Rigel or Aldebaran?*

 Astronomers use H-R diagrams to classify stars and to understand how stars change over time. As you can see in Figure 10, most of the stars in the H-R diagram form a diagonal area called the **main sequence.** More than 90 percent of all stars, including the sun, are main-sequence stars. Within the main sequence, surface temperature increases as absolute brightness increases. Thus, hot bluish stars are located at the left of an H-R diagram and cooler reddish stars are located at the right of the diagram.

The brightest stars are located near the top of an H-R diagram, while the dimmest stars are located at the bottom. Giant and supergiant stars are very bright. They can be found near the top center and right of the diagram. White dwarfs are hot, but not very bright, so they appear at the bottom left or bottom center of the diagram.

Reading Checkpoint What is the main sequence?

FIGURE 11
Orion
Orion includes the red supergiant Betelgeuse, the blue supergiant Rigel, and many other main-sequence and giant stars.

Section 2 Assessment

S 8.4.b, 8.4.c, E-LA: Reading 8.1.0

Vocabulary Skill Suffixes What suffix do you see in the word *constellation*? What part of speech does it indicate? (*Hint:* see Build Science Vocabulary, Chapter 3.) Define *constellation*.

Reviewing Key Concepts

1. a. **Listing** Name three characteristics used to classify stars.
   b. **Comparing and Contrasting** What is the difference between apparent brightness and absolute brightness?
   c. **Applying Concepts** Stars A and B have about the same apparent brightness, but Star A is about twice as far from Earth as Star B. Which star has the greater absolute brightness? Explain your answer.
2. a. **Measuring** What is a light-year?
   b. **Defining** What is parallax?
   c. **Predicting** Vega is 25.3 light-years from Earth and Arcturus is 36.7 light-years away. Which star would have a greater parallax? Explain.

3. a. **Summarizing** What two characteristics of stars are shown in an H-R diagram?
   b. **Identifying** Identify two ways in which astronomers can use an H-R diagram.
   c. **Classifying** The star Procyon B has a surface temperature of 6,600°C and an absolute brightness that is much less than the sun's. What type of star is Procyon B? (*Hint:* Refer to the H-R diagram.)

Lab zone At-Home Activity

Observing Orion With adult family members, go outside on a clear, dark night. Determine which way is south. Using the star charts in Appendix E, look for the constellation Orion, which is visible in the evening during winter and spring. Find the stars Betelgeuse and Rigel in Orion and explain to your family why they are different colors.

Lab zone Skills Lab

How Far Is That Star?

S 8.4.b, 8.9.b

Problem

How can parallax be used to determine distances?

Skills Focus

inferring, calculating, predicting

Materials

- masking tape • paper clips • pen
- black and red pencils • metric ruler • paper
- meter stick • calculator
- lamp without a shade, with 100-watt light bulb
- copier paper box (without the lid)
- flat rectangular table, about 1 m wide

Procedure

PART 1 Telescope Model

1. Place the lamp on a table in the middle of the classroom.

2. Carefully use the tip of the pen to make a small hole in the middle of one end of the box. The box represents a telescope.

3. At the front of the classroom, place the box on a flat table so the hole points toward the lamp. Line the left side of the box up with the left edge of the table.

4. Put a small piece of tape on the table below the hole. Use the pen to make a mark on the tape directly below the hole. The mark represents the position of the telescope when Earth is on one side of its orbit.

PART 2 Star 1

5. Label a sheet of paper Star 1 and place it inside the box as shown in the drawing. Hold the paper in place with two paper clips. The paper represents the film in a telescope.

6. Darken the room. Turn on the light to represent the star.

7. With the red pencil, mark the paper where you see a dot of light. Label this dot A. Dot A represents the image of the star on the film.

8. Move the box so the right edge of the box lines up with the right edge of the table. Repeat Step 4. The mark on the tape represents the position of the telescope six months later, when Earth is on the other side of its orbit.

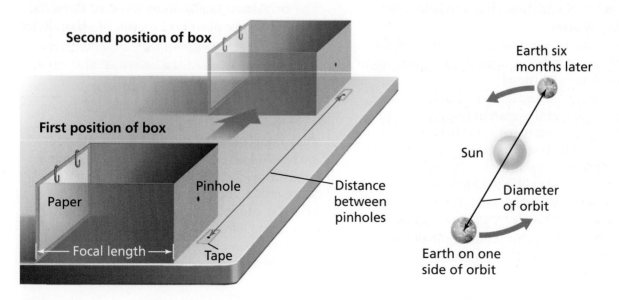

Second position of box

First position of box

Paper

Pinhole

Distance between pinholes

Focal length

Tape

Earth six months later

Sun

Diameter of orbit

Earth on one side of orbit

Data Table						
Star	Parallax Shift (mm)	Focal Length (mm)	Diameter of Orbit (mm)	Calculated Distance to Star (mm)	Calculated Distance to Star (m)	Actual Distance to Star (m)

9. Repeat Step 7, using a black pencil to mark the second dot B. Dot B represents the image of the star as seen 6 months later from the other side of Earth's orbit.

10. Remove the paper. Before you continue, copy the data table into your notebook.

11. Measure and record the distance in millimeters between dots A and B. This distance represents the parallax shift for Star 1.

12. Measure and record the distance from the hole in the box to the lamp. This distance represents the actual distance to the star.

13. Measure and record the distance from the hole (lens) to the back of the box in millimeters. This distance represents the focal length of your telescope.

14. Measure and record the distance in millimeters between the marks on the two pieces of masking tape. This distance represents the diameter of Earth's orbit.

PART 3 Stars 2 and 3

15. Move the lamp away from the table—about half the distance to the back of the room. The bulb now represents Star 2. Predict what you think will happen to the light images on your paper.

16. Repeat Steps 6–12 with a new sheet of paper to find the parallax shift for Star 2.

17. Move the lamp to the back of the classroom. The bulb now represents Star 3. Repeat Steps 6–12 with a new sheet of paper to find the parallax shift for Star 3.

Analyze and Conclude

1. **Inferring** What caused the apparent change in position of the dots of light for each star? Explain.

2. **Calculating** Use the following formula to calculate the distance from the telescope to Star 1.

$$\text{Distance} = \frac{\text{Diameter} \times \text{Focal length}}{\text{Parallax shift}}$$

3. **Calculating** Divide your result from Question 2 by 1,000 to get the distance to the light bulb in meters.

4. **Calculating** Repeat Questions 2 and 3 for Stars 2 and 3.

5. **Predicting** Was your prediction in Step 15 correct? Why or why not?

6. **Interpreting Data** How did your calculation for Star 3 compare with the actual distance? What could you do to improve your results?

7. **Communicating** Write a paragraph that explains how parallax shift varies with distance. Relate each star's parallax shift to its distance from Earth.

Design an Experiment

What would happen if you kept moving the lamp away from the box? Is there a distance at which you can no longer find the distance to the star? Design an experiment to find out.

CALIFORNIA
Standards Focus

S 8.4.b Students know that the Sun is one of many stars in the Milky Way galaxy and that stars may differ in size, temperature, and color.

S 8.4.d Students know that stars are the source of light for all bright objects in outer space and that the Moon and planets shine by reflected sunlight, not by their own light.

🔑 How does a star form?

🔑 What determines how long a star will exist?

🔑 What happens to a star when it runs out of fuel?

Key Terms
- nebula
- protostar
- planetary nebula
- white dwarf
- supernova
- neutron star
- pulsar
- black hole

Lab zone Standards **Warm-Up**

What Determines How Long Stars Live?

1. This graph shows how the mass of a star is related to its lifetime— how long the star lives before it runs out of fuel.

2. How long does a star with 0.75 times the mass of the sun live? How long does a star with 3 times the mass of the sun live?

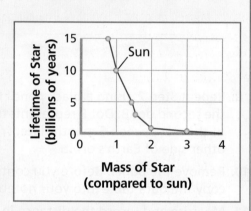

Think It Over

Drawing Conclusions Describe the general relationship between a star's mass and its lifetime.

Imagine that you want to study how people age. You wish you could watch a few people for 50 years, but your project is due next week! You have to study a lot of people for a short time, and classify the people into different age groups. You may come up with groups like *babies, young adults,* and *elderly people.* You don't have time to see a single person go through all these stages, but you know the stages exist.

Astronomers have a similar problem in trying to understand how stars age. They can't watch a single star for billions of years. Instead, they study many stars and other objects in space. Over time, astronomers have figured out that these objects represent different stages in the lives of stars.

◄ **Three generations**

The Lives of Stars

Stars do not last forever. Each star is born, goes through its life cycle, and eventually dies. (Of course, stars are not really alive. The words *born*, *live*, and *die* are just helpful comparisons.)

A Star Is Born All stars begin their lives as parts of nebulas. A **nebula** is a large cloud of gas and dust spread out in an immense volume. A star, on the other hand, is made up of a large amount of gas in a relatively small volume.

In the densest part of a nebula, gravity pulls gas and dust together. As the cloud of gas and dust contracts, it starts to heat up. A contracting cloud of gas and dust with enough mass to form a star is called a **protostar**. *Proto* means "earliest" in Greek, so a protostar is the earliest stage of a star's life, before nuclear fusion has begun.

🔑 **A star is born when the contracting gas and dust from a nebula become so dense and hot that nuclear fusion starts.** Recall that nuclear fusion is the process by which atomic nuclei combine, releasing enormous amounts of energy. In the sun, for example, hydrogen atoms combine to form helium.

Lifetimes of Stars 🔑 **How long a star lives depends on its mass.** You might think that stars with more mass would last longer than stars with less mass. But the reverse is true. You can think of stars as being like cars. A small car has a small gas tank, but it also has a small engine that burns gas slowly. A large car has a larger gas tank, but it also has a larger engine that burns gas rapidly. So the small car can travel farther on a tank of gas than the larger car. Small-mass stars use up their fuel more slowly than large-mass stars, so they have much longer lives.

Generally, stars that have less mass than the sun use their fuel slowly, and can live for up to 200 billion years. Medium-mass stars like the sun live for about 10 billion years. Astronomers think the sun is about 4.6 billion years old, so it is almost halfway through its lifetime.

Stars that have more mass than the sun have shorter lifetimes. A star that is 15 times as massive as the sun may live only about ten million years. That may seem like a long time, but it is only one tenth of one percent of the lifetime of the sun.

 **Reading Checkpoint** How long will a star that is the mass of the sun live?

FIGURE 12
Young Stars
New stars are forming in the nebula on top. The bottom photo shows a protostar in the Orion Nebula. **Applying Concepts** *How do some of the gas and dust in a nebula become a protostar?*

Video Field Trip
Discovery Channel School
Stars, Galaxies, and the Universe

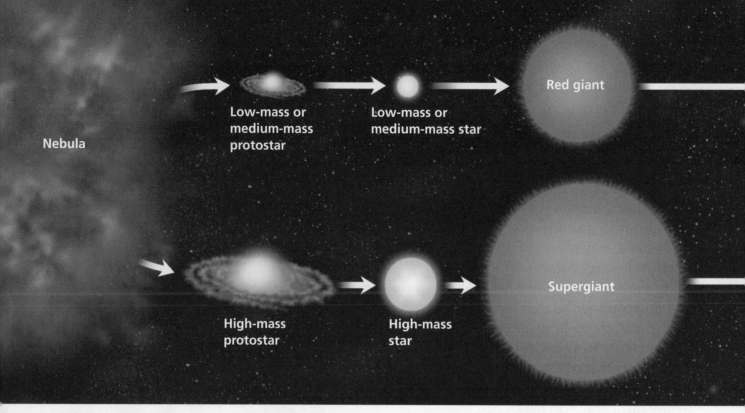

Red giant

Nebula

Low-mass or medium-mass protostar

Low-mass or medium-mass star

Supergiant

High-mass protostar

High-mass star

FIGURE 13

The Lives of Stars

A star's life history depends on its mass. A low-mass main-sequence star uses up its fuel slowly and eventually becomes a white dwarf. A high-mass star uses up its fuel quickly. After its supergiant stage, it will explode as a supernova, producing a neutron star or a black hole.

Interpreting Diagrams *What type of star produces a planetary nebula?*

Predicting

Find Algol, Sirius B, and Polaris in Figure 10, the H-R diagram. What type of star is each of these now? Predict what the next stage in each star's life will be.

Deaths of Stars

As long as a star produces energy through the fusion of hydrogen into helium in its core, the star stays on the main sequence. However, when the star begins to run out of hydrogen, its core shrinks and its outer portion expands. It moves off of the main sequence. Depending on its mass, the star becomes either a red giant or a supergiant.

At this stage, helium begins to fuse in the star's core. The fusion of helium creates heavier elements such as carbon and oxygen. In the most massive stars, elements as heavy as iron are created by nuclear fusion.

All main-sequence stars eventually become red giants or supergiants. As shown in Figure 13, red giants and supergiants evolve in very different ways. **After a star runs out of fuel, it becomes a white dwarf, a neutron star, or a black hole.**

Planetary Nebulas Low-mass stars and medium-mass stars like the sun take billions of years to use up their nuclear fuel. As they start to run out of fuel, their outer layers expand, and they become red giants. Eventually, the outer parts grow larger still and drift out into space. There they form a glowing cloud of gas called a **planetary nebula.** Many planetary nebulas, such as the Cat's Eye Nebula shown on page 621, are spectacular in their beauty.

Reading Checkpoint **What is a planetary nebula?**

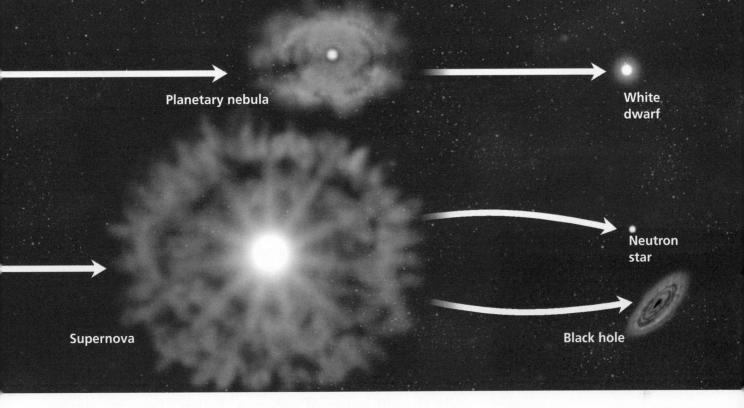

Planetary nebula

White dwarf

Supernova

Neutron star

Black hole

White Dwarfs A blue-white core of a star is left behind a planetary nebula. This core of the original star gradually cools and becomes a **white dwarf.** White dwarfs are only about the size of Earth, but they have about as much mass as the sun. Since a white dwarf has the same mass as the sun but only one millionth the volume, it is one million times as dense as the sun. A spoonful of material from a white dwarf has as much mass as a large truck. Nuclear fusion no longer takes place in white dwarfs. However, they continue to glow faintly for billions of years from leftover energy.

Supernovas The life cycle of a high-mass star is quite different from the life cycle of a low-mass or medium-mass star. High-mass stars quickly evolve into brilliant supergiants. When a supergiant runs out of fuel, it can explode suddenly. Within hours, the star blazes millions of times brighter. The explosion is called a **supernova.**

A supernova produces enough energy to create elements that are heavier than iron, such as lead and gold. These elements, along with other elements that form in massive stars from nuclear fusion, are flung into space by the supernova explosion. This material may eventually become part of a nebula. The nebula may eventually contract to form a new, partly recycled star. Astronomers think the sun began as a nebula that contained material from a supernova that exploded billions of years ago. This means that Earth, and even your body, are made largely of elements that formed inside a star.

Go **O**nline
active art

For: The Lives of Stars activity
Visit: PHSchool.com
Web Code: cfp-5043

Neutron Stars After a supergiant explodes, some of the material from the star is left behind. This material may form a neutron star. **Neutron stars** are the remains of high-mass stars. They are even smaller and denser than white dwarfs. A neutron star may contain as much as three times the mass of the sun but be only about 25 kilometers in diameter, the size of a city.

In 1967, Jocelyn Bell, a British astronomy student, detected an object in space that appeared to give off regular pulses of radio waves. That is, the object seemed to rapidly turn on and then off in a regular pattern. Some astronomers hypothesized that the pulses might be a signal from an extraterrestrial civilization. At first, astronomers even named the source LGM, for the "Little Green Men" in early science-fiction stories. Soon, however, astronomers concluded that the source of the radio waves was really a rapidly spinning neutron star.

Pulsars Spinning neutron stars are called **pulsars,** short for pulsating radio sources. As shown in Figure 14, pulsars do not really give off pulses of radiation. Rather, they emit steady beams of radiation in narrow cones. As a pulsar rotates, these beams also turn, like the spinning beacon of a lighthouse. If the beam happens to sweep across Earth, astronomers can briefly detect a flash of radiation that disappears as the beam turns away from Earth. Thus, astronomers are able to detect a pulse each time a pulsar rotates.

Most pulsars rotate about once a second or so. However, some pulsars spin hundreds of times per second!

 Reading Checkpoint   **What is a pulsar?**

FIGURE 14
Pulsars
Pulsars emit steady beams of radiation. Like a lighthouse beacon, a pulsar appears to pulse when its spinning beam sweeps across Earth.

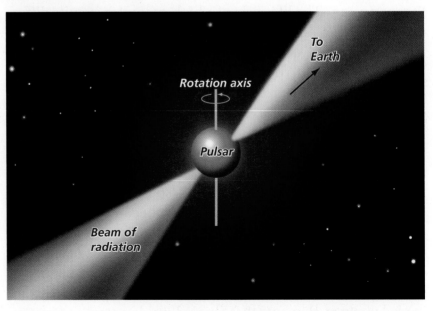

Black Holes The most massive stars—those having more than 40 times the mass of the sun—may become black holes when they die. A **black hole** is an object with gravity so strong that nothing, not even light, can escape. After a very massive star dies in a supernova explosion, more than five times the mass of the sun may be left. The gravity of this mass is so strong that the gas is pulled inward, packing the gas into a smaller and smaller space. The gas becomes so densely packed that its intense gravity will not allow even light to escape. The remains of the star have become a black hole.

No light, radio waves, or any other form of radiation can ever get out of a black hole, so it is not possible to detect a black hole directly. But astronomers can detect black holes indirectly. For example, gas near a black hole is pulled so strongly that it revolves faster and faster around the black hole. Friction heats the gas up. Astronomers can detect X-rays coming from the hot gas and infer that a black hole is present. Similarly, if another star is near a black hole, astronomers can calculate the mass of the black hole from the effect of its gravity on the star. Scientists have detected dozens of star-size black holes with the Chandra X-ray Observatory. They have also detected huge black holes that are millions or billions of times the sun's mass.

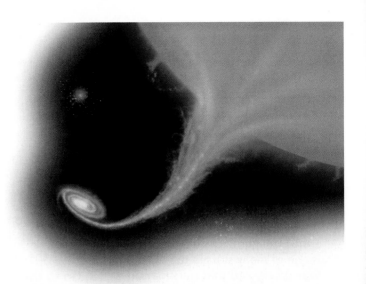

FIGURE 15
Black Holes
The remains of the most massive stars collapse into black holes. This artist's impression shows a black hole pulling matter from a companion star. The material glows as it is pulled into the black hole. **Applying Concepts** *If it is impossible to detect a black hole directly, how do astronomers find them?*

Section 3 Assessment

S 8.4.b, 8.4.d E-LA: Reading 8.2.2; Writing 8.2.0

Target Reading Skill Identify Supporting Evidence Reread the text under the heading *Black Holes*. Create a graphic organizer showing supporting evidence for the hypothesis that black holes exist.

Reviewing Key Concepts

1. a. **Defining** What is a nebula?
   b. **Explaining** How does a star form from a nebula?
   c. **Comparing and Contrasting** How is a protostar different from a star?
2. a. **Identifying** What factor determines how long a star lives?
   b. **Applying Concepts** A star is twice as massive as the sun. Will its lifespan be longer, shorter, or the same as that of the sun? Explain.

3. a. **Comparing and Contrasting** What is a white dwarf? How is it different from a neutron star?
   b. **Relating Cause and Effect** Why do some stars become white dwarfs and others become neutron stars or black holes?
   c. **Predicting** What will happen to the sun when it runs out of fuel? Explain.

Writing in Science

Descriptive Paragraph Write a description of one of the stages in the life of a star, such as a nebula, red giant, supernova, or white dwarf. Include information on how it formed and what will happen next in the star's evolution.

CALIFORNIA Standards Focus

S 8.4.a Students know galaxies are clusters of billions of stars and may have different shapes.

S 8.4.b Students know that the Sun is one of many stars in the Milky Way galaxy and that stars may differ in size, temperature, and color.

- What is a star system?
- What are the major types of galaxies?
- How do astronomers describe the scale of the universe?

Key Terms

- binary star
- eclipsing binary
- open cluster
- globular cluster
- galaxy
- spiral galaxy
- elliptical galaxy
- irregular galaxy
- quasar
- universe
- scientific notation

Lab zone Standards **Warm-Up**

Why Does the Milky Way Look Hazy?

1. Using a pencil, carefully poke at least 20 holes close together in a sheet of white paper.
2. Tape the paper to a chalkboard or dark-colored wall.
3. Go to the other side of the room and look at the paper. From the far side of the room, what do the dots look like? Can you see individual dots?

Think It Over

Making Models How is looking at the paper from the far side of the room like trying to see many very distant stars that are close together? How does your model compare to the photograph of the Milky Way below?

On a clear, dark night in the country, you can see a hazy band of light stretched across the sky. This band of stars is called the Milky Way. It looks as if the Milky Way is very far away. Actually, though, Earth is inside the Milky Way! The Milky Way looks milky or hazy from Earth because the stars are too close together for your eyes to see them individually. The dark blotches in the Milky Way are clouds of dust that block light from the stars behind them.

The Milky Way

FIGURE 16
Eclipsing Binary
Algol is an eclipsing binary star system consisting of a bright star and a dim companion. Each time the dim star passes in front of the bright one, Algol appears dimmer. **Interpreting Diagrams** *When does Algol appear brighter?*

Bright star

Dim companion star

Star Systems and Clusters

Our solar system has only one star, the sun. But this is not the most common situation for stars. ⬤ **Most stars are members of groups of two or more stars, called star systems.** If you were on a planet in one of these star systems, at times you might see two or more suns in the sky! At other times, one or more of these suns would be below the horizon.

Multiple Star Systems Star systems that have two stars are called double stars or **binary stars.** (The prefix *bi* means "two.") Those with three stars are called triple stars. The nearby star Proxima Centauri may be part of a triple star system. The other two stars in the system, Alpha Centauri A and Alpha Centauri B, form a double star. Scientists are not sure whether Proxima Centauri is really part of the system or is just passing close to the other two stars temporarily.

Often one star in a binary star is much brighter and more massive than the other. Astronomers can sometimes detect a binary star even if only one of the stars can be seen from Earth. Astronomers can often tell that there is a dim star in a binary system by observing the effects of its gravity. As the dim companion star revolves around a bright star, the dim star's gravity causes the bright star to wobble back and forth. Imagine watching a pair of dancers who are twirling each other around. Even if one dancer were invisible, you could tell that the invisible dancer was there from watching the motion of the visible dancer.

Eclipsing Binaries A wobble is not the only clue that a star has a dim companion. A dim star in a binary star may pass in front of a brighter star and eclipse it. From Earth, the binary star would look much dimmer. A system in which one star periodically blocks the light from another is called an **eclipsing binary.** As Figure 16 shows, the star Algol is actually an eclipsing binary star system.

FIGURE 17
Invisible Partners
If you saw someone dancing but couldn't see a partner, you could infer that the partner was there by watching the dancer you could see. Astronomers use a similar method to detect faint stars in star systems.

Planets Around Other Stars In 1995, astronomers first discovered a planet revolving around another ordinary star. They used a method similar to the one used in studying binary stars. The astronomers observed that a star was moving slightly toward and away from us. They knew that the invisible object causing the movement didn't have enough mass to be a star. They inferred that it must be a planet.

Since then, astronomers have discovered more than 100 planets around other stars, and new ones are being discovered all of the time. Most of these new planets are very large, with at least half of the mass of Jupiter. A small planet would be hard to detect because it would have little gravitational effect on the star it orbited.

Could there be life on planets in other solar systems? Some scientists think it is possible. A few astronomers are using radio telescopes to search for signals that could not have come from natural sources. Such a signal might be evidence that an extra-terrestrial civilization was sending out radio waves.

Star Clusters Many stars belong to larger groupings called star clusters. All of the stars in a particular cluster formed from the same nebula at about the same time and are about the same distance from Earth.

There are two major types of star clusters: open clusters and globular clusters. **Open clusters** have a loose, disorganized appearance and contain no more than a few thousand stars. They often contain many bright supergiants and much gas and dust. In contrast, **globular clusters** are large groupings of older stars. Globular clusters are round and densely packed with stars—some may contain more than a million stars.

 **Reading Checkpoint** What is a globular cluster?

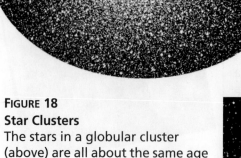

FIGURE 18
Star Clusters
The stars in a globular cluster (above) are all about the same age and the same distance from Earth. The Pleiades (right), also called the *Seven Sisters*, is an open cluster.

Galaxies

Stars are not distributed equally through space. As you have learned, most stars belong to star systems. On a larger scale, many stars belong to star clusters. On an even larger scale, stars are grouped into galaxies.

Galaxies in Space A **galaxy** is a huge group of single stars, star systems, star clusters, dust, and gas bound together by gravity. Many large galaxies, including our own, appear to have huge black holes at their center. There are billions of galaxies in the universe. Each galaxy typically has billions of stars, and the largest galaxies have more than a trillion stars.

Galaxies themselves appear to occur in clusters. For example, our galaxy, the Milky Way, is part of a cluster of 50 or so galaxies called the Local Group. The Local Group is part of the Virgo Supercluster, which contains hundreds of galaxies. Such clusters of galaxies are separated by vast regions of nearly empty space.

Quasars In the 1960s, astronomers discovered objects that are very bright, but also very far away. Many of these objects are 10 billion light-years or more away, making them among the most distant objects in the universe. These distant, enormously bright objects looked almost like stars. Since *quasi* means "something like" in Latin, these objects were given the name quasi-stellar objects, or **quasars.**

What could be so bright at such a great distance from Earth? Astronomers have concluded that quasars are active young galaxies with giant black holes at their centers. Many of these black holes have masses a billion times as great as the sun's mass. As enormous amounts of gas spiral towards the black hole, the gas heats up and shines brightly.

FIGURE 19
Andromeda Galaxy
The Andromeda Galaxy is the nearest large galaxy to our own Milky Way. Andromeda contains hundreds of billions of stars.

Go Online
SCI LINKS™ NSTA

For: Links on galaxies
Visit: www.SciLinks.org
Web Code: scn-0644

Spiral Galaxy

Elliptical Galaxy

Irregular Galaxy

FIGURE 20
Types of Galaxies
There are three major types of galaxies: spiral, elliptical, and irregular.

Types of Galaxies

Galaxies are classified according to size and shape. **Astronomers classify most galaxies into three main categories: spiral, elliptical, and irregular.** Figure 20 shows examples of each major type.

Spiral Galaxies Some galaxies appear to have a bulge in the middle and arms that spiral outward, like pinwheels. Such galaxies are called **spiral galaxies.** The spiral arms contain many bright, young stars as well as gas and dust. Most new stars in spiral galaxies form in these spiral arms. Relatively few new stars are forming in the central bulge.

Some spiral galaxies, called barred-spiral galaxies, have a huge bar-shaped region of stars and gas that passes through their center. Spiral arms extend outward from the bar in this type of galaxy.

Elliptical Galaxies Not all galaxies have spiral arms. **Elliptical galaxies** have shapes that are round, like balls, or oval, like eggs. These galaxies contain billions of stars but have little gas and dust between the stars. Because there is little gas or dust, stars are no longer forming. Most elliptical galaxies contain only old stars. Elliptical galaxies vary greatly in size.

Irregular Galaxies Some galaxies do not have regular shapes. These are known as **irregular galaxies.** Irregular galaxies are typically smaller than other types of galaxies. They generally have many bright, young stars and lots of gas and dust to form new stars. The Large Magellanic Cloud is an irregular galaxy about 180,000 light-years away from our galaxy. At this distance, it is one of the closest neighboring galaxies in the universe.

Irregular galaxies are often located close to larger galaxies. The gravitational pull of these larger galaxies may have distorted the shape of the smaller irregular galaxies.

Reading Checkpoint In spiral galaxies, where are most new stars located?

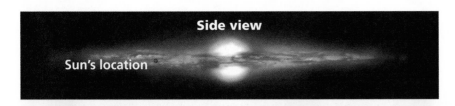
Side view

Sun's location

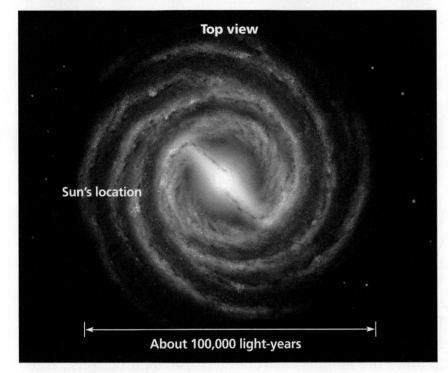
Top view

Sun's location

About 100,000 light-years

FIGURE 21
Structure of the Milky Way
From the side, the Milky Way appears to be a narrow disk with a bulge in the middle. The galaxy's spiral structure is visible only from above or below the galaxy.
Interpreting Diagrams *Where in the galaxy is the sun located?*

The Milky Way

🔑 **Our solar system is located in a spiral galaxy called the Milky Way.** As Figure 21 shows, the shape of the Milky Way varies depending on your vantage point. From the side, the Milky Way would look like a narrow disk with a large bulge in the middle. But from the top or bottom, the Milky Way would have a spiral, pinwheel shape. You can't see the spiral shape of the Milky Way from Earth because our solar system is inside the galaxy in one of the spiral arms. The solar system takes about 225 million years to orbit the galactic center.

The Milky Way is usually thought of as an ordinary spiral galaxy. However, recent evidence suggests that the Milky Way is a barred-spiral galaxy instead.

When you see the Milky Way at night during the summer, you are looking toward the center of our galaxy. The center of the galaxy is about 25,000 light-years away, but is hidden by large clouds of dust and gas. Astronomers can study the center using X-rays, infrared radiation, and radio waves.

Reading Checkpoint How far away is the center of the galaxy?

Lab zone Try This **Activity**

A Spiral Galaxy
You can make a model of our galaxy.

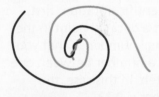

1. Using pipe cleaners, make a pinwheel with two spirals.
2. View the spirals along the surface of the table. Sketch what you see.
3. Next, view the spirals from above the table and sketch them.

Observing The sun is inside a flat spiral galaxy. From Earth's position on the flat surface, is it possible to get a good view of stars in the spiral arms? Why or why not?

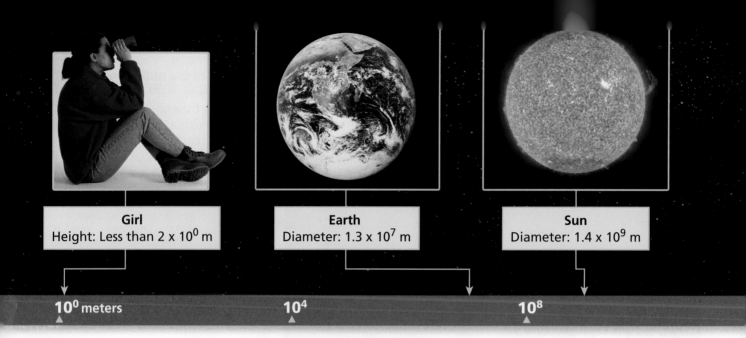

Girl
Height: Less than 2×10^0 m

Earth
Diameter: 1.3×10^7 m

Sun
Diameter: 1.4×10^9 m

10^0 meters 10^4 10^8

The Scale of the Universe

Astronomers define the **universe** as all of space and everything in it. The universe is enormous, almost beyond imagination. Astronomers study objects as close as the moon and as far away as quasars. They study incredibly large objects, such as galaxies that are millions of light-years across. They may also study the behavior of tiny particles, such as the atoms within stars. ⚬ Since the numbers astronomers use are often very large or very small, they frequently use scientific notation to describe sizes and distances in the universe.

Scientific Notation **Scientific notation** uses powers of ten to write very large or very small numbers in shorter form. Each number is written as the product of a number between 1 and 10 and a power of 10. For example: 1,200 is written as 1.2×10^3. One light-year is about 9,500,000,000,000,000 meters. Since there are 15 digits after the first digit, in scientific notation this number is written as 9.5×10^{15} meters.

The Immensity of Space The structures in the universe vary greatly in scale. To understand the scale of these structures, imagine that you are going on a journey through the universe. Refer to Figure 22 as you take your imaginary trip. Start at the left with something familiar—a girl looking through binoculars. She is about 1.5 meters tall. Now shift to the right and change the scale by 10,000,000 or 10^7. You're now close to the diameter of Earth, 1.28×10^7 meters. As you move from left to right across Figure 22, the scale increases. The diameter of the sun is about 100 times that of Earth.

| Cat's Eye Nebula | Andromeda Galaxy | Virgo Supercluster |
| Diameter: 3×10^{16} m | Diameter: 2×10^{21} m | Diameter: 9×10^{23} m |

10^{16} 10^{20} 10^{24}

Beyond the solar system, the sizes of observable objects become much larger. For example, within our galaxy, the beautiful Cat's Eye Nebula is about 3×10^{16} meters across.

Beyond our galaxy there are billions of other galaxies. For example, the nearby spiral galaxy Andromeda is about 2×10^{21} meters across. The Virgo Supercluster of galaxies, which includes Andromeda as well as the Milky Way, is about 9×10^{23} meters in diameter. The size of the observable universe is about 10^{10} light-years, or 10^{26} meters.

FIGURE 22
Scientific Notation
Scientists often use scientific notation to help describe the vast sizes and distances in space.
Calculating *About how many times larger is the Cat's Eye Nebula than Earth?*

✓ **Reading Checkpoint** How large is the observable universe?

Section 4 Assessment

S 8.4.a, 8.4.b, Reviewing Math: 7NS1.1, E-LA: Reading 8.1.0

Vocabulary Skill **Suffixes** What suffixes do you see in the words *elliptical* and *scientific*? What parts of speech do they indicate? Use the term *elliptical galaxy* in a sentence.

⚷ **Reviewing Key Concepts**

1. a. **Defining** What is a binary star?
   b. **Classifying** Are all binary stars part of star systems? Explain.
   c. **Applying Concepts** Some binary stars are called eclipsing binaries. Explain why this term is appropriate. (*Hint:* Think about Algol as you write your answer.)
2. a. **Listing** Name the main types of galaxies.
   b. **Classifying** What type of galaxy is the Milky Way?

c. **Classifying** Suppose astronomers discover a galaxy that contains only old stars. What type of galaxy is it likely to be?
3. a. **Reviewing** What is scientific notation?
   b. **Explaining** How is scientific notation useful to astronomers?
   c. **Calculating** How large is the Cat's Eye Nebula in light-years? (*Hint:* Refer to Figure 22.)

Math Practice

4. **Scientific Notation** The star Betelgeuse has a diameter of 940,000,000 km. Betelgeuse is 427 light-years from Earth. Write each of these figures in scientific notation.

CALIFORNIA
Standards Focus

S 8.2.g Students know the role of gravity in forming and maintaining the shapes of planets, stars, and the solar system.

S 8.4.a Students know galaxies are clusters of billions of stars and may have different shapes.

- What is the big bang theory?
- How did the solar system form?
- What do astronomers predict about the future of the universe?

Key Terms

- big bang
- Hubble's law
- cosmic background radiation
- solar nebula
- planetesimal
- dark matter
- dark energy

Lab zone | Standards **Warm-Up**

How Does the Universe Expand?

1. Use a marker to put 10 dots on an empty balloon. The dots represent galaxies.
2. Blow up the balloon. What happens to the distances between galaxies that are close together? Galaxies that are far apart?

Think It Over

Inferring If the universe is expanding, do galaxies that are close together move apart faster or slower than galaxies that are far apart? Explain.

The Andromeda Galaxy is the most distant object that the human eye can see. Light from this galaxy has traveled for about 3 million years before reaching Earth. When that light finally reaches your eye, you are seeing how the galaxy looked 3 million years ago. It is as though you are looking back in time.

Astronomers have photographed galaxies that are billions of light-years away. Light from these galaxies traveled for billions of years before it reached Earth. From these observations, astronomers are able to infer the age of the universe.

How the Universe Formed

Astronomers theorize that the universe began billions of years ago. At that time, the part of the universe we can now see was no larger than the period at the end of this sentence. This tiny universe was incredibly hot and dense. The universe then exploded in what astronomers call the **big bang.**

◄ Nearly every visible object in this image is a distant galaxy.

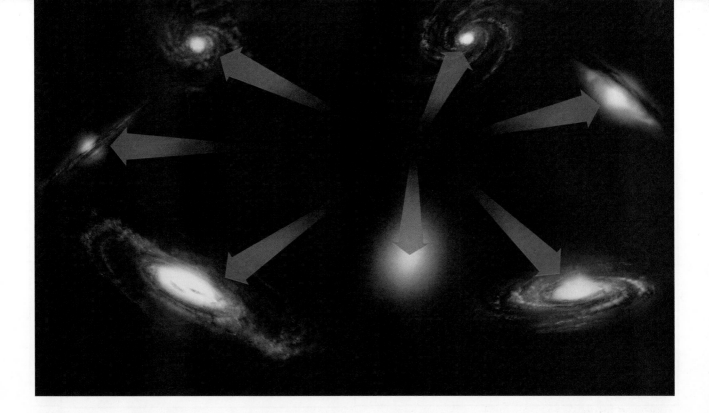

According to the big bang theory, the universe formed in an instant, billions of years ago, in an enormous explosion. Since the big bang, the size of the universe has been increasing rapidly. The universe is billions of times larger now than it was early in its history.

As the universe expanded, it gradually cooled. After a few hundred thousand years, atoms formed. After about 200 million years, gravity caused the first stars and galaxies to form.

If the big bang theory is accurate, what evidence might you expect to find in today's universe? You might expect that the matter that had been hurled apart by the big bang would still be moving apart. You might also expect to find evidence of energy left over from the explosion.

Moving Galaxies An American astronomer, Edwin Hubble, discovered important evidence that later helped astronomers to develop the big bang theory. In the 1920s, Hubble studied the spectrums of many galaxies at various distances from Earth. By examining a galaxy's spectrum, Hubble could tell how fast the galaxy is moving and whether it is moving toward our galaxy or away from it.

Hubble discovered that, with the exception of a few nearby galaxies, all galaxies are moving away from us and from each other. Hubble found that there is a relationship between the distance to a galaxy and its speed. **Hubble's law** states that the farther away a galaxy is, the faster it is moving away from us. Hubble's law strongly supports the big bang theory.

FIGURE 23
Retreating Galaxies
All of the distant galaxies astronomers have observed are moving rapidly away from our galaxy and from each other.

Math Analyzing Data

Speeding Galaxies

Use the graph to answer the questions below about moving clusters of galaxies.

1. **Reading Graphs** How far away is the Bootes cluster? How fast is it moving?

2. **Reading Graphs** Which galaxy is moving away the fastest? Which galaxy is closest to Earth?

3. **Drawing Conclusions** How are the distance and speed of a galaxy related?

4. **Predicting** Predict the speed of a galaxy that is 5 billion light-years from Earth.

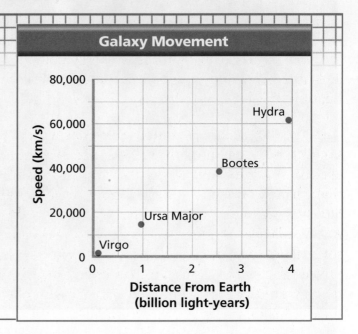

Galaxy Movement

To understand how the galaxies are moving, think of raisin bread dough that is rising. If you could shrink yourself to sit on a raisin, you would see all the other raisins moving away from you. The farther a raisin was from you, the faster it would move away, because there would be more bread dough to expand between you and the raisin. No matter which raisin you sat on, all the other raisins would seem to be moving away from you. You could tell that the bread dough was expanding by watching the other raisins.

The universe is like the bread dough. Like the raisins in the dough, the galaxies in the universe are moving away from each other. In the universe, it is space that is expanding, like the dough between the raisins.

Cosmic Background Radiation In 1965, two American physicists, Arno Penzias and Robert Wilson, accidentally detected faint radiation on their radio telescope. This mysterious glow was coming from all directions in space. Scientists later concluded that this glow, now called **cosmic background radiation,** is the leftover thermal energy from the big bang. This energy was distributed in every direction as the universe expanded.

Age of the Universe Since astronomers can measure approximately how fast the universe is expanding now, they can infer how long it has been expanding. Based on careful measurements of how fast distant galaxies are moving away from us and the cosmic background radiation, astronomers estimate that the universe is about 13.7 billion years old.

FIGURE 24
Rising Dough
The galaxies in the universe are like the raisins in rising bread dough. **Making Models** *How does rising raisin bread dough resemble the expanding universe?*

Formation of the Solar System

After the big bang, matter in the universe separated into galaxies. Gas and dust spread throughout space. Where the solar system is now, there was only cold, dark gas and dust. How did the solar system form? The leading hypothesis is explained below.

The Solar Nebula 🌀 **About five billion years ago, a giant cloud of gas and dust collapsed to form our solar system.** A large cloud of gas and dust such as the one that formed our solar system is called a **solar nebula.** Slowly, gravity began to pull the solar nebula together. As the solar nebula shrank, it spun faster and faster. The solar nebula flattened, forming a rotating disk. Gravity pulled most of the gas into the center of the disk, where the gas eventually became hot and dense enough for nuclear fusion to begin. The sun was born.

Planetesimals In the outer parts of the disk, gas and dust formed small asteroid-like and comet-like bodies called **planetesimals.** These formed the building blocks of the planets. Planetesimals collided and grew larger by sticking together, eventually combining to form the planets.

The Planets When the solar system formed, temperatures were very high. It was so hot close to the sun that most water and other ice-forming materials simply vaporized. Most gases escaped the gravity of the planets that were forming in this region. As a result, the inner planets are relatively small and rocky.

Farther from the sun it was much cooler. As the planets in this region grew, their gravity increased and they were able to capture much of the hydrogen and helium gas in the surrounding space. As a result, the gas giants became very large. Most comets formed near Jupiter and Saturn. They were later flung out to the outer solar system. Beyond the gas giants, a huge disk of ice and other substances formed. Pluto also formed in this region.

Evidence The composition of the inner and outer planets provides strong evidence for the solar nebula theory. Other evidence includes the position of the sun at the center of the solar system and the fact that all of the planets revolve around the sun in the same direction.

 **What is a solar nebula?**

A cloud of gas and dust formed a spinning disk.

Gas in the center of the disk collapsed to form the sun.

The remaining gas and dust formed the planets.

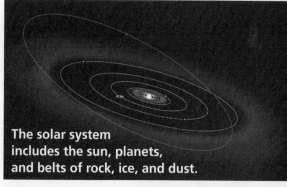
The solar system includes the sun, planets, and belts of rock, ice, and dust.

FIGURE 25
How the Solar System Formed
The solar system formed from a collapsing cloud of gas and dust.

FIGURE 26
Vera Rubin
Astronomer Vera Rubin's observations helped prove the existence of dark matter.

The Future of the Universe

What will happen to the universe in the future? One possibility is that the universe will continue to expand, as it is doing now. All of the stars will eventually run out of fuel and burn out, and the universe will be cold and dark. Another possibility is that the force of gravity will begin to pull the galaxies back together. The result would be a reverse big bang, or "big crunch." All of the matter in the universe would be crushed into an enormous black hole.

Which of these possibilities is more likely? Recent discoveries have led to a surprising new view of the universe that is still not well understood. **New observations lead many astronomers to conclude that the universe will likely expand forever.**

Dark Matter Until fairly recently, astronomers assumed that the universe consisted solely of the matter they could observe directly. But this idea was disproved by the American astronomer Vera Rubin. Rubin made detailed observations of the rotation of spiral galaxies. She discovered that the matter that astronomers can see, such as stars and nebulas, makes up as little as ten percent of the mass in galaxies. The remaining mass exists in the form of dark matter.

Dark matter is matter that does not give off electromagnetic radiation. Dark matter cannot be seen directly. However, its presence can be inferred by observing the effect of its gravity on visible objects, such as stars, or on light. Astronomers still don't know much about dark matter—what it is made of or all of the places where it is found.

An Accelerating Expansion In the late 1990s, astronomers observed that the expansion of the universe appears be accelerating. That is, galaxies seem to be moving apart at a faster rate now than in the past. This observation was puzzling, as no known force could account for it. Astronomers infer that a mysterious new force, which they call **dark energy,** is causing the expansion of the universe to accelerate. Current estimates indicate that most of the universe is made of dark energy and dark matter. Astronomers think that only a small fraction of the universe—less than 5 percent—is composed of "normal matter" that they can see.

Astronomy is one of the oldest sciences, but there are still many discoveries to be made and puzzles to be solved about this universe of ours!

 **Reading Checkpoint** **What is the effect of dark energy?**

FIGURE 27
Dark Matter
Astronomers measured the effect of gravity on light to produce this computer image of how dark matter (in blue) is distributed across a cluster of galaxies.

Section 5 Assessment

S 8.2.g, 8.4.a,
E-LA: Reading 8.2.2

Target Reading Skill **Identify Supporting Evidence** Create a graphic organizer showing the scientific evidence for the hypothesis that the universe will likely expand forever.

Reviewing Key Concepts

1. a. Defining What was the big bang?
   b. Summarizing When did the big bang occur?
   c. Describing Describe two pieces of evidence that support the big bang theory.
2. a. Summarizing How old is the solar system?
   b. Relating Cause and Effect What force caused the solar system to form?
   c. Sequencing Place the following events in the proper order: planets form; planetesimals form; solar nebula shrinks; nuclear fusion begins in the sun.

3. a. Defining What is dark matter?
   b. Explaining How do scientists know that dark matter exists?
   c. Predicting What evidence has led scientists to predict that the universe will continue to expand forever?

Lab zone **At-Home Activity**

Stargazing Plan an evening of stargazing with adult family members. Choose a dark, clear night. Use binoculars if available and the star charts in Appendix E to locate the Milky Way and some interesting stars that you have learned about. Explain to your family what you know about the Milky Way and each constellation that you observe.

The BIG Idea — Astronomers learn about the structure and evolution of the universe by studying stars, galaxies, and other objects in space.

1 Telescopes

Key Concepts — S 8.4.d

- The electromagnetic spectrum includes radio waves, infrared radiation, visible light, ultraviolet radiation, X-rays, and gamma rays.
- Telescopes are instruments that collect and focus light and other forms of electromagnetic radiation.
- Many large observatories are located on mountaintops or in space.

Key Terms

visible light
wavelength
spectrum
optical telescope
electromagnetic radiation
refracting telescope
convex lens
reflecting telescope
radio telescope
observatory

2 Characteristics of Stars

Key Concepts — S 8.4.b, 8.4.c

- Characteristics used to classify stars include color, temperature, size, composition, and brightness.
- The brightness of a star depends upon both its size and temperature.
- Astronomers use a unit called the light-year to measure distances between the stars.
- Astronomers often use parallax to measure distances to nearby stars.
- Astronomers use H-R diagrams to classify stars and to understand how stars change over time.

Key Terms

- constellation • spectrograph
- apparent brightness • absolute brightness
- light-year • parallax
- Hertzsprung-Russell diagram
- main sequence

3 Lives of Stars

Key Concepts — S 8.4.b, 8.4.d

- A star is born when gas and dust a become so dense and hot that nuclear fusion starts.
- How long a star lives depends on its mass.
- After a star runs out of fuel, it becomes a white dwarf, a neutron star, or a black hole.

Key Terms

- nebula • protostar • planetary nebula
- white dwarf • supernova • neutron star
- pulsar • black hole

4 Star Systems and Galaxies

Key Concepts — S 8.4.a, 8.4.b

- Most stars are members of star systems.
- Astronomers classify most galaxies into the following types: spiral, elliptical, and irregular.
- Our solar system is located in a spiral galaxy called the Milky Way.
- Astronomers often use scientific notation to describe sizes and distances in the universe.

Key Terms

- binary star • eclipsing binary • open cluster
- globular cluster • galaxy • quasar
- spiral galaxy • elliptical galaxy
- irregular galaxy • universe
- scientific notation

5 The Expanding Universe

Key Concepts — S 8.2.g, 8.4.a

- According to the big bang theory, the universe formed in an explosion billions of years ago.
- About five billion years ago, a giant cloud of gas and dust collapsed to form our solar system.
- New observations lead astronomers to conclude that the universe will likely expand forever.

Key Terms

- big bang • Hubble's law
- cosmic background radiation • solar nebula
- planetesimal • dark matter • dark energy

Review and Assessment

Go Online
PHSchool.com

For: Self-Assessment
Visit: PHSchool.com
Web Code: cxa-4150

Target Reading Skill

Identify Supporting Evidence
Create a graphic organizer that shows the evidence supporting the solar nebula theory.

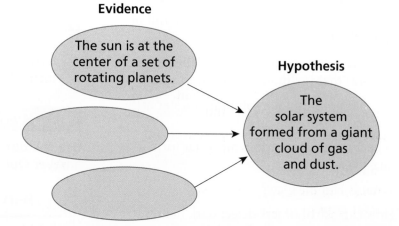

Evidence

The sun is at the center of a set of rotating planets.

Hypothesis

The solar system formed from a giant cloud of gas and dust.

Reviewing Key Terms

Choose the letter of the best answer.

1. Visible light is a form of
   a. spectrum.
   b. electromagnetic radiation.
   c. wavelength.
   d. cosmic background radiation.

2. An H-R diagram is a graph of stars' temperature and
   a. apparent brightness.
   b. main sequence.
   c. absolute brightness.
   d. parallax.

3. A low-mass main sequence star will eventually evolve into a
   a. white dwarf.   b. protostar.
   c. black hole.   d. nebula.

4. A star system in which one star blocks the light from another is called a(n)
   a. open cluster.
   b. quasar.
   c. binary star.
   d. eclipsing binary.

5. Astronomers theorize that the universe began in an enormous explosion called the
   a. solar nebula.
   b. supernova.
   c. big bang.
   d. big crunch.

Complete the following sentences so that your answers clearly explain the key terms.

6. Astronomy was revolutionized by the invention of the **telescope,** which is _____ .

7. More than 90 percent of stars are found on the **main sequence,** which is _____ .

8. Stars are formed in **nebulas,** which are _____ .

9. The Milky Way is an example of a **galaxy,** which is _____ .

10. Evidence for the big bang includes **cosmic background radiation,** which is _____ .

Writing in Science

News Article Imagine that you are a journalist covering current research in astronomy. Write an article explaining what black holes are, how they form, and how they can be detected.

Video Assessment
Discovery Channel School
Stars, Galaxies, and the Universe

Review and Assessment

Checking Concepts

11. Is a light-year a unit of distance or a unit of time? Explain.

12. Why can't astronomers measure the parallax of a star that is a million light-years away?

13. At what point in the evolution of a star is the star actually born?

14. Where in our galaxy does most star formation take place?

15. What is Hubble's law?

16. How can astronomers detect dark matter if they cannot observe it directly?

Math Practice

17. **Calculating** The bright star Spica is about 262 light-years from our solar system. How many kilometers is this?

18. **Scientific Notation** The star Antares is approximately 604 light-years from Earth. Write this distance in scientific notation.

Thinking Critically

19. **Inferring** What advantage might there be to locating a telescope, such as the one shown below, on the moon?

20. **Applying Concepts** Describe a real-world situation involving absolute and apparent brightness. (*Hint*: Think about riding in a car at night.)

21. **Relating Cause and Effect** How does a star's mass affect its lifetime?

22. **Comparing and Contrasting** Compare the conditions that led to the formation of the terrestrial planets with those that led to the formation of the gas giants.

Applying Skills

Use the data in the H-R diagram below to answer Questions 23–26.

Hertzsprung-Russell Diagram

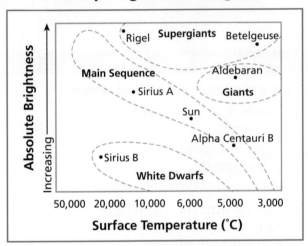

23. **Interpreting Diagrams** Which star has a greater absolute brightness, Aldebaran or Sirius B?

24. **Interpreting Diagrams** Which stars have higher surface temperatures than Sirius A?

25. **Applying Concepts** Which star is most likely to be red: Rigel, Sirius B, or Betelgeuse?

26. **Comparing and Contrasting** Compare Aldebaran and the sun in terms of size, temperature, and absolute brightness.

Lab zone — Standards Investigation

Performance Assessment Check the final draft of your constellation story for correct spelling, grammar, punctuation, and usage. Then decide how you will present your story. For example, you could make a poster, read your story aloud, or perform it as a skit or a play.

Choose the letter of the best answer.

1. You can often see stars at night because
   A they produce light from nuclear fusion.
   B they reflect light from the planets.
   C they reflect light from the sun.
   D they have exploded as supernovas. **S 8.4.d**

2. The most common chemical element in most stars is
   A oxygen.
   B hydrogen.
   C helium.
   D nitrogen. **S 8.4.b**

3. The main factor that affects the evolution of a star is its
   A color.
   B apparent brightness.
   C mass.
   D parallax. **S 8.4.b**

4. An astronomer would likely measure the distance between stars in
   A light-years.
   B kilometers.
   C astronomical units.
   D millimeters. **S 8.4.c**

The table below gives an estimate of the distribution of stars in the Milky Way galaxy. Use the table and your knowledge of science to answer Question 5.

Type of Star	Percentage of Total
Main sequence	90.75%
Red Giant	0.50%
Supergiant	< 0.0001%
White Dwarf	8.75%

5. According to the table, the most common type of stars in the Milky Way are
   A main-sequence stars.
   B red giants.
   C supergiants.
   D white dwarfs. **S 8.4.b**

6. The image above shows a galaxy with few or no new stars. It is most likely a(n)
   A spiral galaxy.
   B barred spiral galaxy.
   C irregular galaxy.
   D elliptical galaxy. **S 8.4.a**

7. Which of the following correctly describes the evolution of a sun-like star from young to old?
   A white dwarf, red giant, main-sequence star, protostar
   B red giant, main-sequence star, white dwarf, protostar
   C protostar, main-sequence star, white dwarf, red giant
   D protostar, main-sequence star, red giant, white dwarf **S 8.4.b**

8. What force pulled matter together in the solar nebula to form the solar system?
   A inertia
   B nuclear fusion
   C dark energy
   D gravity **S 8.2.g**

Apply the
BIG Idea

9. Describe the appearance of the Milky Way as you would see it both from Earth and from a point directly above or below the galaxy. Why does the galaxy look different from different vantage points? **S 8.4.a**

Astronomy
Unit 4 Review

Chapter 12
Earth, Moon, and Sun
The BIG Idea

The motions of Earth and the moon and their position relative to the sun result in day and night, the seasons, phases of the moon, eclipses, and tides.

- How does Earth move in space?
- What two factors combine to keep the moon and Earth in orbit?
- What causes the phases of the moon, eclipses, and tides?
- What are some characteristics of the moon?

Chapter 13
Exploring Space
The BIG Idea

Scientists have learned much about the solar system through various types of space missions.

- How does a rocket work?
- What were the major events in human exploration of the moon?
- What are the roles of space shuttles, space stations, and space probes?
- How has space technology benefited modern society?

Chapter 14
The Solar System
The BIG Idea

The solar system includes the sun, the planets and their moons, and smaller objects such as comets, asteroids, and meteoroids.

- What are the layers of the sun's interior and its atmosphere?
- What characteristics do the inner planets have in common?
- What characteristics distinguish each of the outer planets?
- What are the characteristics of comets, asteroids, and meteoroids?

Chapter 15
Stars, Galaxies, and the Universe
The BIG Idea

Astronomers learn about the structure and evolution of the universe by studying stars, galaxies, and other objects in space.

- How are stars classified?
- How does a star form?
- What are the major types of galaxies?
- What is the big-bang theory?

Unit 4 Assessment

Imagine an adventurous group of astronauts in the far future going on a grand tour of our solar system. They might time their trip to start just after a big event, such as a solar eclipse. They would need a powerful rocket to get them off Earth's surface and beyond Earth's gravitational pull.

The astronauts would visit Mars, pass through the asteroid belt, and then delight at the gas giants Jupiter, Saturn, Uranus, and Neptune. They might spend a lot of time studying Jupiter and its four large moons. And no grand solar system tour would be complete without enjoying a close-up view of Saturn's lovely rings.

After a stop at tiny, cold Pluto, the astronauts would head back toward the center of the solar system, passing Venus and Mercury until finally they would get as close to the sun as they possibly could. They might take note of how well the sun supports life on Earth. Not every star in the galaxy has a system of planets, and of those that do, many may not support life as we know it.

1. For a solar eclipse to occur, what must be the moon's phase? *(Chapter 12)*
   a. new moon   **b.** first quarter
   c. full moon   **d.** third quarter

2. To leave Earth's gravitational pull, the astronauts' rocket had to reach which of the following? *(Chapter 13)*
   a. terminal velocity
   b. orbit
   c. orbital velocity
   d. escape velocity

3. Which of Jupiter's largest moons is thought to have the conditions necessary for life to develop? *(Chapter 14)*
   a. Io   **b.** Callisto
   c. Europa   **d.** Ganymede

4. What kind of star is the sun? *(Chapter 15)*
   a. white dwarf   **b.** main sequence
   c. giant   **d.** supergiant

5. Summary Write a paragraph that summarizes the conditions necessary for a planet to support life as we know it. Give examples of places in our solar system where each of these conditions exist.

Think Like a Scientist

Scientists have a particular way of looking at the world, or scientific habits of mind. Whenever you ask a question and explore possible answers, you use many of the same skills that scientists do. Some of these skills are described on this page.

Observing

When you use one or more of your five senses to gather information about the world, you are **observing.** Hearing a dog bark, counting twelve green seeds, and smelling smoke are all observations. To increase the power of their senses, scientists sometimes use microscopes, telescopes, or other instruments that help them make more detailed observations.

An observation must be an accurate report of what your senses detect. It is important to keep careful records of your observations in science class by writing or drawing in a notebook. The information collected through observations is called evidence, or data.

Inferring

When you interpret an observation, you are **inferring,** or making an inference. For example, if you hear your dog barking, you may infer that someone is at your front door. To make this inference, you combine the evidence— the barking dog—and your experience or knowledge—you know that your dog barks when strangers approach—to reach a logical conclusion.

Notice that an inference is not a fact; it is only one of many possible interpretations for an observation. For example, your dog may be barking because it wants to go for a walk. An inference may turn out to be incorrect even if it is based on accurate observations and logical reasoning. The only way to find out if an inference is correct is to investigate further.

Predicting

When you listen to the weather forecast, you hear many predictions about the next day's weather—what the temperature will be, whether it will rain, and how windy it will be. Weather forecasters use observations and knowledge of weather patterns to predict the weather. The skill of **predicting** involves making an inference about a future event based on current evidence or past experience.

Because a prediction is an inference, it may prove to be false. In science class, you can test some of your predictions by doing experiments. For example, suppose you predict that larger paper airplanes can fly farther than smaller airplanes. How could you test your prediction?

Activity

Use the photograph to answer the questions below.

Observing Look closely at the photograph. List at least three observations.

Inferring Use your observations to make an inference about what has happened. What experience or knowledge did you use to make the inference?

Predicting Predict what will happen next. On what evidence or experience do you base your prediction?

Classifying

Could you imagine searching for a book in the library if the books were shelved in no particular order? Your trip to the library would be an all-day event! Luckily, librarians group together books on similar topics or by the same author. Grouping together items that are alike in some way is called **classifying.** You can classify items in many ways: by size, by shape, by use, and by other important characteristics.

Like librarians, scientists use the skill of classifying to organize information and objects. When things are sorted into groups, the relationships among them become easier to understand.

Activity

Classify the objects in the photograph into two groups based on any characteristic you choose. Then use another characteristic to classify the objects into three groups.

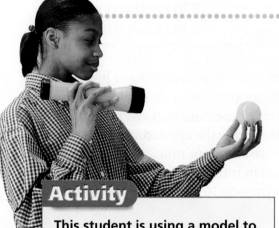

Making Models

Have you ever drawn a picture to help someone understand what you were saying? Such a drawing is one type of model. A model is a picture, diagram, computer image, or other representation of a complex object or process. **Making models** helps people understand things that they cannot observe directly.

Scientists often use models to represent things that are either very large or very small, such as the planets in the solar system, or the parts of a cell. Such models are physical models—drawings or three-dimensional structures that look like the real thing. Other models are mental models— mathematical equations or words that describe how something works.

Activity

This student is using a model to demonstrate what causes day and night on Earth. What do the flashlight and the tennis ball in the model represent?

Communicating

Whenever you talk on the phone, write a report, or listen to your teacher at school, you are communicating. **Communicating** is the process of sharing ideas and information with other people. Communicating effectively requires many skills, including writing, reading, speaking, listening, and making models.

Scientists communicate to share results, information, and opinions. Scientists often communicate about their work in journals, over the telephone, in letters, and on the Internet.

They also attend scientific meetings where they share their ideas with one another in person.

Activity

On a sheet of paper, write out clear, detailed directions for tying your shoe. Then exchange directions with a partner. Follow your partner's directions exactly. How successful were you at tying your shoe? How could your partner have communicated more clearly?

Making Measurements

By measuring, scientists can express their observations more precisely and communicate more information about what they observe.

Measuring in SI

The standard system of measurement used by scientists around the world is known as the International System of Units, which is abbreviated as SI (**Système International d'Unités**, in French). SI units are easy to use because they are based on multiples of 10. Each unit is ten times larger than the next smallest unit and one tenth the size of the next largest unit. The table lists the prefixes used to name the most common SI units.

Length To measure length, or the distance between two points, the unit of measure is the **meter (m)**. The distance from the floor to a doorknob is approximately one meter. Long distances, such as the distance between two cities, are measured in kilometers (km). Small lengths are measured in centimeters (cm) or millimeters (mm). Scientists use metric rulers and meter sticks to measure length.

Common SI Prefixes		
Prefix	**Symbol**	**Meaning**
kilo-	k	1,000
hecto-	h	100
deka-	da	10
deci-	d	0.1 (one tenth)
centi-	c	0.01 (one hundredth)
milli-	m	0.001 (one thousandth)

Common Conversions		
1 km	=	1,000 m
1 m	=	100 cm
1 m	=	1,000 mm
1 cm	=	10 mm

Liquid Volume To measure the volume of a liquid, or the amount of space it takes up, you will use a unit of measure known as the **liter (L)**. One liter is the approximate volume of a medium-size carton of milk. Smaller volumes are measured in milliliters (mL). Scientists use graduated cylinders to measure liquid volume.

Activity

The larger lines on the metric ruler in the picture show centimeter divisions, while the smaller, unnumbered lines show millimeter divisions. How many centimeters long is the shell? How many millimeters long is it?

Activity

The graduated cylinder in the picture is marked in milliliter divisions. Notice that the water in the cylinder has a curved surface. This curved surface is called the *meniscus*. To measure the volume, you must read the level at the lowest point of the meniscus. What is the volume of water in this graduated cylinder?

Common Conversion
1 L = 1,000 mL

Mass To measure mass, or the amount of matter in an object, you will use a unit of measure known as the **gram (g).** One gram is approximately the mass of a paper clip. Larger masses are measured in kilograms (kg). Scientists use a balance to find the mass of an object.

Common Conversion

1 kg = 1,000 g

Activity

The mass of the potato in the picture is measured in kilograms. What is the mass of the potato? Suppose a recipe for potato salad called for one kilogram of potatoes. About how many potatoes would you need?

0.25 KG

Temperature To measure the temperature of a substance, you will use the **Celsius scale.** Temperature is measured in degrees Celsius (°C) using a Celsius thermometer. Water freezes at 0°C and boils at 100°C.

Time The unit scientists use to measure time is the **second (s).**

Activity

What is the temperature of the liquid in degrees Celsius?

Converting SI Units

To use the SI system, you must know how to convert between units. Converting from one unit to another involves the skill of **calculating,** or using mathematical operations. Converting between SI units is similar to converting between dollars and dimes because both systems are based on multiples of ten.

Suppose you want to convert a length of 80 centimeters to meters. Follow these steps to convert between units.

1. Begin by writing down the measurement you want to convert—in this example, 80 centimeters.

2. Write a conversion factor that represents the relationship between the two units you are converting. In this example, the relationship is 1 meter = 100 centimeters. Write this conversion factor as a fraction, making sure to place the units you are converting from (centimeters, in this example) in the denominator.

3. Multiply the measurement you want to convert by the fraction. When you do this, the units in the first measurement will cancel out with the units in the denominator. Your answer will be in the units you are converting to (meters, in this example).

Example

80 centimeters = ■ meters

$$80 \text{ centimeters} \times \frac{1 \text{ meter}}{100 \text{ centimeters}} = \frac{80 \text{ meters}}{100}$$

$$= 0.8 \text{ meters}$$

Activity

Convert between the following units.
1. 600 millimeters = ■ meters
2. 0.35 liters = ■ milliliters
3. 1,050 grams = ■ kilograms

Conducting a Scientific Investigation

In some ways, scientists are like detectives, piecing together clues to learn about a process or event. One way that scientists gather clues is by carrying out experiments. An experiment tests an idea in a careful, orderly manner. Although experiments do not all follow the same steps in the same order, many follow a pattern similar to the one described here.

Posing Questions

Experiments begin by asking a scientific question. A scientific question is one that can be answered by gathering evidence. For example, the question "Which freezes faster—fresh water or salt water?" is a scientific question because you can carry out an investigation and gather information to answer the question.

Developing a Hypothesis

The next step is to form a hypothesis. A **hypothesis** is a possible explanation for a set of observations or answer to a scientific question. A hypothesis may incorporate observations, concepts, principles, and theories about the natural world. Hypotheses lead to predictions that can be tested. A prediction can be worded as an *If . . . then . . .* statement. For example, a prediction might be *"If I add salt to fresh water, then the water will take longer to freeze."* A prediction worded this way serves as a rough outline of the experiment you should perform.

Designing an Experiment

Next you need to plan a way to test your hypothesis. Your plan should be written out as a step-by-step procedure and should describe the observations or measurements you will make.

Two important steps involved in designing an experiment are controlling variables and forming operational definitions.

Controlling Variables In a well-designed experiment, you need to keep all variables the same except for one. A **variable** is any factor that can change in an experiment. The factor that you change is called the **manipulated variable**. In this experiment, the manipulated variable is the amount of salt added to the water. Other factors, such as the amount of water or the starting temperature, are kept constant.

The factor that changes as a result of the manipulated variable is called the **responding variable.** The responding variable is what you measure or observe to obtain your results. In this experiment, the responding variable is how long the water takes to freeze.

An experiment in which all factors except one are kept constant is called a **controlled experiment.** Most controlled experiments include a test called the control. In this experiment, Container 3 is the control. Because no salt is added to Container 3, you can compare the results from the other containers to it. Any difference in results must be due to the addition of salt alone.

Forming Operational Definitions Another important aspect of a well-designed experiment is having clear operational definitions. An **operational definition** is a statement that describes how a particular variable is to be measured or how a term is to be defined. For example, in this experiment, how will you determine if the water has frozen? You might decide to insert a stick in each container at the start of the experiment. Your operational definition of "frozen" would be the time at which the stick can no longer move.

Experimental Procedure
1. Fill 3 containers with 300 milliliters of cold tap water.
2. Add 10 grams of salt to Container 1; stir. Add 20 grams of salt to Container 2; stir. Add no salt to Container 3.
3. Place the 3 containers in a freezer.
4. Check the containers every 15 minutes. Record your observations.

Interpreting Data

The observations and measurements you make in an experiment are called **data.** At the end of an experiment, you need to analyze the data to look for any patterns or trends. Patterns often become clear if you organize your data in a data table or graph. Then think through what the data reveal. Do they support your hypothesis? Do they point out a flaw in your experiment? Do you need to collect more data?

Drawing Conclusions

A **conclusion** is a statement that sums up what you have learned from an experiment. When you draw a conclusion, you need to decide whether the data you collected support your hypothesis or not. You may need to repeat an experiment several times before you can draw any conclusions from it. Conclusions often lead you to pose new questions and plan new experiments to answer them.

Activity

Is a ball's bounce affected by the height from which it is dropped? Using the steps just described, plan a controlled experiment to investigate this problem.

Technology Design Skills

Engineers are people who use scientific and technological knowledge to solve practical problems. To design new products, engineers usually follow the process described here, even though they may not follow these steps in the exact order. As you read the steps, think about how you might apply them in technology labs.

Identify a Need

Before engineers begin designing a new product, they must first identify the need they are trying to meet. For example, suppose you are a member of a design team in a company that makes toys. Your team has identified a need: a toy boat that is inexpensive and easy to assemble.

Research the Problem

Engineers often begin by gathering information that will help them with their new design. This research may include finding articles in books, magazines, or on the Internet. It may also include talking to other engineers who have solved similar problems. Engineers often perform experiments related to the product they want to design.

For your toy boat, you could look at toys that are similar to the one you want to design. You might do research on the Internet. You could also test some materials to see whether they will work well in a toy boat.

Drawing for a boat design ▼

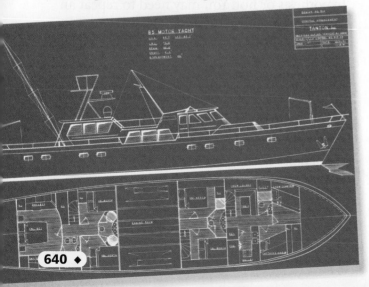

Design a Solution

Research gives engineers information that helps them design a product. When engineers design new products, they usually work in teams.

Generating Ideas Often design teams hold brainstorming meetings in which any team member can contribute ideas. **Brainstorming** is a creative process in which one team member's suggestions often spark ideas in other group members. Brainstorming can lead to new approaches to solving a design problem.

Evaluating Constraints During brainstorming, a design team will often come up with several possible designs. The team must then evaluate each one.

As part of their evaluation, engineers consider constraints. **Constraints** are factors that limit or restrict a product design. Physical characteristics, such as the properties of materials used to make your toy boat, are constraints. Money and time are also constraints. If the materials in a product cost a lot, or if the product takes a long time to make, the design may be impractical.

Making Trade-offs Design teams usually need to make trade-offs. In a **trade-off,** engineers give up one benefit of a proposed design in order to obtain another. In designing your toy boat, you will have to make trade-offs. For example, suppose one material is sturdy but not fully waterproof. Another material is more waterproof, but breakable. You may decide to give up the benefit of sturdiness in order to obtain the benefit of waterproofing.

Build and Evaluate a Prototype

Once the team has chosen a design plan, the engineers build a prototype of the product. A **prototype** is a working model used to test a design. Engineers evaluate the prototype to see whether it works well, is easy to operate, is safe to use, and holds up to repeated use.

Think of your toy boat. What would the prototype be like? Of what materials would it be made? How would you test it?

Troubleshoot and Redesign

Few prototypes work perfectly, which is why they need to be tested. Once a design team has tested a prototype, the members analyze the results and identify any problems. The team then tries to **troubleshoot,** or fix the design problems. For example, if your toy boat leaks or wobbles, the boat should be redesigned to eliminate those problems.

Communicate the Solution

A team needs to communicate the final design to the people who will manufacture and use the product. To do this, teams may use sketches, detailed drawings, computer simulations, and word descriptions.

Activity

You can use the technology design process to design and build a toy boat.

Research and Investigate

1. Visit the library or go online to research toy boats.
2. Investigate how a toy boat can be powered, including wind, rubber bands, or baking soda and vinegar.
3. Brainstorm materials, shapes, and steering for your boat.

Design and Build

4. Based on your research, design a toy boat that
   • is made of readily available materials
   • is no larger than 15 cm long and 10 cm wide
   • includes a power system, a rudder, and an area for cargo
   • travels 2 meters in a straight line carrying a load of 20 pennies
5. Sketch your design and write a step-by-step plan for building your boat. After your teacher approves your plan, build your boat.

Evaluate and Redesign

6. Test your boat, evaluate the results, and troubleshoot any problems.
7. Based on your evaluation, redesign your toy boat so it performs better.

Creating Data Tables and Graphs

How can you make sense of the data in a science experiment?
The first step is to organize the data to help you understand them.
Data tables and graphs are helpful tools for organizing data.

Data Tables

You have gathered your materials and set up your experiment. But before you start, you need to plan a way to record what happens during the experiment. By creating a data table, you can record your observations and measurements in an orderly way.

Suppose, for example, that a scientist conducted an experiment to find out how many Calories people of different body masses burn while doing various activities. The data table shows the results.

Notice in this data table that the manipulated variable (body mass) is the heading of one column. The responding variable (for

Calories Burned in 30 Minutes			
Body Mass	Experiment 1: Bicycling	Experiment 2: Playing Basketball	Experiment 3: Watching Television
30 kg	60 Calories	120 Calories	21 Calories
40 kg	77 Calories	164 Calories	27 Calories
50 kg	95 Calories	206 Calories	33 Calories
60 kg	114 Calories	248 Calories	38 Calories

Experiment 1, the number of Calories burned while bicycling) is the heading of the next column. Additional columns were added for related experiments.

Bar Graphs

To compare how many Calories a person burns doing various activities, you could create a bar graph. A bar graph is used to display data in a number of separate, or distinct, categories. In this example, bicycling, playing basketball, and watching television are the three categories.

To create a bar graph, follow these steps.

1. On graph paper, draw a horizontal, or *x*-, axis and a vertical, or *y*-, axis.

2. Write the names of the categories to be graphed along the horizontal axis. Include an overall label for the axis as well.

3. Label the vertical axis with the name of the responding variable. Include units of measurement. Then create a scale along the axis by marking off equally spaced numbers that cover the range of the data collected.

4. For each category, draw a solid bar using the scale on the vertical axis to determine the height. Make all the bars the same width.

5. Add a title that describes the graph.

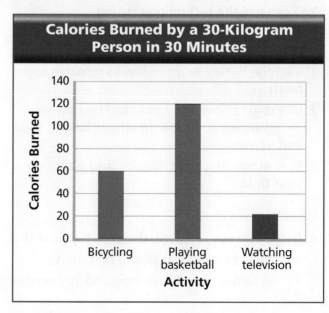

Calories Burned by a 30-Kilogram Person in 30 Minutes

Line Graphs

To see whether a relationship exists between body mass and the number of Calories burned while bicycling, you could create a line graph. A line graph is used to display data that show how one variable (the responding variable) changes in response to another variable (the manipulated variable). You can use a line graph when your manipulated variable is **continuous,** that is, when there are other points between the ones that you tested. In this example, body mass is a continuous variable because there are other body masses between 30 and 40 kilograms (for example, 31 kilograms). Time is another example of a continuous variable.

Line graphs are powerful tools because they allow you to estimate values for conditions that you did not test in the experiment. For example, you can use the line graph to estimate that a 35-kilogram person would burn 68 Calories while bicycling.

To create a line graph, follow these steps.

1. On graph paper, draw a horizontal, or *x*-, axis and a vertical, or *y*-, axis.

2. Label the horizontal axis with the name of the manipulated variable. Label the vertical axis with the name of the responding variable. Include units of measurement.

3. Create a scale on each axis by marking off equally spaced numbers that cover the range of the data collected.

4. Plot a point on the graph for each piece of data. In the line graph above, the dotted lines show how to plot the first data point (30 kilograms and 60 Calories). Follow an imaginary vertical line extending up from the horizontal axis at the 30-kilogram mark. Then follow an imaginary horizontal line extending across from the vertical axis at the 60-Calorie mark. Plot the point where the two lines intersect.

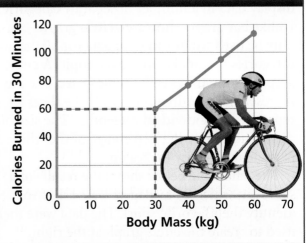

Effect of Body Mass on Calories Burned While Bicycling

5. Connect the plotted points with a solid line. (In some cases, it may be more appropriate to draw a line that shows the general trend of the plotted points. In those cases, some of the points may fall above or below the line. Also, not all graphs are linear. It may be more appropriate to draw a curve to connect the points.)

6. Add a title that identifies the variables or relationship in the graph.

Activity

Create line graphs to display the data from Experiment 2 and Experiment 3 in the data table.

Activity

You read in the newspaper that a total of 4 centimeters of rain fell in your area in June, 2.5 centimeters fell in July, and 1.5 centimeters fell in August. What type of graph would you use to display these data? Use graph paper to create the graph.

Circle Graphs

Like bar graphs, circle graphs can be used to display data in a number of separate categories. Unlike bar graphs, however, circle graphs can only be used when you have data for *all* the categories that make up a given topic. A circle graph is sometimes called a pie chart. The pie represents the entire topic, while the slices represent the individual categories. The size of a slice indicates what percentage of the whole a particular category makes up.

The data table below shows the results of a survey in which 24 teenagers were asked to identify their favorite sport. The data were then used to create the circle graph at the right.

Favorite Sports	
Sport	Students
Soccer	8
Basketball	6
Bicycling	6
Swimming	4

To create a circle graph, follow these steps.

1. Use a compass to draw a circle. Mark the center with a point. Then draw a line from the center point to the top of the circle.

2. Determine the size of each "slice" by setting up a proportion where x equals the number of degrees in a slice. (*Note:* A circle contains 360 degrees.) For example, to find the number of degrees in the "soccer" slice, set up the following proportion:

$$\frac{\text{Students who prefer soccer}}{\text{Total number of students}} = \frac{x}{\text{Total number of degrees in a circle}}$$

$$\frac{8}{24} = \frac{x}{360}$$

Cross-multiply and solve for x.

$$24x = 8 \times 360$$
$$x = 120$$

The "soccer" slice should contain 120 degrees.

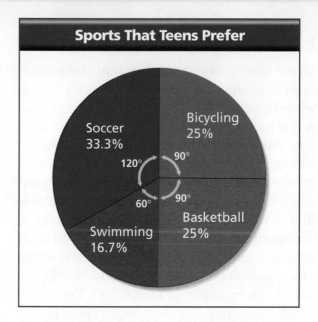

Sports That Teens Prefer

Soccer 33.3% 120°
Bicycling 25% 90°
Swimming 16.7% 60°
Basketball 25% 90°

3. Use a protractor to measure the angle of the first slice, using the line you drew to the top of the circle as the 0° line. Draw a line from the center of the circle to the edge for the angle you measured.

4. Continue around the circle by measuring the size of each slice with the protractor. Start measuring from the edge of the previous slice so the wedges do not overlap. When you are done, the entire circle should be filled in.

5. Determine the percentage of the whole circle that each slice represents. To do this, divide the number of degrees in a slice by the total number of degrees in a circle (360), and multiply by 100%. For the "soccer" slice, you can find the percentage as follows:

$$\frac{120}{360} \times 100\% = 33.3\%$$

6. Use a different color for each slice. Label each slice with the category and with the percentage of the whole it represents.

7. Add a title to the circle graph.

Activity

In a class of 28 students, 12 students take the bus to school, 10 students walk, and 6 students ride their bicycles. Create a circle graph to display these data.

Math Review

**Scientists use math to organize, analyze, and present data.
This appendix will help you review some basic math skills.**

Mean, Median, and Mode

The **mean** is the average, or the sum of the data divided by the number of data items. The middle number in a set of ordered data is called the **median.** The **mode** is the number that appears most often in a set of data.

Example

A scientist counted the number of distinct songs sung by seven different male birds and collected the data shown below.

Male Bird Songs							
Bird	A	B	C	D	E	F	G
Number of Songs	36	29	40	35	28	36	27

To determine the mean number of songs, add the total number of songs and divide by the number of data items—in this case, the number of male birds.

$$\text{Mean} = \frac{231}{7} = 33 \text{ songs}$$

To find the median number of songs, arrange the data in numerical order and find the number in the middle of the series.

27 28 29 35 36 36 40

The number in the middle is 35, so the median number of songs is 35.

The mode is the value that appears most frequently. In the data, 36 appears twice, while each other item appears only once. Therefore, 36 songs is the mode.

Practice

Find out how many minutes it takes each student in your class to get to school. Then find the mean, median, and mode for the data.

Probability

Probability is the chance that an event will occur. Probability can be expressed as a ratio, a fraction, or a percentage. For example, when you flip a coin, the probability that the coin will land heads up is 1 in 2, or $\frac{1}{2}$, or 50 percent.

The probability that an event will happen can be expressed in the following formula.

$$P(\text{event}) = \frac{\text{Number of times the event can occur}}{\text{Total number of possible events}}$$

Example

A paper bag contains 25 blue marbles, 5 green marbles, 5 orange marbles, and 15 yellow marbles. If you close your eyes and pick a marble from the bag, what is the probability that it will be yellow?

$$P(\text{yellow marbles}) = \frac{15 \text{ yellow marbles}}{50 \text{ marbles total}}$$

$$P = \frac{15}{50}, \text{ or } \frac{3}{10}, \text{ or } 30\%$$

Practice

Each side of a cube has a letter on it. Two sides have *A*, three sides have *B*, and one side has *C*. If you roll the cube, what is the probability that *A* will land on top?

Area

The **area** of a surface is the number of square units that cover it. The front cover of your textbook has an area of about 600 cm².

Area of a Rectangle and a Square To find the area of a rectangle, multiply its length times its width. The formula for the area of a rectangle is

$$A = \ell \times w, \text{ or } A = \ell w$$

Since all four sides of a square have the same length, the area of a square is the length of one side multiplied by itself, or squared.

$$A = s \times s, \text{ or } A = s^2$$

Example

A scientist is studying the plants in a field that measures 75 m × 45 m. What is the area of the field?

$$A = \ell \times w$$
$$A = 75 \text{ m} \times 45 \text{ m}$$
$$A = 3{,}375 \text{ m}^2$$

Area of a Circle The formula for the area of a circle is

$$A = \pi \times r \times r, \text{ or } A = \pi r^2$$

The length of the radius is represented by r, and the value of π is approximately $\frac{22}{7}$.

Example

Find the area of a circle with a radius of 14 cm.

$$A = \pi r^2$$
$$A = \frac{22}{7} \times 14 \text{ cm} \times 14 \text{ cm}$$
$$A = 616 \text{ cm}^2$$

Practice

Find the area of a circle that has a radius of 21 m.

Circumference

The distance around a circle is called the circumference. The formula for finding the circumference of a circle is

$$C = 2 \times \pi \times r, \text{ or } C = 2\pi r$$

Example

The radius of a circle is 35 cm. What is its circumference?

$$C = 2\pi r$$
$$C = 2 \times \frac{22}{7} \times 35 \text{ cm}$$
$$C = 220 \text{ cm}$$

Practice

What is the circumference of a circle with a radius of 28 m?

Volume

The volume of an object is the number of cubic units it contains. The volume of a wastebasket, for example, might be about 26,000 cm³.

Volume of a Rectangular Object To find the volume of a rectangular object, multiply the object's length times its width times its height.

$$V = \ell \times w \times h, \text{ or } V = \ell w h$$

Example

Find the volume of a box with length 24 cm, width 12 cm, and height 9 cm.

$$V = \ell w h$$
$$V = 24 \text{ cm} \times 12 \text{ cm} \times 9 \text{ cm}$$
$$V = 2{,}592 \text{ cm}^3$$

Practice

What is the volume of a rectangular object with length 17 cm, width 11 cm, and height 6 cm?

Fractions

A **fraction** is a way to express a part of a whole. In the fraction $\frac{4}{7}$, 4 is the numerator and 7 is the denominator.

Adding and Subtracting Fractions To add or subtract two or more fractions that have a common denominator, first add or subtract the numerators. Then write the sum or difference over the common denominator.

To find the sum or difference of fractions with different denominators, first find the least common multiple of the denominators. This is known as the least common denominator. Then convert each fraction to equivalent fractions with the least common denominator. Add or subtract the numerators. Then write the sum or difference over the common denominator.

Example

$$\frac{5}{6} - \frac{3}{4} = \frac{10}{12} - \frac{9}{12} = \frac{10-9}{12} = \frac{1}{12}$$

Multiplying Fractions To multiply two fractions, first multiply the two numerators, then multiply the two denominators.

Example

$$\frac{5}{6} \times \frac{2}{3} = \frac{5 \times 2}{6 \times 3} = \frac{10}{18} = \frac{5}{9}$$

Dividing Fractions Dividing by a fraction is the same as multiplying by its reciprocal. Reciprocals are numbers whose numerators and denominators have been switched. To divide one fraction by another, first invert the fraction you are dividing by—in other words, turn it upside down. Then multiply the two fractions.

Example

$$\frac{2}{5} \div \frac{7}{8} = \frac{2}{5} \times \frac{8}{7} = \frac{2 \times 8}{5 \times 7} = \frac{16}{35}$$

Practice

Solve the following: $\frac{3}{7} \div \frac{4}{5}$.

Decimals

Fractions whose denominators are 10, 100, or some other power of 10 are often expressed as decimals. For example, the fraction $\frac{9}{10}$ can be expressed as the decimal 0.9, and the fraction $\frac{7}{100}$ can be written as 0.07.

Adding and Subtracting With Decimals To add or subtract decimals, line up the decimal points before you carry out the operation.

Example

```
   27.4          278.635
 + 6.19        - 191.4
 ------         -------
  33.59          87.235
```

Multiplying With Decimals When you multiply two numbers with decimals, the number of decimal places in the product is equal to the total number of decimal places in each number being multiplied.

Example

```
    46.2  (one decimal place)
 ×  2.37  (two decimal places)
 --------
 109.494  (three decimal places)
```

Dividing With Decimals To divide a decimal by a whole number, put the decimal point in the quotient above the decimal point in the dividend.

Example

$$15.5 \div 5$$
```
    3.1
 5)15.5
```

To divide a decimal by a decimal, you need to rewrite the divisor as a whole number. Do this by multiplying both the divisor and dividend by the same multiple of 10.

Example

$$1.68 \div 4.2 = 1.68 \div 4.2$$
```
     0.4
 42)16.8
```

Practice

Multiply 6.21 by 8.5.

Ratio and Proportion

A **ratio** compares two numbers by division. For example, suppose a scientist counts 800 wolves and 1,200 moose on an island. The ratio of wolves to moose can be written as a fraction, $\frac{800}{1,200}$, which can be reduced to $\frac{2}{3}$. The same ratio can also be expressed as 2 to 3 or 2 : 3.

A **proportion** is a mathematical sentence saying that two ratios are equivalent. For example, a proportion could state that $\frac{800 \text{ wolves}}{1,200 \text{ moose}} = \frac{2 \text{ wolves}}{3 \text{ moose}}$. You can sometimes set up a proportion to determine or estimate an unknown quantity. For example, suppose a scientist counts 25 beetles in an area of 10 square meters. The scientist wants to estimate the number of beetles in 100 square meters.

Example

1. Express the relationship between beetles and area as a ratio: $\frac{25}{10}$, simplified to $\frac{5}{2}$.

2. Set up a proportion, with x representing the number of beetles. The proportion can be stated as $\frac{5}{2} = \frac{x}{100}$.

3. Begin by cross-multiplying. In other words, multiply each fraction's numerator by the other fraction's denominator.

    $$5 \times 100 = 2 \times x, \text{ or } 500 = 2x$$

4. To find the value of x, divide both sides by 2. The result is 250, or 250 beetles in 100 square meters.

Practice

Find the value of x in the following proportion: $\frac{6}{7} = \frac{x}{49}$.

Percentage

A **percentage** is a ratio that compares a number to 100. For example, there are 37 granite rocks in a collection that consists of 100 rocks. The ratio $\frac{37}{100}$ can be written as 37%. Granite rocks make up 37% of the rock collection.

You can calculate percentages of numbers other than 100 by setting up a proportion.

Example

Rain falls on 9 days out of 30 in June. What percentage of the days in June were rainy?

$$\frac{9 \text{ days}}{30 \text{ days}} = \frac{d\%}{100\%}$$

To find the value of d, begin by cross-multiplying, as for any proportion:

$$9 \times 100 = 30 \times d \qquad d = \frac{900}{30} \qquad d = 30$$

Practice

There are 300 marbles in a jar, and 42 of those marbles are blue. What percentage of the marbles are blue?

Significant Figures

The **precision** of a measurement depends on the instrument you use to take the measurement. For example, if the smallest unit on the ruler is millimeters, then the most precise measurement you can make will be in millimeters.

The sum or difference of measurements can only be as precise as the least precise measurement being added or subtracted. Round your answer so that it has the same number of digits after the decimal as the least precise measurement. Round up if the last digit is 5 or more, and round down if the last digit is 4 or less.

Example

Subtract a temperature of 5.2°C from the temperature 75.46°C.

75.46 − 5.2 = 70.26

5.2 has the fewest digits after the decimal, so it is the least precise measurement. Since the last digit of the answer is 6, round up to 3. The most precise difference between the measurements is 70.3°C.

Practice

Add 26.4 m to 8.37 m. Round your answer according to the precision of the measurements.

Significant figures are the number of nonzero digits in a measurement. Zeros between nonzero digits are also significant. For example, the measurements 12,500 L, 0.125 cm, and 2.05 kg all have three significant figures. When you multiply and divide measurements, the one with the fewest significant figures determines the number of significant figures in your answer.

Example

Multiply 110 g by 5.75 g.

110 × 5.75 = 632.5

Because 110 has only two significant figures, round the answer to 630 g.

Scientific Notation

A **factor** is a number that divides into another number with no remainder. In the example, the number 3 is used as a factor four times.

An **exponent** tells how many times a number is used as a factor. For example, $3 \times 3 \times 3 \times 3$ can be written as 3^4. The exponent "4" indicates that the number 3 is used as a factor four times. Another way of expressing this is to say that 81 is equal to 3 to the fourth power.

Example

$$3^4 = 3 \times 3 \times 3 \times 3 = 81$$

Scientific notation uses exponents and powers of ten to write very large or very small numbers in shorter form. When you write a number in scientific notation, you write the number as two factors. The first factor is any number between 1 and 10. The second factor is a power of 10, such as 10^3 or 10^6.

Example

The average distance between the planet Mercury and the sun is 58,000,000 km. To write the first factor in scientific notation, insert a decimal point in the original number so that you have a number between 1 and 10. In the case of 58,000,000, the number is 5.8.

To determine the power of 10, count the number of places that the decimal point moved. In this case, it moved 7 places.

$$58{,}000{,}000 \text{ km} = 5.8 \times 10^7 \text{ km}$$

Practice

Express 6,590,000 in scientific notation.

Safety Symbols

These symbols warn of possible dangers in the laboratory and remind you to work carefully.

 Safety Goggles Wear safety goggles to protect your eyes in any activity involving chemicals, flames or heating, or glassware.

 Lab Apron Wear a laboratory apron to protect your skin and clothing from damage.

 Breakage Handle breakable materials, such as glassware, with care. Do not touch broken glassware.

 Heat-Resistant Gloves Use an oven mitt or other hand protection when handling hot materials such as hot plates or hot glassware.

 Plastic Gloves Wear disposable plastic gloves when working with harmful chemicals and organisms. Keep your hands away from your face, and dispose of the gloves according to your teacher's instructions.

 Heating Use a clamp or tongs to pick up hot glassware. Do not touch hot objects with your bare hands.

 Flames Before you work with flames, tie back loose hair and clothing. Follow instructions from your teacher about lighting and extinguishing flames.

 No Flames When using flammable materials, make sure there are no flames, sparks, or other exposed heat sources present.

 Corrosive Chemical Avoid getting acid or other corrosive chemicals on your skin or clothing or in your eyes. Do not inhale the vapors. Wash your hands after the activity.

 Poison Do not let any poisonous chemical come into contact with your skin, and do not inhale its vapors. Wash your hands when you are finished with the activity.

 Fumes Work in a ventilated area when harmful vapors may be involved. Avoid inhaling vapors directly. Only test an odor when directed to do so by your teacher, and use a wafting motion to direct the vapor toward your nose.

 Sharp Object Scissors, scalpels, knives, needles, pins, and tacks can cut your skin. Always direct a sharp edge or point away from yourself and others.

 Animal Safety Treat live or preserved animals or animal parts with care to avoid harming the animals or yourself. Wash your hands when you are finished with the activity.

 Plant Safety Handle plants only as directed by your teacher. If you are allergic to certain plants, tell your teacher; do not do an activity involving those plants. Avoid touching harmful plants such as poison ivy. Wash your hands when you are finished with the activity.

 Electric Shock To avoid electric shock, never use electrical equipment around water, or when the equipment is wet or your hands are wet. Be sure cords are untangled and cannot trip anyone. Unplug equipment not in use.

 Physical Safety When an experiment involves physical activity, avoid injuring yourself or others. Alert your teacher if there is any reason you should not participate.

 Disposal Dispose of chemicals and other laboratory materials safely. Follow the instructions from your teacher.

 Hand Washing Wash your hands thoroughly when finished with the activity. Use antibacterial soap and warm water. Rinse well.

 General Safety Awareness When this symbol appears, follow the instructions provided. When you are asked to develop your own procedure in a lab, have your teacher approve your plan before you go further.

Science Safety Rules

General Precautions

Follow all instructions. Never perform activities without the approval and supervision of your teacher. Do not engage in horseplay. Never eat or drink in the laboratory. Keep work areas clean and uncluttered.

Dress Code

Wear safety goggles whenever you work with chemicals, glassware, heat sources such as burners, or any substance that might get into your eyes. If you wear contact lenses, notify your teacher.

Wear a lab apron or coat whenever you work with corrosive chemicals or substances that can stain. Wear disposable plastic gloves when working with organisms and harmful chemicals. Tie back long hair. Remove or tie back any article of clothing or jewelry that can hang down and touch chemicals, flames, or equipment. Roll up long sleeves. Never wear open shoes or sandals.

First Aid

Report all accidents, injuries, or fires to your teacher, no matter how minor. Be aware of the location of the first-aid kit, emergency equipment such as the fire extinguisher and fire blanket, and the nearest telephone. Know whom to contact in an emergency.

Heating and Fire Safety

Keep all combustible materials away from flames. When heating a substance in a test tube, make sure that the mouth of the tube is not pointed at you or anyone else. Never heat a liquid in a closed container. Use an oven mitt to pick up a container that has been heated.

Using Chemicals Safely

Never put your face near the mouth of a container that holds chemicals. Never touch, taste, or smell a chemical unless your teacher tells you to.

Use only those chemicals needed in the activity. Keep all containers closed when chemicals are not being used. Pour all chemicals over the sink or a container, not over your work surface. Dispose of excess chemicals as instructed by your teacher.

Be extra careful when working with acids or bases. When mixing an acid and water, always pour the water into the container first and then add the acid to the water. Never pour water into an acid. Wash chemical spills and splashes immediately with plenty of water.

Using Glassware Safely

If glassware is broken or chipped, notify your teacher immediately. Never handle broken or chipped glass with your bare hands.

Never force glass tubing or thermometers into a rubber stopper or rubber tubing. Have your teacher insert the glass tubing or thermometer if required for an activity.

Using Sharp Instruments

Handle sharp instruments with extreme care. Never cut material toward you; cut away from you.

Animal and Plant Safety

Never perform experiments that cause pain, discomfort, or harm to animals. Only handle animals if absolutely necessary. If you know that you are allergic to certain plants, molds, or animals, tell your teacher before doing an activity in which these are used. Wash your hands thoroughly after any activity involving animals, animal parts, plants, plant parts, or soil.

During field work, wear long pants, long sleeves, socks, and closed shoes. Avoid poisonous plants and fungi as well as plants with thorns.

End-of-Experiment Rules

Unplug all electrical equipment. Clean up your work area. Dispose of waste materials as instructed by your teacher. Wash your hands after every experiment.

The laboratory balance is an important tool in scientific investigations. You can use a balance to determine the masses of materials that you study or experiment with in the laboratory.

Different kinds of balances are used in the laboratory. One kind of balance is the triple-beam balance. The balance that you may use in your science class is probably similar to the balance illustrated in this Appendix. To use the balance properly, you should learn the name, location, and function of each part of the balance you are using. What kind of balance do you have in your science class?

The Triple-Beam Balance

The triple-beam balance is a single-pan balance with three beams calibrated in grams. The back, or 100-gram, beam is divided into ten units of 10 grams each. The middle, or 500-gram, beam is divided into five units of 100 grams each. The front, or 10-gram, beam is divided into ten major units of 1 gram each. Each of these units is further divided into units of 0.1 gram. What is the largest mass you could find with a triple-beam balance?

The following procedure can be used to find the mass of an object with a triple-beam balance:

1. Place the object on the pan.

2. Move the rider on the middle beam notch by notch until the horizontal pointer drops below zero. Move the rider back one notch.

3. Move the rider on the back beam notch by notch until the pointer again drops below zero. Move the rider back one notch.

4. Slowly slide the rider along the front beam until the pointer stops at the zero point.

5. The mass of the object is equal to the sum of the readings on the three beams.

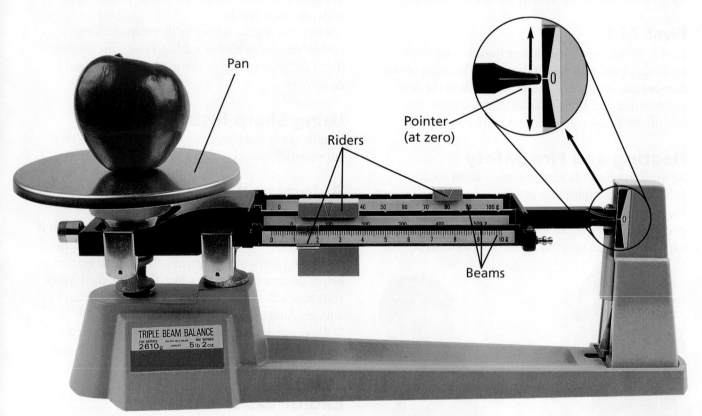

Triple-Beam Balance

Name	Symbol	Atomic Number	Atomic Mass[†]
Actinium	Ac	89	(227)
Aluminum	Al	13	26.982
Americium	Am	95	(243)
Antimony	Sb	51	121.75
Argon	Ar	18	39.948
Arsenic	As	33	74.922
Astatine	At	85	(210)
Barium	Ba	56	137.327
Berkelium	Bk	97	(247)
Beryllium	Be	4	9.012
Bismuth	Bi	83	208.980
Bohrium	Bh	107	(264)
Boron	B	5	10.811
Bromine	Br	35	79.904
Cadmium	Cd	48	112.411
Calcium	Ca	20	40.078
Californium	Cf	98	(251)
Carbon	C	6	12.011
Cerium	Ce	58	140.115
Cesium	Cs	55	132.905
Chlorine	Cl	17	35.453
Chromium	Cr	24	51.996
Cobalt	Co	27	58.933
Copper	Cu	29	63.546
Curium	Cm	96	(247)
Darmstadtium	Ds	110	(269)
Dubnium	Db	105	(262)
Dysprosium	Dy	66	162.50
Einsteinium	Es	99	(252)
Erbium	Er	68	167.26
Europium	Eu	63	151.965
Fermium	Fm	100	(257)
Fluorine	F	9	18.998
Francium	Fr	87	(223)
Gadolinium	Gd	64	157.25
Gallium	Ga	31	69.723
Germanium	Ge	32	72.61
Gold	Au	79	196.967
Hafnium	Hf	72	178.49
Hassium	Hs	108	(265)
Helium	He	2	4.003
Holmium	Ho	67	164.930
Hydrogen	H	1	1.008
Indium	In	49	114.818
Iodine	I	53	126.904
Iridium	Ir	77	192.22
Iron	Fe	26	55.847
Krypton	Kr	36	83.80
Lanthanum	La	57	138.906
Lawrencium	Lr	103	(262)
Lead	Pb	82	207.2
Lithium	Li	3	6.941
Lutetium	Lu	71	174.967
Magnesium	Mg	12	24.305
Manganese	Mn	25	54.938
Meitnerium	Mt	109	(268)
Mendelevium	Md	101	(258)

Name	Symbol	Atomic Number	Atomic Mass[†]
Mercury	Hg	80	200.659
Molybdenum	Mo	42	95.94
Neodymium	Nd	60	144.2
Neon	Ne	10	20.180
Neptunium	Np	93	(237)
Nickel	Ni	28	58.69
Niobium	Nb	41	92.906
Nitrogen	N	7	14.007
Nobelium	No	102	(259)
Osmium	Os	76	190.23
Oxygen	O	8	15.999
Palladium	Pd	46	106.42
Phosphorus	P	15	30.974
Platinum	Pt	78	195.08
Plutonium	Pu	94	(244)
Polonium	Po	84	(209)
Potassium	K	19	39.098
Praseodymium	Pr	59	140.908
Promethium	Pm	61	(145)
Protactinium	Pa	91	231.036
Radium	Ra	88	(226)
Radon	Rn	86	(222)
Rhenium	Re	75	186.207
Rhodium	Rh	45	102.906
Roentgenium	Rg	111	(280)
Rubidium	Rb	37	85.468
Ruthenium	Ru	44	101.07
Rutherfordium	Rf	104	(261)
Samarium	Sm	62	150.36
Scandium	Sc	21	44.956
Seaborgium	Sg	106	(263)
Selenium	Se	34	78.96
Silicon	Si	14	28.086
Silver	Ag	47	107.868
Sodium	Na	11	22.990
Strontium	Sr	38	87.62
Sulfur	S	16	32.066
Tantalum	Ta	73	180.948
Technetium	Tc	43	(98)
Tellurium	Te	52	127.60
Terbium	Tb	65	158.925
Thallium	Tl	81	204.383
Thorium	Th	90	232.038
Thulium	Tm	69	168.934
Tin	Sn	50	118.710
Titanium	Ti	22	47.88
Tungsten	W	74	183.85
Ununbium	Uub	112	(277)
Ununquadium	Uuq	114	*
Unununium	Uuu	111	(272)
Uranium	U	92	238.029
Vanadium	V	23	50.942
Xenon	Xe	54	131.29
Ytterbium	Yb	70	173.04
Yttrium	Y	39	88.906
Zinc	Zn	30	65.39
Zirconium	Zr	40	91.224

[†]Numbers in parentheses give the mass number of the most stable isotope.

*Newly discovered

Table 1: Physical Data for the Planets

Name	Equatorial Diameter (km)	Mass (Earth = 1)*	Surface Gravity (Earth = 1)	Average Density (kg/m^3)	Number of Moons	Axial Tilt (degrees)**
Mercury	4,879	0.055	0.38	5,427	0	0.01
Venus	12,104	0.815	0.91	5,243	0	177.4
Earth	12,756	1.00	1.00	5,515	1	23.5
Mars	6,794	0.107	0.38	3,933	2	25.2
Jupiter	142,984	317.8	2.36	1,326	63+	3.1
Saturn	120,536	95.2	0.92	687	47+	26.7
Uranus	51,118	14.5	0.89	1,270	27+	97.8
Neptune	49,528	17.1	1.12	1,638	13+	28.3

*All masses are shown relative to Earth. Earth's mass is about 6.0×10^{24} kg. To find Jupiter's actual mass, multiply its relative mass by Earth's mass: $317.8 \times (6.0 \times 10^{24}$ kg$) \approx 1.9 \times 10^{27}$ kg. Surface gravity is also shown relative to Earth.
**Axial tilt is the angle that a planet's axis is tilted relative to a line perpendicular to the planet's orbit around the sun.

Table 2: Data for Planetary Motions

Name	Distance From the Sun (AU)	Period of Revolution (Earth years)	Average Orbital Speed (km/s)	Period of Rotation (Earth days)
Mercury	0.39	0.24	47.9	58.8
Venus	0.72	0.62	35.0	244*
Earth	1.00	1.00	29.8	1.00
Mars	1.52	1.88	24.1	1.03
Jupiter	5.20	11.9	13.1	0.41
Saturn	9.58	29.4	9.7	0.45
Uranus	19.2	83.7	6.8	0.72*
Neptune	30.05	163.7	5.4	0.67

*Direction of rotation for Venus, Uranus, and Pluto is opposite to planet's orbital motion.

Table 3: Data for Selected Moons

Name	Year Discovered	Parent Planet	Average Distance From Planet (10^3 km)	Diameter (km)	Period of Rotation (Earth days)
The Moon	–	Earth	384.4	3,476	27.3
Io	1610	Jupiter	421.6	3,642	1.8
Europa	1610	Jupiter	670.9	3,120	3.6
Ganymede	1610	Jupiter	1,070.0	5,268	7.2
Callisto	1610	Jupiter	1,883.0	4,800	16.7
Titan	1655	Saturn	1,221.9	5,150	15.9
Titania	1787	Uranus	435.8	1,580	8.7
Triton	1846	Neptune	354.8	2,706	5.9

Table 4: Data for Small Solar-System Bodies and Dwarf Planets

Name	Type	Year Discovered	Distance From the Sun (AU)	Diameter (km)	Period of Revolution (Earth years)
Ceres	Dwarf planet / Asteroid	1801	2.77	960 × 932	4.60
Pallas	Asteroid	1802	2.77	570 × 525 × 482	4.61
Juno	Asteroid	1804	2.67	240	4.36
Vesta	Asteroid	1807	2.36	530	3.63
Pluto	Dwarf planet	1930	39.24	2,390	248.0
Quaoar	Kuiper Belt object	2002	42	≈1300	285
Sedna	Kuiper Belt object	2003	76–1,000	≈1500?	10,500
2005 FY9	Kuiper Belt object	2005	39–52	≈1500?	307
Eris	Dwarf planet	2005	38–97	≈3000	560

Table 5: Data for the Sun

Mass = 2.0×10^{30} kg	Radius = 7×10^{6} km
Average Surface Temperature = 5,500°C	Absolute Brightness (Luminosity) = 3.86×10^{26} J/s
Average Core Temperature = 1.6×10^{7} °C	Average Density = 1,410 kg/m³

Table 6: Data for Some Well-Known Stars

Name	Constellation	Type	Distance From Sun (light-years)	Apparent Brightness (Sirius = 1)*
Sirius A	Canis Major	White main sequence	8.6	1.00
Canopus	Carina	Yellow giant	313	0.47
Arcturus	Bootes	Orange giant	37	0.278
Alpha Centauri A	Centaurus	Yellow main sequence	4.4	0.268
Vega	Lyra	White main sequence	25	0.258
Capella	Auriga	Yellow giant (quadruple star system)	42	0.247
Rigel	Orion	Blue supergiant	770	0.225
Betelgeuse	Orion	Red supergiant	430	0.175
Altair	Aquila	White main sequence	17	0.132
Aldebaran	Taurus	Orange giant	65	0.119
Antares	Scorpio	Red supergiant	600	0.100
Pollux	Gemini	Orange giant	34	0.091
Fomalhaut	Pisces Austrinus	White main sequence	25	0.090
Deneb	Cygnus	White supergiant	3200	0.084
Regulus	Leo	Blue main sequence	78	0.076

*The apparent brightness of some stars changes over time because of changes in their absolute brightness (luminosity).

Use these star charts to locate bright stars and major constellations in the night sky at different times of year. Choose the appropriate star chart for the current season.

Autumn Sky

This chart works best at the following dates and times: September 1 at 10:00 P.M., October 1 at 8:00 P.M., or November 1 at 6:00 P.M. Look for the constellations Ursa Minor (the Little Dipper) and Cassiopeia in the northern sky, and for the star Deneb, which is nearly overhead in autumn.

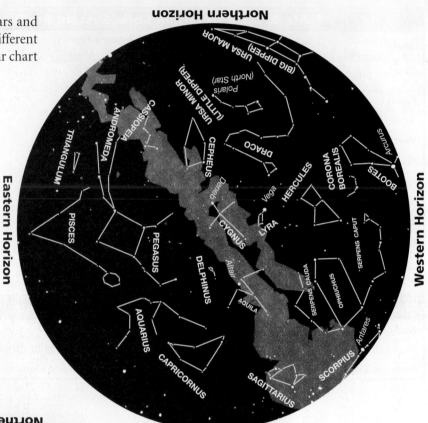

Winter Sky

This chart works best at the following dates and times: December 1 at 10:00 P.M., January 1 at 8:00 P.M., or February 1 at 6:00 P.M. Look for the constellations Orion and Gemini, the bright star Sirius, and the Pleiades, a star cluster, in the winter sky.

Using a flashlight and a compass, hold the appropriate chart and turn it so that the direction you are facing is at the bottom of the chart. These star charts work best at 34° north latitude, but can be used at other central latitudes.

Spring Sky

This chart works best at the following dates and times: March 1 at 10:00 P.M., March 15 at 9:00 P.M., or April 1 at 8:00 P.M. Look for the constellations Ursa Major (which contains the Big Dipper), Bootes, and Leo in the spring sky. The bright stars Arcturus and Spica can be seen in the east.

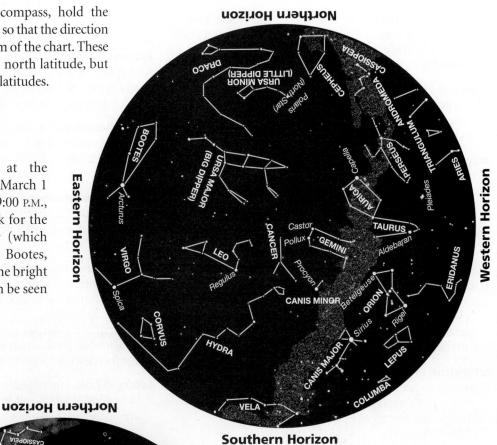

Summer Sky

This chart works best at the following dates and times: May 15 at 11:00 P.M., June 1 at 10:00 P.M., or June 15 at 9:00 P.M. Look for the bright star Arcturus in the constellations Bootes and Hercules overhead in early summer. Towards the east look for the bright stars Vega, Altair, and Deneb, which form a triangle.

English and Spanish Glossary

absolute brightness The brightness a star would have if it were at a standard distance from Earth. (p. 601)
magnitud absoluta Brillo que tendría una estrella si estuviera a una distancia estándar de la Tierra.

absolute zero The temperature at which no more energy can be removed from matter. (p. 26)
cero absoluto Temperatura a la cual no se puede quitar más energía a la materia.

acceleration The rate at which velocity changes with time. (p. 350)
acelaración Razón a la que cambia la velocidad.

accuracy How close a measurement is to the true or accepted value. (p. 31)
exactitud Cuán cerca está una medida del valor verdadero o aceptado.

acid A substance that tastes sour, reacts with metals and carbonates, and turns blue litmus red. (p. 268)
ácido Sustancia de sabor agrio que reacciona con metales y carbonatos, y que vuelve rojo el papel de tornasol azul.

activation energy The minimum amount of energy needed to get a chemical reaction started. (p. 235)
energía de activación Cantidad mínima de energía que se necesita para que empiece una reacción química.

air resistance The fluid friction experienced by objects falling through the air. (p. 387)
resistencia del aire Fricción de fluido experimentada por los objetos que caen a través del aire.

alcohol A substituted hydrocarbon that contains one or more hydroxyl groups. (p. 302)
alcohol Hidrocarburo sustituto que contiene uno o más grupos hidroxilos.

alkali metal An element in Group 1 of the periodic table. (p. 140)
metal alcalino Elemento en el Grupo 1 de la tabla periódica.

alkaline earth metal An element in Group 2 of the periodic table. (p. 141)
metal alcalinotérreo Elemento en el Grupo 2 de la tabla periódica.

alloy A mixture of two or more elements, one of which is a metal. (p. 199)
aleación Mezcla de dos o más elementos, uno de los cuales es un metal.

alpha particle A type of nuclear radiation consisting of two protons and two neutrons. (p. 160)
partícula alfa Tipo de radiación nuclear que consiste de dos protones y dos neutrones.

amino acid One of 20 kinds of organic compounds that are the monomers of proteins. (p. 308)
aminoácido Uno de 20 tipos de compuestos orgánicos que son los monómeros de las proteínas.

amorphous solid A solid made up of particles that are not arranged in a regular pattern. (p. 92)
sólido amorfo Sólido constituido por partículas que no están dispuestas en un patrón regular.

apparent brightness The brightness of a star as seen from Earth. (p. 601)
magnitud aparente Brillo de una estrella visto desde la Tierra.

Archimedes' principle The rule that the buoyant force acting on a submerged object is equal to the weight of the volume of fluid displaced by the object. (p. 428)
principio de Arquímedes Regla que enuncia que la fuerza de flotación que actúa sobre un objeto es igual al peso del líquido que desaloja.

asteroid belt The region of the solar system, between the orbits of Mars and Jupiter, where many asteroids are found. (p. 574)
cinturón de asteroides Región del sistema solar, entre las órbitas de Marte y Júpiter, donde se encuentran muchos asteroides.

asteroids Rocky objects revolving around the sun that are too small and numerous to be considered planets. (p. 574)
asteroides Objetos rocosos que se mueven alrededor del Sol y que son demasiado pequeños y numerosos como para ser considerados planetas.

astronomical unit A unit of measurement equal to Earth's average distance from the sun, about 150 million kilometers. (p. 543)
unidad astronómica Unidad de medida igual a la distancia promedio de la Tierra al Sol; alrededor de 150 millones de kilómetros.

astronomy The study of the moon, stars, and other objects in space. (p. 464)
astronomía Estudio de la luna, las estrellas y otros objetos del espacio.

atom The basic particle from which all elements are made. (pp. 63, 125)
átomo Partícula básica de la que están formados todos los elementos.

atomic mass The average mass of all the isotopes of an element. (p. 132)
masa atómica Promedio de la masa de todos los isótopos de un elemento.

atomic number The number of protons in the nucleus of an atom. (p. 129)
número atómico Número de protones en el núcleo de un átomo.

average speed The overall rate of speed at which an object moves; calculated by dividing the total distance an object travels by the total time. (p. 343)
rapidez media Velocidad general a la que se mueve un objeto; se calcula dividiendo la distancia total recorrida por el tiempo total empleado.

axis An imaginary line that passes through Earth's center and the North and South poles, about which Earth rotates. (p. 465)
eje Línea imaginaria que pasa a través del centro de la Tierra, por los polos Norte y Sur, sobre el cual gira la Tierra.

B

balanced forces Equal forces acting on an object in opposite directions. (p. 376)
fuerzas equilibradas Fuerzas iguales que actúan sobre un objeto en direcciones opuestas.

barometer An instrument used to measure atmospheric pressure. (p. 422)
barómetro Instrumento que se usa para medir la presión atmosférica.

base A substance that tastes bitter, feels slippery, and turns red litmus paper blue. (p. 271)
base Sustancia de sabor amargo, escurridiza y que vuelve azul el papel de tornasol rojo.

Bernoulli's principle The rule that the faster a fluid moves, the less pressure the fluid exerts. (p. 438)
principio de Bernoulli Regla que enuncia que la corriente de un fluido de rápido movimiento ejerce menor presión que el fluido del entorno.

beta particle A fast-moving electron that is given off as nuclear radiation. (p. 160)
partícula beta Electrón de rápido movimiento que se produce como radiación nuclear.

big bang The initial explosion that resulted in the formation and expansion of the universe. (p. 622)
big bang Explosión inicial que dio como resultado la formación y expansión del universo.

binary star A star system with two stars. (p. 615)
estrella binaria Sistema de estrellas con dos estrellas.

black hole An object whose gravity is so strong that nothing, not even light, can escape. (p. 613)
agujero negro Objeto cuya gravedad es tan fuerte que nada, ni siquiera la luz, puede escapar.

boiling The process that occurs when vaporization takes place inside a liquid as well as on the surface. (p. 99)
ebullición Proceso que se da cuando la vaporización se efectúa dentro de un líquido, además de en la superficie.

boiling point The temperature at which a substance changes from a liquid to a gas. (p. 99)
punto de ebullición Temperatura a la que una sustancia cambia de líquido a gas; es lo mismo que el punto de condensación (la temperatura a la que un gas se vuelve líquido).

buoyant force The upward force exerted by a fluid on a submerged object. (p. 427)
fuerza de flotación Fuerza ascendente que ejerce un líquido sobre un objeto sumergido.

C

calendar A system of organizing time that defines the beginning, length, and divisions of a year. (p. 466)
calendario Sistema de organización del tiempo que define el principio, la duración y las divisiones de un año.

carbohydrate An energy-rich organic compound made of the elements carbon, hydrogen, and oxygen. (p. 317)
carbohidrato Compuesto orgánico altamente energético hecho de elementos de carbono, hidrógeno y oxígeno.

carboxyl group A —COOH group, found in organic acids. (p. 303)
grupo carboxilo Grupo —COOH, que se haya en los ácidos orgánicos.

catalyst A material that increases the rate of a reaction by lowering the activation energy. (p. 239)
catalítico Material que aumenta la velocidad de una reacción al disminuir la energía de activación.

cellulose A complex carbohydrate found in plant structures. (p. 318)
celulosa Carbohidrato complejo que se haya en las estructuras vegetales.

Celsius scale The temperature scale on which water freezes at 0 degrees and boils at 100 degrees. (p. 26)
escala Celsius Escala de temperatura en la cual el agua se congela a los 0 grados y hierve a los 100 grados.

English and Spanish Glossary

centripetal force A force that causes an object to move in a circle. (p. 403)
fuerza centrípeta Fuerza que causa que un objeto se mueva en círculos.

chemical bond The force that holds atoms together.
enlace químico Fuerza que mantiene unidos a los átomos. (pp. 63, 177)

chemical change A change in which one or more substances combine or break apart to form new substances. (pp. 70, 216)
cambio químico Cambio en el cual una o más sustancias se combinan o se rompen para formar nuevas sustancias.

chemical energy A form of potential energy that is stored in chemical bonds between atoms. (p. 75)
energía química Forma de energía potencial almacenada en los enlaces químicos entre átomos.

chemical equation A short, easy way to show a chemical reaction, using symbols. (p. 225)
ecuación química Forma corta y sencilla de mostrar una reacción química, usando símbolos.

chemical formula A combination of symbols that represents the elements in a compound and their proportions. (pp. 64, 187)
fórmula química Combinación de símbolos que representan a los elementos de un compuesto y la razón de los átomos.

chemical property A characteristic of a pure substance that describes its ability to change into a different substance. (pp. 61, 215)
propiedad química Característica de una sustancia pura que describe su capacidad para cambiar a una sustancia diferente.

chemical symbol A one- or two-letter representation of an element. (p. 137)
símbolo químico Representación con una o dos letras de un elemento.

chemistry The study of the properties of matter and how matter changes. (pp. 8, 214)
química Estudio de las propiedades de la materia y de cómo cambia.

cholesterol A waxy lipid in animal cells. (p. 320)
colesterol Lípido ceroso que se haya en las células animales.

chromosphere The middle layer of the sun's atmosphere. (p. 548)
cromosfera Capa central en la atmósfera del Sol.

closed system A system in which no matter is allowed to enter or leave. (p. 227)
sistema cerrado Sistema en el cual la materia no puede entrar ni salir.

coefficient A number in front of a chemical formula in an equation that indicates how many molecules or atoms of each reactant and product are involved in a reaction. (p. 228)
coeficiente En un ecuación, número delante de una fórmula química que indica cuántas moléculas o átomos de cada reactivo y producto participan en una reacción.

colloid A mixture containing small, undissolved particles that do not settle out. (p. 258)
coloide Mezcla que contiene partículas pequeñas y sin disolver que no se depositan.

coma The fuzzy outer layer of a comet. (p. 573)
coma Capa exterior y difusa de un cometa.

combustion A rapid reaction between oxygen and fuel that results in fire. (p. 243)
combustión Reacción rápida entre el oxígeno y el combustible que produce fuego.

comet A loose collection of ice, dust, and small rocky particles, typically with a long, narrow orbit. (p. 573)
cometa Conjunto no compacto de hielo, polvo y partículas rocosas pequeñas, que normalmente tiene una órbita larga y estrecha.

communicating The process of sharing ideas with others through writing and speaking. (p. 14)
comunicar Proceso de compartir ideas con otras personas a través de la escritura o el lenguage hablado.

complex carbohydrate A long chain, or polymer, of simple carbohydrates. (p. 318)
carbohidrato complejo Cadena larga, o polímero, de carbohidratos simples.

composite A combination of two or more substances that creates a new material with different properties.
material compuesto Combinación de dos o más sustancias que crea un nuevo material con propiedades diferentes. (p. 310)

compound A pure substance made of two or more elements chemically combined. (p. 64)
compuesto Sustancia pura formada por dos o más elementos combinados químicamente.

compression An elastic force that squeezes or pushes the molecules in matter together. (p. 388)
compresión Parte de una onda longitudinal donde las partículas del medio están muy juntas.

concentrated solution A mixture that has a lot of solute dissolved in a certain amount of solvent.
solución concentrada Mezcla que tiene muchos solutos disueltos en ella. (p. 263)

concentration The amount of one material in a certain volume of another material. (p. 238)
concentración Cantidad de un material en un cierto volumen de otro material.

condensation The change from the gaseous to the liquid state of matter. (p. 100)
condensación Cambio de la materia del estado gaseoso al estado líquido.

conservation of matter The principle stating that matter is not created or destroyed during a chemical reaction. (p. 226)
conservación de la materia Principio que enuncia que la materia no se crea ni se destruye durante una reacción química.

constellation An imaginary pattern of stars in the sky. (p. 598)
constelación Patrón imaginario de estrellas en el cielo.

controlled experiment An experiment in which only one parameter is manipulated at a time. (p. 12)
experimento controlado Experimento en el cual sólo una variable es manipulada a la vez.

convection zone The outermost layer of the sun's interior. (p. 547)
zona de convección Capa más superficial del interior del Sol.

convex lens A piece of transparent glass curved so that the middle is thicker than the edges. (p. 592)
lente convexa Trozo de cristal transparente curvado de tal manera que el centro es más grueso que los extremos.

coordinate A pair of numbers used to determine the position of a point on a graph. (p. 36)
coordenada Par de números que se usa para determinar la posición de un punto en una gráfica.

core The central region of the sun, where nuclear fusion takes place. (p. 546)
núcleo Región central del Sol, donde ocurre la fusión nuclear.

corona The outer layer of the sun's atmosphere. (p. 548)
corona Capa externa de la atmósfera del Sol.

corrosion The gradual wearing away of a metal element due to a chemical reaction. (p. 139)
corrosión Desgaste gradual de un elemento metal debido a una reacción química.

corrosive The way in which acids react with some metals so as to eat away the metal. (p. 269)
corrosivo Forma en que reaccionan los ácidos con algunos metales, como si se comieran el metal.

cosmic background radiation The electromagnetic radiation left over from the big bang. (p. 624)
radiación cósmica de fondo Radiación electromagnética que quedó del big bang.

covalent bond A chemical bond formed when two atoms share electrons. (p. 193)
enlace covalente Enlace químico que se forma cuando dos átomos comparten electrones.

crater A large round pit caused by the impact of a meteoroid. (p. 489)
cráter Gran cuenca redonda causada por el impacto de un meteoroide.

crystal An orderly, three-dimensional pattern of ions or atoms in a solid. (p. 188)
cristal Patrón ordenado tridimensional de iones o átomos en un sólido.

crystalline solid A solid that is made up of crystals in which particles are arranged in a regular, repeating pattern. (p. 92)
sólido cristalino Sólido constituido por cristales en los que las partículas están dispuestas en un patrón regular repetitivo.

dark energy A mysterious force that appears to be causing the expansion of the universe to accelerate.
energía negra Misteriosa fuerza que parece acelerar la expansión del universo. (p. 626)

dark matter Matter that does not give off electromagnetic radiation but is quite abundant in the universe. (p. 626)
materia negra Materia que no despide radiación electromagnética, pero que es muy abundante en el universo.

data Facts, figures, and other evidence gathered through observations. (p. 13)
dato Hecho, cifra u otra evidencia reunida por medio de las observaciones.

data point A point on a graph showing the location of a piece of data. (p. 36)
punto de dato Punto en una gráfica que muestra la ubicación de parte de los datos.

English and Spanish Glossary

decomposition A chemical reaction that breaks down compounds into simpler products. (p. 230)
descomposición Reacción química que descompone los compuestos en productos más simples.

density The ratio of the mass of a substance to its volume. (pp. 24, 425)
densidad Razón de la masa de una sustancia a su volumen.

diamond A form of the element carbon in which the atoms are arranged in a crystal structure. (p. 294)
diamante Forma del elemento del carbono en la cual los átomos de carbono están dispuestos en una estructura de cristal.

diatomic molecule A molecule consisting of two atoms. (p. 151)
molécula diatómica Molécula que tiene dos átomos.

dilute solution A mixture that has only a little solute dissolved in a certain amount of solvent. (p. 263)
solución diluida Mezcla que sólo tiene un poco de soluto disuelto en ella.

directly proportional A term used to describe the relationship between two variables whose graph is a straight line passing through the point (0, 0). (p. 107)
directamente proporcional Término empleado para describir la relación entre dos variables cuya gráfica forma una recta que pasa por el punto (0, 0).

displacement The length and direction of a straight line between starting and ending points. (p. 341)
desplazamiento La longitud y dirección de una línea recta entre los puntos inicial y final.

distance The length of a path between two points.
distancia La longitud del recorrido entre dos puntos. (p. 340)

DNA DeoxyriboNucleic Acid, one type of nucleic acid.
ADN Ácido desoxirribonucleico, un tipo de ácido nucleico. (p. 321)

double bond A chemical bond formed when atoms share two pairs of electrons. (p. 194)
enlace doble Enlace químico formado cuando los átomos comparten dos pares de electrones.

ductile A term used to describe a material that can be pulled out into a long wire. (p. 138)
dúctil Término usado para describir un material que se puede estirar hasta convertirlo en un alambre largo.

eclipse The partial or total blocking of one object in space by another. (p. 481)
eclipse Bloqueo parcial o total de un objeto en el espacio por otro.

eclipsing binary A binary star system in which one star periodically blocks the light from the other. (p. 615)
eclipse binario Sistema de estrella binaria en el que una estrella bloquea periódicamente la luz de la otra.

elastic potential energy The energy of stretched or compressed objects. (p. 360)
energía elástica potencial Energía de los objetos estirados o comprimidos.

electrical conductivity The ability of an object to transfer electric current. (p. 139)
conductividad eléctrica Capacidad de un objeto para transferir corriente eléctrica.

electrical energy The energy of moving electrical charges. (p. 76)
energía eléctrica Energía de cargas eléctricas que se mueven.

electrode A metal strip that conducts electricity. (p. 76)
electrodo Tira de metal que conduce la electricidad.

electromagnetic energy A form of energy that travels through space as waves. (p. 76)
energía electromagnética Forma de energía que viaja a través del espacio en forma de ondas.

electromagnetic radiation Energy that can travel through space in the form of waves. (p. 591)
radiación electromagnética Energía que viaja a través del espacio en forma de ondas.

electron A negatively charged particle that is found outside the nucleus of an atom. (p. 126)
electrón Partícula con carga negativa que se halla fuera del núcleo de un átomo.

electron dot diagram A representation of the valence electrons in an atom, using dots. (p. 177)
diagrama de puntos de electrones Representación del número de electrones de valencia en un átomo, usando puntos.

element A pure substance that cannot be broken down into other substances by chemical or physical means. (p. 62)
elemento Sustancia pura que no se puede descomponer en otras sustancias por medios químicos o físicos.

ellipse An oval shape, which may be elongated or nearly circular; the shape of the planets' orbits. (p. 541)
elipse Figura ovalada, alargada o casi circular; la forma de las órbitas de los planetas.

elliptical galaxy A galaxy shaped like a round or flattened ball, generally containing only old stars. (p. 618)
galaxia elíptica Galaxia con forma de pelota aplastada, que generalmente está formada sólo de estrellas viejas.

endothermic change A change in which energy is taken in. (p. 74)
cambio endotérmico Cambio en el que se absorbe energía.

endothermic reaction A reaction that absorbs energy in the form of heat. (p. 220)
reacción endotérmica Reacción que absorbe energía en forma de calor.

energy The ability to do work or cause change.
energía Capacidad para realizar trabajo o causar un cambio. (pp. 73, 358)

energy level The specific amount of energy an electron has. (p. 127)
nivel de energía La cantidad específica de energía que tiene un elctrón.

enzyme A biological catalyst that lowers the activation energy of reactions in cells. (p. 239)
enzima Catalítico biológico que disminuye la energía de activación de las reacciones en las células.

equinox The two days of the year on which neither hemisphere is tilted toward or away from the sun. (p. 471)
equinoccio Los dos días del año en los que ningún hemisferio está inclinado hacia el Sol ni más lejos de él.

escape velocity The velocity an object must reach to fly beyond a planet's or moon's gravitational pull.
velocidad de escape Velocidad que debe alcanzar un objeto para salir del campo de gravedad de un planeta o luna. (p. 505)

ester An organic compound made by chemically combining an alcohol and an organic acid. (p. 303)
ester Compuesto orgánico formado químicamente al combinar un alcohol y un ácido orgánico.

estimate An approximation of a number based on reasonable assumptions. (p. 30)
estimación Aproximación de un número basado en conjeturas razonables.

evaporation The process that occurs when vaporization takes place only on the surface of a liquid. (p. 99)
evaporación Proceso que se da cuando la vaporización se efectúa únicamente en la superficie de un líquido.

exothermic change A change in which energy is given off. (p. 74)
cambio exotérmico Cambio en el que se libera energía.

exothermic reaction A reaction that releases energy in the form of heat. (p. 221)
reacción exotérmica Reacción que libera energía en forma de calor.

extraterrestrial life Life that exists other than that on Earth. (p. 576)
vida extraterrestre Vida que existe fuera de la Tierra.

fatty acid An organic compound that is a monomer of a fat or oil. (p. 320)
ácido graso Compuesto orgánico que es un monómero de una grasa o aceite.

fluid A material that can easily flow. (pp. 93, 418)
fluido Sustancia que puede fluir con facilidad.

fluid friction Friction that occurs as an object moves through a fluid. (p. 382)
fricción de fluido Fricción que ocurre cuando un objeto se mueve a través de un fluido.

force A push or pull exerted on an object. (pp. 374, 474)
fuerza Empuje o atracción que se ejerce sobre un objeto.

free fall The motion of a falling object when the only force acting on it is gravity. (p. 386)
caída libre Movimiento de un objeto que cae cuando la única fuerza que actúa sobre el mismo es la gravedad.

freezing The change from the liquid to the solid state of matter. (p. 98)
congelación Cambio de la materia del estado líquido al estado sólido.

friction The force that one surface exerts on another when the two surfaces rub against each other. (p. 381)
fricción Fuerza que ejerce una superficie sobre otra cuando se frotan una contra otra.

English and Spanish Glossary

fuel A material that releases energy when it burns.
combustible Material que libera energía cuando se quema. (p. 243)

fullerene A form of carbon that consists of atoms arranged in the shape of a hollow sphere. (p. 295)
fullereno Forma del elemento del carbono que consiste en átomos de carbono colocados en forma de esfera hueca.

galaxy A huge group of single stars, star systems, star clusters, dust, and gas bound together by gravity.
galaxia Enorme grupo de estrellas individuales, sistemas de estrellas, cúmulos de estrellas, polvo y gas unidos por la gravedad. (p. 617)

gamma radiation A type of nuclear radiation made of high-energy waves. (p. 160)
radiación gamma Tipo de radiación nuclear hecha de ondas de alta energía.

gas A state of matter with no definite shape or volume. (p. 95)
gas Estado de la materia sin forma ni volumen definidos.

gas giants The name often given to the first four outer planets: Jupiter, Saturn, Uranus, and Neptune.
gigantes gaseosos Nombre que normalmente se da a los cuatro primeros planetas exteriores: Júpiter, Saturno, Urano y Neptuno. (p. 563)

geocentric A model of the universe in which Earth is at the center of the revolving planets and stars. (p. 539)
geocéntrico Modelo del universo en el que la Tierra es el centro de los planetas y estrellas que giran alrededor de ella.

geostationary orbit An orbit in which a satellite orbits Earth at the same rate as Earth rotates and thus stays over the same place all the time. (p. 524)
órbita geoestacionario Órbita en la que un satélite orbita la Tierra a la misma velocidad que rota la Tierra y que, por lo tanto, permanece sobre ese lugar permanentemente.

globular cluster A large, round, densely-packed grouping of older stars. (p. 616)
cúmulo globular Conjunto grande y redondo de estrellas viejas densamente apretadas.

glucose A simple carbohydrate; the monomer of many complex carbohydrates. (p. 317)
glucosa Carbohidrato simple; monómero de muchos carbohidratos complejos.

graph A picture of information from a data table; shows the relationship between variables. (p. 35)
gráfica Diagrama que muestra la relación entre dos variables.

graphite A form of the element carbon in which each carbon atom is bonded tightly to three other carbon atoms in flat layers. (p. 294)
grafito Forma del elemento carbono en el cual un átomo de carbono se une estrechamente a otros tres átomos de carbono en capas llanas.

gravitational potential energy Potential energy related to an object's height. (p. 360)
energía potencial gravitatoria Energía potencial que depende de la altura de un objeto.

gravity The force that pulls objects toward each other. (pp. 384, 474)
gravedad Fuerza que atrae objetos entre sí.

greenhouse effect The trapping of heat by a planet's atmosphere. (p. 556)
efecto invernadero Acumulación de calor en la atmósfera de un planeta.

group Elements in the same vertical column of the periodic table; also called a family. (p. 136)
grupo Elementos en la misma columna vertical de la tabla periódica; también llamado familia.

halogen An element found in Group 17 of the periodic table. (p. 153)
halógeno Elemento que se encuentra en el Grupo 17 de la tabla periódica.

heliocentric A model of the solar system in which Earth and the other planets revolve around the sun. (p. 540)
heliocéntrico Modelo del sistema solar en el que la Tierra y otros planetas giran alrededor del Sol.

Hertzsprung-Russell diagram A graph relating the surface temperatures and absolute brightnesses of stars. (p. 604)
diagrama Hertzsprung-Russel Gráfica que muestra la relación entre las temperaturas en la superficie de las estrellas y su magnitud absoluta.

heterogeneous mixture A mixture in which pure substances are unevenly distributed throughout the mixture. (p. 65)
mezcla heterogénea Mezcla en la cual las sustancias puras están distribuidas desigualmente.

homogeneous mixture A mixture in which substances are evenly distributed throughout the mixture. (p. 65)
mezcla homogénea Mezcla en la cual las sustancias químicas están distribuidas uniformemente.

horizontal axis (or x-axis) A line that runs left to right along the bottom of a graph, on which the manipulated variable (or independent variable) is labeled. (p. 36)
eje horizontal (o eje x) Recta que va de izquierda a derecha en la base de una gráfica, en la cual se rotula la variable manipulada (o variable independiente).

Hubble's law The observation that the farther away a galaxy is, the faster it is moving away. (p. 623)
ley de Hubble Observación que enuncia que mientras más lejos de nosotros se encuentra una galaxia, más rápido se está alejando.

hydraulic system A system that multiplies force by transmitting pressure from a small surface area through a confined fluid to a larger surface area.
sistema hidráulico Sistema que multiplica la fuerza transmitiendo la presión de un área total pequeña a un área total mayor a través de un fluido confinado. (p. 435)

hydrocarbon An organic compound that contains only carbon and hydrogen. (p. 298)
hidrocarburo Compuesto orgánico que contiene sólo carbono e hidrógeno.

hydrogen ion A positively charged ion (H^+) formed of a hydrogen atom that has lost its electron.
ión hidrógeno Ión con carga positiva (H^+) formado por un átomo de hidrógeno que ha perdido su electrón. (p. 274)

hydroxide ion A negatively charged ion made of oxygen and hydrogen (OH^-). (p. 275)
ión hidróxido Ión con carga negativa formado de oxígeno e hidrógeno (OH^-).

hydroxyl group An —OH group, found in alcohols.
grupo hidroxilo Grupo —OH, que se haya en los alcoholes. (p. 302)

hypothesis A possible explanation for a set of observations or answer to a scientific question. (p. 12)
hipótesis Explicación posible a un conjunto de observaciones o respuesta a una pregunta científica.

indicator A compound that changes color in the presence of an acid or a base. (p. 270)
indicador Compuesto que cambia de color en presencia de un ácido o una base.

inert gas An element found in Group 18 of the periodic table. (p. 154)
gas inerte Elemento que se halla en el grupo 18 de la tabla periódica.

inertia The tendency of an object to resist any change in its motion. (pp. 390, 476)
inercia Tendencia de un objeto a resistir cualquier cambio en su movimiento.

inferring The process of making an inference, an interpretation based on observations and prior knowledge. (p. 7)
inferir Proceso de realizar una inferencia; interpretación basada en observaciones y en el conocimiento previo.

inhibitor A material that decreases the rate of a reaction. (p. 239)
inhibidor Material que disminuye la velocidad de una reacción.

instantaneous speed The speed of an object at any given instant. (p. 343)
rapidez instantánea Velocidad de un objeto en un instante de tiempo.

inversely proportional A term used to describe the relationship between two variables whose product is constant. (p. 109)
inversamente proporcional Relación entre dos variables, cuyo producto es constante.

ion An atom or group of atoms that has become electrically charged. (p. 185)
ión Átomo o grupo de átomos con carga eléctrica.

ionic bond The attraction between oppositely charged ions. (p. 186)
enlace iónico Atracción entre iones con cargas opuestas.

ionic compound A compound that consists of positive and negative ions. (p. 186)
compuesto iónico Compuesto que tiene iones positivos y negativos.

irregular galaxy A galaxy that does not have a regular shape. (p. 618)
galaxia irregular Galaxia que no tiene una forma regular.

isomer Compounds that have the same chemical formula but different structural formulas. (p. 300)
isómero Compuestos que tienen la misma fórmula química pero diferentes fórmulas estructurales.

isotope An atom with the same number of protons and a different number of neutrons from other atoms of the same element. (p. 130)
isótopo Átomo con el mismo número de protones y un número diferente de neutrones que otros átomos del mismo elemento.

Kelvin scale The temperature scale on which zero is the temperature at which no more energy can be removed from matter. (p. 26)
escala Kelvin Escala de temperatura en la cual el cero es la temperatura a la cual no se puede quitar más energía de la materia.

kinetic energy Energy that an object has due to its motion. (p. 359)
energía cinética Energía que tiene un objeto debido a su movimiento.

Kuiper belt A doughnut-shaped region that stretches from beyond Neptune's orbit to about 100 times Earth's distance from the sun. (p. 573)
cinturón de Kuiper Región en forma de disco que se extiende desde la órbita de Neptune hasta alrededor de 100 veces la distancia de la Tierra al Sol.

law of conservation of energy The rule that energy cannot be created or destroyed. (p. 363)
ley de la conservación de la energía Regla que dice que la energía no se puede crear ni destruir.

law of conservation of matter The principle that the total amount of matter is neither created nor destroyed during any chemical or physical change. (p. 71)
ley de conservación de la materia Principio que enuncia que la cantidad de materia total no se crea ni se destruye durante cambios químicos o físicos.

law of conservation of momentum The rule that in the absence of outside forces the total momentum of objects that interact does not change. (p. 397)
ley de la conservación del momento Regla según la cual en ausencia de fuerzas externas, el momento total de los objetos no cambia en su interacción.

lift An upward force. (p. 439)
fuerza de elevación Fuerza ascendente.

light-year The distance that light travels in one year, about 9.5 million million kilometers. (p. 602)
año luz Distancia a la que viaja la luz en un año; alrededor de 9.5 millones de millones de kilómetros.

linear graph A line graph in which the data points yield a straight line. (p. 36)
gráfica lineal Gráfica en la cual los puntos de los datos forman una línea recta.

line of best fit A smooth line that reflects the general pattern in a graph. (p. 36)
recta de mayor aproximación Recta que refleja el patrón general en una gráfica.

lipid An energy-rich organic compound made of carbon, oxygen, and hydrogen. Fats, oils, waxes, and cholesterol are lipids. (p. 320)
lípido Compuesto orgánico rico en energía hecho de carbono, oxígeno e hidrógeno; las grasas, aceites, ceras y colesterol son lípidos.

liquid A state of matter that has no definite shape but has a definite volume. (p. 93)
líquido Estado de la materia que no tiene forma definida pero sí volumen definido.

lunar eclipse The blocking of sunlight to the moon that occurs when Earth is directly between the sun and the moon. (p. 483)
eclipse lunar Bloqueo de la luz solar sobre la Luna llena que ocurre cuando la Tierra se interpone entre el Sol y la Luna.

main sequence A diagonal area on an H-R diagram that includes more than 90 percent of all stars.
secuencia principal Área diagonal en un diagrama de H-R que incluye más del 90 por ciento de todas las estrellas. (p. 605)

malleable A term used to describe material that can be pounded into shapes. (p. 138)
maleable Término usado para describir el material al que se le puede dar forma.

manipulated variable The one variable parameter that a scientist changes during an experiment (p. 12)
variable manipulada Único factor que un científico cambia durante un experimento.

maria Dark, flat areas on the moon's surface formed from huge ancient lava flows. (p. 489)
maria Áreas oscuras y llanas en la superficie de la Luna formadas por enormes flujos de lava antiguos.

mass A measure of how much matter is in an object. (pp. 21, 384, 475)
masa Medida de cuánta materia hay en un objeto.

mass number The sum of protons and neutrons in the nucleus of an atom. (p. 130)
número de masa Suma de protones y neutrones en el núcleo de un átomo.

matter Anything that has mass and occupies space.
materia Cualquier cosa que tiene masa y ocupa espacio. (pp. 58, 214)

mechanical energy An object's combined kinetic energy and potential energy. (p. 361)
energía mecánica Energía cinética o potencial asociada con el movimiento o posición de un objeto.

melting The change from the solid to the liquid state of matter. (p. 97)
fusión Cambio en el estado de la materia de sólido a líquido.

melting point The temperature at which a substance changes from a solid to a liquid. (p. 97)
punto de fusión Temperatura a la que una sustancia cambia de estado sólido a líquido.

meniscus The curved upper surface of a liquid in a column of liquid. (p. 22)
menisco Superficie superior curvada de un líquido en una columna de líquido.

metal A class of elements characterized by physical properties that include shininess, malleability, ductility, and conductivity. (p. 138)
metal Clase de elementos caracterizados por las propiedades físicas que incluye brillo, maleabilidad, ductilidad y conductividad.

metallic bond An attraction between a positive metal ion and the electrons surrounding it. (p. 200)
enlace metálico Atracción entre un ión metálico positivo y los electrones que lo rodean.

meteor A streak of light in the sky produced by the burning of a meteoroid in Earth's atmosphere. (p. 575)
meteoro Rayo de luz en el cielo producido por el incendio de un meteoroide en la atmósfera de la Tierra.

meteorite A meteoroid that passes through the atmosphere and hits Earth's surface. (p. 575)
meteorito Meteoroide que pasa por la atmósfera y golpea la superficie de la Tierra.

meteoroid A chunk of rock or dust in space. (pp. 489, 575)
meteoroide Pedazo de roca o polvo en el espacio.

microgravity The condition of experiencing weightlessness in orbit. (p. 521)
microgravedad Condición de experimentar falta de peso en órbita.

mixture Two or more substances that are mixed together but not chemically combined. (p. 65)
mezcla Dos o más sustancias que están mezcladas, pero que no están combinadas químicamente.

model A representation of an object or process. (p. 14)
modelo Representación de un objeto o proceso.

molecular compound A compound that is composed of molecules. (p. 194)
compuesto molecular Compuesto que contiene moléculas.

molecule A neutral particle made of two or more atoms joined by covalent bonds. (pp. 63, 193)
molécula Partícula neutral hecha de dos o más átomos que se unen por enlaces covalentes.

momentum The product of an object's mass and velocity. (p. 396)
momento Producto de la masa de un objeto por su velocidad.

monomer One molecule that makes up the links in a polymer chain. (p. 304)
monómero Molécula que forma los enlaces en una cadena polímera.

moon A natural satellite that revolves around a planet. (p. 543)
luna Satélite natural que gira alrededor de un planeta.

motion The state in which one object's distance from another is changing. (p. 339)
movimiento Estado en el que la distancia entre un objeto y otro va cambiando.

nanotube A form of carbon that consists of atoms in the form of a long, hollow cylinder. (p. 295)
nanotubo Forma del carbono que consiste en átomos en forma de un cilindro largo y hueco.

neap tide The tide with the least difference between consecutive low and high tides. (p. 485)
marea muerta Marea con la mínima diferencia entre marea alta y marea baja consecutivas.

nebula A large cloud of gas and dust in space, spread out in an immense volume. (p. 609)
nebulosa Gran nube de gas y polvo en el espacio, expandida en un volumen inmenso.

net force The overall force on an object when all the individual forces acting on it are added together.
fuerza neta Fuerza total que actúa sobre un objeto cuando se suman las fuerzas individuales que actúan sobre él. (p. 375)

neutral A word used to describe a solution with a pH of 7. (p. 276)
neutral Describe una solución con pH de 7.

neutralization A reaction of an acid with a base, yielding a solution that is not as acidic or basic as the starting solutions were. (p. 278)
neutralización Reacción de un ácido con una base, que produce una solución que no es ácida ni básica, como lo eran las soluciones originales.

neutron A small particle in the nucleus of the atom, with no electrical charge. (p. 128)
neutrón Partícula pequeña en el núcleo del átomo, que no tiene carga eléctrica.

neutron star The small, dense remains of a high-mass star after a supernova. (p. 612)
estrella de neutrones Restos pequeños y densos de una estrella de gran masa después de una supernova.

newton The SI unit used for the magnitude, or strength, of a force. (p. 375)
newton Unidad del SI que se usa para medir la magnitud o potencia de una fuerza.

Newton's first law of motion The scientific law that states that an object at rest will stay at rest and an object in motion will stay in motion with a constant speed and direction unless acted on by a force. (p. 476)
primera ley de Newton del movimiento Ley científica que establece que un objeto en reposo se mantendrá en reposo y un objeto en movimiento se mantendrá en movimiento con una velocidad y dirección constante a menos que se ejerza una fuerza sobre él.

nonlinear graph A line graph in which the data points do not fall along a straight line. (p. 40)
gráfica no lineal Gráfica lineal en la que los puntos de datos no forman una línea recta.

nonmetal An element that lacks most of the properties of a metal. (p. 149)
no metal Elemento que carece de la mayoría de las propiedades de un metal.

nonpolar bond A covalent bond in which electrons are shared equally. (p. 196)
enlace no polar Enlace covalente en el que los electrones se comparte por igual.

nuclear fusion The process by which hydrogen atoms join together in the sun's core to form helium. (p. 546)
fusión nuclear Proceso por el cual los átomos de hidrógeno se unen en el núcleo del Sol para formar helio.

nucleic acid A very large organic compound made up of carbon, oxygen, hydrogen, nitrogen, and phosphorus; examples are DNA and RNA. (p. 321)
ácido nucleico Compuesto orgánico muy grande hecho de carbono, oxígeno, hidrógeno, nitrógeno y fósforo; ejemplos son ADN and ARN.

nucleotide An organic compound that is one of the monomers of nucleic acids. (p. 322)
nucleótido Compuesto orgánico que es uno de los monómeros de los ácidos nucleicos.

nucleus The central core of the atom. (p. 127); the solid inner core of a comet. (p. 573)
núcleo Centro de un átomo; centro interno sólido de un cometa.

observatory A building that contains one or more telescopes. (p. 594)
observatorio Edificio que contiene uno o más telescopios.

observing The process of using one or more of your senses to gather information. (p. 7)
observar Proceso de usar uno o más de tus sentidos para reunir información.

Oort cloud A spherical region of comets that surrounds the solar system. (p. 573)
nube de Oort Región esférica de cometas que rodea el sistema solar.

open cluster A star cluster that has a loose, disorganized appearance and contains no more than a few thousand stars. (p. 616)
cúmulo abierto Cúmulo de estrellas que tiene una apariencia no compacta y desorganizada, y que no contiene más de unos pocos miles de estrellas.

open system A system in which matter can enter from or escape to the surroundings. (p. 227)
sistema abierto Sistema en el que la materia puede entrar desde el medio que la rodea o salir hacia él.

optical telescope A telescope that uses lenses or mirrors to collect and focus visible light. (p. 592)
telescopio óptico Telescopio que usa lentes o espejos para captar y enfocar la luz visible.

orbit The path of an object as it revolves around another object in space. (p. 465)
órbita Trayectoria de un objeto a medida que gira alrededor de otro en el espacio.

orbital velocity The velocity a rocket must achieve to establish an orbit around a body in space. (p. 504)
velocidad orbital Velocidad que un cohete debe alcanzar para establecer una órbita alrededor de un cuerpo en el espacio.

organic acid A substituted hydrocarbon with one or more of the —COOH group of atoms. (p. 303)
ácido orgánico Hidrocarburo sustituto que tiene uno o más grupos de átomos —COOH.

organic compounds Most compounds that contain carbon. (p. 297)
compuesto orgánico La mayoría de los compuestos que contienen carbono.

origin The (0, 0) point on a line graph; where the *x*-axis and *y*-axis cross on a graph. (p. 36)
origen Punto (0, 0) en una gráfica lineal.

parallax The apparent change in position of an object when seen from different places. (p. 602)
paralaje Cambio aparente en la posición de un objeto cuando es visto desde diferentes lugares.

parameter A factor that can be measured in an experiment. (p. 12)
parámetro Factor que puede ser medido en un experimento.

particle accelerator A machine that moves atomic nuclei at higher and higher speeds until they crash into one another, sometimes forming heavier elements. (p. 144)
acelerador de partículas Máquina que mueve los núcleos atómicos a velocidades cada vez más altas hasta que chocan entre ellas, a veces forman elementos más pesados.

pascal A unit of pressure equal to 1 newton per square meter. (p. 417)
pascal Unidad de presión igual a 1 newton por metro cuadrado.

Pascal's principle The rule that when force is applied to a confined fluid, the change in pressure is transmitted equally to all parts of the fluid. (p. 433)
principio de Pascal Regla que enuncia que cuando se aplica una fuerza a un fluido confinado, el cambio en la presión es transmitida por igual a todas las partes del fluido.

penumbra The larger, less dark part of a shadow surrounding the darkest part. (p. 482)
penumbra Parte de una sombra que rodea la parte más oscura.

period A horizontal row of elements in the periodic table. (p. 136)
período Fila horizontal de los elementos en la tabla periódica.

periodic table A chart of the elements showing the repeating pattern of their properties. (p. 132)
tabla periódica Tabla de los elementos que muestra el patrón repetido de sus propiedades.

pH scale A range of values used to express the concentration of hydrogen ions in a solution. (p. 276)
escala pH Rango de valores usados para expresar la concentración de iones de hidrógeno que hay en una solución.

phase One of the different apparent shapes of the moon as seen from Earth. (p. 479)
fase Una de las diferentes formas aparentes de la Luna según se ve desde la Tierra.

photosphere The inner layer of the sun's atmosphere that gives off its visible light (p. 548)
fotosfera Capa más interna de la atmósfera del Sol que provoca la luz que vemos; superficie del Sol.

physical change A change in a substance that does not change its identity. (pp. 69, 216)
cambio físico Cambio en una sustancia que no cambia su identidad.

physical property A characteristic of a pure substance that can be observed without changing it into another substance. (pp. 60, 215)
propiedad física Característica de una sustancia pura que se puede observar sin convertirla en otra sustancia.

physics The study of matter, energy, motion, and forces, and how they interact. (p. 8)
física Estudio de la materia y de la energía, y de cómo interactúan.

planetary nebula A huge cloud of gas that is created when the outer layers of a red giant star drift out into space. (p. 610)
nebulosa planetaria Enorme nube de gas, que se crea cuando las capas externas de una estrella roja gigante se dispersan al espacio.

planetesimal One of the small asteroid-like bodies that formed the building blocks of the planets. (p. 625)
planetésimo Uno de los cuerpos pequeños parecidos a asteroides que dieron origen a los planetas.

plastic A synthetic polymer that can be molded or shaped. (p. 309)
plástico Polímero sintético que se puede moldear o se le puede dar forma.

polar bond A covalent bond in which electrons are shared unequally. (p. 196)
enlace polar Enlace covalente en el que los electrones se comparten de forma desigual.

polyatomic ion An ion that is made of more than one atom. (p. 185)
ión poliatómico Ión que está hecho de más de un átomo.

polymer A large molecule in which many smaller molecules are bonded together. (p. 304)
polímero Molécula grande en la que muchas moléculas más pequeñas están unidas.

potential energy Stored energy that results from the position or shape of an object. (p. 360)
energía potencial Energía almacenada que es el resultado de la posición o forma de un objeto.

precipitate A solid that forms from a solution during a chemical reaction. (p. 218)
precipitado Sólido que se forma de una solución durante una reacción química.

precision A measure of the exactness of measurement.
precisión Cuán cerca se encuentran un grupo de medidas entre ellas. (p. 32)

predicting The process of forecasting what will happen in the future based on past experience or evidence. (p. 7)
predecir Proceso de pronosticar lo que va a suceder en el futuro, basado en la experiencia pasada o en evidencia.

pressure The force exerted on a surface divided by the total area over which the force is exerted.
presión Fuerza ejercida sobre una superficie dividida por el área total sobre la cual se ejerce la fuerza. (pp. 105, 417)

product A substance formed as a result of a chemical reaction. (p. 216)
producto Sustancia formada como resultado de una reacción química.

projectile An object that is thrown. (p. 387)
proyectil Objeto que es lanzado.

prominence A huge, reddish loop of gas that protrudes from the sun's surface, linking parts of sunspot regions. (p. 550)
protuberencia solar Enorme arco rojizo de gas que sobresale de la superfice del Sol, que une partes de las regiones de las manchas solares.

protein An organic compound that is a polymer of amino acids. (p. 308)
proteína Compuesto orgánico que es un polímero de aminoácidos.

proton A positively charged particle that is part of an atom's nucleus. (p. 127)
protón Partícula con carga positiva ubicada en el núcleo de un átomo.

protostar A contracting cloud of gas and dust with enough mass to form a star. (p. 609)
protoestrella Nube de gas y polvo que se contrae, con suficiente masa como para formar una estrella.

pulsar A rapidly spinning neutron star that produces radio waves. (p. 612)
púlsar Estrella de neutrones que gira rápidamente y produce ondas de radio.

Q

quasar An enormously bright, distant galaxy with a giant black hole at its center. (p. 617)
quásar Galaxia extraordinariamente luminosa y distante con un agujero negro gigante en el centro.

radiation zone A region of very tightly packed gas in the sun's interior where energy is transferred mainly in the form of light. (p. 547)
zona radiactiva Región de gases estrechamente comprimidos en el interior del Sol en donde se transfiere la energía principalmente en forma de luz.

radioactive decay The process in which the atomic nuclei of unstable isotopes release fast-moving particles and energy. (p. 159)
desintegración radiactiva Proceso por el cual los núcleos atómicos de isótopos inestables liberan partículas de rápido movimiento y gran cantidad de energía.

radioactivity The ability of a substance to spontaneously emit radiation; a property of unstable isotopes. (p. 159)
radiactividad Emisión espontánea de radiación por un núcleo atómico inestable.

radio telescope A device used to detect radio waves from objects in space. (p. 593)
radiotelescopio Aparato usado para detectar ondas de radio de los objetos en el espacio.

reactant A substance that undergoes change in a chemical reaction. (p. 216)
reactante Sustancia que participa en una reacción química.

reactivity The ease and speed with which an element combines, or reacts, with other elements and compounds. (p. 139)
reactividad Facilidad y rapidez con las que un elemento se combina, o reacciona, con otros elementos y compuestos.

reference point A place or object used for comparison to describe the position or motion of a person or object. (p. 339)
punto de referencia Lugar u objeto usado como punto de comparación para determinar si un objeto está en movimiento.

reflecting telescope A telescope that uses a curved mirror to collect and focus light. (p. 593)
telescopio reflector Telescopio que usa un espejo curvado para captar y enfocar la luz.

refracting telescope A telescope that uses convex lenses to gather and focus light. (p. 592)
telescopio refractor Telescopio que usa lentes convexas para captar y enfocar la luz.

remote sensing The collection of information about Earth and other objects in space using satellites or probes. (p. 524)
percepción remota Recolección de información sobre la Tierra y otros objetos en el espacio usando satélites o sondas.

replacement A reaction in which one element replaces another in a compound or when two elements in different compounds trade places. (p. 230)
reemplazo sustitución Reacción en la que un elemento reemplaza a otro en un compuesto o dos elementos de diferentes compuestos se intercambian.

reproducibility How close a group of measurements are to each other. (p. 31)
reproducibilidad Cuán cerca un grupo de medidas están entre sí.

responding variable The variable parameter that changes as a result of changes to the manipulated, or independent, variable in an experiment. (p. 12)
variable respuesta Factor que cambia como resultado del cambio de la variable manipulada, o independiente, en un experimento.

revolution The movement of an object around another object. (p. 465)
revolución Movimiento de un objeto alrededor de otro.

ring A thin disk of small ice and rock particles surrounding a planet. (p. 563)
anillo Disco fino de pequeñas partículas de hielo y roca que rodea un planeta.

RNA Ribonucleic acid, a type of nucleic acid. (p. 321)
ARN Ácido ribonucleico; un tipo de ácido nucleico.

rocket A device that expels gas in one direction to move in the opposite direction. (p. 503)
cohete Aparato que expulsa gas en una dirección para moverse en la dirección opuesta.

rolling friction Friction that occurs when an object rolls over a surface. (p. 382)
fricción de rodamiento Fricción que ocurre cuando un objeto rueda sobre una superficie.

rotation The spinning motion of a planet on its axis.
rotación Movimiento giratorio de un planeta sobre su eje. (p. 465)

rover A small robotic space probe that can move about the surface of a planet or moon. (p. 518)
róver Pequeña sonda espacial robótica que puede moverse sobre la superficie de un planeta o sobre la Luna.

English and Spanish Glossary

salt An ionic compound made from the neutralization of an acid with a base. (p. 279)
sal Compuesto iónico formado por la neutralización de un ácido con una base.

satellite Any object that orbits around another object in space. (pp. 403, 511)
satélite Cualquier objeto que orbita alrededor de otro objeto en el espacio.

saturated hydrocarbon A hydrocarbon in which all the bonds between carbon atoms are single bonds.
hidrocarburo saturado Hidrocarburo en el que todos los enlaces entre los átomos de carbono son enlaces simples. (p. 301)

saturated solution A mixture that contains as much dissolved solute as is possible at a given temperature. (p. 263)
solución saturada Mezcla que contiene la mayor cantidad posible de soluto disuelto a una temperatura determinada.

science The study of the natural world through observations and logical reasoning; leads to a body of knowledge. (p. 7)
ciencia Estudio del mundo natural a través de observaciones y del razonamiento lógico; conduce a un conjunto de conocimientos.

scientific inquiry The ongoing process of discovery in science. (p. 10)
investigación científica Proceso continuo de descubrimiento en la ciencia.

scientific law A statement that describes what scientists expect to happen every time under a particular set of conditions. (p. 15)
ley científica Enunciado que describe lo que los científicos esperan que suceda cada vez que se da una serie de condiciones determinadas.

scientific notation A mathematical method of writing numbers using powers of ten. (p. 620)
notación científica Método matemático de escritura de números que usa la potencia de diez.

scientific theory A well-tested explanation for a wide range of observations or experimental results.
teoría científica Explicación comprobada de una gran variedad de observaciones o resultados de experimentos. (p. 15)

semiconductor A material that conducts current under certain conditions. (p. 155)
semiconductor Material que conduce la corriente bajo ciertas condiciones.

semimetal An element that has some characteristics of both metals and nonmetals. (p. 155)
metaloide Elemento que tiene algunas características tanto de los metales como de los no metales.

SI (*Système International d'Unités*) International System of Units; a version of the metric system used by scientists all over the world. (p. 17)
SI (*Système International d'Unités*) Sistema Internacional de Unidades; versión del sistema métrico usado por científicos de todo el mundo.

significant figures All the digits in a measurement that have been measured exactly, plus one digit whose value has been estimated. (p. 32)
cifras significativas Todos los dígitos en una medida que se han medido con exactitud, más un dígito cuyo valor se ha estimado.

sliding friction Friction that occurs when one solid surface slides over another. (p. 382)
fricción de deslizamiento Fricción que ocurre cuando una superficie sólida se desliza sobre otra.

slope The steepness of a line on a graph, equal to its vertical change divided by its horizontal change.
pendiente Inclinación de una recta en una gráfica, igual a su cambio vertical dividido por su cambio horizontal. (pp. 39, 346)

solar eclipse The blocking of sunlight to Earth that occurs when the moon is directly between the sun and Earth. (p. 482)
eclipse solar Bloqueo de la luz solar en su camino a la Tierra que ocurre cuando la Luna se interpone entre el Sol y la Tierra.

solar flare An eruption of gas from the sun's surface that occurs when the loops in sunspot regions suddenly connect. (p. 550)
fulguración solar Erupción de gas desde la superficie del Sol que ocurre cuando los arcos en las regiones de las manchas solares se unen repentinamente.

solar nebula A large cloud of gas and dust, such as the one that formed our solar system. (p. 625)
nebulosa solar Gran nube de gas y polvo como de la que formó nuestro sistema solar.

solar wind A stream of electrically charged particles that emanate from the sun's corona. (p. 548)
viento solar Flujo de partículas cargadas eléctricamente que emanan de la corona del Sol.

solid A state of matter that has a definite shape and a definite volume. (p. 91)
sólido Estado de la materia con forma y volumen definidos.

solstice The two days of the year on which the sun reaches its greatest distance north or south of the equator. (p. 470)
solsticio Los dos días del año en que el Sol está a mayor distancia hacia el norte o hacia el sur del ecuador.

solubility A measure of how much solute can dissolve in a solvent at a given temperature.
solubilidad Medida de cuánto soluto se puede disolver en un solvente dada una temperatura determinada. (p. 263)

solute The part of a solution present in a lesser amount and dissolved by the solvent. (p. 256)
soluto Parte de una solución presente en menor cantidad y disuelta por el solvente.

solution A well-mixed mixture containing a solvent and at least one solute that has the same properties throughout. (pp. 65, 256)
solución Mezcla homogénea que contiene un solvente y al menos un soluto que tiene las mismas propiedades en toda la solución.

solvent The part of a solution that is present in the largest amount and dissolves a solute. (p. 256)
solvente Parte de una solución que está presente en la mayor cantidad y que disuelve un soluto.

space probe A spacecraft that has various scientific instruments that can collect data, including visual images, but has no human crew. (p. 518)
sonda espacial Nave espacial que tiene varios instrumentos científicos que pueden reunir datos, incluyendo imágenes, pero que no lleva tripulación.

space shuttle A spacecraft that can carry a crew into space, return to Earth, and then be reused for the same purpose. (p. 516)
transbordador espacial Nave espacial que puede llevar a una tripulación al espacio, volver a la Tierra, y luego volver a ser usada para el mismo propósito.

space spinoff An item that has uses on Earth but was originally developed for use in space. (p. 522)
derivación espacial Objeto que se puede usar en la Tierra, pero que originalmente se construyó para ser usado en el espacio.

space station A large artificial satellite on which people can live and work for long periods. (p. 517)
estación espacial Enorme satélite artificial en el que la gente puede vivir y trabajar durante largos períodos.

spectrograph An instrument that separates light into colors and makes an image of the resulting spectrum. (p. 600)
espectrógrafo Instrumento que separa la luz en colores y crea una imagen del espectro resultante.

spectrum The range of wavelengths of electromagnetic waves. (p. 591)
espectro Gama de longitudes de ondas electromagnéticas.

speed The distance an object travels in a certain period of time without regard to direction. (p. 342)
rapidez Distancia que viaja un objeto por unidad de tiempo.

spiral galaxy A galaxy with a bulge in the middle and arms that spiral outward in a pinwheel pattern. (p. 618)
galaxia espiral Galaxia con una protuberancia en el centro y brazos que giran en espiral hacia el exterior, como un remolino.

spring tide The tide with the greatest difference between consecutive low and high tides. (p. 485)
marea viva Marea con la mayor diferencia entre mareas alta y baja consecutivas.

starch A complex carbohydrate in which plants store energy. (p. 318)
almidón Carbohidrato complejo en la que las plantas almacenan la energía.

static friction Friction that acts on objects that are not moving. (p. 382)
fricción estática Fricción que actúa sobre los objetos que no se mueven.

structural formula A description of a molecule that shows the kind, number, and arrangement of atoms.
fórmula estructural Descripción de una molécula que muestra el tipo, número y posición de los átomos. (p. 299)

sublimation The change in state from a solid directly to a gas without passing through the liquid state. (p. 101)
sublimación Cambio del estado sólido directamente a gas, sin pasar por el estado líquido.

subscript A number in a chemical formula that tells the number of atoms in a molecule or the ratio of elements in a compound. (p. 187)
subíndice Número en una fórmula química que indica el número de átomos que tiene una molécula o la razón de elementos en un compuesto.

substance A single kind of matter that is pure and has a specific set of properties. (p. 59)
sustancia Tipo único de materia que es pura y tiene un conjunto de propiedades específicas.

English and Spanish Glossary

substituted hydrocarbon A hydrocarbon in which one or more hydrogen atoms have been replaced by atoms of other elements. (p. 302)
hidrocarburo sustituido Hidrocarburo en el cual uno o más átomos de hidrógeno han sido sustituidos por átomos de otros elementos.

sunspot A dark area of gas on the sun's surface that is cooler than surrounding gases. (p. 548)
mancha solar Área oscura de gas en la superficie del Sol, que está más fría que los gases que la rodean.

supernova The brilliant explosion of a dying supergiant star. (p. 611)
supernova Explosión brillante de una estrella supergigante en extinción.

supersaturated solution A mixture that has more dissolved solute than is predicted by its solubility at a given temperature. (p. 267)
solución supersaturada Mezcla que tiene más soluto disuelto de lo que se predice por su solubilidad a una temperatura determinada.

surface tension The result of an inward pull among the molecules of a liquid that brings the molecules on the surface closer together (p. 94)
tensión superficial Resultado de la atracción hacia el centro entre las moléculas de un líquido, que hace que las moléculas de la superficie se junten más; hace que la superficie actúe como si tuviera una piel delgada.

suspension A mixture in which particles can be seen and easily separated by settling or filtration. (p. 258)
suspensión Mezcla en la cual las partículas se pueden ver y separar fácilmente por sedimentación o por filtración.

synthesis A chemical reaction in which two or more simple substances combine to form a new, more complex substance. (p. 230)
síntesis Reacción química en la que dos o más sustancias simples se combinan para formar una sustancia nueva más compleja.

T

telescope A device built to observe distant objects by making them appear closer. (p. 488)
telescopio Aparato construido para observar objetos distantes que hace que aparezcan más cercanos.

temperature A measure of the average energy of motion of the particles of a substance. (p. 74)
temperatura Medida de la energía promedio de movimiento de las partículas de una sustancia.

tension An elastic force that stretches or pulls on the molecules in matter. (p. 388)
tensión Fuerza elástica que aleja o atrae las partículas de la materia.

terrestrial planets The name often given to the four inner planets: Mercury, Venus, Earth, and Mars.
planetas telúricos Nombre dado normalmente a los cuatro planetas interiores: Mercurio, Venus, Tierra y Marte. (p. 552)

thermal conductivity The ability of an object to transfer heat. (p. 139)
conductividad termal Capacidad de un objeto para transferir corriente eléctrica.

thermal energy The total potential and kinetic energy of the particles in an object. (p. 74)
energía térmica Energía cinética y potencial total de las partículas de un objeto.

thrust The reaction force that propels a rocket forward. (p. 504)
empuje Fuerza de reacción que propulsa un cohete hacia delante.

tide The periodic rise and fall of the level of water in the ocean. (p. 484)
marea La subida y bajada periódica del nivel de agua en el océano.

tracer A radioactive isotope that can be followed through the steps of a chemical reaction or industrial process. (p. 162)
trazador Isótopo radiactivo que se puede seguir mediante los pasos de una reacción química o proceso industrial.

transition metal One of the elements in Groups 3 through 12 of the periodic table. (p. 142)
metal de transición Uno de los elementos en los Grupos 3 a 12 de la tabla periódica.

triple bond A chemical bond formed when atoms share three pairs of electrons. (p. 194)
enlace triple Enlace químico formado cuando los átomos comparten tres pares de electrones.

U

umbra The darkest part of a shadow. (p. 482)
umbra La parte más oscura de una sombra.

unbalanced forces Forces that cause an object's velocity to change. (p. 376)
fuerza desequilibrada Fuerzas que producen una fuerza neta diferente de cero, lo cual cambia el movimiento de un objeto.

Universal Law of Gravitation The scientific law that states that every object in the universe attracts every other object. (p. 474)
ley de la gravitación universal Ley científica que establece que todos los objetos del universo se atraen entre ellos.

universe All of space and everything in it. (p. 620)
universo Todo el espacio y todo lo que hay en él.

unsaturated hydrocarbon A hydrocarbon in which one or more of the bonds between carbon atoms is double or triple. (p. 301)
hidrocarburo no saturado Hidrocarburo en el que uno o más de los enlaces entre átomos de carbono es doble o triple.

unsaturated solution A mixture that contains less dissolved solute than is possible at a given temperature. (p. 263)
solución no saturada Mezcla que contiene menos soluto disuelto de lo que es posible a una temperatura determinada.

vacuum A place that is empty of all matter. (p. 521)
vacío Lugar en donde no existe materia.

valence electrons The electrons that are in the highest energy level of an atom and that are involved in chemical reactions. (p. 176)
electrones de valencia Electrones que tienen el más alto nivel de energía de un átomo y participan en reacciones químicas

vaporization The change of state from a liquid to a gas. (p. 98)
vaporización Cambio del estado de líquido a gas.

vector A measurable quantity that consists of both a magnitude and a direction. (p. 341)
vector Cantidad mensurable, tanto con magnitud como con dirección.

velocity Speed in a given direction. (pp. 344, 504)
velocidad Rapidez en una dirección dada.

vertical axis (or *y*-axis) A line that runs up and down along the side of a graph, on which the responding variable (or dependent variable) is labeled. (p. 36)
eje vertical (o eje *y*) Recta que va de arriba a abajo en el lado vertical de una gráfica, en la cual se rotula la variable respuesta (o variable dependiente).

viscosity A liquid's resistance to flowing. (p. 94)
viscosidad Resistencia a fluir que presenta un líquido.

visible light Electromagnetic radiation that can be seen with the unaided eye. (p. 591)
luz visible Radiación electromagnética que se puede ver a simple vista.

volume The amount of space that matter occupies.
volumen Cantidad de espacio que ocupa la materia. (p. 22)

wavelength The distance between the crest of one wave and the crest of the next wave. (p. 591)
longitud de onda Distancia entre la cresta de una onda y la cresta de la siguiente onda.

weight A measure of the force of gravity on an object. (pp. 21, 385, 475)
peso Medida de la fuerza de gravedad sobre un objeto.

white dwarf The blue-white hot core of a star that is left behind after its outer layers have expanded and drifted out into space. (p. 611)
enana blanca Núcleo caliente azul blanquecino de una estrella, que queda después de que sus capas externas se han expandido y dispersado por el espacio.

work A word that describes what is done on an object when a force is exerted on an object that causes it to move. (p. 358)
trabajo Fuerza ejercida sobre un objeto para moverlo.

Index

Page numbers for key terms are printed in **boldface** type.
Page numbers for illustrations, maps, and charts are printed in *italics*.

A

absolute brightness *601*
  surface temperature of star and
    604–605
absolute zero 26
acceleration **350**–355, *351*
  analyzing *352–353*
  calculating 352–353
  changes in force and mass and
    391
  equation 391
  free fall and **386**
  graphing 354–355
  due to gravity 386
  Newton's second law of motion
    and 390–391
accidents, first aid in case of *47*
accuracy *31*
acetic acid *276*, 303
acetylene *301*
acids **268**
  acid-base reactions 278–279
  common *275*
  litmus test for *270*, 275
  organic **303**
  properties of 268–270
  safe use of 277
  in solution 274–275, *276*
  strength of *276–277*
  uses of *272*
actinides *134*, 136, *144*
actinium 144
action force 394–395, *403*, 442
  rockets and *504*
action-reaction pairs *394*–395
activation energy **235**, 236
  for combustion **243**
  controlling rate of reaction
    by changing 239
addition of measurements 32
air
  as fluid 428
  as mixture of gases **95**
  nonmetals in **149**
  as solution **65**
  weight of 418
air bags 232–233
aircraft
  flight of *220*, 437, 439, 442–443
  helicopters 442–443
airplane wing, Bernoulli's
  principle and *439*
air pressure 418–421
  balanced *419*

boiling point of water and **99**
  elevation and *420*, 421
  measuring 422
  at sea level 419
air resistance **387**
alanine *319*
alcohol *302*–303
Aldrin, Buzz 512, 513
Algol *615*
alkali metals *140*, 179
alkaline earth metals *141*
alloys 142, 144, *199*
Alpha Centauri A and B *615*
alpha particle *160*, *161*
aluminum 142
Americium-241 144, *145*
amino acid **308**, *319*, 322
amino group 319
ammonia 275
amorphous solids *92*
Andromeda Galaxy *621*, 622
aneroid barometer *422*
-ane suffix 301
animals, natural polymers
  made by *308*
Antarctica, meteorites in 576
antifreeze 261
***Apollo 11* (spacecraft)** *512*
Apollo program 512–513, 514
apparent brightness **601**
Archimedes 428
Archimedes' principle *428*–429
architecture, metals in *198*
area, pressure and *417*
argon 154
Armstrong, Neil 512, 513, 560
artificial satellites 402, *403*, 511
  space station as **517**
ascorbic acid (vitamin C) 272, 323
astatine 153
asteroids 519, *574*, 575
astronauts 511, 515, 520, 544
  microgravity (weightlessness) of
    521
  moon missions 512–513
  working in space 516–517
astronomers 590, 598
  early Greek 539–540
astronomical unit 543
astronomy **464**.
  See also **galaxies; stars**
  detection of forms of
    electromagnetic radiation
    in 592
Earth in space 465–471

history of 466–467, 538–544
  major figures in 540–541
  observations on future of
    universe 626
  parallax in *603*
  spectrograph used in **600**
  telescopes and **488**, 540, 544,
    590, 592–597, 600
atmosphere 418
  of Earth 553
  of Jupiter 564
  of Mars 557
  of Mercury 554
  of moon 490
  of Neptune 568
  of Saturn 566
  of sun 548, *549*
  of Uranus 567
  of Venus 556
atmospheres (atm) 105
atmospheric pressure.
  See **air pressure**
atom(s) *63*, 124, **125**–130
  chemical bonds between **63**, **177**.
    See also **chemical bond(s)**
  electron cloud model of *63*, *127*,
    128
  particles in 126–128, *129*
  structural models of 125–130
  valence electrons in **176–177**
atomic mass **132**
  average 137
  on periodic table *135*
atomic mass units (amu) 129
atomic number **129**
  of carbon 129, 293
  in periodic table 133, *135*, 137
  of radioactive elements 159
atomic theory 15, 125–130
atomic weight, density and 149
atomizers, Bernoulli's principle
  and *440*
auroras *550*
autumnal (September) equinox
  469, 471
average atomic mass 137
average speed 343
axes of line graph 36, *37*
axis **465**
  rotation of Earth on **465**, 468,
    469, 470
  tilted, of Uranus 567

Index

B

bacteria, nitrogen fixation by 151
baking soda 236
    controlling fire with 244, *245*
    reaction with vinegar 220
    solubility of *264*
balanced forces 376–*377*, 382
    compression and **388**
    in sun 547
balanced pressure 419
ball and stick model of carbon
        atom *293*
bar codes 522
barometer *422*
barred-spiral galaxies 618, 619
bases 268, **271**
    acid-base reactions 278–279
    common *275*
    litmus test for **271**, 275
    properties of 271
    safe use of 277
    in solution 275, 276
    strength of 276–277
    uses of 272, *273*
Becquerel, Henri 159
Bell, Jocelyn 612
"bends, the" 265
Bernoulli, Daniel 438
Bernoulli's principle 438–441
beta particle **160**, *161*
Betelgeuse (star) 599, 600
big bang theory **622**–624
"big crunch" 626
binary stars 615
black holes *613*, 626
    at center of galaxies **617**
Bohr, Niels 127
boiling **99**
boiling point **99**
    of molecular compounds 194
    of organic compounds 297
    of pure water 99, 260
    of solutes and solvents **256**
    solute's effects on 261
bonding. *See* chemical bond(s)
boron 155
Boyle, Robert 108
Boyle's law **108**–109
Brahe, Tycho 541
brakes, hydraulic *436*
brass *199*
    as solution **65**

brightness of stars 600–601
    absolute **601**
    apparent **601**
bromine *153*
"buckyballs" 295
buoyant force **427**–429
    weight and *427*, 428–429
butane 298, 300
butyric acid 303

C

calcium 137, 141
calcium carbonate *64*, *187*
calendars 466–467
Callisto (moon) 564, *565*
cancer, gamma radiation
        to treat 163
carbohydrates *317*–318
    complex **318**, *321*
    simple 317
carbon 150, 151, 292–295. *See also*
        organic compounds
    amorphous form of **92**
    atomic number of **129**, 293
    crystalline forms **92**
    forms of pure **294**–295
    isotopes of *130*
    properties of 292–295
carbonates, reactions of acids
        with 270
carbon compounds 296–304
    hydrocarbons **298**–301
    organic **297**, 316–322
    polymers **304**, 306–315
    substituted hydrocarbons
        302–303
carbon dioxide
    chemical formula *64*, 225
    dry ice as solid *101*
    in soda water *265*, 266
    solubility of *264*
carbon dioxide molecule *63*
    double bond in *194*
    as nonpolar molecule *196*
carbon family 150
carboxyl group **303**, 319
careers in physical science 8
Cassini probe 566
catalysts 239
Cat's Eye Nebula *621*
celestial sphere 539
Cellarius, Andreas *540*
cellulose *308*, 311, *318*
Celsius temperature scale *26*

centimeter (cm) 19, 20
Centralia, Pennsylvania 243
centripetal force **403**
Ceres (asteroid) 574
Chadwick, James 128
Challenger shuttle disaster 516
Chandra X-ray Observatory 596,
        613
changes in matter 68–72, 216
    chemical *70–71*, **216**
    forms of energy related to 74–76
    physical **69**, **216**
changes of state 69, 96–102, 216
    condensation **100**
    freezing **98**
    melting 96, **97**
    sublimation **101**
    vaporization **98**–99
Charles, Jacques 106
Charles's law *106*–107
Charon (moon) 569
chemical bond(s) **63**, **177**
    ability of carbon to bond 293,
        307
    chemical change and *217*,
        220–221
    chemical reactions and 177
    covalent bonds 192, **193**–197,
        293, 307
    double **194**, 301
    energy stored in 75
    ionic **186**, 188, 189, 217
    metallic bond **200**, 201
    periodic table and understanding
        178–182
    stability and 177
    in structural formulas **299**
    triple **194**, 301
chemical change **70**–*71*, **216**.
        See also **chemical reactions**
    bonding and *217*, 220–221
    electrolysis *70*, 76, 219
    electromagnetic energy and **76**
    examples of *70*
    exothermic **74**, 75
    law conservation of matter and
        71–72
chemical energy **75**, 77
chemical equations **225**
    balancing 228–229
chemical formula *64*, **187**, *225*
    of hydrocarbons 298–299
    isomers with same **300**
chemical property(ies) **61**, **215**
    of alloy **199**

Index

Page numbers for key terms are printed in **boldface** type.
Page numbers for illustrations, maps, and charts are printed in *italics*.

of matter 59, *61*
of metals 139
of nonmetals 150
of water *215*
chemical reactions 224–231
  acid-base reactions 278–279
  acids in solution 274–275, *276*
  acids with carbonates 270
  acids with metals 269
  activation energy and **235**, 236
  balancing chemical equations
    228–229
  bases in solution 275, *276*
  in body 322, *323*
  chemical bonds and 177
  chemical equations of **225**
  classifying *230–231*
  combustion **243**
  conservation of matter in **226**–227
  controlling 234–239
  corrosion **139**
  endothermic **220**, *236*
  evidence for 218–221, *218–219*
  exothermic **221**, *235, 236*, 243
  rates of 237–239
chemical symbol *134*, **137**
chemistry 8, 59, 68, **214**
  substances in **59**
**chimneys, Bernoulli's principle
    and** *440*
Chinese rockets *503*
chlorine 153
  reactivity of *179*
cholesterol 320
chromosphere 548, *549*
citric acid 269, 303
classes of elements 136
classifying 635
closed system 226–**227**
clusters, star *616*
coal 150
cobalt 139
cobalt-60 163
coefficient 228–229
"cold war," space race during
    510–511
**collision-ring theory of moon's
    origin** *491*
**collisions, conservation of
    momentum and** *398, 399*
colloids 258
color
  evidence of chemical reaction
    in change of 220
  as physical property *60*

of stars 599
Columbia **shuttle disaster** 516
coma *573*
combining weights of elements 132
combustion 70, **243**
  controlling 244, 245
  as exothermic change **74**
comets 519, *572, 573*, 575
communicating, skill of 14, 635
communications satellites 405,
    524, 526–527
complex carbohydrates 318, *321*
composites 310
compounds 64.
      See also **acids; bases**
  alkali metals in **140**
  alkaline earth metals in **141**
  carbon 296–304
  decomposition of **230**
  ionic **186**–189, 259, 265
  molecular **194**–195, 259, 298
  organic **297**, 316–322
  replacement reactions in
    230–*231*
  semimetals in **155**
  synthesis of **230**
  with transition metals **142**, *143*
compression 380, **388**
computer-aided imaging 523
concentrated solution 263
concentration 238, 262–263
  of hydrogen ions in solution
    276–277
  measuring 263
conclusions, drawing 14, 639
condensation 100
conductivity.
      See **electrical conductivity;
      thermal conductivity**
conservation
  of atoms *71*, 226
  of energy **363**
  of momentum 397–399, *398*
conservation of matter 71–72
  balancing chemical equations for
    228–229
  in chemical reactions **226**–227
  open and closed systems 226–**227**
constellations 539, **598**
constraints 640
controlled experiment 12, 639
controls 12
convection zone (sun) 547
convex lens *592*
coolants 261

coordinate 36
Copernicus, Nicolaus 540, *541*
copper 138, 142
  density of **425**
  replacement reaction to obtain
    230–231
cordless power tools 522
core 546
  of Earth 552, *553*
  of sun 546, 547
corona, solar *482*, **548**, *549*
corrosion 139
corrosive, acids as 269
cosmic background radiation 624
cotton 304
covalent bonds 192, **193**–197, 293,
    307
  double bonds **194**, 301
Crab Nebula *593*
craters 489
creativity 10
crust of Earth 552, *553*
  most abundant element in 152
crystal 188
  diamond **294**
  ionic **188**–189
  metal 200
crystal structure 188
crystalline solids 92
cubic centimeter (cm³) 22
cubic meter (m³) 22
Curie, Marie 137, *159*, 180
Curie, Pierre 137, 159, 180
curiosity 10
curium 137, *144*

Dalton, John 125
dark energy 626
dark matter 626, *627*
data 13, 639, 642
  accuracy and reproducibility of **31**
  collecting 13, *35*
  interpreting 13
  plotting on line graph 36, *37*
data point 36
data table 13, *35*
day and night 465, 470–471
  Earth's rotation and **465**
deceleration 351
decomposition *230*
Deimos (moon) 559
Democritus 125
density 24, *425*–426

atomic weight and 149
buoyant force and *427*, 428
of common substances *25*
comparing densities *425*
floating and *25*, 425–426
of liquid vs. solid *93*

deoxyribonucleic acid (DNA) *321*–322

depth, water pressure and *421*–422

detergents, action of 197

diamond 92, *294*

diatomic molecule 151, 152

digestion
of cellulose **318**
of proteins 319
of starch **318**

dilute solution 263, 277

direction
acceleration and change in **350**, 351
displacement and **341**
of force 374–377
friction and **381**–*383*
momentum and **396**
vector and **341**
velocity and **344**–345

directly proportional variables **107**

displacement *341*

distance 340–*341*
gravity and **384**–385, 475–476
light-year as **602**
speed and **342**–343
to stars, measuring 602–603
work and **358**

distance-versus-time graphs *346*–*347*, *355*

distillation
physical changes in **69**
separating mixture by *66*, *67*

divers, "the bends" in 265

division of measurements *33*

DNA (deoxyribonucleic acid) *321*–322

double bonds **194**, 301

double replacement reaction *231*

double stars 615

drought 234

dry ice *101*

ductile material **138**

ductility of metals *201*

dust tail of comet 573

dwarf planet 563, 569, 574

E

***Eagle* (spacecraft)** 512

ears, air pressure and "popping" in 421

Earth
atmosphere of 553
axis of *465*, 468, 469, 470
gravity and **384**, 385, 475
layers of *552*, *553*
orbit of *465*, 467, 477
revolution around sun *465*, 467, 468, *469*
rotation on axis *465*
seasons on 468–471, *469*

eclipses 481–483
lunar *483*
solar *482*

eclipsing binaries *615*

Egyptians, ancient 464

elastic forces 388

elastic potential energy 360

electrical conductivity 139
of alkaline earth metals **141**
of ionic compounds 189
of metals 139, *202*
of molecular compounds 195
nonmetals as poor at **149**
of organic compounds 297
of semimetals **155**
solutes and 259
of transition metals **142**

electrical energy *76*

electrodes 76

electrolysis *70*, *76*, 219

electromagnetic energy **76**, 77

electromagnetic radiation 591

electron(s) **126**
charge of 128, *129*
covalent bond and sharing of *193*–197
unequal sharing of 194–197
valence. *See* **valence electrons**

electron cloud model of atom *127*, *128*, *129*

electron dot diagram *177*, *178*, *179*

electronics, "heat sink" in 201

element(s) *62*–63.
See also **metal(s); nonmetals**
atomic mass of **132**
atomic number of **129**
classes of 136
compounds from *64*
discovery of 180–181
examples of *62*
from nuclear fusion in stars 610, 611
particles of. *See* **atom(s)**
patterns of properties of 132
periodic table of.
See **periodic table**
predicting new 133
radioactive 158–163
rare earth 142
synthetic 144, *145*

elevation, air pressure and *420*, 421

ellipse 541

elliptical galaxies *618*

elliptical orbit 465, 541
of asteroids 574

emergency first aid 47

Empedocles 62

endothermic change *74*

endothermic reaction **220**, *236*

energy 73–77, **358**–363
activation **235**, 236, 239, 243
from carbohydrates 318
change in matter and change in 73
chemical *75*, 77
chemical change and changes in 220–221
chemical reactions and 235–236
conservation of *363*
electrical *76*
electromagnetic **76**, 77
kinetic *359*, 361, 362, 363
from lipids **320**
mechanical *361*, 363
potential **360**, 361, 362
from sun *76*, 546–547
thermal. *See* **thermal energy**
transforming 77, 362
work as transfer of **358**

energy level 127

-*ene* suffix 301

enzymes *239*

equations, chemical **225**, 228–229

equinoxes *469*, *471*

escape velocity 505

esters *303*

estimate 30

etching with acid 269

ethane 299

ethanol 303

ethene *301*

ethyne *301*

Europa (moon) 564, *565*, 579

European Space Agency 514, 558

Index

Page numbers for key terms are printed in **boldface** type.
Page numbers for illustrations, maps, and charts are printed in *italics*.

evaporation *99*
  separating mixture by *66, 67*
exothermic change 74, *75*
exothermic reaction
  221, 235, *236,* 243
experiment, controlled 12, 639
  See also **investigation and experimentation**
experimental design 639
Explorer 1 (satellite) 511
extraterrestrial life 576, 578–579, 616

Fahrenheit, Gabriel 19
falling objects. *See also* **gravity**
  air resistance and *387*
  free fall **386**
  satellite motion 404
families containing nonmetals 150–154
families (periodic table) 136.
  See also **groups (periodic table)**
fats 320
fatty acids 320
fertilizers 151
fiber 318
fiberglass composites 312
field, safety in 46
filtration
  physical changes in **69**
  separating mixture by *66*
fire 242–245
fire extinguisher *245*
fire triangle *243,* 244
fireworks rocket *503,* 505
first-aid procedures *47*
flammability *61,* 215
  of hydrocarbons **298**
fleece, polyester 314–315
flexibility *60*
flight
  of airplane *220,* 437, 439
  of helicopters 442–443
floating
  Archimedes' principle and *428*–429
  buoyant force and *427*–429
  density and *25, 425*–426
  of ship *424, 425,* 427–429
fluid(s) 93, 418. *See also* **liquids**
  air as *428*
  gas as **95**

fluid friction 382, *383*
  air resistance **387**
fluid pressure 418–422
  Bernoulli's principle and **438**–441
  causes of 418
  moving fluids and 438–441
  Pascal's principle and **433**–436
  sea star movement by *432*
  on submerged object, buoyant force and *427,* 428
  transmitting pressure in fluid *433*
  variations in *420,* 421–422
fluorine *153,* 181
  electron sharing between atoms of *193*
  nonpolar bond in **196**
flying disks, Bernoulli's principle and *441*
fog, as colloid 258
folic acid 272
food
  acids and 269, *272*
  bases and 273
  esters and smell of **303**
  organic acids in **303**
  polymers 306
food, organic compounds in 316–325
  carbohydrates *317*–318
  lipids **320,** *321*
  nucleic acids *321*–322
  proteins *319, 321*
  vitamins *322, 323*
force(s) 374–377, **474.**
  See also **gravity; pressure**
  acceleration and changes in mass and 391
  action-reaction 394–395, *403,* 442, *504*
  balanced **376**–*377,* 382, 388, 547
  buoyant **427**–429
  centripetal **403**
  combining 375–377
  elastic 388
  friction 380, *381*–383
  lift *439,* 442
  motion and *375*–377, 386–388
  multiplied by hydraulic system *434*–436
  net **375,** 376, 391
  Newton's first law of motion and 389–390, **476**

Newton's second law of motion and 390–391
  Newton's third law of motion and 393–399, 403, 442, 504
  thrust 403, **504**
  unbalanced *376,* 389–390, 403
forest fires 234
form, changes in 69
formic acid *303*
formula(s)
  chemical **64, 187,** *225,* 298–299, 300
  structural **299,** 300
fossils on Mars, debate over 578
Freedom 7 (spacecraft) *511*
free fall 386
freezing 98
freezing point 98, 260
  solute's effects on *260*
Freon 302
friction 380, **381**–*383*
  air resistance and **387**
  causes of 381
  types of 382, *383*
Friendship 7 (spacecraft) *511*
fruits, acids in 269
fuel *243*
  carbon in 150
  hydrocarbons as **298**
  rocket 505
Fuller, Buckminster 295
fullerene 295
full moon, lunar eclipse and *483*
fusion, nuclear 546–547, 591, 599, 609, 610

Gagarin, Yuri 511
galaxies 617–619
  Milky Way *614,* 617, *619*
  moving 623–624
  in space 617
  types of *618, 626*
Galileo Galilei 389, 543, 566
  telescope of **488,** 489, 540, 544, 590
Galileo **space probe** 579
gamma radiation (gamma rays) *160, 161,* 162
Ganymede (moon) *564, 565*
gas(es) 95
  inert *154,* 179
  measuring 104–105
  nonmetals as **149**

particles in *95, 104, 105*
pressure and solubility of *265*
temperature and solubility of *266*
gas behavior 103–113
Boyle's law of *108–109*
Charles's law of *106–107*
temperature-pressure relationship *110*
temperature-volume relationship *106–107*
volume-pressure relationship *105, 108–109*
gases, changes of state of 98–101
condensation to liquid ***100***
sublimation of solid to gas ***101***
vaporization of liquid to gas ***98–99***
gas giants 563, 564–568, 625
gasohol 303
gasoline 150, 257, 298
gas tail of comet 573
gems 294
geocentric system *539*
geostationary orbit 524, 526
giant stars *599*, 604, 605
Glenn, John *511*
globular clusters *616*
glucose 317, 318
Goddard, Robert 503
gold 139, 199
alloys ***199***
efforts to make lead into 158
as transition metal 142
gold foil experiment, Rutherford's *126–127*
"Goldilocks" conditions 577
Goodyear, Charles 310
graduated cylinder 22, 23
gram (g) 21
grams per cubic centimeter (g/cm³) 24
grams per milliliter (g/mL) 24
graph(s) *13*, 34–42, 642–644
axes on 36, *37*
of Boyle's law *109*
of Charles's law *107*
distance-versus-time *346–347, 355*
to identify trends 40–41
importance of 35–39
line 35–41
nonlinear *40–41, 355*
speed-versus-time *354*
types of 35

graphite 92, ***294***
gravitational potential energy 360, 361, 362
gravity 380, **384**–388, **474**–476
acceleration due to 386
buoyant force and **427**
dark matter inferred by effect of **626**, 627
distance and *384–385, 475–476*
law of universal gravitation 384, **474**, 475
mass and *384–385*, ***475***
motion and 386–388
orbital motion and *477*
pressure and 416
projectile motion and ***387***
tides and **484**–485
weight and **21**, ***385, 475***
Great Dark Spot (Neptune) *568*
Great Red Spot (Jupiter) 564
Greeks, ancient 539–540
greenhouse effect 556
Gregory XIII, Pope 467
groups (periodic table) *134*, **136**
relating periods and 178
gunpowder 503

halite 188
halogen family 153
halogens 153, 179, 181
compounds containing 302
heat 202. *See also* **temperature; thermal energy**
absorbed in endothermic reaction *236*
as part of "fire triangle" 243
reaction rate and 238
released in exothermic reaction *236*
"heat sink" 201
height, gravitational potential energy and *360*
helicopters 442–443
heliocentric system 540
helium *104*, 154, 428
in gas giants **563**, 564, 566
nuclear fusion producing **546**, 610
hemoglobin 142
Herschel, William 567
Hertzsprung, Ejnar 604
Hertzsprung-Russell diagram ***604***–605

heterogeneous mixtures 65
Hickam, Homer 402
high-altitude balloons, Boyle's law and use of 108
highlands on moon's surface *489*
high tide 484
home fire safety 244–245
homogeneous mixtures 65
honesty 10
horizontal axis 36, *37*
hot-air balloon 103
hot springs, life in *577*
H-R diagram 604–605
Hubble, Edwin 623
Hubble's law 623
Hubble Space Telescope 595, 596
hydraulic brakes *436*
hydraulic lifts 435
hydraulic systems 434–436
hydrocarbons 298–301
isomers ***300***
structural formulas of ***299***
substituted **302**–303
hydrochloric acid *276*
hydrogen *154*, 182
in compounds with carbon 307
in gas giants **563**, 564, 566
isotopes of **130**
nuclear fusion of, in stars 609, 610
in sun 546
hydrogen fluoride *196*
hydrogen ion (H⁺) 274–275, 278
pH and concentration of 276–277
hydrogen peroxide, decomposition of 230
hydroxide ion (OH⁻) 275, 276, 278
hydroxyl group 302, 303
hypothesis 12
conclusions about 14
designing experiment to test 12
forming 638

ice *90*
density of 426
melting of 74, **97**
***-ide* suffix** 187
indicator 270, 277
industry
acids used in *272*
bases used in *273*
tracers used in **162**

Index

inert gases *154*, 179
inertia **390**, 404, 476, *477*
inferring, skill of *7*, 634
infrared radiation 591, 593
inhibitors **239**
inner planets **552–559**, 625
 Earth 552–553
 Mars 541, *553*, *557–559*
 Mercury *553*, 554
 Venus 540, *553*, 555–556
instantaneous speed **343**
insulating materials, new 523
International Space Station 516, *517*
International System of Units. *See* SI units
inversely proportional variables **109**
investigation and experimentation **10–15**
 collecting data 13
 communicating **14**
 controls 12
 designing experiment 12
 developing hypotheses **12**
 drawing conclusions 14
 evaluating accuracy *31*
 evaluating reproducibility of data *31*
 interpreting graphs *13*
 linear vs. nonlinear relationships on graph *40–41*
 planning and conducting 44–46
 safety in 43–47, *44–45*
 slope of linear graph *39*
 variables 12
iodine-131 163
Io (moon) 564, *565*
ion(s) *185*–186
 carbonate 270
 charges *185*
 formation of *185*
 hydrogen (H^+) **274**–275, 276–277, 278
 hydroxide (OH^-) **275**, 276, 278
 polyatomic **185**, 187
 in solution *189*
ionic bond *186*, 188, 189, 217
ionic compound **186**–189. *See also* salt(s)
 in solution 259
 solvents dissolving 265
ionic crystals **188**–189
ion rockets 505
iron *137*

alloys **199**
 atomic number of **129**
 reactivity of **139**
 rusting of 61, *139*, 142, 150, 215
iron oxide (rust) 61, *139*, 142, 150, 215
iron sulfide *226*
irregular galaxies **618**
irregular solids, volume of 23
isomers **300**
isotopes **130**, 137
 radioactive 159, 161–*163*

J

Jansky, Karl *594*
joule (J) **358**
joystick 520, 522
juggling, energy in *362*
Juno (asteroid) 574
Jupiter 562, *563*, 564–565
 moons of 540, 564, *565*, 579

K

Kavandi, Janet *515*
kelvin (K) 26, 107
Kelvin scale *26*
Kennedy, John F. 512
Kepler, Johannes 541
kilogram (kg) 21, 384
kilogram-meters per second (kgm/s) **396**
kilograms per cubic meter (kg/m^3) 24
kilometer (km) 19
kilometers per hour (km/h) 342
kilopascals (kPa) 105
kinetic energy **359**, 361, 362, 363
 calculating 359
 mechanical energy and **361**
 transformations between potential and 362
Kitty Hawk, North Carolina 437
Kuiper belt **573**

L

laboratory safety 43–47, *44–45*
 end-of-lab procedures 46
 first aid procedures *47*
 performing lab 45
 preparing for lab 44
lactic acid 272
lanthanides *134*, 136, 142, *143*

Large Magellanic Cloud 618
lasers, telescopes using 595
Lavoisier, Antoine 71, 226
law(s)
 of conservation of energy **363**
 of conservation of matter **71**–72, 226–229
 of conservation of momentum **397**–399, *398*
 Hubble's law **623**
 of motion, Newton's 389–399, 403, 442, **476**, 504
 scientific **15**
 of universal gravitation 384, **474**, 475
lead 142, *143*, 158
leap year 467
Lecoq de Boisbaudran, Paul-Émile 180
length
 displacement and **341**
 distance and **340**, 341
 measuring 18–*20*
 SI unit of 18, 340
lens, convex **592**
Levy, David 572
life on Earth 577
lift *439*, 442
lifts, hydraulic 435
light
 speed of 602
 visible 76, **591**, 592
lightning *234*
light-year **602**
lignin 311
linear graph, slope on *39*
linear trends *40*
line graphs 35–41
 distance-versus-time *346–347*, *355*
 identifying trends with *40–41*
 plotting 36, *37*
line of best fit 36, *37*, 38
lipids 320, *321*
liquid-fuel rocket 505
liquids **93**–94
 changes of state 96, 97–100
 condensation of gas to **100**
 freezing to solid **98**
 melting of solid to 74, 96, **97**
 vaporization to gas **98**–99
 volume of *22*, *93*
liter (L) 22
lithium 140
litmus test

for acids *270*, 275
for bases **271**, 275
living things, nutrients needed by.
　　See **nutrients**
Local Group 617
long-chain polymers.
　　See **polymers**
Lowell, Percival 557
low tide 484
lubricant, graphite as 294
luminosity 601
lunar eclipse *483*
lunar rover or buggy *513*
luster of metals *202*

Maat Mons (volcano on Venus) *556*
Magellan probe 556
magnesium 141
magnesium chloride 187
magnesium oxide *217*
magnetic field, solar wind
　　particles and 550
magnetic storms 550
magnetism
　　of metals *139*
　　separating mixture by *66*
magnitude
　　of force 374–377
　　vector and **341**
main sequence *604*, **605**, 610
malic acid 303
malleability of metals *201*
malleable material 138, *139*
manipulated variable *12*
　　on line graph 35, 36
mantle, Earth's 552, *553*
maple syrup *262*
maria *489*
Mariner 10 (space probe) 554
Mars 541, *553*, 557–559
　　atmosphere of 557
　　meteorite from 576, 578
　　moons of 559
　　search for life on 578
　　seasons on 558
　　volcanoes on 558, *559*
　　water on 557
Mars Express probe 558
Marvin, Ursula *576*
mass 21, **384**, *475*
　　atomic **132**
　　conservation of. *See*
　　　conservation of matter

density and **425**–426
in galaxies 626
gravity and **384**–385, *475*
inertia and **390**
kinetic energy and *359*
lifetimes of stars and 609, 610–611
measuring *21*
momentum and **396**–399
Newton's second law of motion
　　and 390–391
of particles in atom 129
of sun 545, 546
weight and **385**
mass number 130
materials, space spinoffs of new
　　523
mathematics 30–33
　　accuracy and reproducibility **31**
　　estimation **30**
　　significant figures and precision
　　　32–33
matter *58*–83, **214**
　　changes in. *See* **changes in matter**
　　chemical properties of 59, **61**, **215**
　　classifying 60, 61
　　compounds **64**
　　conservation of *71*–72, **226**–229
　　dark **626**, *627*
　　elastic 388
　　elements. *See* **element(s)**
　　energy and **73**–77
　　mass as measure of amount of **21**
　　mixtures **65**–67
　　physical properties of 59, **60**, **215**
　　properties of 59–61, 215
　　states of 90–95. *See also* **gas(es)**;
　　　liquids; solids
Mauna Kea, Hawaii, observatory
　　on top of 594
measurement 16–26. *See also*
　　units of measurement;
　　　specific measurements
　　accuracy and reproducibility in **31**
　　adding or subtracting 32
　　of air pressure 422
　　of concentration 263
　　of density *24*–25
　　of distance in solar system 543
　　of distances to stars 602–603
　　of gases 104–105
　　history of systems of 18–19
　　of length 18–*20*
　　of mass *21*
　　multiplying or dividing *33*
　　significant figures and precision

of *32*–33
standard system of 17
of temperature *26*
of time *25*
of volume **22**–23
of weight *20*, **21**
mechanical energy 361, 363
medical spinoffs from space
　　program 523
medicine, radioactive isotopes
　　used in *163*
Meitner, Lise 181
melting 74, *96*, **97**
melting point 97
　　of diamond **294**
　　of ionic compounds 188
　　of molecular compounds 194
　　of organic compounds 297
Mendeleev, Dmitri 132–133
meniscus *22*
mercury 139
Mercury (planet) 553, 554
Mercury space program 511
MESSENGER (space probe) 554
metal(s) 138–145, **198**–203
　　actinides *144*
　　alkali **140**, 179
　　alkaline earth **141**
　　alloys 142, 144, **199**
　　chemical properties of 139
　　lanthanides *134*, 136, 142, *143*
　　magnetic *139*
　　in mixed groups 143, *143*
　　in periodic table *134*–135, 136,
　　　140–144
　　physical properties of 60, 138–139
　　properties of *138*–139, *201*–203
　　reactions of acids with 269
　　reactivity of 139, 140, 141, 142,
　　　179, 180
　　transition **142**, *143*
metallic bond 200, 201
meteorites 575, 576, 578
meteoroids 489, **575**, 576
meteors *575*
meteor showers 575
meter (m) 18, 19, 340
meters per second (m/s) 342
methane *71*, 298, 299, 302
methanol *302*
metric ruler 20
metric system 17
　　debate over change to 28–29
microgravity *521*
military rockets 503

Index

Page numbers for key terms are printed in **boldface** type.
Page numbers for illustrations, maps, and charts are printed in *italics*.

milk, as colloid *258*
Milky Way galaxy *614*, *617*, *619*
  structure of *619*
milliliter (mL) 22
millimeter (mm) 19, 20
minerals *322*, 323
Mir space station 515, 517
mixtures 65–67
  colloids *258*
  heterogeneous **65**
  homogeneous **65**
  separating 66–67
  solutions 256–261
  suspensions *258*
models *14*
  of atom 125–130
  of molecules *63*
models, making 635
molecular compounds 194–195,
  298
  in solution 259
molecule(s) *63*, **193**
  attractions between 196–197
  diatomic **151**, 152
  of life *321*. See also **nutrients**
  polar bonds in **196**
  triatomic 152
momentum **396**–399
  conservation of **397**–399, *398*
monomers **304**, 307
monounsaturated oils 320
months, calendar 466
moon, Earth's 478–491
  calendar and **466**
  changing relative positions of
    Earth, sun, and 478–485
  characteristics of 490
  gravitational force between
    Earth and 475
  landings on *512–513*
  lunar eclipse and **483**
  missions to 512–514
  motions of 478–479
  orbit of 475, *477*, 481
  origin of 491
  penumbra of *482*
  phases of **479**–481, *480–481*
  revolution around Earth 478, *479*
  rotation of 478, *479*
  as satellite 403
  size of *490*
  solar eclipses and *482*
  surface of *488*, *489*, *490*, 513
  tides and 484–485
  umbra of *482*

water on, evidence of 490
moon rocks 513
moons **543**
  as components of solar
    system 543
  of Jupiter 540, 564, *565*, 579
  of Mars 559
  of Neptune 568
  of Saturn 566
  of Uranus 567
motion *338*, **339**–341
  acceleration and **350**–355
  describing 339–340
  detecting 394
  distance-versus-time graphs
    346–347, 355
  fluid, pressure and 438–441
  force and *375–377*, 386–388
  friction and **381**–383
  gravity and 386–388
  kinetic energy and *359*
  measuring distance and
    displacement **340–341**
  momentum and **396**–399
  Newton's first law of 389–390,
    476
  Newton's second law of 390–391
  Newton's third law of 393–399,
    403, 442, 504
  orbital *477*
  of planets 541–542
  projectile **387**, *404*
  relative *340*
  satellite *404*
  speed and **342**–343
  on speed-versus-time graph *354*
  velocity and **344**–345
multiplication of measurements
  33
multistage rockets *506–507*

nanotube *295*
National Aeronautics and Space
  Administration (NASA)
  511, 514, 516, 520, 522, 558
natural polymers 306, *308*, 310
natural satellite **543**
neap tides **485**
nebula *609*, 611
  planetary **610**
  solar **625**
neodymium *143*
neon 154

Neptune *563*, 568
net force **375**, 376, 391
neutralization **278**, 279
neutral solution **276**, 278
neutron **128**
  isotopes and **130**
  mass number and **130**
  mass of 129
  in unstable atom 160
neutron stars 599, **612**
new moon 481
  solar eclipses and *482*
Newton, Isaac 375, 384, *389*, 404,
  474, 475
  first law of motion 389–390, **476**
  reflecting telescope built by **593**
  second law of motion 390–391
  third law of motion 393–399,
    403, 442, 504
newton (N) 21, 105, **375**, 475
newton per square meter
  (N/m²) 417
nickel 139, 142
nitric acid-potassium hydroxide
  reaction 279
nitrogen *151*, 194
  in Earth's atmosphere 553
nitrogen family **151**
nitrogen fixation 151
noble gases. *See* **inert gases**
nonlinear graph **40**–41, 355
nonlinear trends **40–41**
nonmetals 148, **149**–154
  chemical properties of 150
  covalent bonds between **193**
  families containing 150–154
  in periodic table *135*, *136*, 150
  physical properties of *149*
  properties of 149–150
  reactivity of *150*, 179, 181
nonpolar bonds **196**–197
Northern Hemisphere 468, *469*,
  470–471
notation, scientific **620**–621
nuclear fusion **546**–547
  new elements from 610, 611
  in stars 591, 599, 609, 610, 611
nuclear power plants 161
nuclear radiation, effects of 160–161
nucleic acids **321**–322
nucleotides 322
nucleus (atom) *63*, **127**, *128*
  size of 129
nucleus (comet) **573**
nutrients 316–325

Index

O

observation satellites 524
observatories 467, **594**, 613
observing, skill of 7, 634
oils *320*
Olympus Mons (volcano on Mars) 558, *559*
Oort cloud **573**
open clusters *616*
open system 226–**227**
operational definition 639
Opportunity rover 558, 578
optical telescopes **592**–593
  advanced 595
oral presentations (to communicate the steps and results from an investigation) 635
orbit 465
  elliptical 465, 541, 574
  geostationary **524**, 526
  of Pluto 569
  of satellite **403**, 404
orbital motion *477*
orbitals 127
orbital velocity **504**
organic acid *303*
organic compounds *297*, 316–322. *See also* **carbon compounds**
  as building blocks of all living things 316–317
  carbohydrates *317*–318
  lipids **320**, *321*
  nucleic acids *321*–322
  properties of 297
  proteins *319, 321*
  vitamins 272, 322, 323
origin of graph **36**, 37
Orion (constellation) *598, 599, 605*
outer planets 562–569, 625
  data on *563*
oxidation *70*
oxygen 152, 181
  atomic number of **129**
  chemical properties of 59
  in Earth's atmosphere 553
  molecule *63*, **194**
  as part of "fire triangle" 243
  physical properties of 59
  reactivity of 181
oxygen family *152*
ozone 152

P

pacemakers 523
Pallas (asteroid) 574
parallax *602–603*
parameter 12
particle accelerators **144**, *145*
particle charges 128
particles. *See also* **atom(s)**
  alpha **160**, *161*
  in atom 126–128, *129*
  beta **160**, *16*
  in colloid **258**
  fluid *418*
  in gas *95*
  in liquid *93*
  in solid *92*
  in solutions 259
  in suspension *258*
Pascal, Blaise 417, 433
pascal (Pa) 105, **417**
Pascal's principle *433*–436
  hydraulic systems and 434–436
payload bay, space shuttle 516
pendulum 362
penumbra **482**, 483
Penzias, Arno 624
Perey, Marguerite 181
periodic table 131, **132**–137, *134–135*
  groups *134*, **136**, 178
  periods **136**, 178
periods (periodic table) **136**, 178
pH, acid-base reactions and 278
phases of moon **479**–481, *480–481*
pH meter 277
Phobos (moon) 559
phosphorus *151*, 162
phosphorus-32 *162*
photosphere 548, *549*
photosynthesis 77
pH scale **276**–277
physical change **69**, 216
  changes of state as 98, 100
  electromagnetic energy and **76**
  law conservation of matter and 71–72
  in solutions **256**
physical models 14
physical property(ies) **60**, 215
  of alloy **199**
  chemical reaction and changes in 218–219
  of matter 59, *60*
  of metals 138–139
  of nonmetals *149*

physical science **8**–9
  big ideas of 9
  branches of 8
  careers in *8*
physical state *60*
physics 8
planetary nebula 610
planetesimals 625
planets
  2003 UB313 569, 655
  ancient Greek observations of 539
  around other stars 616
  elliptical orbit of 541
  formation of 625
  inner 552–559, 625
  outer 562–569, 625
  sun and 542
plants
  complex carbohydrates of **318**
  natural polymers made by *308*
  photosynthesis in *77*
plasma 91, 546
plastics 304, **309**
  recycling *313*
platinum 139
Pluto 563, *563*, 569, 625
plutonium 144
polar bonds **196**–197
polar compounds, solvents dissolving *265*
polonium 159
polyatomic ions **185**, 187
polyester fleece 314–315
polymers 304, *306*–315
  comparing 310
  composites and **310**–312
  development of 310–311
  forming 307
  natural 306, *308*, 310
  synthetic 304, 306, *309*, 310
polyunsaturated oils 320
position, relative to reference point 339
position-versus-time graphs. *See* **distance-versus-time graphs**
positive ion 185, 187
potassium *140*
potassium nitrate 279
potential energy **360**, 361, 362
  elastic **360**
  gravitational *360*, 361, 362
  mechanical energy and **361**
  transformations between kinetic and 362

Index

pounds 21
precipitate *218*
precision **32**
predicting, skill of **7**, 634
predictions, line graphs and making 40–41
prefixes, SI *17*
pressure **105**, 416, **417**–422
  air (atmospheric) 99, 418–421, 422
  area and *417*
  balanced *419*
  Boyle's law on volume and *108–109*
  calculating 417
  fluid. *See* **fluid pressure**
  of gas, measuring 105
  measuring 105, 422
  moving fluids and 438
  from nuclear fusion in sun 547
  solubility and *265*
  temperature-pressure relationship *110*
  transmitted in fluid, Pascal's principle of **433**–436
  variations *420*
  volume-pressure relationship 105, *108–109*
probes, space **518**–519, 544, 554, 556, 558
products **216**
  of acid-base reactions 279
  in chemical equations **225**
projectile motion **387**, *404*
prominences *549*, **550**
propane 298, 299
properties of matter 59–61
  chemical properties 59, **61**, 215
  physical properties 59, **60**, 215
proportionality
  directly proportional variables **107**
  inversely proportional variables **109**
protactinium 144
proteins **308**
  amino acids in **308**, *319*, 322
  cell activities regulated by 322
  DNA and 322
  as nutrients *319*, *321*
  sources of 319
protons **127**, *128*
  atomic number and **129**

charge of 128, *129*
  mass number and **130**
  mass of 129
protostar *609*
Proxima Centauri 602, 615
Ptolemy 539
pulsars *612*

 Q

qualitative data **13**
qualitative observations **7**
quantitative data **13**
quantitative observations **7**
quasars 617
questions, posing 11, 638

R

radiation, forms of 591
  cosmic background **624**
  electromagnetic **591**, 592
  gamma **160**, *161*, 162
  nuclear 160–161
radiation therapy 163
radiation zone (sun) **547**
radioactive decay **159**
  types of *160–161*
radioactive elements 158–163
radioactive isotopes **159**
  using 161–*163*
radioactivity **159**
radio telescopes **593**, 594, 616
  cosmic background radiation detected by **624**
radio waves 591, 593
  from pulsars *612*
radium 159
Ramsay, William 180
rare earth elements 142
rates of chemical reactions **237**–239
ratio **64**
reactants **216**
  in acid-base reactions 278
  activation energy to break bonds of *235*
  catalysts and **239**
  changes in chemical reactions 218, 219
  in chemical equations **225**
  concentration of *238*
  conservation of matter **226**
  inhibitors of **239**
reaction force **394**–395, *403*, 442
  rockets and *504*

reactivity *61*, **139**
  of halogens **153**
  of metals 139, 140, 141, 142, 179, 180
  of nonmetals *150*, 179, 181
  of oxygen 181
  of plastics 313
rectangular solids, volume of *22*, 23
recycling 312–*313*
  polyester fleece from plastics 314–315
red giant *610*
reference point **339**
  relative motion and *340*
reflecting telescope *592*, **593**, 596
refracting telescope *592*
relative motion **340**
remote sensing **524**
replacement **230**–231
reproducibility **31**
responding variable **12**
  on line graph 35
revolution **465**
  of Earth around sun *465*, 467, 468, *469*
  of moon around Earth 478, *479*
Rigel (star) 599, 600
ring (planetary) **563**
  of Saturn 566
  of Uranus 567
RNA (ribonucleic acid) **321**–322
rockets 402, *403*, 502, **503**–509
  development of modern 503
  fuels 505
  how they work 504–505
  lift off 403
  multistage *506–507*
  origins of 503
  space exploration and 502, **503**–507
  on space shuttle **516**
rocks, moon 513
rolling friction **382**, *383*
Roman calendar 467
rotation *465*
rough surfaces, friction and **381**
rovers *513*, **518**, 558, 578
rubber 152
Rubin, Vera *626*
ruler, metric 20
Russell, Henry Norris 604

rust (iron oxide) 61, *139*, 142, 150, 215
Rutherford, Ernest 126–127

S

safety
with acids and bases 277
air bags and 232–233
in field 46, 651
first-aid procedures *47*
home fire 244–245
laboratory 43–47, *44–45*, 651
symbols *45*, 650
salt(s) *279*
common *279*
effect on boiling point of water 261
effect on freezing point of water *260*
as nutrient 323
solubility of *264*
satellite(s) 402, **403**–405, **511**
artificial 402, 403, 511, 517
communications 405, 524, 526–527
geostationary orbit of **524**, 526
saturated fats 320
saturated hydrocarbons *301*
saturated solution 263
Saturn *544*, *563*, 566
Saturn V rocket 507
scale on line graph, creating 36, *37*
scandium 142
Schiaparelli, Giovanni 557
science 7
development of 14–15
mathematics and 30–33
skills scientists use 7
scientific inquiry 10–15
scientific law 15
scientific models 14
scientific notation *620*–621
scientific theory 15
Seaborg, Glenn 181
sea level, atmospheric pressure at 419
"sea of electrons" model of metallic bonding *200*, 201
seasons
on Earth 468–471, *469*
on Mars 558
second (s) 25
semiconductors 155

semimetals 155, *182*
in periodic table *135*, 136
serine *319*
Seurat, Georges *124*
shape, changes in 69
Shepard, Alan 511
ship, floating of 424, *425*, 427–429
Shoemaker, Eugene and Carolyn 572
significant figures *32*–33
silicon *155*
silk 304, 308
silver 142
tarnish (silver sulfide) 61, 64, *132*, 215
simple carbohydrates 317
single replacement reaction *231*
sinking
Archimedes' principle and **428**–429
density and 25, **425**–426
of ship 424
Sirius (star) 464, 466
SI units 17, 636–637. *See also* **units of measurement**
for acceleration 352
of density **24**
of length 18, 340
for magnitude or strength of force 375
of mass **21**, **384**
prefixes *17*
of pressure 105, 417
of temperature 26, 107
of time 25
of volume **22**
of weight **21**
for work and energy 358
skepticism 10
skills in science 7
sliding friction 382, *383*
slope *39*, 346–347
calculating 346
of distance-versus-time graph 346, 347, 355
of speed-versus-time graph *354*
slope on linear graph 39
smooth surfaces, friction and *381*
sodium 137, 139, 140, 141
sodium chloride 323
crystals **188**
formation of *186*, 219
sodium hydroxide 275
solar eclipses *482*
solar flares *549*, 550

solar nebula 625
solar system. *See also* **sun**
components of 543
extraterrestrial life, search for **576**, 578–579, 616
formation of *625*
geocentric model of **539**
heliocentric model of **540**
inner planets 552–559, 625
model of *14*
outer planets 562–569, 625
solar wind 548, 550
solid-fuel rocket 505
solids *90*, **91**–92
amorphous **92**
crystalline **92**
particles in *92*
solid-liquid changes of state 97, 98
sublimation into gas **101**
temperature and solubility of *266*
solstices *469*, *470*
solubility 263–267
of organic compounds 297
solutes 256, 262
effects on solvents 260–261
electrical conductivity and 259
solution(s) 65, **256**–261
acids in 274–275, *276*
bases in 275, *276*
colloids **258**
concentrated **263**
concentration of 262–263
dilute **263**, 277
effects of solutes on solvents 260–261
ions in *189*
neutral **276**, 278
particles in 259
saturated **263**
supersaturated **267**
suspensions **258**
unsaturated **263**
solvent 256, 262
effects of solutes on 260–261
solubility and 265
Southern Hemisphere *469*, 470–471
Soviet Union, space race with U.S. 510–511
space
immensity of 620
as vacuum **521**
space exploration 510–519, 544
challenges of 521

Index

Page numbers for key terms are printed in **boldface** type.
Page numbers for illustrations, maps, and charts are printed in *italics*.

costs and benefits, debate over
 560–561
moon missions 512–514
rockets and 502, **503**–507
space race and 510–511
telescopes in space 544, 596
working in space 516–517
space probes *518*–*519*, 544, 554,
 556, 558
space race 510–511
space shuttles 403, *516*
space spinoffs *522*–*523*
space stations 515, **517**
space telescopes 544, 596
spectrograph **600**
spectrum **591**
electromagnetic *591*
of stars *600*
speed **342**–343, 355
acceleration and change in **350**,
 351, 354–355
average **343**
calculating 343
equation 343
graphing 346–347
instantaneous **342**
kinetic energy and **359**
of light 602
of moving fluid, pressure
 and 438
of transportation 344–345
velocity and **344**–345
speed-versus-time graph *354*
spiral galaxies *618*, 626
Milky Way *614*, 617, *619*
Spirit rover 558, 578
Spitzer Space Telescope 595, 596
spring tides *485*
Sputnik (satellite) 402, 510, 511
square meter (m²) 417
stainless steel 199
standard measurement system.
 See **SI units**
starch 308, **318**
star clusters *616*
stars 598–613
binary (double) **615**
brightness of 600–601
chemical composition of 600
classifying 599–600
color and temperature of 599
deaths of 610–613
giant *599*, *604*, 605
lives of 608, 609, *610*–*611*
neutron 599, **612**

parallax of *603*
size of *599*
supergiants 599, *604*, 605, *610*,
 611, 612
triple 615
white dwarfs *599*, *604*, 605, **611**
star systems 615–616
multiple 615
states of matter **90**–95. *See also*
 gas(es); liquids; solids
changes of 69, 96–102, 216
gases **95**
liquids **93**–94
as physical property 60
plasma 91
solids *90*, **91**–92
static friction **382**, 383
static objects 339
stationary objects 339
steel *199*
structural diagram of carbon *293*
structural formula **299**, 300
of hydrocarbons *299*
sublimation *101*
submarine
buoyant force and *426*, 428
density of *426*
subscript **187**, 299
substance(s) **59**. *See also*
 element(s); matter
chemical property of **61**
physical property of **60**
substituted hydrocarbons **302**–303
subtraction of measurements 32
sucrose 317
sugar 64, 317
solubility of *263*, *264*, *266*
sulfur 152
sulfuric acid 152
summer 268
summer (June) solstice *469*, 470
sun 545–551
age of 609
atmosphere of 548, *549*
features on 548–550
gravitational force of 545, 547
interior of 547, *549*
sunspots 548, *549*
supergiant stars 599, *604*, 605,
 610, 611, 612
supernovas *611*
supersaturated solution *267*
surface tension **94**
Surveyor (spacecraft) 512
suspensions *258*

symbols
chemical 134, **137**
safety *45*
synthesis **230**
synthetic composites 312
problems of 312–313
synthetic elements 144, *145*
synthetic polymers 304, 306, 310
uses of *309*
Système International d'Unités.
 See **SI units**

tail, comet 573
tarnish 61, 64, *70*, *132*, 215
taste
bitter 271
sour 269, 303
technetium 159
technetium-99 163
technology, space spinoffs and
 522–*523*
technology design skills 640
telescope **488**, 590, 592–597
invention of 540, 590
observatories and 467, **594**, 613
in space 544, 596
temperature **74**
boiling point **99**
changes of state and 96–102
chemical reaction rate and 238
freezing point 98, 260
of gas 104
"Goldilocks" conditions on Earth
 and 577
measuring *26*
melting point **97**
solubility and *266*–*267*
of stars, absolute brightness and
 604–605
temperature-pressure
 relationship *110*
temperature-volume relationship
 106–107
tension 380, **388**
terrestrial planets **552**. *See also*
 inner planets
texture 60
theory, scientific **15**
thermal conductivity **139**
of metals 139, 202, *203*
thermal energy **74**, 77, 363
changes of state and flow of
 96–102

heat as transfer of 202
leftover from big bang 624
thermometer 26, 104
Thomson, J.J. 126
thorium 144
thrust 403, **504**
tide cycle 484
tides *484*–485
time
    in distance-versus-time graphs
        346–347, 355
    measuring *25*
    in speed-versus-time graph *354*
    units of 25
tin 142, *143*
Titanic **(ship)** 424
Titan (moon) 566
tracers *162*, 163
transition metals 142, *143*
transportation, speed of 344–345
trends, using graphs to identify
    40–41
triatomic molecule 152
trichloroethane 302
triple bonds *194*, 301
triple stars 615
Triton (moon) 568
Tsiolkovsky, Konstantin 503, 506

umbra *482*, 483
unbalanced forces *376*, 403
    Newton's first law of motion and
        389–390
unbalanced pressure *419*
United States, space race with
    Soviet Union 510–511
units of measurement 17
    for acceleration 352
    of density 24
    to describe motion 340
    joules 358
    of length 18–19
    light-year **602**
    of mass 21
    for momentum **396**
    newton (N) 21, 105, **375**, 475
    pascal (Pa) 105, **417**
    for pressure 105
    of temperature 26
    of time 25
    of volume 22, 104
universal gravitation, law of 384,
    474, 475

universe 620, 622–627
    age of 624
    expanding 623, 626
    formation of 622–624
    future of 626
    galaxies in **617**–619
    geocentric model of *539*
    heliocentric model of *540*
    scale of 620–621
unsaturated fatty acids 320
unsaturated hydrocarbons *301*
unsaturated solution 263
uranium 144, 159
uranium-238 159
Uranus *563*, 567

V2 (rocket) 503
vacuum 521
valence electrons *176–177*
    in alkali metals 179
    in carbon atom 293
    in halogens 179
    in hydrogen 182
    in inert gases 179
    metallic bonding and *200*
    in metals 201, 202
    in nonmetals 181
    number of covalent bonds and
        193
    patterns of 178, *179*
    reactivity of metals and 180
    in semimetals 182
    transfer of 185, 186
vaporization 98–99
variables
    directly proportional **107**
    inversely proportional **109**
    manipulated *12*, 35, 36, 639
    responding *12*, 35, 639
vector 341
    acceleration **350**–355
    displacement *341*
    force **374**, *375*
    velocity **344**–345
velocity 344–345, **504**
    changing 350–351
    escape **505**
    momentum and **396**–399
    of object in free fall **386**
    orbital **504**
    projectile motion and **387**
    of rocket 504–*505*

unbalanced forces and change in
    376
Venera 7 **(space probe)** 556
Venus *553, 555*–556
    atmosphere of 556
    Galileo's observations of 540
    rotation of 555
vernal (spring or March) equinox
    469, 471
Verne, Jules 502
vertical axis 36, 37
Vesta (asteroid) 574
Viking **(spacecraft)** 578
Virgo Supercluster 617, *621*
viscosity 94
visible light 76, **591**, 592
vitamins 272, *322*, 323
volcanoes on Mars 558, *559*
volume 22
    calculating 23
    density and **425**–426
    of gas 104
    of liquids 22, *93*
    measuring 22–23
    of solids 22, 23
    temperature-volume relationship
        106–107
    units of 22, 104
volume-pressure relationship
    105, 108–*109*
von Braun, Wernher 503
Vostok 1 **(spacecraft)** 511
Voyager **probes** 566
    Voyager 2 567, 568

water
    acids in, hydrogen ions produced
        by 275, *276*
    bases in, hydroxide ions
        produced by **275**, 276
    in body 322
    boiling point of **99**, 260, 261
    chemical reaction in formation
        of 235
    density of 93, **425**
    on Earth's surface 553
    electrolysis of *76*
    on Europa, search for 579
    freezing point of pure 260
    on Mars 557, 578
    metals that react with *132*
    molecule 63, *193*, 196
    on moon, evidence of 490

Index

Page numbers for key terms are printed in **boldface** type.
Page numbers for illustrations, maps, and charts are printed in *italics*.

as nutrient 322
pH of pure 276
properties of *215*
solutions with and without 257
states of 90, 93
surface tension of **94**
synthesis reaction to form **230**
tap 256
as universal solvent 257
waterfalls 362
water pressure, depth and *421–422*
water vapor 553
condensation of ***100***
wavelength 591
**weather forecasting, barometer
and** *422*
weight 21, *385*, 475
of air 418
buoyant force and ***427***, 428–429
calculating 385
gravitational potential energy
and ***360***
measuring *20*, 21
white dwarf *599, 604, 605,* ***611***
Wilson, Robert 624
winter 268
winter (December) solstice
469, 470
**wood, synthetic composites
imitating** 311
wool 304, 308
work 358
Wright, Wilbur and Orville 437,
439

xenon 154
X-ray telescopes 596

year 465
leap 467
tracking cycle of 466–467
***-yne* suffix** 301
yttrium 142

zinc 137

Acknowledgments

Science Content Standards for California Public Schools reproduced by permission, California Department of Education, CDE Press, 1430 N Street, Suite 3207, Sacramento, CA 95814.

Activity on page 504 Copyright © Dale Olive/Hawaii Space Grant Consortium/ NASA. Used with permission.

Quote on page 515 by Janet Kavandi is from *Space Shuttle: The First 20 Years,* edited by Tony Reichhardt for Air & Space Space Magazine/Smithsonian Magazine. Published in the United States by DK Publishing, Inc.

Staff Credits

Ernest Albanese, Scott Andrews, Carole Anson, Becky Barra, Peggy Bliss, Anne M. Bray, Katherine Bryant, Michael A. Burstein, Sarah Carroll, Sara Castrignano, Kenneth Chang, Jonathan Cheney, Bob Craton, Patricia M. Dambry, Glen Dixon, Jonathan Fisher, Kathryn Fobert, Robert M. Graham, Anne Jones, Kelly Kelliher, Toby Klang, Russ Lappa, Greg Lam, Dotti Marshall, Tim McDonald, Brent McKenzie, Ranida McKneally, Julia Osborne, Caroline Power, Gerry Schrenk, Siri Schwartzman, Malti Sharma, Laurel Smith, Emily Soltanoff, Paul Ramos, Linda Zust Reddy, Rashid Ross, Marcy Rose, Diane Walsh

Additional Credits

Michelle Chaison, Lisa Clark, Angela Clarke, Brad Conger, Roger Dowd, Paula Gogan-Porter, Tom Greene, Kama Holder, Rich McMahon, Robyn Salbo, Ted Smykal, Laura Smyth, Chris Willson, Heather Wright

Illustration

Morgan Cain & Associates, David Corrente, John Edwards & Associates, Gary Glover, Ray Goudey, Jared D. Lee, Phil Guzy, Kevin Jones and Associates, Steve McEntee, Rich McMahon, Precision Graphics, Ted Smykal, J/B Woolsey Associates

Charts and Graphs

Ernest Albanese, Matt Mayerchak

Photography

Photo Research Sue McDermott, John Judge, Paula Wehde, Kerri Hoar
Cover Images: Front, JPL/NASA; **Back**, Roger Ressmeyer/Corbis.

CHAPTER 1

Pages x1–1, Peter M. Fisher/Corbis; **1 inset,** AGE Fotostock/SuperStock; **3tr,** Image Source/SuperStock; **3tl,** Dorling Kindersely; **3m,** Mark Thomas/Science Photo Library/Photo Researchers; **5 inset,** Richard Haynes; **6,** Kelly/Mooney Photography/ Corbis; **7,** Gail Mooney/Masterfile; **8l,** Mark Thomas/Science Photo Library/Photo Researchers; **8r,** Peter Menzel/Stock Boston; **9,** Peter Arnold, Inc.; **10,** Richard Haynes; **12,** Russ Lappa; **13,** Richard Haynes; **14,** Detlev Van Ravensway/ SPL/Photo Researchers, Inc.; **15,** Shirley Richards/Photo Researchers, Inc.; **16t,** Richard Haynes; **17,** Richard Haynes; **18l,** Bettmann/Corbis; **18m,** Dorling Kindersley; **18r,** The Art Archive/The Picture Desk, Inc.; **19l,** Corbis; **19m,** Science & Society Picture Library; **19r,** Bureau of International Weights & Measures; **20t,** Richard Haynes; **20b,** Richard Haynes; **21 all,** Richard Haynes; **22,** Richard Haynes; **22 inset,** Richard Haynes; **23,** Richard Haynes; **24,** Richard Haynes; **25 all,** Richard Haynes; **26,** Richard Haynes; **30,** Richard Haynes; **31t,** Richard Haynes; **31m,** Richard Haynes; **31b,** Richard Haynes; **35,** Richard Haynes; **38l,** Richard Haynes; **38r,** Getty Images, Inc.; **39t,** Stephen Oliver/Dorling Kindersley; **39b,** Stephen Oliver/Dorling Kindersley; **40r,** Dr. K. S Kim/Peter Arnold, Inc.; **40l,** Mark C. Burnett/ Photo Researchers, Inc.; **41l,** Royalty-Free/Corbis; **41m,** Index Stock Imagery, Inc.; **41r,** Dorling Kindersley; **42,** Richard Haynes; **42,** PH Property Photo; **42,** Russ Lappa; **43t,** Index Stock Imagery, Inc.; **43b,** Index Stock Imagery, Inc./PictureQuest; **44,** Richard Haynes; **45,** Richard Haynes; **46,** Bob Daemmrich.

CHAPTER 2

Pages 52–53, Lawrence Migdale/PIX; **54–55,** Snaevarr Gudmundsson/Nordic Photos/Alamy Images; **55t,** Frans Lemmens/Getty Images; **55ml,** Victoria Pearson/ Getty Images; **55mr,** Photo Researchers, Inc.; **55br,** Walter Hodges/Getty Images;

57 inset, Eastcott-Momatiuk/The Image Works; **58b,** Russ Lappa; **58t,** Richard Haynes; **59,** Russ Lappa; **60r,** Richard Haynes; **60l,** Norbert Wu/DRK Photo; **60m,** Ted Kinsman/Photo Researchers, Inc.; **61l,** Walter Hodges/Getty Images; **61r,** Layne Kennedy/Corbis; **61m,** Richard Haynes; **62tr,** Corbis; **62tl,** Mahaux Photography/ Getty Images; **62bl,** MVR Photo; **63,** Tim Ridley/DK Images; **64b,** Grant V. Faint/ Getty Images, Inc.; **64tl,** Andrew Lambert Photography/SPL/Photo Researchers, Inc.; **64tr,** Ed Degginger/Color-Pic, Inc.; **65t,** Michael Newman/ PhotoEdit; **65b,** Graficart.net/Alamy Images; **66 all,** Richard Haynes; **67 all,** Richard Haynes; **68,** Frans Lemmens/Getty Images; **69br,** Photo Researchers, Inc.; **69,** Richard Megna/ Fundamental Photographs; **69bl,** Tony Freeman/PhotoEdit; **70,** Art Montes de Oca; **71,** Brand X pictures/Getty; **73t,** Russ Lappa; **73b,** Tim McGuire/Corbis; **74t,** Victoria Pearson/Getty Images; **74b,** Snaevarr Gudmundsson/Nordic Photos/Alamy Images; **75,** Dorling Kindersley; **76,** Russ Lappa; **77,** Adam Jones/Photographer's Choice/Getty Images; **78,** Richard Haynes; **79,** Richard Haynes; **80,** Tim McGuire/Corbis.

CHAPTER 3

Pages 84–85, Steve Bloom; **85 inset,** Alfred Saerchinger/zefa/Corbis; **87b,** Charles D. Winters/Photo Researchers; **87ml,** S. Stammer/Photo Researchers; **87mr,** Breck Kent/Earth Scenes; **87t,** James A. Sugar/Corbis; **89 inset,** Richard Haynes; **90t,** Richard Haynes; **90b,** Mike Hewitt/Getty Images, Inc.; **91,** James A. Sugar/Corbis; **92t,** S. Stammer/Photo Researchers; **92b,** Patrick J. LaCroix/Getty Images, Inc.; **93 all,** Richard Haynes; **94t,** Breck Kent/Earth Scenes; **94b,** Herman Eisenbeiss/Photo Researchers, Inc.; **96t,** Richard Haynes; **96b,** Hubert Camille/ Getty Images, Inc.; **97m,** Chuck O'Rear/Corbis; **97l,** Breck P. Kent/Earth Scenes; **97r,** Leslie Harris/Index Stock; **98l,** Richard Haynes; **98r,** Richard Haynes; **99r,** Dorling Kindersley/Science Museum; **99l,** Dorling Kindersley/Science Museum; **100,** Tony Freeman/PhotoEdit; **101,** Charles D. Winters/Photo Researchers; **102,** Russ Lappa; **103,** Carl & Ann Purcell/Corbis; **104b,** MVR Photo; **104t,** Richard Hutchings/Corbis; **105 all,** Richard Haynes; **106 all,** Dorling Kindersley; **107,** Dorling Kindersley; **108,** Richard Haynes; **112,** Russ Lappa; **113,** Richard Haynes; **114,** S. Stammer/Photo Researchers, Inc.

CHAPTER 4

Pages 118–119, Greg Elms/Lonely Planet Images; **123,** Richard Haynes; **124 both,** 1998 The Art Institute of Chicago; **129,** Courtesy of the National Institute of Science and Technology; **131t,** Russ Lappa; **131b,** Richard Haynes; **132t,** Philip Coblentz/Alamy Images; **132m,** Robert Mathena/Fundamental Photographs; **132br,** Richard Megna/Fundamental Photographs; **132bl,** Richard Megna/ Fundamental Photographs; **137,** Photodisc/Getty Images, Inc.; **138,** Richard Haynes; **139t,** Dorling Kindersley; **139bl,** Jeffrey L. Rotman/Corbis; **139br,** Cameron Davidson/ Getty Images, Inc.; **140l,** Richard Megna/Fundamental Photographs; **140m,** Dorling Kindersley; **140r,** Eyewire/Getty Images, Inc.; **141,** Jeff Greenberg/ PhotoEdit; **143t,** Richard Haynes; **143ml,** Christie's Images; **143b,** Richard Haynes; **145l,** Stephen Marks/Getty Images, Inc.; **145r,** David Parker/Photo Researchers, Inc.; **146t,** Richard Haynes; **146b,** Russ Lappa; **147 both,** Richard Haynes; **148,** Kathy Bushue/Getty Images, Inc.; **149bl,** Lawrence Migdale/Science Source/Photo Researchers; **149br,** Dennis McDonald/PhotoEdit; **150t,** Grant Heilman Photography, Inc.; **150b,** Charles D. Winters/Photo Researchers; **150l,** David Porter/Index Stock; **151 inset,** Michael Newman/PhotoEdit; **151r,** Joseph Devenney/Getty Images, Inc.; **152l,** Novovitch/Liaison International; **153l,** Mary Kate Denny/PhotoEdit; **153r,** Richard Megna/Fundamental Photographs; **154t,** Michael Dalton/Fundamental Photographs; **154b,** A & L Sinibaldi/Getty Images, Inc.; **155,** Andrew Syred/SPL/ Photo Researchers **157,** Grant V. Faint/Getty Images, Inc.; **144,** NASA/Johnson Space Center; **143mr,** Russ Lappa; **158,** Jan Van Der Straet/Granger Collection; **159t,** Paul Silverman/ Fundamental Photographs; **159b,** Bettmann/Corbis; **163,** RVI Medical Physics, Newcastle/Simon, Fraser/Science Photo Library; **125,** Royalty-Free/Corbis; **126,** Russ Lappa; **127t,** Dorling Kindersley; **127bl,** Stockbyte; **127br,** Frank Cezus/Getty Images, Inc.; **152r,** Pete Oxford/Minden Pictures; **121tl,** Richard Megna/Fundamental Photographs; **119 inset,** Jane Burton/Dorling Kindersley; **121tr,** Lawrence Migdale/Science Source/Photo Researchers; **121br,** Andrew Syred/ SPL/Photo Researchers; **120l,** Jeffrey L. Rotman/Corbis.

CHAPTER 5

Pages 171–171, Kenneth Eward/BioGrafx/Photo Researchers, Inc.; **171,** Michael Dalton/Fundamental Photographs; **175,** Richard Haynes; **179,** Fundamental Photographs; 180l, Lester V. Bergman/Corbis; 80m, Cecile Brunswick/Peter Arnold, Inc.; **180r,** The Granger Collection, NY; **181t,** Alexander Tsiaras/Stock Boston; **181b,** AP/Wide World Photos; **182,** George Payne; **182 inset,** Sheila Terry/SPL/ Photo Researchers, Inc.; **183,** Russ Lappa; **184t,** Russ Lappa; **184b,** Richard Haynes; **184m,** Russ Lappa; **186tl,** Lawrence Migdale/Photo Researchers, Inc.; **186tr,** Stephen Frisch/Stock Boston; **186b,** Barry Runk/Grant Heilman Photography; **187,** Ric Ergenbright/Corbis; **188,** M. Claye/Jacana/Photo Researchers, Inc.; **189,** Richard Megna/Fundamental Photographs; **191,** Richard Haynes; **192,** Richard Haynes; 197, Richard Hutchings/Photo Researchers, Inc.; **198t,** Russ Lappa; **198b,** Andrea Pistolesi; **199bl,** Diana Calder/The Stock Market; **199br,** Royalty-Free/Corbis; **199t,** Index Stock Imagery, Inc./PictureQuest; **200,** Russ Lappa; **201,** Helene Rogers/ Art Directors; **202,** NASA; **202,** Phillip Hayson/Photolibrary.com; **203,** Dorling Kindersley; **204,** Dorling Kindersley.

CHAPTER 6

213, Russ Lappa; **214,** Ariel Skelley/Corbis; **215,** Tim Hauf/Visuals Unlimited; **216l,** Richard Haynes; **216r,** Russ Lappa; **217 both,** Richard Megna/ Fundamental Photographs; **218m,** Charles D. Winters/Photo Researchers, Inc.; **218r,** Russ Lappa; **218tl,** John Serrao/Photo Researchers, Inc. **218bl,** Michael P. Gadomski/Photo Researchers, Inc.; **219l,** Russ Lappa; **219r,** Russ Lappa; **220,** David Young-Wolff/PhotoEdit; **221,** Aero Graphics, Inc./Corbis; **223,** Richard Haynes; **224,** Russ Lappa; **226l,** Russ Lappa; **226m,** Russ Lappa; **226r,** Russ Lappa; **227t,** John D. Cummingham/Visuals Unlimited; **227br,** Dorling Kindersley; **227bl,** Dorling Kindersley; **233,** Euro NCAP; **234,** Aaron Horowitz/Corbis; **237,** Charlie Neibergall/ AP/Wide World Photos; **238l,** Richard Megna/Fundamental Photographs; **238r,** Richard Megna/Fundamental Photographs; **240,** Russ Lappa; **241,** Russ Lappa; **242t,** Richard Haynes; **242b,** Melanie Duncan Thortis/The Vicksburg Post/AP/Wide World Photos; **243,** The Kevin Keane Archives; **245 all,** Russ Lappa; **246l,** Richard Megna/Fundamental Photographs; **246r,** Richard Megna/Fundamental Photographs.

CHAPTER 7

Pages 251–251, Richard Megna/Fundamental Photographs; **253tl,** Richard Megna/Fundamental Photographs; **253m,** L.S. Stepanowicz/Visuals Unlimited; **254–255,** Jeff Hinter/Getty Images, Inc.; **255 inset,** Richard Haynes; **257,** Digital Vision/Getty Images, Inc.; **258,** Richard Haynes; **260t,** Layne Kennedy/Corbis; **260b,** Onne van der Wal/Corbis; **261,** Paul Barton/Corbis; **262l,** Tim Laman/Index Stock Imagery, Inc.; **262m,** Randy Ury/Corbis; **262r,** Mike & Carol Werner/Stock Boston; **263,** Richard Haynes; **264,** Russ Lappa; **265 all,** Richard Haynes; **266,** Tony Freeman/PhotoEdit; **267 all,** Russ Lappa; **268t,** Russ Lappa; **268b,** Lawrence Migdale/Photo Researchers, Inc.; **269 both,** Russ Lappa; **270 both,** Russ Lappa; **271,** LWA-Dann Tardif/Corbis; **272bl,** Russ Lappa; **272t,** Mark C. Burnett/Stock Boston; **272br,** Russ Lappa; **273tr,** Russ Lappa; **273l,** B. Daemmrich/The Image Works; **273br,** Russ Lappa; **274,** Russ Lappa; **275,** Tom Pantages; **277,** Richard Haynes; **280,** Russ Lappa; **281,** Richard Haynes; **282,** Richard Haynes

CHAPTER 8

Pages 286–287, Gerald D. Tang; **287,** Charles D. Winters/Photo Researchers, Inc.; **291,** Richard Haynes; **292l,** Volker Steger/SPL/Photo Researchers, Inc.; **292r,** SIU/ Peter Arnold, Inc.; **294l,** Cary Wolinsky/carywolinksy.com; **294r,** Barry Runk/Grant Heilman Photography; **295,** Richard Pasley/Stock Boston; **296,** Richard Haynes; **297tl,** Tom Vezo/Minden Pictures; **297tr,** Russ Lappa; **297b,** Richard Laird/Getty Images, Inc.; **298t,** Amana America, Inc.; **298b,** Tony Craddock/SPL/Photo Researchers, Inc.; **300l,** Richard Haynes; **300r,** Russ Lappa; **301r,** Michael J. Doolittle/The Image Works; **301l,** Grant Heilman Photography, Inc.; **302,** Roberto Borea/AP/Wide World Photos; **303t,** R.J. Erwin/Photo Researchers, Inc.; **303b,** Russ Lappa; **304,** Richard Haynes; **305 both,** Russ Lappa; **306,** John Terence Turner; **307,** Russ Lappa; **308m,** Royalty-Free/Corbis; **308r,** Larry Ulrich/DRK Photo; **308l,** Joe McDonald/Corbis; **309,** Superstock; **310l,** Corbis-Bettmann; **310m,** Chris Rogers/ Corbis; **310r,** Terry Wild Studio/Uniphoto; **311l,** David Young-Wolfe/PhotoEdit; **311m,** Jeffrey W. Myers/The Stock Market/Corbis; **311r,** Courtesy of Dow Corporation; **312r,** David Stoecklein/Corbis; **312,** Corbis; **313,** Fred Habegger/Grant Heilman Photography; **314,** Richard Haynes; **315t,** 2004 Richard Megna-Fundamental Photographers; **315b,** Richard Megna-Fundamental Photographers; **316t,** Russ Lappa; **317t,** E.S. Ross/Visuals Unlimited; **318,** Richard Haynes; **319,** Richard Haynes; **320,** Richard Haynes; **322,** Erich Lessing/Art Resource, NY; **324,** Richard Haynes; **325,** Russ Lappa; **326,** Superstock.

CHAPTER 9

Pages 332–333, Mark Barrett/Index Stock Imagery/PictureQuest; **333r,** Rommel/ Masterfile; **334,** Frans Lanting/Minden Pictures; **335bl,** Brand X Pictures/Getty Images, Inc.; **335t,** Eyewire Collection/Getty Images Inc.; **335m,** Andy Wheeler/ Alamy Images; **335br,** Alan Schein Photography/Corbis; **337 inset,** PhotoDisc/ Getty Images, Inc.; **338t,** Richard Haynes; **339t,** Sat Yip/SuperStock; **340b,** Digital Vision/Getty Images Inc.; **340t,** Chris Sorensen; **342,** Russ Lappa; **343l,** Robert LaBerge/ Getty Images, Inc.; **344l,** North Wind Picture Archives; **344br,** National Motor Museum, Beaulieu, England; **344tr,** Topham/The Image Works; **345l,** Bettmann/ Corbis; **345r,** Fritz Hoffmann/documentCHINA; **346,** Bob Daemmrich Photography; **349,** Richard Haynes; **350,** Richard Haynes; **351l,** Ezra Shaw/Getty Images Inc.; **351r,** Nick Wilson/Getty Images Inc.; **351m,** Adam Pretty/Getty Images Inc.; **353,** Kwame Zikomo/SuperStock; **354,** Eyewire Collection/Getty Images Inc.; **356,** Richard Haynes; **357,** Francisco Cruz/SuperStock; **358t,** Richard Haynes; **358b,** Corel Corp./Mike Chambers; **361r,** Paine Stock Photos; **361l,** AP/Wide World Photos; **362t,** Richard Haynes; **362b,** Richard Megna/Fundamental Photographs; **363,** Brand X Pictures/Getty Images, Inc.; **364,** Robert LaBerge/Getty Images, Inc.

CHAPTER 10

Pages 368–369, Sue Ogrocki/AP/Wide World Photos; **371tl,** Ezra Shaw/Getty Images; **373 inset,** Richard Haynes; **374,** Russ Lappa; **375,** Duomo/Corbis; **376 both,** Richard Haynes; **376 both,** Richard Haynes; **377,** Richard Haynes; **378,** Richard Haynes; **379,** Ken O'Donaghue; **380b,** Kindra Clineff/Index Stock; **381t,** B & C Alexander/Photo Researchers, Inc.; **381b,** Jan Hinsch/Photo Researchers, Inc.; **382,** Russ Lappa; **383tl,** Michael Newman/PhotoEdit; **383tr,** Michael Newman/PhotoEdit; **383bl,** David Young-Wolff/PhotoEdit; **383br,** Kelly-Mooney Photography/Corbis; **384,** Joe McBride/Corbis; **385,** NASA; **386,** Megna/ Peticolas/Fundamental Photographs; **387,** Richard Megna/Fundamental Photographs; **388,** Norbert Schaefer/Corbis; **389t,** Russ Lappa; **389b,** Bettmann/Corbis; **390 both,** Richard Haynes; **390 both,** Richard Haynes; **392,** David Madison Sports Photography; **392,** AFP/Corbis; **393,** Richard Haynes; **394tr,** Omni Photo Communications, Inc./Index Stock; **394tl,** David Madison Sports Photography; **394b,** Lawrence Manning/Corbis; **395l,** Syracuse/Dick Blume/The Image Works; **395r,** Michael Devin Daly/Corbis; **397tl,** David Davis/Index Stock; **397tr,** Image Source/Alamy Images; **397b,** Russ Lappa; **401,** Richard Haynes; **402t,** Richard Haynes; **402b,** Courtesy of Homer Hickam; **403,** Jeff Hunter/Getty Images; **404,** Richard Haynes; **406,** David Young-Wolff/PhotoEdit.

CHAPTER 11

Pages 410–411, Getty Images, Inc.; **411,** Russ Lappa; **412,** Russ Lappa; **413b,** Richard Haynes; **413mr,** Runk/Schoenberger/Grant Heilman Photography, Inc.; **415,** Richard Haynes; **416l,** Milton Feinberg/Stock Boston; **416r,** Chlaus Lotscher/Stock Boston; **417 all,** Richard Haynes; **418,** Photodisc/ Getty Images, Inc.; **419bl,** Richard Megna/Fundamental Photographs; **419br,** Richard Megna/Fundamental Photographs; **419t,** Richard Haynes; **420r,** Digital Vision/Getty Images Inc.; **422,** Russ Lappa; **424bl,** Ken Marshall/ Madison Press Ltd.; **425,** Runk/Schoenberger/Grant Heilman Photography, Inc.; **428,** Richard Haynes; **431,** Richard Haynes; **432b,** Stephen Frink/ Corbis; **433t,** Richard Haynes; **437b,** Mercury Archives/Getty Images, Inc.; **437t,** Richard Haynes; **438l,** Richard Haynes; **438r,** Richard Haynes; **441,** Maxime Laurent/Digital Vision; **444t,** Stephen Frink/Corbis; **444b,** Paul Seheult; Eye Ubiquitous/Corbis; **446,** Russ Lappa.

CHAPTER 12

Pages 458–459, Evad Damast; **459br,** Roger Ressmeyer/Corbis; **460,** Gerry Ellis/Minden Pictures; **461t,** Jeff Haynes/AFP/Corbis; **461b,** Dorling Kindersley; **461tl,** Digital Vision/Getty Images, Inc.; **462,** Frank Zullo/Photo Researchers, Inc.; **463,** Frank Zullo/Photo Researchers, Inc.; **463 inset,** Richard Haynes; **464t,** Richard Haynes; **464b,** Eric Lessing/Art Resource, NY; **466l,** Lawrence Migdale/Photo Researchers, Inc.; **466r,** Ancient Art & Architecture Collection Ltd.; **467l,** Janet Wishnetsky/Corbis; **467r,** The Granger Collection; **467m,** Hazel Hankin/Stock Boston; **470l,** Paul A. Souders/Corbis; **470r,** Bill Ross/Corbis; **471l,** Tony Stewart/ PhotoNewZealand.com; **471r,** Dennis Degnan/Corbis; **473,** Richard Haynes; **474–475,** Paul & Linda Marie Ambrose/Getty Images, Inc.; **478,** Richard Haynes; **479t,** E. R. Degginger/Animals Animals/Earth Scenes; **480–481,** Gerry Ellis/Minden Pictures; **480ml,** John Bova/Photo Researchers, Inc.; **480mr,** John Bova/Photo Researchers, Inc.; **480r,** John Bova/Photo Researchers, Inc.; **481tl,** John Bova/ Photo Researchers, Inc.; **481tml,** John Bova/Photo Researchers, Inc.; **481tmr,** John Bova/Photo Researchers, Inc.; **481tr,** John Bova/Photo Researchers, Inc.; **481br,** Dorling Kindersley; **482tl,** Digital Vision/Getty Images, Inc.; **483tr,** G.Antonio Milani/SPL/Photo Researchers, Inc.; **484 both,** Bill Bachman/Photo Researchers, Inc.; **487,** Richard Haynes; **488t,** Richard Haynes; **488b,** Jay M. Pasachoff; **489t,** NASA; **489b,** NASA; **490t,** John Bova/Photo Researchers, Inc.; **490b,** NASA; **492tl,** Paul Sutton/Duomo/Corbis; **492tr,** Jeff Haynes/AFP/Corbis

CHAPTER 13

Pages 496–497, NASA; **497br,** NASA; **498,** NASA; **499,** NASA; **499b,** NASA; **499m,** Reto Stockli/GSFC/NASA; **500–501,** Frank Zullo/Photo Researchers, Inc.; **501,** NASA; **502t,** Richard Haynes; **502b,** Johnson Space Center/NASA; **503,** Jeff Hunter/Getty Images Inc.; **503 inset,** U.S. Civil Air Patrol; **505br,** Reto Stockli/ GSFC/NASA; **508–509,** Richard Haynes; **508b,** Richard Haynes; **509b,** Richard Haynes; **510bl,** TASS/Sovfoto; **511 inset,** NASA; **511r,** NASA; **512 inset,** NASA; **512r,** N. Armstrong/Corbis; **513t,** World Perspectives/Getty Images, Inc.; **514t,** John Frassanito & Associates; **515br,** NASA; **516l,** NASA; **517t,** NASA; **518r,** Roger Arno/NASA; **518l,** JPL/NASA; **519r,** David Ducros/Science Photo Library Photo Researchers, Inc.; **519l,** JPL/NASA; **520br,** Richard Haynes; **521b,** NASA; **522l,** Princess Margaret Rose Orthopaedic Hospital/Science Photo Library/Photo Researchers, Inc.; **522r,** Getty Images, Inc.; **523r,** Pascal Rondeau/Getty Images, Inc.; **523m,** Smith Sport Optics; **523l,** Franck Fife/AFP/Getty Images; **524t,** NASA/ GSFC/Boston University; **525tr,** Russ Lappa; **527r,** Bob Daemmrich/PhotoEdit; **528bl,** World Perspectives/Getty Images, Inc.; **528r,** NASA

CHAPTER 14

537br, Richard Haynes; **538bl,** David Malin/Anglo-Australian Observatory; **539br,** The Granger Collection, NY; **540bl,** Science Photo Library/Photo Researchers, Inc.; **540bm,** Photo Researchers, Inc.; **540t,** Bettmann/Corbis; **540r,** James A. Sugar/ Corbis; **541m,** The Art Archive/Royal Society; **541r,** Corbis Bettmann; **541l,** Explorer-Keystone-France/Gamma Press USA; **545r,** Richard Haynes; **548t,** Dr. Fred Espenak/Science Photo Library/Photo Researchers, Inc.; **549tr,** SOHO/ESA and NASA; **549bl,** National Solar Observatory; **549br,** AURA/STScI/NASA; **550tl,** Ron Sanford/Getty Images, Inc.; **554b,** NASA; **554tl,** Julian Baum/Dorling Kindersley; **555tl,** NASA; **555tr,** JPL/NASA; **555b,** NASA; **556b,** David Anderson/NASA/Photo Researchers, Inc.; **557b,** the Hubble Heritage Team/NASA; **557t,** NASA; **558t,** JPL/NASA; **559t,** U.S. Geological Survey; **560t,** NASA; **560b,** Pat Rawlings/NASA; **561b,** Pat Rawlings/NASA; **562b,** NASA; **564r** Martin Cropper/Dorling Kindersley; **564l,** NASA/SPL/Photo Researchers, Inc.; **565tr,** NASA; **565br,** Corbis; **565tl,** Reuters NewMedia Inc./Corbis; **565bl,** JPL/NASA; **565b,** David Seal/JPL/CalTech/ NASA; **566r,** AFP/ Corbis; **566l,** NASA and the Hubble Heritage Team; **567r,** Kenneth Seidelmann, U.S. Naval Observatory/NASA; **567tl,** Dorling Kindersley/Jet Propulsion Lab; **568r,** NASA; **568l,** Julian Baum/Dorling Kindersley; **569r,** Lynette Cook/ Photo Researchers, Inc.; **569l,** Dorling Kindersley; **570r,** Richard Haynes; **571r,** Richard Haynes; **572t,** Richard Haynes; **572–573,** Jerry Lodriguss/Photo Researchers, Inc.; **573b,** Dorling Kindersley; **574br,** NEAR Project/NLR/JHUAPL/ Goddard SVS/NASA; **575tr,** Frank Zullo/Photo Researchers, Inc.; **576,** Ghislaine Grozaz; **577tr,** Douglas Faulkner/Photo Researchers, Inc.; **578tl,** Calvin J. Hamilton; **578bm,** NASA/SPL/Photo Researchers, Inc.; **579tr,** NASA/Science Photo Library/ Photo Researchers, Inc.; **580,** NASA and the Hubble Heritage Team.

CHAPTER 15

Pages 584–585, Loke Tan/Starryscapes.com; **585br,** Chip Simons/Getty Images, Inc.; **586b,** Bill & Sally Fletcher/Tom Stack & Associates, Inc.; **587tr,** R. Corradi (Isaac Newton Group) and D. R.; Gonçalves (Instituto de Astrofísica de Canarias); **587tl,** Luke Dodd/Science Photo Library/Photo Researchers, Inc.; **587b,** NASA; **589r,** Richard Haynes; **590bl,** Florence Museo delle Scienze/AKG London; **590tr,** Richard Haynes; **592l,** Andy Crawford/Dorling Kindersley Media Library; **592r,** Andy Crawford/Dorling Kindersley Media Library; **593mr,** Jeff Hester and Paul Scowen (ASU) and Mt. Palomar Observatories; **593ml,** C.A.R.A./W. M. Keck Observatory; **593r,** Marshall Space Flight Center/NASA; **593l,** VLA/NRAO; **594l,** Yerkes Observatory Photography; **594r,** Courtesy of the NAIC - Arecibo Observatory, a facility of the NSF; **595l,** David Nunuk/Science Photo Library/Photo Researchers, Inc.; **595m,** NASA; **595r,** JPL/NASA; **596tl,** NASA; **597br,** Richard Haynes; **598tr,** Richard Haynes; **598bl,** Dorling Kindersley Media Library; **601b,** Mark Thiessen/Corbis; **605tr,** Luke Dodd/Science Photo Library/Photo Researchers, Inc.; **608b,** Ariel Skelley/Corbis; **609t,** Anglo-Australian Observatory/Royal Observatory Edinburgh; **609b,** AURA/STScI/NASA; **612l,** Frans Lemmens/Getty Images, Inc.; **614b,** Frank Zullo/Photo Researchers, Inc.; **615 both,** Celestial Image Co./Science Photo Library/Photo Researchers, Inc.; **616b,** Celestial Image Co./ Science Photo Library/Photo Researchers, Inc.; **616t,** David Malin/Anglo-Australian Observatory; **617t,** Robert Gendler; **618t,** David Malin/Anglo-Australian Observatory; **618m,** David Malin/Anglo-Australian Observatory; **618b,** Royal Observatory, Edinburgh/AATB/Science Photo Library/Photo Researchers, Inc.; **620t,** NASA; **620r,** SOHO/ESA and NASA; **620l,** Dorling Kindersley Media Library; **621m,** Bill & Sally Fletcher/Tom Stack & Associates, Inc.; **621l,** R. Corradi (Isaac Newton Group) and D. R.; Gonçalves (Instituto de Astrofísica de Canarias); **621r,** Celestial Image Co./Science Photo Library/Photo Researchers, Inc.; **622b,** NASA; **626bl,** American Institute of Physics; **627t,** Jean-Paul Kneib/Observatoire Midi-Pyrénées, France/Caltech/ESA/NASA; **628l,** Richard Haynes; **630b,** NASA; **631tr,** David Malin/Anglo-Australian Observatory; **633,** Denis Scott/Corbis

Periodic Table of Elements

Key

C	Solid
Br	Liquid
H	Gas
Tc	Not found in nature

1

1
1
H
Hydrogen
1.0079

Group	1	2	3	4	5	6	7	8	9
2	3 **Li** Lithium 6.941	4 **Be** Beryllium 9.0122							
3	11 **Na** Sodium 22.990	12 **Mg** Magnesium 24.305							
4	19 **K** Potassium 39.098	20 **Ca** Calcium 40.08	21 **Sc** Scandium 44.956	22 **Ti** Titanium 47.90	23 **V** Vanadium 50.941	24 **Cr** Chromium 51.996	25 **Mn** Manganese 54.938	26 **Fe** Iron 55.847	27 **Co** Cobalt 58.933
5	37 **Rb** Rubidium 85.468	38 **Sr** Strontium 87.62	39 **Y** Yttrium 88.906	40 **Zr** Zirconium 91.22	41 **Nb** Niobium 92.906	42 **Mo** Molybdenum 95.94	43 **Tc** Technetium (98)	44 **Ru** Ruthenium 101.07	45 **Rh** Rhodium 102.91
6	55 **Cs** Cesium 132.91	56 **Ba** Barium 137.33	71 **Lu** Lutetium 174.97	72 **Hf** Hafnium 178.49	73 **Ta** Tantalum 180.95	74 **W** Tungsten 183.85	75 **Re** Rhenium 186.21	76 **Os** Osmium 190.2	77 **Ir** Iridium 192.22
7	87 **Fr** Francium (223)	88 **Ra** Radium (226)	103 **Lr** Lawrencium (262)	104 **Rf** Rutherfordium (261)	105 **Db** Dubnium (262)	106 **Sg** Seaborgium (263)	107 **Bh** Bohrium (264)	108 **Hs** Hassium (265)	109 **Mt** Meitnerium (268)

Lanthanides

57 **La** Lanthanum 138.91	58 **Ce** Cerium 140.12	59 **Pr** Praseodymium 140.91	60 **Nd** Neodymium 144.24	61 **Pm** Promethium (145)	62 **Sm** Samarium 150.4

Actinides

89 **Ac** Actinium (227)	90 **Th** Thorium 232.04	91 **Pa** Protactinium 231.04	92 **U** Uranium 238.03	93 **Np** Neptunium (237)	94 **Pu** Plutonium (244)